Karl Stieler, Eduard Paulus, Woldemar Kaden, Frances Eleanor Trollope, Thomas Adolphus Trollope

Italy from the Alps to Mount Etna

Karl Stieler, Eduard Paulus, Woldemar Kaden, Frances Eleanor Trollope, Thomas Adolphus Trollope

Italy from the Alps to Mount Etna

ISBN/EAN: 9783743331679

Manufactured in Europe, USA, Canada, Australia, Japa

Cover: Foto ©ninafisch / pixelio.de

Manufactured and distributed by brebook publishing software (www.brebook.com)

Karl Stieler, Eduard Paulus, Woldemar Kaden, Frances Eleanor Trollope, Thomas Adolphus Trollope

Italy from the Alps to Mount Etna

TABLE OF CONTENTS.

FROM THE ALPS TO THE ARNO.

	PAGE
SONNET	1
THE GREAT ROADS TO ITALY	1
THROUGH THE MONT CENIS	1
THE VIA MALA	6
ACROSS THE ST. GOTHARD	9
ACROSS THE BRENNER	14
IN THE TRENTINO	19
ON THE LAGO DI GARDA	26
VERONA	35
FROM VERONA TO THE MOUNTAINS OF VENETIA	48
FROM VERONA TO THE ADRIATIC	55
VENICE	60
TO TRIESTE AND MIRAMAR	78
MANTUA	83
MILAN	87
THREE LAKES	99
LAGO DI COMO	99
LAGO DI LUGANO	105
LAGO MAGGIORE	108
TURIN	111
GENOA	117
ON THE RIVIERA DI PONENTE	128
ON THE RIVIERA DI LEVANTE	141
IN EMILIA	149

FROM THE ARNO TO THE TIBER.

FLORENCE	157
FLORENTINE ART	170
FLORENTINE NATURE	177
PISA	183
SIENA	187
THE LAKE OF THRASYMENE	192
THE ROADS TO ROME	199
BESIDE THE ADRIATIC	199
BESIDE THE TYRRHENE SEA	204
THE MIDDLE ROADS	205
TO ROME	208

TABLE OF CONTENTS.

FROM THE TIBER TO ETNA.

	PAGE
WITHIN THE CONFINES OF LATIUM	215
ROME	215
THE ETERNAL CITY IN A MODERN TOGA	231
AMONG THE RUINS	246
PIOUS PILGRIMAGES AND PROFANE PROMENADES	253
A WORD ABOUT CICERONI	275
THE NORTHERN WANDERER IN THE ROMAN CAMPAGNA	280
FROM THE SHORES OF LAGO FUCINO TO THE PONTINE MARSHES	300
MOUNTAIN MONASTERIES AND A PAINTER'S PARADISE	332
FROM THE BANKS OF THE LIRIS TO THE SHORES OF THE SIRENS	343
COMPANION LANDSCAPES	343
EXCURSION FROM THE GRAN SASSO D'ITALIA TO VESUVIUS	343
"KNOW'ST THOU THE LAND?"	354
ANCIENT AND MODERN CAMPANIANS	362
THE EVER YOUNG PARTHENOPE	373
THE BEAUTIFUL, DANGEROUS NEIGHBOUR	384
AMONG GRECIAN RUINS	392
A SEA VOYAGE FROM BAIÆ TO SALERNO	404
THE THREE SISTER ISLANDS	414
THE ISLAND OF TIBERIUS	420
FROM THE SHORES OF THE SIRENS TO THE MOUNTAINS OF CALABRIA	430
GRÆCIA MAGNA	430
A PROCESSION ACROSS THE COUNTRY	439
LUCANIA, APULIA, AND CALABRIA, IN THE PAST AND PRESENT	434
FROM THE SILA TO ETNA	447
SICILIAN LANDSCAPE	447
THE ISLAND UNDER THE VEIL OF LEGEND AND HISTORY	447
A VOYAGE ROUND THE ISLAND	453
TO ETNA	463

FULL PAGE ILLUSTRATIONS.

	PAGE
ORNAMENTAL BORDER	1
VIA MALA. "LE TROU PERDU"	7
MAKING THE TUNNEL THROUGH THE ST. GOTHARD	13
PALAZZO SARDAGNA IN TRENT	19
OLIVE GROVE ON THE SHORE OF THE LAKE OF GARDA, NEAR TORBOLE	29
VERONA	35
VIEW FROM THE GIARDINO GIUSTI, VERONA	45
PIAZZA DEI SIGNORI IN VICENZA	57
PIAZZA OF ST. MARK, WITH THE PIAZZETTA. VENICE	63
FISH-MARKET NEAR THE RIALTO	67
COFFEE-HOUSE ON THE RIVA DEGLI SCHIAVONI	69
CANOVA'S TOMB IN SANTA MARIA GLORIOSA DEI FRARI. VENICE	73
SCENE IN CHIOGGIA	77
TRIESTE	79
MIRAMAR	83
THE CATHEDRAL OF MILAN	93
MILANESE LADY	97
THE CERTOSA, NEAR PAVIA	99
COMO	101
MENDICANT FRIAR IN THE BRIANZA	104
LAGO MAGGIORE, WITH ISOLA BELLA AND ISOLA PESCATORE	109
SALITA SAN PAOLO, GENOA	119
VIA SAN LUCA, GENOA	123
PEGLI ON THE RIVIERA DI PONENTE	129
SAN REMO	131
FROM A VILLA NEAR BORDIGHERA	133
MONACO	135
SEASHORE NEAR SAVONA	137
NICE	139
PORTO VENERE, GULF OF SPEZIA	145
MARBLE QUARRIES NEAR CARRARA	149
CANOSSA	151
MARKET-PLACE, WITH THE FOUNTAIN OF NEPTUNE. BOLOGNA	155
FLORENCE, FROM SAN MINIATO	159
VIA DEGLI STROZZI	163
LOGGIA DEI LANZI	165
ORLANDINI'S BEER-GARDEN, FLORENCE	167
SAN MICHELE	169

FULL PAGE ILLUSTRATIONS.

	PAGE
COURTYARD OF THE PALAZZO VECCHIO, FLORENCE	173
CHOIR OF SANTA MARIA NOVELLA, FLORENCE	177
VINTAGE IN TUSCANY	181
CAMPO SANTO, PISA	203
CASCADES OF TERNI	205
ORVIETO	207
RUINS OF THE PALACE OF THE CÆSARS ON THE PALATINE	217
CAMPO VACCINO, ROME	221
ROME FROM THE CONVENT GARDEN OF SANTA SABINA ON THE AVENTINE	229
FOUNTAIN IN A ROMAN COURTYARD	233
PIAZZA MONTANARA, WITH THE THEATRE OF MARCELLUS	239
ROMAN FLOWER-SELLER	243
COLISEUM, FROM THE PALATINE	247
FORUM ROMANUM	249
A SERMON IN THE COLISEUM	251
ST. PETER'S, FROM THE VILLA DORIA PAMFILI	253
EVENING ON THE PINCIAN	255
INTERIOR OF ST. PETER'S, ROME	259
ROME, FROM THE VILLA CORSINI	263
POUSSIN'S VALLEY	273
ON THE PINCIAN	275
AFTER THE MASS IN S. TRINITÀ DE' MONTI, ROME	277
FOUNTAIN OF TREVI, ROME	279
ACQUA ACETOSA IN THE ROMAN CAMPAGNA, LOOKING TOWARDS MOUNT SORACTE	281
NEAR NETTUNO	285
BRETHREN OF THE MISERICORDIA BEARING THE BODY OF A MAN WHO HAS BEEN KILLED IN THE ROMAN CAMPAGNA	289
ON THE WAY TO CERVARA. ARTISTS' FESTIVAL IN ROME (1ST MAY, 1869)	293
VIA FLAMINIA ON THE ROMAN CAMPAGNA	295
SHEPHERD BOY IN THE CAMPAGNA	299
BATTLEFIELD NEAR TAGLIACOZZO	303
OLEVANO	307
FROM THE VILLA OF HADRIAN, NEAR TIVOLI	319
CAMP OF HANNIBAL NEAR ROCCA DI PAPA	325
ARICCIA	329
BY THE WELL AT OLEVANO	339
TERRACINA	343
FALL OF THE LIRIS NEAR ISOLA	347
OLIVE GROVE NEAR VENAFRO	349
VAL DI SANGRO	351
SUMMER NIGHT AT POSILIPPO	355
TRIUMPHAL ARCH OF KING ALFONSO	359
NAPLES, WITH VESUVIUS, FROM POSILIPPO	363
CORSO AT NAPLES	365
PORTA CAPUANA, NAPLES	367
DOLCE FAR NIENTE	369
CEMETERY. FEAST OF ALL SOULS, NAPLES	371
VIEW OF NAPLES FROM THE CORSO VITTORIO EMANUELE	375
PORT OF NAPLES	379

FULL PAGE ILLUSTRATIONS.

	PAGE
THE LAVA COMES	385
EXCAVATIONS IN POMPEII	397
PINE-WOOD NEAR TORRE DEL GRECO	405
A VILLA AT SORRENTO	407
FROM A VILLA, CASTELLAMARE	409
BATH OF DIANA	411
VIEW OF AMALFI FROM THE CAPUCHINS' GARDEN	413
CORAL FISHING	417
CAPRI, FROM THE HOTEL PAGANO	421
A GARDEN SPRING IN CAPRI	425
ARRIVAL OF A MARKET BOAT, CAPRI	427
ENTRANCE TO THE BLUE GROTTO	429
BATTLEFIELD OF CANNÆ	435
PLATANI NEAR MONTALLEGRO	453
ON THE ORETO IN THE CONCA D'ORO, NEAR PALERMO	455
PALERMO	461
ETNA FROM THE SOUTH	467

ILLUSTRATIONS IN THE TEXT.

	PAGE
ROAD OVER THE MONT CENIS	3
THE DEVIL'S BRIDGE	10
ON THE BRENNER, BELOW GOSSENSASS	15
WANDERERS ON THE BRENNER PASS	17
THE CASTLE OF TRENT	19
FOUNTAIN IN THE CATHEDRAL SQUARE AT TRENT	22
FRUIT-SELLERS IN TRENT	23
PEASANT WOMAN FROM THE NEIGHBOURHOOD OF TRENT	24
RIVA	26
CASTLE OF ARCO IN THE VAL DI SARCA	27
PIETRAMURATA IN THE VAL DI SARCA	28
LAKE OF CAVEDINE IN THE VAL DI SARCA	29
MILL IN THE BUCO DI VELA	30
DEPARTURE OF A STEAMBOAT FROM PESCHIERA	32
DESENZANO	33
TORBOLE	34
SANTA ANASTASIA, VERONA	35
FONTANA DI FERRO, NEAR VERONA	36
PIAZZA D'ERBE	37
JULIET'S HOUSE	38
DRAW-WELL	39
THE AMPHITHEATRE	41
COURT-YARD OF A HOUSE IN VERONA	42
BRIDGE OF THE BORGHETTO, NEAR VALEGGIO	43
VALSTAGNA	45
CASTLE OF VILLAFRANCA	47
BASSANO	48
PORTA RUSTERI, FELTRE	49
NEAR PRIMOLANO IN THE VAL SUGANA	51
ON THE CORDEVOLE	52
CITTADELLA	52
MOUNTAIN FORTRESS OF COVOLO	53
COTTAGE IN THE VALLEY OF THE BRENTA	54
VILLA GIUSTINIANI, PADUA	55
THE OLD SEMINARY, VICENZA	56
CHURCH OF ST. ANTHONY, PADUA	58
RIVA DEGLI SCHIAVONI, VENICE	60
VENETIAN FISHING-BOAT	61
ARRIVAL OF A MILK-BOAT	62
SAN PIETRO, CASTELLO	64
ON THE ISLAND OF TORCELLO	65
BRIDGE OF SIGHS	67
GHETTO	68

	PAGE
MONUMENT OF GENERAL FARNESE IN THE JESUITS' CHURCH	70
STREET IN VENICE	71
ON THE GIUDECCA	72
STREET SCENE	73
STREET IN VENICE	74
A GONDOLA	75
FROM THE LAGOONS	76
ON THE ROOFS	76
GROTTO OF SAN SERVOLO NEAR TRIESTE	80
WINCKELMANN'S MONUMENT	81
VIEW OF MANTUA FROM THE BRIDGE OF SAN GIORGIO	83
RIFLEMEN WAITING FOR A TRAIN	85
MONUMENT TO LEONARDO DA VINCI	88
COLUMNS OF SAN LORENZO	89
SANTA MARIA DELLE GRAZIE	91
CORSO VITTORIO EMANUELE	94
MONK AT THE WELL IN THE CERTOSA	95
LAKE OF COMO—VIEW OF MALGRATE FROM LECCO	97
BELLAGGIO, SEEN FROM VILLA GIULIA	99
STREET IN TREMEZZO	101
TAVERN IN LUGANO	102
THE RAVINE OF THE PIOVERNA, NEAR BELLANO	103
MONTE SALVATORE, ON THE LAKE OF LUGANO	105
ROTUNDA OF HERCULES ON ISOLA BELLA	106
BAY OF PALLANZA	107
MONCALIERI, NEAR TURIN	111
FOUNTAIN IN THE GIARDINO REALE	112
MONTE DEI CAPPUCCINI	113
ROAD TO THE CHURCH OF SUPERGA	114
PORTA PALATINA	115
FOUNTAIN IN THE ACQUA SOLA	117
PORTA VECCHIA DELLA LANTERNA	119
EVENING AT THE MOLE	120
MARKET IN THE PIAZZA DI PESCHERIA	121
AT THE PORT	122
BEFORE THE CONFESSIONAL IN SAN LORENZO	123
HARBOUR OF GENOA	125
SCENE ON THE SHORE	128
NEAR BORDIGHERA	129
OBELISK IN VILLA PALLAVICINI	130
PROCESSION	131
BORDIGHERA	132

ILLUSTRATIONS IN THE TEXT.

	PAGE
HARBOUR OF MONACO	133
VIEW NEAR SAN REMO	133
CONVENT GARDEN AT PESIO	135
MENTONE	136
INTERIOR OF A PEASANT'S COTTAGE IN BRIGA	137
ON THE SHORE OF THE LAVENZA, NEAR BRIGA	138
STREET IN TENDA	139
CASTLE OF MONACO	140
LAVAGNA—RETURN FROM FISHING	141
SEASHORE NEAR QUINTO	142
JEZZANO, IN THE BAY OF SPEZIA	142
ON THE PENINSULA NEAR SESTRI LEVANTE	143
THE ISLAND PALMARIA, IN THE BAY OF SPEZIA	144
FOUNTAIN OF THE SIREN IN CARRARA	145
LERICI, NEAR SPEZIA	146
SIESTA	147
ON THE RIVIERA	148
MONKS PLAYING BOWLS	149
PIFFERARI	151
THE LEANING TOWERS IN BOLOGNA	152
TOMB OF THEODORIC, RAVENNA	153
PONTE VECCHIO	158
FOUNTAIN OF NEPTUNE IN THE PIAZZA DELLA SIGNORIA	159
PALAZZO PITTI	161
LOGGIA NEAR MERCATO NUOVO	163
FOUNTAIN OF THE PORCELLINO IN THE MERCATO NUOVO	167
IN FRONT OF THE LOGGIA DE' LANZI	169
COURTYARD OF THE BARGELLO	171
BRONZE FOUNTAIN IN THE PIAZZA DELLA SANTISSIMA ANNUNZIATA	173
VIEW FROM THE BOBOLI GARDENS	174
FOUNTAIN IN THE BOBOLI GARDENS	175
VIEW IN THE VAL D'ARNO	179
SAN MINIATO AL MONTE	180
COLOSSAL STATUE OF THE APENNINE IN THE PARK AT PRATOLINO	181
STREET LIFE IN PISA	183
PIAZZA DEL DUOMO	185
TAVERN NEAR SAN FREDIANO, LUCCA	186
CHURCH OF SAN DOMENICO	187
ST. GALGANO NEAR CHIUSDINO	188
CONFIRMATION IN THE CATHEDRAL OF SIENA	189
PORTA AUGUSTA, PERUGIA	193
INTERIOR OF AN ETRUSCAN TOMB NEAR PERUGIA	197
ASSISI	199
DEPARTURE FOR THE MOUNTAINS	200
CATHEDRAL OF ANCONA	201
SAN MARINO	202
AQUEDUCT OF SPOLETO	203
PRELATE FUGGER'S TOMBSTONE	206
ETRUSCAN ROCK-TOMBS AT CASTEL D'ASSO, NEAR VITERBO	208
THE GREAT FOUNTAIN IN VITERBO	209
HOUSE IN VITERBO	210

	PAGE
LAKE OF NEMI	217
ROMAN FORUM	219
WELL NEAR ARICCIA	221
SANTA CROCE IN GERUSALEMME, AND NERO'S AQUEDUCT	222
PORTA FURBA, IN THE ROMAN CAMPAGNA	223
CIVITA LAVIGNA	224
WELL BENEATH OLIVE TREES NEAR TIVOLI	225
CASCADES AT TIVOLI	226
OLD TREES IN THE VILLA D'ESTE	227
ROMAN GIRL	230
IN THE VILLA BORGHESE	231
SEGGIOLA DEL DIAVOLO IN THE ROMAN CAMPAGNA	233
VILLA LANTE ON THE JANICULUM	234
COURTSHIP	235
IN VILLA MASSIMO	237
CHURCHYARD AT MONTE SERRONE	239
STELLA, A ROMAN MODEL	241
PEASANT OF THE CAMPAGNA	242
WOMAN OF TRASTEVERE	243
SEMINARIST	244
ROMAN MODEL	245
TEMPLE OF MINERVA IN THE FORUM OF NERVA	247
SCENE IN THE RUINS OF THE TEMPLE OF VESPASIAN	249
THE PANTHEON	251
ARCH OF TITUS	252
A GROUP OF HOUSES IN THE GHETTO	254
ENTRANCE TO THE GHETTO	255
OLD JEWESS	257
THE CONFESSIONAL	259
CLAUDIAN AQUEDUCT IN THE VILLA WOLKONSKY	262
VIA APPIA	264
GAME OF MORA	267
ON THE CAMPAGNA	268
CYPRESSES BY THE WELL OF MICHAEL ANGELO	269
WOOD AND GROTTO OF EGERIA IN THE CAMPAGNA	271
THE PONTE NOMENTANO	273
VIA APPIA	275
SCALA SANTA	277
BROCCOLI-SELLERS IN TRASTEVERE	278
PEASANTS IN THE ROMAN CAMPAGNA	281
VELLETRI	282
VALMONTONE	283
CASTLE OF PALO	285
HERDSMAN IN THE CAMPAGNA	286
THE SHEPHERD'S RETURN HOME	287
OSTIA	289
CIVITA CASTELLANA	290
BRACCIANO	291
SHEPHERD OF THE CAMPAGNA	293
MIDDAY IN POUSSIN'S VALLEY	295
GOATHERD	298
CECCANO	299
CELANO, ON LAGO FUCINO	301
CIVITELLA	304

ILLUSTRATIONS IN THE TEXT.

	PAGE		PAGE
CYCLOPEAN WALLS NEAR ALBA FUCENSE	305	ON THE SHORE BY CUMÆ	393
CAPISTRELLO, IN THE VALLEY OF THE LIRIS	307	TEMPLE OF VENUS NEAR BAIÆ	395
ARPINO	309	LAGO DI FUSARO NEAR BAIÆ	398
THE ITALIAN FAMILY UMBRELLA	311	IN THE STREET OF TOMBS, POMPEII	400
VILLA FALCONIERI, NEAR FRASCATI	312	TEMPLE OF NEPTUNE AT PÆSTUM	401
GENAZZANO	313	ON THE SHORE AT BAIÆ	405
TEMPLE OF THE SIBYL, TIVOLI	316	ROAD NEAR MASSA. VIEW OF CAPRI	407
TIVOLI	317	GORGE NEAR SORRENTO	409
ROMAN BEGGAR CHILD	319	TASSO'S HOUSE, SORRENTO	410
ROMAN PEASANTS	321	RAVELLO	411
MARINO ON THE LAKE ALBANO	323	SALERNO	412
GENZANO ON THE LAKE OF NEMI	325	ISCHIA	415
VIEW OF CASTEL GANDOLFO FROM THE VILLA DORIA	326	POZZUOLI, WITH CAPE MISENUM AND THE ISLANDS	
NINFA, WITH NORMA	327	OF PROCIDA AND ISCHIA	417
LA MAMELLE, NEAR CIVITELLA	329	AT THE WELL	418
GIRL OF THE SABINE HILLS	330	COURTYARD IN ISCHIA	419
BOY OF THE SABINE HILLS	331	OLD "SCALINATA" IN CAPRI	421
SUBIACO	333	NATURAL ARCHWAY	424
CHARACTERISTIC HEAD FROM THE SABINE HILLS	334	MARINA, CAPRI	425
ROAD FROM CAVI TO GENAZZANO	335	ROCK OF TIBERIUS, WITH THE JUPITER VILLA, CAPRI	427
SAN GERMANO AND MONTE CASSINO	337	A TOILET IN CAPRI	429
PEASANTS OF SORA.—SUNDAY REST	338	MONTE VERGINE	431
PEASANTS OF SORA PREPARING POLENTA	339	MILL NEAR ARIANO	433
THE SERPENTARA NEAR OLEVANO	341	PETRA ROSETE, ON THE CALORE NEAR BENEVENTO	435
BOY OF THE ABRUZZI	344	RUINS OF THE ABBEY OF THE HOLY TRINITY,	
GIRL OF THE ABRUZZI	345	VENOSA	436
ALBA	347	CATACOMBS OF SIPONTO, NEAR MANFREDONIA	437
STREET SCENE IN THE ABRUZZI	349	STREET IN MONTE SANT' ANGELO	438
GRAN SASSO D'ITALIA	352	JEWISH CATACOMBS NEAR VENOSA	439
VIGNETTE	354	CANOSA ANTICA	440
GIRL OF THE MOUNTAINS NEAR SALERNO	355	LAKES OF MONTICCHIO	441
FOUNTAIN IN THE VILLA REALE, NAPLES	357	TAVOLA DE' PALADINI	442
FISHERMAN OF GAETA	358	ON THE BUSENTO NEAR COSENZA	443
THE BAY OF NAPLES FROM CAMALDOLI	359	REGGIO CALABRO	444
NEAPOLITAN FISHER-GIRL	360	FISHERMAN'S COTTAGE	445
ON AN ERRAND	365	STRAITS OF MESSINA	448
GROTTO OF POSILIPPO	367	RUINS OF THE ANCIENT THEATRE AT SYRACUSE	449
OYSTER-BEDS AT SANTA LUCIA	370	SHIPPING OFF CAPTIVE BRIGANDS	451
ZAMPOGNARO	371	THE ROADSTEAD, NEAR LICATA	454
ON THE MOLE, NAPLES	374	NEAR ALCAMO	455
GIPSY TINKERS IN NAPLES	375	LATOMIE DEL PARADISO, NEAR SYRACUSE	457
THE CUSTOM-HOUSE DOCK, NAPLES	377	RUINS OF THE TEMPLE OF HERCULES, NEAR GIR-	
SANTA MARIA IN PORTICO, NAPLES	379	GENTI	459
IN FRONT OF A BAKER'S OVEN IN NAPLES	381	CONVENT OF SAN MARTINO, NEAR PALERMO	460
POMPEII	385	CATHEDRAL OF PALERMO	461
DRAW-WELL AT THE FOOT OF VESUVIUS	387	PALAZZO CORVAJA, IN TAORMINA	464
IN THE HARBOUR OF PORTICI	390	EVERGREEN OAKS, NEAR SCIACCA	465
EVENING IN THE STREET OF TOMBS, POMPEII	392	ON THE ROAD FROM MESSINA TO TAORMINA	467

Oh land of Beauty, garlanded with pine
 And luscious grape-vines, 'neath whose
   vaulted skies
Of blue eternal, marble mansions rise,
And roseate flowers from every lattice shine,
Still have the Nations striven from of yore
For thy fair fields, lovely as Eden's plain;
Thy temples; and thy cities by the main
Throned hoar and grey upon the rocky shore.
Who hath seen thee,—oh never in his breast
The heart grows wholly old! Some youthful
   zest
Of life still lingers; some bright memory!
And when the nightingales in Autumn chill
Fly forth, a yearning stirs his spirit still
To fly with them toward sunny Italy!

FROM THE ALPS TO THE ARNO.

BY

KARL STIELER.

ITALY.

THE GREAT ROADS TO ITALY.

THROUGH THE MONT CENIS.

ITALY has been called the Land of Wonders; but even the very ways into Italy have something of wonder about them—a kind of enchantment which no other roads or paths can pretend to. The road to Italy seizes powerfully on our imagination as we wend on our pilgrimage towards that great goal, and impresses us before we know the land to which it leads.

As far back as historic records reach, Italy has always been the Paradise of the earth. It almost seems as though nature herself were desirous to screen and protect this sanctuary of her beauties, for on three sides she has protected it by the sea, and to the north has built up a gigantic wall. But this barrier has been stormed by the passion of almost all nations, and the historic foot-prints which they have left behind them are these mighty Alpine roads! In this lies their grandeur and their charm : they were not constructed by this or that powerful individual, but the longing, the envy, the vengefulness, of whole nations, have traced these paths. Italy was the soul of the world, and all were wooing her; she was the focus of all ancient culture, and this focus each nation desired to possess as its own. To speak without metaphor, the various incursions into Italy have been the result of great historic tides, or mighty passions, and the traces of these great movements remain in the colossal construction of the Alpine roads.

One of the most ancient and mighty of these is the Mont Cenis, *Mons Cinerum*. According to the legend, it derives its name from the fact that thousands of years ago the woods which covered it were burnt to ashes. Let us place ourselves in the narrow mountain-walled gorge. We are among the Cottian Alps. The peaks of Cima del Caro, La Levanna, Monginevro, and Gran Paradiso, rise before us, and in the midst of them is the solemn, world-famed, Mont Cenis. It forms the point at which the Graian and Cottian Alps meet. Here lies the barren, long-drawn plateau over which led the ancient military road from France to Italy. High above the pass rise jagged peaks of rock, almost always veiled in grey clouds, almost always covered with deep snow : Rocciamelone, and La Rouche, and others. They rise to an altitude of eleven thousand feet, the height of the plateau itself being seven thousand five hundred feet.

Cardinal Bentivoglio, writing his memoirs in Venice in the year 1648, speaks of the Mont Cenis as the King of the Alps, and in truth there is something majestic in these titanic outlines, these gloomy features, in the brooding solitude, through which we are passing. Between the rocks spreads a thicket of luxuriant shrubs, interspersed here and there by a slender birch tree; glowing Alpine roses peep through the dark green, and in the clefts blooms the fragrant *Viola cenisia*, but it blooms only to fade unseen. No human eye meets ours on this pilgrimage; we hear only the fluttering of the ptarmigan in its flight, or the shrill whistle of the marmot; and when the air is still we can hear great stones fall, loosened from the rocks above. We can see the eagle tracing his airy circles; but these are all the signs of life we encounter. All else is dead.

Hard by the road lies the dark little lake, from whose depths the Cenisia rises. During seven months of the year the lake is covered with thick grey ice. But even when the tardy spring loosens these bonds, when the trout once more rises towards the sunlight, still there remains something sinister in the aspect of the scene, like the feeling of an eternal prison. Nor are the dumb waters the only prisoners here; for on the eastern shore of the lake, amidst this barren solitude, stands the little hospice founded in the time of the Carlovingians, and restored by that Bonaparte who loved to call himself the successor of Charlemagne. He established barracks here for thousands of soldiers, and we feel oppressed as we conjure up in fancy the procession of those long columns: the weary, ragged guard, laden horses, and rolling artillery. Here they may rest an hour before descending on the battle fields of Italy: here draw breath before the final words, "*Ave, Cæsar, morituri te salutant.*"

Only a few squalid buildings exist here close to the hospice. There are no other inhabitants except the men charged with the maintenance of the road. Six-and-twenty houses have been erected at the most dangerous points of the road, the use of which is to provide a shelter for wanderers overtaken by the snow. The watchmen pass their lives in combating danger for themselves and others; for fearful storms rage here when the winds from Lombardy and Savoy meet, and rush together like two howling wolves.

Such is the landscape of the Mont Cenis: we have endeavoured to sketch it in slight outline. And yet what memories of great deeds hang round that dreary stony spot! Of what antiquity is the first track across these heights,—from the days of Hannibal and Constantine, of Charlemagne and the journey to Canossa! We possess a description of the latter by Padre Bresciani, and our blood boils as often as we read it.

When the excommunication was pronounced against Henry the Fourth, and the princes in Tribur had resolved to drive him from the imperial throne if he were not absolved before the spring, the young man of twenty-six years—once so proud—rose up and set out on his pilgrimage, accompanied only by his noble wife, his child, and a few faithful followers. They passed through Burgundy to Geneva, and thence across the Alps to the Comté of Maurienne. It was near Christmas time, and the winter was so severe that the vines were frozen even to their roots, and the Rhine was covered with ice during four months. The particulars of this journey are calculated to make one's hair stand on end. The Emperor offered thousands for a guide to accompany him across the mountain; but not a man could be found to accept the task. All declared the thing to be an impossibility. And yet Henry's throne and life depended on its accomplishment. Outlawed and poor as the wretchedest man in his dominions, the Emperor climbed the rocks of the Mont Cenis. The sumpter mules, which had been furnished him by his relative, Count William, in Besançon, were mostly lost by falling over the precipice long before the travellers reached the summit. They endeavoured to proceed on little sledges made of pine boughs lashed together, but in a short time this mode of conveyance became impracticable. Then Bertha and Conrad, the little Imperial prince, were strongly stitched into huge furs and skins, which were now pulled onward, now held back, by means of two ropes attached to them. Henry walked by their side in ragged garments, with bleeding feet and a bleeding heart!

From the close of the seventeenth century, the Mont Cenis really belonged to the French: at least in every historic sense. In all the bitter struggles that they waged with the House of Savoy, in all wars whose goal and object lay in the south, Mont Cenis was their natural highway. Up to that period it had seemed to be desired that the road should be kept almost secret, and so narrow as to be scarcely practicable for a beast of burthen. But now the object was precisely opposite. Already in 1693 Marshal Catinat had widened it sufficiently to admit the passage of small vehicles and the lighter kind of artillery. But the first who transformed it into a modern military road on a grand scale, was Napoleon, whose engineer was the ingenious Giovanni Fabrane.

The history of the origin, and carrying out of the gigantic work of the Mont Cenis tunnel, is singularly remarkable. It has, like all great works in the world, its tragic

ROAD OVER THE MONT CENIS.

story; nay, this colossal idea has even had its martyr, who sacrificed his whole life to it without ever being understood. This man was the engineer Joseph Medail, of Bardonèche, who already in the year 1832 laid before King Charles Albert a plan for the piercing of the Cottian Alps, almost identical with the one at present adopted. The plan was admired, as one admires and wonders at something entirely out of one's reach, but no one dreamt of carrying it into execution. But the courageous son of the Alps was not yet daunted. Ten years later he laid his project before the Chamber of Commerce at Chambéry; it was examined, and there also was deemed in the highest degree ingenious, but its lot was the same as before; no one dreamt of carrying it into execution. Medail died long before the great conception of his life was fulfilled. He left it as a legacy to posterity.

It was long ere the fulfilment came; but at length, under the direction of the engineers Grattoni, Grandis, and Sommeiller, the tunnel was completed after nine years' labour, and on the 17th of September, 1871, the line was publicly opened for traffic; a new pledge of union between the nations of Europe.

It was about the beginning of October when I began the journey through the Mont Cenis. Nature begins to assume a sterner, more rugged aspect as soon as we leave the south of France and enter Savoy. The mountains take bolder forms and rise to loftier heights. Instead of the soft golden colouring of the Provençal landscape, we find deeper and more sombre tones. Firwoods crown the heights, and mountain streams pour themselves down in cool crystalline floods. Isolated huts of dark brown bark, stand by the wayside here and there; rarely we came to a weather-stained village, more rarely to a patch of shady woodland, and tinkling herds of cattle. We are in the real bold mountain-world; the old hunting-ground of the hardy Piedmontese. Still narrower, and more shut in grows the picture, the farther we travel. Mere straitened footpaths lead to the side valleys which seem to open and shut again as we fly past. The struggle of man's handiwork against the forces of Nature is already visible in a hundred tokens. Closer and wilder press the mountains around us, until the road is walled on either hand by colossal rocks. It is not possible to proceed further! The locomotive whistles shrilly, the iron wheels jar and creak: this is Modane, the last station just at the foot of the Mont Cenis.

Here the train halts for nearly an hour. Out of the wide opened doors of the first-class carriages pours a stream of people of many nations, Italians and Frenchmen, Englishmen and Russians, all costumes, all tongues, mixed confusedly together! As the real frontier is in the middle of the tunnel, the custom-house examination takes place here. We are motioned with courteous wavings of the hand to enter the hall, and open our trunks. "*Prenez garde!*" shout the porters as they push trucks full of luggage into the *Douane*. "*Sangue di Cristo!*" swears an Italian who has lost his wife in the crowd. A prima donna on the way to the Scala at Milan has nineteen huge trunks, and her luggage is the last to be examined!

Modane lies in a rocky basin, barely an hour's walk in circumference. Dry torrents of rubble—the *talus* of the mountain—descend to the very edge of the rails, and while it is yet early in the afternoon, the mountains cast their blue shadows down into the valley. Here is the entrance into the Mont Cenis. In this wilderness now stands the big railway station which forms the dividing point between France and Italy. Instead of the French train which has carried us thus far, an Italian one is now drawn up in front of the platform: the carriages are painted a dark colour outside, and lined with light-coloured cushions, and each compartment carries eight passengers. The lamps were already lighted; the workmen gave a last tap to an axle here and there; the second locomotive that was to help us on our way, came puffing up; one jerk, and we were off!

We were all now in a state of feverish excitement, and the more so as we were unable to discern the object of the general curiosity, for the entrance into the world-renowned tunnel lies about two hundred feet sheer above the station, and the line makes two huge curves before reaching it. The gradient is something really tremendous. The locomotive no longer rolls smoothly onward, but absolutely climbs upward, seeming to fight its way foot by foot, and soon we look down on the grey shingle roofs of Modane lying far below us. The engine gives a loud yell, like the cry of a man suddenly hurled down into the darkness; the steam twists and writhes low down on the ground; a moment's dim twilight, and then utter blackness.

We were really rolling through the Mont Cenis tunnel, and most of us experienced a strange sensation. It was not fear, but an awe-stricken sense of being so delivered over to the powers of Nature, that no human hand could help us should any accident occur during those dark miles. We feel that we are removed out of the reach of aid. Any stone in the vault above us might be lord of our lives. And Nature sometimes is vindictive! We opened the windows. A warm damp air, which oppressed the respiration, poured in. It was impossible, on looking out, to see either the walls of the tunnel or the next carriage, so tremendous was the darkness; we could perceive only the vaporous masses of smoke as they glided past the lighted windows. There was something weird and almost diabolic in these formless apparitions, which now were gliding under the wheels, now rising to the roof, ever melting away and being reproduced. The noise of the engine became terrible. We were conscious, as it were, of the Herculean labour that it was performing; we heard it pant and groan; for there is an ascent of more than four hundred feet within the tunnel! Sometimes it seemed almost as if the locomotive would come to a standstill, as if it had no more strength left in it. Then came a great impetus and the labour began again. I looked at my watch. We had been but ten minutes in this dungeon; barely a third of the whole way had been traversed.

Since there was no outlook possible, I turned my glance inward: that is to say not into my own soul, but into the interior of our compartment, and examined a little more attentively the neighbours whom fate had given us. The ladies who sat opposite to us held a handkerchief over their eyes and coughed. They did not wish it to be perceived that they were crying—so greatly did this Tartarus affect their spirits. Some Frenchmen seized on the situation with the utmost liveliness; they were all eye and ear, and recounted all manner of details. They naturally looked upon the Mont Cenis tunnel as their own peculiar work, and felt themselves bound to do the honours in the railway carriage. Another ten minutes passed by, the air became still more sultry and oppressive, it was impossible to read or sleep, yet we felt that the highest point of the tunnel had been reached; for suddenly the way beneath us changed,—it became level,—it sank. Then the locomotive began to rush onward with frantic speed, as though it were resolved to make up for lost time. The tiny stations—or niches rather—in the interior of the tunnel, appeared like so many will-o'-the-wisps; for the signalmen stood there with dazzling lanterns in their hands to certify that they were at their posts. As to seeing the men themselves, that was quite out of the question. Involuntarily the thought suggested itself, "If a collision were to take place here! If we were to run off the rails!" So far as I know, the Mont Cenis has hitherto been exempt from serious accidents, Only once, on the 24th of May, 1873, it is said that two trains entered the tunnel at the same time, coming in opposite directions. But by a timely application of the break, they were stopped, and remained motionless fronting each other. Whether this really happened as described, I was not able to learn on official authority, and therefore I can but rely on the assertion of the travelling companion who narrated it. My only doubt of his veracity is occasioned by the circumstance that he continually declared " I was present. I saw it myself!"

Nevertheless the narration did not fail to produce an effect. The Frenchmen handed about a little bottle of ether. Thirty-one minutes had elapsed, and already we began to have a far-off glimmering of the twilight which heralded the end of our captivity. The locomotive rushed on towards the opening like a wild beast seeking its freedom. As on shipboard one hears the cry "Land, land!" so now on every countenance was written "Light, light!" We were in the open air once more, the sunshine poured its full rays over the mountain peaks, green fir trees and slender birches were seen, we heard the torrents dashing down the rocks, everything was living around us! Over the station were displayed the arms of Italy. "*Bardonecchia!*" shouted the guard. "*Cinque minuti di fermata!*" And now we looked back upon the vast stone portal which forms the entrance to the tunnel;—upon this fortress of the human intellect. We saw the whole mountain range, through whose entrails we had passed, with the white cross still standing on the summit; the white cross which marked the point at which the workmen from the two sides of the mountain were to meet at its centre underground.

In truth it was not merely the sensation of being once more free which expanded our breasts at that moment, it was also a feeling of pride and satisfaction that we lived in days when such a work was possible. It may be called a miracle; but it is a miracle wrought by our own hands, and not by invisible powers.

THE VIA MALA.

WHICH of us has not seen some being whose beauty enchants us, and yet in whom a strain of evil is found that strikes us as diabolical? Nature, too, has such shapes, and some of them she has placed as sentinels between the lands of the Teuton and the Italian. Even in the name some demoniac suggestion arises, every time we utter the words "*Via Mala.*"

The Via Mala is the finest portion of the Splügen Pass: the Alpine road that leads from Coire to Chiavenna, and although certain resemblances to the St. Gothard may be found in it, yet this pass has its own different glories. As on the St. Gothard the Reuss, here it is the Rhine whose course we follow. But it is not yet that broad Rhine in whose flood minsters are mirrored, for whose shores nations contend, but the wild child of the mountains dashing through the narrow gorge, recking nothing of the world in its solitude! No other river presents so striking a contrast between the wildness of its youth, and the dignity of its later time; and the Lake of Constance forms the mysterious alembic in which the transformation is effected. On leaving the Lake, and after taking one bold leap, the Rhine belongs to serious and active life; but all that it leaves behind it in the mountains bears the impress of childhood's untamed glee.

As we follow the ascent of the road, we meet with records of the great old Alpine passes. In the village of Felsberg we see the traces of a vast landslip. In Oberems are memories of the terrific combats by means of which the " Tricolours " forced their way

VIA MALA. "LE TROU PERDU."

here. On a steep height stands the castle of Rhäzüns; and at Reichenau, a few miles further down the valley, at the spot where the "Hinter" and the "Vorder" Rhine meet, there is the residence of the Planta family. In the last-named château two pictures are shown, which a former tutor sent thither as a souvenir of himself. The old folks in the village speak of him to this day as Monsieur Chabaud: history calls him Louis Philippe the Citizen King.

It is not long before we enter into a beautiful sunny valley, called in the Romansch dialect Val Domgiasca. It lies considerably below the true mountain region, and is protected from rough winds by forests, and from flood by huge dams; so that a rich vegetation is enabled to flourish here. Numerous castles, and many villages whose houses climb the slopes, enliven the scene, on which the lofty snow-crowned Piz Beverin looks down. All around the mountains are richly wooded, and the air we breathe is full of the odours of the pine. But often enough there has been wild work in these woodlands; for during the Thirty Years War feuds arose here; men, and even boys, flew to arms, and many of the foreign rulers lay gasping in their blood.

As is the case with most of the Alpine passes, the history of this road goes back to a remote antiquity; and that portion of it as far as Thusis, is peculiarly rich in traditions. The noble monastery at Katzis was founded in the time of the Merovingians by (it is said) the *wife* of a bishop of Coire! But the fortress of Hohenrhätien, which overhangs the Rhine at a dizzy altitude, and whose ruins still declare its ancient might, is attributed to the sixth century before Christ. The Tuscian Prince Rhætus is supposed to have been its builder, and the town of Thusis is said to derive its name from the same ancient nation.

One may look upon the rock on which this fortress is built, and the corresponding one opposite to it, as forming together the colossal portal of the Via Mala which begins here. For immediately behind Thusis, which lies a bright smiling village in the valley, the landscape begins to become more sombre, and narrow; its stony limbs are contracted, all fresh bloom disappears, the rocks are grey of hue, and as a stream of words breaks from an overcharged soul, so break the waters of the Rhine from their stony prison,—foaming, raving, irresistible! All that usually makes a landscape attractive, is lacking here. The rocks seem to grow before our eyes, as a man's form dilates in anger. Only the naked passion of one of Nature's wrathful moods, stares full upon us. It is the wicked, demoniacal trait in the beautiful aspect of the Splügen, which now strikes us.

But the spirit of Man was not cowed, he dared to affront even this wrathful mood of Nature,—and he conquered it. It is now just four hundred years since the first road was made through these rocks; a road not more than four feet wide, however. Previous to that there was only a wild footpath across the Alpine pastures. Then in the fortieth year of the last century some stone bridges were begun, and still much later was the tunnel blasted, which now bears the name of the "*Trou Perdu*." On the hottest summer days the stones here drip chill drops upon one: and the dampness and the darkness seem to repel one despite oneself. The landscape still wears a gigantic character; the rocks on either side rise to the height of two thousand feet, and are divided by a space of little more than thirty feet in width, and, in precipitous depths below, the stream foams past. One shudders to behold the bridges thrown across this chasm, and boldly spanning it backwards and forwards, until after a long wandering we reach the end of the Via Mala. The fit of rage has spent itself, Nature grows milder before our eyes, a gentle breath seems to soften her aspect which glared on us before like to a stony Medusa, and life and laughter revive again. Only a few paces more and we find ourselves in the sweetest valley that can be imagined, amid a whole Idyll of green meadows, and dark woods, interspersed with Alpine huts; whilst the Rhine flows by, crystal clear, with a gentle murmur.

The name of this valley is Schams. It is hard to believe that its inhabitants have ever exchanged their peaceful shepherd-life for the clash of arms; and yet even this plot of earth has been the theatre of bloody strife. For the lords of Bärenburg who ruled over the valley of Schams, were so stern and cruel as to remind us of Gessler; they trampled down the property and the liberties of the people, and many traditions are alive to this day, which give some idea of this tyranny; for example, that of the peasant Johannes Caldar:—his feudal lord entered his poor cottage one day, and in brutal scorn, spat into the cauldron where the mess of soup for the poor people's dinner was being prepared. The outraged peasant seized the arrogant miscreant by the throat, and shouting, "Eat thyself, what thou hast seasoned!" held him down with an iron grasp in the seething liquor, until he was choked to death.

Under Hans von Rechberg, and Heinrich von Rhäzüns, the troopers of the allied nobles, pressed onward towards the valley of Schams; it having been given out that a great hunting expedition was in progress, in order to deceive the peasants. In an ever narrowing circle the enemy surrounded the valley, until at length some herdsmen, on their way to the mountains in the early glimmering dawn, perceived the threatening peril. Swift action was now needful. Breathlessly, unrestingly, hastened the messengers by secret paths to Rheinwald, and the neighbouring valleys, and soon came well-armed allies to the rescue; nor rested until the troops of the tyrants had succumbed to their blows, and the fortresses had been reduced by famine. One of the leading nobles, Heinrich von Rhäzüns, was condemned to death, and as he showed signs of terror at sight of the sword of justice, the executioner reassured him (!) by splitting a hair at one stroke. Nevertheless the noble's life was after all spared, on the intercession of an old servant of his!

What we have here narrated happened some four hundred years ago; but traces of the same sturdy antique spirit may be met with to this day in Zillis, Fardün, and Andeer.

If we consider the plastic formation of the Splügen road, it presents itself to us in a series of terrace-like steps. The Val Domgiasca is situated on the first step, and is separated from the valley of Schams by the rocky portal of the Via Mala; which represents the next step, and this in turn is divided from the topmost step, the Rheinwald Thal, by the stony walls of the gorge of Rofila. Above these lies the village of Splügen, and the summit of the pass: some seven thousand feet above the level of the sea. Of course, the vegetation is not so rich here, as in the two lower valleys; but a full and healthy life breathes all around us. The blue blossoms of the flax stand in the meadows, the rye grown here ripens only in the late autumn; but man lives at peace with nature, and his labour brings a blessing. The enormous traffic at Splügen (for here the roads to Bellinzona and Chiavenna divide) give this pass a great air of animation.

Martinurè (1740) states that there is a small lakelet on the Splügen, deep among the mountains between Rheinwald and Schams, which he calls Calandari. It is only a stone's throw wide, but of depth unfathomable. The legend of the lake recounts that it has the magic power to draw into its depths all creatures that approach it. A young woman who had lost her way, and, overcome by fatigue, lay down to sleep upon its shore, disappeared altogether and left no trace behind; but four miles away, her girdle and her keys were found. The Rhine had cast them up upon its banks. And when some daring youth once drove seven horses into the lake, although the animals were restored living to land (after three hours) yet every beast had lost the iron shoes from its feet.

Now the post carriage descends at a rapid trot past the Lira, and the foaming cataract of the Madesimo, through vast galleries which protect the road from avalanches, and at length a long distance below Campo Dolcino, we perceive the fine old town crowned with southern gardens; the old town with its defiant walls, and its defiant name:—Chiavenna. The word is derived from *clavis*. It is the *key* to that rugged pass, and the key to the golden treasures of Italy.

ACROSS THE ST. GOTHARD.

LADEN with a light knapsack we step along the high road which begins at the southern shore of the Lake of the Four Cantons. We pass onward through the streets of Fluelen and Altdorf, where the charm of ancient legends still lingers; here Tell fitted his arrow in his bow; the waves that flow beside our path and break against the rocks of the Rütli yonder, have borne his skiff upon their bosom; we see the great monument to him which rises high above the market-place at Altdorf. No matter that the learned have banished his figure from history, we believe them not. In the hearts of the people, it will live for ever!

As soon as we have left the last houses of Altdorf behind us (the town was devastated by a fearful fire in 1799), when the last passer-by in his old-fashioned costume, has disappeared, the scene grows wild and solitary. The road begins to mount very soon. We are on the old world-famous St. Gothard Pass. Our eyes no longer stray across dark roofs to blue waters; right and left the rocks press hard upon the road, and straight ahead rises the mighty Bristenstock, as though he would bar our further passage. The Reuss dashes on its way foaming through the narrow gorge. But we are not yet fully in the wilderness; for where the narrow valley widens out a little, green meadows and neat villages are spread, shaded by limes and maples, or hidden amongst gigantic walnut trees. Heavily laden waggons stand to rest before the doors; playing children, and gossiping groups seated on the stone doorsteps, are the figures which animate this Idyll. From beneath the brown eaves, a maiden peeps forth and listens to what they are saying down there about her sweetheart. We have wandered thus through Amsteg and Inschi, through Wasen and Göschenen. Foaming waterfalls scatter their spray on to the road; great larches that have been carried down by an avalanche and cling with tough roots to the lower soil overhang us on the rocks; in their shadow grow broad dock-leaves and low bushy shrubs; all plants produced by culture become rarer and rarer, and finally disappear. Already at Wasen the finer sorts of foliage have died out. Only a few straggling cherry-trees surmount the slopes, and the last yellow fields wave in the sunshine. In the tiny gardens surrounded by fences of heavy stone, the rough tall hemp grows, and a few poor flowers, scarcely sufficing to deck a shrine, or the grave-stone of a parent, or to make up a nosegay for a lover's hand. Beyond Göschenen the scenery grows bolder, and here a gloomy valley opens on our right. It is no longer a landscape: it is a chaos of grey, splintered fragments, with the white dazzling glacier of the Galenstock high above us. It seems to have attracted every ray of light towards itself and to glare down

THE DEVIL'S BRIDGE.

threateningly into the dreary waste at its foot. The slight grasses which grow between the loose stones, tremble softly in the wind. Other movement there is none. A sort of dread seizes on us as we advance into this wilderness, and see how all life disappears, how the rocks press closer, and feel a twilight chill around us. No wonder that the legend tells us the bridge which crosses yon dizzy chasm was the work of the Fiend. The road turns a sharp rocky angle; the thundering voice of falling waters sounds in our ears as though it cried "Halt!" And in the next instant we stand before the Devil's Bridge.

This is the culminating point of the famous road. Not absolutely the highest as regards the level above the sea, but the highest in respect of man's skill and daring. It is truly a wonderful work; especially when one considers that a path has been carried over this abyss for centuries back. The spot is striking and remarkable in the highest degree. The Reuss has absolutely forced its way through masses of granite. The narrowness of the channel increases the raging fury of the waters, and this channel appears merely like a deep slit in the steep ascent of the St. Gothard. Who could dare to bridge it over? The tradition runs that when the inhabitants of the Ursener Thal were asking themselves and each other this important question, the Devil appeared to them, and promised to build their bridge, on condition that the soul of the first living being who crossed it, should be devoted to him. The cunning men of the Ursener Thal accepted the condition: but no sooner was the bridge completed than they sent a dog across it, and the animal was instantly torn to pieces. So enraged was his sable Majesty at being thus cheated, that he seized vast blocks of granite from the mountain with the intention of hurling them down and destroying his own work. But even here, the *Urseners* were too many for him. Just as he was in the act to throw they shouted a hearty "God bless you!" in his face, and the Fiend let the stones fall aimless from his hand. One of them, called to this day the *Teufels-stein* (Devil's stone), rolled down the valley as far as Göschenen, and lies by the side of the road there. This old original devil's bridge, the subject of the legend, is still perfectly visible; it stands in a partially ruined condition beneath the bold arch which now carries the road across the ravine.

One might stand here for hours gazing down into the gulf upon the foaming waters, which now rear themselves up threateningly from the yeasty whirl, now plunge deep down into the bed of the river. With what a restless eager, *resentful* tone, they rave and mutter! But centuries and generations pass above them one after another, and understand nothing of what they say. This wilderness enjoys but a few bright moments daily, when the rays of the sun shine over the mountain wall, and reach the stream; then a thousand glittering drops appear, tinted with rainbow hues; then the noise of the flood becomes a rejoicing song, and it scatters its silvery spray high in the air. But soon again comes the shadow; the moss on the old ruined bridge becomes blackish-green once more; the spray of the waterfall, which was gilded but for a few brief moments, grows grey and cold, and drenches us with its fine, invisible particles. How swiftly the shadow deepens into night! How swiftly the year deepens into winter! The pallid moon illuminates the snow-covered bridge with uncertain rays. A train of smugglers passes noiselessly along the road, with loaded guns and blackened faces; they search slowly about for the railings at the edge of the precipice, which the storm has blown down, and lead their trembling beasts by the bridle; the frost has made the road slippery and split the masonry; they listen, they grope,—the foremost man falls into the torrent! That is an appropriate crossing of the Devil's Bridge.

In the year 1799, when the French, Russians, and Austrians, fought at this spot, the old bridge was partially blown up, and, though it has been said that the soldiers of Suwarrow crossed the yawning chasm upon rotten beams of timber hastily laid across it, the fact is the ancient arch is not only extant but perfectly passable. The new bridge was constructed between the years 1828-1830; its span is shorter than that of the old one; and it crosses the torrent at an altitude of ninety-five feet above it.

Soon after the Devil's Bridge comes the "*Urner-Loch*," (literally the Uri Hole). Here again has man made his way *vi et armis* through barriers which Nature opposed to him: as he has bridged the abyss yonder, so here he has broken through the rocks,— and rocks of the hardest granite. Before that, there was merely a wooden gallery hanging by chains to the surface of the steep cliff. The man who undertook to pierce the rock was one Pietro Moretini, of Locarno, who began the daring work in 1707, and completed it in eleven months. To be sure it was narrower and lower than it is now, (the road through the tunnel at the present day measures more than sixteen feet in width,) but, nevertheless, it was nearly two hundred feet long; and everywhere, in those days, people were talking of the wonderful tunnel that had cost fully eight thousand gulden! Who could have guessed that, a hundred and fifty years later, seventy-five millions of francs would be expended on piercing the Mont Cenis? Nay, that the hammer would be already sounding on the flanks of the St. Gothard! The Urner Loch forms not only a boundary for the road, but for the landscape. When we have passed with echoing footsteps under its dark vault and out into the free daylight again, we have a new scene before us; Andermatt (On-the-meadow) is the sunny name of the village on which we enter, and its name is a reality; a green carpet appears to be spread out before us, the Reuss, which we have just beheld raving and foaming, streams gently and silvery through the fields, the wild spectacle is changed to a smiling Idyll. This is the Ursener Thal whose wonderful contrast with the neighbouring wilderness Schiller has described in his "William Tell;" and which appeared so strange to its ancient inhabitants themselves, that they accounted for it by saying it had arisen out of the rocky deserts at a miraculous bidding of St. Colomb.

In pre-historic times there is no doubt that the Ursener Thal was a lake shut in by that granite rock which Moretini pierced. But at the time when that work was executed, the inhabitants of the valley, about four hundred in number, formed a little republic of herdsmen, who governed themselves freely and independently; a council chosen from the whole valley carried on the government; fifteen judges were appointed from among the inhabitants; and only on occasions of great importance did they descend into the lower lands to take counsel with the *Landrath* of Uri. But even then the ultimate decision rested with themselves; it was not until the beginning of this century that the little free state became subject to the authority of the Canton.

That which makes the scenery of the Ursener Thal so peculiar, is its absolute isolation. There is rich pasture-land, but no woodland, no luxuriant foliage; all the great mountains which surround these meadows are bare and dreary, only one dark, triangular patch of forest overhangs the village: it is the so-called "*Bann Wald*" which was, for generations, looked upon as especially sacred. It was forbidden on pain of death to cut down a tree here, inasmuch as these green walls formed the only protection of the village against avalanches; but during the wars of 1799, the axe pierced this forest for the first time, and the wounds made then, are visible to this day! Often, on digging deeply, blackened knots of wood are found, and colossal twisted roots; confirmations of the tradition which says that the original inhabitants set fire to the forests of the whole region, —either to gain more pasture-land, or to get rid of the numerous beasts of prey.

As soon as we have passed through the Ursener Thal, and left Hospenthal behind us, the landscape becomes wild and barren once more: it grows stony beneath our feet, it grows lifeless before our eyes; this is the last huge step of the heights of the St. Gothard. The road winds along in bold curves, and at length we find ourselves in front of the famous hospice. We have reached the summit of the pass, and yet, nevertheless, still higher peaks rise all around us; the Stella, and Monte Prosa, Fibia, and Fiento, close the prospect with their gigantic walls. The old hospice, which was already established, and served by Capuchins, in the thirteenth century, was destroyed by a terrific avalanche in 1777. In the present building something like ten thousand strangers are refreshed and sheltered during the year; no payment is taken, only a free gift, if it is proffered. The former stable, an octagon, around whose walls ran eight mangers, and whose roof was supported by a single pillar, was destroyed in the war at the beginning of the present century; Suwarrow's Cossacks threw its rafters into their camp-fires.

On the summits of the St. Gothard is the Lago Lucendro; a dark, shining sheet of

MAKING THE TUNNEL THROUGH THE ST. GOTHARD.

water, surrounded by icy, almost perpendicular, rocks; it reminds one of the Avernus of the ancients, at the entrance to Hades. From its depths the Reuss takes its source; and from one of the smaller neighbouring lakes rises the Ticino, which follows the road as far as Milan. But no matter how wild and rough the scene without, we sat snugly enough in the guest-room,—men who had never met before, and probably would never meet again, who had nothing in common save the passing minute, and the spot of earth on which the sole of their foot rested. Each had something to narrate: this one of the campaign of 1799, the other of the avalanches, which are especially frequent on the southern side of the mountain. As late as the summer of 1801, might still be seen, all along the route, the skeletons of horses and mules lying at the bottom of the precipice where they had been thrown because they were exhausted and because fodder was scarce. All around the Lago Lucendro, and the little lake of the Oberalp, the earth was strewn for many a long year with broken muskets, the butt-ends of pistols, and whitening bones; nay not unfrequently bullets were found of which it was easy to distinguish the Austrian from the French. Two great butt-ends of muskets did duty for oars in an old boat drawn up near the shore, and near it you might see a newly-made mound, surmounted by a splendid cross. So said an old man who sat with us at table. His beard was hoary, but his eyes sparkled when he spoke of these things; as a boy he had been an eye-witness of that bloody time. For a long period, during the Napoleonic times, you could hardly stop at an inn on the St. Gothard route without meeting with French officers; they lorded it over the company, and led the conversation, they prated of the wars of the great Emperor, of their vengeance against England, of their love-adventures in foreign lands. Thus our chat lasted deep into the night. When the talk slackened, we heard the wind beating against the windows:—that howling mountain-wind that tears the avalanches from the rocks, and overwhelms whole villages at one swoop. The most perilous spots are La Piota, St. Antonio, and the valleys of Tremola and Bedretto; in the latter place on the sixth of February, 1801, an avalanche fell upon Osacco, and crushed thirteen persons. Only in one house the beams of the roof fell so fortunately as to protect the dwelling from being utterly smashed: it was night, a mother and child were sleeping in the house, and it was three days before they were dug out of the ruins; both, however, eventually recovered.

At length we separated, each to his bed. How strange it seemed to be going to rest among sights and sounds so widely different from all our daily life had been accustomed to, and which seemed to have merely flitted past us dimly. I could see the climbing mules and the weary soldiers; I heard the thundering avalanche; but the thunder grew more distant, the words more confused, man and horse were veiled in a sort of mist, they seemed to stand still from utter weariness, and then—I fell asleep.

After such a night how glorious is the morning with its dewy brightness! It brought back the strength and the desire to pursue our wanderings. Now we were going downwards, southwards, to the land where the "citrons bloom;" now for the first time we realized that we were travelling to Italy: for on no other road does the heart beat with such longing for the goal. The road descends in sharp zig-zags through the Val Tremola, crossing numerous bridges on the way; the landscape grows richer, more animated; far beneath our feet yonder lies Airolo—lies Italy! Still, however, the temperate strength of the north struggles with the lavish luxuriance of the south, the fir tree flourishes side by side with the yew, and the avalanches have made hideous furrows down the leafy slopes. But finally the sun gets the mastery. In place of the ash and alder, appears the chesnut. The Ticino, which has hitherto accompanied our path in headlong haste, now begins to flow with a mild and gentle current, and not far below Airolo we meet with the first vines, although we are still two thousand five hundred feet above the sea level; but then the soil on which we stand is the soil of Italy.

In the little inn at Faido we made our last halt, before setting out for the lakes and the fair city of Milan. How delicious is the flavour of the purple grape and the red wine after our pilgrimage! and how the black eyes of the pretty Giannina sparkle as she chatters to us of all imaginable things and people! how her small white teeth shine, and her long dark tresses! It was almost hard to part from her, despite all the splendours towards which our journey was tending. As we set off once more on our southward way, a voice cried after us from the vine-wreathed balcony, "Addio!"

ACROSS THE BRENNER.

THERE may perhaps be other and bolder roads, but the Brenner railway was the first with which the mind of man achieved a victory over the spirit of the mountains, and scaled the highest wall which nature opposes to his progress—the Alps. The Brenner railway really opened that epoch of Titanic works which now follow swiftly one upon the other, and which some day will be recognised as the distinctive mark of this century; for if the Gothic art created churches, and the Renaissance palaces, the present epoch makes railways; which—"they too—almost reach to Heaven!" Of course any path that climbs among the heights is more attractive than one which leads amongst the lower valleys, but the charm is here greatly increased by the fact that the wild and singular character of the road presents itself to us at the very first; the landscape does not gradually unfold itself, but is there before our eyes in full perfection as soon as the train begins to ascend.

Let us cast one glance back at the ancient city on the Inn: to the right, a splendid abbey extends its two wings; in the background rise the blue summits of the Solstein, and the Martinswand; then the great tunnel through the Iselberg swallows us up. It is, so to speak, the gateway through which we enter upon this daring road; we are to feel the mighty power exerted in making it, at the very threshold. When we again emerge into the light, the glaciers of Stubai are looking down upon us. The Sill, wild child of the mountains, brawls impetuously along, and if a wider glimpse of landscape than our narrow course is opened into some side valley, we catch sight of white houses nestling under the rocks. High aloft stands a ruined castle, or a tiny chapel, the sound of whose bell is almost lost in the noise of our journey. Threateningly hang great stones overhead; threateningly yawns the precipice underfoot; the grey rubbly soil appears so loose, that one trembles to think of a heavily laden goods train passing over it; we see little pebbles roll swiftly down the slope of the cutting, the soil of which is barely held together by a lattice-work of dry bushes and branches. When there is a clearing in the forest, we can see across to the old post road, which is now so quiet and deserted, and which nevertheless once counted amongst the great roads of the world; Roman milestones of Caracalla and Septimius Severus have been found there; Charles the Fifth took this road when he travelled out of Italy to the Imperial Diet at Augsburg; Kaiser Max, the last knight of chivalry, hunted in these gorges.

The longest of the twenty-seven tunnels of the Brenner railway is that of Muhlthal, (two thousand eight hundred feet long) which brings us to the station of Matrey. This was the ancient Matrejum, a permanent camp of the Roman legions, of whom its soil still covers many relics; it was a noble seat in the rude times of the German Empire, as the walls of its castle still record. The tower greets us silently from the height, and the iron rails are laid almost among its rocky foundations. It is now deserted; the

ON THE BRENNER, BELOW GOSSENSASS.

Princes of Auersperg, to whom it now belongs, living far away. Amongst the great personages whom the village has received and sheltered, was Pius the Sixth, when he was on his way to Germany in 1782, and a baker on that occasion conceived the happy thought of obtaining the blessing of his Holiness on all his bread! When Charles the Fifth came to Matrey in the year 1530, he found the whole place in flames, so that he was obliged to take shelter in an isolated house, the Grieshof. Since then the village has been seven times destroyed by fire.

Steinach turns its back on the railway, the fronts of its houses looking westward. Now it is left on one side, looking sullen and neglected; and yet it was, once upon a time, one of those flourishing old-fashioned post stations to which the last ten years have put an end for ever. In the old days the road was frequented day and night; sixty horses stood in the stables, and the gay frescoes with which the houses were adorned witnessed to the well-to-do condition of the burghers. Max Emanuel and Andreas Hofer knew this place, but now it is all deserted; and the great world-history has turned into other routes! On the stretch of road between Steinach and the Brenner post, occurs one of the worst curves which the railway has to pass; for the ascent is so steep that it was impossible to attempt it in a direct line. The line, therefore, instead of continuing its course southward, turns suddenly towards the east, returning to its old direction after a long détour. Many important tunnels mark this bit of the line, which after Gries becomes more and more picturesque, and more and more steep, until at length we reach the summit of the pass. "Brenner Station!" cries the conductor all along the train. "Brenner!" the traces of two thousand years of history are embedded in the word. The Legions of Augustus crossed the Brenner, and so did the world-wide traffic of the German Empire. Here too is the point at which the waters divide, flowing towards the Black Sea and the Adriatic. But the neighbourhood has no attractions for the stranger; the few houses which make up the hamlet are insignificant and poverty stricken; the little lake which rests upon the summit, is dark and stagnant. According to the most recent computations, the Brenner is four thousand four hundred and twenty-four feet high. It is the least elevated of all the passes which cross the Alps, and to one looking from a high mountain peak, it appears like a notch in the blue chain. Not far off is the Brennerbad; it possesses springs which formerly burst boiling from the earth; but which, owing to some unexplained chance, have become mingled with cold waters. Its fame is of ancient date, and numerous pilgrims sought healing here.

Between Schellenberg and Gossensass there are one or two striking points. Gossensass lies nearly in a perpendicular line below Schellenberg, at a depth of five hundred and sixty feet, and in order to accomplish the descent it was necessary to spread it over a stretch of nearly nine miles. Once more the train changes its course, and plunges deep into the Pflerschthal, until it resumes its old direction, in a tunnel that brings it out at the Gossensass station. Whilst foot travellers can go from the one place to the other in little over five minutes, the locomotive occupies nearly half an hour in doing so. Amongst the passengers who are awaiting the train on the platform, we now begin to see many inhabitants of the neighbouring valleys. To be sure they scarcely ever go farther than to the next station, but they serve to give a delightful *couleur locale* which is in agreeable contrast with the cosmopolitan crowd of travellers. Who does not find it pleasant to look upon those tall stalwart figures; those dreamy, yellow-haired damsels with black bodice and broad-brimmed hat? They were unwilling enough to admit the railway into their peaceful, remote homes; and many of them, to this day, are not reconciled to the good fortune that was thus thrust upon them.

Franzensfest, which we pass soon after Sterzing, gives a warlike character to the scene. Heavily accoutred soldiers crowd into the train, and the foreign tongues they speak, seem to deepen the impression that their service is hard and compulsory. Several officers, too, get into the train at this point; mostly fine-looking fellows. Many a one is accompanied to the carriage door by a woman who looks after the departing train with wet eyes; to Hungary, to Poland, to Trieste, they are dispersing in various directions. But not only the men, all the memories, in this locality bear a military stamp. Here, where the ways part to the Pusterthal and the Brenner, where lies the key of the approach to Italy, much noble blood has flowed; we have reached that part of the pass which is strategically the strongest, and forts were erected to protect it. Here, at this point which commands the gorge of Brixen, there have been bitter struggles for the mastery, nay it almost seems as though Nature herself took sides, and fought for the defence of the pass. She grows rougher and sterner than heretofore, and piles up on

WANDERERS ON THE BRENNER PASS.

giddy heights a store of rocky projectiles which, in the combats of 1809, crashed down upon the foe; the bloodstain of 1809 is the stamp and token, the distinctive symbol, of this road! In Mittenwald, where there is a solitary post-house, the bullets are still sticking in the walls. More than a thousand men of one German regiment were slain at a spot still called the "Sachsen Klemme," or Strait of the Saxons. The trees were torn from the heights, and the stones from the rocks, to be hurled down on the invader. The enraged people fought as in the old heroic times; they had been disarmed, but Nature herself furnished an inexhaustible armoury; *she* was their ally and their refuge; *she* gave to the combat that elemental fury which we cannot think of without a shudder. Every People has its Thermopylæ.

Now, in the central point of the defile stands the threatening fortress of Franzensfest, upon a colossal substructure of granite. Gigantic walls and gateways frown upon us, but in the background rises a mightier fortress, the mountain itself. Thirteen years (from 1833 to 1846,) elapsed between the beginning and the completion of the work.

Once past the gorge of Brixen, the valley widens, the road descends rapidly, the air grows milder and the vegetation richer. Brixen is our next halting-place; here we have one more specimen of the genuine little Tyrolese town, with all the qualities and defects involved in the phrase. Botzen is touched with a breath of the south; but here the antique hostelry of the Elephant, the narrow streets adorned with oriel windows and glimpses of foliage, the wide spaces that suddenly open out before the numerous churches, the priests, who breviary in hand walk surrounded by a swarm of children, these things are characteristic of the German Tyrol. Brixen is a town belonging to the Church; it has for centuries been the seat of a Prince Bishop; and this fact has stamped itself on every detail. Monks and nuns are met with everywhere, piety absolutely lives in the streets, even trade is imbued with it; for the only manufactury that Brixen possesses makes cowls for Capuchin friars. Even after the railway was opened, the stage coach from Brixen to Botzen journeyed daily alongside of the rails, and was daily well-filled.

But our readers will probably rather remain true to the iron road, which now carries us onward through Klausen and Atzwang. Many a remembrance of song and story greets us from the mountains; we see the gables of the convent where Haspinger once dwelt; the long white walls of Seben, where the Romans had built a fortress, and, crowning a rocky eminence, the castle in which Oswald von Wolkenstein the Minnesinger, was born. But near Atzwang there is yet more work to be done to subjugate this untrained nature; for here, not only earth and rock, but the river offers its opposition to the great attempt. In several places the course of the Eisack was turned, and the rails run in the former bed of the stream; or it was imprisoned in the so-called water tunnels, between whose walls of masonry it rushes darkly. Atzwang is the last pretty village that we see before entering the wide flat valley in which Botzen stands. Already the chestnut tree flourishes on either side of us, and an air of greater industry and cultivation announces the neighbourhood of an important city. One more struggle has to be made; once more the stormy Eisack must be bridged over; once more a lowering rock must be pierced, that stands as the last portal guarding the way, and then we speed out into freedom, into a very Paradise. The gigantic wall of the Dolomite mountains stands before us in all its vastness and majesty crowned with a thousand airy pinnacles; the train runs among vineyards where the ripe grapes are hanging; crowds of slender gables and flat roofs meet our view. "Bolzano!" shouts a voice. Everywhere we hear Italian accents.

Can this be Italy, the southern land with its magical colouring, we ask ourselves with a start? But we are as yet hardly on the threshold of those delightful plains now opening before us. It is not *Bolzano*, it is only *Botzen*.

PALAZZO SARDAGNA IN TRENT.

THE CASTLE OF TRENT.

IN THE TRENTINO.

THE Adige is one of the rivers that are consecrated by the legends and the love of the people, around whose shores the great militant figures of history group themselves, in whose bed lies a treasure of golden memories. The Adige seems to have impressed somewhat of its own character upon the country it traverses; even as the river foams down from the mountains in wild impetuous windings, so is the land cleft into bold ravines in its upper portions; and when the stream begins to flow with a broader, calmer current, the valley spreads itself out into wide plains laden with wine and oil, with corn and silk. And all this bounty, these rich gifts, are in a manner expressed by the habitual phrase used by the people in speaking of the river. The inhabitants of these parts talk of the " Padre Adige," just as the Germans speak of " Father Rhine."

The most interesting district in the course of the Adige is undoubtedly the so-called Trentino; for if at Botzen the river is still a thoroughly Tyrolese mountain stream, yet by the time it flows through Verona, its waters are completely Italian. But just at the point where it reaches Trent the transition from one character to the other is completed.

One feels at once that two contrasted forces are merged in one another in the waves of the Adige; its surface seems to reflect a singular double image. If this species of psychological and national conflict, amid which the inhabitants exist, is peculiarly interesting, the natural phenomena are not less worthy of notice; since the mild south which predominates in the valley changes through varied gradations to the roughness of the north which crowns the topmost heights. Nature does not spread out her treasures one beside the other, but one above the other, up to the last and highest stages of all, which bear only a coarse kind of corn and *gran turco*, (Indian maize).

The tree which certainly contributes most to the Italian character of the landscape, is the olive; but the wide, silver-grey olive woods which clothe the slopes of the Lago di Garda, never reach a higher altitude than seven hundred feet above the sea-level. The fig ripens at fifteen hundred feet, and the grape at two thousand feet above the sea: although, to be sure the vines are stunted, and by no means the finest of the twenty-six different kinds which the Trentino produces. But then the south suddenly shuts her lavish hand. Upon the highest cultivated platforms, (four thousand four hundred feet above the sea-level) are golden fields of rye, and all that is above them, is rock and wood: —a thoroughly Alpine country. Wild creatures haunt its depths; it is scarcely thirty years ago, since the trace of bears was found in the Val di Sarca, and the last wolf killed, and to this day the eagle builds his eyrie on the top of the rocks.

Looked at, not with regard to finer details, but as a mass, the whole country may be roughly divided into three constituent parts, nearly equal in extent. The first division is covered with forest; the second consists of rock and water; the third, and smallest, is cultivated, fertile land. This last division is moreover limited in extent, in consequence of the opposition, which has endured for centuries, between free proprietors and those peasants who cultivate another man's acres, and receive in return only a small fraction of the net produce. In this struggle for existence,—in which the one party is endeavouring to obtain immediate returns regardless of consequences, and the other is anxious to preserve for the future,—the Agro Trentino has suffered severely. Important tracts of country have been nearly destroyed by this ruthless system, and the woods, too, have been much injured: so much so that the consequences of the devastation committed are already felt in sharp changes of climate, although the law now does its utmost to protect the woods. Books are distributed in the schools, setting forth the evil of such reckless destruction, but printed words influence the peasant much less than spoken ones; and at all times destruction moves faster than enlightenment.

Any *res litigiosa* (if I may be allowed to use that ugly word) is interesting beforehand, from the very fact that there is a contest about it, and, for this reason, the little land that is called the Trentino, and in which, for centuries, two powerful national elements have been struggling against each other, has attracted the attention of observers to the singular conditions of its existence. The following numbers, which we take from statistics, do battle on one side or the other. Every figure is an armed combatant:

The population of the Trentino amounts at the present day to about three hundred and forty thousand souls. It has increased since 1810 (when the first trustworthy census took place) exactly one hundred thousand. The "circle" of Roveredo, to which the Val di Sarca, and the northern shores of the Lago di Garda belong, is the most populous. The number of schools is about five hundred; of churches three hundred and fifty; of priests more than a thousand. The spiritual supremacy is exercised by the Chapter of the Cathedral at Trent. If we run through the list of Prince Bishops, the changes of the times are, as it were, reflected in them; in the beginning we find antique, powerful types: Gerhard and Burkard, Atto and Udalrich, thorough Germans; then come a few Italian sounding names here and there; and finally the famous names of the Austrian nobility predominate,—the Harrachs, Thuns, and Wolkensteins. The Bishop was assisted by a council of five Doctors, and the Capitano of the city, named by the Counts of Tyrol. Matters of supreme importance were referred to—Wetzlar!

So at every point German history is intermingled with the Italian annals of the country. It seems to us like a myth when we consider that in the beginning of the nineteenth century Trent and Riva were Bavarian cities, and that Val di Non and Val di Sole sent their representatives to the Parliament at Frankfurt! The Trentino lies before us like a great vestibule of Italy; the outlines of the country, and the architecture of the towns, the atmosphere and the colouring, are impregnated with the breath of the south; we begin to feel that we are foreigners here. This is the broad strip of land that lies between Germany and Italy, divided from the former by the Alps, from the latter by the mountains of the Veronese;—the spot where Nature pauses after having taken leave of the chaste severity of the Alps, and, before assuming the fulness of southern beauty, she stands still at the parting of the ways. A few steps further, and she becomes the idol of millions, the spoiled darling that bears the enchanted name of *Italia!* The rocky summits which surround the Trentino in a wide semi-circle are steep and rugged; their forms are frequently harsh, but the air which streams through the valleys below them is mild and caressing; and though the waves of the Adige be stormy at times, yet they run between trellised vines and sunny terraces, and flow with the soft swell of an ancient melody. As we have said, Nature here seems to be a creature struggling between two conflicting feelings; but, in truth, it is scarcely a struggle, for the definitive choice has in reality been made. It is the same with the inhabitants. They seem to fluctuate between Germany and Italy; but they, too, have made their choice; it is the blue south that they mean when they speak proudly of "la patria."

Such is the Trentino. And in the midst of it stands the ancient Roman city of Trent. The best view of its wide-spread walls is obtained by mounting to the Dos Trento; half way up the hill, even, you see far into the valley and over the rushing Adige; near to the present bed of the river lies the ancient one, now dry and deserted; that grey wall, which is now cut in two by the railway, was built by Theodoric, king of the Goths; the rugged towers which rise above the level of the dwellings, have witnessed the passage of twenty centuries. The memories of old, old times overlie this place, even as geological strata are superimposed one upon the other in the earth; but men pass by, and see only the sod on which their own feet rest. "Veda! Il Buon Consiglio!" said a man who had accompanied us unasked, pointing with his hand towards the mighty castle which bears this name; its battlements, which masterfully dominate the city, were glowing in the evening light. High above them the mountains stretched in noble outlines. The castle was built in days when every palace was a fortress, and all power manifested itself defiantly. Here dwelt the Prince Bishop with his Chapter; the latter claimed the privilege of having only nobles or the most renowned men of learning among its members. Above the long ranges of windows rises the battlemented masonry wherein hawks make their nests. The whole building is surrounded with a warlike-looking rampart, and at present it does indeed belong to Mars. "E una caserma," said our man, with lowered voice and an air of mortified pride. And then he began to tell of the ruined glories of the great saloon;—of the noble staircases, of the majolica, and the frescoes of Giorgione and Giulio Romano. "E una caserma!"

"And that building," we asked, "whose cupola is seen above the house-tops, close to the two slender towers?"

"Il duomo," he answered, with a kind of pathos. It seemed to him incomprehensible that any one could be ignorant of things so important; for here lie the bones of the famous martyr Vigilius, who once upon a time, built the first church in Trent, and was murdered by the heathens because he attacked the worship of Neptune to which god the city once was dedicated. Many derive the name Trent from Neptune's trident, and the trident was found engraved on a Roman boundary stone which is carefully preserved to the present day; but others think that the town derives its name from the confluence of three rivers which meet near it. Pliny and Strabo are both of this latter opinion. The builder

FOUNTAIN IN THE CATHEDRAL SQUARE AT TRENT.

of the duomo, or cathedral, is said to have been Adamo di Arogno. Its reddish squares of marble have been blackened by time; at a considerable height the wall is broken by airy arcades where pigeons flutter in and out, and the long nave is divided from the side aisles by pillars. Much simpler, but with more of historic interest, is Santa Maria Maggiore where the Council of Trent was opened in the year 1545. The predominant colouring of the church is of white and red marble. There are statuettes in the niches and delicate bas-reliefs on the walls. The magnificent organ of the church, which was celebrated for its rich tone, was destroyed by a thunder-bolt on the 13th June, 1819. A huge fresco painting in the choir of the church perpetuates the memory of the Council, and contains numerous portraits of those who took part in it. The Virgin with her child floats above the disputants and mitigates the asperity of their words. It is well known that the sittings of this assembly continued at Trent fully eighteen years. Twenty-nine ambassadors from secular princes attended it, nay there was even a special "Physician to the Council," the famous Fracastoro.

It was already twilight before we descended, and took a turn or two in the streets which were filled with a motley crowd, as is nearly always the case in Southern cities in the evening, but the population had little to recommend it to the sympathies of a foreigner. Among the lower classes we saw plenty of examples of the squalor of outward appearance and the mobility of gesture, which are so characteristic of the South; but without that *grandezza* with which a poor man in Italy accosts a foreigner; and even the more cultivated classes are puzzled to find a middle term between their sympathies, which draw them southward, and the experience which teaches them how much solid good

FRUIT-SELLERS IN TRENT.

comes to them from the North. But this latter view appears to have acquired strength latterly.

My volunteer guide assured me that it was worth while to pause a moment in front of the Palazzo Galasso, since it was one of the finest private buildings that Trent could boast of. "Who built it?" asked I, in astonishment. "George Fugger of Augsburg," was the answer. After Fugger, it came into the hands of the Counts Thun and Gallas, until at last the Zambelli became the proprietors of it.

We passed on, crossing the Cathedral Square. The heavens were gradually decking themselves with sparkling stars; the water in the great marble fountain standing in the middle of the piazza, murmured and plashed over the god Neptune with his trident and

PEASANT WOMAN FROM THE NEIGHBOURHOOD OF TRENT.

sirens. In the suburb on the other side of the Adige we saw the dark cypresses that surround the old garden of the Franciscan monastery. "Trent, too, has its Saints," said my companion, "and one of them may be counted amongst the youngest in the calendar, for it was a child barely two years old, named Simon, whom the Pope canonised to make amends for his sufferings." People will still tell you that he was stolen and tortured by the Jews. The corpse, which is buried in San Pietro, was fished out of a stream; and thirty-nine inhabitants of the old Ghetto (Jews' quarter) who were accused of having been accessory to the child's murder, were punished with death.

The increase in material prosperity which has come to the "Agro Trentino" of recent times has been essentially due to the railway; but the direction of its commerce is towards

Germany. There, and not in the sunny South, Trent lays up her treasures of fruit, and silk, and wine, and if among the articles she receives in exchange a little German morality should slip in, she will be no loser by the bargain.

After Trent, Roveredo is the most important town of the Italian Tyrol; but here industry already preponderates over agriculture. There are more than fifty manufactories devoted to silk-spinning alone. The founders of Roveredo, which was called "Rovereith" in the language of the Middle Ages, were the Counts of Castelbarco. The name of the town, which now sounds so soft and southern, was formerly harsh and German; and the symbol of the town, which is still seen in its coat of arms and whose trace we find in the name itself, was the oak. From *robur*, from the oak-wood which once grew in Val Lagarina, Roveredo is named. Here, too, Nature has left traces of her destructive powers in the great chaos of rocky fragments not far from San Marco, which formerly was called the "Stony Sea." The landslip which strewed the huge fragments here, took place in the time of the Carlovingians in 883; and it presented, even in 1319 so fearful a picture that Dante introduced it into his *Divina Commedia*. He had come to this neighbourhood on being exiled by the Florentines, to enjoy the hospitality of the Counts of Castelbarco. For a brief period Roveredo belonged to the Republic of Venice, until it was united to Tyrol by Kaiser Max. The characteristics of the south are more striking here than at Trent, dazzling white walls meet our eyes on every side, cypresses and fig-trees become more numerous, in the gardens blooms a more varied and gaily coloured Flora; and even the abundant waters which sparkle everywhere in wells and fountains furnish a symptom of southern proclivities. It makes the heart beat quicker when we see the women of Roveredo, who enjoy the reputation of being peculiarly beautiful, moving along the Corso Nuovo towards the long avenue which is the general promenade on cool evenings. They glide along chatting and whispering, draped in black silk, their brilliant eyes half concealed behind their fans; and the beggar who implores them for a trifling alms, calls them "Madonna."

Near Pacco a ferry crosses the Adige. From this point we cast a last look back at the pretty town; then our road lies far away; the next evening we are looking at blue murmuring waters, as the moon rises slowly behind Monte Baldo. These are the waters of the Lago di Garda.

RIVA.

ON THE LAGO DI GARDA.

TWO roads lead through the Trentino to the Lake of Garda. The one (known to thousands of tourists) branches off from Mori to Riva: the other much less betravelled but finer and bolder, leads from Trent through the Val di Sarca.

Not long after leaving Trent we enter a gigantic rocky gorge called Buco di Vela. Above its rugged walls only a strip of blue sky is visible, and the trembling aspen clings to the clefts of the rock: here and there a mountain-stream murmurs over a stony bed, and turns a solitary mill-wheel in the valley. We emerge from the ravine close to the little lake of Terlago, whose waters reflect a world of stone all around it. There are many similar lonely mountain tarns in the Val di Sarca; they form indeed a characteristic feature of it and, as it were, prepare us to approach the vast basin in which the ebb of prehistoric centuries has left behind the Lago di Garda. Scarcely has Terlago disappeared, when we come to Lago Toblino, out of whose silent depths an ancient castle rises, built by the Romans, and on whose shores all the luxuriant vegetation of the south unfolds itself. But soon Nature resumes her stony and defiant aspect, when we reach the Lago di Caverline passing Pietramurata by a high winding road.

A rocky eminence crowned by a fortress shows itself in clear colours as we look towards the south; that is the castle of the old powerful Counts of Arco, and the last great milestone on our way. When we have left it behind us, we have reached our goal and stand on the shores of the shining Lake of Garda.

* * * * * * *

The flood spreads itself out before our eyes in apparently limitless extent, its deep blue colour seeming to give a foretaste of the charm of the still distant Adriatic. We sit upon a little terrace built up high above the lake, and watch the boys playing on the shore, and the slight barks whose sails melt away into vapoury distance. We are in

CASTLE OF ARCO IN THE VAL DI SARCA.

Riva; in the very sound of the name one feels some subtle enchantment of the South. The Lago di Garda, which we purpose exploring from this point, is the largest of all the Italian lakes; with its circumference of a hundred and twenty-four kilometres, it surpasses the extent of Lago Maggiore by one third. Three great provinces meet on its shores, the Trentino, Venetia, and Lombardy; and though the streams which feed it come mostly from the high mountains, from Val di Sarca, Ledro, and Tavolo, the river which flows out of it is the broad bright Mincio, whose name has a warlike sound in the ears of the men of this generation. It is one of the important lines along which we trace the course of history, the great "Quadrilateral" was intrenched behind it, and its waters nourish the marshy lands that surround Mantua. How much blood had to be shed before these regions heard the victorious cry "Viva l' Italia!"

The shape of the country around the Lago di Garda, when we look down upon the huge basin from a height, is uncommonly picturesque and varied. At the northern end of the lake the shores are steep; the threatening rocks of Tyrol still tower here, and, as it were, oppose themselves to all that is foreign and strange: Monte Baldo and Monte Adamo are designed in bold outlines against the blue sky, little creeks and inlets sharply cut into the banks, and the surface of the lake is narrow. But the farther we advance towards the south, the more does the picture change. It seems to grow before our eyes, the waters spread themselves out in all directions, softly swelling hills stretch on either hand, until at length the landscape becomes flat and tame and the waters predominate over the whole scene. The Lago di Garda has now entirely lost all the characteristics of a mountain lake. We appear to be gliding over a Lombard plain covered with water. It is not difficult to believe, here, that the lake is barely sixty-four metres (about two hundred feet) above the level of the sea, and the tradition which declares its basin to be the ancient bed of the Adige. The islands, which rise here and there, are not high, and have none of those jagged forms by which so many an island declares the struggle it has had for existence.

PIETRAMURATA IN THE VAL DI SARCA.

Even Sermione, the long peninsula at the southern border of the lake, is covered with thick olive woods, more gentle than majestic in their aspect, and rythmic as the waves that ripple past them.

Here begins the history of the lake;—not a history in the dry and compressed style of the ancient chroniclers, but a history in sweet sounding song; for Catullus lived here. Two thousand years ago the conquerors of the world had found in their path the azure jewel that we call the Lago di Garda; and though the stormy spirit of the Cæsars passed on unmoved towards Gaul and the Germanic forests, the spirit of the poet paused here in silent ecstasy, and asked for nothing more. The little city which stood here at that period, and of which some remains of walls are still extant, was called Sirmio. It was Sirmio that Catullus greeted in exulting verses, when after a long absence he returned to tarry there, and to exclaim:

"O quid solutis est beatius curis?"

And whoso knows the songs written by that wondrous hand can feel in them even to-day the light pulsing of the waves which gave them their form and spirit.

It is a picture from the antique world with which we begin:—the great poet in the midst of this smiling Idyl, his eyes lovingly beholding every detail which the beauty of

OLIVE GROVE ON THE SHORE OF THE LAKE OF GARDA, NEAR TORBOLE.

Nature presents to them, with no ambition but to comprehend them; with no wish but to sing them.

The Lago di Garda is mentioned also in the poems of Virgil and in the Divina Commedia. But the hands of many powerful personages were rudely stretched to grasp this jewel, and fought for its possession. The most noble families of Verona and of Venice met here in arms; the Kaiser and the Church, Guelph and Ghibelline contended for it, and not seldom the history of the beautiful lake is as stormy as its

LAKE OF CAVEDINE IN THE VAL DI SARCA.

waters. The peaceful times of which Catullus sang here soon came to an end. Upon the Monte Rocca, whose double summit rises above Garda, the ruins of a grey old tower are still to be seen, where Adelaide, the widow of Lothair, was imprisoned. Barbarossa gave and Henry sold away the land; until again new races came whose better right was but their better sword. But the conflict raged highest in the period during which the power of Venice brooked no opposition; when cities, great and small, made war upon one another, and when every noble was a free lance. It was in the year 1439 that the Duke of Milan, Filippo Maria Visconti, was at war with the Venetians;—he the more powerful on land, they on the sea. He had occupied nearly the whole territory of Garda with his soldiery, and was already master of the district, when the Venetians, commanded by Gattamelata, conceived the bold idea of sending a portion of their fleet to the lake!

The difficulty of surmounting the heights that lie between Garda and the country of the Adige, and of bridging over the chasms which yawn amid that stony mountain wilderness was enormous; but Venice was then all-powerful. The project was jeered at, at first, but soon thousands of busy hands were at work to make a way for the squadron, which consisted of more than thirty ships. The fleet was towed down the Adige as far as

Ravazzone, and from thence was brought by land to the lake of Loppio; two thousand draught animals being employed to move the tremendous weight. The water-shed was reached: from Monte Baldo they came down on the Lago di Garda like a migration of prodigious monsters. It was a "moving wood" that advanced towards the foe;—but a wood of masts and flapping sails. The inhabitants of the shores were terror-stricken at

MILL IN THE SUCO DI VELA.

the aspect of these huge forms which all at once appeared upon their lake. But the audacious armada was soon completely destroyed; and the Venetians were not victorious over Milan until they had prepared a second fleet, built on the spot.

But this was not the last blood shed here, nor the last fleet that fought here. We are speaking of Italy; and Italy is not a peaceful heroine. Not only did the wars of the first Napoleon, and those of '49, rage on these shores, but later, towards the beginning of 1860, daring little steamers cruised about these waters, manned by volunteers, and carrying the flag of Italy. Their guns, which commanded nearly the whole of the lake, frequently put a stop to the communication between Riva and Peschiera. From many a silent boat gliding peacefully through the blue waters, would come suddenly the shrill shout of "Viva l' Italia!" "Viva Garibaldi!" The young fellows who leant against the mast, wore the red shirt, and it was then that I heard for the first time the well-known song "Camicia rossa!" We may speak openly of these things now; they are forgotten and forgiven, but in that day they weighed heavy on men's spirits and even the stranger perceived the smouldering agitation.

In penetrating a little into the streets of Riva, we soon feel that Nature has done much better for the place than man. The streets are a narrow labyrinth of angles, for the most part; although it is true that every neglected corner, every coloured rag that flutters upon the roofs, every lazy vagabond sleeping under a doorway, bears the stamp of the picturesque. At a few points the streets widen out into stately Piazzas, of which the finest is without doubt, the Piazza looking on the port. Here the daily life of the place is seen in a motley crowd, and the houses are adorned with long rows of pillars; here too the artistic unity of the town with the landscape is best perceived. All the lines are distinct and firm; the ruinous walls seem to have grown out of the stony soil rather than to be built upon it. The gigantic rocks of Monte Giumella, the blue distance of the lake, the fine old olive trees which seem to press around the city in serried ranks, all harmonise wonderfully together in form and colour. The picture is complete, and it is so new and exciting, that one's heart begins to beat with the delightful sensation of roaming freely in foreign lands. And if now and then our ears are pierced by the shrill yells of the urchins who struggle for a stray lemon that has fallen to the ground; if occasionally we are splashed by the spray from a dirty boat full of red-capped rowers, we cannot be angry with them. Nay, even the Italian dandies, who give themselves great airs in front of the Caffè Risatti, excite only an indulgent smile. There must be fellows like these!

Certainly we already perceive the difference (noticeable throughout Italy) between the impression produced by the upper and lower classes of the people. That the latter gain, and the former lose, our sympathy the closer our acquaintance with them becomes, is an observation continually confirmed on our progress, from Verona to Naples. The frank, frequently noble, air of the common people, contrasts very favourably with the *blasé*, frivolous manners so often met with among the "Signori" of the great cities.

Of all the roads leading out of Riva, that which is called the Via Ponal, is the most beautiful; it is named from the fine waterfall which it passes before reaching the Val di Ledro. Here, as so often in the high country around Benaco, we find a small dark green mountain tarn, whose steep rocky walls hint of the neighbouring Alps, whilst the vegetation on its shores luxuriates in Southern exuberance. How willingly we loiter here, and dream away one more day in this solitude, before returning to noisy little Riva!

The steamboat which traverses the lake from end to end, four times a week, stops at the most important stations on either bank, and many a smiling Idyl, many a glorious memory rises before us on the voyage. As we reach the middle of the lake, we realize for the first time the luxuriant fertility of the country. On the sunny slopes we see carefully cultivated lemon gardens; we see vineyards richly enough laden to adorn a procession of Bacchus with their fruit; and between these again, groves of olive trees with their delicate, tender, silver-grey foliage. Few trees are so noble. From Limone to Gargnano the banks are steep, the rocks rise almost perpendicularly from the water, which is here of considerable depth; but from Gargnano to Desenzano, stretches the long, fruitful shore, which the Italians call the "Riviera." Gardens and elegant villas alternate with arable land. Many of the houses have the lintels of the doors and the window-sills of marble from the quarries of Tremosine. The nobles of Verona and Brescia have their country houses here; but besides that, there is frequently a gathering of the populace, gaily dressed and merry folks, on market days at Gargnano, when the fishing-boats run into the harbour of Salo to take refuge from bad weather.

The most important point on the eastern shore is Torbole, sheltered by a snug little port around which the angry winds contend with each other. Two winds chiefly predominate on the Lago di Garda: the north wind which comes across the Alps and is here

DEPARTURE OF A STEAMBOAT FROM PESCHIERA.

called "il Sover," and the "Ora," which blows from the south. Their alternations, and the brilliant calms which succeed them, give to this lake that inexhaustible richness of colouring which makes it quite unique. When the smooth surface displays a fathomless blue tint, with the sky like a tender veil above it, it will change on a sudden as by the stroke of a magic wand to dark steel-colour directly a storm begins to agitate its depths; until this too, abruptly disappears to make way for a pale green, with white, foam-crested waves. Then the black tempestuous sky will grow lighter, a rosy evening gleam will steal over the wide waters that rock themselves slowly to rest whilst the moon appears amid the torn wrack of clouds and pours forth a stream of silver. It is like a human countenance on which anger and joy succeed each other; which is now full of rage, now pale with terror, until at length silent peace overspreads its features.

The two islands which we come upon soon after Malcesine, are the only steep ones in the lake, and their fortress-like appearance is heightened by the bold ruins of ancient castles, which take us back to the days of the Scaligers. But in a brief while the soft blue waters wash away these rugged memories, and we are held by the charm of the delightful present. We steam on past Garda, the little hamlet of the ancient countship, which gives its name to the lake. Here too, stand a few ruined towers, but their sternness is subdued

DESENZANO.

and hidden beneath a heap of odorous flowers and leaves; camellias and oleanders, wine and oil, adorn the terraces. The legend runs that here was the site of the ancient town of Benacus, of which the inscriptions tell that have been dug out of the rubbish. Many a charming village seems to rise out of the waters, and sink down into them, as we glide quickly past;—usually built in semicircular form round a bay, like Bardolino, or girdled with antique walls like Lazise whose salutary springs were known to the ancients. Then, when we have lost sight of Sermione, we are near to the southern shore of the lake. Those white houses, shining there in the west, belong to the village of Desenzano; the blackened walls beneath which we walk, bear the proud name of Peschiera; this is the limit of the lake.

Let us cast one look back over its blue surface before we go.

A light fishing bark rocks on the waves; the white sail swells in the evening breeze; the crew is going in the twilight to fish. The spot at which the Mincio runs out of the lake, is a good fishing ground. They cast their nets, leaning far over the boat's side

F

and singing at their work. Their dark bright eyes, full of that enthusiasm which dwells only in the south, look attentively at the clouds rising above Monte Baldo, and at the evening star breaking through them. The wind carries their song to the distant shore, so that wife and children can hear it. Which are the happier here, they or we? We feel the charm that surrounds us, with conscious self-investigation: but in their hearts it has grown up unconsciously. We gaze perplexed on these foreign wonders: but to them all this beauty is home!

We cannot understand the words they sing; they are carried away by the wind and the waters,—but perhaps that is the very soul of their song!

TORBOLE.

VERONA.

SANTA ANASTASIA, VERONA.

VERONA.

FROM Santa Lucia, where the railways into Verona meet, the eye can already embrace the enchanting prospect of the city. In the foreground stand the threatening fortifications with their sharp strong angles surmounted by dark cypresses between which you catch glimpses of little white villas scattered on the heights. Amid the rattle of the train and the rush of the Adige we are carried swiftly nearer to the goal; and our hearts beat high with expectation. For, though the Italian landscape that we have hitherto seen, captivated us, Verona is the first real Italian *city* that we have greeted. And what memories awake as we draw near to her gates,— those gates behind which stands one of the finest monuments of antiquity,—behind which Dietrich von Bern and Alboin intrenched themselves,—where Dante lived an exile, and where Romeo grew pale beside Juliet's coffin.

But soon the dreamy past fades away, for the train rushes with a shrill whistle into the station at Porta Nuova, and gives us back to the present. Out of the throng in the lofty arched station, out of sound of the shouts of facchini and railway guards who are showing the way to the stream of passengers, we push our way to where "Uscita" is written above a door; and then, when we have reached the free space without, we begin to breathe freely.

"Torre di Londra!" "Aquila nera!" "Colomba d'oro!" resound on all hands in a sing-song tone. The porter who stands at the door of each omnibus with a brass badge on his cap, seizes not only on one's travelling bag but on one's person, and we find ourselves thrust bodily into an omnibus! Verily it was a true saying of Stephen the German postmaster-general; "In these days people don't travel, they *are travelled.*"

FONTANA DI FERRO, NEAR VERONA.

The trunks are hauled on to the roof, "Avanti!" cries the porter to the driver, and then off we go along wide interminable streets leading from Porta Nuova into the interior of the town. The pace is that peculiar hurried trot which all Italian nags have. We fly along carelessly over stocks and stones; if the bay stumbles now and then, it is hardly noticed amidst the rattle of the pavement and the tinkle of the bells on the harness. A man, standing at a street corner, and who has barely time to jump aside out of reach of our wheels, shouts after us "Canaglia!" But the word sounds as melodious as if it were a compliment.

We soon come out of the hot, dusty road to the railway, into the narrower, cooler streets of the town, turn several sharp corners, and finally roll under the wide open portal of the hotel. The airy staircase, the marble floors, and the great oleanders in the entrance-hall show us already that we are in an Italian household. The guests seated at table who dispute with lively gestures about politics, bear the same stamp, as we take our places among them refreshed and comforted after having got rid of the dust of travel.

We soon feel at home, and after strolling about here and there, making pause before some sudden street picture, we find ourselves on the Piazza d'Erbe: the point where the city life flows in the most varied stream. In the time of the Romans, this was the Forum. Now the Piazza is surrounded by fine mediæval architecture, under whose open arcades the crowd throngs. A marble fountain murmurs in the centre; the figure surmounting the basin is ancient, and represents the city of Verona with an open roll in her hand setting forth the immemorial renown of her citizens. A pillar, hewn from a single stone, stands here, but its summit is empty; and the remarkableness of the column consists in the fact that it *is* empty. For here in old times stood the Venetian lion of St. Mark, and looked down arrogantly upon the oppressed populace below, until it was destroyed in the battles of the Revolution (1797.) So stormy history and every-day life take hands here; an every-day life that seems to belong to the trivialities of the hour.

Hundreds of buyers and sellers swarm beneath the white awnings over the stalls. Fruit and vegetables are piled up on the low boards; a load of the most splendid flowers fills the heavy baskets; numberless voices rise one above another. The moving crowd divides itself everywhere into distinct groups. On this side we hear

PIAZZA D'ERBE.

"Piselli, fagiuolini, cavolfiori!" On the other re-echoes the cry "fragole, uva, limoni!" "Scusi, Signore!" cries a third, who has pushed against us by a sudden movement. Under the arcades of the Casa dei Mercanti, the younger generation of Merchants is assembled: each one with a flower in his button-hole and a Cavour cigar in his mouth. On the walls over their heads you may read gigantic placards; and here and there political watchwords scrawled—such as, indeed, are seldom wanting on walls in Italy. Every one is bargaining—this one for thousands, that other for twenty *centesimi;* but the smaller the sum, the bigger the noise! Only look at that pedlar, with what contemptuous glances he measures from head to foot the customer who offers him ten *centesimi* whilst he demands twelve! He steps back in inexpressible indignation, but almost immediately reason gets the upper hand, and with persuasive gestures he cries out once more "Dodici!" "Dieci!" replies the other as quick as lightning. And now begins a dialogue, which consists of but two words truly, but is conducted with such a wealth of tone and action, that one could see nothing better acted on the stage. "Dieci!"—"Dodici!"—"Dieci!"—"Dodici!"—"Dieci!" roars one against the other, as though they were dealing sword-thrusts; until at length the seller suddenly cries "Va bene!" and flings his wares into the buyer's hand.

Meanwhile a new group appears from the Via Pellicciai, accompanying a street singer with shouts of laughter. Where the throng is thickest, the fellow takes his stand, makes a circle, and begins to burlesque with admirable mimicry a new prima donna who has lately succeeded at the opera. Hideous grimaces accompany the *pianissimo* to which he slowly lets his voice sink. The people keep running to him from all quarters, and laughing faces show themselves at the high, arched windows, until the whole train disappears into a neighbouring street. But we hasten through the picturesque gate of the Volto Barbaro, to the Piazza dei Signori, where the spirit of the old days of the city, and the power of her later rulers, are petrified in wonderful shapes.

JULIET'S HOUSE.

Without doubt there can be but few towns in which the great epochs of history are embodied in such noble architectural memorials as here; for in the *arena*, classical antiquity has bequeathed to us a monument scarcely surpassed in beauty by the Roman Coliseum. And although only a few striking memorials of Gothic times remain, yet these become richer as soon as the rule of the Scaligers begins, and the struggle between Guelph and Ghibelline. From that epoch date the mighty castles, and the houses defended by towers which still to this day mark the physiognomy of Verona. And then came the Renaissance, and gave to the town two such men as Sanmichele and Fra Giocondo, to whom some wondrous palaces, and a few of the most beautiful churches, owe their origin. But the warlike character of the town, which is the central point of the famous Quadrilateral, soon resumed the upper hand, and the battles at the close of last century, and the later conflict between Austria and Italy, are betokened by the fortifications of to-day, with their staring cannon.

So the past of Verona reveals itself to our eyes. The Piazza dei Signori, however, on which we stand, belongs exclusively to the Middle Ages: here dwelt the rulers of the city, Mastino and Alberto of the race of Scaliger; here stands the Palazzo del Consiglio, where the Council of Five Hundred sat, and in front of whose hall are ranged the statues of five worthies of antiquity who called Verona their home. These are Pliny, Catullus, Cornelius Nepos, Macer Æmilius, and Vitruvius. The pure forms of the noble building are very attractive. Not without awe do we stand before the monument of Dante, which adorns the middle of the Piazza, for the sublime singer dwelt four years within these walls as the guest of Can Grande. He himself was a Ghibelline who held immoveably by the Emperor, and the Scaligers also followed the same side. The eagle which rises on their coat of arms above the ladder, was the Imperial eagle.

Wheresoever in Verona you come upon noble historic monuments, they are almost sure to be connected with the name of this family,—with their lives or their death; but the finest of all is their tomb. It is hard by the Piazza dei Signori, and may be considered as an appurtenance of the church of Santa Maria Antica, in whose courtyard it stands surrounded by iron railings; not hidden in a dark gloomy vault, but rising high and free in the midst of life. According to Villani, the Scaligers had their origin from a petty tradesman of Montagna, who dealt in ladders, (in Italian, *scala*; hence the name, *Scaligeri*,) and were simple citizens when they settled in Verona. But those happened to be the times in which the burghers of the cities were involved in bitter strife with the nobles, and the influence which the Scaligers acquired was such that it led the populace to elect their Podesta from among that family, in the year 1260. This was Mastino; and when an assassin's dagger destroyed his life, he was succeeded in power by his brother Alberto. The latter soon made himself an independent prince, and was succeeded in turn by three sons, of whom the most important bore the name of Can Grande. With him really began a brilliant period, such as fell to the lot of many small Italian states after the time of the Hohenstaufens. His fame as a soldier, his encouragement of

DRAW-WELL.

science, the liberal way in which he cherished the arts, contributed to raise the *Veronese* (the district around Verona) to the highest pitch of prosperity. The best people in the land reposed their hopes on Can Grande; Dante sang of him that he would make the Ghibelline cause triumphant; but the higher the flight, the deeper the fall. As in most of the great Italian families, the passions of certain individuals were fatal to the rest. Murder and lust raged unchecked among the members of this race; three times, brother was slain by brother, until at length the thirst for undivided power led to the extinction of the family. Antonio was the last of his race. After one hundred and thirty years of brilliancy, the star of the Scaligers set at last;—one of the brightest that Italy has ever seen. Even their tomb bears witness that it was so.

The monument of Can Grande is placed above the portal of the church; a heroic equestrian figure. On either side of him are the sarcophagi of Mastino and Giovanni. Over another sarcophagus rises a Gothic spire, enriched with numberless pinnacles and figures, and surmounted by a horse and rider, all so magnificent that one almost overlooks the exquisite little sarcophagi niched in among them. It is perhaps the finest tomb that any Italian ruler ever had; but the activity of life, and not the peace of death, reigns here; in their graves they are still lords of the city, and their corpses are throned high above the heads of the living generation.

No other church of the city, therefore, is so rich in historical associations as Santa Maria Antica. Still in many of the others are to be found traces of an eloquent past—as indeed is the case with nearly every inch of Verona's soil. There is a tradition that the old cathedral was erected on the ruins of a temple to Minerva, and the figures which adorn the great door date from the time of the Carlovingians. Among them stand Roland the Brave, and Queen Bertha the mother of Charlemagne. But he who passes through the long cloister to the learned halls wherein are preserved the archives and the library of the cathedral chapter, plunges still deeper into the past. The most precious works of the Roman classic authors, manuscripts of the time of the Emperor Constantine, were found here; and there are few towns to which European erudition is more indebted. In San Zeno Maggiore there are many artistic treasures; the nave of the church was built before the days of the Hohenstaufens, and the reliefs in brass on the doors, the pillars resting on the backs of strange monsters, even the frescoes, indicate a remote antiquity. The chapel of the Pellegrini is renowned for its architecture; San Giorgio possesses a masterpiece of Paolo Veronese; but the oldest church of all is said to be San Siro, where to this day you may read an inscription purporting that here the first mass ever said in Verona was performed. Tradition says that it was built by permission of King Berenger, with the stones taken from the ancient theatre.

From thence we proceed to the ruins which the world of antiquity has left to us in Verona—that world in which Catullus and Pliny lived. But little remains of the theatre, situated on the left bank of the Adige, beneath the rocky fortress of Castel San Pietro. It was a meritorious work—begun in the last century—to remove and dig out the enormous masses of rubbish, and reveal the theatre to the eyes of the present day. At all events in the open space of the stage, and the fragments of seats, we gain an interesting picture, which is enhanced by the surrounding landscape; for the theatre lies just between the river and the rock of San Pietro, so that the latter forms a background to the scene.

If the impression made by the theatre is incomplete, and requiring to be filled up by knowledge or imagination, on the other hand the aspect of the mighty arena produces a most powerful impression. In order to reach it we cross the Piazza Brà (now Vittorio Emanuele), one of those vast squares whose wide space makes the surrounding buildings appear almost stunted, except where a tower rises here and there above the red roofs. But the Piazza itself is dwarfed, nay disappears, before the huge colossus which we now behold,—before this remnant of the universal power of the Cæsars.

Who built the amphitheatre is unknown to this day; and no stone has yet been discovered bearing any elucidation of the mystery. It is a mere supposition that the building dates from the reign of Trajan. It is constructed, for the most part, of the reddish marble found in the quarries of the Veronese and brought down on the Adige: so that no other amphitheatre can be compared with this for costliness of material. Maffei, the renowned historian of the city, dedicates a copious examination to the arena, and leads us with an experienced hand amid all the changes which the wondrous work

has passed through in the course of ages. From its inexhaustible masses were taken the
stones for the building of the city walls, when Verona was threatened by the barbarians;
during civil conflicts it became the fortress in which rival parties entrenched themselves;
ordeals and executions took place here, and women of notoriously bad character lodged at
one time in the deserted walls. But during all, there was something dark and mysterious

THE AMPHITHEATRE.

in the immense space, with its cages for wild beasts and slaves. People felt themselves to
be in a "Labyrinth," as the arena was called in the days of King Pepin; until finally
the idea began to dawn that this was a wondrous work of antiquity that ought to be preserved. Thereupon it was forbidden, as early as the sixteenth century, to remove any
stones from the arena, the inhabitants who had taken up their abode in the arched
corridors were strictly watched, and at length there was even a public tax imposed to
pay for the repair of dilapidations. In this way alone has it been possible to preserve
the famous monument—at all events as a whole—although but few of the marble
benches are the original ones, and although the external wall has been broken away,
all but four mighty arches. The lead and iron which formerly bound the huge blocks

of stone together, continued still to be pilfered by thievish hands, and were changed under the hammer into weapons with which new generations were to destroy each other.

How the architectural form of the amphitheatre arose is declared by its name, and ancient authors add numerous explanations of it; the semicircles of *two* theatres were merely joined together, so as to form a complete circle. Nearly all the important cities of Italy built similar theatres, at first of wood, but afterwards of stone; and the size of

COURT-YARD OF A HOUSE IN VERONA.

them gives one a surprising glimpse of the population and traffic of the provinces in those days.

According to Maffei's measurements the arena of Verona is four hundred and fifty feet long, and three hundred and sixty feet wide, and the forty-four rows of seats which rise step by step one above another, could accommodate more than forty thousand spectators. The seats were divided by passages which spread like rays from the centre of the arena to the topmost gallery, so that the crowd, which entered by no fewer than seventy arched doorways, could easily disperse itself over the enormous space. As a protection from sun and rain, a colossal awning of sail-cloth was spread over the spectators; and under its shelter the many-headed public could sit at ease, listening breathlessly to the growl of the panther as it crouched beneath the feet of the elephant; or watching the sword of the gladiator as he gave his adversary the coup-de-grâce. *Habet! habet!*

What a frightful picture is conjured up by these recollections! We see the blood-thirsty masses, intoxicated with excitement, who once sat upon these marble steps; now watching the games in the strong tension of expectation, now bursting into shouts of

exultation. Prætors and Ædiles, men in flowing togas, and women with golden
ornaments in their hair; and above these, pressed in a closer throng, the wild populace
ragged, hungry, rough, but insatiable in their thirst for blood! They cower together,
each in himself a beast of prey. *Panem et circenses* is their threatening watchword.
Hecatombs of noble animals have already fallen, the most renowned gladiators of the
schools, which existed in Imperial times all over Italy, have already displayed their

BRIDGE OF BORGHETTO, NEAR VALEGGIO.

prowess in the arena, but still there has not been slaughter enough. Like the shout of
a storming army, like the *Evoe!* of a bacchanalian orgie, a cry goes through the thousands
and thousands of spectators, until the last Herculean champion sinks upon the earth.
We shudder! But when we, as it were, awake, and look around us, everything is silent
and empty; the seats deserted, the blood dried up from the earth, and the generations
who exulted here buried beneath the ruins of a thousand years! Only the artizan who
has fixed his workshop under the shelter of the great arches, hammers with assiduous
hand. The little day-theatre erected in the midst of the vast space, looks, with its
painted boards, like a toy put there by a child's hand to serve for the exhibition of its
puppets. No man, save the stranger gazing curiously about him, enters this deadly silent
circle; but the sun with his eternal calm passes slowly through it, gliding from step
to step, and like a gigantic dial that marks, not hours but centuries, the shadow of
them falls upon this sepulchre of Roman greatness.

But we hasten from the spot where the power of the human race displayed itself in
a feverish squandering of force, where even to think on those burnt out passions excites

us. The charm of Nature works upon us with soothing silent power, when we take refuge with her in a wondrous garden of Verona. It is the Giardino Giusti, of which I am speaking: that fine symbol of the city itself, where Art and Nature are singularly blended. The ground, flat at first, rises gently for a space until at length it terminates in sudden heights, and here, amid broad pathways and narrower twilight ways, stand the oldest spires of Verona:—more than two hundred cypresses! They rise high as the towers of the city, and older than the oldest palaces, whilst among them flourish laurels and myrtles, oleander and acanthus. The marble statues in the thicket stand veiled with a dreamy shadow; fallen gods who have taken refuge in this fair asylum which shelters them with its eternal green. Eighteen of the statues are said to be antiques, and to have come from the Museo Molin; and there are also many Roman inscriptions, let into the rocks and grottoes. A perfect flood of flowers fills the garden beds; every green alley is overgrown with roses, which seem striving to hold us back as we advance, but the finest point of the Giardino Giusti, is the terrace at the end of the garden, which we reach by means of a winding staircase. There lies before us an immeasurable circuit, whose edge at the horizon disappears in mist,—the delicate chain of the Apennines, and, to the north, the Alps; then, somewhat nearer to the eye, spreads the great Lombard plain. The golden fields, which shine in the evening light, are full of maize; the mulberry trees stretch in long rows, bound together by garlands of vine, and those dark lines are the little ditches which serve to irrigate the plain. The cupola of Sant'Andrea in Mantua rises above the flat surface, and yonder we see the Euganean Hills, that still keep their old classic name, where the ashes of Petrarch repose. The more the eye withdraws itself from the distance to the nearer foreground, the thicker grow the villas, until the gaze is fixed by the central point of the panorama—the city at our feet.

From hence the peculiar and individual character of the construction of Verona is best observed. One sees how the river and the protecting rocks marked out, as it were, the limits of the site for the ancient city, and how the building of it went on under the hand of Roman, Goth, and Ghibelline; in the spirit of servitude, or of freedom! High above the roofs rise elegant towers,—not only those with which the churches point heavenward, but those erected by the chiefs of powerful families in days when every house was a fortress. Many of them, to be sure, have perished with the necessities of the time which created them; the memory of them remains in a poem of the eighth century, which enumerates forty-eight of such towers. Scarcely any other place in Verona is so adapted to plunge us into historical reminiscences as the Giardino Giusti:—the tranquil grove under whose trees perhaps Dante wandered, whose cypresses rise above the graves of a thousand perished years, whose silence divides us from the noise and bustle of the outer world.

Here we can appreciate the rightfulness of the appellation "Verona la degna" (Verona the worshipful); here one should loiter at the evening hour when the wide sea of dwellings is swimming in light, when every wave of the Adige is like molten gold, when under the bowery foliage the nightingales begin to stir in the twilight. No rough footstep, no stranger's eye, disturbs us. Only a pair of lovers passes slowly along, pressed close together, side by side, and touching with dreamy hands the boughs as they go. Laurel and myrtle! It was in Verona that the deepest of all love tragedies began and ended;—where Romeo and Juliet loved. The material remains, truly, do not consecrate these memories in our minds; but what are they compared with the ineffaceable associations connected with this spot for three centuries? It is not the ruinous house which

VIEW FROM THE GIARDINO GIUSTI, VERONA.

awakens in us the love-charm of those images; it is not the broken sarcophagus which makes that death-scene present to our minds. All these things have long been a perfect picture in our souls, and haunt us with a secret spell wherever we see a long range of lighted palace windows. These recollections belong to the whole town of Verona, and not alone to the deserted street to which tradition has banished them.

The house which is now said to be the palace of the Capulets stands in the Via San Sebastiano, and a hat (*capello*) hewn out of stone is said to be the confirmation of the

VALSTAGNA.

legend. But the wild noises that resound from within, and the utensils piled pell-mell in the courtyard, show that the place is now a tavern. It is in bad repute even among the inhabitants, and we gladly turn our backs on it. "La tomba di Giulietta," the coffin which once contained the bodies of both the lovers, stands in the former courtyard of the convent of Franciscan nuns; it is of red granite, and the edges of it are much crumbled away. The cover, on which the names were once to be read, has disappeared years ago; for during a long time the empty sarcophagus served as a trough for water, and strangers' hands were at liberty to break off fragments of the stone as relics. At the present day a sharper watch is kept, and a couple of withered wreaths, placed there by unknown hands, lie upon the cracked edge of the coffin.

The first time I saw Verona,—before 1866,—it was still in the possession of the Austrians; and if one did not feel oneself to be precisely in a fortress, for which the extent of the town is too wide, yet the military element was noticeably predominant.

The place was garrisoned by Croat regiments, and whoever crossed the Piazza Brà of an evening was sure to see the white-coated soldiery strolling about in numerous groups; smart Uhlan officers sat in front of the cafés, sipping their sherbet, and listening to the regimental band, playing—Radetzky's march, and the Emperor's hymn! But the Signora who passed by in black silk with a long black veil, turned her head aside without smile or greeting, for " Verona la degna" languished in the grasp of the foreigner.

Now the eagle has freely loosed his talons from the city, after holding her for two thousand years:—the eagle of the Roman legions, and of the German Empire, the eagle which soars above the ladder in the arms of the Scaligers, the double-headed eagle which fell from his proud height at Magenta and Solferino!

The caffè where the officers of the Imperial cavalry once caroused, is now called by the name of Victor Emanuel; and the citizen reeling home under the delightful influence of *vino della riviera*, may shout with impunity " Viva l' Italia ! "

The neighbourhood of Verona is rich in associations, and in fine landscape scenery; although the latter is more remarkable for large grandiose outlines, than for charm. Many of the names one meets here are written with blood in the page of History,—Custozza, Solferino, Novara, Montebello; and any one who has travelled this way in company with soldiers, must have perceived the gloomy effect which these names produce on their spirits. I have seen them—the weather-beaten heavy-laden figures,—crowding to the windows of the railway carriage, pointing to the hot fields, and then to the old scars on their foreheads. The sun was scorching, when under his fierce rays they trudged along uphill, with fixed bayonets, half hidden in a cloud of dust; marching on towards death. How many thousands of their comrades lie under those mounds,—how many thousands more will fall there if there should come another war! One could read all that in the glittering eyes and knit brows of the rough, tired soldiers. They looked wistfully into the distance, as though they could see the threatening cloud on the horizon, as though they felt the unquiet blood that was then beating in the heart of Europe;—it was just before 1866.

Towards Mantua lies Villafranca, the little town where, on the 11th of July, 1859, the two Emperors met together, to arrange the conditions of peace; whilst the French fleet was already before Venice, and the Quadrilateral was being prepared to sustain a long siege with all the terrors of Sebastopol. The lightning flash from that cloud which had lowered over the plains of Lombardy had penetrated far and wide; and boundless was the amazement when, on a sudden, Peace was given to Europe!

It was cradled in the walls of the old castle which commands the town from a distance, and was erected by the Scaligers to threaten Mantua. The towers rise boldly with sharply cut battlements, into the blue sky; a veritable falcon's eyry. The soil, although frequently stony, is intersected by ditches and canals, often dating from the days of the Hohenstaufens; Arrigo d'Egna, the great Podestà, caused one such " Fossa" to be made which runs as far as Somma Campagna.

Although Villafranca owes its name to free commerce, yet it was always one of the best fortified townlets in the Veronese Province. But it was renowned especially for its " Muraglia," a fortress wall which extended to Valeggio, a distance of six kilometres. This, too, was erected by the Scaligers in the fourteenth century, and defended by battlements, turrets, and gateways. Borghetto is famous for the ruined bridge which spans the Mincio; Gian Galeazzo Visconti built it to defy the princely house of the Gonzagas, and to turn aside the waters of the Mincio which defended Mantua. He did not succeed in this aim, although he expended more than a hundred thousand *zecchini* on the work. The whole of the deep valley which divides Borghetto from the castle of Valeggio, was bridged across; the length of the erection was five hundred metres, the breadth, twenty-five and a half; and fourteen great towers rose threateningly above it. The conflict which these battlements appeared designed to call forth was not wanting; but battles raged fiercest here in the time of Bonaparte,—not the great, taciturn, soldier-Emperor, but that fiery

CASTLE OF VILLAFRANCA.

youth who crossed the Alps as General of the Republic, and stood on the bridge at Arcola with flying banner and flying hair!

On examining closely the crumbling masonry of the bridge at Borghetto, fragments were found precisely similar to the Roman buildings at Sirmio, and in the neighbourhood of the Lake of Garda; deep down amongst the rubbish of the embankment, coins were found bearing the image of Consuls and Emperors; in a word, it can scarcely be doubted that the bridge is erected on the ruins of an ancient Roman viaduct. Long before Bonaparte led his legions into battle, "Ave, Cæsar!" had been uttered here by Roman lips. "Ave, Cæsar!" Word of evil omen which has drenched the soil of Verona with blood!

BASSANO.

FROM VERONA TO THE MOUNTAINS OF VENETIA.

THE great railroad which now runs from Trent to Venice, has attracted all the traffic of Venetia to itself, like a mighty river, for it, alone, possesses that magic quality which enchants the present generation,—namely, speed; and therefore it obtains the preference. All the millions of hasty pilgrims, and precious freights which go from Germany to Italy, follow this route. The Venetian mountains are half forgotten and deserted, with their bold fortress of Covolo, their rivers, Brenta and Cordevole, their defiant Citadella, their fragrant valleys, Val Stagna, Carpané, and Val Sugana. On their steep rocky heights lies that singular Island, as it were, of the German language, called "I Sette Comuni" (*i.e.*, The Seven Communes); ancient German settlements which stand like outposts of the Empire, in Italy. Formerly, before the railway had marked out the present path for travellers, a curious enquirer would make his appearance now and then among the lonely hill-farms; and the inhabitants were enchanted to hear his greeting in the familiar tongue, like a message from their distant fatherland. But now that has nearly ceased; father and sons have yielded to the foreign language, and only an old woman may be heard here and there singing a German lullaby over the cradle of her grandchild. Whoever climbs now into the villages of the "Sette Comuni," visits "the death-bed of the German tongue."

But before mounting thither, we will take a look around the remarkable district which divides Venetia from the Trentino.

PORTA RUSTERI, FELTRE.

Nearly all the towns in it have an air of hoary antiquity, and in their history we find the traces of the destroying hordes of Attila, the hand of Alboin, Odoacer, and Theodoric.

"Ho, Marcoman and Vandal, Swabian, Goth!
Up, Attila, up gloomy scourge of God!
Heel down this half-dead city in thy wrath!
Her cup is full, she sinks beneath the sod."—H. LINGG.

These lines occur to us here, and yet a new life has arisen out of the ruins.

There is Feltre with her turretted battlements ; squeezed together on a hill-side, with her ancient Porta Imperiale, which recalls the Roman processions of the German Emperors, her Casa Guarnieri, a specimen of the finest Gothic architecture, and the little Byzantine church erected up aloft there on Miesna, by the Crusaders. The situation of Belluno is almost the same :—on a delightful slope, half hidden among the Alps, with its gigantic stone gateway, and slender campanile (bell-tower). The Gothic Palazzo Municipale has a dignified ancient look ; so has the Palace of the Bishops, which was founded in the time of Barbarossa. Legends hang themselves about these walls like garlands of creeping plants. One legend goes back to the age of Pliny and Ptolemy, and informs us how a wild boar ravaged the mountains all around, until a warrior of Celtic race overcame him ; and then for the first time the city began to enjoy uninterrupted prosperity.

Bassano is a much more quiet place ; it lies on the bank of the Brenta at the point where the stream leaves the mountain for the plain. The Arts and Sciences have adorned the little town of which the Da Pontes (the painters more generally known under the name of Bassano) were natives ; whilst Canova was born in the immediate neighbourhood. With that proud reverence which Italians have for their great Masters, the citizens have collected all the treasures of the above-named artists, that they could lay hands on. Every fleeting sketch, every incomplete design, has been held sacred by them.

And in the same way almost all the little towns of the Venetian Alps, possess a hidden interior attraction, notwithstanding their rough and solitary outside. They are like certain persons whose harsh appearance repulses us, and who only allow us to find out by degrees, how many beautiful thoughts, how many weighty memories, their souls contain. But still the fairest of all is still Nature ; the noble landscape spreading silently around us, that *tells* us nothing of its wonders, but only lets us dimly guess them. Loiteringly we follow the course of the dark Brenta, and hear Tasso's song :

"Corre la Brenta al mar, tacita e bruna."

We are upon the limits that divide the Trentino from Venetia. Val Stagna still smiles upon us clear and free ; but soon the landscape narrows to a frowning mountain-pass, and when we come to Primolano, the ruins of a castle of the Scaligers look down on us, and presently we enter that terrible rocky gorge, once commanded by the threatening little fortress of Covolo.

The old main road from Germany to Venice passes by here. The castle is niched into a sort of rocky cavern ; eagles and hawks built in it and swooped down on any prey that chanced to fall from the road bordering the precipice, into the depths below ; until man displaced them, and built an eyry of his own wherein to wait for his enemy. We find Covolo mentioned for the first time in the year 1004, when Arduino Duke of Ivrea entrenched himself in the pass to bar the way against the Emperor Henry. Later the Scaligers became lords of the place, (as a ladder carved in the rock still testifies) until finally the Carraras came. But the mastery did not remain with them, either ; for all the powerful families of Italy whose names fill the Middle Ages with a clash of arms, vied with each other for the fine bold eagles' nest,—the Viscontis of Milan, and the Doges of Venice, and even Kaiser Max himself, the latter of whom conquered it in 1509, and united it permanently with Tyrol.

Dal Pozzo, who visited the fortress at the end of last century, has given us a lively picture of it. At that time the only means of entrance within its lofty walls was a rope, to the end of which a broad girdle was attached, and which was wound up by a cog-wheel,

Every chamber was hewn out of the solid rock:—the armoury and the casemates, the little chapel, and the dungeon for prisoners. Deep, dark corridors lead into the interior of the cavern, where two springs of water spurt out from the rock, and are received into

NEAR PRIMOLANO IN THE VAL SUGANA.

stone reservoirs. In the chapel, dedicated to St. John the Baptist, the holy sacrament is kept; and when we leave it, we come upon a double door—the outer of oak, the inner of iron—behind which powder and lead are stored! Muskets and carronades, old field-pieces that once stood in the loop-holes, and thousands of grenades lie piled up here. In one corner is a chaos of sharp-cornered stones, which were to be used for throwing down on the besieging foe. The number of the garrison must always have been but small, for the casemates could accommodate but a few hundred men. At the time of which Dal Pozzo writes there were sixteen habitable chambers.

ON THE CORDEVOLE.

In the days when Covolo belonged to Venice, the defence of the fortress was confided to that spirited little mountain people whom the Doge spoke of as "I nostri fedelissimi Sette Comuni" (our most faithful Seven Communes). It was German faithfulness that had earned this epithet; for the Seven Communes that linger on high up among the Venetian mountains are sprung from an ancient German stock, although how they came there is a riddle to enquirers.

CITTADELLA.

Already, in the earliest times in which we have any record of them, the "*homines Teutonici*" are mentioned as dwelling in the Seven Communes among the mountains of the Vicentino; and they were then held to be the descendants of those blonde Cimbri whom Marius defeated near Verona. In the last century, the answer of these people to any enquiry as to their race and name would be "Ich pin an Cimbro" ("I am a Cimber"). The Seven Communes which embrace a population of about thirty thousand souls in their scattered farmsteads, and the central point of which is the hamlet of Asiago, had early

FROM VERONA TO THE MOUNTAINS OF VENETIA.

formed themselves into a brave little republic, which existed rather under the protection, than the rule, of Venice. They had their own constitution, founded upon certain ancient special rights, the compilation of which reaches back to the time of Ludwig of Bavaria; and they were always looked upon by the surrounding populations as something peculiar, foreign, and mysterious. The name of the chief place in the Seven Communes is in their own dialect "Sleghe," and thence the inhabitants of the whole district were called "Sleghers," or, with an Italian turn of pronunciation, "Slaperi." That some ironical meaning should have slipped into this word could scarcely have been avoided; it was the old conflict between the German and Italian spirits. But the little republic held unshakeably by its Germanism, no matter how temptingly the South assailed its constancy. It was the women, above all, who most faithfully preserved the old traditions; and church and school-house worked with them in this sense for a long time. Only German was allowed to be spoken in the pulpits of the Seven Communes, and if there were no priests forthcoming from among themselves, they sent for them from Silesia and the Rhine. Nay, in the Church register is written after the names of most of them the addition

MOUNTAIN FORTRESS OF COVOLO.

"d'Allemagna." But the Curia soon adopted another system: whenever the Communes asked for a German priest the Canons sent them an Italian one, who forbade the children to talk their mother tongue. Indeed it soon came to refusing absolution to those who wished to confess in German. Hence it is not surprising that the enquirers who visited the "Sette Comuni" about thirty years ago found only scattered, erratic traces of the old energetic speech. They drew their picture from a few poor fragments, not from the full and living reality.

For the rest, all the investigations into the peculiarities of this singular little country, and, especially, into the origin of its inhabitants, are not of recent date. Leibnitz mentions these strange "islands of language" with amazement; and the King of Denmark who

COTTAGE IN THE VALLEY OF THE BRENTA.

visited Italy in 1709, himself climbed up into the Seven Communes to hear and investigate their speech. At that time many held the polite opinion that the inhabitants were of Danish origin! Some think that they are descended from the Huns; others from the "Longobards." Some incline to the opinion that their dialect approaches that of the Alemanni,—others think it resembles Low German. But, although we are unable to settle these disputes, thus much is clear, that the people that greet us here with blue eyes and golden hair, is of German race. Truly these characteristics are almost all that remain to testify to their ancient origin, and in another ten years or so, it is probable that even this trace may have disappeared.

It was with a strange feeling that I climbed slowly up to the Seven little Communes in a green solitude of pine woods. There came into my head the fairy tale of the seven dwarfs who watch over a glass coffin in a lonely forest. In the glass coffin sleeps a fair maiden with closed lips. All day long the dwarfs go out to labour in the forest, and in the silent evening hour they return and wait and watch to see if her eyelash does not quiver, and the breath come from her lips. But all is still, sleeping, dead ;—and this "Little Snow-white" is the German speech!

VILLA GIUSTINIANI, PADUA.

FROM VERONA TO THE ADRIATIC.

JOURNEYING from Verona towards Venice, the traveller finds the hills of Monte Berico almost stopping the way; and at the foot of the said hills, a city somewhat mean and straitened in its outward aspect, and yet rich within, in artistic treasures. This is Vicenza, the "City of Palladio." She, too, possessed a great master whose pride it was to adorn his native place with his best works, and for whose sake many a visitor seeks her walls.

Palladio, born in Vicenza in the year 1518, was originally a sculptor; until being impressed by the grandeur of ancient architecture in Rome, he was won over to that art. Among the plans for the completion of St. Peter's, one by Palladio still exists; and it was on its final rejection that he returned home, and erected there the pillared edifices which have become models for Europe.

In the construction of Vicenza we still find distinct traces of antiquity; but on the gigantic Piazza which was once the Forum, now stand the town hall, and the famous "Basilica," the Palace of the Prefect, and the "Loggia del Delegato," and the marble statue of Palladio reminds us who it was that created all this beauty.

When we use the word "basilica" now-a-days, it suggests to most persons a splendid ecclesiastical building, but such was not the most ancient meaning of the word. The oblong halls used for the assembling of the public, bore this title; and Greek philosophers and Roman judges were wont to meet in similar places, long before the Church used them for her worship. In this antique sense the Basilica of Palladio must be understood. It is the real public palace of the city, the centre of her public life, and the apex of her public pride. The wide halls with their double row of columns were intended to express these thoughts and sentiments, and the artist's mastery is shown in the brilliant manner in which that intention is carried out. Vicenza is but a small town, with a population of barely forty thousand inhabitants, yet how powerfully the sense of conscious strength, and the sentiment of freedom, strikes us here! A sentiment which may be sometimes overpowered, but never humbled.

THE OLD SEMINARY, VICENZA.

The same impression is produced on visiting the Museo Civico (Civic Museum) which contains many curiosities; or the Olympic theatre, founded in the middle of the sixteenth century, to reproduce the antique stage. But the same artistic spirit has reached beyond the immediate limits of the city; for example there is the Villa named "La Rotonda," of which Goethe says in his "Italian Journey," that architecture has never reached a higher point of luxury. The noble building was not intended for a permanent dwelling, but merely for temporary occupation, and the important point was not so much the interior accommodation, as the external effect of the edifice which shows on all sides the magnificence of a classic temple. The great saloon, roofed by a cupola, is lighted from above; unfortunately the bullets of the Italian war have done much mischief to it.

The proud Vicenza, once able to cope with Venice, and the Viscontis, is now but a quiet provincial town, and her chronicles record rather "being" and "suffering" than "doing." Only the old memories still survive. May they be fruitful in the minds of the young generation!

PIAZZA DEI SIGNORI IN VICENZA.

We are in Padua, in a town whose narrow nooks and alleys are surmounted by gigantic domes and towers. Presently we come out of the neglected ways into great solitary Piazzas and wide streets, added by later times to the original city; but these, too, lose themselves in deserted gardens, and then all around becomes still and lonely. A priest in a broad-brimmed hat reproving some children, itinerant vendors shouting their wares with loud echoing voices, and an artizan hammering at his work under an open doorway, were the first living figures we saw. Frequently the doors are replaced by a torn curtain, through whose rents we can look into the life going on in the dwelling, where a greenfinch twitters in a cage suspended from the ceiling. At the corners of the walls you may still read the relics of the "demonstrations of '66." "*Vogliamo Vittorio Emanuele! Vogliamo l'Italia Una!*" &c. &c. Then again we wander further past long rows of dusky houses close by the water's edge, and connected with each other by old fashioned bridges; for the old town, which was formerly a fortress, is intersected by canals of the Brenta, and shows frequent traces of its ancient origin. Indeed it is this antiquity which chiefly strikes us at first, and we are uncertain whether reverence for its dignity, or disgust at its squalor, predominates in our minds.

At length after some further wanderings we reach the Piazza dei Signori, where stands the Loggia del Consiglio, and where the Past still meets us in all its ancient pride. Let us pause here, and think of the famous names connected with these walls, which Antenor founded, which Livy called his home, and which in Roman times could send out (as Strabo assures us) an army of two hundred thousand men. It is not to be wondered at that one's thoughts involuntarily recur to the history of the past, in these Italian cities; for the secret of their attractiveness consists partly in the consciousness that these cities are connected with the earliest development of European society;—that there was scarcely any great epoch in the history of human culture, but found here its theatre and its heroes. And however frivolous the Italians may be, yet they are all penetrated with this sentiment of historic continuity. The pious worship of past greatness, is a noble trait in the character of the modern Italian. How proud is Mantua of her Virgil, Verona of Catullus, and Padua of Livy!

Certainly, however, Padua was no exception to the curse which rested on the whole history of Italy in the Middle Ages. Civil wars, and noble feuds, devastated her territory, power was won and lost by treachery, and her Princes used the policy of Macchiavelli long before Macchiavelli had written his "*Principe.*"

But Padua did not belong to these princelings only: there was yet another Master here, who bears the sounding title "Il Santo!" and whose name is inextricably connected with that of the city. The colossal temple dedicated to his honour, is almost the symbol of Padua; streets, Piazzas, and schools, are named after him, and the name of Saint Anthony is on every tongue. Thus we have here before our eyes the three great factors which have principally prevailed in the building of all these cities;—in the splendid palaces dwells the pugnacious spirit of the old Republics: in the temples filled with master-pieces of Art, and all manner of treasures, the ostentatious magnificence of the Church early exhibited itself: and in the crowd of dusky houses, thickly pressed together to make room for the expansion of these two powers,—in the squalid alleys along the canals of the Brenta, swarms the People,—the weary care-laden masses, who live for centuries under an oppressive yoke, until all at once *they*, too, leap into power, and prove themselves a more formidable force than any other! Nearly all Italian cities, and Padua not the least, have experienced this in times of blood.

Amongst the palaces which belong to the public life of the Commonwealth, the Palazzo della Ragione is remarkable. It was built about the time of the Lombard League, and has a wonderful hall with a wooden roof, which is said to be the largest in Europe. Its colossal dimensions may be conceived when we state the fact that the

CHURCH OF ST. ANTHONY, PADUA.

paintings in it contain more than three hundred separate subjects, and the extent of the floor is reckoned at 16,500 square feet. On the whole, although this huge space contains several curious objects (as the "Horse of Troy," some Egyptian statues, and tolerable pictures), yet the striking thing is undoubtedly the external architecture. But even in this respect the Loggia del Consiglio, with its noble rows of columns, far surpasses it; nor is the Palazzo Giustiniani inferior, a palace which recalls to us classic names, for Falconetto was its builder, and its owners were the Cornaro family, who had come hither after Padua had acknowledged the supremacy of Venice in 1405. The courtyard of the Palazzo Giustiniani is charming; but still more charming is the garden in the midst of which delightful wilderness stands a lonely villa.

Now we approach the "*Santo;*" we are near to the famous church of Saint Anthony. The surprising impression which this colossal edifice produces, is due rather to the enormity of its masses, than the skill with which they are combined; for the seven cupolas which overarch the nave and transepts, are rather oppressive than elevating in their effect.

Opposite to us rises the splendid brazen equestrian statue of Gattamelata, erected by the Venetians in honour of their hero; a master-piece of Donatello. And then we enter the interior of the church by the great main doorway. Some veiled figures are praying, indistinct in the dim light which softens the hard outlines of the bronze bas-reliefs, and the crude tints of the pictures. The length of the nave appears to stretch away almost immeasurable before us, while on the other hand the side chapels seem too narrow and limited to contain the fulness of their treasures. The richest of these is, of course, the "Capella del Santo"—the chapel of Sant' Antonio himself. Here the bones of the saint are preserved in a consecrated shrine, and marble bas-reliefs represent the miracles which he worked; heavy silver candlesticks, and hanging lamps, in which a never-extinguished flame is burning, gilt carvings, and statues of saints in the niches, all unite to form a grand expression of religious pomp, especially as we see almost everywhere the work of some master hand.

Master hands have left their impress also in other parts of the church: for instance in the chapel of San Felice, or in the chancel, with its fine bronze works by Riccio and Donatello. The chapel of San Giorgio which belongs to the church of the "Santo," but is divided from it by a certain space, was discovered to be precious in an artistic sense only in the year 1837, in which year Ernest Förster, celebrated for his Italian researches, released its paintings from their tomb of dust.

Amongst the other churches of Padua, the chief are the Duomo (cathedral), the church of the "Eremitani," and the Carmine; but in point of Art, the Madonna dell' Arena is undoubtedly the most important. Its singular name is due to the fact that it was erected on the ruins of a Roman amphitheatre: its value to artists lies in the precious frescoes by Giotto, which fill nearly the whole oblong space.

To the fame of arms which Padua enjoyed, there soon was added the fame of letters. The high school, founded by the Emperor Frederick the Second in 1222, assembled the studious youth of all European countries. One is astonished on entering the splendid courtyard with its colonnades, to behold the shields of red marble which bear the arms of many noble families, and to see amongst the statues which adorn the university-buildings that of a woman. It is the portrait of Lucretia Cornaro Piscopia, who died in the year 1684, and who received academical honours in Padua. Hers is not the lowest among the famous names which Padua has handed down to us; but Padua has had but one Livy!

RIVA DEGLI SCHIAVONI, VENICE.

VENICE.

MIDNIGHT is past; a boat glides through the narrow canals, the figure of the gondolier shows like a black shadow, and a sepulchral cry "Giaè, giaè!" sounds as the gondola shoots past the sharp corners. The moon is high in the heavens, but her light reaches not to these narrow watery ways. Only a few twinkling stars peep between the tall houses, and now and then a tardy light glimmers behind some barred window. Hark! Who goes there? Behind a half-opened door that is nearly on a level with the water, a girl peeps forth, and then hurriedly scuds away; ours is not the gondola she was waiting for. On the marble steps that lead down from noble doorways to the water, sleepers are lying stretched. From time to time a boat glides past us, so close that the sides almost graze each other; the gondoliers greet each other with secret signs, and we peer curiously at the masked figures reclining on the cushions. Then all is still again, and we hear nothing save the lapping of the water against the keel, and the splash of the oar.

We listen, and now strange sounds meet our ears. Far away there, beyond the Lido, murmurs the sea in which the Doge was wont to throw his golden ring in token of betrothal; it is the hour of flood, and the tide slowly rising, fills the Lagoons and flows into the Canal Grande among the palaces of the proud old names.

VENICE.

> " All is still; the sea breathes only.
> Sighing deep, lamenting sore,
> Knocks the Doge's bride deserted
> At each lordly palace door."

And that, really, is what we seem to hear; we feel the power of the great deep, but we do not see it; we are imprisoned in a labyrinth of narrow watery paths, which cross, and are tangled endlessly in one another, and lead,—who knows whither?

VENETIAN FISHING-BOAT.

Some such impression as that above described, is felt by a traveller arriving at night by the train from Mestre, and then rowing from the station into the city. No horse, no carriage, is to be seen; nothing but the dark throng of gondolas which thread their way in and out with snake-like agility. All firm foundations seem to sink away from one's feet, and we see only the black pliant waters, from which the weather-stained houses rise up perpendicularly. The sad gloomy hues which they display even in broad daylight, become more dreary darkness by night, and the long intricate voyage has, in truth, something Stygian about it! Disappointment makes us dumb.

We went in the boat to the hôtel of the Luna, where we were to take up our quarters, and that dark journey I shall never forget. We were a curiously mixed party;—a German Professor with a long intelligent face, a stout old lady (an Italian from the Provinces), and a young married couple on their wedding tour. At first there was plenty of chatting; but as the minutes seemed to grow longer and the ways narrower, a sort of oppression settled down on us. I gazed at the face of the pleasant young wife, framed in golden curls, but I could only catch a glimpse of it at

ARRIVAL OF A MILK-BOAT.

intervals when a stray beam of light from a window fell upon her. What charming features, noble and beautiful as the countenance of a Madonna, and yet still retaining the unconscious enchantment of a childlike soul. She drew her cloak tighter about her, and pressed closer to her husband, whilst her large bright eyes glanced timidly around.

"Why is it all so black here?" she asked, half aloud. "The walls, and the gondolas, and the water! Only look at those long trunks there under the cloth. They are just like coffins!"

Her husband comforted her smilingly and unloosed the little white hand with which she had grasped him. We saw her fingers move uneasily, and then again she gazed about her, up at the walls of the houses, and down at the canal.

"Fiesco and the Moor were in Genoa, were they not? Ah! but there was a Moor of Venice, too. And—and the Bravo, hidden behind the door with his dagger!"

The Professor grinned. The husband answered quietly, "I almost believe you are frightened! Ah Maria!"

The Italian matron from the provinces began to feel uneasy. Fear is infectious, and she rolled her black eyes anxiously. It might, perhaps, have been better if her husband —whom in general she could very well dispense with,— had been with her; and

catching the last words of the young bridegroom's sentence, she nodded her head and ejaculated, "Ave Maria!"

At length a full stream of light poured out upon us from a doorway, and the boat stopped at the Albergo della Luna. With the agile strength common to Italian *Facchini*, the trunks were unloaded from the boat; we mounted the handsome staircase adorned with green plants, and found no Bravo waiting for us behind the door; in a word, all was well again. Even the stout matron was satisfied that her husband had not accompanied her after all, and she called out a smiling "Felice notte!" to the young couple.

The May sun was shining brilliantly when we entered the Piazza of St Mark the next day. Who has not felt the enchantment of such sunshine, breathing of spring and morning, penetrating the soul with an awakening power? Now the dark veil was lifted that lay last evening over Venice; now the sea was blue, and the old grey blocks of stone of which the palaces are built looked bright and strong, and the delicate open-work of the façades glittered in the light. She is still alive, the silent city of the Doges! With full hands she pours out her treasures; with wondering eyes we contemplate her marvellous form; but St. Mark's is the very heart of her.

The Piazza di San Marco is closed in on all four sides; and although the Piazzetta adjoins it on the north-east, the unity of the picture is not destroyed by it. On the right and left stretch out the huge rows of buildings called the *procuratie*. The lower stories consist of open arcades under which the crowd throngs; the upper have rows of columns whose structure combines grace and vigour. The *procuratie* are joined by a cross wing, (the edifice called the Ala Nuova) which terminates the Piazza on the west. At the opposite end there lies before us St. Mark's church with its great cupolas and porches, its marble minarets, and mythic figures,—the wonder of Venice! Immediately in front of it stands the colossal mast, or flag-staff, from which once floated the banners of conquered kingdoms; and the Campanile, where the bells of St. Mark's sound.

Here for the first time we realize the wide-spread power of Venice: that fairy city which sprang not from the earth, but the sea; still touched with the glamour of the East, and yet mistress of all Western culture—so rich in arts and arms in loves and hatreds! Venice is a sphinx whose enigma we never wholly penetrate. In vain we strive to find an image that shall express her mysterious essence. The Unique brooks no comparisons.

As in the old times, even so to-day, the centre of life and movement is the Piazza of St. Mark's, although it offers but a pale shadow of the life of former days. Here, on sunny mornings, all the foreigners assemble; here lounge the *ciceroni*, and on the neighbouring Piazzetta, the gondoliers. Itinerant vendors of all kinds push their way amongst the chairs that are set out in front of the cafés under the open arcade. But the most brilliant spectacle is at night, when hundreds of gas-jets are alight in the huge bronze candelabra—when the gold sparkles in the jewellers' windows, and the sound of gay music is borne across the Piazza. Then the crowd gathers from all sides. Here come the *nobili* with their wives. The gondolas throng to the Piazzetta, and the Merceria seems far too narrow for the press of people. But the Piazza di San Marco seems almost to grow and widen in the blue moonlight that peeps down into the dazzle of gas, and then hides coyly behind the pillars of the Procuratie. It seems as if its rays had touched the faces of the fair women, whose delicate pallor is renowned. They trail their rustling garments over the marble pavement, leaning carelessly on their husbands' arms, whilst their glowing glances stray far and wide above the rim of the black fan they carry.

The noise and the passion which run through the publicity of Italian life, continue deep into the night; then last hasty words are spoken, yet one more stolen glance is shot from beautiful eyes, and the happy individual for whom it is intended understands the farewell. Around the steps of the Piazzetta—all of white marble, so that you cannot miss them even at night—the gondolas gather again, and then separate on their different ways through the dark and dead-silent canals. On the great Piazza the lights are extinguished in the candelabra, the music ceases, and stray boatmen stretch themselves to sleep on the bases of the columns. Further and further the moonlight advances into the centre of the Piazza, the echo of the last footstep dies away in San Moisé, and then all is silent throughout the vast space.

And now we hear again the murmur of the sea upon the Lido yonder. Venice

SAN PIETRO, CASTELLO.

Queen of the Seas, is alone in her forsaken beauty; all her children are sleeping, weary of noisy revelry and trivial mirth, but she sits like a musing widow, looking away beyond the cradle that she rocks. What is this present generation? These, the youngest of her sons, preserve no memory of the former glories of their race—of the beauty of their mother, of the passions that thrilled through her when the great ones of the earth were vying with each other for her favour. They are like children who sport artlessly amid the ruined splendours of their ancestral home.

It was thus that the city appeared to me one solitary night; the setting moon hung low in the heavens like a lamp that faintly illuminates a sleeping chamber; the rocking cradle was the sea, and a faint movement in the air seemed to be the sighs of the beautiful widowed Venice.

But morning succeeds to night. At an early hour next day, when everything was full of life and sunshine, we stepped beneath the portal of the church of St. Mark, which stands alone amidst all temples of the world. Although age, and the moist sea air, have spread their veil over these walls, yet the brilliant colouring and the mighty outlines shine through all the grey dimness of the past. The bronze horses above the great door are

rearing : the cupolas and arches stretch their great curves in intensity of power : each
portion of the huge building seems alive and animated, yet in the whole, reigns the profound and noble peace proper to the house of God.

It is difficult to shake off the grand impression of this whole, sufficiently to examine
the rich abundance of details which are displayed before us—almost every one of deep
historical interest, almost every one of perfect beauty. It is now exactly eight hundred
years ago since the building of St. Mark's was completed; its ecclesiastical sanctity is
bestowed on it by the relics of the great Evangelist; its historical sanctity consists in its

ON THE ISLAND OF TORCELLO.

intimate connection with the fortunes of the city and of her rulers. It was the theatre of
their triumphs and the refuge for their cares; all that she has achieved and suffered,
Venice has done under the protecting wing of St. Mark. On looking towards the main
façade we are overpowered by the mass which has been piled up by the wealth of the city,
and the fertility of her creative power. Five mighty arches, supported on noble columns,
form the entrance to the outer vestibule, and the bronze doors leading into the interior,
the mosaics upon a back-ground of gold, the many-coloured marbles—all these make so
profound an impression on us, that we stand still and gaze upward in bewilderment.
Each by itself is a wonder! It is known that the famous group of four horses, which
stands above the main portal, is of the antique Roman period, and was for a long time in
Byzantium, the capital of the Empire of the West. The Doge Dandolo, at the age of
ninety-five, led on the Venetians to the storming of Constantinople (1203). He was
nearly blind, but a fiery life still glowed in his veins; his name indicates the apex of the

Venetian military power; his monument consists of the noblest architectural treasures of the city.

The church of St. Mark contains trophies from all parts of the world: every stone has a history. Those two great pillars at the entrance to the Baptistery, were part of the booty of Acre. The bronze folding doors were once in the church of St. Sophia at Stamboul. The marble columns, which stand right and left of the main portal are said to have been taken from the Temple in Jerusalem. The broad flag-stones on which we stand—three squares of red marble—still narrate to us how Barbarossa once prostrated himself before Pope Alexander: "*Non tibi, sed Petro.*" "*Et Petro et mihi!*"

In examining the mosaics which fill the vaulted roof, we find ourselves in the midst of the Old Testament history; among forms which, with all their hardness, are yet not devoid of fervent expression, and with all their Byzantine stiffness, have still much earnest dignity; Paradise, the First Blessings, and the First Sorrows of Man, are the subjects of them. But let us pass beyond this outer vestibule into the interior of the church, in whose half-twilight a richer depth of colour glows. All is covered with a mass of mosaics and sombre marbles. On the parapet which divides the choir from the nave, stand figures of the Apostles in blackened bronze, and above the high altar, where the bones of St. Mark repose, rises a baldaquin upon twisted columns. How wondrous is the effect of the whole when the sunshine streams through the windows; when the organ fills every corner of the church with its invisible flood; when we seem to realize the fervour of all the past generations who have knelt here in prayer and praise—offering them up with different minds from ours of to-day, but with hearts so like to our hearts!

What St. Mark's is as the expression of the religious spirit, that the Ducal Palace is for the secular power, of Venice; it has scarcely a rival even in Italy. The Doge's palace, as it stands before us now, was begun in the 14th century, and completed in the 15th after a long interruption, for the earlier building, which dated from Carlovingian times, fell a prey to the flames. Two mighty ranges of columns, one above another support the broad massive upper buildings—a huge, clear, flat surface, whose peaceful unity is only broken by the gothic arched windows which admit light into the noble halls within. Here every line is classic. The very position of the palace, its relation to the church of St. Mark, its two fronts—one commanding the Piazzetta and the other the sea—declare the inner significance of the building; it is the foundation, the very corner-stone, of all Venetian splendours. The court, into which the Porta della Carta leads, is princely, and has something colossal about it even before we perceive the Scala dei Giganti;—that marble staircase, with the figures of Mars and Neptune, on whose topmost step the Doge was wont to be crowned. And now let us mount by the Scala d'Oro to the wide, echoing, gold-encrusted halls, where the Great Council held its sittings, where are the statues of the famous men who have sprung from the Republic, and the portraits of the Doges who ruled over it.

But yet a little shadow rests on these splendours. A slight shudder mars the enchantment, for the hands of Venice are stained with blood—much noble blood sacrificed to unworthy passions. There is the Bocca di Leone, into which Envy threw its secret accusations. We pass by the door that leads to the prisons and the Bridge of Sighs; we see amidst the line of Doges, the black space from whence Marino Faliero's portrait was effaced when his head had fallen beneath the axe of the executioner. In the Sala del Maggior Consiglio, the Great Council held its sittings. All the members wore scarlet robes. Here the die was cast for war or peace, for honour or disgrace; and the pride

FISH-MARKET NEAR THE RIALTO.

that uplifted their hearts is, as it were, embodied in the masterpieces which adorn walls and roof. Everywhere Victories, coronations, gods,—nay, Tintoret who produced in this hall the largest painting known in the history of art, chose no meaner subject than the World of the Blessed! Venice dreamt only of Paradise. We pass on through a long series of saloons. Here the Doge was elected by the Nobili; there he received ambassadors from foreign lands; yonder was his bedchamber; and here the guards paced to and fro watching over the most precious jewel of Venice—the Doge's life.

The triumphal arch through which we entered, was erected for Morosini, the hero who subjugated the Morea, the barbarian whose cannon destroyed the Parthenon, burying hundreds of Athenians under the most magnificent ruin that the earth has ever seen. We come to a little chapel on our way, in which the Doge was accustomed to hear mass every morning. He was accompanied during the ceremony by the Council of Ten, and in the last room which we enter, this council held its bloody tribunal. "*Consiglio de' Dieci!*" That was a word of terror to all citizens of Venice; and whatsoever pains her defenders may take to prove the contrary, it must be allowed that though the Republic might be free in other respects, yet in this tribunal she had a power which could only be compared with that of Robespierre or the bloodthirsty Marat. All crimes against the security of the state—(and, therefore *all* crimes?)—were subject to their jurisdiction. The Doge himself, was liable to feel their mysterious power. In secresy and silence the witnesses were examined; in secresy and silence the sentence was carried out; and, in order still further to simplify their proceedings, three Inquisitors were moreover named of whom no one was allowed to know the persons or the residence. But they existed; and their invisible omnipresence lay like a dark ban upon men's spirits.

BRIDGE OF SIGHS.

The complete truth about Venice cannot be learned in the lofty Ducal Palace where the ceilings are full of gold, and where art, free and untrammelled, created her masterpieces. We must go down even as far as the Pozzi, into the dungeons below the level of the water; or we must mount into the hot leaden cells (the Piombi); then we begin to conceive what was the secret canker gnawing at the root of all this beauty—then we feel with unspeakable horror what is the shadow on the conscience of the proud Queen of the Adriatic. But this shadow is necessary to the perfect portrait. Who does not know whence the Bridge of Sighs derives its name? that wondrously elegant arch which spans the Rio del Palazzo, leading from the noblest beauty to the deepest misery! And who could see the fearful Piombi unmoved? It was a smiling May morning when we first visited them; first the prisons, and then the torture chamber, on whose ceiling the hook may still be seen to which the unfortunate wretches were hoisted up; and whose floor is paved with smooth stones in order that the blood should easily be wiped from it. We shuddered.

I thought of the times of Dandolo and Morosini. I pictured to myself the last night of one condemned to death here, and the tortures of those from whom a confession of guilt was wrung. The Piazza of St. Mark is almost at our feet, we can hear in the evening the swell of the music and the murmur of the crowd of masquers. It is a Festa night, and up there beneath the leaden roof, a man lies brooding, whom to-morrow the executioner will awaken. Perhaps the friend who betrayed him is in the merry throng, and that moon whose rays glimmer through the bars, perhaps is shining on the gondola wherein his beautiful wife receives the homage of a stranger's love. He groans, he strikes his forehead with his hand—"*nessun maggior dolore che ricordarsi del tempo felice, nella miseria.*" (Dante, Divina Commedia.)

And that, too, was Venice!

With a sensation of relief we return to the open air, to the grand Piazzetta where the sea-breeze blows, where the "Zecca" opens its pillared halls; that ancient mint, which as early as the year 1280, coined gold sequins. And what a press of gondolas! On every side is heard the cry "La barca, Signore!" "Commanda la barca?" The gondolier

GHETTO.

COFFEE-HOUSE ON THE RIVA DEGLI SCHIAVONI.

greets us, his oar in his left hand, his right raised with a slight gesture of salutation; the blue shirt bound at the waist by a red sash, reveals his open breast, and his sunburnt face looks frankly at us. A moment, and the picturesque, sinewy figure is in full movement; the oar dips deep into the wave, and the bark shoots like an arrow along the Grand Canal.

It is the largest of the four hundred watery ways which intersect Venice. Nearly four miles in length stretches the broad stream from Santa Chiara to the Giudecca. Along the Canal Grande rise the noblest palaces of those great old families whose names were written in the "Libro d'Oro"—the Golden Book—of the Republic. That book was burned on the open Piazza in 1797, when the Western Tempest broke over Venice: it was a hurricane such as even those children of the ocean had never yet witnessed, and its name was—*Egalité!*

On the narrow point of land exactly opposite to the steps of the Piazzetta, are the Dogana di Mare (Sea Custom House) and the Seminary of the Patriarch, both dominated by the fine church of Santa Maria della Salute. This church was built as a votive offering by the Venetians in the time of the plague, after more than 40,000 persons had fallen victims to the pestilence, and has come to be one of the great landmarks of the city, with its gigantic cupola, and white mass of building shimmering in the morning light. In almost every pictorial representation of Venice you see Santa Maria della Salute.

We glide onwards until we come opposite to the Palazzo Contarini Fasan, and here the gondolier pauses. It is one of the finest façades in Venice: the marble balconies are as delicate and slender as if worked in precious metals, tall and narrow rise the arched windows with their columns opening on to the balcony; and yet amidst all this elegance there is a strength which shows us that mighty times and mighty men once reigned here. Now great names throng upon us. Here is the Palazzo Corner; and there are the houses of the Foscari, the Balbi, Mocenigo, Grimani, and Loredan. Before each princely door are white marble steps leading down into the water, and great wooden posts—painted with the colours of the family—which serve to moor the gondolas to.

We pursue our voyage, and a splendid arch is suddenly seen spanning the Canal Grande; it is the Bridge of the Rialto, for a long time the only one which crossed the Grand Canal, and still by far the most interesting of all the bridges that Venice possesses. A busy tide of life flows hitherward, for it is the central point for retail dealers. Here the fishermen bring their wares to market; here the laws of the old Republic were published at a column which bears the name of the "Gobbo di Rialto" (the hunchback of the Rialto), and on the bridge itself stands a double row of little *botteghe* (shops) built of marble and roofed with lead. As the story goes the first of them were erected because it was feared that the bridge might be forced upwards in the centre, and Da Ponte, whose opinion was asked, advised in his last moments that the two ends of the bridge should be weighted in this manner. Thus the Ponte di Rialto obtained the upper buildings which give it almost an inhabited air, but deprive it of the imposing boldness which once distinguished the unencumbered arch. It is nearly one hundred and fifty feet wide, and its foundations under water rest upon a platform of twelve thousand piles.

In the same manner, as is well known, all the houses and palaces in Venice have arisen out of the sea; the whole city is the most colossal edifice upon piles, that the world has ever seen. In order to support the enormous weight put upon them, it was necessary to choose only the mightiest trunks, and the finest sorts of wood, which were brought from foreign lands by the enormous sea commerce of Venice; and it happened in the last century that a noble family resolved to pull down their splendid palace on the

Canal Grande in order to get at the precious cedar stems on which it is built, and thus rescue themselves from a slough of debt. But the Republic forbade this desperate measure.

Amongst the palaces on the Grand Canal two have an international importance. That is to say, they reveal to us not only the enchantment of beauty, and the luxury, to which Venice attained at home, but the world-wide commerce which the city of the Lagoon once commanded. The Fondaco dei Tedeschi, close to the Rialto Bridge, was the chief place of meeting for the German merchants, and the central point of their commerce. The whole traffic of the Levant with the north passed through Venice, and the Turks, as well as the Germans, had their national house on the Canal Grande; the Fondaco dei Turchi. This house too was the property of the Republic, and was by its hospitality dedicated to the use of the Mussulmen. Here the Koran was read, and the praises of Allah recited; it was the focus of Oriental life in Venice. The building is tolerably well preserved (it has now, in the year 1875, been entirely and carefully restored); but it shares the fate of all the palaces on the Grand Canal, it has fallen into the hands of strangers.

MONUMENT OF GENERAL FARNESE IN THE JESUITS' CHURCH.

When the gondola has glided on beneath the Ponte di Rialto, we come upon yet more beautiful palaces;—the Ca' d'Oro, with its wonderfully richly sculptured façade, and the Palazzo Pesaro, with its heavy, massive walls; but the finest of all is the Vendramin-Calergi. The gondola silently pauses before the marble steps; we enter the colossal doorway and a porter shows us the way, and greets us in the most undeniable French. This is the palace of the Duchess de Berri,—now the property of the Count de Chambord. No other of the splendid buildings of Venice which I visited produces so deep an impression of decay,—of the mixture of a glorious past with a squalid present. We walked onward through corridors and saloons, past noble statues and muffled pictures. Here a splendid mirror showed a long crack; there the yellow damask was all moth-eaten; and even our guide looked as grumpy and regretful as though all the fine things decaying before our eyes had been his own. The lilies show proudly on the golden cradle that we pass by in our progress, but the ancient race of its owners is desolate; all sorts of utensils and articles for the performance of religious ceremonies lie about in the little chapel, but no bell sounds there, and no taper is lighted. Impotence and stagnation declare themselves painfully in the midst of this splendour. It would be foolish to calculate the worth of such a building by the price that it fetches; but to show the deep fall from its glories of former days which Venice has experienced, I know no more striking comparison than that furnished by the figures concerning the Palazzo Vendramin. This palace, which was sold *three hundred years ago* for sixty thousand ducats, came into the possession of the Duchess de Berri in recent times, for six thousand ducats!

And so we hasten onward between the long rows of palaces, to the end of the Grand Canal, to the island of Santa Chiara, where the Lagoon opens out and the sea begins. Great red buoys, which serve to mark the way for navigators, balance themselves on the waves, and the arches of the huge railway bridge reach across to where Terra firma shows dimly in the distance. It is the longest bridge in the world, for it measures nearly twelve thousand feet in length, and has more than two hundred arches. Xerxes' idea of bridging over the Hellespont has been, as it were, realised by modern Venice; for we roll on iron rails over the waters right into the interior of the town.

Nearly all that we have hitherto seen shows us but the traces of past greatness; princely buildings silently decaying, and princely families sharing the fate of their palaces. We have been passing through a worn-out world, whose pulse has ceased to beat for generations, where

STREET IN VENICE.

Life scarcely defends itself against Death. But a very different aspect of Venice reveals itself to us when on leaving the Piazza of St. Mark,—always the point of departure,—we plunge into the commercial parts of the town. We pass through an archway in the clock-tower, that forms so characteristic a feature of the north side of the Piazza, with its great bronze figures that strike the hours, and get into the *Merceria* leading to the Ponte di Rialto. Here we are in the midst of the Present, with its manifold requirements and feverish haste. The watchword here is not "to be," but "to have"; not the dignity, but the keenness of the old Venetians predominates here. It is well known that

ON THE GIUDECCA.

the first idea of great financial transactions originated in Italy, but in this field of commerce also Venice ranked foremost; she had the oldest bank in Europe, which dates back to the days of Barbarossa, and the development of which is a considerable factor in the city laws. All enactments having reference to this bank were proclaimed from the steps of the Rialto; here was the Exchange; here the great commerce in the treasures of the East was carried on; here Venice bartered the wealth of her industry for the wealth of natural products, before England and Holland became the mistresses of the trade of the world.

CANOVA'S TOMB IN SANTA MARIA GLORIOSA DEI FRARI. VENICE.

Not far from the Rialto stands the oldest church in Venice, San Giacomo, erected in the sixth century, if we may believe an inscription over the doorway. Nearly every church in Venice (and there are one hundred and two of them) is rich in art treasures, but we are unable to do more than indicate a few of them here. The church of the Frari produces a great impression, both by the amplitude of the space which surrounds it, and the largeness of its dimensions. Its interior contains the proud monument to Titian, and the imposing pyramid beneath which Canova rests. The religious order to whom the church belongs is that of the Franciscans. The church of Saints Giovanni e Paolo (called, in the vernacular of the Venetian populace, "Zanipolo") belongs to the Dominicans, and

STREET SCENE.

has, like the Frari and San Marco, an official character; for the victory of Venice over Cyprus was annually celebrated in this church; the funeral mass for the Doge was always performed there; and many Doges chose it for their last resting-place. We may cite Morosini and Mocenigo, Giustiniani and Loredan; but the finest tomb of all is that of Andrea Vendramin. The sarcophagus is placed in a lofty arched niche, adorned with columns supported by eagles; a sleeping figure of the mighty Doge lies on it, and the Virtues, whose figures surround him, watch over his eternal repose.

Of the other churches we may name San Rocco with its famous "Scuola;" Il Redentore on the Giudecca is a master-work of Palladio, who also built St. Giorgio Maggiore. Where it is possible, the churches are surrounded by a free space, but some of them are in the narrowest corners of lanes and alleys. Nay, behind the Scalzi, the Ghetto stretches out. It may be now some seven hundred years ago since the Ghetto was populated with its present inhabitants; for formerly the Jews were banished to the island of the Giudecca, and even in the time of Charles the Fifth, they were compelled to distinguish themselves by a red sign on the hat. At the present day they are not interfered with. Numerous chattering groups line the narrow streets of the Ghetto, which on the great festival days of Israel are changed into real gardens of greenery. The leafy garlands reach from one window to the other, and red carpets and hangings adorn the balconies, and many a Shylock may be seen wandering amongst the throng of laughing girls.

Rich as Venice is in beauty, however, one thing is wanting to her,—Nature. Whosoever wishes to enjoy nature must take refuge in the Giardini Pubblici, on the Lido, or on the little islands of Chioggia and Torcello, where the fishermen's huts stand, built out of the beams of wrecked ships. The public gardens of Venice are the creation of Napoleon, who pulled down hundreds of buildings, even consecrated buildings, in order to give this space for recreation to the Venetians: making them thus the most rare and singular of presents, a solid piece of dry land, a promenade amongst trees! You go along the Riva de' Schiavoni, which leads from the Piazzetta in the direction of the Lido. This Riva is a noble quay paved with broad flag-stones, over which throngs of people move, and in front of which are anchored rows of ships. Some have their flags flying; the star-spangled banner of the United States, or the proud colours of the German Empire. Others are having their sides newly pitched, while the idle sailors lie sleeping on the decks. Every now and then we come upon a bridge with shallow broad steps, crossing a canal. To the left lies the Arsenal, with its huge docks and magazines, watched over by the stone lions which were brought from Athens by Morosini. Centuries long this arsenal enjoyed a great European reputation, and no other in the world was considered comparable to it. The superintendence of it was entrusted to three "Patroni," who were chosen from the ranks of the nobles, and were changed every night at the same time with the sentinels on guard. The *Ammiraglio dell' Arsenale* had to watch over and protect the ducal palace during the election of the Doge; he commanded the Bucentaur on which the newly-elected Doge put out to sea to drop his ring into the Adriatic; a swarm of workmen was under his orders. During the time when the Republic was at the height of its power, ten thousand noble oak stems lay constantly steeping in the water, to serve for the construction of new ships. Every rope and every pulley had its private mark, and the theft of even a nail was punished with five years of the galleys. Here too lay the world-renowned "Bucentaur" at anchor—the pompous vessel of the Doge, all overhung with gold and red velvet, and with a deck inlaid with ebony and mother-of-pearl. Eighty-four golden oars propelled the bark over the blue waters; and the shouts of an exultant multitude accompanied her course!

STREET IN VENICE.

The collection of arms in the arsenal had formerly a great reputation, and offered a rich fund for historical observations. But the hand of the foreigner has in all times been busy amongst its treasures, and every victor helped himself from these trophies.

But in a short time we step out of this iron circle into the fresh green of the gardens, which chiefly charm us by the exquisite view to be seen thence. One should gaze from this spot at the roofs and towers of the wondrous sea-city, when they are gilded by the evening light, or when the twilight throws its veil around Santa Maria della Salute. The Lagoons open out widely before us, often crested with foaming waves ; and the figures we meet slowly pacing the broad alley, have frequently something of the stateliness of the old "Nobili." In all Venice there is not a single horse. Only here on a soft road running parallel with the main path, a rider is occasionally seen, and the street boys leave off their games to stare at the wonderful animal. The *Gardini Pubblici* are situated at the extreme point of Venice, on that sharp promontory which stretches out into the Lagoons. If you proceed beyond this point in a boat, you reach the Lido, a long stretch of sandy shore which divides the Lagoons from the open sea ; and beyond that again are the " Murazzi," the

A GONDOLA.

tremendous sea-walls which protect the town against the Adriatic. From hence is obtained the best idea of the extraordinary position of Venice ; how that shallow flood which goes by the name of *Laguna morta* and *Laguna viva*, stretches between the sea and the dry land, and how from its surface arose the most marvellous city in the world. The Lagoon is divided from the moving sea, as well as from the solid land, by sand-dunes, like gigantic dams. But there are great portals opened seawards by which ships can reach the free Adriatic. *Porto di Lido, Malamocco, Porto dei tre Porti* are the names of these three outlets. The Lagoons cover a superficies of more than a hundred and seventy square miles ; the *murazzi* alone which are erected to ward off the sea close to Palestrina, are over eighteen thousand feet long, and more than forty feet thick, and thirty feet high.

At Porto di Lido the soft sands are covered with stunted shrubs, and little trembling grasses grow close to the edge of the sea that washes over them with its encroaching waves. The waters are dark as blue steel ; the great steamer disappears on the misty horizon, and the light bark returns homeward with its sail fluttering in the wind. We gaze out into the boundless expanse. Far away a white-winged seagull is circling, but at length it too is lost to sight in the infinite distance. In front of the little *osteria* (tavern)

FROM THE LAGOONS.

which stands on the Lido, and under the green acacias bedecked with coloured lanterns, revelry goes on deep into the night. There the merry boatmen drink and laugh until the last bark pushes off from the Lido and returns homeward across the flowing Lagoon which, at flood-tide, rises nearly six feet. A distant music enchants our ears as we land at the Piazzetta. It is the gondoliers upon the Canal Grande, singing their old songs— songs which have never yet been written down by a stranger's hand, but which live in the memories of the people.

ON THE ROOFS.

But at length the hour of departure approaches. Our last walk leads us to the same goal as our first; that is to say, to the Piazza di San Marco. In front of the gilded church stands the proud *campanile*, the bell-tower, which we mount by a steep winding way.

SCENE IN CHIOGGIA.

From the low chamber of the guardian of the tower, from among the beams where the bells hang—(formerly these bells sounded only in accordance with the commands of the Doge)—we step into the open air, and, as by enchantment, we behold land and sea stretched out before our eyes. The mountains of Verona, and the far mists of the Adriatic; the spires of palaces, and the points of masts; a sea of houses and waters lies before us! Now again it is flood-tide, and, as it rises, the city seems to sink into the advancing waves. We might almost fancy that she must sink on for ever, down, down, deeper and deeper—into her grave.

TO TRIESTE AND MIRAMAR.

WE looked after the steamer which was putting out to sea through the *Porto di Lido*, one moonlight night. Already we can scarcely see the long pillar of smoke which marks her track, nor the red light at her masthead. She plunges onward through the foaming waves, and her destination is Trieste. Nearly every night one of the splendid steamboats of the Austrian Lloyd makes this voyage, and it is an enchanting scene that one contemplates leaning against the mast, looking forth, feeling, hearing, seeing, the Infinite all around one: the limitless vault of Heaven, the immeasurable waters, the great solitude of the sea!

In the sunny morning hours, when the fresh early breeze is blowing over the deck, the steamboat enters the harbour of Trieste, whose colossal buildings declare, even at the first glance, what a world-wide traffic meets here. Ships bearing the flags of countries in high northern latitudes, and the "*vapori*" bound for the Levant, lie side by side. The number of vessels bound on long voyages that cast anchor off Trieste, is calculated at more than thirteen thousand annually. What Venice was for the sea commerce of old times, that is Trieste to the modern world. The enterprising spirit of the present day, the riches accumulated by ceaseless toil, the easy inter-communication of all imaginable nations (brought together by self-interest, not sympathy), are the principal constituent elements in the present condition of the city. More than four hundred millions of francs pass through the hands of its inhabitants every year. Well may they be proud and lavish, well may they build and display their wealth!

Despite its modern character, Trieste is really of very ancient origin, and was the battle-ground of Illyrian and Celtic tribes long before the Romans completely subdued it, one hundred and seventy-seven years before Christ. It was then called Tergeste, and was Romanised with incredible rapidity. The old city, situated on the heights (not close to the sea), was rebuilt in a square form and fortified with towers, so as to keep in check the refractory races between the Alps and the Adriatic. From the hands of Attila and Alboin, Trieste passed into those of Charlemagne, until, at length, all-powerful Venice became supreme over all her neighbours. Trieste had to pay a yearly tribute, and for centuries the jealous Doges endeavoured to destroy her commerce. But presently the Kaiser came forward in opposition to the Venetians—for Trieste was a town of the German Empire. In the year 1508, Maximillian the First expelled the enemy that was pressing around her, and the liberties of Trieste were repeatedly made the subject of discussion in the "Reichstag." The Imperial supremacy changed by degrees into a purely Austrian supremacy, until at length the double-headed eagle obtained the mastery altogether.

Its commercial prosperity, which Venice looked upon with deadly hatred, Trieste owes to the great Maria Theresa. Her laws liberated trade from its shackles, and it was she who opened to the traffic of foreign nations that free path which, previously (owing

TRIESTE

partly to religious intolerance), had been closed to them. The stream of Greeks and Mussulmen from the Levant, now pours in unchecked, and the temples of all confessions stand peacefully near to one another. The chief point of interest in the town is, of course, the port, from whence is obtained the best view of the singular situation of Trieste. Here one seems to see the confluence of those many streams which bring riches to it, and here begins the wonderful Canal Grande, which carries ships of heavy burden right into the centre of the town. The origin of the harbour dates from shortly after the beginning of the Thirty Years' War, although at first it was merely a basin fit to receive small barks. The present colossal erections belong to this century. The lighthouse, which stands on the extreme point of Santa Teresa, was built in 1834.

Without doubt, the finest point in the interior of the town is the Piazza della Borsa, and that is characteristic of Trieste: for her commercial interests evidently predominate everywhere,—her architecture, her Corso, even her churches, are made subservient to these. Close to the Borsa (Exchange) stands the Tergesteum, a gigantic palace erected in 1840 on the site of the old Custom House, and destined to be the gathering point of all the commerce of the South. It contains the offices of the Austrian Lloyd, splendid reading-rooms, and printing-offices, and in the glass-covered galleries which run through the building and serve for public promenades, it is easy to recognise the southern tendency towards publicity and living under the eyes of all beholders. Certainly, however, the Austrian Lloyd is by far the most important of all the great institutions which have been created here. And the history of its origin is in some sort the prototype of those great creations of public utility in which Europe is now so rich. Baron Bruck, afterwards Austrian Finance Minister, was one of the founders and promoters of it. At the commencement, its action was confined to matters connected with insurance (1831), until the necessity was felt of systematically arranging and publishing the important news about trade and shipping which constantly reached the company. Thus arose a second undertaking,—the "Giornale del Lloyd Austriaco," which soon appeared also in the German language, and was the beginning of that colossal literary activity which the " Lloyd " now displays. Magnificent geographical works, maps, woodcuts, engravings, as well as numerous periodical publications, appear from its offices.

But the third, and most important branch of its undertakings, began with the establishment of those great lines of steamers which now command the whole traffic of the East, when it was perceived that not only the rapid diffusion, but the rapid acquisition of news was important; when, in a word, it was acknowledged that the possibility of utilizing any commercial facts depended on the facilities of communication. Once the idea was conceived, the means of carrying it out were not difficult to find. The vessels were built in London, and on the 16th of May, 1837, the first Lloyd's steamer started for Constantinople. That was the turning-point. It is almost impossible for the uninitiated to form an idea of the enormous power of expansion which the company at once developed, of the sharp-sightedness with which it increased its range of business, and of its widespread connection with other great commercial institutions. The Levant, and the west coast of the Black Sea, the lower Danube and the Po, have now regular communication with Trieste. The original capital, which amounted but to a million and a half, had increased tenfold in 1870; the number of steamers was close upon seventy, and the material used for heating their engines alone, cost over two millions of gulden per annum. To understand these facts one must be acquainted with the particulars of the service—one must consider that in the course of a single year, more than one million one hundred and eighteen thousand miles were traversed, more than three hundred thousand passengers conveyed, and that the goods transport reached nearly to six million *centners* (hundredweight). "Avanti" is the proud device of the company, and with good right is it borne.

The Tergesteum strikes us with a sense of the active intelligence and brain-power

GROTTO OF SAN SERVOLO NEAR TRIESTE.

which guides the undertaking. But in the Arsenal of Lloyd's—completed in 1857, and valued at four million nine hundred thousand gulden—we see, in the thousands of busy hands at work there, the evidences of external and physical force. One thing more— whence comes the singular name of the company? What is meant by that word "Lloyd"? It is not known to every one that Mr. Lloyd was originally the keeper of the Exchange Coffee-house in London, where brokers and agents were in the habit of meeting together to discuss business and strike bargains. As early as the beginning of the eighteenth century, the place passed into the hands of a commercial company, which used it as a regular place of meeting, and soon had representatives in all parts of the

WINCKELMANN'S MONUMENT.

world. The advices received from these various quarters were posted up at Lloyd's, and, later on, published in "Lloyd's List," a journal which has appeared daily since the year 1800. In this manner arose the world-renowned English institution, and the Austrian Lloyd was modelled on it.

From the Tergesteum, the Corso leads into the old town, where are very strong fortifications, and many traces of antiquity. There is little to be said about the churches of Trieste; but one grave we must visit, which every German looks upon with veneration. It is the sepulchre of Winckelmann, the great man who gave new light to the study of antiquity, and who was murdered in Trieste, in 1768, at the moment when he was showing to his guide Arcangeli, a collection of ancient gold coins. (Arcangeli was himself the murderer.—Translator's Note.) Lessing, although he had frequent disputes with Winckelmann, nevertheless declared that he would willingly have given two years of his own life to save that of Winckelmann, so highly did he esteem his merit.

But the ghost of yet another man rises up before us as we explore Trieste and its neighbourhood. Not far from Grignano, a castle stretches out into the sea: it is Miramar, the knightly citadel, the Tusculum of Maximilian before he met his tragic fate at Queretaro. The battlements of the castle are sheltered from the sea by huge dams built of Istrian stone; broad flights of steps lead down beneath alleys over-arched with green foliage to the soft, sandy shore, whence you look over marble balustrades across the wide expanse of the blue Adriatic. Even the stranger who wanders beneath these leafy shades, and listens to the nightingales that ever haunt them, feels his heart drawn towards the place; how dear then must it have been to the ill-starred Prince who passed his happy youth there! He has fallen by the bullets of an enemy whom he tried to combat with the higher weapons of intellect; his wife, the noble king's daughter, is sunk in madness, and desolate by the sea-shore stands the Castle of Miramar.

MIRAMAR.

VIEW OF MANTUA FROM THE BRIDGE OF SAN GIORGIO.

MANTUA.

IN the winter of 1809 a hero was executed by the muskets of French soldiers in the fortress of Mantua, and we may almost say that the sound of those shots still echoes in the memory of the people. The bloody deed then accomplished, so outraged the feelings of contemporaries, that it left, as it were, an ineffaceable stain upon the town itself, for whosoever now speaks of Mantua, another name immediately rises to his lips,—the name of the patriot Andreas Hofer. So entirely does the world of to-day sympathise with the feelings of those who indignantly beheld Hofer's cruel fate, that we run some risk of forgetting, in the contemplation of this heroic man, who belongs so entirely to our modern history, how many other great names are at home in Mantua.

This town shares in full measure the peculiarity we have pointed out as belonging to most of the Italian cities: namely, that its civic records are more important than the history of many states. Almost each one of them counts great families which treated as equals with the rulers of Europe; almost each one has its heroes of antiquity, who still live in the popular imagination. As in Verona we met with the traces of Catullus, and in Padua with those of Livy, so here we find Virgil, the great singer of the Æneid, who celebrates the reed-crowned Mincio in his "Georgics," and longs for the Muses to lead him back once more to his native home.

But Mantua, too, had her full share in all the storms that followed the destruction of the Roman Empire, and in the stirring events which marked the Middle Ages in Italy. Here it was that Alboin and Autharis swayed the sceptre; here the German Emperors were wont to halt for a day of rest on their Imperial progress through Lombardy; here Henry the Fourth and the Countess Matilda, Hildebrand's powerful patroness, contended bitterly for the possession of the city; and the great nobles, who all were striving for mastery, waged bloody warfare in her streets until at length Gonzaga obtained the supremacy. His race continued to rule over Mantua for more than three hundred years. It was strong and valiant; ever ready for the fray when war knocked at the city gates, and liberal in encouraging the fine arts whenever there was an opportunity of beautifying the city and ministering to the patriotic pride of the citizens. All that Giulio Romano painted in the fine old castle, all that Alberti has built, arose under the princely patronage of some Gonzaga Mæcenas. It was not Florence only who could boast of her Medici.

Mantua is built on two islands of the Mincio, which here widens out considerably and surrounds the town like a lake. Five great gates lead out on to five high roads to north and south; a huge mill-dam forms a pathway from the town to the citadel, and in Porto Catena, there lie at anchor numerous black sailing-ships deeply laden, that ply to the shores of the Adriatic. The town and its tremendous fortifications rise up out of the waters with a grim and defiant aspect. The spirit of the golden Renaissance has fled from it long ago, and is replaced by a spirit of warlike sternness. Strength, and not beauty, is the key-note of its modern development; and in truth Mantua is at the present day one of the most formidable fortresses in Europe: for whilst the town itself counts scarcely more than twenty-eight thousand inhabitants, the casemates can accommodate an army of forty thousand men! Strong bastions are built deep down into the water, which is crossed by clanking iron draw-bridges, and every gate is armed to the teeth. All approaches to the city are commanded from hence for a long distance. The French besieged the place fruitlessly in July, 1796, and the enemy had to make tremendous sacrifices in 1797, 1799, and 1814, before Mantua yielded. Indeed, those years have ploughed the stern furrows into the physiognomy of the town which strike us to-day; and as in 1809, it was the scene of a tyrannous injustice, when the courier from Milan came riding in with the death-sentence of the noble-hearted Tyrolese Hofer; so in the sad years which followed 1848, it was again the theatre of those dark political trials wherein not individual transgressions but the liberty of nations was ruthlessly condemned. The gloomy impression made by these reminiscences, is increased by the heavy and unhealthy atmosphere of the surrounding marshes, whose exhalations become the terrible allies of the garrison against a besieging—especially a foreign—foe.

But we soon forget such dispiriting sensations, when, turning our backs on Mantua the fortress, we enter Mantua the town, and pass through her streets before palaces and theatres, and masterpieces of another time, that are almost unequalled. Here we are led onward by the creative hand of Art instead of the destructive hand of War. The Piazza San Pietro may be looked on as the principal point in the city, containing as it does the Duomo, and the old Palazzo Ducale. From hence, as far as the Via della Croce Verde and the Teatro Sociale, flows the thickest traffic; and the original and singular aspect of the scene is enhanced by the fact that one of those lakes, formed by the broadening out of

RIFLEMEN WAITING FOR A TRAIN.

the Mincio, reaches nearly to the Piazza, and is crossed by a single bridge leading to the *Lunetta*.

Giulio Romano is the presiding genius in the old Castle of the Dukes of Mantua.

He completed the artistic significance of Bonaccolti's building, and has made its internal walls renowned for all time by his Trojan frescoes. The *Palazzo del Te* is still richer in works of this master; it contains eight rooms, adorned by his hand, inexhaustible in fulness of details, and incomparable for grace as well as grandeur. The former quality is especially remarkable in the so-called Hall of Psyche, the second in the Sala dei Giganti, or Hall of Giants, where the heaven-storming Titans appear almost terrible in their might. The enormous power of growth and expansion which that period (the Renaissance) possessed is best evidenced by the choice of artistic subjects which were taken by preference from the antique world of gods and goddesses. Every little Prince in duodecimo would have his gallery full of Olympians, and his halls full of giants. Perhaps this mania might appear laughable to us, were it not that the carrying of it out fell into the hands of artists who put all their own artistic greatness at the service of this striving after political greatness, and thus surrounded these little courts with an eternal halo. That which a great minister or a great general has done for other dynasties, was accomplished for the Italian Princes of the sixteenth century by the great artists whose names are linked imperishably with theirs. And this was felt by a people who have so keen a sense of public honour and public disgrace as the Italians have. The position which Giulio Romano held with relation to the Court of the Gonzagas and the citizens of Mantua was a brilliant one; for not only the nobles by birth, but the aristocracy of intellect, attained to a certain sovereignty in those "Republics." Giulio Romano was not the servant but the friend of the Duke who employed him; his house was honoured by the people almost as a sacred place; his death was mourned as a national calamity. "We have lost our Giulio Romano, our right hand," writes Hercules Gonzaga in the year 1546.

And in truth the artistic life of the city ceased almost simultaneously with that of the inimitable Master. The last of the line of Gonzaga died in 1707, amid the decadence and degradation which is the heritage of the closing generations of such a line, and left behind him as an apple of discord the mighty citadel for whose possession Germany and France, Austria and Savoy, contended. The contest endured for more than a century; but now the tricolour of a United Italy waves over the spot where Andreas Hofer shouted his last "Hurrah!" for Kaiser Franz before giving the fatal word—"Fire!"

MILAN.

IT is not by its external aspect but in virtue of its intrinsic worth that Milan counts among the most important cities of Italy. Its *sobriquet* of the "moral capital of the country" is more than a mere phrase. What deeds had to be done, what sufferings to be endured, before the nation was united! And although enthusiasm for this aim was diffused throughout the whole country, yet the lion's share of the *labour* fell to Northern Italy. Here principally, in Piedmont and Lombardy reigned that strong and sober spirit which adds action to will, and which shrinks intimidated from no endurance; and in power of endurance at all events no other Italian city can be compared with Milan. It has been besieged forty-eight times, and stormed twenty-eight times. As often as the stormy flood of war poured over the Lombard plains, it beat its angry waves against the walls of this city. Milan rises out of the tempestuous history of the Middle Ages like a rock out of the ocean. But together with all these warlike surroundings, and the manly boldness which was the distinguishing characteristic of the city, arts and sciences, wealth and love, continued to flourish.

Two thousand years have passed over the capital of Lombardy, and we can hardly realise to ourselves that this same city, in which we have seen Radetzky's white-coated soldiery, and heard in 1859 the enthusiastic shout of "Viva Vittorio Emanuele!" was besieged by the Romans 200 years B.C., that Theodosius held his court here, and Attila wasted it with fire and sword. But most terrible of all was the chastisement inflicted by Barbarossa, who, angered by the repeated revolts of Milan against his authority, swore to level the city to the earth, and in fact caused all the public buildings, with the exception of one or two churches, to be pulled down with great iron hooks, and the woodwork of them set on fire. Two hundred years later we find the Visconti in full possession of the town; the means by which they established and maintained their power being the same that were then used by all the rulers of Italy, the same that are set forth by Macchiavelli in the "Principe," with the sole difference that some were able to apply them more boldly than others. Cruel times of bloodshed and tyranny had to pass by before the Sforzas won the Dukedom of Milan. This family was of low, nay peasant, origin, but the founder of its dignities possessed at least personal valour, and showed what could be accomplished by belief in a high destiny, but his descendants finally sank into degradation beneath the curse of worn-out traditions. But Milan first felt the real yoke of despotism, when Charles the Fifth gave her into the hands of the Spaniards, in whose clutches she remained until the beginning of the eighteenth century. How she felt under the rule of Austria, is known to all contemporaries; in vain were German *savants* and German artists summoned to give new glory to the city, Milan would not be German, she would be nothing but a portion of United Italy! And terrible years had to be lived through before there finally came the Peace of Villafranca, and the King entered Milan amid universal and joyful enthusiasm.

It is singular enough that a town which has ever been so constant to the national cause, should show so little that is nationally characteristic in its external aspect. Every one who knows Italy will admit that the Italian element is less visible in Milan than elsewhere. The life, the whole physiognomy of the town, has much more of the cosmo-

MONUMENT TO LEONARDO DA VINCI.

politan air which belongs to every large capital; and, indeed, several of the streets might be in Paris for all one can see to the contrary. The newer streets (above all the *Galleria Vittorio Emanuele*) are those which bear a more southern stamp. The desire for vast, brilliant spaces, which is expressed in these, is an essential characteristic of the Italian, whose whole life tends to external show. One should arrive in the Lombard capital on the evening of a Festa, and walk through this arcade where thousands of people throng, and thousands of gas-lights flare, to understand what night means in Italy, and to realize that we are on Italian soil.

The foundation stone of the Galleria Vittorio Emanuele—a building perhaps unequalled in Europe in its way—was laid on the 4th of March, 1865. In the centre of

COLUMNS OF SAN LORENZO.

the huge cross formed by the building, rises a dome of glass, and the octagon which is overarched by this dome is richly adorned with frescoes and caryatides, and the statues of famous Italians. Here are Raphael and Dante, Savonarola and Arnold of Brescia. Here too Macchiavel has his monument, and opposite to him—his equal in political wisdom, and his superior in political liberality—stands Cavour. The whole arcade, lighted by twelve hundred jets of gas, wears the aspect of a southern bazaar, and contains ninety-six magnificent shops full of all manner of luxuries; sparkling ornaments, rich carpets, statues, and pictures. The doors of the cafés are wide open, displaying crimson velvet divans, and huge mirrors, and the sellers of newspapers push their way among the chattering groups within, calling out "*Perseveranza, Nazione, Fanfulla, cinque centesimi!*" Everything combines to make the *Galleria* the brilliant focus of public life : the massive grandeur of the building, and the careless ease of intercourse, busy diligence, and leisurely finery. In the tympanum of the dome are frescoes representing the four quarters of the world, Europe, Asia, and the rest; but the solid ground we tread on, and from which this masterpiece has arisen, is the soil of ancient, historic Milan. In no other town of Italy is civic patriotism combined with the cosmopolitan spirit as it is here.

When you visit the offices, the shops, the banks, and manufactories of Milan, you find everywhere serious busy men, carrying on their occupations with almost northern earnestness; and it is only in the evening when working hours are over, and the population flocks out on to the Corso, or into the Galleria, that the Milanese appear to us as Italians in the full sense of the word. Rapid talk flows freely, the characteristic black veil hangs in graceful folds round fair faces and throats, gay silks trail and rustle. Even among the women of Milan is to be found an energetic spirit that interests itself in public affairs, and Aleardi spoke from his heart when he addressed to them his poem entitled "Le Donne Veneziane alle Milanesi" (The Women of Venice to those of Milan). Milan, at the date of this poem, already made part of a united Italy, but Venice still languished in the power of the foreigner, and sighed in plaintive tones for the star of Italy to shine on her lagoons.

The key-note running through all life in Milan is *moderness*: despite the memories of a great Past which surround us on every side, the spell of the Present is omnipotent. Even when expressed by antiquated forms, modern life is triumphantly dominant. The Piazza dei Mercanti, from whence the draconian edicts of the Podesta were formerly issued, now echoes with the tumult of the Exchange: and in the Loggie where theological disputations once resounded, the Chamber of Commerce sits in council, and notwithstanding that the foundation of the Ospedale Maggiore (Great Hospital) is of ancient date, yet the full development of its original purpose, the absolute equality of all sufferers within its walls, is in truth the work of modern progress. Such results may have been foreboded and aimed at in former centuries, but it was reserved for the present day to work them out in conscious freedom and completeness. About the year 1784 all the charitable institutions which Milan possessed were combined in one fund, on which all the necessitous had a claim,— from the impoverished widow of a princely house, to the beggar rocking her child on her care-laden breast. Besides this fund, there are three thousand beds at the disposition of the sick poor, and all these large means are administered in a spirit of the noblest benevolence, under the ceaseless supervision of the patrons, and in accordance with the wishes of the benevolent donors, whose portraits are exhibited every two years in the hall of the Ospedale. The extent and importance of this institution may be judged from the fact that it possesses more than forty-seven millions, and that about one and twenty thousand sick persons and ten thousand little children (these latter chiefly in the country), are yearly relieved by it.

If we cast a glance on the realm of politics, we shall find at once innumerable reminiscences of the Bonapartes,—but this too is a trait of entirely modern history. With no other Italian city had the Bonapartes such intimate personal relations, as with Milan: here it was that the man who had stood with waving banner on the bridge of Arcola, placed the iron crown upon his own head; here the viceroy Eugène kept a luxurious court; and here the third Napoleon made a triumphal entry after the battle of Magenta, and received homage as the Saviour of Italy. Such recollections have an indescribable power over the generations who have witnessed the circumstances; for it is action not reflection which influences the masses, and it is the concrete fact which appeals to them as they look upon the proud *Arco della Pace*. To this is added a certain sentiment of gratitude;—for nothing is falser than to deny to Italians the possession of this good trait,—since the people feel that the foundation stone of their Unity was laid by the French Emperor at a period when no other but himself *could* have laid it. These considerations may serve to excuse the

Napoleon-worship, the traces of which we meet with here; it may have had something repulsive about it when it was addressed to the all-powerful Emperor, but its aspect is changed and ennobled when it is dedicated to *fallen* greatness.

But everywhere we find a hundred instances of the warmth with which the Italians cling to all the names of those who have played a friendly part in the history of their country;

SANTA MARIA DELLE GRAZIE.

and with what liveliness they nourish the memory of all the men who have contributed their own renown to the glory of Italy. In every large town the streets and squares are named after the chief citizens whose monuments have been erected by posterity; and the children playing at their base learn unconsciously that patriotic pride which they retain in manhood. Everywhere the sense of kindred with the national heroes is enthusiastically cherished; and as a type of all, we may name one,—the great Cavour. In Milan he has a noble monument, but his popularity is evidenced even in the smallest trifles; on the bank-notes that pass through the citizens' hands is engraved the portrait of the famous minister, looking statesmanlike and sage through his spectacles; the favourite cigar which the cabmen smoke, and the gentlemen by no means disdain, is called the 'Cavour.'

We saunter onward through the Contrada di Brera, and enter a pillared courtyard with fine statues in it. The scientific treasures of Milan are collected here; and the picture gallery in the same building contains some fine specimens of the old masters. Who that has ever seen Raphael's 'Sposalizio' (the marriage of the Virgin) can ever forget it? or who could attempt to describe it as he saw it? We feel indeed that in a series of slight sketches such as the present it is impossible to do any sort of justice to artistic things; for it were too presumptuous to emit a trenchant judgment in a few words, and to give to the subject all the attention it ought to claim, would require, not pages but volumes.

On the way towards the Porta Ticinese,—one of the twelve city gates—we are held fast by a strange spectacle, that transports us suddenly from this modern world into the antique: these are the Colonne di San Lorenzo, sixteen Corinthian columns of wonderful beauty, which belonged to some Roman Thermæ, and are mentioned in the poems of Ausonius. Yonder is the Duomo—the Cathedral,—with its white marble pinnacles, its cool twilight aisles, its world-wide historical reminiscences. For a long time poor squalid houses pressed close around its marble walls, and greatly injured the effect of the whole; but now a wide space has been opened all around the cathedral, and the view of it is unimpeded.

The huge building rises before us, gigantic in its massive whole, yet of almost fairy lightness in its manifold details. We were standing at the corner of the Via Capellari gazing upward in dumb admiration, when an Italian, who had been watching us for some time, seized my arm and pointing with an enthusiastic gesture to the Duomo, exclaimed, "*Ecco ciò che poteva il* 1386!" "Behold what the year 1386 could accomplish!" It was indeed in that year that the Cathedral of Milan was commenced by Gian Galeazzo Visconti, and although there needed years, nay centuries, for its completion, and although the hands of many nations have co-operated in the production of this masterpiece of man's art, yet the glory of the original conception belongs to that remote epoch. We mount the broad marble steps that give access to the five portals in the main façade, and a blind man leaning against a pillar murmurs in a hollow voice, "*Misericordia per un cieco;*" neglected children playing on the steps cry after us, "*Un soldo, signore, un soldo!*" and stretch their hands eagerly; a guide who has followed us from the corner of the street comes slily up and whispers in our ear "*La cattedrale, signor, una guida per la cattedrale.*" Such annoyances meet you on every threshold in Italy, but you can easily shake them off by the expenditure of a few centesimi and the use of a persuasively expressive forefinger; but above all use few words or you will infallibly be worsted.

The main entrance is closed, not by a jarring door, but by a huge curtain, and pushing this aside we stand within the enormous nave with its solemn twilight and its columns rising upward in lofty sublimity. A little silver bell tinkles from a distant sidechapel, and women sink devoutly on their knees whilst a priest in rich vestments, who has just stepped forth from the sacristy followed by two acolytes, pauses and beats his breast reverently. In a niche yonder beside a confessional box kneels a girl in black garments; her cheeks are flushed, her eyes raised to heaven; she has forgotten the world around her, she sees and hears nothing, she knows not that she is murmuring her confession half aloud—acknowledging a transgression like that of the fair Francesca da Rimini—"*Al*

THE CATHEDRAL OF MILAN.

tempo dei dolci sospiri, ..." Somewhat further on sits an aged woman on a bench, her grey hair showing beneath her black veil, and she too is absorbed in her own thoughts, she too has her heartache. A glance at the handsome, care-laden old face reveals its story. She has lost a beloved child for whom she has murmured a daily petition in this spot for years past—"*Misericordia!*"

A wondrous and almost inexplicable sensation of awe and reverence overpowers those who enter these sacred aisles; even the careless stranger, even the frivolous and irreligious, are affected by it. It is not merely the vastness of the space and the beauty of the proportions; it is not merely the lofty pillars and the "dim religious light" which have this mystic power; no, it is some spiritual force whose current carries us away, something *soulful* that speaks to the soul! In the consciousness that millions have wept and worshipped here, that as they kneel and pray now before our eyes so they have knelt and prayed here for centuries, lies the secret of this mysterious influence. This is the true consecration of the Duomo; this is its invisible wealth, more precious than silver lamps and golden chalices; this it is that speaks in the flood of sound from the mighty organ!

The ground plan of the church marks a cross; the length of the nave is about four hundred and fifty feet, and it has two aisles on either side. The whole of the floor comprises more than a hundred and ten thousand square feet, so that it is quite a long excursion to traverse it from end to end. An extremely ancient church formerly stood on the site of the present Duomo; but no fragment of its materials was used in the construction of the newer temple. For there was an inexhaustible supply of marble from the quarries of Condoglio, and the gifts which flowed in for the splendid building were at first almost embarrassing in their richness and number. Galeazzo Visconti himself sacrificed a great portion of his booty and jewels to it, Marco Carelli offered a gift of thirty-five thousand ducats, and Pope Boniface the Ninth promised to all Lombards who should make a pilgrimage to Milan, the same indulgences as those promised to a pilgrimage to Rome, on condition that they should devote one-third of the sum thus saved to the building of the Duomo. Certainly the original plan of the church was simpler than its development in subsequent times; the five great portals and the fifty-two octagon columns were already begun, it is true, but it was intended to have only one altar, according to the Ambrosian rite. All the side-altars now in the church date from the time of San Carlo Borromeo, and were for the most part designed by Pellegrini, who also constructed the subterranean passage to the Archbishop's palace.

After passing between two pillars of red granite which majestically adorn the main entrance, we step at once on to the meridian which runs through the church, and was inserted into the marble pavement in 1786. Then further on we perceive many proud monuments such as the Popes and their nephews were wont to enrich Italian temples with. Statues and pictures crowd every altar; among the former a repulsively anatomical St. Bartholomew carrying his own skin over his shoulders! And to this æsthetic enormity the "artist" has had the good taste to add an inscription setting forth that the figure is *not* by Praxiteles, but by himself, "Marcus Agrates"! The seven-armed candelabrum which has belonged to the Cathedral of Milan since the middle of the sixteenth century, is world-renowned; but its origin is still a mystery. Its arms come out from the huge stem like the twisted branches of a tree, on which strange figures of animals are climbing. Near at hand stands the statue of the Madonna dell' Albero, and at her feet sleeps Cardinal Borromeo, whom Manzoni has immortalized in the "Promessi

Sposi." The tomb of his great ancestor, St. Charles himself, is beneath the choir; the coffin that contains his remains was made at the cost of King Philip the Fourth of Spain;

CORSO VITTORIO EMANUELE.

it is of pure gold, and if Ignazio Cantù is to be trusted, the chapel of San Carlo contains the value of more than four millions of francs.

But noble and solemn as is the interior of the Duomo, we receive perhaps an even more striking impression when, after having climbed the hundreds of steps, we emerge into the open air on the roof of the huge building. The thousands of marble statues surmounting airy pinnacles, seem to be the work of enchantment ; and, fairy-like in the distance, we see the blue chain of the Alps with Mont Blanc shining whitely aloft, and with the great passes, which serve for the intercourse of nations, in their shadowy depths. The

MONK AT THE WELL IN THE CERTOSA.

number of statues on the exterior of the Duomo is reckoned at two thousand ; among which a statue of Eve is very celebrated. Canova too has contributed three master-pieces ; Rebecca, St. Dasius, and Napoleon the First. The latter is, without doubt, the finest ; of colossal size, and bold as a hero of antiquity, the Cæsar of our century stands there holding in his clenched hand the lance with which he overthrew Europe. Motionless and marble cold, he looks down upon the city which he once ruled over, and where his stepson Eugène held a brilliant Court. But the Fates have made him serve as a symbol of their irony; for there are fourteen lightning conductors intended to protect the roof from thunder-bolts, and—in order not to spoil the artistic harmony of the whole—these wires are so arranged as to be held in the hands of figures armed with lance and shield, among them the great Corsican. He who caused his warlike lightnings to devastate whole nations, is now become the dumb instrument to disarm the lightnings that glide harmless through his hands.

One may spend hours on the broad platform of the roof wandering among the grove of marble figures that rise on every hand, and still find something new :—wreathed flowers and foliage, dragons' heads, from whose mouths the water pours in the rainy season, all of dazzling marble, all so dumb and yet so eloquent! The walls are scribbled over in all languages in the world, and although the scribblings mostly consist of ill-written names, yet here and there you come upon a sentence showing what strong emotions have been awakened by the influence of the place. There are quotations from Byron and Dante, Rousseau and Goethe; and patriotism expresses itself in numberless "*Evvivas*" for United Italy. There is undoubtedly a certain exaltation of spirit felt on this airy height; but prosaic handicraft intrudes itself into the midst of the poetry. In that smoking metal pan yonder they are melting lead to repair the roof, and when the mid-day hour of rest arrives, the sun-burnt workmen crowd together in a circle and pull the dice and the copper "soldi" out of their pockets. I saw them sitting cross-legged at their ease, gambling away with eager, flashing eyes: "*Cinque—sei—dieci!*" "*Accidente!*" (Palsy seize ye!), cried one who had lost. I turned away and leant for a long long time over the marble balustrade, gazing at the distant Alps, or down upon the red-brown roofs of the town ; the spirit revels in the view of yonder immeasurable horizon!

Amongst the other churches of Milan, the most worthy of notice is the basilica of Saint Ambrogio, which dates from the fourth century, and owes its origin to that great Father of the Church, St. Ambrose, founder also of the so-called Ambrosian rite. St. Ambrose seems to have impressed some of the noble simplicity of his own character upon the church; for the whole building bears this stamp, notwithstanding the alterations made in it by later times. Without being specially beautiful, it is full of dignity, and of that solemnity which belongs to a great past. Before the high altar in this church took place the conversion of St. Augustine, and the coronation of the Italian Kings Berengar and Otho the Great, and the two emperors, afterwards excommunicated by Rome, Henry the Fourth and Louis of Bavaria. The church contains valuable objects in gold and silver, and many interesting antiquities, but its most precious treasure is the history that belongs to it.

The fame of Santa Maria delle Grazie rests chiefly on its possession of Leonardo da Vinci's Last Supper: which, however, is not in the church itself, but in the refectory of the convent belonging to it. The story of the vicissitudes this great fresco has undergone, and the noble figures which fill it, are known to everybody, even to those who have never visited Italy. But despite all the injuries it has sustained, the original makes an impression which no copy can approach. Barbarous generations, whether clothed in coat of mail or monkish cowl, have cruelly assailed it ; but the traces of a sacred genius have not been utterly effaced, nor will they be, so long as but one outline of the great design remains visible.

In the evening hours, when noise and movement awake throughout all Italy, the

MILANESE LADY.

pulse of life begins to beat quicker in Milan also; and then a phenomenon, which we have scarcely named hitherto, but which is of high importance in Italy,—I mean the Theatre,— presses itself on our attention. It must be owned that people do not so much go thither with an idea of seriously enjoying art, as attracted by the excitement of a crowd; but however this may be, actors and singers are an indispensable element among these people. And the artists themselves are more sensitive to this fact, than to the supercilious indifference

LAKE OF COMO. VIEW OF MALGRATE FROM LECCO.

with which the public chatters throughout their performances; they do not place their pride in being attentively listened to, but in the consciousness that the public cannot do without them. During the time when Venice was the only city excluded from United Italy, her chief theatre, "Là Fenice," was closed and silent; and this circumstance was the most eloquent possible protest against the state of things then prevailing. This sense of their own importance runs through all circles of the Italian stage, and the meanest supernumerary shares it with the first artists. I shall never forget once meeting with a couple of singular-looking figures in the railway station of a small town; they were promenading up and down the platform attracting much curious attention by their pantomimic gestures. The man's garments were ragged and squalid, but those of his wife were still more so, and her grey hair, unacquainted with the comb, fell in tangled locks about her forehead; she reminded me of Hecuba. My hand was already in my pocket, and I was just about to say, "You are street-singers, I presume;" when the man anticipated my question with the words "*Siamo artisti drammatici,*" accompanied by a gesture worthy of Talma. As to Hecuba, she measured me with a look that I have never seen surpassed by Ristori herself!

The Eldorado of Italian artists, the high object of their ambition, is the Scala in Milan. Whoever has won laurels here, is welcome on any foreign stage; whoever has been able to fill this vast space with his voice, is certain of triumphs everywhere. The Scala is incontestably the first opera-house in Italy; so that in this respect also, Milan remains the "*moral capital.*" The singular name, La Scala, is derived from a church that bore the same title, and on the site of which the present theatre is erected: after San Carlo in Naples, the largest theatre in Europe. There are five rows of boxes, which, together with the pit, are capable of containing nearly four thousand spectators. All the decorations are in the costly and lavish style of the first empire; Napoleon and Josephine, Eugène and his marshals, have sat here surrounded by a brilliant court. Those were days of heavy oppression for Italy; but she was forced to wear an appearance of gaiety and prosperity, for such has ever been the will of all Cæsars!

But after all the sights and sounds of brilliant gas-lighted Milan, I could not repress a yearning for a glimpse of nature. This yearning sent me forth out of the noisy city, and was not stilled even by a visit to the exquisite Certosa, which lies barely fifteen miles from Milan, and rises solitary and majestic out of the Lombard plain. We must devote a few words—they can be but few—to this masterwork.

The Certosa di Pavia was erected almost contemporaneously with the Duomo of Milan; it contains a church and cloister, and numerous conventual buildings. But these are all designed in the same style, and offer a perfection of artistic unity such as scarcely another edifice in Italy can boast of. We stand dumb with admiring astonishment before the exquisite façade. A spirit of holiness seems to breathe through these halls, through these solitary alleys, to whose influence we involuntarily resign ourselves. There does not reign here that empty idleness, weary of existence itself, which we find in so many monasteries: but on the contrary, a dignity and strength which concentrates life into silent reflection instead of squandering it in the bustle of the outer world. It is fulness of thought, and not poverty of intellect, which characterizes this solitude, and glorious works of art exalt the spirits of the pilgrims who approach these gates. That, too, is a kind of worship. We lingered nearly a whole day in the classic halls of the Certosa, and then returned to Milan. To-morrow we start from thence for the beautiful Lake of Como, where the bustle of the capital changes softly into a moonlit Idyll!

THE CERTOSA, NEAR PAVIA.

BELLAGGIO, SEEN FROM VILLA GIULIA.

THREE LAKES.

LAGO DI COMO.

NEAR Cadenabbia there is a road winding along beneath green arches of the vine, or under the blue canopy of heaven, now hidden from a view of the landscape, now opening out so as to allow the mountains mirrored in the soft waters to be seen. The natives call this road "*Via del Paradiso*,"—The road of Paradise; and the words linger in our memory all the while we tarry here, for truly the whole enchanting district of the three lakes is a Paradise. We have seen many a masterpiece of man's handiwork during our pilgrimage, but here nature has set her masterpiece; and as we see certain stars that surpass all the others in their lustre, so shines pre-eminent in beauty this triple star of the Three Lakes, amid the heaven of Italy. How exquisitely refreshing is this soft air to one coming from the crowded town! As we wander by steep ways through the little villages perched high above the shore, the peasant who passes us with his laden mule, and the children peeping over a crumbling wall, grin and nod and look at us with great dark eyes:—the very beggar by the way-side has fallen asleep in the soft spring afternoon, and is dreaming, perhaps, that he is a king! And what a balsam is this air, how we feel the coolness it has stolen from the waters in its flight, and rejoice as we hear it *soughing* and surging amid the clefts of the rocks! The heart expands, the soul exults, and we feel inclined to cry aloud and joyfully, "*Via del Paradiso !*"

Such are the impressions offered to one who clambers actively amongst the heights above the three lakes; but also to him who keeps to the more level high-ways along the margin is offered a delightful series of pictures by the alternations of pretty townlets, with solitary landscape. Nowhere do you find villas combining in so high a degree rustic peace, with classic elegance; nowhere else do you so easily forget the world, nor find it again so easily when you need it.

We make halt first at the Lake of Como, which is a long deep basin measuring more than forty miles in circumference, and divided into two arms, called respectively, Lecco and Como, from the towns upon their shores. The latter, Como, whose northernmost houses are washed by the waves of the lake, is the very ideal of a little Lombard town; with a certain sternness about its architecture, rich in beauty and warlike reminiscences, full of life and movement. The citizens possess a neat little theatre, and a Lyceum, which recalls the great men who called Como their home:—the two Plinys, Pope Innocent the Eleventh, and Pope Clement the Thirteenth, Jovius, and Rezzonico. Volta also was of Comascan origin. The Duomo is amongst the finest cathedrals of Northern Italy; perhaps, indeed, it may be said to be the finest of all after Milan. It is distinguished by severe Gothic architecture, and by a singular air of dignity and solemnity, only alloyed here and there by a touch of the Renaissance, as in the façade (which is of later date than the rest) and portions of the choir. The great round-arched portal is surrounded by exceedingly rich ornamentation, full of figures of saints framed in carved stone-work, and mellowed into that rich tone of colouring which the breath of centuries alone can give to a building. But mingled with the freedom of artistic power is the sense of an intellectual freedom which does not insist on compressing all that is noble within the limits of one form of faith; for amidst the saints you may see German Emperors and antique heroes, and, one on each side of the portal, stand two men who were in their way apostles of light —I mean the elder Pliny, who lost his life in the service of science, and his nephew, the author of those wonderful letters which still delight us! Their residence was the Villa Pliniana, which is situated among peaceful groves upon the heights near Torno. In the courtyard the spring still murmurs, of which the younger Pliny writes to his friend that it rises and falls three times a day, with a regular ebb and flow. Pliny carefully relates how a ring which he laid on the dry ground there was first slightly sprinkled over, and then entirely concealed by the waters, until on their sinking again it was once more brought to light. The sage loved to rest beside this fountain, whose eternal rising and falling offers a profound symbol of our existence; and he wrote some of his finest pages here. His heart was at ease, although his brain might be struggling with hard problems; for he says in his first book, "Here I am assailed neither by hopes nor fears; I regret no word that meets my ear, nor any that issues from my lips; and I hear no bitter invectives against mankind."

The landing-place in Como is the head-quarters of all the varied traffic of the lake, which the steamboat daily traverses throughout its entire length, and offers a busy and lively spectacle, with its noise, and crowd, and bustle of coming and going. How pretty,

CORK.

too, it is to see the little boat put off from some village on the shore at which the steamer does not stop, and dance along on the foaming waters until it reaches the side of the big ship, and a ladder is lowered to enable passengers to descend into the wavering bark! The steamer has paused, but every one on board is in a state of restless bustle. *"Aspetti, aspetti!" "Partenza Signori!" "Corpo di Bacco!"* we hear resounding from every side, and the next moment the machine begins to puff and pant, the paddle-wheels churn the waters into foam, and the steamer is off again. Meanwhile the little boat is being slowly rowed towards the shore, where a retired *Osteria* peeps invitingly from a green nest of vines and olives; a pair of sweethearts sit side by side in the boat, and their friends on board the steamer smilingly wave hats and handkerchiefs to them as they are rowed away, but they see only each other, and the light breeze carries their voices away out of hearing.

STREET IN TREMEZZO.

Long after the boat with its freight of happy lovers has disappeared in the distance, we continue to see spread out before us all the enchantment of an Italian shore. Villa after villa rises from the midst of dark green foliage, cool grottoes are seen laved by the blue waters, a little white chapel glitters on the heights, and the road turns sharply round the threatening angle of the rock. The most celebrated of all the villas is the Villa d'Este, built by Cardinal Pompeo Gallio, who was born in the village of Cernobbio, hard by, and was the son of a poor fisherman. Here he passed his childhood; and in later years, when he was robed in the purple, and oppressed by the cares which the purple brings with it, he frequently returned to these scenes, and built a palace where his father's hut once stood. Often of an evening the stately figure clad in scarlet silk would be seen pacing beneath the shade of the yew-tree alleys, followed at a respectful distance by his clerical attendants, chatting together in subdued tones; perhaps weighty news may have arrived from Rome, from the *Gesù*, or the Vatican! But

TAVERN IN LUGANO.

Pompeo doubtless paused whenever the breeze dividing the branches of the trees opened a glimpse of the blue lake, and listened to the song of the fisherboy returning homeward, and thought of the days when he himself sat careless and light-hearted in a humble fishing-boat. Now he sits in the bark of St. Peter—close to the helm, too!—and navi-

THE RAVINE OF THE PIOVERNA, NEAR BELLANO.

gates a stormy sea, for Charles the Fifth has wearily resigned the Empire, and Luther's fiery words are penetrating to all ears. The echo of them sounds threateningly even in Italy; and Rome and its future seem enveloped in a lurid cloud, even such a one as is rising above the ridge of mountains yonder. Pompeo pauses, looking darkly before him, whilst the priests whisper together and the waves murmur low.

Centuries passed, and there, where once the Cardinal walked, dwelt the repudiated wife of a King of England,—the Princess Caroline with her suite. It was about this period—from 1815 to 1820,—that the present extensive pleasure-grounds were begun, a charming little theatre built, and numerous outbuildings for the accommodation of those attendants who had followed the princess in her exile.

We soon have an instance of the cosmopolite-international character which marks the border of the Lake of Como ; all nations, all forms of riches and renown, meet here. As we pass beneath a castle crowning a high point of rock, one of the sailors shows a double range of dazzling teeth and pointing to the building exclaims, "*Troubetzkoy, Principe Russo!*" The next name comes much more trippingly off his tongue, as he exclaims eagerly "Villa Taglioni," at the same time raising himself on his toes, and perceiving in an instant from our nod, that we foreigners knew something of the fame of the great dancer. All these villas have something of a classical grace about them ; some trace still lingers on these shores of the spirit in which the ancients built their villas, and were wont to pass their lives in the country ; that is to say not with an idea of enjoying for a while a rude, rustic kind of ease, but surrounded by all external elegances to cultivate their minds amid the charms of nature. The Villa Pliniana, mentioned above, is truly the great ancestor of all these country seats ; and perhaps something of its influence may have insinuated itself even into the dwellings built by foreign pilgrims in the land,—albeit they know nothing of it ! The paths traverse marble terraces where stand Apollo and Aphrodite ; orange and cypress trees shade the gardens ; the flower-beds are rich with all imaginable hues from the glow of the rose to the purple depth of the violet ; the waters murmur softly, and we are overcome by an almost irresistible conviction that all the beauty and sweetness of the earth are concentrated on this soil.

The finest of all the villas which the State of Como possesses, the "*Regina del Lario*," is the Villa Carlotta, not far from Cadenabbia. Nature and Art have combined to adorn this princely residence, which possesses amongst other treasures the bas-relief by Thorwaldsen, representing the Triumph of Alexander, and Canova's exquisite group of Cupid and Psyche. But the first rank, so far as landscape beauty is concerned, must be assigned to Bellaggio, situated at the point where the two arms of the lake divide ; its name is celebrated throughout the world. High above the village which advances close to the water's edge, rises the Villa Serbelloni, its gateway hidden by pines and cedars, and commanding a wide view in all directions of shining waters, houses in nests of verdure, and light barks on their way to Melzi. Here and there a valley opens, into whose depths you give a brief glance as the little boat glides past them, and out of which a foaming torrent dashes into the lake. "*L'Orrido di Bellano*," cries one of our rowers, pointing to the water which tumbles in silvery spray from the rocks, and forms the waterfall of the Ploverna, the finest on Como. The main stream which flows through the lake is the Adda, which is first perceived near Malgrate, opposite Lecco ; a large stone bridge that dates from the days of the Visconti unites the two shores, for the lake here is narrow, and the intercourse between the two banks of it lively and continuous. A splendid road leads from hence to Como, and a broad canal reaches as far as Milan, but our path does not lie in that direction ; the district of the three lakes still holds us for a time, and we cheerfully obey the invitation shouted to us as we stand on the steamboat at Menaggio, "Per Porlezza, signori! Per il lago di Lugano!"

MENDICANT FRIAR IN THE BRIANZA.

MONTE SALVATORE, ON THE LAKE OF LUGANO.

LAGO DI LUGANO.

DURING my stay in these parts I am often reminded of the fairy tale of the King who had three fair daughters, whose wooers were constantly disputing as to which of the three carried off the palm of beauty. Finally the youngest is adjudged to be the fairest : for although she has neither the tall and princely stature of the eldest sister, nor the depth of intellect which distinguishes the second, she possesses nevertheless, a certain amiable grace, a winningness, a charm, that are all her own, and are more powerful than the gifts of the others. It is almost the same with those three marvellous lakes which lie close together on the southern slope of the Alps. Grand and majestic, pre-eminent even in its name, the Lago Maggiore stretches itself out before our eyes ; the Lake of Como is distinguished for its traditions of genius and art ; but the pearl of beauty belongs to that pale blue flood which nestles timidly between the two larger lakes, and is called the Lago di Lugano.

Only a few villages on the lake belong to the kingdom of Italy ; the greater part of its shores is in Switzerland, and the mixture of different elements which is quite perceptible in its population, is expressed, also, in the features of the landscape. Intercourse with the inhabitants of this district leaves a most agreeable impression of their character: they have the pleasant vivacity belonging to even the meanest Italians, something, too, of their *grandezza*, but they are devoid of the serious drawback to these advantages,—that which is euphuistically termed the "*dolce far niente.*" The sterner spirit of the Swiss has influenced them with its energy and activity, and they seem to possess the best qualities of both races. As I have said, the charm of the landscape lies partly in this blending of different elements that complete each other. The beauty of the South is lavished on this lake, and yet its mountain peaks rise bare and jagged, and wherever a ravine opens, its rocks are as stern and grey as in some mountain lake in Switzerland; orange and myrtle, silver olives and golden vines bloom here in luxuriant richness, but high above them we

ROTUNDA OF HERCULES ON ISOLA BELLA.

see great woods of misty pine-trees dark of hue;—a northern forest under an Italian sky! Innumerable windings mark the course of the lake;—such deviations as we see in the current of a rapid and impatient stream; but this circumstance is the secret of the great variety in the scenery, since we are continually coming upon a new and unexpected view. Suddenly the road turns a sharp corner of the cliff down which a foaming stream is pouring, and all at once we find ourselves close to a gigantic bridge which spans the lake in an oblique line. This bridge is at Bissone, is two thousand five hundred feet long, and offers a charming view from its centre, of the manifold branches of the lake. Indeed the singular formation of the narrow basin is best seen and understood from this point; and not less strange than its visible configuration are the relative depths of its various parts. For example, whilst at Oria and other places, the water is nearly a thousand feet deep,—

BAY OF PALLANZA.

thus rivalling the depth of the Swiss lakes,—here, where the bridge of Bissone leads across it to Melide, it measures but a few fathoms! The grandiose bridge, designed by Lucchini, was opened to the public in 1847.

The town of Lugano is perhaps the most interesting point on the lake. It is the capital of the Canton Ticino, and of Italian Switzerland. It was sold in the sixteenth century to the Confederation by the Duke of Milan; and is at the present day a prosperous and thriving little town. Its climate possesses a large share of southern mildness, as the position is an admirably sheltered one; commerce flourishes, arts and sciences are not neglected, and guests flock from all parts of the world to this smiling Paradise. The stranger who intends to linger a few days in Lugano, generally takes up his quarters at the Hôtel du Parc, which is really an ideal hôtel with delightful gardens at the free disposition of visitors, where you may feel as entirely at home as though all the beauty that surrounds you were your own, and with a broad stone terrace looking down upon the blue waters with Monte San Salvatore mirrored in them.

At a very short distance from the hôtel is the church *Degli Angeli*, with the famous fresco by Bernardino Luini,—a noble and touching representation of the Crucifixion. This is undoubtedly the most precious possession that the town can boast of; but we find traces everywhere of artistic culture, and many of the neighbouring villas built by rich strangers, contain collections of good modern pictures. The most agreeable promenade by the margin of the lake is the quay, where on market-days you may see interesting specimens of the popular life and manners : a motley throng of country folks in gay-coloured national costume, mountaineers and boatmen, Swiss and Italians, all mingled together and all chattering, bargaining, greeting—or cursing, as the case may be! Amongst the strangers to whom Lugano has given hospitality, are many distinguished men, who have sought repose and refuge here from the storms of active life. Mazzini dwelt for years in a villa near Lugano, on foreign soil, but close to the mother country, whose greatness and unity were the aim and object of his life. Whosoever has met him in his solitary walks here, must retain an ineffaceable impression of his simple, noble dignity of aspect :—an impression much at variance with the general (and erroneous) notions entertained by strangers about this great man. But Time has been more just to him. He strove not for his own glory but the glory of his nation, and remained magnanimous and poor, virtuous and faithful, to his last hour. An almost antique temperance and moderation of spirit, was the keynote of his character; and this was acknowledged after his death by the general voice not only of Italy, but of Europe, and is confirmed by the citizens of Lugano among whom he lived. His outward aspect had something of old-fashioned aristocracy. He wore a high black cravat framing his delicately cut face, that was expressive of benevolent mildness; men took off their hats as he passed, children smiled at him confidingly, and the poor knew him for their most untiring friend. Such was Mazzini! The grave in which he lies at Pisa (where he passed the last days of his life) gave him the only gifts he ever received from his country —a few handfuls of his mother earth.

LAGO MAGGIORE.

THE Lago Maggiore stretches before us in all its imposing extent; over thirty miles long, and concealing tremendous depths beneath its waters. Its northern shores touch the rugged mountains of Switzerland, where the Simplon road comes down, and snowy peaks are seen rising above the fir woods; but as its blue waves stream onward towards the sultry plains of Lombardy the tints grow richer, the air clearer, and the fertility of the South displays itself in unchecked luxuriance. The banks are thickly inhabited; here is a humble cottage on the slope of the hill; yonder a splendid modern palace adorned with every elegance: there again, are some remains that recall to us the times of the Romans who built here temples to their gods and villas for their luxurious rich. Nature too has built here with wild volcanic forces; the broken chain of rocks which crowns the shore not far from Pallanza is continued under the blue depths of the lake, and wherever a peak rises above the surface it forms

one of those marvellous islands which lie like enchanted gardens in the midst of the waters. The little towns dotted along the edge of the lake have an air of old-fashioned simplicity;—there is a tiny port with dark-coloured boats, a broad stone quay, the houses have open arcades in front of them, and attractive-looking gardens; the streets are steep and narrow, and the heights above are crowned with crumbling ruins. The busiest moment of the day is that when the steamer stops at the landing-place, and the inhabitants crowd round the newly arrived strangers. At other times only the heavy-laden diligence passes by, or the vetturino with jingling bells to his horses. The town-hall, the post-house, and so forth, are the principal buildings in every little town, and their occupants the most important personages; the population is lively, good-natured, and industrious. Such is the aspect of the hamlets and townlets on Lago Maggiore,—Pallanza and Angera, Locarno, and Canobbia.

In Pallanza we took a boat and were rowed across to the Isole Borromee. Two of these, San Giovanni and the Isola dei Pescatori are poor and unadorned, and inhabited only by fishermen and their families. One narrow street of low houses runs through the island; fishing-boats with their nets are moored to massive piles; half-naked children play about in the soft sand, and of an evening you may hear the fishermen singing an ancient song whose tune is marked by primitive simplicity as he sails homeward before the light breeze. But in strong contrast with this idyllic poverty is the formal stateliness of the Isola Bella, which rises in a series of terraces from the blue waters. The gardens which now adorn it were laid out in the seventeenth century by Count Vitaliano Borromeo, who created shady grottos and leafy alleys on the rocky islet. The earth in which the trees were planted was brought hither in boats from the mainland, and now after two centuries have passed, the vegetation has reached a high degree of luxuriance, and the barren rocks are transformed into a fairy-like garden. Near to the shore on the lowest terrace, is a broad walk all overshadowed by orange and pomegranate trees, citron, and myrtle, whose stems have attained a gigantic thickness, and amidst which wild roses bloom and singing birds make their sheltered homes. This walk leads to a shrubbery of laurels; and here, more than seventy years ago, a young man paced, lost in ambitious dreams, and cut upon the bark of a laurel tree, the one word—'*battaglia*'; the man was Napoleon Bonaparte, and the time a few days before the battle of Marengo! Above there, in the deserted palace that turns its front towards the Simplon, we find yet other traces of the great conqueror: the bed is shown on which Napoleon slept, and which has been used by no one since that time. But with the pride in harbouring so great a guest, was mingled a considerable dose of fear and uneasiness: and travellers who visited the Borromean Islands in 1803, narrate how the greater part of the costly pictures and statues were removed from the palace, and carried safely away "out of the clutches of the art-loving (!) French."

The whole palace is built in a *barocco* style according to the taste of the day when it was designed, and reminds us in its old-fashioned formality and stiffness, of the French *châteaux* of the period. The so-called throne-room is really splendid; and even the other saloons with their marble pavements and columns, and their white statues glimmering out of dim recesses, have something stately and princely about them,—albeit the stateliness smacks of a time that is no more.

Much less artificial, and therefore much more attractive is the Isola Madre, whither we proceed in a light bark one brilliant morning. The soft wind blows the perfume of the blooming gardens into our faces; silver fishes leap out of the waters; the whole enchantment of the morning freshness seems to pervade the air. The Isola Madre is the largest of the Borromean Islands. All is still and solitary here; only a castellan who keeps watch and ward over the gardens and the uninhabited palazzo, reigns over the islands, and opens the gate to us as we mount the tall flight of steps. The gardens of this island offer specimens of the vegetation of every zone; one portion is set apart for tall northern pines and firs, whilst on the opposite side flourish palm-trees and cedars, sugar-canes and tea-plants.

At the southern extremity of the lake is Sesto Calende where the Ticino flows out of it; but the most important town in this part of the lake is Arona, a cheerful, prosperous little place, where commerce and traffic flourish, and are daily flourishing more and more. There are one or two good frescos in its churches, but undoubtedly its chief 'lion' is the colossal statue of the Saint whose home was Arona. Upon a lofty hill rises a pedestal formed of blocks of granite, and nearly fifty feet high; upon this stands the statue of St. Charles Borromeo, Archbishop of Milan, and one of the most zealous champions of ecclesiastical supremacy. The monument, which was completed in the seventeenth century, and cost more than a million of francs, was erected out of the private means of the Borromeo family and the voluntary contributions of the inhabitants of the district. As we are told, the design was made by Cerano and the execution was confided to Falconi and Zanella, who gave to the statue its present aspect. The figure of the saint is about seventy feet high; he has one hand stretched out in blessing over the town where he was born; his head is bare, and in his other hand he holds the book of Eternal Truth. His features bear the impress of that deep and enthusiastic earnestness which marked his whole life. His battle-cry was the power of the Church, but it did not make him deaf to the voice of humanity; for this man climbed up to the rugged mountain villages in order to comfort the poor and needy, and during the terrible plague that devastated Milan, he was to be found everywhere by the bedsides of the sick and dying. The statue is impressive by reason rather of its colossal proportions than of its artistic value; but still it never fails to produce a powerful impression. On the eminence that rises above it, stand the ruins of the feudal castle where San Carlo was cradled; the massive contours of the figure stand out darkly against the pale evening sky, and even at a great distance from Arona we can still perceive the gigantic hand extended in benediction. Farther and farther in the distance the great statue dwindles and finally disappears. The Present holds no such figures; it is one of the giants of old days!

MONCALIERI, NEAR TURIN.

TURIN.

WE are on the banks of the Po. From the balustrade outside the Capuchin Monastery we look down upon the wide-spreading city with its vast piazzas, rectangular streets, and great domes rising out of a sea of reddish, tiled roofs. Then come verdant gardens, and far in the background the blue chain of the Alps with their snowy summits. High above all the others tower Monte Rosa and Monte Viso, and through the gaps of the jagged outposts of the Alps, you get glimpses, here and there, of savage Savoyard vallies. The air which blows from thence is sharp and keen; it has no touch of southern softness in its breath, but rather the stern vigour which is expressed in the material aspect of the city:—active energy overpowering dreamy fancy.

This is the old valiant home of the Sards who have made Italy free and united; this was for centuries the capital of little Piedmont, upon whose energy the mother country staked her best hopes; this is the birthplace of the great statesman Cavour. Although Turin was already, in the time of the Romans, a strongly fortified place (as may be proved by the plan and disposition of its streets to this day) yet its chief historical importance dates only from the eleventh century, when it came into the possession of the House of Savoy,—to which it belongs up to the present time. Indeed there are very few cities which are at once so true to dynastic ties and traditions, and so full of intense patriotism for the great mother country. We naturally find the traces of the House of Savoy in

FOUNTAIN IN THE GIARDINO REALE.

every palace and monument throughout Turin; and its influence is felt everywhere. The names of Amadeo and Emanuele, of Philibert and Carlo Alberto, meet us at every step; amidst these eighteenth century buildings we seem to see Prince Eugène striding along as when he saved the town from the French by one of his victories. And however much modern hands may have modified the old forms, they cannot efface their impressions. It is true that Turin does not possess the charm of many another southern city, yet nevertheless she stirs our sympathies profoundly, and we feel for her—if not admiring enthusiasm, yet—heartfelt esteem and respect.

The most important streets in Turin are the Via del Po, Via di Roma, and Dora Grossa,—a remnant of the old Roman Road which led from hence to the mountains:

MONTE DEI CAPPUCCINI.

these streets all converge to the Piazza Castello, a huge square space on which stands the Palazzo Madama, and near to which are the chief public buildings. The Palazzo Madama is a strange looking edifice, less like an elegant palace than a gloomy fortress; and is overgrown with ivy. We wander round its dark walls, whose towers look desolate enough for birds of prey to build in, until we come to the façade opposite to the Via Dora Grossa, when the picture changes on a sudden. This façade was designed by Juvara and built with lavish costliness, and the rude fortress that frowns on three sides of the building here is turned all at once into a princely castle displaying all the pomp of the eighteenth century. The royal palace also, with its splendid gardens, is approached from the Piazza di Castello. In addition to the splendid saloons and dwelling rooms, most of them decorated with paintings on subjects relating to the history of Piedmont, the palace contains, moreover, a famous annoury—perhaps the finest collection in Europe. In addition to a rich variety of arms of general historic value, it contains many curiosities of more personal interest: for instance the armour of Prince Eugène, the sword used by Napoleon at Marengo, and the banner which the papal troops lost at Castelfidardo. As

Q

might have been expected, the more recent events which have culminated in the resuscitation of Italy, have left distinct traces on the aspect of Turin; for nowhere can you read contemporary history in the public streets, so clearly as in Italy, and whosoever has fought with a bold hand or a dauntless brain for "*la Patria*" may be sure of the recognition of a

ROAD TO THE CHURCH OF SUPERGA.

public monument. "*Gl' Italiani d'ogni Provincia*," is inscribed on the monument to Vincenzo Gioberti, erected in 1860; although the means by which Gioberti endeavoured to attain his country's independence were singularly ill-chosen, inasmuch as he hoped to gain that end by the assistance of the Papacy! But the Italians forgave their great man this radical error, and remembered only that the aim and object of his life was "*L'Indipendenza d'Italia*."

Despite the removal of the capital southward, the streets of Turin are still very lively and full of traffic. The houses are lofty, with elegant balconies; and the ground-floor is generally shaded by open arcades containing handsome shops. In the narrower streets

PORTA PALATINA.

you frequently come upon interesting glimpses of old-fashioned court-yards overgrown with creeping plants; at the street corners you find *kiosques* after the Paris fashion, filled with newspapers and caricatures from all parts of the world. A motley population of passers by is mirrored in the splendid plate glass of the shop fronts, and yonder, where you see a huge beehive stuck up over the door as a sign, is the savings-bank.

On Sundays the churches are well filled; *La Gran Madre di Dio* and *La Consolata*, and above all the cathedral in which the young Rousseau, once upon a time made profession of the catholic faith. At three o'clock one Sunday afternoon we strolled into the cathedral just as a troop of children had assembled for religious instruction. They were all seated on low benches arranged in a hollow square, the boys on one side and the girls on the other. The lessons had not yet begun when we entered, and the young rascals were chattering at the full pitch of their lungs as energetically as though they had to settle the politics of the nation; only two out of the whole number seemed at all shocked at this profane levity, and looked round triumphantly at the delinquents whenever an ecclesiastic chanced to pass by, and to hiss out an angry "*sh—sh—sh!*" to the noisy crowd. Finally came the teacher in his cope and stole, stepped, catechism in hand, into the centre of the square, and began to examine the children. The very first boy gave him a wrong answer, and the priest took him by the ear to lead him off to the dunce's stool; but the little fellow began hotly to argue the point, and to maintain that the matter was as he had stated it. It was impossible to permit himself to be blamed publicly! When, however, his powers of argument failed to justify him, he despairingly appealed to the compassion of a higher tribunal: "*Misericordia di Dio!*" he roared out as he sank down sobbing on to the seat of ignominy. The little girls showed a charming array of pretty childish faces; some had their chins propped thoughtfully on their hands, others let their dark eyes stray abstractedly in all directions, the elder children—girls of from twelve to fourteen years old—wore black veils and fluttered their fans nervously at the difficult questions. I shall not easily forget the indignant glance which the tallest of them threw after the priest who, when she had failed to answer three successive questions, was ungallant enough to shrug his shoulders contemptuously at her ignorance. After the catechism was over, a prayer was said. The children fell lightly on their knees like a flock of pigeons alighting on a field, and when the prayer was over, they rose again like a flock of birds fluttering, chirping, and chattering, and swarmed out through the great doors of the Duomo.

Now all is still again in the cool dim space, and the monument to those members of the house of Savoy who are buried in the Capella del Sudario, stands silent and solemn before us. The *kings* are buried in the Superga, a solitary church on an eminence, a few miles from Turin, commanding a wide view over the surrounding country. It dates from the stormy times when hostile armies were assembled under the walls of Turin; Victor Amadeus vowed to build a church if little Piedmont were but saved; he kept his vow, and Juvara was the architect of the votive temple. Who could guess, then, that within a hundred and seventy years the capital of the Savoyard Kings would be called—Rome!

FOUNTAIN IN THE ACQUA SOLA.

GENOA.

WE stand here in presence of a Princess enthroned in robes of marble whiteness, whose forehead nature has wreathed with laurel and myrtle and decked her breast with roses, to whom belonged the great race of Doria, and whose title is "*La Superba*." Much of her glory has departed, truly; but the last passion that dies in a proud nature is pride, and her pride Genoa has preserved to the present hour! She has lost her world-wide power, but she cannot be dethroned from the supremacy of her great past; the diadem of mountains that crowns her head no victor can take from her, nor the daily homage of the blue seas that murmuring kiss her feet;—she is to-day, as she was centuries ago, La Superba!

The aspect of her material and external life is certainly much changed since Genoa lost her independent sovereignty, and was incorporated with the little kingdom of Sardinia. Civic industry replaces the far-reaching plans of the Doges; the pomp of power has ceased; the nerves and sinews of public life in Genoa now are commercial, and not political interests. Nevertheless, although the sphere of their activity was narrowed, yet the energy, acuteness, and ambition of the Genoese soon found new aims to strive for; and they bent all the strength, both of their defects and their qualities, to the effort to shine—to advance—to preponderate! They had not forgotten that their symbol of old was the griffin—the mythic creature that combines sharp claws with soaring pinions. Every bold enterprise which the unquiet spirit of the times brought to light was keenly followed and observed in Genoa; every political idea which seemed to serve the greatness and glory of Italy made the blood of the old "Superba" course more quickly through her veins, and her prudence never quenched her enthusiasm. Nowhere was "Italia Una" greeted with heartier acclamations; nowhere was Garibaldi's hymn sung with more exulting delight than on the strand where Andrea Doria's palace is mirrored in the waves. It is true that with all her wonderful beauty certain parts of Genoa convey an impression of decay, and of having seen better days: but you feel at once that new and vigorous life is circulating through her marble limbs, and that it may be reserved for her alone of all the splendid cities which Italy possessed in the middle ages, to fulfil the fable of the Phœnix. The statue of her great Columbus stands at the gates of the town like a silent promise for the Future.

The view of Genoa from the sea is indescribingly striking. The bay in which the town lies presents no soft curving semi-circle, but is a deep jagged notch made by the sea in the rocky shore, from whose edge the tall mansions and palaces rise, terrace after terrace, up the steep slope of the mountain, which towers gigantic behind the town. Nature has raised a fortress here which offers a terrible resistance to any possible attack; and man has added still more threatening fortifications to her handiwork. He has built out great stone piers into the sea—the Molo Vecchio and Molo Nuovo—near to which stands the lighthouse, and he has planted batteries upon the rugged heights; but the beauty of the scene is such that even these frowning forts cannot destroy it; they seem to harmonize with the bare rocks above them, and to add to the soft charm of the lower landscape, a character of self-sufficing strength that is very imposing.

In the harbour there stretches a perfect forest of masts bearing flags of all countries; here are two formidable ironclads of the Royal Navy; yonder is a merchantman from America, and a sailing vessel from the Indies. You hear a babel of all languages, and see little barks and row-boats threading their way amidst the larger craft. There are two thousand of these small boats in the harbour of Genoa. The immense traffic of the port, and the restless vivacity of Southern life are here brought visibly before our eyes with a movement and noise, a never-ending variety of groups and figures, that really defy description. On the broad stone quay that runs along by the water's edge, and from whence flights of steps lead down at intervals, are crowds of boatmen and *facchini* (porters), with bare breasts and sunburnt faces; poor, patched, ragged, and dusty, yet bearing many of them traces of a high type of manly beauty. Half-naked urchins play and clamber about on the edge of the quay; there goes a train of sober-paced mules, heavily laden with sacks of grain; yonder a couple of lads are fishing, perched astride upon a floating barrel; here comes a black visaged fellow, unlading coals from a little collier. "*Un batello, Signore! un batello!*" cries a boatman, unloosing his little craft from the iron ring to which she is made fast. We step in, and are steered with wonderful swiftness and accuracy through a labyrinth of floating walls. It is only by thus coming close to their huge flanks that one realizes what gigantic bodies these big ships are. Who knows

SALITA SAN PAOLO, GENOA.

what bottom the anchor last rested in, which they have cast here ?—what rocks may have
threatened their massive sides ?—how many hundred lives may one day sink to destruction
within one of these huge bulks? The mystery of the great deep, and the bold adven-
turousness of those who first ploughed its surface, strike our imaginations forcibly here.
Many of the ships bear a statue of Columbus at the prow, others an image of the Madonna,
others again the lion-like bust of Garibaldi. On all sides they are lading or unlading,

PORTA VECCHIA DELLA LANTERNA.

hammering cases or weighing bales. One begins to have some conception of the immense
scale on which goods that we are accustomed to see in minute quantities are imported or
exported, and also to realize the yawning gulf that divides wealth from poverty: for upon
these very bales and sacks worth millions, the poor *facchini* sleep, worn out with their
daily toil, and awake to look longingly at the galley fire on board the ship yonder, where
they are cooking polenta, or at the casks of sweet wine that are being sent off to foreign
shores. Early and late, summer and winter, there is nothing for the *facchini* but toil
and poverty; yet poor as they are they still possess one thing—a home, a country.
How much more to be pitied are those emigrants upon the great ship that sails to-day
for the Brazils!

Thus we wind our way among a thousand different objects, until we reach the limit of the harbour which the two great moles embrace in a crescent-shaped line, and now the throng begins to diminish. The dazzlingly white lighthouse shines in the sunlight, the waves foam around huge blocks of stone, and at length we are out in the open sea. With what a different motion our bark now rocks and dances on the water! The difference between the sea here, and inside the harbour, is that between the pulse that beats in

EVENING AT THE MOLE.

freedom, or in a prison! We meet few boats; a rich merchant propelled by eight stout rowers, darts swiftly past us on his way to meet his ship that has just been signalled from the port: further away lies a great steamer newly arrived from the Levant and undergoing quarantine, with the clothes of the crew fluttering from the rigging in the fresh, purifying breeze. We are already a good distance from Genoa, and the dolphins are playing and leaping all around us, when we catch sight of something rising and falling and rocking strangely ahead, and hear a broken sound of bells. On nearing this curious object, we find it to be a *sound-signal*, to warn mariners off some dangerous rocks. A kind of raft painted red, is anchored here, and in a pyramid erected on it hangs a colossal bell. The furious haste with which the invisible hand of the storm sounds this bell, the rage of the roaring waters that strive to drown its voice, the frenzied violence with which the huge beams seem as though they would tear themselves free from the chains that hold them together,—all this has something weird and terrible in it. How wild and ghostly must this floating bell sound in a tempestuous winter's night!

The port of Genoa is separated from the town by a long sort of colonnade, or pier, which forms one of the pleasantest promenades imaginable; and underneath which, in vaulted chambers, there are enormous magazines and storehouses. At every hundred

MARKET IN THE PIAZZA DI PESCHERIA.

yards or so, a gate opens from the port to the town; iron tramways cross each other in all directions, to facilitate the transport of heavy loads, hundreds of little carts stand ready, drawn by mules and donkeys which fill the air with their brayings; they are often harnessed three or four nose to tail, for the streets are too narrow to permit of their going abreast, and they are generally furnished with a set of bells that tinkle cheerfully as the animals clatter over the pavement.

As soon as we leave the neighbourhood of the port the whole aspect of the town is altered: it has a different physiognomy and a different expression. Instead of the ceaseless, almost slavish toil of the porters and boatmen, we find in the principal streets an air of easy and pleasant bustle and occupation. The maritime element has disappeared, and we are on dry—nay mountainous—land. The narrow lanes climbing the heights between rows of lofty houses, paved with bricks, and only practicable for the sure feet of mules and donkeys, give the street commerce of Genoa a peculiar stamp, and offer a series of striking pictures which Rome or Venice could not surpass. I mounted up the Salita San Paolo; the people were washing and cooking in the open air; under a doorway sat a pedlar-woman chattering to a swarm of women with their babies in their arms. An

AT THE PORT.

Abbate passed by with a grave and laborious step, and the women looked after him curiously; I fancied he must be some great dignitary, and asked who he was. "*I* don't know," answered the pedlar-woman, shrugging her shoulders with an air of sovereign disdain and indifference: "*Non lo so! Un prete,—un fanatico!*"

The great centre of trade is in the immediate neighbourhood of the Loggia dei Banchi, where the Exchange is, and where the Strada degli Orefici (Street of the Goldsmiths,) begins. Here you see the delicate gold and silver filagree work for which Genoa is famous, spread out in profusion, for the most part on a background of blue velvet which shows it off to great advantage. But this is a species of wealth created by industry: Genoa is not lacking in another sort of riches which have been the inheritance of the great princely families for generations, and are petrified into marble palaces, or bloom in enchanting gardens. We find such in the Via Balbi, the Strada Nuova, Strada Nuovissima, and Via Carlo Felice, which are the resort of the fashionable world; and when we enquire who are the occupants of the elegant equipages that roll past, every name that is told us, is, as it were, a fragment of history. There stands the Palazzo Ducale in which the Doge once dwelt; the magnificent Palazzo del Municipio formerly belonged to the Dorias; then come the Spinola, Pallavicini, Durazzo, Balbi,—one more splendid than the other. In these Genoese palaces the court-yards are usually very handsome; they are invariably high above the level of the streets, and are approached by a broad flight of marble steps. The court-yard is surrounded by a colonnade, also of white marble, is hand-

VIA SAN LUCA, GENOA.

BEFORE THE CONFESSIONAL IN SAN LORENZO.

somely paved, and has a fountain in the middle, round which orange-trees and oleanders are planted. From hence the main staircase leads up to the reception-rooms; the banisters are of gilt bronze, and there is generally a huge hanging lamp, which is lighted at dusk. The state rooms are magnificent, with folding doors of the costliest woods, and their walls hung with masterpieces of art. A *festa* in these halls, when they are filled by crowds of the beautiful Genoese ladies, with the eloquent fan in their hands, the gold arrow in their hair, and whole love-stories in their dark eyes, must be an enchanting spectacle.

The building whose entrance is guarded by two stone lions, is the University, the court-yard of which is reckoned one of the finest in Genoa. It was formerly the College of the Jesuits, and was built almost entirely by a member of the Order, who belonged to the rich and noble Genoese family of Balbi. Here comes a swarm of students flooding the wide staircase, ascending with a lagging step, descending with a swift one. The walls are adorned with numerous stone tablets which record some memorable date, and with the statues of learned men, and allegorical representations of various virtues, which are probably only to be found thus in effigy among the students! Every wall and pillar is scribbled over with numerous inscriptions; for the demonstrative tendency which characterizes Italians in general, appears to reach its climax among the Academic Youth. *Evviva Garibaldi, Re della Repubblica!*" was scrawled in long letters on one marble-slab; and for ten whole years no one had found time,—or thought it worth while,—to efface this expression of political opinion. Others were more subjective, and contented themselves with a "*lungo addio*," before they departed. It was striking to see several inscriptions in English: "Farewell for ever!" was to be read in more than one place.

The Palazzo Brignole-Sale is renowned for its picture gallery; but its exterior is remarkable enough to attract attention, for it is of a glowing red colour, and looks, sometimes, in the sunset light, as if the whole building were on fire! The populace call it the *Palazzo Rosso*. The most remarkable of the many churches which Genoa possesses are perhaps Santa Maria di Carignano, and the Santissima Annunziata:—the first for the fine view to be had from its cupola, the second for the wonderful richness of its internal decorations. The roof is covered with gold, even to the capitals of the white marble columns; and this has a wonderful effect when the light streams in through the purple curtains that screen the windows in the dome. This church is not usually opened until four o'clock in the afternoon, but even then it is generally silent and deserted, and devoid of that hum and movement which destroy the solemnity of most Italian churches. I had the wide nave almost to myself one afternoon: there was only a monk who had taken refuge there from the glare of the hot street, and was pacing up and down reading his breviary, and a young girl with a white veil on her head, kneeling in front of an empty confessional box and waiting for the priest. On the very steps of the confessional lay a beggar-boy with an exquisite Raphaelesque face, fast asleep.

From the Annunziata the way lies through the most fashionable streets to the *Fontane Amorose*, where the ascent begins to the *Acqua Sola*, the most favourite promenade in Genoa. The plateau on which these gardens are laid out is nearly one hundred and fifty feet above the sea, so that you have a limitless view beyond the roofs of the town and its rocky bastions, over the blue waters. I descended from the Acqua Sola to the sea-level again, by stony and deserted paths where chance was my only guide. A threatening storm was gathering in the heavens as I came out from these winding ways in the immediate neighbourhood of the Palazzo Doria. The mass of white houses was relieved in marble pallor against the black clouds swiftly rolling up behind it; and now for the first time I realized the bold character of the physiognomy of the town, and the correctness of her appellation, "La Superba," as she stood there majestic and defiant, with

HARBOUR OF GENOA.

the angry sea rolling dark foam-crested waves at her feet! I hastened down a steep street by the *Muro dei Zingari* (Gipsies' Wall), which leads through a western suburb of the town, but the stormy wind blew clouds of dust in my face with such violence that at length I was fain to take refuge in a dirty little *osteria* which I found by the road-side.

Here, under a vine-covered porch in front of the house, a party of grimy-visaged fellows, workmen employed in the arsenal, were sitting drinking; for it was Saturday evening, and the wages had just been paid. They clinked their glasses, and quarrelled, and sang, and added a most diabolical riot to the noise of the howling wind. However one must allow that they displayed the merits which are in general characteristic of the Italian workmen: —sobriety and frugality. It is only the noise that is greater with them, not the consumption; for three Italians will make a greater row over one poor bottle of wine, than would thirty Englishmen or Germans in emptying a barrel! Their enjoyment consists in the companionship, the chatter, the discussion, the noise; and the circumstance that they drink a "*bicchier' di vino*" at the same time, is merely an adjunct—a means, not an end. It is therefore neither so unpleasant nor so dangerous to mix with them as it seems from a distance; on the contrary, the stranger will be courteously and willingly received, room will be made for him, and care taken to avoid saying anything that might offend him; and if he is able to converse in Italian with tolerable fluency he will be welcomed with pleasure. Such, at least, are the impressions I brought away with me from the tavern by the *Muro dei Zingari*.

There are yet two points of interest which every traveller in Genoa visits, and whither we should like to accompany the reader before leaving the town. The first of these is the noble cemetery, a long parallelogram of marble arcades shaded by dark cypresses. There is always a certain melancholy charm to one who is a traveller in foreign lands, in leaving the busy haunts of men now and then, for consecrated spots like this, where only our common humanity is appealed to, and we are moved by feelings far above any passing antipathy that may arise towards foreign customs and people. How much beauty, how much happiness, and how much suffering lie at rest here in the Campo Santo of Genoa! One might wander for hours in its marble cloisters and muse on the history of the unknown dead.

The last, and most attractive pilgrimage for all foreign visitors to Genoa, is the Villa Pallavicini, close to Pegli. Nature has beautified the spot so lavishly that one might willingly dispense with the artificial additions on which the owner has spent millions. For, although it is true that much art has been expended in laying out the park, and leading you from one surprise to another, yet the real charm of this delightful domain does not lie in such aids;—the blue sea, of whose limitless extent you get a glimpse from marble terraces whenever a soft breeze parts the branches of the tall camellias, the nightingales that sing all day, the flowers that fill the air with perfume,—these are the real treasures of the Villa Pallavicini! And in presence of these the artificial mediæval ruins, the kiosques, and grottos, inevitably sink into triviality; but at the same time the generosity and public spirit which the princely owner displays in allowing strangers free access to his Villa, cannot be too highly prized, or too warmly acknowledged. In this connection I would record a noteworthy contrast between people of the Latin and northern races, which I observed here: the latter, namely, turn towards the sea and the view, the former crowd noisily and eagerly through the narrow doorway of the "*cabane rustique;*" in the one, silent admiration is the chief sentiment, in the other, pure curiosity. The majority of the company, on the occasion when I visited the Villa Pallavicini, happened to be French people; and as they were very free in expressing their sentiments, I enjoyed some amusing scenes. "*Ah, quel séjour de paix et d'innocence!*" cried a hollow-eyed elderly gentleman, who entered the pretty Swiss Cottage with a very showily-dressed lady on his arm. One stout matron pinched all the flower-buds with her fingers, and discovered that the

"Italian flowers" were miles behind the French. "*Ticus, nos boutons sont beaucoup plus avancés,*" said she complacently to her son, a pert youth, who certainly looked like a very forward bud indeed! Every minute one heard an exclamation—"*charmant, ravissant, gracieux, majestueux,*" etc., etc. In short it was an excessively comic spectacle, and sent us back to Genoa in a very cheerful humour, there to dream away one more day.

Beautiful cities never seem more beautiful than at the moment when we are obliged to leave them! The sky and the sea and the marble palaces were bathed in a flood of light, as we took our last look at Genoa; and we acknowledged that, although the whisper of a sigh may be heard in the word now-a-days, yet she is still worthy of the proud epithet she bore of old ;—*La Superba!*

SCENE ON THE SHORE.

ON THE RIVIERA DI PONENTE.

THE little hamlet of Pegli, close to the Villa Pallavicini, lies on the Riviera di Ponente. From Genoa to Nice stretches this wonderful road, to which, perhaps, no coast scenery in the world is comparable for beauty, along the edge of the changing sea. Every village has its own special distinction: in this one a Roman Emperor was born; in that one a Pope; a third boasts of its palm-trees, and another of a famous battle that was fought near it in old days.

Until quite lately the only way to travel from Genoa to Nice was along this high road. Heavily laden diligences and swift *vetturini* crossed each other all day long with much jingling and rumbling and cracking of whips, and the tired traveller was glad to arrive at his halting place for the night in Loano or Albegna. But now all this is changed: the railway train goes from Genoa to Nice in seven hours, passing through more than seventy tunnels on its way, and sometimes so close to the sea that the foam of the waves is thrown on to the swift wheels. But it must be owned that we lose in beauty what we gain in speed. From Genoa as far as Savona the coast is little varied. In nearly every considerable place there are great shipbuilding yards, where hundreds of busy hands are hammering; and on more than one occasion we counted thirty vessels lying close together. Lower down on the sandy shore that the waves had left smooth and moist, we saw bands of fishermen, ten or twelve together, hauling in their nets, whose place was marked by a red barrel floating at some distance on the sea, whilst others were

PEGLI ON THE RIVIERA DI PONENTE

manning a little sailing boat and putting off to fish. They were all bare-legged to the knee, and the boatmen wore scarlet Phrygian caps. Presently a donkey driver passed by, tramping barefooted through the soft sand, and singing lustily as he went; besides his laden beast he had charge of a rough cart drawn by a mule, and my curiosity was excited by an inscription in chalk on the side of the cart. I examined it and found it to consist of the singular motto, "*Morte ai Stupidi!*"—"Death to the Stupid!" Certainly a singular device for a donkey driver.

The little villages on the shore (or sometimes perched half-way up a high cliff) are

NEAR BORDIGHERA.

enchanting, half hidden among gardens and vine-trellises, fig trees and olives. In almost every garden there grows a gigantic species of hemp, which shoots up to the height of the first floor windows, and looks like some huge sea-weed, and the aloe shows its stiff sharp leaves in every crevice of the rock where there is room for a handful of soil.

One striking feature of the railway journey along the coast, is the frequency with which the tunnels succeed each other. The contrast between looking out at the boundless sea one instant, and being plunged into utter darkness the next, is more strange than agreeable; light and darkness succeed each other with absolute suddenness and lightning speed, and a ray of sunshine strikes you with its dazzling brightness, and is then withdrawn, just like a glittering dagger which some dæmon or genii should keep rapidly sheathing and unsheathing. Sometimes, however, we come to a long stretch of open ground, from whence we can contemplate the wondrous play of colour in the Protean sea. Now, when the horizon of the sky is of a pale yellow tint, the waves below it are dark as blue polished steel; again, when gloomy clouds are gathered in the heavens and pile themselves up threateningly, the waters turn livid, and roll in pale green billows crested with curdling foam; anon the whole expanse shimmers into a soft silvery grey, then comes the rosy hue of evening, and at last the glorious gold and purple of the sunset pours itself upon the flood. But these changes are not to be seen every day: sometimes months

OBELISK IN VILLA PALLAVICINI.

pass, during which a blue cloudless sky is stretched clear and dazzling above the equally blue Mediterranean for as far as the eye can reach.

The narrow strip of land that lies between the sea and the mountains, and is all covered with dark rocks and green olives, is itself of such a nature as to make the position of the towns and villages all along it peculiarly picturesque. The little place on the hill yonder, surrounded by ancient walls, is Finale; then comes Oneglia, where Andrea

SAN REMO.

Doria was born, and then the little town of Porto Maurizio, celebrated for its harbour. At a window looking on to the sea sits a young mother singing, spindle in hand, with the sunset light upon her face, whilst her brown-skinned, black-haired little ones are playing under the orange trees in the garden. Even in the prosaic railway stations, what life and

PROCESSION.

movement, what charming figures! It is a pity to rush through such scenes in an express train; but really the railway is becoming master of the whole road, and it is surprising to find what numbers of persons, even of quite the lower orders, have taken to using it. The notion that "time is money" seems to have taken root even among the Italians. In the coupé where we sat, we had a fellow-traveller who amused us all mightily. He was a stout priest from the French side of the frontier, just started on a holiday trip, and looking the very ideal of good humoured jollity. At every station at which the train stopped his mouth widened into a broad grin as he jumped out hastily "to enquire how long we were to halt there." The answer was usually "*Cinque minuti;*" whereupon he would hurry off to the buffet to have his flask filled with red wine of the country. This flask was regularly found to be empty by the time we reached the next station, when the whole manœuvre was accurately repeated.

The first of the three famous places of resort for invalids which we come to on the Riviera di Ponente, is San Remo, a little town of nearly twelve thousand inhabitants. It owes the shelter it enjoys from harsh winds to the rocky promontories which shut in its deeply curved bay to the east and west. The original town is built far back inland, but the newer edifices, palaces, villas, and hôtels which are intended for the use of strangers during the winter, are much nearer to the shore; so that San Remo is clearly divided into the Old Town and the "*Quartiere Marittimo.*" The former is a sort of architectural chaos, of which I have never seen the like, a labyrinth of steep alleys and old archways, built partly to prop up the crumbling old town walls that have suffered much hard usage at the hands of Saracenic pirates. The climate of San Remo is renowned for its mildness and evenness; and the vegetation—luxuriant all along the Riviera—here attains a higher point of lavish fertility. Here we see palm-trees for the first time, many of them are as much as eighty feet high, and the palm branches used in the solemnities of Palm Sunday at Rome are all sent from hence, and all by one family, the Brescas, who received the privilege from Pope Sixtus the Fifth. The story goes that the origin of this privilege dates from the raising of the great granite obelisk which stands on the Piazza of St. Peter's, on which occasion, when the workmen employed had got into difficulties, and there seemed scarcely any hope of the huge mass being successfully raised into its place, the sailor Bresca of San Remo rendered good service by hauling at the ropes at the peril of his life.

BORDIGHERA.

But the most famous plantation of palms on the whole coast is at Bordighera, where these splendid trees are so numerous that palm branches form a regular article of export to France and Holland. Soon after Ventimiglia, where the French frontier is passed, we arrive at Mentone, renowned throughout Europe for its sanitary advantages. The position of the town is similar to that of San Remo, for the bay is enclosed by rocky heights at each end, and sheltered at the back by the great mountains of the Maritime Alps. The plan, too, of building is the same; the old town lies as far as possible inshore, and on the

FROM A VILLA NEAR BORGHERA

ON THE RIVIERA DI PONENTE.

slope of the hills, whilst at the margin of the sea you find numerous elegant and spacious new houses erected for the winter visitors, and often let for large sums. The vegetation

HARBOUR OF MONACO.

here is, if possible, more magnificent than that we have hitherto seen on the Riviera. The lemon trees are especially luxuriant and vigorous. Every street boy who idles about dirty and ragged may have a fragrant white blossom in the button hole of his buttonless jacket. The climate of Mentone is one of the finest in Europe. During forty-three years the thermometer only went down below zero four times, and then but for a few hours; whilst the summer heat is scarcely ever so intense as that which is commonly felt every season in

VIEW NEAR SAN REMO.

Paris and St. Petersburg. Mentone was formerly an appanage of the princeling whose territory we shall enter on at the next station; now it is the chief town of a French

Canton, since the Prince of Monaco was paid four millions of francs in 1860, "*pour céder une ville qui ne lui appartenait pas.*"

Monaco is the next important place we come to, and there is a visible excitement among the passengers as we approach it, for there in the gaudily gilt Casino is the gambling table which is the chief and most peculiar feature in this miniature state. "It would be worth while to get out here and win a thousand *napoléons d'or* whilst waiting for the next train," says a traveller, who looks as if it would puzzle him to stake a hundred! The principality, whose entire length can be traversed in the railway train in thirty minutes, and which at many points only measures a hundred and fifty metres across, nevertheless lies in a position of wonderful, almost unique beauty. A huge rock that advances boldly from the shore, and falls almost perpendicularly into the sea, bears upon the plateau on its summit the princely castle, and the houses of the little town. The gardens that surround it are full of stone-pines and cypresses, and on the natural terraces of the rock bloom the vine and the aloe. The battlemented walls and ramparts which enclose the town give to the whole a bold, fortified air, which reminds us of the old pirates' nest which once crowned these heights. Its shadow makes a deep blue spot upon the sea, and the road winds in sharp zig-zags downward to the shore.

Nearly opposite the town lies Monte Carlo with the Casino, to which an admirable road leads, as smooth as a drawing-room *parquet*, amidst plantations of the finest exotic shrubs and flowers, and with indications on every hand that millions are expended in making the place attractive. The Casino stands on an open space, and is adorned with marble pillars; it contains fine saloons, used for balls and concerts, a reading-room furnished with newspapers from all quarters of the world, and, lastly, the magnificently decorated "Salons de jeu." All the arrangements are strictly after the French fashion; you hear scarcely a word of any other language, and see no coin of any other country on the green tables. Access to these latter is only possible on certain conditions, which are rigidly adhered to; it is forbidden, for instance, to minors, to persons in a menial position, and to the "negligently dressed!" Good manners are *de rigueur* here; and it is considered as necessary to ruin oneself with a good grace, as it was to an ancient gladiator to die with dignity. Nevertheless, unpleasant circumstances will occasionally happen, as was proved a winter or so back, when a poor wretch shot himself through the head in the middle of the saloon. There is a tolerably strict control exercised over the entrance into the gambling rooms, even of those persons whose toilet is of the most unexceptionable kind. No one is admitted without a ticket issued and signed by the "*Commissaire spécial,*" nor can such a ticket be obtained except on giving one's full address. It is made evident in the politest manner in the world that people here have a right to look on you with suspicion. A swarm of liveried lackeys fills the halls and corridors, and even their smooth-shaven faces have assumed the *blasé* air which is considered good style in the "Cercle des Étrangers." This is the name under which the whole meritorious gambling institution is included, and "Cercle des Étrangers" is written on the green ticket of admission, *valable pour un jour*, which the visitor receives. The authority which rules and regulates everything, and whose edicts are seen everywhere, is an invisible entity denominated "l'Administration," the general factotum of Monaco, and the good genius of its finances if of nothing else. Not without reason did the old saying arise :—

"Son Monaco sopra un scoglio
Non semino ne raccoglio
Ep'pur mangiare voglio."

MONACO.

(I am Monaco perched on a rock; I neither sow nor reap, but I mean to eat nevertheless! The means by which it ate and lived formerly was piracy; now it is gambling;—evidently a considerable moral progress!

The excitement of gaming, like all other fevers, grows more intense towards evening, when the rooms are ablaze with wax-lights and the throng presses so closely around the green tables that those in the front rows,—the old inhabitants,—glare round indignantly.

CONVENT GARDEN AT PESIO.

No sound of exultation or disappointment is to be heard; nothing but the hard clink of the money. Eyes and not lips are eloquent here, for any display of emotion would be contrary to *bon ton*, and to the laws of the all-powerful "Administration;" but how expressive are the silent glances! How terribly eloquent is all this dumb show! The *grande dame* yonder with dark brows and massive features sets her twenty-franc piece time after time indefatigably on the same number, but it is never the winning one, and you see the calculation of her losses pass across her face like a thunder-cloud every time the croupier coolly sweeps away the gold coin. "*Cinq mille francs*," she whispers to a lady near her;—evidently the sum she has lost that evening. But there are still two rouleaux of gold before her, there wants still an hour of midnight! Behind her stands a young gentleman of the first Parisian society, who certainly if he be not a minor has only just ceased to be one; but who would cavil about a week or two with a person who can lose fifteen thousand francs in half an hour? Fifteen times running the young Vicomte has set a thousand franc note on number seventeen, (it is whispered that that number represents a lucky day in his, not very ancient, history,) and fifteen times running has the croupier raked up the crisp white note with its blue letters as if it were a mere worthless scrap of paper. A sort of shiver ran through the crowd at last; they were touched on a tender point,—the love of gain. But the young Vicomte went out sullenly by himself on to the marble terrace where the throng of careless non-gambling visitors was assembled under rose-bowers and orange-trees. What will the noble father of this hopeful aristocrat say when he receives the young gentleman's next letter? This had been a good evening for

MENTONE.

the bank; only one of all the players won constantly: he was a repulsive looking man who persistently staked his silver five-franc piece (the lowest stake allowed) and received gold napoleons in exchange for it.

Each of the buildings which flank the Casino contains a magnificent Café got up in the highest style of Parisian luxury, with wide doorways, columns, carpets, mirrors, etc., etc., of the costliest kind. There are single tables surrounded by elegant screens, so as to shut off select parties from the profane vulgar, and only leave room for the entrance of the *garçon* with the champagne. From behind these screens is heard the laughter of silvery voices and the rustling of silken dresses; possibly the party numbers among it some elegant leaders of Parisian *ton*, ladies who have their box at the "Italiens," and drive magnificent equipages in the Bois de Boulogne. They are gay despite their losses at the

SEASHORE NEAR SAVONA.

green table, and possibly console themselves with the saying that those who are unlucky at play are fortunate in love.

One may pass some very delightful days in Monaco, but after a while one is glad to get away from it; and one would be glad even if the next station were not Nice, "the Pearl of the Mediterranean" as it is called. The aspect of this town is attractive in every direction. The landscape in which it is placed is enchanting, and in Nice itself there is the piquant contrast,—one might almost say *conflict*,—between the element of the real

INTERIOR OF A PEASANT'S COTTAGE IN BRIGA.

Italian populace and that of French—"civilization," which has entirely taken possession of the superficial part of all social intercourse. In addition to this there are the contrasts between the numerous other nationalities which crowd Nice from October to the middle of April, and which are sufficiently indicated by the names of many public buildings and streets. Here is the German Protestant temple, and there the Russian Church; yonder is the *Promenade des Anglais*, and close by a shop which announces itself as a branch of a great Parisian house. A magazine of children's clothing bears the sign "*Aux grâces enfantines*," and the poorest little stall where flowers are sold has written above it "*Maison spéciale pour l'exportation de fleurs en France, Belgique, et Angleterre*." Everywhere Parisian manners and Parisian fashions dominate, and the Theatre where they are performing the "Fille de Madame Angot" sticks up on its playbills as *the* attraction *par excellence* "*Grand succès parisien!*"

ITALY.

Nice lies close to the sea, but there is no bay as at San Remo or Mentone, and the port, situated to the east side of the town is so insignificant that marine commerce has never reached any flourishing point there. On this eastern side also lies the old town, huddled together close to the castle in the form of a triangle; and here is a labyrinth of dirty narrow streets, through which traffic on wheels is exceedingly difficult. But the western part of the town and the whole of the shore belong exclusively to the foreign colony who occupy more than eighty splendid villas hereabouts. We see English

ON THE SHORE OF THE LAVENZA, NEAR ERIGA.

matrons and their daughters very calm and self-possessed under a fire of eye-glasses from the officers of the *grand' armée*, gouty noblemen in Bath chairs with the "Times" in their hands, and the population of nomad fine ladies and gentlemen,—a little the worse for wear, but delightfully fashionable—proper to a foreign place of resort such as Nice. One can wear a straw hat and white linen coat even in November. What an odd anachronism this costume appears to us northern folk, who know that our friends and relations are sitting at home over the fire with snow on the roof and mud on the pavement! The chief place of assembly for the fashionable world is—besides the *Promenade des Anglais*, begun in 1822 by the British colony in order to give employment to a number of poor distressed workmen,—the *Jardin Public*, which lies near the sea and is filled with the finest exotic plants. It contains myrtles of truly colossal proportions and the noblest palm-trees in Nice. The palm in the centre of the garden, however, was "planted in honour of the annexation!" Quite close to the Jardin Public a little river runs into the sea, called the Paillon, which is distinguished above all its fellows, even in these parts, by the fact that it

scarcely ever has any water in it. Its dry pebbly bed stares up at the sunshine; but it is crossed by several bridges, nevertheless. The whole nomenclature of Nice is impressed with an air of almost comic grandeur: for instance there are Boulevards, Avenues, Quays and Squares, and all baptised with the high-sounding but somewhat ephemeral title

STREET IN TENDA.

"Imperial." In a word, there are many other things besides the great palm-tree in the *Jardin Public* that have been "planted in honour of the annexation."

Although Nice itself is wanting in that air of *picturesque neglect*, if I may so express it, which gives a peculiar charm to the aspect of many thoroughly Italian cities, and although French civilization has covered it with the sort of varnish which makes modern Europe so monotonous, nevertheless the excursions to be made in the neighbourhood,—especially towards the mountains,—offer all the attractions of unsophisticated nature. Peculiarly beautiful is the road over the Col di Tenda towards Valdieri, a favourite hunting seat of King Victor Emmanuel; snowy peaks rise above the crumbling walls of the little town, and although there remain but few vestiges of the fortresses erected in the

Middle Ages to resist the incursions of the Saracens, yet that wild people has left other traces of its presence in these parts, in the shape of manifold traditions. Not far from Tenda lies the little village of Briga, picturesquely situated on the banks of the Lavenza nearly three thousand feet above the sea level, and surrounded by the wildest solitudes. The men of Briga lead a nomad sort of life with their flocks and herds in the mountains, whilst the young girls, whenever they can be spared from home, go down into Nice, there to earn their marriage portion in service.

Another point of interest much renowned in this district, is the Certosa of Pesio; an ancient monastery, in whose inner courtyard great trees grow and cast cool shadows on the cells of the monks. Many a pilgrim has sought refuge there, and endeavoured to lighten the load of sins that lay heavy on his conscience by penance and solitude: but now it is a place of cure for bodies instead of souls, and physicians strongly recommend its pure bracing air to invalids. The sea and the mountains are in truth Nature's best and mightiest works, for in them lie the hope and the secret of health.

CASTLE OF MONACO.

LAVAGNA. RETURN FROM FISHING.

ON THE RIVIERA DI LEVANTE.

N both sides, to the west and the east, the gulf whose central point is the fair city of Genoa, stretches its blooming shores; hence the names that distinguish the wondrous coasts that lie east and west of Genoa,—*Riviera di Levante*, and *Riviera di Ponente*. We are now about to follow the former, or eastern, road which, like its western neighbour, is carried along through the rocky cliffs by means of various tunnels, and affords here and there glimpses of the soft blue Mediterranean peeping between olive and myrtle groves where pretty villages and villas are nestled. The first station of any importance that we come to, is called Nervi, a little town much resorted to in winter by invalids and delicate persons, with gardens blooming all the year round, that reach down to the sea, and sheltered from rough winds by high mountains in its rear.

These mountains front us in a grand semicircle when we reach Lavagna, a tiny white townlet that looks like something on the stage. Nor is it lacking in heroes; for Lavagna is the home of the *Fieschi*, who possessed it as a countship as early as the eleventh century, and of whose blood came the well-known conspirator against the power of the Dorias. Two Popes, Innocent the Fourth, and Adrian the Fifth, also belonged to this town and to this family; and even in the present century, the well-known name has once more been mixed up with a bit of European history, on the occasion of the attempt on the life of Louis Philippe, which took place in the year 1835 on the Boulevard du Temple. Whether the criminal really had a right to the name of Joseph Maria Fiesco which he

SEASHORE NEAR QUINTO.

assumed, is uncertain to this day; but this much is known: namely, that he had been already twice condemned to death as a conspirator, and thus at all events shared something of the dark fatality which has seemed to rest upon the name of Fiesco for three centuries.

Soon after Lavagna, Sestri di Levante seems to rise up out of the sea as we approach it; it is situated on a narrow tongue of land with a steep rock rising at the extremity of it

JEZZANO, IN THE BAY OF SPEZIA.

which rock is called Isola. The golden evening light is shining on the battlement of an old tower that crowns the rock, and touching the summits of some dark pine trees around it; the waves break softly on the beach, and away in the distance we see the road climbing

ON THE PENINSULA NEAR SESTRI LEVANTE.

a steep ascent amid olive groves. Wherever a valley opens the parched bed of a mountain torrent is visible, dried up by the fierce sunshine and full only of dazzling white pebbles; poor little hamlets lie scattered on the slopes, their squalid houses still watched over by a ruinous tower or castle. The first of these villages that we come to is called Moneglia, above whose roofs rises an ancient fortress which once commanded the entrance into this rocky gorge; for here the road grows ever wilder and steeper, and leaves the sea-shore for the inland mountain fastnesses. Already we are nearly two thousand feet above the blue mirror of the Mediterranean when we come to a solitary hostelry that bears the name of Bracca, which is also the name of the whole valley through which the road is carried here, and finally we reach the highest point of the pass. We have made a wide detour, and are at a considerable distance from the sea in the midst of a wild mountainous country; but now we begin to descend again, and the hard poverty to which this stony, sterile soil condemns its inhabitants, gives place to smiling ease as soon as we descend into the valley of Borghetto. In Cassana close at hand, are several caverns renowned for the discovery of numerous fossil bones in them. The wild burnt-up torrent bed by which the

THE ISLAND PALMARIA, IN THE BAY OF SPEZIA.

road passes to go to Cassana belongs to the little mountain streamlet the Vara; we pass through one more grey solitary village called San Benedetto, and then come once more to the coast.

That is the old mountain road which we have been describing, but now,—like many another similar pass,—it is almost deserted; for the railway is now open from Sestri to Spezia. It cost years of labour to win this railway from the rocky cliffs and sandy shore, but it is at length completed, and thousands of strangers traverse it yearly. Here, as we speed along with the swiftness of the wind, we get a glimpse of a blue chain of mountains delicately outlined on the distant sky, and are told that those are the mountains of Carrara; and presently in the bay that opens beautifully before us, we come in sight of Spezia. The town itself is small, and devoid of splendour or attraction, although they are building new palaces there every year, but its position amid a green background of olive-trees is enchanting.

The harbour of Spezia, lying between two fortified points of rock, is renowned all over the world, and is said to be one of the finest harbours for ships of war in Europe. The first Napoleon ordered surveys to be made, and occupied himself with strengthening the defences of the place from whence he thought he could command the whole of the Mediterranean. Now a fleet of the Italian Royal Navy lies at anchor there; and whenever the political

horizon looks stormy in Southern Europe, Spezia becomes once more a word of power. Amongst the historical reminiscences of the place may be reckoned the stay made there by Garibaldi after he was taken prisoner at Aspromonte. He had, as is well known, been

FOUNTAIN OF THE SIREN IN CARRARA.

wounded by a bullet which had penetrated through his boot into the bones of the foot; and the Hotel of the Città di Milano in Spezia, where the wounded hero was laid up, was crowded by surgeons from all parts of the world. There were the famous Italians Albanese and Cipriani, the Englishman Partridge, and the Russian Perigoff, but none of them were able to relieve the patient's sufferings, or to agree about a diagnosis. At length by Garibaldi's own earnest wish Nélaton was sent for, arrived about the end of October, and then and there laid the foundation of that European reputation which

LERICI, NEAR SPEZIA.

belonged to him ever afterwards. On the first examination of the wound he differed from the opinion of the majority of his colleagues, of whom only two out of the seventeen surgeons assembled, believed the ball to be still in the wound. He has himself narrated the transaction in a published account as follows:

"I examined the wound with a probe; and at the depth of about two centimeters and a half, I struck against some hard body which gave a dull sound; .... passing to one side of this obstacle, I probed further, and at the depth of from five to six centimeters came to the bone. The first obstacle clearly was the bullet. I told this to the General, and begged him to assure himself of the fact, and for this purpose gave him a probe to the point of which was attached a minute fragment of Sèvres porcelain rough at one side. The General put the instrument into the wound with his own hand, struck against the obstacle which I had found, pressed upon it lingeringly, and then withdrew the probe. The tiny morsel of porcelain was no longer white, but marked with a dark, metallic-looking stain. This was analysed and found to be lead. There was no longer any doubt about the matter. We had found the bullet!"*

As may be supposed the circumstances above narrated have taken an important place

SIESTA.

in the annals of Spezia, and whenever the 'Hermit of Caprera' is mentioned, you are sure to hear all the inhabitants, young and old, begin to recount the story of the wound.

The neighbourhood of the town is famed for its beauty, and one of the most beautiful spots in it is Porto Venere (or the Port of Venus) named from a temple of the goddess that stood here long before the Pisans built a church and convent on the same site. At the distance of a few miles from Spezia the Isola Palmaria lies out in the sea; it is an island composed almost wholly of marble; and further on along the coast is Lerici, half hidden amid olive woods, and echoing with the ship-builders' lusty hammer on the shore.

* This account of a scene in which all Europe was deeply interested, is—in so far as it leads the reader to infer that M. Nélaton extracted the ball—inaccurate. It is true that Nélaton concurred with the two or three surgeons who declared, contrary to the opinion of the majority, that the ball was still in the wound. It is also true that to him is due the credit of inventing the probe with a fragment of porcelain attached to it, which was the means of positively determining the fact that the ball was there, and its exact position. But the operation of extracting it was performed by Zanetti (one of the most eminent surgeons whom Italy has ever produced), and Nélaton was not even present on the occasion. It may be stated, moreover, in contradiction to sundry pamphlets and newspaper articles published at the time, that the only woman present in Garibaldi's room when the bullet was taken from his ankle, was the Signora Jessie White Mario, who held the General's hand during the operation.—*Translator's note.*

ITALY.

The next large town that we meet with on the Riviera di Levante is Sarzana, which although it counts barely ten thousand inhabitants, can boast itself rich in proud memories. Nicholas the Fifth, one of the greatest Popes who ever filled the throne of St. Peter, came from Sarzana; and to Sarzana, too, the family of Bonaparte belonged, before they migrated to Corsica in 1612. Behind Avenza the railway branches off to Carrara. Veins of marble run through the whole coast-line that we have been traversing: they glitter in the mountain gorges, they rise up from the waves in the numerous little islands that lie off the shore, but here at Carrara they are gathered together into one colossal and inexhaustible quarry.

Carrara is the marble-treasury of the world, from whence, even since the days of Augustus, the white marble has been obtained which was destined to be animated by the artist's hand. The quarries from which it is cut lie deep among the hills in wild, savage-looking gorges; there are more than four hundred of these quarries in active operation, and you constantly hear detonations echoing among the mountain peaks, as the great masses of marble are blasted from their native rock, and see on all hands troops of sun-burnt workmen busy with the dazzling white stone. On every side we have proof how rich Carrara is in this precious material; not only in churches and palaces, but in far humbler buildings it is prodigally employed; every petty tradesman decks his doors and windows with it, and you enter a miserable tavern by a staircase made of—*Carrara marble!*

Amongst the other towns on the Riviera, Massa and Pietra Santa are perhaps the most worthy of notice. Great veins of marble pierce the soil in all directions; the slopes are crowned with vines and olives, and from amidst the green peep out ruined castles, the homes of a thousand fantastic legends. Then to the right spreads itself the illimitable blue of the Mediterranean, veiled with the softest haze; the fresh sea-breeze blows upon us as we pursue our way along that golden pathway, whose very name suggests the murmur of waves upon the shore, and the play of morning sunbeams—Riviera di Levante!

ON THE RIVIERA.

MARBLE QUARRIES NEAR CARRARA.

MONKS PLAYING BOWLS.

IN EMILIA.

IN no country is travelling so rich in delightful objects as in Italy, but in no country are the limits of time and space more oppressively felt. In most other lands the intermediate spaces between great cities or famous points are comparatively devoid of attraction, but here almost every tiny town that we pass on our way to the great centres is important, either historically or picturesquely. Art has everywhere scattered pearls of price; the number of petty potentates who held their courts in the various subdivisions of Italy, created a hundred centres of interest for the traveller. One would desire to see everything, and yet it is impossible to halt everywhere! Without much sacrifice of one's inclinations, and without neglecting a thousand beauties, it is absolutely impossible to travel through Italy and to describe it.

The district we are now hastening through is the ancient Emilia; the district of the Romagna, and of the Legations, whose cities flourished centuries before Christ, and upon whose soil the dying Roman Empire painfully drew its last gasp, and made way for the new era that was to arise out of its ashes. Where is a city to be found so rich in treasures of early Christian art as Ravenna? Parma was the home of Correggio's immortal genius; and of Ferrara, where the house of Este ruled, it has been truly said:—

"No mighty name is named in Italy,
But has been on a time our house's guest."—GOETHE.

But the other cities of Emilia are lacking neither in glory nor great men who cultivated arts and sciences under the fostering patronage of princely races. And a storm-tossed moving story is that of this whole province, from the days when Gauls and Goths contended here in arms, and Belisarius took Ravenna, down to the revolution of 1849, when Garibaldi trod this soil with his legions! Nearly every great family which ruled over Italy in the Middle Ages, from the Visconti in Milan to the Borgias in Rome, have extended the theatre of their feuds over Emilia, and side by side with the conflict of material weapons raged the deadlier conflict of spiritual warfare, which latter we may convey in a word,—here stands the Castle of *Canossa*.

All these great events have found characteristic expression in the monuments and architecture of the series of cities which we now come upon. The first of them is Piacenza, which, behind a bulwark of twelve mighty forts, contains half a hundred churches and half a thousand palaces; but in the sound of its name lingers some trace of the pleasantness of the town in the eyes of bygone generations:—*Piacenza*, how delightfully the word sounds! The central point of such traffic as the town still possesses, is the Piazza dei Cavalli, where stands the Palazzo del Comune which served the citizens for a town-hall. The façade of the ground-floor offers a series of five open arches, beneath which, in old times, the tribunals were held, and public business transacted, whilst the upper story served for the meetings of the town council, and even, during one period, was used as a theatre. Despite the elegant architecture of the central part of the building, with its windows surrounded by richly decorated arches, the effect of the whole is stern and warlike, owing, partly, to the bold battlements which crown the Palazzo. Two bronze equestrian statues of members of the Farnese family, which stand in front of the palace, harmonize admirably with its general tone.

But this town-hall of Piacenza is far surpassed, and almost sinks into insignificance, when we behold the ducal castle of Ferrara rising before us in gloomy majesty. Time has blackened these walls that rise, fortress-like, from out a wide moat filled with water, and defended by frowning towers, battlements, and bridges; all of so stern and threatening an aspect, as to impress one with a vague sentiment of terror. In looking on this castle we can believe in the power, but not in the happiness of the race that ruled here; we seem to feel something of the oppression which weighed on Tasso's spirit when he dwelt at the court of the Estes. And yet in those days the town was animated by a lively varied population of some hundred thousand inhabitants: whereas now its streets are empty and deserted, and the threatening castle looks down upon poverty and solitude.

The present population of Bologna is about the same as that which Ferrara possessed in the time of its highest prosperity; but Bologna could easily contain three times that number of inhabitants, on such a colossal scale is the city planned. It almost seems as if the wide-spreading plain which here surrounds us on all sides had inspired the eyes and hands of the builders with large and grandiose projects: palace succeeds palace, and street after street opens on to a wide piazza framed in by lofty walls and turrets. Nay, even the statues that stand in the public places are of gigantic dimensions; the statue of Neptune, which adorns a fountain in the *Piazza di Nettuno*, is nearly ten feet high, and together with the smaller bronze figures which surround the sea-gods, weighs more than twenty thousand pounds. Adjoining the Piazza di Nettuno is the Piazza Maggiore (now named Piazza Vittorio Emanuele, after the King) where the market is held, and where a number of interesting buildings are crowded together. This is an impressive spot to visit when the noise and bustle of the day are over, and the full moon rises behind the Palazzo Apostolico. *Palazzo Apostolico!* this name, too, is now obliterated from the building that bore it so long, but at the sound of it rise up a thousand reminiscences of the stormy history of Bologna; for the crown worn by the city's rulers, was the triple tiara of the Vatican. The influence of the ecclesiastical power in Bologna is displayed in the numerous churches which are distinguished not only by important works of art, but also by

CANOSSA.

PIFFERARI.

their enormous dimensions; especially is this the case with San Petronio, the principal church of Bologna, whose gigantic size positively astounds one at the first glance; but there are many other churches built with a similar lavish prodigality of means. Few cities of Italy were so rich as Bologna, which bore the epithet of *La Grassa* (The Fat) in consequence of her easy opulence; but notwithstanding the tight grip which Mother Church always endeavoured to keep on so wealthy a city, the burghers maintained a spirit of proud independence throughout all their vicissitudes. Among the churches, that of Santo Stefano is distinguished, not so much for its artistic treasures, as for containing a sort of museum of ecclesiastical curiosities of all kinds, pictures, and statues, gold and silver jewelry, and relics of saints.

THE LEANING TOWERS IN BOLOGNA.

But all these temples with their splendid bell-towers, all these turrets and battlements of princely palaces, are not so distinctively characteristic of the general aspect of the town as are the two mighty monuments which are visible for miles above the sea of roofs, and with which the traditions of seven centuries are entwined. These are the leaning towers, each named after its founder:—the larger *Asinelli*, the smaller *La Garisenda*. The view from the summit of the former (which overtops its neighbour by a hundred and thirty feet) reaches from the Paduan hills to the Apennine, and from the Adriatic to the towers of Modena; all the treasures which Nature and Man have lavished on this soil, lie beneath our gaze,—the happy fields through which, as far back as two thousand years ago the *Via Æmilia* led northwards to Milan.

As we advance eastward towards the sea, however, the plain grows marshy and desolate, and close to the sandy shore we come upon a city which surpasses most towns of central Italy in renown, though not in prosperity;—I mean Ravenna. Who has not pictured to himself the old Gothic King Theodoric?—here is his tomb. Whose heart does not ache to read of the great Dante sadly departing into exile?—here it was that he found rest for time and eternity. In Ravenna Thumelicus, the son of the barbarian Prince Hermann, grew up to be a gladiator; in Ravenna Gaston de Foix fell in one of the bloodiest battles which Europe had yet seen; in Ravenna Byron sought peace and repose beside the beautiful Countess Guiccioli. Yet these are but a few of the more salient memories of the city which for centuries led so stormy an existence, and then again for centuries so stagnant and solitary a one! The foundation of her political importance and prosperity was the harbour which Augustus caused to be constructed for

TOMB OF THEODORIC, RAVENNA.

his fleet close to Ravenna. This prosperity decayed and fell with the decay and fall of the Roman Empire; but Ravenna has another indestructible importance which is assured to her as long as her stones stand one upon the other: she is, namely, the treasury and metropolis of all Europe for the study of early Christian art. Almost everywhere else the works produced by the painter and sculptor and architect in the fifth and sixth centuries of the Christian Era have been hopelessly damaged or ruthlessly destroyed by the vandalism of succeeding generations; a basilica such as the church of *Sant' Apollinare in Classe*, is almost unique amongst the monuments of the world. It is supposed to stand upon the site of an ancient temple of Apollo; the saint to whom it is dedicated is said to have suffered martyrdom in the reign of the Emperor Vespasian. The church stands about an hour's drive away from the town, and the road to it lies, for some portion of it, close to the enchanting *Pineta* (pine-wood), which made so profound an impression on Byron; but when it was built (A.D. 534—549) it stood, as its name imports, close to the busy harbour where the Roman *classis* (fleet) lay at anchor. The sea has now receded many miles from the spot, and tall pine trees grow above the sandy bottom where once the galleys of Augustus rocked upon the waters of the inconstant Adriatic.

The task of playing *cicerone* through Ravenna should be undertaken not by a mere unlearned recounter of his travels, but by a profound student of ancient art; and the visitor who really desires to see and understand her treasures, will find that he must devote himself very seriously to his aim. The whole neighbourhood of the town is full of forlorn melancholy, and the town itself still suffers for the centuries during which she lay neglected and forgotten, apart from the great highways of traffic. But yet she has wonderful compensations—at least in the eyes of an artist! Ravenna is a new tint in the wondrous picture,—a new chord in the wondrous concert—that we call Italy. She furnishes another proof of the inexhaustible artistic treasures of this land; and therein we find much consolation! For in taking leave of the gentle reader we are conscious of many short-comings, but then we say to ourselves, " Who could be so mad as to undertake the task of exhausting the Inexhaustible?"

MARKET-PLACE, WITH THE FOUNTAIN OF NEPTUNE, BOLOGNA.

FROM THE ARNO TO THE TIBER.

BY

EDWARD PAULUS.

FLORENCE.

'Mid deserts dimly through the mists descried
We speed across the barren Apennine,
Or, plunged deep down where never sunbeams shine,
Pierce arrow-swift the mountain's mighty side.
Sudden we feel soft spring-like breezes blowing,
Down from the sky that shimmers crystal clear,
And at our feet there opens far and near
A wide green land where laurel groves are growing.

Fair Florence, we salute thee 'mid thy bowers
Beside the yellow Arno's storied stream,
Thy wondrous marble dome that towers supreme,
Thy stern old walls all garlanded with flowers,
And, hid within the solemn cypress glade,
Thy silver fountains whispering in the shade.

AFTER a somewhat gloomy journey through innumerable tunnels, and amidst the arid, bare, rocks of the inhospitable Apennine, we suddenly get a glimpse— whilst we are still high on the mountain—down into wide-spreading, verdant Tuscany. Milder airs play around us, and we feel an intense longing to be down there in that realm of all ancient culture,—culture of art, of commerce, and of land. Even as seen from the railway the extraordinary fertility of the soil strikes us. It is cultivated with minute industry, and scattered over in all directions with cottages, farm-houses, and villas: these latter generally situated on the slope of a sunny hill, surrounded by cypress groves, and within reach of a fresh stream or fountain. It is a happy, beautiful, peaceful-looking land, covered with the very emblem of peace, the silver-leaved olive, which grows and thrives everywhere. Even on the stoniest soil you may see great ancient olive trunks, twisted, hollow, and decayed, but still bearing a crown of silvery foliage that trembles in the breeze and makes a glory in the sunlight.

This first town we come to on the plain, with a marble bell-tower and lofty dome,— is it Florence? No; we dart past; this is only Pistoia. It is surrounded by an evergreen garden where the garlands of vine are slung from tree to tree. The country grows still richer and lovelier as we advance; here is Prato, a pleasant smiling little town, and already we catch glimpses above the trees, of castles, and mansions, and groups of statuary. Suddenly uprises Brunelleschi's gigantic dome looking almost silvery in the sunshine, and all around it, flowing out even to the slopes of the olive-green hills, spreads the town, magnificent with soaring towers and noble buildings. This, *this* is Florence!

From the very first day of our acquaintance with the fair city, it inspired us with sympathy; it is so pleasant and home-like despite its thousand years of historic greatness! The houses are pressed close together in a neighbourly fashion, and are mostly crowned by an open, shady *loggia*, or arcade, with slender stone pillars; and the peculiar Florentine broad eaves stretch out from the roof and shelter the streets below from sun and rain.

There is an air of tranquillity and contentment in the narrow streets with their lines of sober, brownish-grey houses, broken here and there, by a church, or an open Piazza decorated with monuments and elegant open arcades. Three-fourths of the town lies on the right bank of the Arno, the remaining fourth, with the Boboli Gardens and the gigantic Pitti Palace, lies on the left. Six bridges, two of them modern iron ones, cross

PONTE VECCHIO.

the yellow Arno; the finest of them, the *Ponte della Trinità*, is built of sandstone and marble, and forms in its entirety one long, graceful curve from shore to shore, with which the smaller curves of the arches harmonize admirably. A very different aspect is presented by the *Ponte Vecchio*, an ancient bridge with houses and shops on it, which carries across the river a large part of the city's traffic; and this is not inconsiderable, for Florence has now a population of nearly a hundred and fifty thousand inhabitants. Seen from this bridge the shores of the Arno on each side present a series of lofty, irregular buildings, many of them with open *loggie* on the roofs, and some of the more ancient bearing towers: whilst in the distant background rise olive-covered hills sprinkled over with churches, villas, and ancient convents shaded by tall cypresses.

A short distance above the Ponte Vecchio, we turn to the left and find ourselves in

FLORENCE, FROM SAN MINIATO.

FLORENCE.

front of the Uffizi, the buildings of which enclose a narrow oblong space opening, at its upper end, on to the Piazza della Signoria. Outside the arcade, which extends along the whole length of the ground floor, are niches at regular intervals, and in these niches stand marble statues of the most famous Tuscans. Here are Andrea Orcagna, Nicolo Pisano, Giotto, Donatello, Leon Battista Alberti, Leonardo da Vinci, Michael Angelo, Dante, Petrarch, Boccaccio, Ferrucci, Machiavelli, Guicciardini, Amerigo Vespucci, Galileo,

FOUNTAIN OF NEPTUNE IN THE PIAZZA DELLA SIGNORIA.

Benvenuto Cellini, Cosmo the First, Lorenzo the Magnificent, and many others; truly a series of names for any country to be proud of! Passing by these we reach the Piazza della Signoria, where, in close proximity to the mighty mass of the Palazzo Vecchio, stands the beautiful Loggia dei Lanzi. The Piazza is moreover adorned with numerous statues and monuments, and the great fountain of Neptune, where marble sea-horses, and listlessly reclining marine goddesses, fling showers of silvery water at each other in sport.

Many tragical and cruel reminiscences are connected with this Piazza, and with the great pile that stands here—the Palazzo Vecchio. First came the fierce and ruthless struggle between the Guelphs and the Ghibellines, which endured for centuries: for, as Dante says, the commonwealth of Florence was like a sick man who restlessly changes his posture without ever finding ease or rest. But out of these times of conflict grew up the bold and profound ideas, on which even to-day the State and society are founded, and from the contending ranks emerged the pure and noble figures of immortal artists, poets, and men of science ; until at length, almost imperceptibly, and without any act of violence, the rule of the Medici was firmly established—the rule of not merely the richest and most powerful, but the best and most cultivated citizens in Florence. Arts and Sciences begin to flourish in hitherto unheard-of fulness and beauty, the Golden Age seems to have returned with Cosmo the First,—*Pater Patriæ*,—and his high-souled grandson, Lorenzo the Magnificent. Nevertheless there occur at intervals wild outbreaks of the old Florentine passion and vindictiveness. The 26th of April, 1478, is the date of the conspiracy of the Pazzi. On the morning of this day, Lorenzo the Magnificent, together with his younger brother Giuliano dei Medici, a chivalrous youth of two-and-twenty, is attending mass in the cathedral, at the moment when the officiating priest (who happens, on this occasion, to be Cardinal Raffaele Riario, nephew of the Pope) is in the act of elevating the host, and when at the sound of the bell all the congregation bows itself to the earth, one of the hired assassins stabs Giuliano with his dagger. Giuliano staggers and falls, and Francesco de' Pazzi, throwing himself upon him, stabs him again and again with such blind fury that he actually wounds himself in the thigh. At the same time two priests, Maffei of Volterra and Bagnono, attack Lorenzo. Maffei wounds him in the throat, but not mortally, and Lorenzo flies to the sacristy, the brazen doors of which are at once shut and bolted, and defy all attempts to break through them. The populace rushes from the fatal scene confused, terrified, and horror-stricken, as if the Day of Judgment had arrived. Outside, on the Piazza, old Jacopo de' Pazzi unfurls the banner of Liberty, and the Archbishop of Pisa (deeply implicated in the conspiracy) forces his way into the Palazzo Vecchio with an armed band ;—all in vain ! The indignant people tears the two priests to pieces, hangs the Archbishop of Pisa and the two Pazzi high on the stone cross of a window frame in the Palazzo, flings down other of the conspirators from an upper storey on to the stones of the Piazza, and carries their mangled remains stuck on pikes in triumph through the city.

But later, after the too early death of Lorenzo, terrible dissensions once more convulse fair Florence. There arises in the midst of the people the haggard, pale, enthusiastic figure of Savonarola, the Dominican monk of San Marco, like a threatening prophet of old, full of dire forebodings. The vanity of this world, the seductions of the flesh, the immoral and enervating beauty of all arts and sciences, form the theme of his penitential preachings. And with the force and fierceness of a flame fanned by storm-winds, he sweeps the calculating, sensual, intellectual Florentines along with him into the fantastic "kingdom of God" which his fanatical brain has imagined. Pietro de' Medici is expelled, Jesus Christ the Saviour of the World is proclaimed King of Florence, and the monk's power knows no limits. On the last day of Carnival in the year 1497, and on the same day of the following year, Savonarola causes a huge pyramidal pile to be erected on the Piazza della Signoria. Its foundation consists of masquerading garments, masks, false beards, and so forth ; above these are works of Latin and Italian poets, priceless parchments and manuscripts with miniatures and illuminations ; then come women's adornments, jewels and articles of the toilet ; higher still musical instruments, chess-boards, and playing cards ; at the summit of all, paintings, especially such as represented female beauty. When this pile was set alight, the Piazza resounded with the blaring of trumpets, the ringing of bells, and the singing of many voices. Afterwards there was a procession to the Piazza San Marco, where a very curious round was danced. Those who took part in it stood in three concentric circles : the inner one consisting of the monks of St. Mark's Convent alternating with boys dressed to represent angels, the next of acolytes and young men of the laity, and the outer one of old men, citizens, and priests, the latter crowned with olive-branches.

But—on Ascension Day of the following year, another pile stood in the Piazza della Signoria, and with it the body of Savonarola, after being seven times put to the torture and finally strangled, was burnt to ashes!

The old historic Piazza contains buildings so bold and grandiose in conception as to recal the ancient Roman architecture. Here we see the daring idea of Arnolfo who erected the tower of the Palazzo Vecchio; that is to say, he carried up the broad, massive, ancient tower of the Fornaboschi to a dizzy height above the roof of the building, and

PALAZZO PITTI.

crowned it with a sort of stone baldacchino resting on four huge round stone pillars, so that this tower commands a view over Florence only rivalled by that from the dome of the Cathedral. Yonder we behold the great work of Orcagna, after whose design the Loggia de' Lanzi was built, (subsequent, however, to Orcagna's death) the noblest and most beautiful open arcade in Italy. Only three wide arches rise upon rich pillars; but *what* arches! How perfect in symmetry and proportion! The Loggia was completed in 1387, and one may date from thence the commencement of the "Rinascimento," the new birth of classic art and architecture. In truth, however, it was quite a new art that then arose, as distinct and different from the old, as is the modern world from the ancient. This building has ever been the delight of connoisseurs. When Lorenzo de' Medici begged Michael Angelo to design him a supremely magnificent palace for the magistracy, to be erected on the Piazza, the great artist advised him to carry the Loggia de' Lanzi entirely round the Piazza, since nothing finer could possibly be invented! The prince, however, shrank from the expense of such an undertaking.

It is pleasant to stand under the shelter of the beautiful Loggia, and to look down from the steps of it into the lively, populous Piazza. Many Florentine loungers may generally be seen assembled here amidst the wondrous groups of statuary which fill the arcade. Your Florentine lounger is not beggarly, half-naked, and insolent like the

Lazzaroni of Naples, neither does he stun you like him with discordant senseless noise; no, he is peaceable, placid, well dressed, and reposes very comfortably on the luxuriant laurels of his great fore-fathers!

Among the statues in the Loggia de' Lanzi are some of the finest creations of antique, mediæval, and modern art. In the centre stands the fine classical group in marble, of Ajax with the body of Patrocles, and close to it the modern group of Achilles and Polyxena by Pio Fedi;—an admirable work despite all that can be said against it, instinct with passion, and a brilliant example of the indestructible talent for sculpture which the Italians possess. Here, too, is the beautiful meditative Thusnelda, her head drooping dreamily as though she were sadly thinking of her native Germanic forests; and near her are five other antique female figures. At the distance of a few paces stands Donatello's Judith in bronze; she holds aloft the grinning ghastly head of the Philistine warrior Holofernes, and is evidently rejoicing in the bloody deed just committed. The greatest work—at least if greatness be measured by size—of Benvenuto Cellini is also here under the Loggia: it is the bronze figure of Perseus, about the casting of which he has so much to say in his autobiography. The smooth-limbed son of the gods, displays triumphantly Medusa's head with its horrible snaky curls and awful deadly beauty. The pedestal on which the statue stands is adorned with marvellous richness, and reminds one of innumerable other works due to the chisel of this fantastic, self-willed, genial artist, who, notwithstanding all his defects, literally overflowed with talent, and who boasts loudly of his triumphs throughout his singular autobiography: adding to the description of nearly every one of his numerous productions "this was the most beautiful and divine of all!"

Proceeding onward from the Piazza, through the lively and crowded Via Calzaioli, past the square colossal mass of Or San Michele, in whose niches stand the noblest statues of Ghiberti and Donatello, we reach the *Piazza del Duomo*,—the Cathedral Square. On the left we have the Baptistery where the world-renowned bronze gates are; to the right the Duomo with its blank, unfinished façade, and close to it Giotto's Campanile (Bell-tower) all clothed with coloured marbles. The origin of the Baptistery is lost in almost mythical obscurity. It was once the principal church of the city; and many Italians declared it to have been originally a temple dedicated to Mars. This is, no doubt, an error; but the materials of the building which consist in part of genuine antique pillars, and blocks of stone, point at least to a very early period in the Christian era. The interior of the building is very solemn; it is dimly lighted, surrounded by pillars, and surmounted by a dome, in which strange Byzantine mosaics glimmer on a golden background. The exterior, with its delicate coloured marble panellings, is remarkable as showing an attempt in the direction of modern art,—a sort of anticipation of the Renaissance by two hundred years! And one of the greatest among the creators of the Renaissance of art in Europe,—the Florentine Brunelleschi,—diligently studied this monument from his youth upwards. His statue stands but a few paces from it on the south side of the Duomo. Brunelleschi is represented as looking up joyfully at the cupola of the Duomo, his grandest and boldest work which dominates with its noble outline the whole of towered Florence, and her villa-besprinkled suburbs. It is a never-to-be-forgotten sight that breaks upon the traveller along the sunny slopes of the Val d'Arno, when he first beholds fair Florence amid her garland of gardens, bristling with towers, and surmounted by the glorious dome of Brunelleschi rising noble and serene in the brilliant rays of a southern sun.

But seen nearer, the dome loses nothing of its imposing effect; especially when viewed from the eastern side, where it rises like a huge mountain above the cluster of

VIA DEGLI STROZZI.

LOGGIA NEAR MERCATO NUOVO.

chapels around the choir. The drum is pierced by huge round windows, above it is the
dome formed by eight marble ribs converging together, and above that again, the lantern,
more than seventy feet high. If this lantern were placed on the flat earth, it would form
of itself a beautiful temple,—a marble rotunda in which the taste of the Renaissance, so
rich in ornamentation, has begun to display its elegant luxuriance. Brunelleschi the great

master, lived to see the completion of the dome which he constructed with a double shell, —one over the other,—to be the admiration of all subsequent ages, and the beginning of the lantern, which was carried out in strict accordance with his design.

When the last rays of the sun which gild so lingeringly the summit of the Duomo have died away, when the birds have ceased their graceful wheeling and skimming around the mighty cupola, and when the moon begins to pour her magic light over the marble pile, then the town at its feet begins to live and move after the hot summer day. Then the numerous little tables set out in front of the Caffès are filled with chattering groups, drinking coffee, lemonade, or syrup and water. There they sit, smoking, talking, disputing,—but always with moderation and courtesy,—until a cold breath of wind, blowing from the Arno, scatters them. Next morning, however, there they are in the Caffè once more, with the unfailing cigar and a newspaper. The waiters run about with coffee and smoking hot rolls soaked in butter, which I can pronounce from experience to be excellent, and flower-girls—with nothing blooming about them except the bouquets they sell—peep in, and insist upon sticking a flower into the button-hole of any stranger who may happen to be present, whilst a single glance from a native will suffice to repulse them. As the heat increases, the upper classes take refuge behind the massive walls of their cool palaces, and wait patiently until the evening, when they go to an open-air theatre, and then drink coffee again in the Piazza del Duomo.

The Duomo, with its clothing of fine coloured marbles, is built in what may be termed the Florentine-Gothic style; and the most perfect specimen of this style stands near it in the shape of Giotto's graceful Campanile. It rises in five storeys, each one loftier than the other, broken by exquisite pointed-arched windows,—a wonderfully simple square tower; but the panels of marble which clothe it with most harmonious colouring, the delicately cut festoons, ornaments and statuettes, which adorn it, make the colossus marvellously light and elegant. In the month of May, in the year 1865, on the occasion of the Dante Festival, the whole city, including the Duomo, was illuminated; and then the fairy-like beauty of these enormous masses of building was fully brought out. The Campanile with its polished marble pillars seemed absolutely suffused with light, and transfigured: an image of the majestic figure of the great poet to whose immortal memory the festival was dedicated, glowing with a flame of holy and exalted love.

The interior of the Duomo is most impressive at twilight, when its great painted windows admit a soft, enchanted light,—when its proportions seem to grow and grow in the dimness,—when tapers begin to glimmer here and there upon the altars, grey dusk silently invades the solemn consecrated space, and from the world without there sounds through the lofty vaults the deep tone of the great awful-voiced bell! How often has it rung to summon the burghers of Florence to fight against their fellow-citizens, or—more nobly—against the common foe!

The greatest, and the last, deed of the free commonwealth of Florence, was the defence of the city against the troops of Charles the Fifth. In a spirit of magnanimous self-sacrifice the Florentines destroyed their suburbs, burning to the ground country-houses adorned with frescoes by the greatest painters, and surrounded by blooming gardens, lest they should afford shelter to the enemy. Michael Angelo fortifies the tower of San Miniato al Monte, which is standing to this day, and strengthens it to resist all attacks. Food becomes scarce, fresh troops of Spaniards and Germans keep strengthening the Imperial army, yet the courage of the besieged is not to be bowed; and, far away from the city, behind the Cyclopean walls of old Volterra, the last hero of the Republic,

LOGGIA DEI LANZI.

the fiery Ferrucci, is bravely fighting and repulsing the Spanish storming parties. But the position of Florence becomes daily more desperate; the plague rages fearfully in this sultry July weather, throughout the low-lying, shut-in valley; corpses lie in the public streets, and Malatesta, the commander of the troops hired by Florence for her defence, is engaged in secret negotiations with the enemy! Then in that moment of extremest need, the victorious Ferrucci is commanded to return to Florence with his whole army, and approaches slowly, being reduced by fever, and having to take circuitous routes. He is already as far on his way as Pistoia, when, on the third of August, towards evening, the news suddenly flies lightning-swift through the sultry, plague-stricken city, that a battle has been fought, Ferrucci is victorious, the Prince of Orange the commander of the Imperial army, sent out to meet Ferrucci, is killed! Indescribable rejoicings, boundless hopes arise; but, alas, meanwhile the truth is that all is lost! Ferrucci has been indeed victorious at first, and the Prince of Orange is slain; but the fight continues in a townlet close to Pistoia, they fight in the fields, in the streets, and at length, overpowered by superior numbers, Ferrucci with a few followers is pressed into a house and taken prisoner. He is led before the Spanish leader, Maramoldo, the man over whom he has so often been victorious, and the Spaniard seizing a pike, with a curse strikes it into the breast of the defenceless wearied hero. "You are only killing a dead man," are Ferrucci's last words.

On the fifth of August the crushing truth is at last known in Florence, and all who hear it understand that the ground is sinking beneath their feet. As at the end of a dark and stormy day the sun sinking below the edge of the horizon sends out one final, fiery gleam, so shines, at the close of Florentine history,—Ferrucci! Then the night sweeps down on it; miserable treachery and intrigues weave a net-work which stifles the freedom of the city, and the freedom of Italy.

When all is lost, Michael Angelo returns sad, silent, and solitary, to his studio, where soon afterwards he carved the renowned figures of Morning, Evening, Day, and Night, which are still to be seen on the tombs of the Medici, in the Sacristy of San Lorenzo, which Sacristy was entirely designed by Michael Angelo.

> Lo! those four reclining figures;
> Morning, Evening, Day, and Night,
> Then it was the sculptor drew them
> From the marble's depths to light;
>
> All his bitter indignation,
> All his sorrow's deepest moan,
> Breathed Prometheus-like within them,
> And inspired the lifeless stone.
>
> Till the sparks flew from his chisel
> Day by day he toiled with might,
> Raising up his troubled spirit
> Into Art's clear realms of light.
>
> And at length the work was ended.
> Round the forms divinely fair
> All the people crowded breathless,
> Dazzled, as by sunlight's glare;
>
> Saw the marble limbs majestic,
> Gazed upon the brows sublime;
> Then outspake the poet Stromi
> To Night's statue thus in rhyme:

The Night that here reposing thou dost see
An Angel from the stone hath new created.
She sleeps; but by Life's flame is animated.
What, dost thou doubt? Wake her, she'll speak to thee!

But great Angelo,—his spirit
Striving still with bitter pain,—
From the burning depths of feeling,
Hurled this answer back again:

Sweet 'tis to sleep; and sweeter to be stone,
In days which shame and vilest wrongs deprave.
Neither to see nor hear is all I crave;
Therefore speak low, and let me slumber on! *

The figures are indeed beyond all description noble and beautiful; there is something of mysterious and superhuman grandeur about them. Here is revealed to us the whole titanic nature of the greatest of the Moderns, with its enormous creative force, and fiery aspirations. Michael Angelo was more than sculptor, painter, architect, and poet; yet he was all these, and no one of the Arts seemed sufficient to absorb his vast genius. There is a sublime and inextinguishable sadness in him—an unspeakable restlessness; and therefore his art often delights in wild and daring creations, and many of his works are unfinished. But when he does design with clear and complete lines, he leaves all competitors a thousand miles behind him; and he displays a consummate knowledge of the human body, and a mastery of the chisel, such as none have attained since; and such as were only attained before him by the Greeks in their greatest period of art.

The Medicean Chapel is contiguous to the Basilica of San Lorenzo, another masterwork of Brunelleschi. In its pillared aisles may be perceived the spirit of a new, reforming time, which strove after the noble simplicity of early Christendom, and the return of the Master towards the forms of the ancient Christian basilicas; which, however, he reproduced with an added beauty and freedom of his own.

The site of the most ancient part of Florence lies between San Lorenzo, the Duomo, and the Palazzo Vecchio. Here are the two markets, the Mercato Vecchio where there is the greatest crowd and the worst odour, and the Mercato Nuovo, with its fine market-hall in the style of the Renaissance, and the bronze fountain of the "Porcellino"—the well-known Florentine boar, which the natives call by that affectionate diminutive of "little pig" or "piggy"!—hard-by, noble Corinthian columns run through the length and breadth of the lofty, rectangular hall of the Mercato Nuovo. Here, in the old town, stand numerous palaces, but the finest of all are undoubtedly the Palazzo Strozzi and the Palazzo Riccardi. One of the most difficult tasks which the Florentine builders had to cope with, was the transforming the old, gloomy, mediæval castle, into a noble city

---

* The stanzas printed in italics were really addressed to the Statue of Night by Giovanni Battista Strozzi, and replied to as above by Michael Angelo. Perhaps it may be worth while to lay before the reader the Italian originals.

"La Notte che tu vedi in sì dolci atti
Dormire, fu da un Angelo scolpita
In questo sasso, e perchè dorme, ha vita;
Destala se nol credi, e parleratti."

To which Michael Angelo replies:

"Grato m' è il sonno, e più l' esser di sasso;
Mentre che il danno e la vergogna dura
Non veder, non sentir m' è gran ventura;
Però non mi destar; deh parla basso!"—*Translator's note.*

ORLANDINI'S BEER-GARDEN, FLORENCE.

palace. And this task most persons who have visited Florence will own that her architects have successfully accomplished. The ancient city dwellings—of the nobles at least,—were frowning fortresses, surmounted by battlements and towers, and with massive limestone walls, in which, at a great height, a few Gothic arched windows divided by a central column were sparingly introduced. The finest specimen of such an urban fortress is the Bargello, the old town-hall, in the very heart of Florence. We enter it through a magnificent courtyard partly surrounded by open arcades, or *loggie*, and richly adorned

FOUNTAIN OF THE PORCELLINO IN THE MERCATO NUOVO.

with coats of arms in carved stone-work. A broad and noble external staircase leads from this courtyard to the upper halls, which are now rich in the original colouring of their frescoes. (Some years ago these were entirely hidden beneath a coating of *whitewash!*) They are spacious apartments with huge Gothic fire-places, and surmounted by roofs of carved rafters, or else by vaulted ceilings. In the chapel of the palace is to be seen in fresco a portrait of Dante at thirty-five years of age. It is a mild countenance of remarkably delicate outline, and does not yet wear the eagle aspect of the author of the Divina Commedia, worn by suffering, sorrow, and patriotic lamentations over the decay of his native land.

Brunelleschi was a creator and originator in architecture. He designed the Pitti Palace,—the first and most colossal attempt on record, to construct an artistic façade out of unhewn blocks of stone. The masses of stone are only cut at the corners, the rest of them being left rough and are of incredible size and massiveness. They recal the genius of the old Etruscans who surrounded their cities with Cyclopean walls. Brunelleschi's successors somewhat softened this aspect of rugged strength, by confining the rough stonework—a style called technically 'Rustica'—to the lower storeys of the building, and adorning the upper ones with elegant arched windows, above which the whole was crowned by the broad projecting eaves which form so striking a feature in Florentine architecture. From the mighty blocks of rough stone that form the basement storey, project great lanterns, rings, and sockets to hold torches and banners, all in magnificent wrought ironwork; and the majority of the palaces contain a fine interior courtyard with a well or fountain.

What a contrast to these pompous and magnificent edifices is presented by the dark little Gothic house where Dante was born! It is in a narrow obscure street close to Or San Michele. Yet never did Florence wear a nobler or more impressive aspect than when she celebrated the six hundredth birthday of her Dante, and placed upon that poor little dwelling the inscription: "In this house was born the Divine Poet Alighieri." The whole city was decked with flags, every house was covered with tapestry, garlands of flowers, and laurel-wreaths. From the massive iron rings in the hoary old palaces the gay tricolour of Italy was fluttering; but perhaps the most impressive sight of all, were the verses from Dante's divine poem affixed to buildings, bridges, and various monuments all over the town. Wonderful it was to remember that most of these grey old palaces were standing in Dante's stormy life-time! And as the people read, and were moved by the mighty verses, how clear it was that Dante's poetry, although it grew until it reached the Heavens, yet had its root and origin here deep in this very soil! The massive blocks of stone spoke of a bloody, violent, wildly agitated history:—the history of old Florence with her Guelphs and Ghibellines, her unsleeping feuds, her beautiful women who were drawn into the fatal strife, and raised cruel discord between the noblest families, waging war upon each other from their fortress-dwellings.

This Dante Festival was one of the grandest commemorations that a people ever solemnized;—a people once more free, united, and powerful after long centuries of shame and wrong, and honouring in Dante, at once the boldest champion of her unity, her greatest poet, and her most unfortunate patriot.

As a poet Dante surpasses all his contemporaries, nay, all poets whom Italy has yet produced. His "Vita Nuova" strikes a chord which no one before him had touched; it unveils the deepest mysteries of the human heart; never before had Love been treated in so grandly ideal and spiritual a manner. But in the Divina Commedia the author rises to still higher heights of passion and the purified contemplation of divine beauty. The "Vita Nuova" is the germ from which sprang that gigantic plant the Divina Commedia, whose roots reach deep down into the lowest *bolgia* of hell, while its summit blooms transfigured in the pure light of Eternal Love. It is a mirror of the whole Universe, and, again, the history of Humanity; more peculiarly the history of that paradise of the earth, Italy, torn and divided as it was by fraternal feuds, and of the heart of Italy, Florence, from whence the poet was banished for ever.

"Ungrateful Country," exclaims Michael Angelo in one of his sonnets:

> Ungrateful Country, who hast nursed his woes
> And killed his better fortune! Well I see
> How on the Best, worst evils still are poured:
> Let his example this hard truth disclose:
> No greater hast thou ever bred than he,
> Yet bitt'rer exile hath no man endured!

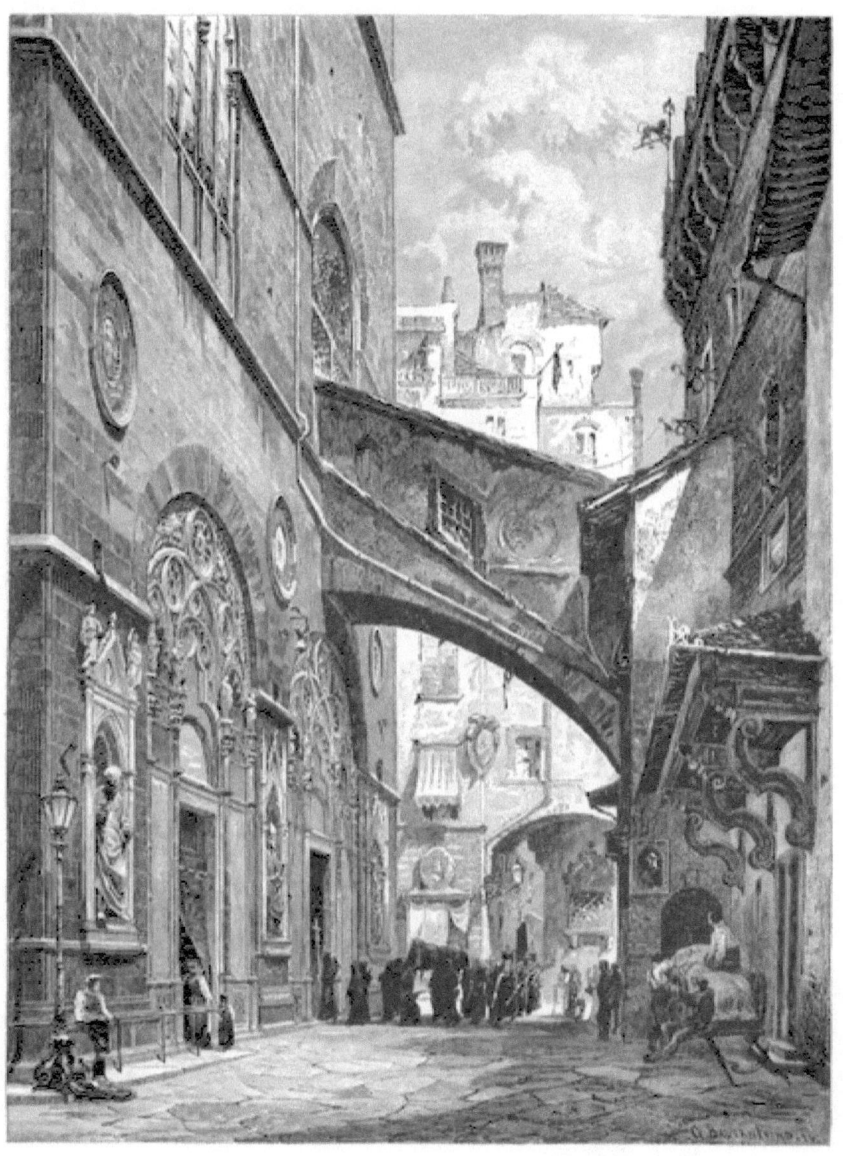

SAN MICHELE.

A marble statue of Dante, which was uncovered for the first time during the Festival of 1865, stands on the Piazza of Santa Croce. And within quite recent years the façade of Santa Croce, which, like the fronts of so many Florentine churches, had been left unfinished, has been covered with dazzling white marble.* Santa Croce is the oldest and finest of all the churches belonging to the mendicant orders; it contains a noble monument to Dante, and is, in fact, the Pantheon of Florence. In the colossal space of the nave, which

IN FRONT OF THE LOGGIA DE' LANZI.

is only the more impressive by reason of its extreme simplicity, are buried, under splendid monuments, some of the greatest Italians: Michael Angelo, Galileo, Alberti, Alfieri, Macchiavelli. Dante's bones rest in far-away Ravenna. Santa Croce contains, moreover, some tombs of the earliest Renaissance period, the frescos of Giotto in the chapel behind the choir, and the exquisite marble pulpit adorned with delicate sculpture, by Benedetto da Majano. In the exterior cloister is the chapel of the Pazzi, designed by Brunelleschi. It was built in the year 1420, and is one of the earliest, as well as one of the finest, specimens of the revival of classical architecture.

* At the expense of an Englishman, the late Mr. Sloane.—*Translator's note.*

FLORENTINE ART.

FLORENCE, the modern Athens! There is a great similarity between both these most important nurseries of culture:—a similarity in their deeds and works, their struggles and victories, their good and bad fortunes; but, above all, in the spirit of mildness and peace which emanated, and still emanates, from them, a spirit of the purest and noblest humanity. And lo! the symbol of peace, the grey-green olive-tree, still crowns both cities, and makes them sacred soil, garlanded and consecrated to the gods. Corinth and Sparta, Delphi and Olympia, with their marble temples glistening with votive offerings, their shady groves, and their colossal ivory and golden statues of the gods, are now mere heaps of ruin. But Athens is still the "eye of Hellas;" and though often wasted, devastated, and barbarously plundered, her holy temples yet stand above Theseus' ancient city, and the gods of Olympus still hover protectingly around them, mindful of the divine votive offerings of Intellect which have been made to them here.

When Sylla, after a long siege, overcame Athens, and prudence counselled him to destroy her, he spared the city for the sake of her glorious dead; and when, in our own day, in the year 1859, the commandant of the Fortezza di Belvedere in Florence received from the last Grand Duke of Tuscany the order to bombard the town, he made answer: "One may cannonade the rest of the world, but one cannot cannonade Florence."*

Athens, it must be owned, is utterly ruinous in comparison with the so much younger Florence, where the development of art during four mighty centuries, is still clearly to be seen:—an art which has been illustrated by some of the greatest geniuses the world has ever seen, and in which the most exalted ideas of modern humanity have expressed themselves. Eternal Rome might vie with Florence in the magnificence and number of her works of art, but not in the continuous and unbroken heritage of progress bequeathed by one age to another. In Florence the development proceeds steadily from the first grey, struggling dawn of the Middle Ages to the full noon-day lustre of the modern intellect; art in Florence rises step by step in one homogeneous edifice, whose ideal beauty has been a joy and refreshment to the noblest spirits in all times. In Rome, thanks to the counter-reformation of the Jesuits, the pure specimens of early-Christian architecture, the severe frescos of Giotto's school, and the delicate works of the first masters of the Renaissance period, were in great part destroyed. They gave place to stiff, ungraceful pilasters, and lumpy masses of stucco, thoroughly tasteless and *barocco*. The roofs are painted with huge cloudy heavens, in which crowds of saints, painfully cramped in their limbs, and expressing a very incomprehensible amount of agitation in their countenances, are floating. Gigantic tabernacles constructed of gilded bronze and marbles of every colour in the rainbow, rise up to the vaulted ceilings in pompous masses, bearing chubby-cheeked angels, who blow big trumpets with a manifestly painful

---

* This answer is "*ben trovato*," but alas, "*non è vero!*" The reply of the commandant to the Grand Duke simply was, that his soldiers would refuse to obey any such order.—*Translator's note.*

exertion of lungs. In Florence, on the other hand, everything—or nearly everything—
remained unspoiled and unaltered, each work in the place it was originally destined for,

COURTYARD OF THE BARGELLO.

and still instinct with the spirit of the ancient founders, who rest in their tombs near to
the votive offerings they made to religion and to art. From the earliest Christian times
down to the latest times of the Renaissance, Florentine art extends in an unbroken
sequence ; the horrors of the *Barocco*-style were in a great measure avoided by the artistic

instinct of the Florentines; and at the present day the tendency of her artists is to return to the best of the early models.

Let us now cast a rapid glance at the Florentine School of Painting.

Cimabue may be considered the founder of the Florentine School of Painting; he was born of a noble family in the year 1240, and worked much in Pisa (the choir of the Duomo) and still more at Assisi, where he covered the upper church of the cathedral dedicated to St. Francis with frescos. He broke away from the stiff conventionalities of the Byzantine Mosaics; and his pictures display a good deal of the serene and cheerful beauty of the Antique, without losing the solemnity and seriousness of the intensely religious early Christian Art. One of the most famous works of Cimabue is to be seen in Florence in the church of Santa Maria Novella;—the Madonna and Child. The Virgin is seated under a canopy, and above her head six charming angels are floating. She is clothed in a dark, rich garment with gold borders, which falls in long straight folds. The expression of divine maternal love on her countenance is rendered with wonderful vividness. This picture was so enthusiastically admired when it was first painted, that it was carried in procession from Cimabue's house to the church.

Next in succession to Cimabue comes Giotto, painter, sculptor, and architect. Vasari relates that Cimabue found him one day keeping the sheep of his father Bondone; the boy, only ten years old, and utterly without instruction, was drawing one of the sheep on a fragment of stone; whereupon Cimabue took him as his pupil. Giotto, the awakening genius of the fourteenth century, soon originated the most bold and animated designs, crowded with a great variety of figures. He filled whole churches and chapels in different parts of Italy with his frescos, which are still well-preserved in the church of the Madonna dell' Arena in Padua, in the lower church of the Duomo at Assisi, in Florence, Rome, and Naples. Besides all that, he covered the exterior of the Duomo of Florence with splendid marbles, built the enchantingly beautiful campanile, and adorned it with exquisite statuettes. The school of painting which he founded, both frescos and paintings on wood, branched out widely in various directions. On many an altar in the Florentine churches may still be seen his slim, narrow-shouldered saints on a gold background, with their pale, gentle, yearning faces, their soul-fraught, pensive eyes, delicate, expressive hands, and rich brocaded garments. They glimmer from afar through the solemn twilight of the Gothic aisles.

After Giotto and his disciples comes Orgagna, painter, sculptor, architect, and poet. He carried on for a time the construction of the Florentine Duomo, and being dissatisfied with the proportions of the span of the roof, as designed by Arnolfo and Giotto, carried the arches to their present huge dimensions. His whole genius tended towards the grand and powerful, the stirring and terrible in art, which he carried out in enormous frescos imbued with Dantesean intellect and Dantesean boldness. The traces of his genius may be seen in the Campo Santo of Pisa, in Santa Maria Novella, in the tabernacle in Or' San Michele, and in the Loggia dei Lanzi. Power and passion animate all his figures; but yet he reaches a point of ideal religious serenity, such as Florentine art only attained to by going through all the phases of actual life and suffering. And this it is which is so wonderful and admirable in his works. Soon after Orgagna's death, the Florentine artists embraced the Real unconditionally; and yet—with few exceptions—not to extravagance. The soft and gracious blue skies of Florence have never been favourable to exaggerated enthusiasm, and seem able to produce only delicate and judicious minds. The later artists remove their creations from the ideal spheres wherein the figures of Giotto

COURTYARD OF THE PALAZZO VECCHIO, FLORENCE.

and Orgagna still stand or float, into the realms of the actual;—into the full, every-day life of Florence, with all its realities. The Madonna is represented as a graceful Florentine maiden, and set in a rose-garden with the villas, walls, and fantastic towers of the town for a background. The Holy Family descends into this work-a-day world, and its members wear the splendid, becoming, and many-coloured costume of the day. The delight in portraiture,—which Giotto shared,—grows stronger and stronger, and the artists represent well-known figures of the people, and graceful youths belonging to the noblest families of Florence. The young Masaccio, Brunelleschi's friend, points the way with his frescos in the church of the Carmine, and is followed by a string of first-rate names; among them Ghirlandajo, Michael Angelo's master.

Sculpture advances at an equal pace with painting. Giotto, Orgagna, and other masters, are themselves sculptors as well as painters; and in the year 1330, Andrea Pisano, after two-and-twenty years of labour, finishes his bronze gates for the Baptistery:—somewhat stern and stiff, perhaps, but full of dignity. Then in the years 1427, and 1452, Lorenzo Ghiberti completes his two great bronze gates for the other portals of the Baptistery, of which gates Michael Angelo says that they are worthy to stand at the entrance to Paradise. A whole world of thought, the fulness of the spiritual life of that day, is fixed into exquisite forms in these bronze gates.

BRONZE FOUNTAIN IN THE PIAZZA DELLA SANTISSIMA ANNUNZIATA.

Ghiberti joins the old art to the new, which latter tends entirely to the representation of Nature; and such men as Brunelleschi, Quercia, Donatello, active workers in marble and bronze, and many more besides, are his worthy compeers.

But so great is the productive power of this time, that shortly a third species of art arises, which *combines* painting and sculpture: the art, namely, of working in *terra-cotta*, baked and coloured clay. It was invented by Luca della Robbia, and carried on after his death by his nephews and great nephews. Luca della Robbia also worked in marble. One of his productions, which is worthy to be compared with the finest in this kind, stands above the organ in the Duomo at Florence, and consists of bas-reliefs representing groups of children dancing, singing, and playing on musical instruments. He has richly endowed his native city Florence, and other parts of Tuscany with his terra-cottas; works full of simplicity, sentiment, and piety. For the Art of the Renaissance had its source in religious enthusiasm; but it was enthusiasm which soon got beyond the limits prescribed by the priests, and to which the Beautiful in and for itself is sacred. "True painting,"

VIEW FROM THE BOBOLI GARDENS.

says Michael Angelo, "is pious and noble in itself; for the mere striving after perfection elevates the soul to devotion, inasmuch as it brings it into closer communion with God."

The Art of the Florentines had continued to grow ever richer, more many-sided, more accurately faithful in its delineations of actual life, when,—perhaps at the moment that the turning-point was nearly reached, and Art ran some risk of falling into the petty and commonplace, —the greatest geniuses of all appeared upon the scene. These men, from their heritage of three centuries of unflagging struggle and aspiration, from the great and earnest ideas of the old masters, from the gigantic artistic progress of the early Renaissance, and lastly from their own gifted intellects, evolved the splendid results which will be the standard and measure of Art for a thousand years to come. They are Leonardo da Vinci, Michael Angelo of Florence, and Raphael of Urbino.

Leonardo da Vinci was richly gifted. He sought to penetrate the secrets of Nature in all directions, and studied the laws of optics, mechanics, statics, &c. His mind was surprisingly versatile. Wherever he went he attracted crowds of enthusiastic disciples and was the friend of kings. But a strangely unfortunate star seemed to rule over the fate of all his productions, nearly every one of which perished either during his lifetime or shortly after his death. The colossal model for an equestrian statue of Ludovico il Moro in Milan (for the casting of which Leonardo demanded a hundred thousand pounds' weight of brass) was chosen as a mark to shoot at by the archers when the French

FOUNTAIN IN THE BOBOLI GARDENS.

entered Milan in 1499, and utterly destroyed. His great cartoon of a battle-piece, which he designed in competition with Michael Angelo for the great Sala del Consiglio in Florence, was cut up and lost. It represented soldiers and knights engaged in deadly contest round a standard; even the horses were struggling and raging against each other in wild confusion. The cartoon was admired and studied by the greatest masters of the day. Lastly his world-renowned Last Supper is nearly effaced from the wall of the Refectory in Milan, which was long used as a stable for horses! But even in its decay it testifies to the almost superhuman depth and creative power of the Master; and stands to this day an unapproachable wonder, and one of the highest developments ever attained by Art. The influence which Leonardo—the inventor of *chiaro-oscuro*,—had upon his contemporaries, is incalculable; and everything that remains from his hand bears an irresistible charm.

At the very time when Leonardo and the young Michael Angelo were competing for the palm of victory with their cartoons, a beautiful youth of twenty years old entered the city—it was Raphael of Urbino. Florence was then at the summit of her power and glory, and the young painter received impressions then which lasted him his whole life. Many of them were contradictory impressions, no doubt, but he combined, and harmonized, and transfigured them with his own peculiar grace.

Thenceforward the Florentine painters—a Fra Bartolomeo, an Andrea del Sarto, and others—followed in the path of one or other of those three greatest ones. The apex is reached; but even the descent—even the latter summer and autumn—produce many delightful and beautiful flowers. The list is closed with Giorgio Vasari, who was at once painter and writer, and who, himself the personal friend of many of the great masters, and having before his eyes their masterpieces in their first freshness, wrote the history of Florentine art. He gives us the whole long list of Tuscan artists, from Cimabue down to Michael Angelo, and a catalogue of their works. His book is full of errors, nay, often of downright inventions and old wives' tales; but the glamour of that wonderful Art-world is upon every word of it! His style is forcible and picturesque, his information often most precious; and old Vasari may be said to be the father of all modern histories of art.

* * * * * * *

We must not omit all mention of the great collections of pictures, made during several centuries by the princes and the people, the national treasures of Florence. The two huge palaces of the Pitti and the Uffizi, are connected together by a long gallery, which crosses the Arno above the Ponte Vecchio; and in these two palaces are displayed to the public a splendid series of works of art, from the Antique, through all the changes and fluctuations of Christian art, down to the *second* classic period, which may fairly be ranked as equal with the first—the Renaissance. Here the northern stranger, who has crossed the Alps for the first time, makes acquaintance with Raphael, Michael Angelo, Andrea del Sarto, Fra Bartolomeo,—and yet there are people who fancy they can see all these wonders in the course of one afternoon, and who probably think there ought to be donkeys ready saddled and bridled at the top of the Uffizi stairs, to enable visitors to ride through the galleries, and thus view them even more expeditiously than they do at present!

Besides these, the churches are full of works of art; and there is, moreover, the Accademia di Belle Arti in the immediate vicinity of the beautiful Piazza della Santissima Annunziata, with its arcades and elegant bronze fountains. In the Accademia a collection of Tuscan painters is arranged in strict chronological order; and there is, too, an artistic museum in the Bargello.

CHOIR OF SANTA MARIA NOVELLA, FLORENCE.

In the old Dominican convent of St. Mark, from whence Savonarola scattered his fiery words, the corridors, the cells, and the refectory, are adorned with the frescos of Fra Giovanni Angelico da Fiesole. His contemporaries gave him, even during his life-time, the title of Beato, or Blessed; and in truth, in looking upon these slender figures, and these sad, yet glorified faces, we feel something of that peace which passeth understanding. We seem to see the form of the pious monk as one who has conversed more with angels than with men, transfigured by the serene light of heaven, standing on the threshold of that turbulent agitated time—full of innovations in religion as in art— the Renaissance.

FLORENTINE NATURE.

"The hyacinths were blooming fresh and fair,
In Boboli, what time with flute-like note
The nightingale poured music from her throat,
And Spring's sweet spirit filled the morning air."

MIST still broods over the towers and palaces of the town, above which the cupola of the Duomo, divinely illumined by the golden rays of the rising sun, soars into the clear ether. Here in the gardens of Boboli we look upon the back of the Pitti Palace, glowing redly in the morning light; a huge, massive, gloomy, almost awful-looking pile! Yet the rosy little clouds float peacefully above it, swarms of swallows dart joyously hither and thither, and from the olive-grown depths of the garden comes the clear note of the nightingale, dying away at times, and then sounding again fuller, sweeter, and more thrilling than ever.

A cypress alley leads right through the gardens, and as it rises, a beautiful and widespread view is obtained of the city and the fruitful valley with its scattered villas, and the bare summit of Monte Morello in the background. How the great, gnarled, solemn cypresses rise up into the soft blue of the morning sky! Marble gods gleam out of the shadowy myrtle thickets. Down in the lower part of the gardens a stream of water is trickling from the great fountain surrounded by a fragrant bower of laurels. Orange and oleander trees bloom in great vases on a little island in the midst of a lake, and above them rises the graceful form of Giovanni Bologna's beautiful marble fountain, where colossal river-gods let the water drip gently from their urns. The soft murmur of the fountain, the luxuriant growth and bloom, the stillness of the place, the pure, perfumed air, the consciousness of the near neighbourhood of Florence—all these make up an atmosphere of delight and beauty which fills and soothes the soul unspeakably. As we wander onwards we catch glimpses of the city, or look down into little olive-grown dales, where stone cottages stand half hidden by almond and mulberry trees, and where children are playing beneath vine-trellised bowers, calling and laughing with their silvery little voices.

A great contrast to these beautiful tranquil poetic gardens of Boboli is presented by the *Cascine*, quite on the flat ground beyond the city, on the right bank of the Arno. The Cascine is a long dusty sort of park, with lawns and fine trees—some of them mantled with ivy to the top—commanding but little outlook, and containing a few uninteresting buildings in the modern style. But this is the daily rendezvous of the

Florentines. Handsome carriages roll up and down the drives, or stand by hundreds on the space before the great café, when the band is playing. Here the fashionable world is to be found unfailingly at certain times and seasons; and at the door of every smart carriage may be seen a group of Florentine dandies, chatting with airs of intimacy to the fine ladies within. There is nothing stirring, nothing exciting in the scene; it gives one the impression that all these people will go on doing exactly the same things day after day until the sky falls!

Formerly the King of Italy, Vittorio Emanuele, the *Re Galantuomo*, might be seen driving here occasionally, but never stopping his carriage. A strong, indomitable looking kind of man, with his bronzed face, keen eye, and massive throat; reminding one of some of the valiant captains whose swords were doughtily wielded in the service of the old Florentine Commonwealth.

A much more agreeable promenade than that through the Cascine may be made on the opposite side of the river, to a cypress-crowned hill, where stands the convent of Monte Oliveto, or to the heights of Bellosguardo, with its pleasant villas and pine-trees. From hence a most exquisite view of the city may be enjoyed. The Pitti Palace, with the Boboli Gardens sloping up behind it, appears in all its tremendous mass; and the effect of its huge rough blocks of stone is imposing even at this distance.

*   *   *   *   *   *

Outside the Porta Romana begins the splendid new road which has cost the Florentines some millions of francs. It leads between villas and gardens up the hill by a series of zig-zags to the new Piazza di Michel Angelo. Here, where formerly an olive-wood grew, now stands a fountain, and the great copy in bronze of Michael Angelo's "David."

> "There on the bright enchanting plain
> Fair Florence 'neath the sunshine lies;
> And towering high o'er roof and fane,
> Her Duomo soars into the skies."

Further on we come to the Campo Santo, the burial-ground of San Miniato al Monte. It is made in a succession of terraces on the hill-side, and glitters with white marble. How still is everything around! The dazzling white grave-stones, the melancholy monuments, the dark cypresses, the ancient black and white façade of the venerable basilica of San Miniato, with its mosaic pictures on a gold background—all steeped in the infinite silence of a sultry noon. Nearer and nearer a funeral procession approaches; six men carry the coffin, and others go before with lighted tapers. They all wear black garments, and black hoods drawn completely over the head and face, from which their eyes sparkle strangely through two round holes. They are members of the confraternity of the *Misericordia*, an institution which has existed in Florence for several hundred years.

The interior of San Miniato is like one huge grave-yard, and is literally paved with tombstones, on many of which bunches and wreaths of flowers may often be seen. The windows of the choir are made of semi-transparent plates of alabaster, and admit a pale, softened light. In the apse above is a grandiose mosaic, representing the Saviour. The whole basilica is surrounded by columns, and has an ancient roof of rafters; and to the left of it opens that celebrated chapel of St. James, which contains treasures of architecture, sculpture, fresco-painting, and terra-cotta, in the highest style of the Renaissance;

amongst them a fine monument to a cardinal of Portugal, whose statue reclines on an exquisitely carved sarcophagus.

The ancient Etruscan city of Fiesole seems to invite us from the hill on which she is throned, with her tall campanile and Capuchin convent on the topmost summit of the height. Halfway up the steep road to Fiesole, on a sunny olive-covered slope, stands the favourite creation of Cosmo the First, the *Badia*, built by Brunelleschi. All the surroundings are in harmony with each other. Around a peaceful cloistered courtyard are built the church, the refectory, the library, and other halls; and towards the city and the smiling landscape opens a delightful pillared *loggia*. In the sunny, deserted rooms

VIEW IN THE VAL D'ARNO.

we may fancy ourselves surrounded by the spirits of those illustrious men who were so far in advance of their age, and who hastened the dawn of that most flourishing epoch in Italian history, the Renaissance, the time of a new intellectual birth; until the powers of darkness and priestcraft, supported by French and Spanish swords, trod down the ripening harvest! In those days noble and profound ideas grew up amidst a refined and joyous society; Art and Philosophy were marked by sublime tendencies, and at the same time by the purest humanity. In those days well might a Pico della Mirandola exclaim : "God made man at the end of the six days of creation, in order that he might acknowledge the laws of the universe, love its beauty, and admire its grandeur. God bound man to no special spot of earth, to no fixed action, to no iron necessities; but gave him movement and free will. 'I have placed thee in the centre of the world,' says the Creator to Adam, 'in order that thou mightest look around thee and behold all that it contains. I created thee a being neither heavenly nor earthly, neither wholly mortal nor wholly immortal, in order that thou mightest educate and conquer thyself. Thou mayest degenerate into a beast, or develope thyself into a godlike being. The brutes

A A 2

bring with them from their mother's womb all that is needful for them; higher spirits are from the beginning that which they continue to be throughout eternity. Thou alone hast a power of development and growth according to thy free will, thou hast within thee the germs of a manifold existence.'"

From Fiesole there is a most striking distant view, especially towards the south. At our feet lies the city, shut in by hills of varied outline; and beyond it you see far and wide over the land, over pine woods, fruit orchards, arable fields, and ancient towns rising

SAN MINIATO AL MONTE.

from rocky eminences. Long drawn lines of mountains stretch out far, far away in the distance, looking misty and unreal as they recede, and above them the clouds of heaven sail peacefully.

An hour beyond Fiesole lies a favourite point for excursions, the Park of Pratolino, which combines the advantages of fine woods with pure mountain air. Here amidst noble oak trees crouches the colossal figure of the Apennine, built up with stone and mortar after the design of Giovanni Bologna. This giant has a beard seven yards long!

But what traveller has ever exhausted all the beauties of the Florentine Campagna? As we penetrate into the folds of the hills, which seem absolutely secluded from the world, we find ever new beauty, and delicious peacefulness. Here are gardens on every hand; flowering rose-bushes peep over the high walls, oleanders and pomegranates glow in their rich bloom beside stately villas, pine woods crown the higher summits of the hills, and ever and anon we catch the silvery glimmer of some olive-grown slope shadowed by dark tall cypresses; like one melancholy note which serves but to enhance the fulness of the joyous concert of the spring.

VINTAGE IN TUSCANY.

COLOSSAL STATUE OF THE APENNINE IN THE PARK AT PRATOLINO.

Blooming defiles lead into stern stony valleys. In the valley of the Ema, on an abrupt eminence, stands the Certosa, glittering white in the sunshine. It contains delicately carved cloisters, ornamented with paintings in the interior courts, and marble fountains which betray the hand of some great master of the *Cinque Cento;* and from the cells the eye roves enchanted over hill, and dale, and rugged mountain. The valley of the Arno immediately above Florence offers another picture full of cheerfulness and beauty. Villa succeeds villa, gardens rise on terraces one above the other, little villages nestle down by the river's brink, on the mountain ridges stand ruined castles. We are far from the city, in a solitude, but the brightest and most blooming solitude imaginable, with pillared edifices, fountains, gay-coloured garden-beds, ancient cypress trees, and groves of evergreens!

As we advance up the course of the river the valley grows narrower and more lonely, the gardens disappear, mill-wheels churn the water amid the sallows, and the great woods come down to the edge of the road. After a long and toilsome pilgrimage the wanderer reaches the far-famed monastery of Vallombrosa—the shady valley—and further still, high up in the wild rugged Val d'Arno, close to the source of that river and to the source of the Tiber, we come to Camaldoli, the retreat of the holy Saint Romualdo. Here upon the bare, treeless summits of the mountains—with the woody meadows of the convent at our feet—here from this backbone of Italy, we look down upon a whole confused, deeply cleft, rocky labyrinth, through which the Arno and the Tiber have pioneered green pathways. There they lie, the infinitely varied hills covered with pine woods, and, sloping down on either hand, the fruitful smiling valleys; then come marshy plains, from whence mighty cities have arisen—yonder, lost in the misty blue of distance, stands old Ravenna, near the Adriatic, and there, towards the Tyrrhene sea, rise up the towers of Pisa. The eye roves from sea to sea, and beholds a limitless extent of storied earth, inhabited for thousands of years by artistic, warlike, and commercial populations, and rich in temples of ancient worship, and homes of immortal culture.

STREET LIFE IN PISA.

PISA.

PISA la Morta! Dead or asleep, since the days when the Florentines robbed her of her liberty, she lies idly dreaming on the sandy plain, a few miles from the sea-shore, in the soft, slumberous, misty air. The proud merchant ships have disappeared that once carried on a flourishing trade with the East, or bore across the salt seas valorous Crusaders to the wondrous land which the Saviour's foot has trod, and where the Christian knights seized kingdoms from the unbeliever. Gone, too, is the pompous fleet of war-vessels, allies of the Hohenstaufens, which once received Conradin, the last of his race, with a concert of flutes and cymbals; and which so often went forth to fight against the Genoese, and returned with many captured galleys and thousands of prisoners. The day of Meloria (1284) broke away the first jewel from Pisa's diadem. The Genoese came in force, commanded by Uberti Doria; the fight lasted all day until long after sunset, five thousand Pisans were slain, sixteen thousand taken prisoners and carried to Genoa. Soon after that a horrible incident happened in Pisa,—the death of Count Ugolino, with his four sons, in the *Torre della Fame*. Kaiser Henry the Seventh, the Luxemburger—the emperor for whose coming Dante so ardently longed—intended to make Pisa the capital of Italy; but he died in 1315, in the neighbourhood of Siena, and was buried in the Campo Santo of Pisa, where his monument may still be seen. Again and again the city's fortunes fluctuated; she was the theatre of ferocious civil war, but enjoyed at intervals some better and more tranquil days; until at length, after a heroic resistance which lasted fourteen years, she fell finally into the power of Florence in the year 1509.

All tells of past greatness, of departed splendour! And even the exquisite buildings which Pisa erected in the highest period of her maritime supremacy—the Cathedral, the Baptistery, the Campo Santo, the Campanile—are threatening to sink into ruin. Not only has the famous Leaning Tower sunk to one side, but the other edifices have sunk considerably, and it is striking to see how firmly their marble frames hold together. But the soil is treacherous, and the great buildings stand at a threatening angle of inclination on the treeless sandy plain, over which a southern sun pours its burning rays, reflected from the yellow soil with dazzling power on to the great marble walls. It is hard to say which is grander and more beautiful, the wide aisled Duomo, or the Leaning Tower close by, with its rows of airy columns; or again, the massive circular Baptistery covered with dainty Gothic carving, surmounted by a bell-shaped cupola, and surrounded by a girdle of pillared arches. In the interior of the Baptistery, every tone spoken or sung is reflected from the lofty vaults into waves of wonderful music; it is as if the lightest whisper could awake the dreaming Spirit of Harmony with which the whole building is imbued.*

The Duomo is a real museum of precious works of art, especially those of the school of Niccolo Pisano, which, even earlier than the Florentines, emancipated sculpture from rudeness and rigidity, and showed a remarkable tendency to return to the best models of antiquity. There are, in the apse of the choir of the cathedral, fine mosaics representing the Saviour, the Madonna, and St. John; the latter the last work of Cimabue.

But still richer is the Campo Santo, which lies to the north of the Cathedral and Baptistery. It is an oblong, rectangular building, with smooth, unadorned marble walls on the outside, and within consisting of long open arcades, surrounding a space of ground overgrown with rose bushes:—

"Sacred is the soil around us;
All across the stormy ocean
From Jerusalem the Pisans
Brought it with profound devotion.

"'Tis the soil of that dread mountain
Where the Saviour's cross once stood,
Where the earth grew darkly crimson
Moistened with His precious blood.

"Thence they brought it unto Pisa,
Deeming that in mould so blest
Their belovèd dead would slumber
In a doubly hallow'd rest.

"And from out this earth fresh springing
Purple roses bud and bloom,
Breathing o'er the wanderer's spirit
Memories of the Holy Tomb;

---

* The peculiarity of the echo in the Pisan Baptistery consists in the sounds being wonderfully *prolonged;* so that three harmonious intervals—such as the notes of the common chord, for example—sung one after the other, are echoed back blended into one harmonious sound, which has an indescribably beautiful and unearthly effect.—*Translator's note.*

"Breathing of the Love immortal
Which o'ercometh mortal strife,
Rising o'er the grave victorious,
Glorifying death and life!"

Each of the four colonnades that surround the central space is filled with fine works in marble, ranging from Greek and Roman times down to the present day. Here are antique sarcophagi and pillars, mediæval monuments adorned with gold mosaics,

PIAZZA DEL DUOMO.

severely religious sculptures by Pisano, and splendid tombs of the Renaissance period; all mingled together in beautiful variety, and standing out upon the finest background in the world. For the walls of the loggia are covered with an unbroken series of frescoes by the greatest masters of several successive centuries; from the representation of the Last Judgment, and the Triumph of Death in Orgagna's grand and gloomy manner, to Gozzoli's pictures full of unspeakable life and cheerfulness. Perhaps the fresh joyous spring-tide spirit of the early Renaissance is nowhere so vividly presented to us as in these four-and-twenty designs with their crowds of noble animated figures, and their delightful backgrounds full of temples and turrets, lofty mountains, and valleys watered by winding streams. The most famous of these frescoes are Noah's Vintage, the birth of Jacob and Esau, the marriage of Jacob and Rachel, and Joseph recognised by his brethren. Beneath the last-named stands Gozzoli's tomb, erected in 1478 by the Pisans. In the Campo Santo, too, may be seen the huge chains of the Port of Pisa, which were taken in battle by the Genoese in 1362, and by them given to the Florentines, who hung

ITALY.

them up in the Baptistery of Florence, where they remained down to a quite recent period. But the new times brought reconciliation, and the trophy was given back to Pisa as a token that henceforth there was to be peace amongst the sister cities of Italy.

A few hours' journey north-west from Pisa, lies Lucca, an important city of sixty-five thousand inhabitants. The ramparts which surround the town are planted with shady trees, and afford a delightful promenade, whence the eye enjoys a view of the picturesque flat-roofed towers of Lucca, or ranges over the charming landscape, backed by the jagged line of the Pisan mountains. From this range of hills stretches a mighty aqueduct, which, supported on five hundred arches, was constructed in the year 1834, but is built with truly Roman solidity and massiveness. Lucca, founded by the Ligurians, was a Roman colony 200 years B.C. The remains of a great amphitheatre are still to be seen there, and the ancient basilicas of the city,—especially San Frediano—contain numerous richly wrought columns taken from the amphitheatre. Lucca is not very rich in famous artists, and yet she claims one of the greatest for her son : Matteo Civitali (1435—1501) the sculptor, whose immortal works, full of simple, noble beauty, adorn the cathedral.

TAVERN NEAR SAN FREDIANO, LUCCA.

CHURCH OF SAN DOMENICO.

SIENA.

HIGH above the green, fruitful plain, upon a group of isolated hills Siena sits enthroned. The town is still entirely surrounded by walls and towers; in the little ravines between the hills, and on the slopes, the houses are crowded together in picturesque disorder;—time-darkened palaces in the heart of the city, great churches crowning the summits, and the dazzling marble duomo dominating all. How fertile and pleasant is the whole country round! The soil is in part clay, in part sand; and the latter has a yellow—almost golden—hue. There are gardens everywhere:—gardens which produce corn, wine, and oil, and all sorts of vegetables and fruits; and scattered amongst them, you come upon groups of sunny farm-houses, all built of solid stone, and inhabited by a kindly, pleasant, industrious population. Then come plantations of the evergreen oak (or ilex) and beech; and at about an hour's walk from Siena there is a fine wood composed entirely of ilex-trees, where many an ancient

188   *ITALY.*

trunk is twined about with glistening ivy, and where a long-deserted convent stands at the outskirts of the forest. Still more poetic and impressive are the ruins of the Abbey

ST. GALGANO NEAR CHIUSDINO.

of San Galgano, near Chiusdino, several miles to the westward of Siena, where a stranger's foot scarcely ever treads. The noble columns of the purest gothic, the soaring arches, the whole mighty mass of ruins, are silently crumbling to decay, neglected, and, as it were, effaced from the memory of men.

CONFIRMATION IN THE CATHEDRAL OF SIENA.

The harmonious Italian language is heard in Siena to perfection; the soft Florentine accent, with its lazy aspirates, being tempered here by somewhat of Roman strength and vigour. And the inhabitants are as refined, cultivated, and agreeable, as their speech worthy in all respects of their beautiful mediæval city, which, for fine public edifices, works of art, temples, and the charm of the surrounding landscape, may dispute the palm with Florence herself. Siena, indeed, seems to the stranger a smaller Florence:—only more tranquil, more idyllic, more remote from the clash and conflict of this work-a-day world.

In the most central and the loftiest position in the city, rises the duomo. It is built in alternate stripes of black and white marble, and has two fine façades, one to the east, and the other to the west. The eastern transept remains in an unfinished and almost ruinous condition, its colossal proportions having rendered its completion impossible, by reason of the great cost involved in it; and the empty arches of its gigantic windows overlook the semi-circular market-place which lies beneath them. This market-place is adorned by the celebrated Fonte Gaja, with its charming bas-reliefs in marble:—a fine work of Jacopo della Quercia, erected within the years 1402—1419. All around the market-place, in a wide semi-circle, stand the palaces of the Sienese nobles, built of brick, in a fine early gothic style, and the chord of the arc is entirely formed by the Palazzo Pubblico, or Town Hall. This picturesque gothic building has a tower somewhat like that of the Palazzo Vecchio in Florence, rising to a dizzy height. Its façade is adorned with fine arched windows, and its interior halls contain several remarkable frescoes, some of great antiquity, and the fine colossal figures of Sodoma. Both these towers,—that of the Palazzo Pubblico in Siena, and that of the Palazzo Vecchio in Florence,—are distinctively characteristic of their respective towns; the Sienese soars higher and bolder, but at the same time more slender, slight, and graceful, than its massive, gloomy, and threatening rival of Northern Etruria.

Among the palaces, besides those of gothic brick-work with their richly pillared arched windows, may be observed several elegant edifices of the Renaissance period, built of sand-stone, and having their lower stories decorated with magnificent wrought iron-work:—arabesque designs full of palm-branches, griffins, lanterns, serpents, and heads of oxen and sheep. The development of art in Siena is almost as rich as in Florence, and of quite equal antiquity, handed down through the centuries of a long series of Great Masters, from Duccio, the highly gifted contemporary of Cimabue, to Balthasar Peruzzi, who was driven back to his native city by the famous sack of Rome in 1527. This Peruzzi, one of the greatest architects of any period, and at the same time a painter and decorator, worked in Rome at St. Peter's, built the Palazzo Massimi there, and has, moreover, adorned his native city with several of his most exquisite works. The most recent investigations have brought to light an incredible number of previously unknown—or at least unnamed—Sienese artists, whose works still beautify the old city. In this respect the cathedral, the very marble pavement of which is rich with fine designs in a peculiar kind of etching, holds the first rank. Amongst the best known masters who worked in the cathedral, may be mentioned Niccolo and Giovanni Pisano, Quercia, Michelangelo, Sodoma, Pinturicchio, and Peruzzi. As long ago as in the Middle Ages, the purely Greek group in marble of the Three Graces,[*] was discovered in Siena, and the town still preserves this treasure. Sienese art has at all times been distinguished by an inimitable grace and elegance, and especially during the period of the early Renaissance. The eye

---

[*] This beautiful group, which for many years stood in the building called the Library, annexed to the Cathedral, was removed at the desire of the present Pope, who deemed it an unfit ornament for a Christian church, and is now preserved at the "Academia delle belle Arti."—*Translator's note.*

is never weary of admiring the charming little churches with their well-proportioned cupolas, nestling in the ravines that intersect the group of hills on which the town is built, or perched picturesquely atop of the steep slopes. Within them are to be seen frescoes and oil-paintings, sculptures and friezes of quite Grecian elegance. In striking contrast to these are the huge, unadorned masses of the two great churches of the mendicant orders, built of dark brown brick ;—San Bernardino, and San Domenico, frowning down from their heights like Saracenic fortresses. At the foot of San Domenico lies the ancient fountain, Fonte Branda, sung of by Dante.* These fountains are a specialty of Siena ; they are huge cisterns, or reservoirs of water covered by a lofty vaulted arch, and situated in the lower parts of the city, where the waters from the upper lands are gathered together. Elegant pointed arches rise over the clear surface of the fountain, and wild roses and ferns flourish in the interstices of the walls. Hither come troops of women and young girls every evening to fetch water; and the whole scene recalls a picture from the biblical history, where the young maidens at the well of the city refresh the thirsty traveller with a cool draught from their slender earthen pitchers.

* The good people of Siena doubtless cling firmly to the tradition which makes their Fonte Branda the Fonte Branda mentioned by Maestro Adamo in the 30th Canto of the "Inferno." But the best opinion of the more recent Dantescan scholars is that the Fonte Branda, 'so piteously recalled by the parched tongue of the suffering Adamo, is a fountain or rill in the Casentino, just above Prato Vecchio.—*Translator's note.*

THE LAKE OF THRASYMENE.

HE grey Cyclopean walls on which Hannibal's warlike gaze rested still look down from the mountain cities around the lake. Thrasymene lies tranquil, shrouded in a slight veil of mist, unfurrowed by the keel of a boat, dotted with green islets, and surrounded by shores covered with oak-woods.

Once long long ago the mist spread thickly over the waters, and over the narrow shore near Passignano, where now the railway runs, and hid the position which Hannibal had ingeniously taken up to lie in wait for his enemies. Eagerly and unsuspiciously the Roman troops, under the command of the Consul Flaminius, pressed on into the gap that opens between the lake and the rocky prominence close to Passignano. The heavy morning fog completely concealed the foe from them. As the head of the Roman column approached this hill, Hannibal gave the signal of attack; at the same time his cavalry closed and guarded the entrance to the pass, and the dispersion of the mist suddenly showed all the neighbouring heights bristling with Punic arms. It was no combat, but a total rout. All those who had remained without the narrow pass were driven into the lake by Hannibal's cavalry, the van of the column in the pass itself destroyed almost without resistance, and the majority of the soldiers, including their Consul, were absolutely cut down in the act of marching past.

But the sounds of strife and bloodshed have long ceased to disturb these scenes. A profound peace reigns over the wide and singularly beautiful landscape;—one of the most beautiful even in Italy. Above the almost circular basin of the Lake the blue mountain pyramids of Monte Amiata and Monte Cetona rise in the south-west, and offer a spectacle of unparalleled grandeur. On the northern shore of the lake is seen Cortona on her rocky slopes, surrounded by Cyclopean walls, and containing a labyrinth of dark, narrow, and steep lanes, in which the gloomy, haunted-looking old sand-stone palaces are crumbling to decay. Above the town, upon a sunny eminence planted with olive trees, stands the gothic church of Santa Margherita, from whence there is a wonderful panoramic view of the surrounding country. Below Cortona, again, in a deep gorge formed by a little mountain stream, overgrown with fruit trees, and affording a charming peep of the mirror-like surface of the lake, lies the church of the Madonna del Calcinajo. This church is entirely unknown to the great majority of travellers, yet it is one of the noblest specimens of the early Tuscan Renaissance, built by Cecco di Giorgio in the form of a Latin cross, and surmounted by a lofty cupola. Upon its altars are still to be seen pictures by no less a hand than that of Cortona's greatest citizen, Luca Signorelli, the creator of the frescoes in the Lady chapel of the Duomo at Orvieto.

The shores of Thrasymene are traversed in great part by a high road, but are but thinly populated. On the western side, on a narrow tongue of land that stretches far into the lake, stands Castiglione del Lago, almost an island city, with alleys and streets as strait and confined as those of Venice. Here, forgotten and neglected by the world still stands the palace that once belonged to the victor of Lepanto, the conqueror of the Turk, Don John of Austria. Its halls are still adorned with frescoes representing his doughty deeds; especially the ceilings are fine, painted by Giulio Romano in his best and happiest period.

PORTA AUGUSTA, PERUGIA.

If any one wishes to enjoy them he has but to take a little boat and get himself rowed across the lake to Castiglione. A subtle enchantment seems to fill the spirit in the midst of this wide sheet of waters; the still, shining lake, the blue sky, the utter solitude, the girdle all around of wood-covered hills, crowned with hoary ancient cities, from whence the matin bells are chiming,—all combine to make a singular and delightful impression. It is a wondrous country! Hill-city after hill-city, on the jagged rocky ridge; Perugia, Montepulciano, Pienza, Radicofani, San Quirico, Castiglione dell' Orcia, and others. In the extreme distance lies Siena; and high above all these stony peaks towers from a belt of clouds the massive bulk of Monte Amiata, from whose top the cupola of St. Peter's may be descried. Even in former days, when the great high road to Rome passed through these towns, they were sleepy and deserted enough, but since the railway train has puffed along the lower plains, and beside the beautiful lake of Thrasymene, they have become still more remote and unvisited. They are all still surrounded by walls and towers, and seem to have grown into one with the brown rocks on which they are built. Very often in the midst of the town a yawning chasm is seen splitting the crag, and spanned by the arch of a stone bridge picturesquely overgrown with ivy and the wild vine.

For hours at a time your travelling carriage, with a yoke of oxen in front to help the horses—grand-looking beasts, these oxen! sleek, long horned, and of a soft dove-colour—will have to crawl and toil up the steep way to some mountain city; passing the cisterns cut deep into the overhanging rocks by the roadside, and the girls coming down to fetch water with a huge earthen pitcher of antique form carried on the shoulder, and a scarlet kerchief bound over their abundant black hair. Who could over-praise the beauty of the maidens of Montepulciano, or the merits of its noble vine that ripens here in the pure mountain air, upon the sun-baked chalky soil? And then the view from the city walls! Who can describe that view over the heaped-up hills, rising ever higher, step after step, until they reach the Alpine altitudes that glitter in eternal snow, the mirror of Lake Thrasymene with its islets, and, nearer to our feet, the shining little lakes of Montepulciano and Chiusi set in the greenness of the fruitful Val di Chiana?

Close by that Lake of Chiusi, where Porsenna once dwelt, and where his half-ruined colossal tomb is still pointed out, rise several hills of coagulated sand, shaded by a few scattered oak trees. These hills are perforated in all directions with passages and chambers, the last resting places of ancient Etruscans. They were the common burying-place for the entire population. Here are winding galleries filled with niches to contain the cinerary urns, of which hundreds have been found. Where several such galleries converge to one point, there is generally a loftier space like a chapel; and the whole bears a striking similitude to the Christian catacombs. In the precipitous ridge of rock that looks over the valley, have been found single chambers, which served for the tombs of distinguished families. Heavy folding doors of stone closed the entrance to each roomy chamber, whose roofs, cut in the sandstone, either flat or sloping in shape, are adorned with coffered panels painted red. All around the chamber are ranged the sarcophagi, or, as the case may be, smaller oblong urns containing only ashes. At about the height of the eye there runs around the wall a sort of frieze, representing incidents from the life of the deceased;—how they drove abroad in a chariot drawn by four horses, or how they went forth to the chase, all painted in pure colour on the natural surface of the wall. The figures are clearly and sharply designed, and full of expression; and the animals especially are admirably drawn.

In the valley behind Montepulciano stands the solitary church of San Biagio, built by Giuliano da San Gallo, entirely of blocks of limestone. It is one of the most remarkable domed churches of the Renaissance. A great cupola rises in the centre of the Greek Cross, in which shape the church is built, and the light is admitted only through the windows of this cupola. All the lines of the edifice are severe, and of antique simplicity; the exterior looks like what St. Peter's might have been had the designs of Bramante and Michael Angelo been faithfully carried out.

At the distance of a few hours' journey from Montepulciano, rises the mountain town of Pienza, the native place of the great Pope Æneas Sylvius Piccolomini. The pontiff filled the poor, obscure, little mountain town with splendid palaces, which although once more solitary and deserted, are still standing in full preservation; so that Pienza transports the beholder into the midst of the most flourishing period of the Italian Renaissance. The greater part of these edifices were constructed within a few years, —1460, to 1464,—and the highly cultured, art-loving Pope, assisted the architect with his personal advice. The papal palace is square in form, and surrounds a courtyard with arcades and richly painted walls. Its façade, looking towards the Val d'Orcia, displays three ranges of pillars, one above the other, which pillars are surmounted by exquisite capitals of carved foliage. The view from this side, looking across the valley of Orcia to the wood-crowned eminence of Monte Amiata, is indescribably impressive. In the summer of the year 1462, when the plague and the excessive heat were making the lowlands terrible, Æneas Sylvius took up his abode in these mountains, as he has himself so well described. Midway up the hill on which Pienza stands, he established his head quarters, together with the Roman Curia, in the ancient Longobard convent of San Salvatore. From hence, looking from among the chesnut trees at the edge of a rugged precipice, the whole of Southern Tuscany may be descried; and in the distance the towers of Siena. Here, in the exquisite summer weather, under the shade of mighty oaks and chesnuts, upon fresh, smooth lawns free from thorny briars, or troublesome insects, or dangerous reptiles, the Pope enjoyed the most serenely cheerful days. Every week he himself chose out some new shady spot for the *Segnatura** which was held on certain fixed days. Once during such an assembly it happened that a huge stag was roused by the dogs from his lair in the neighbouring thicket, and after valorously defending himself with hoof and horn, was seen to flee away into the higher mountains. Of an evening the Pope would sit in front of the convent overlooking the valley of the Paglia, and hold cheerful converse with the cardinals. Some of his Holiness's suite who ventured to descend the mountain in the ardour of the chase found the heat in the lower districts insupportable, and all the vegetation scorched and burnt up;—a real Inferno! whilst the convent in its green shade of woods seemed to be a habitation of the Blessed.

To the southward of Lake Thrasymene, upon a bold and rocky eminence, stands the ancient Città della Pieve,—now a poor insignificant little place,—the birthplace of Perugino, Raphael's master. But to the east, on a long isolated back-bone of hills rising from the plain, higher than any of these hill cities, and dominating them all by virtue of her position, is enthroned Perugia (the ancient Perusia), the mightiest of all the Etruscan cities, still an important town, and once so strong a fortress that even Hannibal after his victory at Thrasymene dared not attack her. The town somewhat resembles Siena with its fine churches and picturesque groups of houses; but it is much sternerlooking; the streets are narrow, steeper, darker; the air is keener and rougher, the

---

* The Segnatura, or Signatura, was a supreme tribunal of the Roman Curia, consisting of seven prelates and a cardinal, which latter presided over it under the title of Prefetto. It was called *Segnatura di Giustizia e Grazia*, because it not only emitted sentences, but enjoyed the sovereign privilege of according a free pardon.—*Translator's note*.

scenery around wilder and more grandiose;—a noble Alpine style of scenery in the immediate vicinity of the snow-crowned central range of the Apennine. Perugia has none of the gentler charms of Siena, and its history is more troubled, stormy, and wild. The tradition still lingers of the Bloody Wedding of Perugia, in the family of the whilom rulers of the town, the Baglioni. A conspiracy was entered into, at the head of which were two distant connections of the family, Grifone and Carlo Barciglia, against their relatives Guido and Ridolfo Baglione, with their sons Gianpaolo, Simonetto, Astorre, and Gismondo. The plot was carried into effect suddenly on the wedding day of Astorre Baglione with Lavinia Colonna, in the summer of the year 1500. The feast began and continued amidst signs and tokens of sinister augury. In the night of the fifteenth of July, Guido, Astorre, Simonetto, and Gismondo were murdered in their respective houses: the rest managed to escape. As the body of Astorre, together with that of Simonetto, lay out in the open street, the beholders (and especially the foreign students who frequented the then famous university) compared him to an ancient Roman, so noble and dignified was the aspect of his lifeless form. Simonetto, on the other hand, looked bold and defiant, as though death itself had failed to subdue him. But on the following day those Baglioni who had escaped from the city, collected a large following and, with Gianpaolo at their head, forced their way back into Perugia, where other adherents speedily joined them. Grifone fell into the hands of his cousin Gianpaolo, and the latter ordered him to be killed. Atalanta, Grifone's mother, a still young and beautiful woman, who had some days previously retired to her estate in the country, together with Zenobia, Grifone's wife, and two children of Gianpaolo, now returned with her daughter-in-law to see her dying son. All made way for the two women as they passed along; those who had struck down Grifone shrunk out of sight, fearing to draw upon themselves the mother's curse of vengeance. But, contrary to expectation, Atalanta conjured her son to pardon those who had given him his death wounds, and Grifone expired amidst her prayers and blessings. Then the two sad women in their trailing garments stained with Grifone's blood, went slowly away across the Piazza, amidst the awe-stricken silence of the crowd. This Atalanta is the same for whom Raphael painted the famous Entombment, now in the Borghese Palace, in Rome. The picture was a sort of votive offering to the highest and holiest example of maternal grief.

But even in these latter days the history of Perugia displays one page of blood and horror: the storming of the city by the Swiss Papal troops, under Colonel Schmidt. Together with the whole of the Romagna, Perugia had risen up to join herself to the kingdom of United Italy, under Victor Emmanuel. Everywhere the annexation had been proclaimed without the slightest act of violence; but Colonel Schmidt thought it incumbent on him to wrest back the town into the power of its old rulers *at any cost*. It would be difficult to imagine any place more adapted for defence than Perugia, with its strong encircling walls built on the living rock, its massive stone houses, its narrow, steep, and winding streets defended by long flights of steps, and great arches of solid masonry. On this occasion every window became a loop-hole; children hurled down showers of stones, and the heavy Roman tiles, women poured hot oil on to the heads of the advancing soldiers; it was a conflict without a parallel, obstinate, unchristian, blind, and pitiless! House after house had to be stormed singly. In their chambers, in their beds, before the pictures of their saints, men and women were seized by the infuriated Swiss, and butchered. And then, once more, Perugia lay gagged and bound at the feet of the Pope King, and—Colonel Schmidt was made a General!

But the blood of those so ruthlessly slain, cried aloud to Heaven, and only a few years had passed before the States of the Church broke up and crumbled to pieces, like an edifice of rotten timber. The stern fortress which was built to terrorize and oppress

INTERIOR OF AN ETRUSCAN TOMB NEAR PERUGIA.

the city by the fierce Pierluigi, son of Pope Paul the Third, is levelled to the earth; and on its site is a charming promenade planted with flowers, and commanding a splendid view over the mighty range of mountains and the broad valley of the Tiber to Assisi, which sits aloft upon a buttress of the great hills.

* * * * * * *

"Cast away everything, and become a beggar," spake Bouddha Sakya Muni centuries before the birth of Christ. A powerful Indian King took off the golden diadem from his brow, went out into the wilderness, and preached to the poor lessons of love and long-suffering. "Cast away everything, and become a beggar!" These words, which found an echo in the profoundest depths of the peoples' nature, seized powerfully upon the East, and have kept firm hold on it even to the present day.

And the same words were uttered many centuries later from the innermost heart of a young man in the distant western world of Europe,—one Francis, the son of a well-to-do merchant in Assisi, born in the year of the Redemption 1182. In the midst of a luxurious life he suddenly flung away his gold-embroidered garments, wrapped himself in rags, and went away into solitude. At first he was held to be crazy; but he soon won disciples by his fervent faith and the burning eloquence which seemed to spring from the immediate influence of a Divine power upon his frail mortal frame. Francis was no gloomy ascetic; he embraced the whole creation in a spirit of unwearying love and gentleness and compassion, communing even with the beasts of the forest and the birds of the air, that were not scared by his peaceful presence. Soon the whole western world was covered with colossal churches of the Mendicant Order, wherein the merits of voluntary poverty were preached to the people. And to this day those vast, unadorned, early Gothic choirs, with their bold and lofty vaultings, bear testimony to the intense earnestness, the pure enthusiasm, which emanated from the influence of St. Francis of Assisi;—an incredible contrast to the condition of the Papacy, which at that period was sunk into mere outward show and luxury, and yet in the course of time, destined to do that Papacy incalculable service.

Two years after the death of Francis he was canonized, and the Duomo of Assisi (which consists really of three churches erected one above the other) was built above his tomb. The Duomo and Convent of San Francesco are situated at the lower end of the town, and are built upon enormous foundations and substructures of solid masonry at the edge of the precipice, looking towards the river Teschio. In the background is the city, looking as if it were one with the rock it stands on; above that again, the ruins of an old castle, and the range of treeless chalk hills, overgrown with juniper bushes, and wild thyme, and parched tufts of grass. Fearful chasms split the great mountains in their loftier regions; the autumn rains eat deep channels in them every year; at the bottom of the ravines the larger rivers wind along:—now rushing swollen and angry in a flood of terribly destructive power; now showing only an almost dry bed of baked white pebbles in the hot droughts of summer. Amidst these solitudes St. Francis dwelt for many years, and their grandeur entered into his soul.

The Cathedral of Assisi is almost a little world apart, full of consecrated works of art, and sublime memories. The body of the Saint rests in the lowest part of it, in a tomb cut in the living rock. Above that rises the lower church, a vaulted, massive building with rows of thick, low pillars, and pierced so sparingly with windows that the eye needs some time to accustom itself to the 'dim religious light' sufficiently to distinguish Giotto's solemn frescoes, typifying the vows of Chastity, Poverty, and Obedience, whilst in the side chapels ancient painted glass windows admit coloured rays that sparkle like jewels on the stone pavement. The upper church is a wide, free, cheerful space, full of light, and roofed by a vault that seems made of palm branches laid together. Here are the world-renowned frescoes of Cimabue.

ASSISI.

THE ROADS TO ROME.

BESIDE THE ADRIATIC.

HERE once passed the important *Via Flaminia*, where now the railroad runs for miles along the shore. The blue waves of the sea break into white foam against the stone dam on the top of which the train rattles and puffs. On one hand is the ever-moving expanse of the Adriatic, its horizon melting mistily into the silvery belt of clouds above it: white sea-gulls wheel and swoop on swift, strong pinions, and the little Dalmatian fishing boats cut their way doughtily under a press of canvas through the sunny waters. On the other hand are blooming valleys between softly swelling hills, backed by the rugged lines of the higher range of chalky mountains, from whose heights old battlemented towns look down. Again, on the shore itself, are lively, industrious, populous seaside places, set amidst the richest gardens of the plain :—Rimini, Pesaro, Sinigaglia, and so on till we reach the " elbow of Italy," Ancona. This town is piled up against the steep hill's side, in a way that reminds us of Genoa. It stretches in a semi-circle round the fine harbour, at the entrance to which the Triumphal Arch of the Emperor Trajan is still standing in a state of excellent preservation.

But let us return to Rimini, the ancient Ariminum, where the ruins of Sigismund Malatesta's threatening fortress-castle are crumbling to decay. Rimini lies at the mouth of the Marecchia valley, which is still spanned by the five-arched bridge built by the Emperor Augustus; and on the opposite side of the town, looking towards the mountains, stands a fine triumphal arch, erected in honour of the same Emperor. Rimini bears, unmistakeably, the aspect of a place that has seen better days. A population of old women, distaff in hand, sits in waiting under the wall of the Duomo, and levies black

DEPARTURE FOR THE MOUNTAINS.

mail on the traveller who approaches to view a building splendid even in its incompleteness;—the great monument which Sigismondo Malatesta caused to be erected to his former mistress, the beautiful Isotta, by one of the greatest masters of the dawning Renaissance, Leon Battista Alberti of Florence. This Alberti was the friend and admirer of Brunelleschi; he designed the façade of Santa Maria Novella, and the Palazzo Rucellai in Florence, and the supremely beautiful church of Sant' Andrea in Mantua.

Further on is Pesaro, renowned for its figs, and its villas in the taste of the later Renaissance, set in a wilderness of gardens. Tasso and Ariosto once sung of them: now they are silent and neglected, but from the laurel thickets, which encroach even on to the marble steps, the nightingale is heard to pipe her sweetest songs, and away across the placid sea, in the warm summer night, the stars of this southern heaven rise large and glowing. Close to the railway station, on the shore, the Swan of Pesaro has at length found a resting place! I allude to the monument of the great maestro Rossini; there he sits, snuff-box in hand, with his pleasant, smiling, shrewd, rather Epicurean face,—the man who never travelled on a railway, now exposed henceforward to the close vicinity of yelling locomotives!

Then comes Sinigaglia, the birth-place of Catalani; a clean, industrious, well-to-do little town, where one of the greatest fairs in all Italy is held. Many Jews are to be found here. Count August von Platen, one of the most indefatigable of Italian travellers, says that he found at the fair of Sinigaglia very little German merchandise, but a great number of Nuremberg toys, which he proceeds to apostrophise sentimentally as a symbol

CATHEDRAL OF ANCONA.

of his Fatherland! But Sinigaglia has other and less trivial reminiscences: amongst them the destruction of one of the greatest Peoples of Antiquity. The battle of the Metaurus fought against Hasdrubal, Hannibal's brother, took place close to this spot. The victory of the Romans, although hardly won and bloody, was complete; the Carthaginian army, unable to retreat, was utterly destroyed and its encampment taken by storm. Hasdrubal, when he saw that the bravely-contested battle was lost, sought and found, like his father, Hamilcar, a soldier's death. The day after the battle, the Consul Nero broke up his positions, and after an absence of less than fourteen days, once more confronted Hannibal in Apulia. Hannibal had received no tidings from his brother, and was ignorant of his fate. The first news was brought him by the Roman Consul, who caused the head of Hasdrubal to be thrown into the enemy's outposts. Then Hannibal perceived that he had hoped in vain, and that all was lost.

Much more interesting and attractive, however, are the mountain towns:

San Marino, the ancient Republic, perched on a precipitous ledge of rock; a state which covers a superficies of some four square miles, and contains a population of eight thousand inhabitants! (The town itself counts only sixteen hundred.) There is a strange air of serenity in the quaint narrow streets of the town, with their little houses built of

SAN MARINO.

rough-hewn limestone. Within the houses are stored up furniture and utensils of a hoar antiquity; and even some of the inhabitants look as though they belonged to a past geological period! They dwell here from generation to generation, proud and content on their airy height. The whole world seems to belong to them as it lies stretched in endless beauty and variety at the foot of their native rock. The Republic of San Marino once sent a message to Napoleon the Great, which has become classical: "We accept," said the Republic, "the friendship of the First Consul. We will pay for the cannons. We desire no extension of territory."

Urbino, Raphael's home, is a town of seven thousand inhabitants, full of reminiscences of high intellectual culture; an oasis beloved of the gods. High above the stream of

CAMPO SANTO, PISA.

Time, it stands yet almost unaltered. The palace of the great Montefeltro family is a splendid building of the Cinque Cento time. It contains halls with noble friezes, and carved chimney-pieces, all painted in blue and gold upon the white marble. And all round the city there open out grand views over the solemn mountains, the fertile shores, and the eternal sea. In several of the churches of Urbino are to be found altar-pieces painted by Giovanni Santi, Raphael's father. The aspect of his native town, the surrounding scenery, and family influence, all combined to foster the budding genius of the boy Raphael. His pictures are steeped in the serene and pure atmosphere of this mountain city, elevated high above all low mists and exhalations of the common world.

Behind Loreto, the renowned place of pilgrimage whose *Casa Santa* is as important for the history of Italian sculpture as the Campo Santo in Pisa is for that of painting, stands Recanati, on a barren rock. Here was born Count Giacomo Leopardi, the greatest Italian poet since Dante, and, like Dante, the faithful mirror of his own times. Nay, Leopardi was, perhaps, the stronger of the two! Dante lived in the exciting and swift-moving days of Guelph and Ghibelline: Leopardi in the most nerveless and degraded period of Italian history;—the beginning of the nineteenth century (from 1798 to 1837), doubting and despairing, but full of a grandly antique spirit. Never has utter hopelessness been expressed more profoundly, nakedly, grandly, and touchingly, than in Leopardi's poems. Sickly, weak, and lonely, from his youth upward; crushed beneath the sorrows of Italy, and yet clinging desperately to the idea of her ultimate liberation, he withered and drooped untimely, like a plant of the southern sunshine amid bleak Alpine winds. We give one passage from his poems:

> Love, love, thou hast departed from this bosom
> So warm and glowing once. With chilly hand
> Misfortune grasped it, and it froze to ice,
> Even in the very springtide of my years.
>
> * * * *
>
> And yet if sometimes, when o'er smiling slopes
> The dawn arises silently, or when
> The village roofs and fields in sunshine glow,
> I meet a youthful maiden in her beauty;
> Or when amidst the placid quietude
> Of summer nights, I wander forth alone
> And pause beside some rustic home, and gaze
> Upon the solitary landscape, listening
> To one shrill girlish voice that sings within
> The while its owner plies her busy wheel;
> Oh then, even yet, my heart will stir and beat!
> But soon, alas, it turns to stone again.
> All soft and sweet emotions are estranged
> From my unhappy breast for evermore.

BESIDE THE TYRRHENE SEA.

AT present the railway follows nearly the same line by the sea shore which the *Via Aurelia* of the Romans formerly traversed. But long before the existence of the Roman road, an ancient Etruscan road passed through these regions amidst blooming gardens and populous cities, whence various artistic products were exported—mainly ornaments of brass and gold—by bridle-paths across the Alps, even into the very heart of Germany. Or the Etruscan ships sailed between the pillars of Hercules, carrying to the shores of the North Sea precious and eagerly-sought-for freights of amber, which were bartered for the bronze weapons of the Huns. In those times the land was more flourishing and fertile than it has ever been since. Large and massive conduits, built of cuneiform stones, assured a regular current to the rivers, which would otherwise have been apt to stagnate in their course through the lower lands, and afforded the means of beneficial irrigation during the heat of summer. The cities were mostly built on rocky eminences—often artificially scarped—and were surrounded by gigantic Cyclopean walls.

Now all these things are destroyed or deserted. From Leghorn downward, even to the very gates of Rome, there is scarcely a trace of cultivation, and the soil has become rotten and worthless. Broad sedges, marsh-cypresses, great bilberry-bushes, heather that grows to the height of a man, and is full of purple blossoms in the Spring, stiff, flowering thistles, odorous thyme, all manner of wild thorny creeping plants, which twine around the huge Cyclopean walls whose strength defies Old Time to utterly destroy them, and choke the disused conduits, and mantle the resting places of the dead,—all these have overgrown the land. And this wilderness is inhabited by wild boars, black-muzzled buffaloes, the venomous steel-grey viper, the crane, the snipe, the plover, and the melancholy booming bittern.

Opposite to Elba lies Populonia, now a miserable village, once the emporium that received the inexhaustible stores of iron obtained in Elba. Beyond and behind Grosseto is the ancient Rusellæ, completely ruined, Vetulonia, Saturnia, Vulci, and, behind Corneto, Tarquinii, the vastest of all the Etruscan burying places. The number of tombs there is reckoned at two millions. And then, far away across the greyish-brown waste, and the low rolling hills overgrown with shrubs, you catch a glimpse of the dome of St. Peter's, looking solitary and mysterious on the horizon.

Several islands rise out of the Tyrrhene Sea: Elba, fertile, well-cultivated, with prosperous towns, and rich mines of iron-ore, and, nearer to Sardinia, little, unproductive, rugged Caprera. Yonder, in the Island of Elba, once resided his Imperial Majesty the Emperor Napoleon the First, placed there against his will by the European powers, after he had ruined his own people, but still keeping a Court, and a regiment of soldiers! Here, in Caprera, Garibaldi voluntarily retired (after having given freedom to *his* people), without rank or wealth, and peacefully cultivated his fields.

CASCADES OF TERNI.

THE MIDDLE ROADS.

NE of these is a railway, running eastward from Arezzo past the Lake of Thrasymene, passing below Assisi, and joining the line from the Adriatic coast at Foligno. From hence it proceeds nearly parallel with the ancient *Via Flaminia*, which reached the Adriatic at Fanum, the modern Fano. The line passes through a hilly district, by Trevi, with its grey stone houses hanging on the steep slope, to Spoleto. This town is built up on a rugged height, crowned by its great fortress castle, backed by great mountains covered with ilex woods, and commanding a fine view of the valley of the Tiber. It is the boldest of all the mountain towns perched defiantly on their rocks, which we pass by this route to Rome. In approaching Spoleto from the railway, we come first to the *Porta della Fuga*, the self-same Etruscan gateway before which Hannibal turned back after the battle of Thrasymene. Within the town are many remains—most of them in a ruinous condition—of mediæval buildings: buildings of the time of the Hohenstaufens, who placed the Swabian Knight, Conrad of Irslingen, here as Duke of Spoleto. The ancestral castle of his race may still be seen, ruined and weedgrown, in a remote valley of the Wirtembergian Black Forest.

AQUEDUCT OF SPOLETO.

The rule of these Swabian barons did not endure very long. But between the years 1342 and 1351, a scion of this race, his mind filled with old traditions and hatreds, undertook to avenge the expulsion of his ancestors by carrying warfare and rapine throughout Italy. This was Werner von Irslingen, known as Duke Guarnieri, the leader of a famous band, and styled by himself "the enemy of God, of pity, and of mercy!" The last of the family, Reinald by name, lived a beggared noble in his castle of Schiltach, in the Black Forest, and when he died was under the weight of grave accusations brought against him by the Imperial courts of justice, in the year 1446.

Castello, once the residence of the most fascinating woman of the fifteenth century, Lucrezia Borgia, stands at a great altitude, and commands an extraordinary view of the amphitheatre of mountains, and down into the rocky valley. This valley is spanned by the highest stone aqueduct in the world; it is more than seven hundred feet long, and about three hundred feet high, and has ten arches resting on gigantic pillars. It was built by the Lombard dukes, who ruled here during several centuries. The water that runs through its broad channel is collected among the silent, ever-green oak-woods of Monte Luco, where one or two deserted hermitages and the Capuchin Monastery of San Giuliano stand.

PRELATE FUGGER'S TOMBSTONE.

Below Spoleto the railway passes through a long tunnel, underneath the heights that form the watershed of the Clitumnus and the Nera; and reaches Terni, situated between two arms of the Nera. Terni is the birthplace of Tacitus. About an hour and a half from Terni, the Velino falls over masses of tufa into the tremendous gorge of the Nera, and forms the famous cascades. The principal fall is six hundred feet high. We saw it one evening when the sun was sinking behind the mountains. The purple light glanced between the rich foliage of the trees, and illuminated the bold outlines of the yellow tufa rocks. Tremendous was the fury of the waters as they came thundering down into the gulf, whirling, quivering, hissing, roaring, and foaming! And from the wild, yeasty, snow-white mass, there kept rising clouds of mist, growing thinner and purer, until they were mingled with the arch of peace that spanned the tumult with its heavenly colours. Then the light clouds of spray passed onward, wonderful in variety and beauty, like troops of celestial and immortal forms, and high in air a royal eagle circled in his slow and stately flight.

The ancient Narni lies below Terni, just at the entrance to a wild gorge, through which the Nera has forced its passage. Above is the Cyclopean citadel, and in the fore-ground, crossing the torrent, a half-ruined, gigantic Roman bridge. The railway here passes through a gorge which recalls the Via Mala in its dark and threatening aspect. The rocks overhang the road, and are clothed with laurel bushes and dwarf ilex. The Nera dashes impetuously along in its narrow course, until at length the rocky walls open out into the valley of the Tiber, and we behold the plains of Latium stretching fair in the sunlight.

The second of the roads through central Italy is also a railroad, which pretty nearly follows the course of the ancient *Via Cassia* coming from Chiusi, passes westward by the Lake of Thrasymene, and so on to Orvieto. Orvieto is built upon an isolated rocky hill, and looks down with its weather-blackened palaces into thinly-populated valleys overgrown with ilex woods. It was once a Papal residence. The traveller approaching

ORVIETO.

Orvieto can discern from a considerable distance the west front of the Cathedral—one of the wonders of the world. It is in the purest Gothic style, and nearly covered with mosaics upon a gold background, wonderfully symmetrical, grand, and, above all, splendid. Adjoining the cathedral is the Lady Chapel with the renowned frescoes of Luca Signorelli and Beato Angelico of Fiesole;—the finest works of both. The Resurrection of the Dead, and Paradise, are by Signorelli. The first-named picture especially displays a quite enormous power of passion, and wonderful mastery in the representation of the nude ;—a foretaste of Michael Angelo. Opposite to this the pyramidical group of Prophets by Beato Angelico enchants the eye. Signorelli gives us powerful, even violent, movement and action : here, on the contrary, all is peace and rest, and the faces shine with a divine serenity ;—a foretaste of Raphael. But neither of these two great and immortal geniuses, despite the master-pieces they have given to the world, have ever surpassed in certain respects the work of their predecessors in the Lady Chapel at Orvieto.

A pleasant excursion may be made from Orvieto to the little Lake of Bolsena, on whose southern shore lies Montefiascone, the famous place where the muscadel wine known as Est Est is grown. The tombstone of the prelate Fugger of Augsburg—a rude but undoubtedly genuine Gothic work—is still shown in the Church of San Flaviano at Montefiascone.

> Propter nimium Est Est
> Dominus meus mortuus est.

The noble churchman was travelling through Italy, and being much disgusted at the quantity of poor sour wine he found on his journey, he sent a trusty henchman on before him as *avant-coureur* to investigate the hostelries on his route, and to taste the wine. If the liquor were found satisfactory, the faithful servant was to chalk the word Est on the tavern door. In due course he arrived at Montefiascone, and tasted the muscadel. So delicious did he find it that one single Est appeared to him but poorly to set forth its merits :—so he chalked up two !

> Then with chalk of ruddy hue
> On the tavern door he drew
> In great letters his device,
> " Est " twice over—some say thrice.
>
> Came the bishop, saw, and drank,
> Till upon the ground he sank.
> Tapster, cellarer, host, and all
> Gave him pious burial.
> *Propter nimium Est Est*
> *Dominus meus mortuus est.*
>
> WILHELM MÜLLER.

ETRUSCAN ROCK-TOMBS AT CASTEL D'ASSO, NEAR VITERBO.

TO ROME.

Lo, as the rosy morning light is growing,
Soracte's sevenfold peaks are redly glowing;
And ere that selfsame sun sink in the west,
On great eternal Rome thine eyes shall rest.

HERE begins already the great waste of the Roman Campagna, covering wonderful ruins, of which a few here and there peep up above the soil. Sometimes we come upon a group of miserable huts made of reeds, or a crumbling mediæval tower. Poisonous weeds grow luxuriantly around them; thistles, and the noble acanthus, looking as though the capitals of the Corinthian columns buried in the soil had sprouted into leaf!

Here is Viterbo, the ancient city, with its beautiful murmuring fountains and sombre palaces, and, outside its gates, singular rocks full of caverns, and gardens of Renaissance villas running wild. Viterbo is the city of the Popes, who frequently took refuge here either from German Kaisers, or from their own turbulent Romans. The huge Papal palace still stands stern and fortress-like, the old time-stained town walls look much as they looked when many a legion of foreign soldiers marched past them in the Middle Ages, on their way to the Roman Campagna to encounter battle, wounds, malaria fever, and death. Conradin, the last of the Hohenstaufens, passed this way on his road from Pisa through Toscanella, whose singular marble churches, covered with Gnostic figures,

THE GREAT FOUNTAIN IN VITERBO.

existed even then. Pope Clement the Fourth, Conradin's bitterest enemy, watched the troops march past from the wall of the town.

Whilst their banners flutter lightly,
On they march with warlike din,
And of all that troop so knightly,
Handsomest is Conradin.

Hark, the trumpets blaring loudly !
Hark, the northern shout and song !
Helm and hauberk flash out proudly
Sunlit, as they prance along.

HOUSE IN VITERBO.

Watching from the rampart tower
Glares Pope Clement gloomily.
Words of hatred, words of power,
Prophet-like, thus speaketh he:

"Go, poor fool ! Like smoke-wreaths flying
Soon shall fade each vain device;
And thyself art blindly hieing
Victim to the sacrifice !"

Loud he calls, but all unheeding
Conradin leads on his band.
Soon his fair young head lies bleeding
In the dust on Naples' strand.

Further to the south, passing by the Lake of Vico in the crater of an extinct volcano, we approach nearer to Monte Soracte. In the distance we had descried it as a long misty blue mountain with seven peaks: seen closer it shows itself to be a lofty, wide, spreading wooded height, furrowed by many gorges, and bearing ancient convents that peep out from amid the trees on its undulating slopes. On the side fronting towards Rome, stands the very ancient monastery of Sant' Oreste (Soracte is now popularly called

Mont' Oreste) founded by the Longobards. In the year 747, Carloman, the eldest son of Charles Martel, renounced the pomps of his princely rank, and retired hither to become a monk. Yet another and more poetic historical figure is connected with the neighbourhood of Soracte;—Otho the Third, the last scion of his great race. He was an enthusiastic youth of barely two-and-twenty, dreaming of restoring the universal empire to Rome, and awaiting his bride, the daughter of the Greek Emperor, whom his envoy Archbishop Arnolfo of Milan, was to conduct to him across the Ionian Sea from Byzantium. But surrounded by enemies and blockaded in the little castle of Paterno at the foot of Soracte, he turns his dying gaze across the wide Campagna to Rome, now risen in revolt against him; and from the other side of the Alps come the tidings that the Germans, whom his ancestors had made the most powerful people in the world, intended to set him aside and crown another prince in his stead. He dies, poor, crushed by misfortune, and comprehending the vanity and emptiness of all mundane things.

If there be on earth a prospect calculated to enchant the spirit and fill it with aspirations unspeakable, it is that which is seen from the summit of Soracte. All around us the amphitheatre of grandiose and finely-shaped hills; at our feet the great rolling plain of the Campagna, teeming with the wondrous ruins of so many centuries; on the horizon a shimmer of the sea; in the midst of the plain the Tiber rolling majestic on its winding course; and lo! upon its banks, framed in by leafy gardens, red in the sunset-glow, Eternal Rome!

FROM THE TIBER TO ETNA.

BY

WOLDEMAR KADEN.

WITHIN THE CONFINES OF LATIUM.

ROME.

Oh scene sublime ! Yet stern and sad enough
To make us shudder with an icy breath
From times for ever past. And oh, what times !
The glorious days of Rome's supremacy.
From every ruin sounds a wond'rous voice
Like the invisible rush of eagle's wings.
And Rome's great spirit ghost-like walks the earth
Which once she ruled in uncontested might.

H. LINGG.

OMA! Roma! Thus shouts the wanderer from northern lands, in whose mind a longing to behold the Eternal City has grown with his growth from earliest youth, when he first catches sight of the Dome of St. Peter's rising from the plain and towering into the intense blue of the sky.

Rome! Rome! Even although we may not articulate it with our lips, yet in our hearts the mighty name sounds and echoes; and we feel an awe-stricken shudder as the memories of the classic past come upon us with resistless enchantment, and a thousand years of history seem concentrated into that supreme moment when we first see Rome. The gift of *seeing* in its true sense is not given to all; but even to those who possess it, Rome is too vast, too mighty, to be seized on at once in its entirety.

Rome is a broken mirror whose fragments and splinters still reflect the colossal images of heroes, citizens, populace, and nations, in glory and splendour, in devastation and decay, in blood and misery. The dust of centuries and the ashes from many a funeral urn lie thickly on the broken fragments, and hide their pictures from the eyes of most of us; but after long and patient gazing, the ruins combine themselves into a whole, the colossal images are united into one vast world-picture, so a-blaze with glory that the soul is filled with awe and wonder, and even the eyes of the wisest are dazzled.

The traveller from the north feels himself suddenly transported into a new world as soon as he passes the barrier of the Alps. This Italy is in truth a land of sunshine and delight. The sun beams more brightly than with us at home; the moon has a more silvery lustre; other stars shine above us and light us to pleasant paths. A rich luxuriant vegetation surrounds us, and fills the air with perfume. We seem to be wandering in a garden hedged in by laurel and myrtle, over-arched by roses and vines. A charming melody accompanies the traveller on his way—a melody that fills and cheers his heart —Spring sunlight, Summer breezes, wine and flowers, dark eyes, brilliant landscapes— these form the theme of the melody, and there needs but to have a sympathetic human heart in order thoroughly to enjoy it.

ITALY.

But soon as we approach nearer to Rome there is mingled harmony with the melody, and it sounds ever fuller and stronger. The tones grow and swell into a great symphony, in whose rolling depths the pleasant butterfly-winged melody is overwhelmed; but from its waves the spirit arises in tempestuous strength, and is wafted on eagle's pinions through the wide, wide Past to sunny heights from whence it contemplates a majestic vision of the World and of Humanity.

Such is Rome! Such are the first impressions of Rome!

Even the greatest minds are confused at first by the immensity of this symphonic sea. They are stunned—bewildered; they grope after a beginning; they seek a standpoint from whence to behold the spectacle before them; they are hurried restlessly from one object to another; many mornings, many evenings, make up a long series of days; and only when these are passed is the classic repose of mind attained to which is so peculiarly essential in Rome. Goethe himself long sought for it in vain.

We cool our fevered brow in the refreshing waters of the Fontana di Trevi, and collect our thoughts into an attitude of solemn reverence beneath the dome of Agrippa, the incomparable Pantheon, which, once dedicated to all the gods, now hospitably receives any worshipper whose heart retains some feeling for the ancient deities.

And then begins to arise from its grave, amid dust and ruins, rank greenery, and modern buildings, out of the mists of history and the veils of the past, great imperial Rome—the complete and perfect Rome of Hadrian! In gorgeous raiment, sword in hand and diadem on head, she shines from her throne upon the Seven Hills, proud mistress of the earth from the sunrise to the sunset. The sun looks proudly down upon her!

> High sun, thou dost pause to look with lingering gaze on thy Rome!
> No greater hast thou beheld : no greater shalt ever behold.

In a flood of rosy light, the sun comes forth and illuminates the city. Let us, too, gaze upon the glorious scene, and try to conjure up a vision of the shining marble city in all her antique beauty!

But whither shall we first direct our eyes in this sea of graceful temples, mountainous amphitheatres, solemn mausoleums, and vast baths; amid the labyrinth of shady porticoes and populous forums, of royal palaces full of golden halls, and colonnades, and triumphal arches? Yonder stride the mighty aqueducts from the blue mountains to the plain, filling countless fountains, wells, gardens, and villas with their silvery water in profusion. From hill to hill of the city proud arches are boldly stretched; and the valleys between them are groves of marble. Here is a forest of pillars of all kinds : Doric, Ionic, Corinthian, Roman, polished monoliths glancing in the light, and capitals adorned with all variety of richest fancy. And then between these, on wall and frieze, in niche and grotto, in garden and square, from every shady nook, shines out a second populace in stone, the great army of statues in noble marble or gilded bronze. All the deities of Olympus, all the ancient kings and heroes, seem to have descended to partake in some great Festival of Art! It is almost too much of beauty!

The yellow, legend-laden Tiber seems to linger as he flows beneath the grandly-arched bridges; Phœbus seems to linger as he drives his team towards the neighbouring sea, unwilling to depart. But Spring never leaves the city : here is his eternal kingdom!

Covered with the deep green of the new wheat, with vine and olive, with pine and cypress, the wide Campagna stretches towards the hills in which the Tiber takes its rise;

RUINS OF THE PALACE OF THE CÆSARS ON THE PALATINE.

towards Nemi with its charming lake, the Speculum Dianæ, and Alba Longa. Great paved high roads intersect the plain; and on either side of them, the wealth, ostentation, or affection of the survivors have raised rich monuments to their dead. Villa upon villa

LAKE OF NEMI.

as far as the eye can see! Their marble walls are delightfully relieved against the dark greens and browns of the landscape: the farthest of them look like flowers upon the rich plain,—like white magnolia blossoms amid their lush foliage. Above the whole is the light of this clear Olympian ether, silvery even in the shadows, and gilding even the meanest things with an enchanted ray. The perfume of a divine Spring-tide fills the air, and kisses away care. The nightingales never abandon these gardens and ever-green groves; their love-songs sound the whole year through. They warble in the gardens of the Esquiline, where poets dwell: and mingle their sweetest lays with the strophes of Horace, Virgil, and Propertius. Here, too, the violets bloom eternally.

It is only in this clime that man can be entirely happy and enjoy the full flavour of the draught of life. So thought Cicero in his exile beneath the skies of Asia, and wrote longingly to his friend: "Oh, thou mayest dwell but in Rome, and live only in that air."

That sun looked down, too, upon a powerful people whose spirit had an eagle's wings:—a people of leonine strength and leonine courage. Thus Rome became the proud heart, the thinking head, and, above all, the powerful arm, of the world. Every Roman, whithersoever he might wander along the roads that led to all the nations of the earth, could see in fancy written in letters of flame above the gates and triumphal arches of his native town, the Virgilian:

"Tu regere imperio populos, Romane, memento!"

And this proud and lofty feeling of self-reliance and daring, developed itself in the domestic polity of the city, as well as in its foreign rule. Thus Rome conquered the world.

The beginning was small: and might be compared to the grain of mustard seed of the Evangel. One poor hill was once large enough to contain the cradle of the Roman people. Look yonder! In the midst of the six other heights that seem to girdle it about, you behold the Palatine. It is the hill of Romulus; the first foundation of the Imperial city. The other mounts surround it like sentinels; and a series of five kings completed the strong chain, by joining hill to hill with castles and towers. The Sabine Titus Tatius joined the Palatine to the Capitoline hill: the Quirinal was added to the chain under Numa Pompilius: the Cœlian, under Tullus Hostilius: Ancus Marcius added the Aventine: and finally, under the sixth king, Servius Tullius, the seven hills were united into an armed whole by the addition of the Esquiline and the Mons Viminalis. The town was finished. The Seven Hills had become one fortress; and Servius Tullius encircled it with a huge girdle of walls. From this period begins the real history of Rome, which up to then consists of mythic shadows and misty, nebulous legends. Those are but dim ways which lead the enquirer into the endless maze of races and localities, such as the Volscians and Sabines, the Marsi and Rutuli, Tibur and Latium. All the accounts of the Aborigines are fabulous. They were finally pressed upon by the powerful Sabines and withdrew to the neighbourhood of Alba Longa, from whence they colonized the Seven Hills by the banks of the Tiber. They called the whole district in which their cities were situated, Latium, and Jupiter Latiaris was the presiding deity of the Federation. His Olympus was on the Mons Albanus, popularly called at the present day Monte Cavo. It is the Latin "Mountain of the Gods," and from its summit a glorious view is to be descried. On a clear sunny day it is sometimes possible to see distant Corsica in the glittering sea. All around us lie the localities of the ancient Latin Confederation, whose "Rütli" may be found in the waving groves of Marino near the sweet waters of the Ferentina. Near Ariccia, close to the lovely little Lake of Nemi, was worshipped the moon-goddess Diana Nemorensis, who yet on summer nights contemplates her own fair image in the waters of the lake, called, as we have said above, Speculum Dianæ, or Diana's Mirror. Yonder stands the Arx, the citadel of the old Confederation, now called Rocca di Papa.

Amongst the other Latin towns are Ardea, many-watered, richly wooded; more inland, Tusculum, founded by the son of Ulysses and Circe; further westward the proud Præneste (Palestrina), ancient city of the oracle; on the *Via Prænestina* Gabii; and on the soft, vine-covered Sabine hills, the beauteous Tibur (the modern Tivoli), with her silver girdle of waterfalls, and evergreen groves where the prophetic nymph Albunea wandered by the Anio's banks. Here was the sacred wood of the founder of Tibur, the holy Tiburnus; and here the most ancient rites of Hercules were celebrated. But Lavinium

ROMAN FORUM.

is the real holy place and unique symbol of the Latin Confederation. Alba Longa was for some time its chief town; but after Rome was founded and was growing ever mightier under the rule of the Tarquins, great Jupiter descended from the Capitoline hill of Alba Longa, and emigrating across the plain, enthroned himself upon the Roman Capitol, where a splendid temple was built and dedicated to him; and so the earlier shrine fell into neglect. The Romans and the Latins continued for some time to be distinguished from each other as separate peoples: but only as one sees two rivers that have flowed together keep each for awhile his own hue and current, until at length the mightier of the two absorbs the lesser, and they are mingled into one homogeneous stream. The elder stream of the Latin race was soon lost in the great ocean of Rome. And thus it comes to pass that in the twilight of myth and legend the Latin and Roman histories are constantly entwined with one another, like two laurel-stems springing from one root.

The ancient legendary story of Rome meets us in various enchanting aspects throughout the limits of Latium. It murmurs in the white-foaming waves of the sea that break in their monotonous rhythm upon the desolate sandy shore; it sighs in the shuddering pine trees standing like grave sentinels to guard the coast; it whispers among the reeds of the Anio and the Tiber; its breath rises in the mist upon the sultry Campagna; the she-wolf lurks in the rocky caverns overgrown with ivy—faithful companion of the legend always,—and with prickly bramble bushes; in sunny woodland glades, gay with golden gorse, and draped with the graceful wild vine, the bird of Mars, the party-coloured woodpecker taps and hammers his ancient uncomprehended oracles; soft south winds blow from the sea and lisp melodious Grecian names into the listening ear. And the air and the odours, the movement of the breeze, the murmur of the leaves, and the solitude of the forest, take prisoner our soul, twine around it the fascinations of a fairy tale, carry it far away upon the wings of a dream,—far, far away from modern times and people, into the old enchanted realm that we loved in our boyhood, ignorant and innocent of keen-edged criticism!

The land is empty and barren; its coasts are sandy, or covered with thorns and dwarf myrtle shrubs. Dark woods clothe the inner country. A rude race dwells in its caverns and rocky clefts:

"*Gensque virum truncis et duro robore nata.*"

They know neither restraint nor culture, but roam aimless and lawless through the woods, nourishing themselves on bitter acorns and the raw flesh of animals killed in the chase. But a better time, a golden time, was to come.

Jupiter had thrust out his father Saturn from the celestial heights. The latter, wandering in search of an asylum, seeks refuge in this poor earth among the unhappy sons of men. The old god lands upon the desolate shores of Italy, and hides himself timidly amidst the recesses of her mountains; and names the district Latium: the land of concealment. But he could not live inactive, and the Golden Age began on earth. The blessed sickle began its reign; the exiled god taught the wandering tribes to cultivate fruit trees and the vine; gathered them together within walled towns upon the hills even as far as to the river Liris; and was, in a word, their Saviour. The wretched and care-laden found peace with him. There was neither service nor slavery; but all enjoyed cheerful peace and happy liberty. Saturn is not a king; he is the pious father of the shepherds. In the end he disappears in a cloud. His son, the first king of the law-abiding people, is Picus,—the mysteriously prophetic woodpecker, the king of the woods. From him descends Faunus, who loves the charming nymph Marica. Marica dwells amid the forests beside the waters of the Liris, and is a grand-daughter of Circe and the Sun. From her divine blood and that of Faunus, springs Latinus, who, proud of such ancestry, wears the glittering diadem.

This Latinus gives his name to the Latin nation. His people lifts itself more and more out of the darkness of the tangled woods, into higher, clearer paths; but its sacred trees, its consecrated groves, bear witness that it retains some memory of its Olympian ancestry. Thus, Laurentum is built around a sacred laurel tree, and King Picus, changed into the mysterious woodpecker, utters oracles in the Laurentian woods. The manners of the people are pious and simple; and the daughter of Latinus, Lavinia, grows up a pious and simple princess, amid these solitudes, of an age to be a happy bride.

About this time it comes to pass that Æneas, tossed hither and thither by winds and waves, approaches the Latin coast with his high-beaked Grecian galleys. In the golden light of morning he beholds before him a great dark wood, between whose tree-

roots flows a broad, swift stream, turbid and yellow with sand from the distant hills. Thick reeds nearly choke up the entrance to it, and many birds flutter around it, cheering

WELL NEAR ARICCIA.

with their songs the home-sick hearts of the Greeks. This river is the Tiber, and on its banks Æneas lands. He and the other chiefs of the wandering band pitch their tents under the shadow of the oaks at the forest's edge, and prepare their meal. But the food is scant; and at length they are impelled to eat up the flat loaves which have served them for table and platter. But in this very circumstance Æneas sees the fulfilment of a prophecy of his father, Anchises, which has hitherto appeared incredible to him:

> When, oh my son, in a strange and foreign country
> Hunger shall force thee to eat the board as well as the viands,
> Then, after weary toil, expect thou to found a dwelling.
> Draw the lines with thine hand, and plan out, thyself, the entrenchments.

Æneas blesses his true Trojan Penates, and sends a hundred youths, their brows bound with the olive branch of Minerva, to the royal dwelling of Latinus to beg leave to make a permanent settlement in his land. But in the night a new prophecy is revealed to him.

SANTA CROCE IN GERUSALEMME, AND NERO'S AQUEDUCT.

He has fallen asleep, troubled with many cares, lulled by the murmur of the stream. The waters part, and between the poplar trees that line the river banks uprises the god, and comforts him with a promise; "Take this as a token: where thou shalt find the wild sow of the woods, lying beneath an oak with her thirty young ones, there, in that spot, be the place of thy settlement." Next morning brings the fulfilment of the token, but it brings also the disturbing tidings that Turnus, the mighty Turnus, the bridegroom chosen for her child by Lavinia's mother, learned in magic lore, is in arms against Æneas and his companions. In his anxiety Æneas seeks for allies. Travelling along the banks of the river about mid-day, he espies under the flaming sunshine, seven wooded hills, and on the summit of one of them a castle with towers and turrets. The houses round about are poor and humble. Here reigns Evander, who receives his high guest with royal honours, gives him to eat and to drink, and promises him his help. He wanders with Æneas and his companions along the steep paths, along the hills all overgrown with shrubs, and in the midst of cheerful converse, shows him the "traces of man's disposing hand" amidst the thicket;— the remnant of a past time.

There, where the masses of rock are wildly strewn about, and where furze and thorns grow rankly, in that rocky dwelling once lived the hideous Cacus, whom Hercules slew in his divine wrath. Here is the Porta Carmentalis, built in honour of the prophetess mother of the king; there the gloomy woods of the Palatine. This wood-grown, water-dripping cave is the Lupercal, dedicated to the Lycæan Pan; yonder is the Tarpeian Rock. He tells of the Capitol, surrounded by an impenetrable thicket; Jupiter dwells there, and many of the country folk have seen him standing amid the trees and swinging the dark Ægis in his hands to call down awful tempests. Up aloft there rises the Janiculus, and there Saturnia! Fallen masonry, grey fragments of old time, tell of the days of Janus and of Saturn.

Fair white herds of cattle graze in the meadows, and sun-browned herdsmen stand

PORTA FURBA, IN THE ROMAN CAMPAGNA.

near them leaning on their staves. The old king leads his guest past them into the shelter of his hospitable roof.

The gods give him aid, and, though the conflict is fierce and furious, Turnus and his unwilling ally Latinus, are conquered. Æneas makes a treaty with Latinus, weds the fair Lavinia, and founds and fortifies the holy city of Lavinium. But at length Æneas is removed from this changeful life, and Lavinia, fearing her husband's son Ascanius, flies to Tyrrheus. Tyrrheus, the faithful servant of the royal house, dwells deep amid the woods, and watches over flocks and herds. Here stands his rude hut guarded by huge dogs, and the wild woodland folks come hither with their children to play and sport, whilst the axe of the wood-cutter, felling the knotty oak, awakes the echoes of the mountains. In this forest solitude Silvius sees the light; and is therefore the "wood-born" son once promised to Æneas. He is bred up in the forest, and in time comes to rule over the town of Alba Longa, sharing his throne with Julus, the son of Ascanius.

Then ruler follows ruler. In the daring Romulus Silvius the old hereditary Titan nature awakes again. He defies the gods, and strives to equal them, dreaming how to obtain mastery over the lightning and the thunder-bolt, so as to make them obedient in his hands; until at length indignant Jupiter darts an angry flash and destroys the royal rebel and Titan together with his stronghold. At the same time the Lake of Albano rose and swelled until it covered with its silent waters the proud castle whose Cyclopean walls the legend says may still be discerned beneath the lake on moonlit nights.

After him follows the good Aventinus whose tomb gave the name to the hill near the Palatine; and then come Procas and his two sons, the virtuous Numitor, and the wicked Amulius. Numitor's daughter is the beautiful Rhea Silvia, an Albanese vestal. Silvia goes down from the holy temple of Vesta one evening to fetch pure water from the spring. The shadows are already dark beneath the trees. All is silent and still. The

CIVITA LAVIGNA.

sun sets, and the twilight rapidly descends from the mountains, whilst an evening breeze goes shuddering through the foliage. Suddenly, in the path of the girl returning homeward, a wolf appears and frightens her into taking refuge in a neighbouring cavern. Here the god Mars is awaiting her and compels her to his embrace. The god comforts the weeping Rhea Silvia by promising her immortality for herself and her children, but the vestal is terror-stricken, for she knows that for her—a sacred priestess of Vesta,— love means death. When the birth-hour of the twins arrives, the holy fire in the temple goes out, the altar of the goddess quakes, and her image angrily hides its countenance. Thus Silvia's fault becomes known to Amulius, who without hesitation condemns mother and offspring to death in the river Anio. The god of the stream receives the sinking princess in his arms, and makes her his consort. Meanwhile the two children, exposed in a wooden shield, are borne on and on by friendly currents towards the sea. The Anio gives them to the Tiber, and the latter—whose waters are overflowing at the time,— carries them into a quiet haven amid reeds and foliage between hills. A wild fig tree growing at the foot of the Palatine spreads out its roots compassionately, and holds fast the frail bark that bears the children of the god. Then the waters subside from the shore and leave the weeping infants among the roots of the fig tree. A she-wolf, whose young ones have been taken from her, hears their plaintive cry, and hastens to carry the forlorn babes into the neighbouring cavern of the Lycæan Pan. Here she tends them and suckles them, and lays them on a bed of leaves and moss. The sacred woodpecker, their father's bird, the magpie and plover, famous in auguries, fly to them with fruits and sweet berries, and singing birds flutter round the mouth of the cavern. This crowd of feathered creatures attracts the attention of Faustulus, the guardian of the king's herds, as he passes

WELL BENEATH OLIVE TREES NEAR TIVOLI.

by that way, and hastening to the cave he is astounded by the strange spectacle of the two babies sucking the she-wolf. He takes them home with him to his humble straw-built hut on the Palatine Hill. His wife receives the little ones, and is a faithful foster mother to them, and so they grow up strong and healthy amongst the twelve sons of Acca Larentia. Early accustomed to deeds of daring and the use of arms, they hold their own and defend their rights against man and beast,—against robbers, or the fierce creatures of the forest. And sometimes, with a foretaste of the true Roman nature, they make might do duty for right. At other times they lead the life of their supposed parents, watch the herds and flocks, cultivate the soil with the gifts of Ceres, and make offerings in brotherly unity to the good gods, with wreaths of wheat-ears bound with white ribands on their brows. The followers of Romulus are called Quinctilii, the friends of Remus Fabii.

Then arise dissensions between these and the herdsmen of Numitor and Amulius; and at the harvest festival of the Dea Dia, the hostile neighbours fall upon Remus from an ambush, seize him, and carry him to Alba to Amulius. The bold Romulus calls his followers and friends around him, hastens to Alba and kills Amulius, whom he does not know to be his mother's slayer. Numitor, reinstated in his rights, assigns to the im-

CASCADES AT TIVOLI.

petuous youths a tract of ground beside the Tiber, there to found a permanent abiding place. But two hills appear to offer equal advantages for the building of a city, and the choice of one or the other of them gives rise to a fierce conflict between the brothers, until fratricide terminates the dispute, and the city is named Roma!

OLD TREES IN THE VILLA D'ESTE.

Romulus, gazing with his eagle glance from the towers of his Rome, looked through the purple veils of sunset towards a great time, and a golden future: saw the turret-crowned Rome clad in the Imperial toga, and borne aloft upon the car of victory.

> "Blest in her Godlike sons, embracing a hundred descendants;
> Celestial citizens all, and dwellers on heights Olympian!"

And so Rome grew—grew—grew.

Centuries have flown past with sounding pinions. Their mighty wings have overthrown temples, walls, the city, and the throne. The spirit of Old Legend sits half hidden in a grey veil, timid and silent, amidst the ruins of the Palatine Hill, and bows her face on to her knees. The ivy creeps noiselessly around her, and the pine trees sigh to her in the south wind.

Centuries have flown past, and we of this modern generation stand and gaze among the ruins. Our wandering feet stumble amid the fragments of a great past, and Fancy endeavours with child-like hands to reconstruct from fallen pillars, crumbling marbles, and blackened masonry, the ancient Rome, the seat of all the gods. We walk as strangers along the paths of Legend and History, and guess at bygone glories.

This is the Palatine. Yonder, its course marked by thick-growing reeds, the Tiber still flows. Houses and ruins are crowded together in the valleys and on the heights. The mighty dome of St. Peter's dominates the city with Christian serenity; and it, too, is growing old. This is the Palatine; and above there, on yon smiling sunny eminence, is the *Auguratorium* from whence Romulus spied the prophetic vultures. The place is tranquil, and one in which to interrogate Nature, and enquire into her holy secrets. But she remains mysteriously silent; no breeze moves the dark branches of the ilex; the flowers are motionless; bright lizards marked with strange hieroglyphs lie upon the broken marbles; the heavens are deeply blue, but empty,—empty and void; no eagle, no dove will give an augury thence for evermore. All seems dead,—dead! Rome has fallen, and is falling slowly; she falls like the dying gladiator whose sword has dropped from his hand, and whose mouth is closed in silence. The proud head has not yet touched the earth, but it is bowing lower and lower towards the dust. Yes; all is dead! And the sorrowing Spirit of Legend nods a grim affirmative with her veiled head!

But the bright summer sun shines calmly over all this. The flowers rejoice, and the white butterflies flutter gaily above them. Nature is beautiful, and heeds not our regrets; she sends her Spring-time, and strews the graves with odorous roses, with violet and myrtle.

> "Thou smil'st on ruin and despair,
> Great, eternal Nature, fair
> As at the first creation!
> Thy calm eyes see everywhere
> Only renovation.
>
> "Whether to the troubled breast
> Thy smile bringeth pain or rest,
> That thou heedest never.
> Thou, in changeless beauty drest,
> Smil'st serenely ever."—H. LINGG.

Yes; fair is the sunshine, the sky, the atmosphere, of Rome! They refresh the heart and elevate the mind, transporting it far beyond these crumbling ruins, into the contemplation of the mighty Spirit of the universe. Rome is a great poem, of which we possess only the broken tablets and half-burned parchments in the ruins amid which

ROME FROM THE CONVENT GARDEN OF SANTA SABINA ON THE AVENTINE.

we tread on the Palatine. But we build up a whole world of thought out of these fragments, and rejoice in the depths of our soul when the mighty spirit of the past is revealed to us even though but in a transient glimpse. The hand of a god seems to touch our brow, and consecrate us to live in Eternity, and to retrace the course of long centuries in hours of wrapt and delicious contemplation. And this god dwells only in Rome. Feel him, acknowledge him, open thy heart to his influence, and thou shalt return to thy cold northern clime, changed and elevated, and initiated into the worship of the Eternally Beautiful!

The Palatine Hill is, more perhaps than any other spot in Rome, rich in historic charm, and is a delightful place in which to while away the silent hours of a summer midday. We descend from the Auguratorium to the edge of the steeply-sloping hill, all overgrown with rich southern vegetation. We see the locality of the steps of Cacus, and beneath us there, where ivy and clematis, blackthorn and wild roses, cluster amid tall, palm-like reeds,—there, where the air blows cool and moist, is the cave of the she-wolf, the Lupercal! There stood the sacred fig tree. Look to the left: here, under the oak trees in a thicket of brambles, once stood the humble hut of Faustulus, which was preserved and tended late into Imperial times. Guide posts bearing inscriptions mark the place. We will approach them unquestioningly; we will read them as credulously as children read a fairy tale, and dream undisturbed by criticism.

For the rest, as regards all the ruins and fragments recently brought to light, their "name is but sound and smoke." We will rejoice in what remains, and ask no questions. We mount the broad flight of steps to the height whereon a great temple once stood, and let our eyes wander beyond the peaceful waters of the Tiber, to the remotest distance of the Campagna:—to where the Tyrrhene Sea is glistening, and the horizon is a deep purple line. Then, turning away, we approach the neighbouring Aventine Hill, once covered with the traces of busy life, and bearing temples, tombs, and monuments dating from the remotest antiquity. Now it is silent and deserted; and out of all the past splendours there have arisen three Christian convents. The largest of these is called Santa Sabina, and it stands beneath the trees with the two lesser convents near it, like a pious mother leading her children to worship. This convent-church and its surroundings form a perfect picture; the tower, the roof, and white walls are admirably relieved against the green foliage, and one part of the building is half-hidden by pines, ilexes, and cypresses. It is surrounded by vineyards and cornfields, where on this heathen soil the materials for the Christian's sacred and mysterious sacrifice are growing.

We turn and seat ourselves upon the steps of the Academy, once brave with shining marbles, and enjoy, as did the old Romans, the soul-stirring verse of some classic writer. Before us lies the city in her wide extent, and as far as the hill of the Vatican stretches a pure deep-blue sky, whilst the sun's rays are tempered by the shadow of the tall, black, aromatic cypresses that lift their proud spires above the wall. This was a spot for assemblies of the noblest and most cultivated, and here the grand lines of Virgil seemed to take bodily shape and to be realized:

> " . . . . inclyta Roma
> Imperium terris, animos æquabit Olympo,
> Septemque una sibi muro circumdabit arces,
> Felix prole virum!"

Yes; splendid, glorious Rome, thou whose power was only limited by the limits of the world, whose daring knew no ruler under Heaven, whose Seven Hills were circled by one wall, rejoice, and be proud of thy heroic race! With what exaltation did that race once celebrate the day of the uniting of the Seven Hills! Fires rose from every height and filled the dwellings of the gods with the smoke of incense. What a beautiful festival was this of the Septimontium! But to-day we celebrate a yet nobler one: the festival of the *Venti Settembre*,—the 20th of September, the date on which this ancient seven-hilled city after long waiting and hope deferred, was placed as the noblest jewel in the royal diadem with its hundred pearls of Italian cities. Not only seven hills, but all mountains and valleys, from the distant Alps to the Adriatic, rejoice upon this day. The Present shines with a bright and wondrous light, and sky and sun, land and sea, seem to sympathise with its gladness.

Lo, there, an aged, venerable priest descends the temple steps; he unlooses the sacred fillet from his silver hair, and disappears with bowed head, and lingering step.

But on the Capitol is seen once more the purple-bordered toga, and it is worn by the King of Italy. No sacrifice smokes on the altars, but the shouts of the people ascend to the vault of Heaven. They shout and exult manfully, "*Evviva la Roma nuova!*" And high in the clear firmament shines a radiant star, "la Stella d'Italia!"

ROMAN GIRL.

IN THE VILLA BORGHESE.

THE ETERNAL CITY IN A MODERN TOGA.

> "Thou lead'st us back into the upper world,
> O spirit of this nineteenth century!
> Thou tellest of new races that arise,
> Of noble edifices springing up
> From ruin, and of holy temple-columns
> Built for eternal worship of the gods."—J. D. FALK.

HIS wonderful modern time of ours puffs and thunders along on his fire-horse over iron roads that cross the ancient Roman ways, on, across the bare, brown, uncultivated plain, past the antique milestones, towards the Eternal City. The rolling Campagna spreads to the right and the left of the railway like a petrified sea whose swelling waves have been suddenly arrested in their movement. The Tiber flowing between grey willows, lingers lazy and sullen far behind the flying train. A purple mist hangs over the horizon, and the heavens are as brass above us. Light and heat reign here, unchecked and untempered, with tremendous power. No sign appears to betoken that we are approaching the former mistress of the world. We dream ourselves back into the time of Evander, when only a wild population of herdsmen trod this plain, and the landscape lends itself completely to such dreamings. Now, as then, white herds of cattle roam over the brown hillocks, followed by a sunburnt herdsman mounted on a swift horse. He reins in his steed as he looks with a scowl after the train,—no friend, clearly, to modern "Progress;"—and then with a shout and a flourish of his long lance disappears in a whirl of dust across the Campagna. A herd of young horses stands down yonder by the water. The handsome beasts stare for an instant with raised heads at the steaming locomotive, and then fly like the wind from the river's brink over the parched plain. At every station you see the rural population of Latium, browned by the sun, or blanched by fever.

Onwards! Here on a hill stands an old ruined tower overgrown with ivy;—there is a miserable dwelling, smoke-blackened and windowless;—huge hayricks and wheat stacks; —melancholy remains of a long-ruined aqueduct;—long stretches of uncultivated land;— onwards, always onwards across the plain, and always the same pictures! The traveller stretches his head out of the carriage window and peers eagerly into the misty horizon: surely he must soon get a glimpse of the city! Ah, see yonder! Is it an illusion? Is it a cloud rising up from the sea?—for the sea lies over there. He looks more keenly. No; it is no illusion, it is in very truth the great dome of St. Peter's that he sees! There is Rome! His heart beats faster. There is Rome! He can no longer bear to remove his gaze from that direction. But the dome disappears, hidden by hills; it rises again to view, still apparently at the same distance; once more it sinks, and his feverish impatience must endure yet a long delay before the whole picture is fully revealed to the traveller out of its veil of mist. Yes; that is Rome, surrounded by softly-rounded hills covered with pine and cypress. White villas stand on the outskirts of the city, around which the grey wilderness of the Campagna flows, even to its very threshold.

With a piercing shriek from the steam-whistle, the train rattles into the new Roman railway-station, adorned with paintings typical of many of the chief Italian cities. There is a loud babel and confusion of many tongues all around, even as in the old Imperial days. No trace remains, truly, of many ancient peoples whose language was once wont to be heard here: the proud Syrian, the rude Sarmatian and Sicamber, the sun-ripened Ethiopian, the dignified Egyptian, and obsequious Greek,—all, all, have disappeared. But in their stead are the stalwart sons and fair daughters of the blond northern barbarians, whose strong forefathers did battle with the conquerors of the world, or rendered service as soldiers and sentinels,—a kind of antique Swiss Guard to antique Bourbons! Here they come in crowds, easily recognisable by the scarlet-bound volume of the well-known cicerone of Coblenz. There descends from the carriage, *nil admirari* in his eye, the proud Briton looking silently upon this world of ruins. His fair-haired wife is on his arm, and they are followed by a Junonian troop of daughters. Yonder a son of Gaul flits through the crowd, as lithe and sinuous as his own flexible tongue. But they all pass on unhindered. No threatening police officer of the all-powerful Sejanus enquires their name, their rank, or their business. Modern Rome keeps open doors, and the stranger wanders through the city as freely as the wind. The air has grown lighter here, and we seem to breathe more easily, we who remember the manifold obstructions and vexations of a tyrannous government which the traveller had perforce to suffer with patience in former days.

The whole town has grown airier, cheerfuller, and more habitable; but as to the imperial purple hem on her new toga,—that has yet to be sewn on by some tailor of the future! The town is, as yet, in a state of growth and transition. This is obvious the moment we pass out of the precincts of the railway station on to the wide piazza in front of it. The trees and plants in the newly laid out garden are in an embryonic condition, and the pavement consists more of good intentions than solid stone. It is difficult to say of the masses of cut and uncut stone piled up all around us, whether they have already served for old buildings, or are waiting to serve for new ones. To the right is a mass of

FOUNTAIN IN A ROMAN COURTYARD.

ruinous constructions:—the gigantic Baths of Diocletian, in which, and out of which, numerous modern churches, convents, houses and halls, have been built. And these latter again,—as though infected by the contact of ruin,—are already themselves almost ruinous; as may be seen by their dusky, dusty hue, their cracks and crevices, their blind windows unopened for many a long year, and their rotting doors. Here, as at the *Porta Viminalis*, Rome consisted solely and wholely of ruins but a few years ago:—ruins

SKOGIOLA DEL DIAVOLO IN THE ROMAN CAMPAGNA.

antique, mediæval, and modern! Nothing but ruins. And the population born and brought up amid these ruins let things perish as they would. In papal Rome no hand was stirred to repair the universal decay with hammer or mortar.

But in every corner of the city, in every courtyard, on every piazza, the fountains plashed with so sweet a lullaby, the three hundred and sixty-five churches offered so welcome a refuge where weary souls might sleep and dream, that in this atmosphere of secular slumber men were scarcely aware of the decay around them, and wandered like somnambulists amidst the ruins, leading an existence scarcely more animated than that of the ivy which covered them.

Then came a fresh breath of autumn, and one morning the cannons thundered at the gates of the city. Their sound overpowered the plash of the fountains, the bells of the churches, and the voices of the chanting monks. The smoke of the great guns entered in at the open doors of the temples, and was more powerful than the sensuous sweet odour of incense.

And the Roman awoke!

He awoke, rubbed his sleepy eyes, and perceived that he was dwelling amid ruins; he perceived that his paternal roof-tree was ready to fall on his head and crush him, and he aroused himself thoroughly. He addressed himself manfully to the task of preparing a new garment for the old city, and the time will soon come when the wealth of water and the superfluity of churches will cease to be the only distinguishing characteristics of Rome. In a few years Rome will stand on a level with the foremost European capitals. But as yet she has not reached that level;—a fact of which we may convince ourselves by our very first walk through the city. In the course of time the wilderness had invaded her

VILLA LANTE ON THE JANICULUM.

very streets, the waste landscape of the Campagna pressed close around her gates, like a swarm of beggars before the marble steps of a palace; so that the proud old patrician city with her palaces of counts and dukes, her villas of barons and cardinals, was absolutely in danger of becoming utterly ruralized, and of being over-run by rude shepherds and cattle-drivers. Had not the buffalo and the white ox long since been seen—growing bolder and more numerous day by day,—on the Forum, in the Capitol, desecrating the sacredest ruins? "Picturesque!" you say? Yes; picturesque enough, but scarcely in accordance with modern conceptions of the civilization of a great metropolis, such as Rome desired to appear before all eyes! Grass grew on every piazza, goats were pastured in front of the Lateran, and the lazy, dirty, insolent beggar of the Campagna encamped himself with wife and children wheresoever it seemed good to him. "Picturesque" also these street groups;—admirable compositions for the pencil of a sketching tourist, but—everything in its place! And such like vermin are not for a city about to don her modern holiday attire. Whosoever does not attend to the workman's cry:

"No more of slothful leisure! Hasten, quick,
Bring stones and lime, bring here the binding mortar!"

whosoever does not follow that behest, let him go hence, out of the city. Rome must and will be remodelled by the spirit of the times; her obsolete toga will be exchanged for the

costume of the Boulevards and the "West End." But never fear! She will still be
Rome, and her ruins will not be painted red, white, and green, but will keep their hoary
time-stained colour, such as we shall continue to see in numerous streets and alleys of the
town for many a year to come.

COURTSHIP.

Do but plunge into some quarter where the fresh air of the *Venti Settembre* has not
penetrated, and you will be unable to find any difference between Rome and the obscurest
little hole in the Volscian or Sabine Hills. It seems strange that artists should undertake inconvenient and costly journeys to those mountain places in order to bring home,
after months of labour, a sketch-book full of old doorways, crooked staircases, broken
window-arches, and other subjects stamped with the mark of destroying Time, when
they can have all that and more, still older, still more ruinous, and therefore still more

picturesque in the obscurer quarters of their own holy city, together with all the Volscian and Sabine smells into the bargain! Look as you walk, and wonder at the homes of industry amid the filthy narrow lanes of the metropolis. Gaze in astonishment at the black edifices with rusty iron gateways, whereof you are puzzled to know whether they have been splendid palaces or gloomy mediæval prisons. The foot stumbles over slippery and uneven pavements, the eye turns with disgust from dark window-holes draped with miserable rags hung out to dry, with a shudder you hasten past the cavernous-looking dwellings of the poor, past the *botteghe*,—the wretched shops,—where the people buys its food and drink. Surely all this is at least as "picturesque" as the pig-populated street-corners of Subiaco and Olevano! But let even these quarters be pulled down: let light and air make a triumphal and princely entry even here, nevertheless Rome will still be Rome,—beautiful, mighty, wonderful, *picturesque* Rome!

The ordinary traveller, who neither comprehends the greatness of the past nor can conceive of the future from that which he sees around him, is, for the most part, disappointed in Rome, and is enthusiastic only about St. Peter's, or the general view of the city as seen from a distance. But whoso has ears may *hear the city growing*. Whoso has eyes may see shining in the eyes of the Romans the promise of a sunny future; and above the prosaic odours of broccoli and maccaroni, you may scent the breath of a newly awakened Spring. But another breath floats above the city even now as it ever has done,—the sweet, soft atmosphere of philosophic repose, the ease of noble contemplation, the serious and attractive beauty of intellectual labour. For these no town in the world affords such opportunities as Rome. And the stranger who in Rome can follow the path of common frivolity, can stand idly amid this spectacle of life with his hands folded, or can use them only for trivial toying with some form of Art,—such a one deserves not to be in Rome at all. The silent past teaches us with the melancholy eloquence of its ruins to turn our eyes within; and no noisy diversions, no unworthy excitements need trouble our spirit. In these garden-houses into which no murmur of the tide of daily life can penetrate, where the winds from the Campagna whisper low, in whose courtyards clear fountains trickle softly,—in such places as these, dwells a peace which might be vainly sought for elsewhere throughout the world: a peace unknown in the remotest and most solitary island: a peace worthy of the gods!

Whoever wishes to devote himself to serious brain work, whoever desires to penetrate into the spirit of the Beautiful, or to live amidst the enchantments of a stupendous past, and bask in the magic light of history, whoever seeks happiness in the serene regions of intellect, should live in Rome. But even to those who have known sorrow in the cold dreary world, to those whom the dark waves of misfortune have nearly overwhelmed, Rome offers peace of mind, and consolation for woe and tears. For what is our love betrayed, our heart deceived, upon a soil whose very dust is the ashes of great nations? And what are our tear-drops compared with the torrents of blood shed in the gloomy night of Rome's decline and fall?

> "Behold the Pantheon, and think: in Rome
> The death of one man is of small account."

Aye, truly is it of small account! The soul learns here to comprehend the great afflictions and miseries of the world, and to forget her own pettier griefs. The sweet celestial-hued blossom of Lyric Poetry blooms not on this soil: around the ruins are twined the tendrils of the solemn passion-flower. This sombre historic colouring must for evermore belong to the city; *it* will not change with the changing banner that flaunts from the Castle of St. Angelo. Let the aspect of the modern city vary as it will, let them alter the transient adornments, as they once were wont to change the head-dress upon the

IN VILLA MASSIMO.

marble busts of Roman Empresses,—still, still the solemnly beautiful features must remain the same, immutable for ever!

The Rome of to-day is divided into two conflicting portions, as in a huge balance; one scale contains the Vatican, the other the Quirinal, and History stands like Nemesis holding the balance aloft in her mysterious hand. The scales waver and fluctuate this way and that; perhaps the iron sword of some modern Brennus may once more decide the question and turn the scale. *Væ victis!* But we will hope that civic virtues may prevail.

> O Rome, Rome, all too long hast thou been lying
> Low in the dust, a by-word, and a jeer!
> But now once more upon thy forehead clear,
> Gleams thine old crown, all enemies defying.
> Fair wert thou in thy woe; but weak as fair.
> Now is thy beauty joined with noble strength,
> And after patient suffering, lo, at length
> Thy tear-stained eye a cheerful beam doth wear,
> And now, down-swooping on thy sacred soil,
> Should some transalpine horde in arms assail thee
> Seeking to spoil thy harvest, 'twill recoil
> Met by stout hands and hearts that shall not fail thee;
> And Tiber's wave with alien blood shall flow,
> Ere thy bright sword of Freedom shall lie low!

The spirit of Antiquity and History—which here are one and the same,—has incorporated itself in this Roman People, and made of them, not merely the most handsome physically, but the most intellectually capable, and worthiest race of the Peninsula. The Roman People has comprehended the high responsibility laid upon the foremost city of Italy, and is thoroughly capable of fulfilling its task: the task, namely, of giving a good example, of taking the initiative, and of championing and maintaining the national dignity even with its blood if need be. And whoever unblushingly maintains that this people is degraded and corrupted to the core, speaks falsely, and is utterly devoid of insight into the popular life and sufferings. During long dark years of miserable misgovernment, the German People, also, had much to suffer, and to shed much blood and many tears; yet it retained its vitality, and awoke, when the time was ripe, to a new existence. But such sufferings as were endured by the Romans, who were stricken even unto the soul, the Germans have never experienced: and the fact that the former still live and live worthily, is a testimony that they too possess a robust vitality,—even more robust than that of the Germans. If hitherto they have deserved our pity, now, when in their suddenly acquired freedom they display so excellent a behaviour, they certainly merit our highest esteem.

> " Or che del proprio brando ti sei cinta,
> T' ammireranno le straniere genti
> Vincitrice del Mondo, e non più vinta!"

One leading characteristic is indelibly stamped upon this people: their deeply serious outlook upon the world. Rome never was a frivolous, wanton city, living gaily through the sunshiny days, and caring for nothing but merry-makings: and now she has somewhat the air of a convalescent looking hopefully towards the rosy spring-time, and feeling the healthful breeze of heaven dry the tears of pain on his cheek. This trait of seriousness is found in the lowest peasant of the Campagna; but the long centuries of barbarous misgovernment and ill-treatment have not been able to destroy the original, grand, and noble type of the race, and the antique traditions still live even among the lowest of the people, who all know something of the great ancestors whose pride they inherit. To the present day the Roman race is as distinct in form and type from its neighbours of Upper Italy, Tuscany, and Naples, as the population of some remote island, and shows the unmistakeable impress of the antique Romans. Their frames are powerful and well-knit,

PIAZZA MONTANARA, WITH THE THEATRE OF MARCELLUS

the head round, the eyes and hair black, the complexion slightly bronzed. Their limbs are in admirable proportion to the body, but their hands and feet are small and fine, denoting a high-bred race. The glance of the Roman is fiery, lively, and penetrating as his speech which he uses with agreeable and facile eloquence. Removed alike from obsequiousness or affectation, his manners are remarkably graceful. His carriage displays a certain solemnity, such as he might have worn when his Seven-Hilled City was mistress of the world. Is this air the result of the sombre surroundings amid which he has lived, or is it innate in him? Certainly the melancholy of the ruins around him may have contributed to it, since it powerfully impresses even the stranger who is a temporary sojourner in the city. With a mixture of this seriousness and a strong sense of self-esteem, the Roman contemplates all events from a high and dignified point of view; and with the same dignity he opened his gates to the new order of things and offered to its ambassadors a princely hospitality. Such feelings are not confined to the dwellings of cultivated citizens, they may be found beneath the open sky upon the waste Campagna, and the poor shepherd preserves an attitude of dignity even beneath the ragged folds of his miserable mantle.

CHURCHYARD AT MONTE SERRONE.

It was this sense of self-esteem which kept up the Romans during times of darkness, and preserved the main mass of the people sound, despite the deplorable education which was always endeavouring to chip the fine marble into paltry puppets. This self-esteem kept him from vain and weak complainings, restrained him from cowardly revenge, and taught him to despise death. Even to-day the *Quirites* know how to die as proudly and tranquilly as their forefathers, who ever looked Death manfully in the face. You may call it rude harshness, that the Romans of to-day, as those of old, are destitute of the amiable germanic sympathy with nature, that they are ready with the knife as their fathers with the sword, that they have little feeling for the sufferings of the brute creation:—but there is character in all this; more character than in the effeminate youths who turn pale if a pigeon has to be slaughtered, and break out into cowardly lamentations, if they feel the least pain. The Roman Republic cultivated and created this stern character, and through it old Rome grew strong and mighty and able to rule the nations: through it she may again become strong and powerful, when once the effect of the years during which this natural quality was forcibly repressed and perverted, shall somewhat have passed away. For between a Decius Mus rushing upon death for a noble cause, and the youth who sacrifices his life for an unworthy one, there is only the difference of education and aim.

The Roman women offer an equally fine picture. They are the direct opposite of a German Gretchen whose blond tresses are wound round a gentle dreamy little head, and whose blue eyes look even by day as though they were full of the soft glimmer of moonlight. The Roman woman typifies clear decision. She is the representative of serious and majestic womanhood. Her beauty is celebrated all over the world, and has no rival throughout the rest of Italy. The Milanese may be amiable, the Venetians graceful, the Florentines fascinating, the Neapolitans animated, but they none of them possess the antique calm and classic beauty of the Roman women, nor their high soul and strength of mind. It is possible that those who admire only the Greek style of beauty, and who identify the beautiful with the graceful, may contest the Roman woman's right to the palm of superiority; but the fact is that the Roman beauty differs from the Greek as much as the language and poetry of the two great ancient peoples differed from each other. The Roman female countenance displays none of the gentle softness, the lyric tenderness, the attractive loveliness of a Greek head; it is more firmly moulded, stronger, more epic. The Greek form of the girlish Venus has ripened on this soil, under the sun of Italy, into the fully developed woman behind whose broad brows lie, not merely love-dreams, but the consciousness of a certain spirit of sovereignty: the woman whose splendid frame and ample breast were framed to bear and suckle a Romulus and Remus. Those full round arms are able, not only to wind themselves in an affectionate embrace around her husband, but, if need be, to wield sword and lance, and avenge an injury without man's assistance, like the grand Camilla of Virgil. The Roman woman has never been a slave. In her house she rules royally, like the spouse of Ulysses, free and self-asserting. Her large beaming eyes have nothing of that soft appealing expression of timidity which seems to implore the protection of the stronger sex; her features are devoid of the sentimental tenderness which seems to invite love. When I have learned to understand the Roman Woman

" —— then first I understand the noble marbles."

Goethe's favourite Juno of the Villa Ludovisi, before which he stood in wrapt adoration so many a morning, has much of this grandeur, in the firm, goddess-like, enchanting mouth, the decided chin, the broad forehead, and the nostril slightly raised with a touch of disdain.

Goddess and woman at once, and both in the highest perfection;
Say, which is chiefly divine,—where reigns the woman supreme?
Feminine beauties attract and charm thee to warm admiration,
But, lo, the goddess prevails, and silent thou bendest in worship!

Fair-haired Roman women are very rare. But the wealth of black locks suits magnificently with the rich brown of their complexions mellowed by a southern sun, and with the pomegranate-flower red of their lips. Such liveliness as that of the Neapolitan women, and coquetry, are foreign to Roman female nature. These women move like queens, with fine broad-shouldered and broad-hipped figures, well-proportioned throats, and flexible waists. They do not bend, or wave from side to side as they walk, but glide

STELLA, A ROMAN MODEL.

along with sweeping draperies, like so many wandering goddesses. In them we find united,—like the seven hues in the rainbow,—the seven beauties of which the popular rhymes sing throughout Italy :

"Sette bellezze vuole aver la donna,
    Prima che bella si possa chiamare ;
Alta dev'esser senza la pianella,
    E bianca e rossa senza su' lisciare,

" Larga di spalla, e stretta in centurella,
    La bella bocca, e il bel nobil parlare.
Se poi si tira su le oscure trecce,
    Ecco la donna di sette bellezze!"
        Tigri, Canti popolari Toscani.

Which may be roughly but faithfully rendered thus :

A woman, to be truly beautiful,
Must have seven beauties which I now recite :
She must be tall of stature, and her skin
Must bloom with Nature's colouring, red and white.

The shoulders wide, the girdle small and thin ;
Her mouth, well-shaped, all hearers must delight
With noble speech. Now add thick raven tresses,
And all the seven beauties she possesses !

These physical attractions are accompanied by a dignified, gracious bearing ; and the "*bel nobil parlare*," the noble speech of the Roman women, is peculiarly fascinating. No one who has once felt the charm of this eloquence whose deep full tones and flowing vowels are as harmonious as fine music, can ever forget it. The Italians have a proverb which shows that they themselves consider their language to sound best in a Roman mouth : *Lingua toscana, in bocca romana!* And amidst all this dwells a noble soul, an aspiring mind, long repressed, but destined yet to soar high in the rosy light of the new dawn.

PEASANT OF THE CAMPAGNA.

Of course the possibilities of all these beauties, mental and physical, are only in a latent condition among the poor peasant-women of the Campagna, and the female population of the Trastevere (literally ' Beyond-Tiber,' the quarter of the city which lies on the same side of the river as the Castle of St. Angelo and St. Peter's) ; who seem like fine plants checked in their growth by unfavourable surrounding conditions. The rich high-born beauty blooms and flourishes like the flowers and shrubs in the luxuriant Roman gardens : the wretched peasant woman of the Campagna is poor, haggard, tanned by sun and weather. But *her* gait, too, is proud, *her* eyes also flame brightly ;—they flame, alas, with hunger and fever, two maladies hereditary in her blood ! There is character in her features : and even when her countenance shall be utterly withered and wrinkled, and discoloured by years, hard work, and weather, it will yet be full of character, though it be as ugly and hag-like as that of an old witch. The bluntness, or disagreeable sharpness, which age impresses upon the women of other European countries is not seen among them. They are all fit to serve as painters' models. And let it not be supposed that the gaily dressed, dark-eyed girls, and the sham shepherds with dishevelled locks, whom one sees in the Via Sistina, and on the steps of the Trinità de' Monti, or theatrically grouped in the neighbourhood of the painters' studios, are the only models worth looking at. Indeed the best, and most really beautiful, are not to be found among them. Roman girls are utterly devoid of sentimentality, and women of the Roman populace talk as familiarly of the latest tragical stabbing-case, as our women

ROMAN FLOWER-SELLER.

talk of the last new novel. And whenever a man has been killed they immediately take the part of the wretched assassin. There is nothing to be done for the dead man, but the other, interesting, much to be compassionated criminal who has had the 'misfortune' to kill somebody, he, indeed, may have need of help and sympathy. For the accursed *carabinieri* are after him, and he must not be let to fall into their hands. Wheresoever he goes and relates his bloody story, he is sure to meet with shelter. The women press round him full of pity and curiosity, the children stare on him as a hero, the men admire him, and help him as best they can. But even in this apparently cruel and barbarous trait there is a certain,—how shall I say?—a certain practical way of viewing life, which directed to proper ends might lead to good.

WOMAN OF TRASTEVERE.

For the rest, the people is really harmless and good-natured, and we state this opinion after a pretty close acquaintance with them. They never lose sight of what is naturally fitting and becoming. Everyone will readily acknowledge this who has watched them in their popular festivals, or at their games either in the city or outside the gates. The foreigner is never insulted, and all women, natives and strangers alike, enjoy a peculiar amount of consideration from the men, in word and deed. This is no light praise to give a people, and justifies, if there were nothing else, the highest hopes of its capacity for receiving education; for where nature has bestowed tact and good feeling, the task of education will be comparatively easy.

A tendency to satire is observable among the educated classes; and three figures, which have come to be absolutely popular characters, were for a long time the bearers and representatives of this satiric spirit. Every city has such a one: in Naples it is lu cuorpo de Napole, in Milan l'Uomo di Pietra, in Venice Sior Nioba, and in Rome Pasquino, Marforio, and the Abate Luigi. These are three decayed stone statues, of uncertain origin, which were for centuries as well known to the populace as the Apollo, the Capitoline Venus, and the Antinous are known to lovers of Art, and which served for satires of all sorts to be stuck on to. The streets where they stood were called after them, and you may still find the Via di Pasquino, the Via di Marforio, and the Vicolo dell' Abate Luigi. Pasquino originally promulgated the well-known *mot* "Quod non fecerunt Barbari, id fecerunt Barberini." This was levelled at Pope Urban the Eighth of the family of Barberini, who plundered the venerable monuments of Rome right and left in search of building materials, and was truly in his way more destructive than the barbarians.

On another occasion, when an insignificant priestling had been turned by a stroke of the magic-working Papal sceptre into a Cardinal, and his sister, a poor washerwoman, released from her tubs and soap-suds, Marforio one day appeared bedaubed with dirt from head to foot, and Pasquino enquired of him "Why are you so dirty, Marforio? And, what do I see? You have not even changed your shirt!" "Be quiet," answered Marforio. "Yesterday they made a princess of my washerwoman." When Gregory the Fourteenth had set off on a journey through the provinces, and left behind a government of regency composed of much-hated individuals, Pasquino asked Marforio: "Why are you weeping?" And Marforio answered: "How can you ask? Have we not lost our shepherd?" "Blockhead!" answers Pasquino, consolingly, "don't the dogs remain behind to look after the fold?"

SEMINARIST.

These, and a thousand similar utterances, serve to show the secret hatred of the then existing order of things, which must find vent in some way. It was impossible that it should do so by means of the press, for the one or two public journals that existed were mere pale shadows of newspapers; and no book which excited thought, or broached new ideas could hope to receive the "Nihil obstat" of the all-powerful Censor Theologus. Thus the freedom of the press had to take refuge on the marble breasts of the old statues of Pasquino and his friend Marforio. Now that is all changed. Thousands of printed leaves flutter about, political birds of every feather, satirical bats, and quarrelsome sparrows, fly around the windows of the Vatican, the exclusive mansions of sullen pride, and the dwellings of the cit. They croak, and screech, and pipe, and chirp, and flute, in the morning sky. Many a one stops his ears, but the sound penetrates even through his dreams. In these days the black robe of the priest is seldom seen amid the crowd; the carriage of a cardinal rarely rolls along the Corso (never with pomp and state), and a promenade on the Pincian Hill is no longer agreeable to high dignitaries. They used to take such pleasure in listening to the French military bands there,—and it is a year or two since the French have made music among the laurel trees of the Pincian!

Another circumstance has given a new and not unbecoming colour to the aspect of Rome: the increase, namely, of trade and commerce and civil industry. The Roman is not slothful by nature, but his all too huge calendar of festivals placed itself like a barrier as wide as a church door between him and his work, and accustomed him to spend his time with folded hands, or in some trivial game. The Piedmontese invaders have cut and curtailed the aforesaid calendar in all directions, and no one seems to long for its restoration to its former completeness. Labour has already put forth a hopeful blossom, and

ROMAN MODEL.

Rome may expect a rich harvest. But serious labour "suffers not the lyre's sound," endures not dance and song, and some day we shall see play wholly driven out by work, as the varied national costumes of Europe have been almost utterly superseded by French and English printed calicos. Our children's children will read wonderingly in some old book of travels that there once was a Carnival, horse-racing, and a Tombola in Rome, and that the games of *boccia* (bowls), *pallone* (a kind of tennis), quoits, and *mora*, and the national Saltarello, were rife here. But then they will be permitted to see, what we can only faintly guess at and imagine,—glorious old Rome in her Modern Toga.

AMONG THE RUINS.

"Deep is your sleep, ye centuries, how deep!
Departed years, how sombre is your night!
These columns, once with regal splendours dight,
Are prisoned now as in some dungeon keep,
Sharing the fate of stars whose light is gone.
Greatness dwells only in the soul, whom Fate,
Though it afflict, has made immortal. Great
Are human souls. Ye centuries, sleep on!"

H. Lingg.

STEP softly, oh traveller, for our walk leads us to a great graveyard; to the Roman burial place of classic art! The spot on which thou standest is sacred soil. Here, where once the Highest and Noblest was revealed visibly to the soul of man, we still feel the breath of the gods upon us, and can reconstruct a world of beauty by earnest contemplation. One thought grows clear as we gaze: how grand, how infinitely splendid and luminous, must this dead antique world have been in the fulness of its youth, when even the broken fragments of its tomb can so impress us! Still stands the goddess Roma on the Capitol, but she is the queen of a desert, the mistress over an empty kingdom. Proud columns, mighty walls and arches, towers and gateways, still surround her, but they are all shattered, fallen, broken, and blackened by fire, smoke, and blood. History, bent beneath the weight of thousands of years, sits in the Pantheon, and dreams of the divine sunset-light of the past, and stares with hollow eyes into the gloomy world of ruin. The terrible words of the prophet are realized here. Her glories are departed with the sound of her harps. Her bed is on ruins, and her covering is of ashes. "How art thou fallen, oh Lucifer, Son of the Morning!"

And yet,—if nothing remained of all the former splendours, save the Pantheon, the Apollo, and the Capitoline Venus, there would still be enough to enable us to conceive the ancient beauty, to reconstruct the city, and to people it with a god-like race. And had we nothing but the mountainous mass of the Coliseum, it would suffice to give us an idea of the vastness of that antique world. Greatness and beauty are stamped upon all the works of ancient Rome. And greatness and beauty harmoniously combined, are in truth the ideal of the human mind, ever striving at once upward and onward. This world once possessed them, but they have departed; we seek them painfully amid the wrecks of classic art, and all our prying and peering, all our modern criticising and burrowing, all our efforts, in a word, are like the wanderings of a sleep-walker. The gates of that golden house are closed against us cultured moderns; we wait and watch in the atrium, like door-keepers in a royal palace, who peep through the golden gratings to catch a glimpse of the gods enthroned within.

Evening has just extinguished the bright torch of the sun, and is descending on dream-like purple wings, from the glimmering heights into the streets of the city. With light, soft hand, he effaces the bright transient tints of day from palace and painting, from

COLISEUM, FROM THE PALATINE.

flower and tree, and darkens the last white gleams upon tower and cupola. Wherever he wings his flight, loud life is hushed. His companion, the moon, comes forth with soft

TEMPLE OF MINERVA IN THE FORUM OF NERVA.

illumination, and beneath her rays the scars of a thousand years are healed. The splintered column rises again proudly as of yore, and is linked to its solitary sisters by a silver chain of light; stone is joined to stone, and all the monuments live anew. The green moss, symptom of solemn age, becomes a golden decoration upon roof and cornice.

The moon rises higher, and the streets grow more silent: only the tireless fountains plash coolly through the night, filling their marble shells and basins. Moon-rays and star-rays play upon these waters; they creep over garden walls and mingle with the mysterious breath of flowers. All the city sleeps, and night is here. The night has glided on us so softly and so sweetly. What ails thee, oh soul? Why art thou so sad? A caged nightingale is singing yonder:—it is like the heart imprisoned in this mortal breast, that beats restlessly and would fain sing away its sorrows. Nothing stirs in the streets but the silent breeze of night. It blows white mystic clouds down from the moon to earth; they glide over the roofs and come nearer,—the purple hems of their long robes sweep majestically over the broad steps,—golden diadems glitter,—is it a dream? Behold them, the immortal gods, all assembled to take their places in the mighty temple dedicated to them. Here is the Pantheon, noblest dwelling of the gods, rising, itself almost god-like, out of the darkness. No longer sad and mournful as it appears in the bright light of day, like a forlorn stranger in the midst of a new, many-coloured, unknown world, but a giant full of majesty, a mythic hero, unwearied by his two thousand years' combat against the storms of barbarians, and the rigours of the hostile sky. Here dwells for evermore Jupiter Tonans; here stands his brazen altar, and from hence he rules over the world. He knits his dark brows, and the ambrosial locks fall over his royal forehead, mighty enough to bear all the crowns of the earth. That is the Jupiter of Otricoli; we know him well. But all the divinities approach:—Venus comes, ancestress of the Augustan race, and Mars girded for battle, and Apollo the protector and helper, with his sounding bow, Juno and Vesta, Ceres and Minerva—all, all are here. The gates of the Pantheon are opened wide, and Hebe, the ever youthful, marshals the silent Olympians to their golden chairs.

The moonlight, as it plays between the gigantic columns, weaves strange myths out of light and shadow. Ye gods, permit a mortal to approach!

> "Lo, what wondrous bliss vouchsafed to me, a mortal!
> Dream I? Or am I a guest in Jupiter's house ambrosial?
> Here I prostrate myself, here at thy knees, oh Father,
> Stretching forth suppliant hands. Jupiter Xenius, hear me!"—GOETHE.

The old gods have disappeared, but before they departed they gave into the hands of one of the later born of Time all their celestial grandeur, their beauty, their mystical charms, and the secret of Olympian poesy. And since they could not endow his perishable body with eternal life and youth, they granted them to his spirit manifested in the works of his hand, and, as a last boon, permitted the great master to sleep his long sleep within their temple. Raphael's bones repose in the niche by yonder chapel, and his tomb makes the Pantheon once more a place of pilgrimage for future generations.

Let us hence from the temple once more into the night. The nightingale is still singing, the fountains murmur in their sleep, the white clouds are floating away to the sea. We wander through the deserted streets, past sentinels, past the consecrated doors of many a church and chapel, past the flare of yellow street-lamps, past dark alleys, where a glimmering light shows us the image of the Madonna of many sorrows, with a handful of fresh flowers before it, through the deserted streets we wander—and suddenly find ourselves on the wide moonlit space of the Forum Romanum. A fresh odour of leaves, and grass, and flowers, is blown across it from the Campagna, but it is the damp cool odour of a graveyard. Do you seek the sarcophagus of ancient Rome? Behold it! Her head reposes on the Capitoline Hill, where the Dioscuri, and a brazen emperor high

FORUM ROMANUM.

on his horse, and two great lions, are keeping watch. Tall pillars stand like funeral torches around the bier, but the tapers are burnt out, and the noblest candelabra over-

SCENE IN THE RUINS OF THE TEMPLE OF VESPASIAN.

thrown. The marble cerements have been torn away, and the corpse lies all uncovered in its mouldering coffin. But at midnight life returns into its heart. The dead one stirs not, but she hears the great bell of St. Peter's sound in the silence. The Apostle is enthroned upon the Vatican hill, and his handmaidens, the Christian churches, decked with modern splendour, press around the graves of ancient Rome, whose temples are forlorn and dedicated to decay. The priests sing hymns to Mary in the choir, and chattering ciceroni come at every moment, telling the children of a northern clime old legends of Roman beauty, and prating of Roman art. Barbarians have seized on her heritage, broken open the casket, and scattered gold and marbles, beauty and wealth, abroad throughout the world, or placed them as remembrances of the great Mother in cold museums. Alas, poor Rome!

> "Another has won the sceptre,
> And thou art Queen no longer,
> And thine eye is dim and torpid,
> And thy lily-white arm is nerveless,
> And thy vengeance can never reach them,
> The blessèd Maiden Mother
> And her wondrous Son Divine."—HEINE.

Yonder stands the Coliseum. How grandly gloomy it is! A ruined mountain—a crater of the terrible burnt-out Roman volcano, split by the thunderbolts of Heaven—great enough to hold the night and all her terrors within it! It is like a broken sacrificial vase, once filled to the brim with blood of men and beasts, now overflowing with the scent of flowers, and lighted by the gentle moon, and the tender pitiful stars. But in its midst, thrust into the soil like a sword with its hilt uppermost, stands the Cross, symbol of conflict and of peace. All the huge lonely arena is consecrated to the passion of the greatest Conqueror of the world, the Crucified Jesus.

> "Thou hast vanquished, Galilean!"

We wander in shadow through dark vaults and corridors, and a cold shudder thrills us. Something seems to glide amid the blocks of stone, swift and noiseless—up above there how it sighs and whispers amid the tendrils of the sombre ivy, waving ghostlike to and fro! The stone benches are being filled; a pale silent crowd presses through the eighty arched portals:—the soldiers of the legions with rusty weapons, vestal virgins wrapped in mouldering veils, priests, senators, they all climb into their seats, and stretch their arms, and hastily arrange their garments, grey with the dust of centuries. From the sand of the arena—see, see!—they rise up slowly and painfully, wretched, haggard, hollow-eyed men, pale women, innocent little children—they drag themselves to the cross and embrace it with their arms, *"Morituri te salutant, O Christe!"*

Then the bell of St. Peter's sounds solemnly, and the bells of the other Christian churches respond to the sound. Their voices go trembling through the dark corridors of the Coliseum, and one great gleaming star shines high above the cross; it is the same that once stood above the humble house in Bethlehem, the star of Love Eternal. *Ave Maria!* The murmur of prayer is mingled with the sound of the bells; a troop of monks, the soldiers of modern Rome, advance to exorcise the ancient spectres. In fourteen chapels, dedicated to the sufferings of the Saviour and of His most faithful followers, the incense smokes, and the people kneel, scarcely understanding how much blood their Faith once cost in this place. They mutter their child-like prayers with child-like thoughtlessness; and the words of the preacher, telling how transient are earthly things, and how abiding the divine ones, echoes every Friday from the hoary walls.

Thus, at least, a Pope ordered it should be a hundred years ago; but now that too

A SERMON IN THE COLISEUM.

is over. Science has excavated the arena, inquiry has invaded all the vaults of the Coliseum, and the sermon is silent. But what matters this change? Greater changes still attract our gaze,—wondrous changes! The proud emperor who erected this mighty show-house for Rome had destroyed a city which was flourishing many a century before

THE PANTHEON.

Rome,—Jerusalem the Golden. He built the Coliseum, and it, too, was conquered and destroyed by Time and Christianity. And Christianity piled high into the heavens the modern Pantheon, a monument of imperishable faith for all Catholic nations of the earth! Yet the day will come when the gigantic dome of St. Peter's must fall in its turn; and later generations will wander amid its ruins, and listen to tales of its old splendour, and gather coloured fragments of marble from the rubbish. Then St. Peter's will be admired as the Coliseum of Christianity, wherein neither sword nor lance, but the spirit

of a world-subduing idea, did battle. And as the names of powerful Cæsars cling to
heathen ruins, so in the marbles of this edifice are engraved the proud and ineffaceable
traces of men who ruled here in Faith, and in whose hand the humble cross of Golgotha
grew mightier than the earth-compelling sword of Antique Rome.

By faith, and faith alone, men are able to accomplish great deeds, let it be in the

ARCH OF TITUS.

temple of Jerusalem or the Pantheon, in the church of St. Peter's or the cathedral of
Cologne. And our own times? Our times, too, fight with the sword of the Spirit, and
struggle on, hopeful of a glorious freedom. And our temples? We care not for temples,
but let us erect what we may, our Faith and cry shall be, " Room and Light for All !"

ST. PETER'S, FROM THE VILLA DORIA PAMFILI

PIOUS PILGRIMAGES AND PROFANE PROMENADES.

> "From peace to war the unstable nations turn,
> And carve their deeds on many a monument,
> So that the latter times their fame may learn,
> Reading these records as a testament.
> Fruits ripe, and rot, and crumble back to earth;
> Heroes march proudly past, and disappear;
> But blossom, growth, and fruit, and foliage sere,
> Are one in Life's great story,—Death and Birth."
>
> H. Linon.

IT is a dull, rainy, April day. Clouds of mist brood over the Tiber, and veil the towers of the churches, from whence no bell may sound to-day; for this is the day on which the Crucified Redeemer was laid in the tomb.

How dreary is Rome on such a rainy day! How dirty, and how dull! Nowhere is the filth more abundant, or the misery, forlornness, and lifelessness more strongly marked, than in that portion of the shore of the Tiber which lies between the bridge of Fabricius, opposite to the island, and the Pons Aurelius, opposite to Trastevere. This quarter of the city is low, and unprotected against the muddy waters; its streets are the narrowest, its houses the darkest, its dirt the most overpowering. Nevertheless it holds within its gloomy precincts the most ancient of all Rome's antiquities—one that has outlasted all changes, braved all deaths, and preserved its existence amid the fall of thrones, temples, and palaces, amid fire and slaughter, and beneath the yoke of the bitterest oppression and fanaticism; one that still walks among us like a living mummy, like Ahasuerus treading over graves and corpses, and smiling at death; one that will still live on, even when the proud dome of St. Peter's shall have fallen in ruin—the community of Roman Jews!

And here is the Ghetto. Yes, this quiet, obscure community is truly the most ancient of Rome's antiquities, older than the wall of Servius Tullius, and it is fitting that we visit it first.

As children, long before we made acquaintance with the heroes of Roman history, we had wandered beneath the palm-trees of Sichem, had journeyed from Jerusalem to Jericho, and had diligently learned the songs of the inspired singer, which he sang in the golden house at Jerusalem upon the psalter with ten strings. The God of Jacob was also our God, and his people had become our people, and their sufferings our sufferings. How deep are such early impressions! No wonder, then, that we still preserve an intense sympathy, nay more, an intense admiration, for this people. Where is another race to be found, where another faith, which, oppressed with a thousand woes, amidst grief and lamentation, trodden down into the dust, cursed, and frequently almost destroyed, living in an eternal martyrdom, considered lower than the beasts of the field, deprived of wife and children and Fatherland, its possessions scattered to the winds, yet *never* relinquished hope? The hope of the promise sustained them; they wept and wept, but still they hoped! Years went by slowly and sadly, hundreds, thousands of years, and the consolation and the Messiah came not. Yet at every Paschal feast, on the vigil of the fourteenth day in the first moon, when the liberation from Egyptian bondage is celebrated, are heard from the lips of the father of the house the words, "Behold, this is the food which our fathers partook of in Egypt! Let everyone that hungers come and eat. Let everyone that sorrows come and share in our feast. This year we make the feast here, but next year we shall make it in the Land of Israel! This year we celebrate it as bondsmen, but next year as sons of freedom!"

A GROUP OF HOUSES IN THE GHETTO.

Thus sounded the comforting words of hope, whose arid buds have not yet been quickened by the Spring. The waves of the Tiber rolled on indifferently towards the sea; dirt and misery grew in the narrow alleys on the shore, watched narrowly by hate and covetousness; and still the "chosen people," the people of the inheritance, lived on. History, with shame upon her brow, has graven with a bloody stylus the story of the Jews upon the marble pillars of Rome. We can read it from the proud Arch of Titus to the Portico of Octavia, a story of shame and violence. What sufferings! What a Titanic struggle, in a silent resistance of mingled defiance and humility, against the kings and gods of the world! What an appallingly dreary stretch of road in the history of a nation's life lies between the Babylonian Captivity and the present time! We behold the wild

EVENING ON THE PINCIAN.

Antiochus Epiphanes erect an image of Jupiter Olympus in their holy temple, in audacious scorn of their God; what tears and anguish of heart! Then follow the days of Judas Maccabeus and the Jewish heroes, days full of noble striving, and resounding with the clash of swords; what blood and cruelty! Pompey vanquishes the holy city, and the Roman toga sweeps over the altar of Jehovah; Marcus Licinius plunders the temple with robber-like hands; and lastly comes the decisive period of the stern Titus. Jerusalem

ENTRANCE TO THE GHETTO.

falls, and Israel, homeless, but still not hopeless, is carried into exile upon Italian soil. During the triumphal procession in which Olympian paganism celebrated its victory, the last hope of Israel, the bold leader, Simon Bar-Cochba, was strangled in the Mamertine prison at the foot of the temple of Jupiter Capitolinus. And then the Arch of Titus was erected as an eternal shame and stigma on the vanquished. Later on there followed the oppressions of Trajan, Hadrian's fresh destruction of Jerusalem, and the subjugation and utter treading under foot of the Jews' native land: it is laid waste, and the people have no longer a permanent abiding place. After Constantine, a new and hydra-headed enemy attacks them; fanatical Christendom, which clothes them with the robe of the Pariah in jeering scorn, and brands the mark of Cain upon their brow. More terrible even than to be thrown to the beasts in the arena was exposure to the fury of the zeal-inflamed Christians, who raged with fire and sword against the homeless ones for centuries long, and attacked their trembling communities either by means of odious laws or utter lawlessness. And yet they lived on and on, full of hope, in the foul and ill-famed alleys of the Ghetto! With pathetic tenacity these outcasts, to whom no Heaven peopled with angels smiled consolation, clung to life. It is the same profound love of life which speaks from the shade of Achilles in the joyless Orcus :—

> "Rather in daily toil would I till the fields as a hireling,
> Poor, and needy, and stripped of heritage and possessions,
> Than rule over all the host of the shadowy dead, in Hades."

They have seen the temples totter, the pillars crack, and paganism fall; they have seen thrones overturned and sceptres broken; they have seen the Roman power decline, and Christianity,—the teaching of the Carpenter's Son,—grow up into a mighty church; they have seen a temple erected by this church greater, loftier, more magnificent, than the temple of Solomon;—and they have seen, too, how in the middle ages, the walls of this splendid temple were split and shaken by the hammer-strokes of a northern monk. They live, and will live!—Will the papacy offer so stubborn, so iron a resistance to the course of time, and the onward flight of the intellect?

A feeling of wonder overcomes us when we behold at this day the unmixed posterity of those Jews whom no persecutions have availed to extirpate;—a living page of Ancient History. We cannot but admire and sympathise with such indomitable strength amidst unspeakable sufferings. Verily I say unto you, such faith is only to be found in Israel, and their Jehovah is no vain imagination.

In this frame of mind we stand musingly in front of the remains of the Portico of Octavia, the proud sister of the Emperor. Here, eighteen hundred years ago, Titus and Vespasian offered up a prayer of thanksgiving previous to that triumphal procession in which the captive Jews were the principal figures. Here, at the present day, the foulest dirt of Rome seems to be concentrated. The Pescaria, the evil-smelling fish-market stands here close to the Ghetto, with its often overflowed, and muddy streets. Here, too, is the notorious church of St. Angelo, into which the Jews were driven to be "*converted*" by zealous monkish preachers, like beasts into the shambles. Here is the "Place of Tears,"—the Piazza del Pianto, reminding us of the words of the Prophet Jeremiah, "I stretch out mine arms and weep, I weep and mine eyes are filled with water, and there is none to comfort me." We wander through the Ghetto, and see the pale descendants of Abraham cowering before their dark dens of dwellings, bargaining and working. They deal in the antique shreds and fragments of a brilliant by-gone world, and patch with parti-coloured rags, the garments of the modern one. Deep-set, melancholy eyes look up at us. No one smiles. From a gloomy corner house comes the sound of a cracked guitar, and a nasal voice singing a monotonous, fragmentary song. We cannot hear the words, but we think involuntarily of the sorrowful verse of the psalmist : "By the waters of Babylon we sat down and wept, when we remembered thee, O Zion. As for our harps we hanged them up upon the trees that be therein."

Many generations have disappeared and been buried; and up yonder, in the Circus Maximus, which once contained an exultant crowd of a hundred and fifty thousand men, lies the Jewish burial-place. It is a solitary, cheerless spot. Here the muddy waters of the Marrana flow lazily between sighing reeds; and wretched stones overgrown with sun-browned weeds and grasses among which the cicala sings, show the places where the dead repose. But the hour of consolation has at length sounded, even in the Ghetto : United Italy reaches forth to them a humane hand, and offers them equal air and light, and equal laws, with her own sons. The Jews of to-day are free. Have they as yet accustomed themselves,—will they ever accustom themselves to the new light? Their eyes have grown weak and are dazzled by it, and they still hold a shielding hand over them.

> "When the Lord shall release the captives of Zion,
> Then shall we be as dreamers."

It requires some little trouble to discover the next oldest monument of the past which Rome has to show : the small remains of the fortress wall of Servius Tullius on the southern slope of the Aventine.

OLD JEWESS.

Not that they are, in truth, particularly well worth looking at : for we see only a fragment of hoary wall, grey with age, built of large square blocks of tufa, and overgrown with brambles and all manner of weeds and creeping plants. The direction of the wall may be traced by a continuous mound of rubbish, which divides the alleys of the dirty quarter of the Velabrum from the Tarpeian Rock. More interesting are the records of the old Priest-King who built it and reigned over it, and who may be compared in so many points with the first king of Italy in our own day. Servius Tullius was elected by a *plebiscitum*, by the will of the people, without regard to the customary formalities, to be the national king. With a strong hand and ripe experience he set about making thorough reforms in the constitution, and was the first who made patricians and plebeians into one united people. He was the darling of his people, who gave him the name of "*Fortunæ filius*," and attributed his constant good luck (always excepting his tragic end) to the favour of Fortune, who visited her protégé every night in the royal palace. The plebeians were admitted into the national assemblies, and mild and benevolent laws established the rights and duties of all the citizens. The blending of the Seven Hills into one whole, and the establishment of a common system of defence for all, were due to him ; and he was also fortunate in war. That was two thousand five hundred years ago. Exactly two thousand years after Servius Tullius, there sate in the villa among the vineyards above the wall of Servius, in the spot where the colossal statue of Minerva stands under the shadow of black cypress trees, another powerful man, who was preparing himself to bear the dignity of a Priest-King. This was the Cardinal Montalto, originally Felix Peretti, a poor herd-boy on the pastures of Montalto in the March of Ancona, who, as Pope Sixtus the Fifth, became one of the most powerful of all the wearers of the triple tiara. Gifted with an iron nature, a character of adamant, he imbibed from his contemplation of the ruins of past greatness, that spirit of insatiable ambition, that ruthless sternness, and that practical intelligence, which once distinguished ancient Rome, and which he manifested on every occasion when he saw an opportunity of glorifying God's Kingdom,—or his own. In this spirit he erected the mighty obelisk of Heliopolis upon the Piazza of St. Peter's, caused the vast dome of that Christian Pantheon to rise into the air, and created the aqueduct which he named after himself, "*Acqua Felice.*" He was resolved to make all things conduce to the glorification of Christianity over paganism, and over every classical tendency. For this reason he wished to destroy the fine tomb of Cecilia Metella on the Appian Way, and was only restrained from that barbarous act with infinite trouble; for this reason he wanted to cast the two most important representatives of pagan art,—the Laocoon, and the Apollo Belvedere,—out of the sacred halls of the Vatican.

On the same vine-covered slope stands a humble little church. It is called Santa Prisca, and according to the old Christian legend, is built on the site of the dwelling of Aquila and Priscilla, a married couple of Jewish race who were friends of the Apostles, and lived here, and followed the trade of carpet weaving. Paul found them on his travels in Corinth. According to the Acts of the Apostles, they were newly arrived there from Italy, because the Emperor Claudius had ordered all Jews to quit Rome. Paul laboured with them. Peter dwelt in their house during the period of his captivity in Rome, and baptized the converted Christian couple in the fountain of Faunus. Here, and everywhere in Rome and its neighbourhood, we meet with the legendary footsteps of St. Peter, and can trace them even to the gates of his cathedral. Even amidst the chill darkness of the Mamertine prison, hard by the Forum, sounds the name of the poor fisherman's son, Simon Peter. In this most horrible of all prisons Manlius was once confined, the adherents of Caius Gracchus, and the fellow conspirators of Catiline were strangled. Forty-three Ætolian princes, Jugurtha, the bold Numidian, Simon Bar-Cochba, the Jewish leader, were all put to death here. In these dungeons Sabinus was beheaded, and the all-powerful favourite of Tiberius, the handsome Sejanus, languished; blood flowed upon blood, and Despair dashed its head against the impenetrable walls and expired amid curses.

But look on this widely different picture: we see Peter, first of Martyrs, prepared for death and preparing others to meet it, announcing the Gospel of Love to a small company of his fellow prisoners. By the power of his faith, a silvery stream of water trickles out of the stone walls, and in it those who already stand on the threshold of death, bow their heads and are baptized into life eternal. The fragment of a pillar, a little altar, and a stone basin, remain as memorials of that day. We climb up again from the darkness into the light, overleap in thought the long space of eighteen hundred years, and raise our eyes from the depths in which the mustard-seed of the Gospel was planted, to the lofty cross that surmounts the Church of St. Peter.

"*Tutti convengon qui d'ogni paese!*"—DANTE.

We are upon the Piazza of St. Peter's. The colonnades of Bernini embrace the wide space like an angel's outspread wings, where the people may be gathered together as chickens beneath the wings of their mother. But all is still and silent; the vast piazza is

INTERIOR OF ST. PETER'S.

filled with the sunshine of an autumn afternoon, and the fountains plash sleepily as though in a dream. Groups of weary, dusty peasants who have made a pilgrimage hither from the Sabine, Volscian, or Hernician Hills, lie in picturesque groups upon the broad steps in front of the church. They have come, full of faith, to kiss the brazen toe of the Apostle within there. They bring their little children and their sick with them, hoping for comfort and healing from the hands of him who was once poor and barefoot, who wandered hither

THE CONFESSIONAL.

from the fisherman's hut by the far-away Lake of Genesareth, a beggar and an outcast, and to whose glory the most splendid temple of the earth has been erected. "*Tu es Petrus!*"

Here once stood the Gardens and the Circus of Nero, the blasphemer of Christ, who caused the martyred bodies of the Christians to be dipped in pitch, and to serve as torches to light his orgies. He deemed his power and his kingdom to be eternal, and looked on the wretched Christians as dust before the wind, as a fleeting shadow in the desert. How could these ascetics who despised death, and relinquished pleasure, be of any importance in the eyes of him who made it the study of his life to enjoy to the utmost every sensual delight, and to deny all higher love?

Peter comes to Rome borne on the wings of Truth, upheld by the power of an idea that reconciles the human with the divine, and dies a martyr's death in the Circus of Nero. But the seed has fallen on good soil, and springs up plentifully watered with blood. His body is laid by pious mothers and sisters,—with tears, but still in the hope of a joyful resurrection,—within the dark catacombs. Twenty-four years later, Saint Anaclete builds a small subterranean chapel on the spot of the Apostle's martyrdom. Later still, the body is removed from the catacombs by the care of the pious Emperor Constantine and his mother Helena, and above the sacred bones is raised a beautiful basilica, which the piety of those days hastens to adorn, in chapel, altars, roof, and pavement, with the richest ornaments of gold and silver, marble and mosaics. The Christian Empire is removed to Byzantium, and the old heathen glories of Rome sink day by day into deeper decay. Silence spreads over the City of the Seven Hills, the valley of the Tiber, and the deserted Campagna. And then amidst this forlorn solitude, no longer dazzled, no longer injured, by Imperial splendours, the Papacy slowly grew and grew. Soon it rose to a lofty height, draped itself in the sovereign purple, seized, together with the Keys of Heaven, upon the sword of Peter, and commanded the world! As, during the interval, the original magnificence of the shrine of St. Peter had been sadly dimmed, it came into the mind of one of these vice-regents of Heaven, to build a worthy temple to the Saint,—a temple which should stand through all time, and receive all the nations of the earth within its walls. Nicholas the Fifth was this Pope. He ordered that the ancient basilica in which Charlemagne had been crowned by Leo the Third should be destroyed. Then followed a hundred and thirty years, during which many great masters worked in faith, and not for show. During this time eight-and-twenty Popes succeeded each other on the throne of St. Peter. And, contemporaneously with the completion of the Reformation on the northern side of the Alps, Raphael, the great reformer of art, was working. What times those were!

Julius the Second and Leo the Tenth were the chief patrons, and Bramante, Raphael, and Michael Angelo, the chief architects of the edifice; but countless others with hand and head contributed to set aside the original design, and to dissipate its unity by their subsequent execution. Platen was certainly quite right in saying of St. Peter's:—

"Mighty masters designed me for earth's most glorious building ;
But soon 'neath bungling hands my noble form was distorted.
The Greeks did well, who erected no such colossal temples :
For the work that is spread over ages can never be truly harmonious."

One idea, however, is thoroughly and brilliantly expressed in this edifice,—the idea of the Papacy. Yes, the Papacy has expressed itself here with all its world-swaying pride. It is not Christianity in its sublime humility, it is not even Catholicism; both are buried under these huge masses of stone. No! the church of St. Peter's is a work like the Coliseum, like the gigantic Egyptian pyramids, sprung from a haughty spirit of ambition, and not from the wish, the will, the heart, of a believing and devout people. We cannot *pray* here, beneath this cold gilded vault: we cannot open our hearts to a Saviour who writes up in gold letters above the door of His Father's house, the proud words : "*Christus vinxit, Christus regnat, Christus imperat !*" A far different inscription should adorn *His* temple; and how much sweeter would it be to read there, "*Christus amat, Christus docet, Christus exaltat !*" We can pray in the poorest village church, wherever the soul, undisturbed by wonder, can lay itself humbly before the Highest. But here—there is wonder and nothing else! We admire, we measure, and compare, but those depths of the heart which ever keep some memories of our childish faith, the simple hymns of Christmas-tide, the joyful Easter chimes—these sacred depths of the heart remain unstirred. The solemn self-communings of the spirit, which transport even the most sceptical back for a time amidst the rosy paths of innocent childhood never visits us in Rome. The exaggeration of luxury drives out faith, or changes it into superstition.

> "In Rome, in Rome, in the holy town,
> They are singing and ringing loudly.
> Here comes the procession trailing on,
> And the Pope in the midst walks proudly.
>
> "'Tis the pious Pope Urban; on his brow
> The triple tiara he's wearing;
> His purple vestments amply flow,
> And Barons his train are bearing."—HEINE.

"My kingdom is not of this world," saith the Lord. And yet these men, aged for the most part, approaching the verge of the grave, sometimes trembling beneath the weight of years, clung fast to the earthly kingdom. They wrapped the imperial mantle around their feeble bodies, girded themselves for war and conflict, and the whole vast circle of this globe from sunrise to sunset—heaven and hell, death and the devil—the realms of darkness with purgatorial fires, and deliverance from them, ban and blessing—all the thunderbolts of Zeus to pierce the souls of the living as well as the departed, to strike at the head of the most distant rulers, and at their people—all this, and yet more, was grasped in one hand, the Pope's! He was to be as a god, even though he were the greatest of sinners. He was emperor of the world, even though he were the son of a beggar. The furies of war as well as the angels of peace were his obedient messengers, whom he sent forth with sword or olive-branch as it seemed good to him, without right or justice, amongst the nations cowering at his feet. He was a prince of this world, and his temple was his throne; but Christ dwells not in that house!

A walk through its pillared aisles lead us as along a "Via Appia of the Papacy," past many tombs of these rulers who preached the vanity of all the things of this world, and whose names call up associations little adapted to the sanctity of the place. All of them awaken historic interest, some of them artistic interest, but not one of them delights a thinking mind.

> "'Tis true, were the mind not free, then, perhaps, the idea were lofty,
> That a monarch of thought should rule supreme over every spirit."

Yonder, above the door of the chapel of the choir, stands a simple marble sarcophagus; it awaits the successor of the Pope who last died, and bears the name of the latter, being intended merely as a provisional resting-place for the body of the deceased until his successor also shall descend from the throne. A powerfully eloquent *Memento mori!* An appeal, too, for brotherly love!—But who has learned from it?

The tombs of the two Popes most distinguished for their intense love for, and zealous patronage of the Arts,—Julius the Second and Leo the Tenth,—are not amongst the dead in St. Peter's. The first, the bold champion of the unity of Italy, "the liberator of Italy from foreign and domestic tyrants," whose strong character sympathised with the titanic genius of Michael Angelo, and to whom we owe the foundation of the cathedral, the paintings in the Sistine Chapel, the Loggia of Bramante, the Stanze of Raphael, and many more things of beauty, lies in the church of San Pietro *ad Vincula*. Leo the Tenth is buried in the church of Santa Maria sopra Minerva. He was of the House of Medici, devoted to the worship of the beautiful, and loving Raphael above all artists, as the high priest of beauty. Leo's motto was, "Since God has given us the Papacy, let us enjoy it!" And he did enjoy it with every refinement of pleasure.

The eighteen years which elapsed between the accession of Julius to the death of Leo, contain whole centuries of progress in Italian art and culture; and indeed form the most brilliant epoch in its history. We would willingly give to these two patrons of art the most splendid tombs in St. Peter's, which, however, are occupied by comparatively insignificant pontiffs.

But it is not only Popes who rest here. Protestants may well contemplate musingly the tomb of Christina, the apostate daughter of Gustavus Adolphus, who died for the

CLAUDIAN ACQUEDUCT IN THE VILLA WOLKONSKY.

cause of the reformed faith ;—the heedless queen, and accomplished woman, of the seventeenth century. Germans will find food for thought in the bas-reliefs with which Urban the Eighth has adorned the monument to the Countess Matilda, on which they see one of their native sovereigns represented in the deepest humiliation, bare-foot, and clad in a penitential garment,—Canossa! Musicians may interest themselves in the tomb of Palestrina, the great reformer of music. Artists are delighted with the early effort of Michael Angelo's genius in front of the chapel near the entrance, which is named after the master's work, "la Pietà." It seems to have been sculptured by the chisel of a Greek who had embraced Christianity. The faithful can stoop to kiss the foot of the bronze statue of the Prince of the Apostles, worn and polished by the lips of generations of believers. And those who love the pomps of the Church should come here on the day on which the Papacy still displays all its mediæval splendour;—the holy festival of Easter. Those of a romantic temperament, whose heads are intoxicated by the fumes of the incense, and whose senses are transported by the splendours around them, may perhaps think of Tannhauser, how he appeared in the sacred edifice in the days of Urban the Eighth: they may recal their own perils from the demoniac power of earthly beauty, and exclaim:

"Like Tannhäuser, my ancestor,
Around my brows I'd twine
A thorny wreath, and wander forth
To Rome's immortal shrine.

ROME, FROM THE VILLA CORSINI.

> "There would I fall upon my knees,
> And humble prayers would falter,
> Imploring God to show me grace
> Before St. Peter's altar.
>
> "I'd kiss the Holy Father's foot,
> And pay him homage duly,
> And ask him if the withered twig
> Could ever blossom newly."
>
> *The New Tannhäuser.*

But the branch of Mother Church itself will grow dry and withered now that the waters of life no longer refresh it with a pure stream; and even as the arch of Titus commemorates the fall of the temple at Jerusalem and the triumph of paganism over Judaism,—even as the arch of Constantine commemorates the fall of the temples of Jupiter, and the triumph of Christianity over paganism, so, to-day, when the free spirit of the nineteenth century has prevailed over the old bondage, the Porta Pia* has become the triumphal arch of the new epoch, and St. Peter's is shaken to its foundations.

A real sense of careless enjoyment, the full and free pulse of life, is not to be felt in Rome. Easy gaiety does not belong to this atmosphere. We wander among tombs, we tread upon the resting places of the dead. Let us turn which way we will, our thoughts are inevitably diverted from the images of vigorous life. How different it is farther southward in Naples! There, no man thinks on death; amid the roses and vines of to-day, the tears and sorrows of yesterday are forgotten; there men live in the moving present, and leave the dead to bury the dead. In Rome, even when we would fain rejoice and make merry, it is in vain: the glasses do not clink, the wine does not sparkle, the very roses look pale;—they have been growing out of the ashes of broken urns!

Monte Testaccio is the paradise of the Roman populace. Here are vast cool cellars full of great casks of wine,—the finest wines of the Romagna, the delight of topers. In front of the cellar-doors spreads a sunny meadow with shady oaks and plane-trees scattered over it, under which benches and tables are placed, and these are always well-filled. For, notwithstanding that the city can boast of excellent water, and despite the tempting murmurs of the Fontana Trevi, your genuine Roman much prefers the poorest wine to the best water; and the wine here is excellent. On sunny summer days, and at the time of the ancient feasts of Bacchus, in the genial October, this "Prato del popolo Romano" resounds with song and dance, the loud voices of the players at *Mora* fill the air, and the red and white wine flows in streams. The wines of the Roman Campagna suffice to supply the citizens of the town, as well as the peasants of the neighbourhood. Genzano, Frascati, and Albano, but especially Genzano and Velletri, afford excellent vintages, and are, so to speak, casks which one may tap the whole year round. The vineyards on the hills of Albano receive the most diligent and careful cultivation from their owners, and the vine-dresser is a *persona grata* in every house. The Roman wines are not extraordinarily powerful, nor apt to overcome one suddenly; but they are agreeable, pleasant to drink, and soft to the palate. Besides the above-mentioned, there is the Montefiascone, which enjoys a distinguished reputation from of old. It grows upon the slopes of the hills which are mirrored in the lake of Bolsena, and is known under the legendary name of

---

* It was by a breach in the city wall, close to the Porta Pia, that the Italian troops of King Victor Emmanuel entered Rome on the 20th of September, 1870.—*Translator's note.*

Est-est. All connoisseurs in the noble liquor agree in declaring that the town takes its name, not from the people called the Fisconi, as the learned pretend, but from the flask, —*fiascone*,—which is its chief glory! And they cannot refuse a tribute of sympathy to the prelate Johannes Fugger (*of course*, a German!), who tarried under the verandahs of Montefiascone to sip this noble wine, and who sipped and sipped till he died! The wine of Orvieto is scarcely less excellent. It, as well as the former, is the product of a

VIA APPIA.

volcanic soil, and joins subterranean fire with the sunny perfumes of the upper world. The same may be said of the Aleatico, and of the *vino santo* of Ascoli.

But however great votaries of Bacchus the Romans may be, they voluntarily give up the palm for drinking powers to the fair-haired barbarians of the north. And although the German language is in general too rough and harsh for their tongues, yet they have learned one word from it which may be heard in every tavern to the further slopes of the hills; the word "*Trinken's Wein!*" Every Roman,—from the Pope down to the beggar who lurks and loiters near the tables of the jolly topers on Monte Testaccio,—understands "*Trinken's Wein!*" But the words have a Roman addition tacked on to them: —"*alla Tedesca!*" In the German fashion! The complete phrase is "*Trinken's Wein alla Tedesca!*" and it is to be met with even in a popular rhyme:—

" Sora Francesca !
Voglio venir alla cantina vostra
Per far un Trinken's Wein alla Tedesca."

A German poet who followed this invitation but too often, and whose poems "Flowers of Idleness, from Rome," were too often gathered on the summit of Monte Testaccio, is not far from us here. Up above there, where the dark cypresses peep over the wall, is the *Ghetto* of the Protestant dead;—not a churchyard, not a cemetery, for churchyard and cemetery are not permitted to heretics. In this burial ground, at the foot of an old pine tree, stands a broken pillar; the grave which it once adorned has become quite neglected and weed-grown, and beneath this pillar sleeps Friedrich Wilhelm Waiblinger, who died, aged only twenty-six years, on the seventeenth of January, 1830. Possessed of a poetic nature, which but too easily runs into wild scepticism and cynical enjoyment, he hastened his own death by dissipation. His poems, at least the greater part of them, are real pearls of German poetry, and are too little known. He understood Italian life better than any other, and has expressed better than any other the various fluctuating feelings to which it gives rise. How did his soul exult when he beheld visions of the past in the gold of sunset, the rosy light of the morning! When his gaze wandered over the laurel groves to the storied mountains and the shining sea! And as he sings:

"When newly wakened from a dream
By sound of many a jubilant voice,
I hear the clash of tambourines,
I hear the happy folk rejoice;
And when upon the sunny mead
Where golden grape-vines richly glow,
There dance, all crowned with rosy wreaths,
The loveliest women earth can show.

"Then would my panting spirit learn
How on their clear Olympian heights,
Careless of Fate, in youth eterne,
The gods enjoy supreme delights.
Then do I deem those only wise
Who reck not of the dark To-be,
Those only bless whose childlike eyes
The present hour alone can see."

Such was the philosophy of Waiblinger; and so we can scarcely sorrow over his grave, nor over the graves of any of those who have found a resting-place in this lovely spot. It seems, in truth, to be the sweetest spot on earth, a real Poets' Corner filled with the murmur of waving trees, the song of the nightingale, and the odour of flowers. Surely it must have seemed thus to the Ancients also, and Caius Cestius must have had a poetical nature, to have erected his pyramidal monument just on this spot. Besides Waiblinger and Cestius, however, others of far higher renown lie here close to the ivy-grown wall of Aurelian: the poets Shelley and Keats, Emil Braun the archæologist, the painters Reinhard and Elsasser, and two persons connected with one who loved Rome above everything :—Goethe. These persons are his son Julius Augustus Walter von Goethe, and the son of "Lotte," the Hanoverian Minister President L. Kestner. To Goethe himself the prayer which he made to the gods was not granted:

"Jupiter, let me dwell here! And lead me, O Hermes, hereafter
Onward past Cestius' tomb, lead me down gently to Orcus!"

Thus we are once more among the graves, and our way leads from the flower-grown "Protestant Ghetto," to the lonely Via Appia, where the crumbling ruins of antique tombs line our path on either hand. Yet we do not feel sad. These departed ones were fortunate, in that they lived in Rome's great days; and their last abiding place is so beautiful that the living might almost envy it. The Via Appia has been called the *regina viarum*, the queen of roads, and so it truly is; not merely on account of its majestic grandeur, but far more because of its landscape beauties. And then, what road inspires such thoughts and dreams as this one?

We leave Rome by the Porta Caprea; one association follows close on another all along the route. Here once was the grove and temple of the Muses. Here are the remains of the Arch of Drusus, the tombs of the Scipios, the few fragments of the temple of Mars, the tomb of Priscilla. Here, to the left down in the valley, once flourished the ancient grove of Egeria, so rich in legends, where Numia was wont to meet the nymph, and whither the Emperor Domitian once exiled the miserably poor Roman Jews, who formed a sort of gipsy settlement here. Onward! We come into the open country and feel the fresh scent of grass and herbs on the Campagna. Nature, ever cheerful, has long ago overpowered the odour of the tomb with flowers. We have arrived at the tomb of Cecilia Metella, that stands like a sentinel overlooking the Campagna, and from whence there is an enchanting view. The green plain stretches away to the Sabine hills; the aqueducts stride across it like cohorts in broken lines; here and there an isolated group of trees crowns some low mound, and yonder lies fair Tivoli in the sunshine. Numberless other localities may be seen and recognised from hence; mountain tops crowned with golden light rise into the blue sky; deep shadowy valleys open. Then comes a rain-cloud, and shifting streaks of colour glide over the plain. How it changes! Yonder the Albanian mountains look black as night, whilst the Sabine range is smiling in sunshine; now the ruined aqueducts show pale yellow on a dark background, and anon the background grows light, and the aqueducts take a deep colouring, whilst the windows of Albano and Frascati glitter in the sun.

Herds of cattle roam across the plain, followed by mounted herdsmen, hawks wheel in the clear air, and croaking ravens fly around the old stones of the massive tower-shaped tomb of Cecilia Metella. What a delicious stillness all around us! At our feet are marble monuments relieved against the green, or burial mounds overgrown with aromatic mint and myrtle bushes. Laurels shoot up amidst the fragments of fallen capitals, vases, and urns:—laurels growing, perhaps, on the grave of some classic poet. A cool breeze murmurs plaintively in the cypress-trees, and gaily painted butterflies, happy children of the sun, sport among their dark branches. Lizards sun themselves upon marbles covered with half defaced inscriptions, or slip through the chinks into coolness and shadow. This stone seat here was sacred to the *Diva Quies*, the kind goddess of rest, and peaceful withdrawal from the cares of life, and the weary bustle of the city. Here we will sit down, surrounded by whispering voices of the past, and re-people in imagination the now solitary Appian Way.

A cloud of dust arises before the city gate. We hear the sound of flutes and of women's voices singing the *nænia*, the mournful dirges for the dead. The body of the departed one is accompanied by his relatives draped in mourning garments, by his friends and fellow-citizens, and slaves. The dead man lies upon a bier, adorned with flowers, with his face upturned towards the sky, dressed in his richest robes, and surrounded by the last gifts of those who loved him,—wreaths, locks of hair, flowers, ribbons, images, and coins. The procession makes a halt: this mass of masonry is the *Ustrinum*; and here the funeral pile is heaped up, strewn with flowers and twined with ivy. The eyes of the corpse are opened once more, and it is prepared with sweet-smelling ointment and spices as if for a festival. Festal robes cover him, ornaments bedeck his arms and forehead,— and then the torch is set to the heaped-up pile, and the dirges, weeping, and lamentations resound again. Meanwhile, the ashes crumble and sink lower and lower, and a libation of wine extinguishes the last glowing embers. All that remains of the dead is gathered into

GAME OF MORA.

an urn; the living hasten to return to the city, and give the last greeting as they look back once more: "*Salve! Ave! Vale!*"

Upon a fragment of marble lying amongst the weeds, we can read the pious inscription: "*Ave, anima candida!*" On another: "*Terra tibi levis sit!*" Who wrote it? And for whom? The earth has been but too light above these dead; the wind carries it away mingled with their ashes, and scatters it in grey dust over the leaves of the laurel and thorn and wild rose bushes.

That height yonder, above the main road that leads to the Neapolitan provinces, is Monte Cavo, where the temple of the Latian Jupiter once stood. Those to whom a triumphal entry into the capital was not granted, might, nevertheless, celebrate their triumph on this mountain. Then the road echoed with the clash of weapons, and the shouts of soldiers and civilians. The glitter of armour and golden embroidery could be seen from afar off. Clouds of incense curled around the ivory chariot of the victor; and he himself was the most splendid of all in his *tunica palmata* and purple toga. He was preceded by the *Tubicines*—trumpeters blowing a warlike blast; by the bearers of the trophies, standards, and spoil won on the field; and the white sacrificial bull that had often bathed in the waters of the Clitumnus. After the chariot came the singers, the musicians, and the legions wearing wreaths of myrtle. The victor himself here wore only a crown of myrtle. The laurel-crown was denied to him, eagerly as he might desire it.

ON THE CAMPAGNA.

Ah, how many a one has eagerly desired and striven for the laurel in mighty Rome! Above all, one poet, whose grave we will now visit.

Flora, the flower-garlanded goddess, seems almost to have abandoned Rome since the destruction of her temples, so few are the gardens and flowers that bloom here.* If we would refresh ourselves with the perfume of flowers, and at the same time enjoy the fine panoramic view of Rome, we must ascend the slopes of either the Pincian Hill, or the Janiculum. The latter rises on the southern side of the Tiber; it was once the place of sacrifice to Janus, then the tumulus, or burial-mound of the holy Numa. Later still, it bore the luxurious gardens of Cæsar; now the convent of St. Onofrio stands on it, and within St. Onofrio there is a grave that holds beneath its marble the mortal remains of one whose fame lives immortal in the realm of genius,—Torquato Tasso.

We cross the Tiber, and proceed through the quarter of Trastevere, in whose dark and narrow streets mediæval Rome seems to have taken refuge from the glare and gas-light of modern Rome. We admire here and there a beautiful woman, clothed in the rags

* It is true that a passer-by will not see many flower-gardens in the city itself; such as there are being hidden behind stone walls. But the supply of flowers in Rome shows no falling off in the favour of the goddess Flora. Not even in Florence—the *Città de' Fiori*—are they more beautiful and abundant.—*Translator's note.*

of a beggar, but with the bearing of a queen, in whose eyes the beams of that sun which once shone on antique beauty are brightly reflected, and pass through the Via Lungara, which is, truly, remarkable for nothing but its length, to the heights of the Janiculum. A vigorous vegetation sprouts from every chink in the walls, and overspreads the gardens and all the place. Flowers give out their sweet smells everywhere. This is an advantage

CYPRESSES BY THE WELL OF MICHAEL ANGELO.

which the Janiculum enjoys over most of the other hills; the marble-dust of ruins is not favourable to flowers. They grow abundantly on the graves of the beloved dead, as if the loving thoughts buried with them rose again out of the tomb at every spring-time. But let us cast our eyes down from this blooming world of flowers on to the city, and behold ancient, mediæval, and modern Rome as in a picture. There are the storied hills, which seem to reach each other the hand, and encircle the city; there was the plain of Mars; there Tarquin's field traversed by the Flaminian Way; yonder lies St. Peter's and the great mass of the Vatican, and to the right and the left on the shores of the Tiber spreads the Rome of our own day, crowned with church towers, and dressed in a priestly garb. How the windows glitter in the sunshine, how the bells jangle, how the noise of the streets ascends to our ears, mingled with the ear-piercing trumpet notes of the gladiators of the Italian King as they march along! It is a sea; and one individual human life is but as a drop that falls into its depths; sometimes a tear-drop which grows into a shining pearl, precious and beautiful for all time. The convent of St. Onofrio once contained such a pearl.

Many thoughts arise in our minds as we stand before its portal. We recall the image of Charles the Fifth waiting before the door of the monastery of St. Just, having just withdrawn from an empire on which the sun never set, and resigned his proud crown and sceptre in humility and weariness of spirit. We seem to see the unhappy poet, sick in mind and body, flying from the heat of the day, abandoning a realm whose eternal possession, whose eternal sunshine the Muses had once bestowed on him, leaving everything behind in the city, in the world without there, and seeking no light save that of the torch reversed and soon to be extinguished. It was in the winter of 1594. The young spring was preparing to revisit the Seven Hills, just as Tasso sought refuge here, a weary pilgrim. Even so a child, tired with the glare and noise of day, seeks rest at twilight in his mother's bosom. How sultry had the poet's day been! How eager his race in the dusty arena of life! How his heart beat, how his cheek glowed! Love smiled down on him from its lofty balcony; the laurel of victory tempted his ambitious soul; fame beckoned him. "Give me to drink of thy cup," he cries, "thou mocking apparition! Thou risest higher! Thou disappearest!" He clutches at a shadowy robe,—love hides his face, and the laurel-crown is scattered to the winds.

> "Blessèd is he who dares the world disdain;
> For it is falser far than words can paint.
> It offers to our thirsty souls that faint,
> A chalice filled with bitter woe and pain."

Behind the convent, to the southward, stands the aged oak beneath which Tasso often sat gazing over the Campagna. Here, too, Saint Filippo Neri often preached in the open air, teaching Christian humility to his hearers, and warning them to despise self, and all the vanities of this world. The tree was injured by lightning many years ago; but the spot is consecrated for ever. We love to entwine memories and associations with trees, and although the way from hence is long to the body, it is but a short flight for the spirit from Tasso's oak to the cypresses of Michael Angelo beside his well in the cloister garden of Santa Maria degli Angeli. The two men were contemporaries.

Who does not know this most beautiful of the smaller churches of Rome, which has arisen at a stroke of Michael Angelo's magic wand, like an exquisite flower of architecture, from amidst the ruins of the Baths of Diocletian, built by bleeding Christian hands? Nowhere, perhaps, does the splendour of antiquity appear so striking as here; and later times have emulously endeavoured to surpass it by adorning the walls of the church with a rich treasure of pictures by the greatest masters. Salvator Rosa is buried here. A monastery is connected with the church, which monastery is inhabited by Carthusian monks. Their cells enclose a wide and handsome courtyard, surrounded by one hundred elegant columns of Travertine marble. Michael Angelo built this courtyard, and at the same time made the designs for the church, his latest work. He placed a well in the midst, and planted around it four cypress trees of which three are still existing. We will take the cypresses as symbols of the "four souls"[*] which dwelt in this wonderful genius,

[*] This expression was applied to Michael Angelo by a contemporary, who declared him to possess *four* souls; the soul of a sculptor, a painter, an architect, and a poet.—*Translator's note.*

and dedicate one to the painter of the Sixtine Chapel, the second to the sculptor of the Moses, the third to the architect of St. Peter's dome, and the fourth to his poetical works. The deepest silence formerly reigned here; and the brethren in their white robes used to sit beside the well and listen to the murmur of the dark, three-centuries-old cypress branches. But modern times have invaded even this spot; the jingle of spurs and the loud notes of the trumpet re-echo in the quiet cloister-cells; and where the white-cowled

WOOD AND GROTTO OF EGERIA IN THE CAMPAGNA.

monks were wont to sit, you may see the gay uniforms of a regiment of Lancers. And the old cypresses shake their heads wonderingly over the change!

Little that is new and little that is beautiful is created in these modern times; and we must content ourselves with admiring the ruins of the ancient times. Barracks, manufactories, Parliament houses, and railway stations, are the chief works of the present day. The present day, too, has shown itself to be very little conservative, and looks with indifference upon the fall of ancient splendours. There is the Villa Madama on Monte Mario, where Peace seems to have taken up her abode amongst green trees, and creeping plants, and tall reeds, and vines ;—well, the Villa Madama makes us sad when we look at it, for it is doomed to speedy destruction. And they are really things of beauty which are on the point of perishing here; masterpieces of painting. How much happier is the poet whose fame is daily renewed by the press! whilst the fame of the painter crumbles slowly with the crumbling plaster on a wall, and is faded by the sun, and washed away by the rain of Heaven. The glorious crowns of Raphael, Guilio Romano, and Giovanni da Udine, will lose some leaves by the fall of this Villa. No hand is stretched to save it.

The building is at this moment nothing but a huge poultry-house, where hundreds of cackling cocks and hens flutter about the visitor and strut up and down the great saloon, like so many enchanted Medicean or Bourbon princes and princesses! The cheerful old custodian of the place, who lives contentedly amidst weeds and manure-heaps, thinks he has done wonders in washing the once rosy faces of the exquisite cupids and nymphs in the hall above with a damp broom! Poor cupids and nymphs! They continue to smile, gracefully indeed, but they look sadly pale and sickly; and they cannot cling on to the roof, but every now and then they tumble down piecemeal among the "princes and princesses" below,—who immediately gobble them up, thinking no doubt that the whole arrangement is a special provision of Providence, who sends supplies of chalk and mortar for the better production of eggs, after this fashion. It is really melancholy to behold. A cyclops of Giulio Romano's above the door could not endure the spectacle any more, and has become entirely blind: only the pale shadow of his former self still lingers on a bit of wall green with damp. We pass out by the rickety wooden door, into the courtyard. Broken statues are lying among the nettles, and ferns are growing from the walls. The fountain in a niche drips out a scant supply of water from the trunk of an elephant, which is completely overgrown with grass and weeds; and a wild fig-tree is growing in the reservoir.

On the terrace, however, we can forget the decay of man's handiwork, and enjoy an enchanting view over the grand landscape. The eye ranges with delight over Monte Rotondo and Soracte, Palombara, Mentana, Monte Flavio, Monticelli, Tivoli, the heights of Subiaco and Olevano, as far as Frascati, Genzano, and Monte Cavo. Immediately at our feet the Tiber flows upon its winding course, and is here crossed by the Ponte Molle. This whole locality is inexhaustible in landscape beauties; and when you think you have seen everything, you have only to take ten steps in any direction to discover a new picture. The painters of former days, before there were railways in the land, did well to receive their comrades arriving from the north at the Ponte Molle, and to initiate them at once into the merits of Roman wine, and the secrets of Roman landscape. All that is over now. Art travels by railway now-a-days, wears a dress coat, and is no longer found sitting amongst the jovial topers of the Roman populace.

> "O Ponte Molle, thou bridge renowned,
> Where out of many a flask straw-bound,
> Full glorious draughts I've taken,
> O Ponte Molle, what ails me now
> That here I sit and sip so slow,
> And feel myself forsaken?"—H. SCHEFFEL.

And yet both wine and landscape are as golden and heart-delighting as of yore; and we may intoxicate ourselves with them as often as we will!

In the immediate neighbourhood is the favourite valley of Poussin, who came to Rome in 1624, a poor wandering painter. He was a treasure-finder, who knew how to discover and raise the most precious treasures of Nature with his magic wand. He and his friend Claude Lorraine were the great prophets of landscape painting, and they both knew how to breathe upon the canvas the sweet mysterious charm of Italian nature as no other has ever done; and so that when we see their pictures far from Rome, our soul seems to move its wings, longing to fly back to the sunny land of Art.

We are nerving ourselves for our departure from beloved Rome. We are bound for the Campagna and the mountains, and our hearts are heavy. But they will be heavier

FOUNTAIN VALLEY.

still when we shall be far away in the midst of a northern winter, or sultry, colourless summer. Therefore, oh spirit, drink thy fill of air and light and sunshine, of forms and images, and carry a rich store of memories over the mountains and their cloudy summits, to thy home! And if the gods will, thou mayest some day return hither, and feel once more the ever-new aspirations amidst the ever-young beauties.

We will speak our farewell greeting to the city from the Monte Pincio. There are

THE PONTE NOMENTANO.

no graves here; only a blooming, joyous life among flowers and music and ever-green foliage. Here the northern pine-tree mingles its branches with those of the palm; and here the melancholy longing of the north, is changed to deep contentment and serenity of soul. Here Time gives us minutes to which we would fain say: "Tarry awhile; ye are so fair!" We lean upon the balustrade and look down upon the amphitheatre-shaped space at our feet, the Piazza del Popolo. A gay throng of people is pressing out at the city gate, bound either for some noisy *osteria* or for the pleasant woodland shades of the Villa Borghese. As the mild evening approaches, busy life withdraws from the streets of the city over which twilight is already drawing her veil. As the sun sinks towards the sea, all the world hastens up hither to catch his last rays from beneath the trees of the Pincian, and to feast their eyes on the rosy glow of a southern sunset. Already the heights behind the Vatican are in deep shadow; already night is invading the villas beneath the pines yonder; but the mighty dome of St. Peter's still catches the light of Heaven from a thousand golden shafts; and the brightness shines down from the gilded cross on its summit like a message of peace and good-will. The world seems reconciled with Heaven in this hour of sunset light. Then, upon the farthest horizon towards the sea, a deep violet cloud arises from the wild Campagna, and folds itself about the hills, and floats above the sinking sun. A breeze of evening comes shuddering through the oaks and laurels, and blows the breath of flowers far and wide over the city. Cool fountains murmur amongst the garden-beds, and in the east, a clear sky suffused with a rosy flush reflected from the setting sun, makes a wondrous background for the sharp delicate outlines of cedar, pine, and palm-tree. Meanwhile the violet cloud has taken a deeper hue; but from the spot where the god of day sank to rest, the light of his diadem still rises, and touches the peaks of the mountains once more with mellow gold: then comes pale green:—then the shadows of the night. But there where all daylight is already dead, the dark red streaks still glow behind the Vatican, like the purple borders on an imperial toga :—a last farewell!

Night is here, and the lamps are being lighted down in the streets. Among the paths here on the Pincian, the stately forms of fair women move, silken dresses rustle, and the melody of the sweetest language on earth fills our ears. The city lies like a dark dream at our feet. Yes; that is Rome! So it looked and lived, long before we had beheld it even in longing fancy. That is the ideal city which we figured to ourselves from the pictures of poetry and history. That is the great arena on which, for the last two thousand years, a politico-religious-social drama of Humanity has been played. There is the old glorious theatre; and strange new dramas are being prepared behind the scenes. This is the sky which defied alike Nero's incendiary torch and the smoke of papal tapers, to dim its purity. To-morrow the same sun will rise, bright as the sun that dazzled Homer. This is the same perfumed air in which the victorious banners of the legions fluttered of old, and whose warm caresses have been fatal to so many monarchs. The kingdom of this world and the kingdom of the Cross were cradled in this little shadow-filled valley, watered by a lazy, inconsiderable stream. Both sovereignties are lost to Rome now :

> "For when thy sword had won and mastered all,
> Thou sank'st again with all in barbarous night.
> But thence arose anon new blood, new life ;
> In vain hast thou destroyed, in vain hast striven ;
> Only the echo of the clasking chains
> With which thou once didst blind and fetter Europe
> Lives in the speech of France, Spain, Italy !"

In this latter tongue, one of thy noblest ornaments, I give thee, beloved city, my farewell greeting. But it shall not be "*Felice notte!*" for thy long night has changed into clear and cheerful daylight. I wish thee "*Felice giorno! Felicissima eternità!*"

ON THE PINCIAN.

VIA APPIA.

A WORD ABOUT CICERONI.

 LETTER to the publisher, which the author desires to present to the public also.

NAPLES.

MY DEAR SIR,

"Ac ne me foliis ideo brevioribus ornes,
Quòd timui mutare modos, et carminis artem."—HORACE.

When I had the gratification of serving as a sort of cicerone to you through the most enchanting localities of this classic land, I could not help admiring you in my own mind as the very ideal of a traveller in Italy. Especially I admired your contemplative calmness, and the wise moderation with which you enjoyed the pleasures around you. Of course I speak here of such pleasures as are conveyed to the mind through the eye; the purest and most innocent of pleasures:—those bestowed by the beauties of landscape and of art. Without bewildering yourself amongst a labyrinth of details and particulars, you rather strove to obtain a harmonious conception of the whole,—to keep a complete image in your mind, so that on your return home you could analyse the component parts at your leisure, or people the beautiful scenes stored in your memory with the personages, details, and circumstances described in books of travel. You remember those unfortunates who, when the wide world lay steeped in sunshine before us, and whilst we were enjoying the exquisite sky, the sea, the perfume of orange-blossoms, were gazing on the far blue mountains, or giving ourselves up to the marble poem of some divine statue,—you remember, I say, those unfortunates, who, whilst we were thus enjoying existence, were seated on a bench in front of some Greek marble studying their 'Murray' or 'Baedecker' for hours together, or rushing about with perspiring faces in order to get through their allotted daily task before the bell should ring for the *table d'hôte*?

You were not as these; and, thank Heaven, there are thousands more who do not resemble them. And it was the thought of you and of other persons like you who understand how to enjoy travel, which I had chiefly in my mind in writing my share of our work, the portion concerning Rome. I did not wish to play the part of one of those tiresome and over-anxious guides who will not let one pass over a single fragment of a ruin or a single work of art: I did not wish to be either one of those painters who paint men and things with the utmost minuteness, even to a wart on the face or a fly on the wall! Nor yet a colourless photographer; nor yet—still less!—one of those pompous individuals who deliver lectures on art with an "*ex cathedrâ*" air, and spoil our pleasure by continual comparisons between what we have and what we have not, and contrive, with their dry talk, to take the bloom off all beauty.

Or, how should you like, on your first entrance into the little cabinet which contains the Capitoline Venus, to have to endure such a sermon as this: "This figure is very celebrated. If you observe, the conception of it is very similar to that of the Venus de' Medici in Florence; only, as you no doubt remember, the turn of the head is more coquettish in the latter."

Or, again, one of these official ciceroni, in describing the enchanting gardens of Sorrento, says: "The shape of the country bears a striking resemblance to that of the new-fashioned arm-chairs with high backs. The two promontories running out towards the sea are the two arms of the chair, nearly equal in height; and the seat is represented by the celebrated plain of Sorrento, perfumed with orange flowers!" &c. &c.

Now, my respected friend, I would not consent to play the part of such a cicerone as these are, for any sum that could be offered to me! I will consent to be a guide to grand and characteristic scenery, and to grand and characteristic works of man's hand; and as a painter, I have endeavoured to give a poetic tone to all my representations of such scenes and things. With these feelings I wrote my "Rome" and "Southern Italy," striving to teach my readers to see Art and Nature with an intelligent enjoyment, and leaving to each one to fill in minor details for themselves as they pleased; when all of a sudden your request to write one more complementary chapter comes on me like a thunder-clap. "For," you write to me, "our public will miss a great many things—a very great many things." And then you begin to enumerate: Sant' Angelo, the Vatican, the galleries, the papal gardens, the villas, the Lateran with its museum, the Catacombs, the Baths of Caracalla, the Scala Santa, San Paolo fuori le Mura, the Carnival, &c. &c. &c.; all things on which I have not touched. And you are so kind as only to mention twelve items; whilst, alas, I count on and on, and find with a shudder that at a rough estimation, and according to the best Roman guide-books, there are about two thousand famous, important, or at least interesting, objects to be seen between the *Valle dell' Inferno*, and the Porta San Sebastiano; a formidable list from A to Z: from the Academy of France, or the charming anemone-grown lawns of the Villa Doria Pamfili, to the Zeus of Otricoli. These things, many of which would require the observation and study of several days— nay, in some cases of several weeks—to understand them thoroughly, are all described in the famous little books, "How to see Rome in three days," and "Rome visited in eight days." These works have a great sale, just as those other philanthropic productions have, which promise to make you "A perfect Englishman in twelve hours."

AFTER THE MASS IN S. TRINITÀ DE' MONTI, ROME.

Rome in three days!! Forgive me if I heave a sigh! Shade of Winckelmann, you knew, even in your day, the dreary kind of traveller who comes to Rome with the firm resolve to see *everything*, and who then plunges into this sea of wonders on the arm of a strong swimmer, ordinarily called a *valet de place*; like children who want to learn swimming, and are with difficulty enabled to keep on the surface of the water with the help of the master's supporting hand! Yes, these hasty tourists remain always on the surface. And if the surface be bright and shining, and such as to catch the eye, it is all very well; but if by chance this surface should be dimmed by time and misfortune, it is surely permitted (at all events when there is no one there to see!) to shrug one's shoulders and hurry on to something else! An exception is to be made, however, in favour of such things as *must*, positively, be beautiful because they are so famous. These are to be enthusiastically admired and be-praised —of course only in public. This class of travellers finds Rome by no means inexhaustible, although extremely fatiguing; and requires to be refreshed in the evening at the *table d'hôte* of a first-rate hotel, after the exhausting effort of "enjoying art."

"*Table d'hôte*"—that puts a thought into my head. Since our travels have come to be a series of pilgrimages from one hotel to another, we have ceased to be able to gratify our individual gastronomic preferences. The *table d'hôte* compels us to suit our taste to whatever is brought us, and patiently to swallow down our allotted portion every day. We do not dine, we are fed, and indigestion lurks

SCALA SANTA.

menacing in the background. "What then?" do you say. Oh, you must understand that by this allegory I intend to set forth the numerous books on art and art-criticism with which our travelling public is crammed until its mental digestion is so injured that it can really admire nothing; its natural healthy appetite being destroyed, and moreover every object of interest being docketed with someone else's ready-made opinion. I have no

BROCCOLI-SELLERS IN TRASTEVERE.

desire to add my little ticket to the rest; and, indeed, I have already, in saying this much, forfeited my right of entrance into the paradise of Fine Art criticism. And I am glad of it. I should really be unable to say anything new about what has already been so much praised—still less anything brilliant. What would it profit you, my good friend, or what would it profit our respected public—which has cost both of us some sleepless and anxious nights—if I were to begin making phrases about the church of San Paolo fuori le Mura, for example?

I find the following entry in my note-book: "This church was built by a Christianity in a state of decomposition; a Christianity manifesting itself in petrified dogmas, and for this reason it is cold, stiff, sceptical, void of faith, as are the dogmas of the latter half of this century, and over-ornamented with tinsel, as the dogmas are over-laden with learned glosses. It is intended to dazzle and surprise by its newness and glitter; and it does indeed dazzle the merely curious, but does not bear the serious examination of the cognoscente or the earnest inquirer. The Church has sought after new dogmas to set them above the cross on her domes and spires; architecture has obediently followed her lead, and the result is the dogmatic, Jesuitical style of building that we see! Old Catholics, either in art or religion, would never have built so. We seem to perceive the odour of decay and ruin,—a chill air from bygone times, amidst these shining rows of pillars. The poor ignorant people stand and wonder. This is a 'national monument' they are told. It is rather the official commemoration of something which is rapidly becoming extinct."

Thus much I had written in my note-book. But on coming home I found the whole thing expressed much better, more wittily, and above all, more shortly, in Louis Ehlert's

FOUNTAIN OF TREVI, ROME.

"Roman Days." Listen. "A glaring ugliness that makes one's eyes ache. Five naves ('*ships*' as the Germans call them, preserving the metaphor in their own language) and no captain. Dishonourable falsifications in the execution."

In Santa Maria Maggiore, original Christianity seems to have a stronghold. This church gives an impression of solidity, almost like a mediæval fortress with tower and battlements. The atmosphere here smells less of dogmatic incense than of the real odour of sanctity. The tone of colouring in the interior is religious and historical. But alas, the saint has not been able to prevent architectural frivolity from tacking on all kinds of mundane frippery to her sober vestments. San Lorenzo fuori le Mura was truly once upon a time a splendid basilica. Even now it seems to cling painfully to the past. But it may be compared to a nut with a gilded shell, which has been preserved from Christmas to Christmas, but whose sweet kernel of hearty and sincere faith has long ago become dry and withered. The antique columns, walled into the church like grafts of pagan architecture, have not taken kindly to the Christian soil. In the Campo Santo, the burial ground, close to the church, there are tombs covered with rich but tasteless ornaments, such as a peasant would choose, to whom the heaviest is always the best. They bear witness to the fact that riches and good taste do not always go hand in hand, and that idle show is more prevalent than simple faith. We pass these monuments coldly by. What a different effect is produced by a simple little marble slab in the catacombs, with the inscription, dictated by joyful faith, "Flora vivas!"—"Aurelia vivas in vita æterna!"— "Donatus homo Dei."—"In pace!" And who can help feeling a melancholy sympathy, when he reads on the dark walls, out on the Via Appia yonder, that old love-story of the third century, graven by the hand of a lover who follows the path of his lost one step by step, in undoubting faith? "Sophronia, thou livest with thine own ones!—Thou livest in God!—Sophronia, thou livest for ever!—Sweet Sophronia, thou livest for ever, ever livest thou in God!" If this faith could sprout again out of the catacombs, like a seed in Spring-time, we should have beautiful ecclesiastical architecture once more!

Are you still reading on? I hope not, and confess that I have been somewhat malicious in boring you with my poor Roman note-book. I might have continued the amusement still longer, only that to say truth I get weary of it myself! I cannot make mere dry descriptions. I look at everything with the *heart*, and care only for that which appeals to the heart. I hold, too, with the Horatian "*dulce est desipere in loco.*" And hitherto, in my former Italian sketches, such as the "Days of Wandering," the critics seem not to have been discontented with me. Karl Braun speaks of them as "bright, facile, rich in form, and brilliant in colour." R. Gottschall, in his "Leaves for Literary Entertainment," pronounces them "thoroughly charming; sketches full of fresh poetic feeling, rich in perfume, in harmony, and in sunshine. The wandering poet is found in every line of them," &c. And Schweichel understood me when he wrote: "W. K. has no idea of playing the official guide, or enchanting æsthetic tea-parties. Nature and Life are the sources whence he draws."

You know that I am not thirsty for praise, and the above opinions are only intended to show that my way of writing has been found to please. And, in fact, I neither can nor dare attempt to change it. A stiff and ceremonious style would please nobody—neither you, nor the public, nor the critics. As a poet who loves wandering, I commenced my journey from the Tiber to Etna; as such I shall lay down my staff at the end of our work. A god compels me, and you will kindly tolerate "*quidquid corrigere est nefas.*"

In conclusion, when I look around for some one who shares my Roman point of view, I find him once more in the witty Louis Ehlert, whose words express my heartfelt sentiments, and therefore I give them here: "My nature is not so insatiable as that of most travellers who are spurred on from enjoyment to desire. I do not care for a compendium; I would far rather content myself with *one full general impression*, than run the risk of destroying its spontaneity by mixing it up with other things. This kind of *economy* is nowhere more necessary than in Rome."

So let your traveller wander on in peace through the Roman Campagna, and see what images you can people this vast canvas with for yourself.

Grateful Italy, for whose praise you have done so much, greets you as a friend. So also does

Yours truly,

WALDEMAR KADEN.

P.S.—Pray adorn my letter with some pleasant pictures, that it may look more attractive.

THE NORTHERN WANDERER IN THE ROMAN CAMPAGNA.

"Down to the shore where the sea-waves are flowing,
E'en from the Sabine Mountains far and blue
Where the sun's rays with fiery heat are glowing,
Where the soft ether takes a deeper hue,
And where sparse woodlands shadow-like are showing,
Destruction's cruel traces meet the view,
And whispering voices say with mournful tone,
Here Melancholy reigns and has her throne."

W. VON HUMBOLDT.

CASTEL FUSANO, *August*, 187—.

DEAR FRIEND,—I send this letter, and the accompanying papers containing the description of the Roman Campagna which you desired to have, from the most forsaken corner of the earth. You tell me with great delight of your journey through the pleasant Baden country, through charming Thuringia, and the legendary dreamy Harz. You have refreshed your eyes, wearied with the gaslight and coal-smoke of cities, in the joyous summer greenery of woods and meadows; have cheered your spirits with the sight of rich waving cornfields, and the merry faces of the country folks; have probably shouted down a light-hearted song from the heights, in answer to the girls singing in the gardens below; and are now doubtless full of excitement and enthusiasm about your journey to Rome and the Roman Campagna, which latter seems to be illumined in your imagination with the most brilliant light of Romance.

Friend, thou art only preparing for thyself a gigantic deception, as long as thou wearest the blue or green spectacles which belong to a lyric or idyllic frame of mind! That is to say, so long as you look at landscape with the eyes of a German holiday traveller. For what is it which rouses the enthusiasm of such a one? Just look into any collection of German lyrical poetry; turn over any popular choral song-book, and what do you find over and over again? "Who has built thee up so high, fair wood?" "Oh valleys wide, oh hills, oh beautiful green wood!" "Through fields and beech-grown

ACQUA ACETOSA IN THE ROMAN CAMPAGNA, LOOKING TOWARDS MOUNT SORACTE.

aisles," "In a cool dell," "Oh wood, thou well of coolness," and so on, and so on. There is nothing but singing and praising of the murmur of leaves, and the gold-green shadows on velvet moss beside the bubbling stream; of wood-birds, and wandering "Burschen" on their travels, and of the harvest songs in vale and hill, in the cheerful village, or on the fruit-bordered country road. And the German character is expressed in all this, and loves it, and cries "How beautiful!"

Now with one stroke of fancy's magic wand, take away all the woods, fields, and

PEASANTS IN THE ROMAN CAMPAGNA.

meadows, strip the mountains of their royal mantle, let the streams and rivulets be dried up in one night, and the cheerful, hospitable villages fall into dreary ruins; let poverty stalk in rags through the depopulated land, all sound of song and joyfulness die into silence beneath the brazen sky, and thorns and thistles sprout from the soil,—then make a journey through the so highly-praised Thuringia, and see what impression it makes on you! Try seriously to picture to yourself such a landscape;—you certainly would not admire it. And yet such—accurately such—is the Roman Campagna: or at all events the portion of it which is understood by most persons under that name. And there is only one difference to be noted,—certainly a very important and characteristic one,—and that is the sky, the light, the atmosphere, of the Roman Campagna. A grey, cloudy, rainy sky would make such a disfigured German landscape as I have imagined, appear still more sad and wretched; whilst here the brilliant heavens transfigure even this desert into Homeric clearness and illumination. Here we have a bronze epic: the German wilderness would be more comparable to a tearful elegy.

I advise all tourists who do not care about classical poetry, who feel no enthusiasm for the Iliad and the Odyssey, and prefer under all circumstance a sweet lyric to a serious epic,—or such as only look upon the country with the eyes of a utilitarian economist,—by no means to visit the Roman Campagna. Let him not come to the Campagna, for he would simply not understand it, and would find this landscape stretching out before him bare and withered as a beggar's hand, the most wearisome thing under the sun. Whilst the painter, the poet, the thinker roam here and gaze with the deepest delight, and read ancient oracles in the deeply furrowed lines of this dry outstretched plain, as in the palm

VELLETRI.

of a hand, those other travellers would but yawn and think of the song about the journey from Leipsic to Halle:

"Once from Leipsic to Halle a man set out ;
'Ha!' thought he, 'I shall see something new, no doubt!'"

but all that he saw was "poplar trees, nothing but poplar-trees!" And even poplars are not to be found here: only thistles the height of a man, gnarled thorn-bushes, low herbage all burnt up in summer, dust, heat, and the murderous *malaria* into the bargain:—that hydra which raises its hundred heads out of the marshes to destroy the wanderer! The messengers sent out by Moses to view the land of Canaan declared that the country devoured its inhabitants. And the same might emphatically be said of the Roman Marshes.

How many travellers have I met with who were enraged at having been sent into the Roman Campagna! And how few who could discover and appreciate its solemn beauty! In order to do so it is necessary to look at it seriously and reverently; those who are incapable of doing so can find absolutely nothing in the landscape; although, perhaps, at home they had been attracted by the numerous pictures of the Campagna in which the painter has represented some picturesque bit, with interesting details of still life, and a favourable disposition of light and shade. The English, at least, get some practical benefit out of the locality, and ride and hunt in all directions over the rolling plain. And yet I do not say that one may not educate one's eyes and ennoble one's perceptions. When the traveller once has the green North fairly behind him, and in his progress from the Alps Southward has grown accustomed to the Italian atmosphere and the Italian vegetation,—which in its colour and the stiffness of its forms has also somewhat of an epic character,—as soon as he becomes aware that the commonplace conception of what is

VALMONTONE.

"pretty and pleasant," is entirely foreign to this soil, and that in its stead the tragic and serious are met with everywhere, so soon will his eyes be opened to the glory of the ruins and the beauty of this dead earth. And the view of the wilderness spreading around the walls of Rome will awaken thoughts in him which could never have been aroused among the rich cornfields under the shady beeches and oaks, or upon the well-kept roads of his cultivated home. When once we have made a journey through the Campagna from the mountains to the sea, with seriousness and reverence, we understand the spirit of history; we understand history itself,—not merely its small unimportant marginal notes which concern individuals, but its complete, grand, universal significance. We have read the most important leaf that has remained from the burning of the Sybilline books.

The conclusion of these general remarks is, I think, the right place in which to quote a few words of Winckelmann, from a fragment of his "Letter on the journey to Italy." How truly he says: "Travelling in Italy is like the view over a great wide plain. Most people observe it with their eyes or their hands; very few with their intelligence. Some persons remark in the grand landscape a cloud of smoke or dust, an ass-driver with his beasts, rather than a beautiful Villa, &c., &c." I do not place you in the number of such; so see how you like the Campagna when I bring it a little more accurately before your eyes.

To this end, I must first of all make you acquainted with my present abode. It lies quite in the Campagna, but forms, with its surrounding woods, an oasis in the desert. As to my life here, I might almost begin with the traditional story-book phrase, "Once upon a time—," for I am dwelling in an old, old enchanted castle by the sea, which, by the kindness of its proprietor, Prince Chigi, in Rome, has opened its iron portals and given me a hospitable reception. You have read the name of it at the top of my letter,—"Castel Fusano." If we were living in the antique times, I should probably have written "Fusano near Laurentum"; but the post-office officials know nothing about that, now-a-days. You will find the enchanted castle if you continue in a direction almost due South from Rome along the *Via Ostiensis* or *Laurentina* towards the sea-shore until you come to Ostia, and from thence turn to the left across a sandy flat. You will see a pine-wood rising in sudden and unexpected beauty from the dead plain. In the midst of this wood, upon a sandy space where there are still some traces to be seen of a garden long ago overwhelmed by the wilderness, stands the feudal, mediæval castle. It has long ago taken the grey hue of the desert around it, but it looks, with its four corner towers, only so much the more defiant, and savage;—like a nobleman turned brigand.

A deeper woodland solitude than surrounds this place could scarcely be found. One seems to be cut off from the whole world here, and to be the last man left alive. And the silence is so overpowering that one is tempted to give a shout or a whistle (which, however, finds but a brief fluttering echo among the stems of the pine-trees) in order to assure oneself that one still lives and breathes! No bird sings here; they fly hastily across the wilderness. No sound of murmuring waters is heard here in fountain or rill. The two or three *Campagnoli*, who are the guardians of the woods and the cow-houses, but who look like robbers, wander shy and silent as if they had almost forgotten the use of speech, past the hoary walls. In silence the great black ants follow the path of their caravan among the dry pine-needles that strew the ground, and the dumb tortoises move slowly between the brittle sand-weeds followed by the stealthy fox in search of his prey. At mid-day the god Pan sleeps, and Nature, too, sleeps. No breeze stirs; the resinous woodland odours rise in thick clouds around the doors and windows of the castle. The air quivers and trembles above the heath, dazzling the eye, and fantastically transforming all objects. Then one thinks that a thick hedge of roses ought to arise around the castle, and that the King and Queen should be slumbering in its dim halls, and the princess high up in one of the corner turrets. The pretty old fairy tale haunts me here, and grows real in my fancy, —and this is the palace of the Sleeping Beauty.

Towards evening, when the sun is sinking into the sea, the silent landscape is animated for a brief while with sounds and voices. The lowing of cattle is heard, and the tinkling of their bells, and the rough herdsman, spurring his smoking steed, gives out short hoarse cries, now to his half wild dogs, now to some untamed bull rushing fiercely along. The osprey answers him with bent head from the rosy evening sky; the sea wind brings flocks of piping sea-gulls flying landwards over the tops of the pine-trees;—and when all is silent again, and the clouds of dust are dispersed in the twilight, you hear the soft and soothing surge of the neighbouring sea, like the breathing of a sleeping Titan through the darkening solitude.

Then the moon rises above the shrub-grown hills of Laurentum, Orion's silvery lamp beams over the sea, and the charm is complete. Beloved legends float in shining draperies, and whispering ancient names, above the glimmering heath, from whence in answer to the call, departed forms arise noiselessly with the night mists. Strange

NEAR SETUBAL

mysterious sounds meet the listening ear,—a cry,—a harsh croaking,—a distant shot,—
a shudder in the soughing pine-trees. There is in all this a mixture of the weird and the
beautiful which powerfully excites the imagination. From the thickets of Ardea to the
forlorn mouths of the Tiber, which loses itself sullenly in the sand, and whose outgoing is
blessed by no human hand,—from thence to this place there spreads a dreary wretched
shore, forgotten by spring and love, whose sandy soil only affords nourishment to a few

CASTLE OF PALO.

shrubs. Heather, lentiscus, wild myrtle and olive-bushes, and dwarf oaks surrounded by
aromatic-smelling weeds, find a scanty living here. The soil is in part marshy; for the
little streams which meander through it in the rainy season, are absorbed by the sand
before reaching the sea, and thus form steaming pools, out of which rise mists and swarms
of gnats, and, as the summer advances the grey, ghostly *malaria*. It knocks with its
bony hand at the few miserable huts of the shepherds and peasants and implacably
demands its yearly tribute of human lives. The pallid herd-boy who has withstood its
influence for sixteen or seventeen poverty-stricken years, the lean, brown girl before she
can wear her marriage wreath of scanty blossoms, the weather-beaten, hardy man and his
wife amidst her joyless and toilsome existence,—all these the malaria takes year after year
and drags them pitilessly to death, and hunts them, dying, across the sun-burned heath,
and returns ever greedier of prey again and again. Thus the grim reaper strides over the
Campagna, and passes no threshold by. In a few years the hut is empty, the fox glides
in at the broken door, and the rain and the wind beat in at the unglazed windows.

Reeds and rank grass spring up all around, and bye and bye a light-hearted painter comes and finds a delightfully picturesque "bit" of ruin. He paints it and whistles gaily the last new song,—and next year a storm blows away the last remnant of the poor dwelling, "and their place knows them no more."

There was a time, indeed, when all this coast was flourishing, when the sea-sand did

HERDSMAN IN THE CAMPAGNA.

not girdle the land with its deadly silver band, and when a thriving healthy population inhabited it down to the very edge of the blue waves that washed the marble thresholds of their cities. And when they turned their gaze back from the sea, they looked upon a green, well-cultivated land, that stretched away to the mountains of the Tiber's source. The people called themselves Laurentians, and the chief cities of that time were Antium, the hoary sea-town of the Volscians; Ardea, the home of the bold Turnus and the valiant Rutuli; and Lavinium, the splendid and venerable mountain city. In Laurentum the sacred laurel grew, and seafaring folks landed here from far and near to bring their offerings and gifts from foreign lands to the sacred shrine of Mars. The sailors encamped under the consecrated trees, enjoying their friendly shade, and listening to the oracles of the tapping woodpecker, that promised them a prosperous voyage home. All that is past and gone, buried beneath the white sea-sand; and no ship anchors more before the shadeless and inhospitable coast. Yonder, far out at sea, the lateen sails of the Neapolitan fishermen glide past, but there is nothing to tempt them to a shore which has not even a stream of fresh water to offer them. In the early days of Spring the sacred woodpecker may still be heard tapping at the stems of the pine trees, but the childlike mouth of antiquity, which knew the language of the birds, is shut for ever, and we cannot understand the woodland oracle.

Before the time of the Roman Emperors the locality had already become more deserted

THE SHEPHERD'S RETURN HOME.

and uncultivated, and all efforts to put new life into this decaying nature were unavailing. It was attempted by means of canals—those arteries of life to the soil—by making roads, and granting special privileges—all in vain! As early as in Nero's time Lavinium, the last remnant of the Latin Confederation, was so ruined, and had such a bad reputation, that every Roman shrunk from making even the briefest sojourn there. And the senator of those days who was compelled to pass a night in Lavinium in order to attend the yearly religious ceremony held there, no doubt cursed from the bottom of his heart Numa, who had founded these rites. Many Roman villas were still standing along the coast as far as Ostia; but they quickly fell into decay. Pliny gives a charming sketch of his Villa Laurentina by the sea. I can reach the site of it in a quarter of an hour from my castle in the wilderness. The sea is still the same, its shining shores stretch out on the blue horizon to Castrum Novum, and the promontory of Circe; the sky is still the same, the myrtles smell as sweetly now as then, and that peace, so dear to the student, still reigns here far and wide. But where is the violet-scented cystus, the palm-grown garden of Pliny, his favourite retreat when he dwelt in Laurentum? Where are the plashing fountains, the murmuring springs and streams? The cheerful colonnades have fallen; the gaily painted chambers, whose steps were washed by the waves when the south wind blew, have been swallowed up by the eternal sea, and drawn down into its dark depths; and no trace of the old splendour remains, save perhaps a handful or two of bright-coloured fragments of mosaic and glass, which the Nereids throw at our feet in idle sport. All the other villas, too, which showed like towns to the sailor on the sea, and the wanderer on the shore, and where mirth and jest once resounded—where are they? The foot of the solitary traveller strikes not one stone of them on this strand strewn with broken shells and dry seaweed.

For long centuries Ostia,—the rich ancient Ostia, once the flourishing port of Rome, now a second Pompeii beside the Tiber,—lay hidden from all eyes beneath a huge mound of earth and rubbish. No place transports the visitor so completely into the antique days as this recently excavated city, larger and more important than Pompeii. Nowhere do we feel more strongly the influence of a pensive melancholy, than upon these silent banks overgrown with willows, which once witnessed the landing of golden treasures from all parts of the earth. Pompeii is smiling even in death,—she died amidst the joys of Campania; Ostia's ruins are sombre and sad,—they were the witnesses of Rome's decay. Ostia may be reached from the castle in about a quarter of an hour. We walk silently and musingly through those halls covered with thistles, through those streets once populated with the busy life of a sea-port, but where now not a soul is to be seen, except perhaps a fierce-looking shepherd, or an overseer of the excavations who begs for tobacco. The Tiber has broken impetuously into the city and has carried away great pieces of the basalt pavement from the main street, and spread clammy slime over the mosaic flooring of the rich dwelling and temples, whose columns lie broken into a thousand fragments on the ground, and whose white and coloured marbles are strewn far and wide. The poisonous swamps press around the walls of the present town, and their fever-laden breath has almost depopulated it. A thicket of low shrubs surrounds the marsh, and here herds of half wild oxen roam about. Upon the road, somewhat raised above the surrounding level, you seldom see a living creature. Formerly salt used to be strewn upon the site of a destroyed city; and salt is to be found all around Ostia, produced by the evaporation of the sea-water which is brought in artificial canals, and left to stagnate in the sun. Salt indeed is the only crop which the soil produces; no ear of corn bestowed by bounteous Ceres bends beneath the reaper's sickle, no ripening fruit blesses the gardener's hand. As I traversed that dreary road one midsummer day, and compared the past with the present, the lines came into my head :—

* * * * * * *
"And when five hundred years were o'er,
I passed the self-same way once more.
But of the town I found no trace;
A lonely shepherd piping played,
And flocks were grazing on the place.
'When was the town destroyed?' I said.
He answered, and piped on full clear,
'My flocks have always pastured here.'"—RÜCKERT.

The town * still looks imposing from a distance, by reason of its bold and threatening mediæval castle, which once protected the town, the fruitful Campagna, and the mouths

---

* That is to say the modern, or rather the mediæval town of Ostia, which stands within a stone's throw of the ancient city.—*Translator's note.*

BRETHREN OF THE MISERICORDIA BEARING THE BODY OF A MAN WHO HAS BEEN KILLED IN THE ROMAN CAMPAGNA.

of the Tiber, and on whose walls six Popes one after another have placed their marble
scutcheons. But seen near, Ostia is unable to dissimulate the beggar's garment she now
wears. Her streets and alleys are empty and deserted. A dozen or so of half-starved
inhabitants, carefully wrapped in shawls and mantles even at midday, glide trembling with
fever between the houses which threaten speedily to fall in ruins. Alas, the change! All
is in fragments; the foot treads on nothing but fragments:—fragments of coloured
mosaics, fragments of glass showing prismatic hues, fragments of vases, lamps, ornaments

OSTIA.

and marbles. These form the soil on which the silent town behind the castle is built.
Every clod of earth which the traveller's staff breaks from the mounds all around contains
some relic of the dead city. We stand and gaze; we stoop and pick up handfuls of the old
perished splendours; but we cannot re-construct a complete picture by means of them.
The street of tombs must certainly have been more splendid and grandiose than that of
Pompeii, as is attested by the remains of its pillars, marbles and mosaic pavements. The
temple of Jupiter must have been equally fine. It stands on a low hill above the city,
and must have had an imposing effect from the surrounding plain, both by reason of its
noble architecture and its brilliant marble facings. The interior walls of brick-work are
still in good preservation, and a flight of marble steps leads up to the golden house of the
Father of the Gods. The huge slab of African marble which forms the threshold in front
of the principal entrance is also well preserved. The lofty niches in the interior which
once served to hold the assemblage of marble gods, are absolutely intact, but they look
hollow and empty like the eye-sockets of a skeleton.

The landscape which you behold from the steps of the temple is exquisite beyond all expression. It stretches before us with its tender, delicate outlines and wonderfully harmonious colouring, and the distant mountains serve as a frame for it. Not one harsh touch spoils its perfection. A master-hand has sketched the outlines with an unfailing pencil, the sun has coloured it with a full and glowing brush, and the picture is absolutely perfect. From Civita Castellana beyond Soracte, over the Sabine mountains to those of Albano, the eye roams with ecstasy in an enchanted circle which takes the senses prisoner. In the centre of this circle lies the Eternal City, with the golden sunlight playing on its towers. There is nothing to distract the eye from the distant view;—no poor and small details disturb the grandeur of the general impression. The strong sun-

CIVITA CASTELLANA.

browned tints of the foreground melt by gentle gradations through the faint green of distant foliage, and the silvery tone of the horizon, into a soft grey, taking from the glimmer of the distance and the blue of the atmosphere that indescribable colour which looks like real absolute silver on the broad slopes of the sun-illumined hills, and becomes a silvery azure in their folds and ravines.

But what a rich variety of changes these lights and shades, these tones and colours, are capable of affording! They appear very different under the sunlight of spring or summer from what they look in autumn or winter. What a powerful effect is produced by the sunrise and the mid-day glow! And how overpowering, although entirely different, is the impression of the sunset! During the warm days of the first spring or autumn rains, what kaleidoscopic transformations from one minute to the other! The sky is clear and blue; little tender, rosy cloudlets float through the ether,—when lo, the clouds begin to gather, and a dark mass rises behind the Sabine mountains, which look from summit to foot as if they had been built out of chalk under the sudden weird side light that falls on them. Then the rain traverses the country in dark, oblique lines, whilst close beside it,—often even in the midst of the rain,—golden rays of sunlight fall in strange contrast upon the land that knows not whether it shall laugh or weep. The rain moves onward, and covers one village, hill, or villa after another, with its grey veil; and then the instant after they spring back into dazzling light, like children leaping from the bath. One must have seen the sunrise—and still more the sunset,—from the summit of Somete, the castle-hill of Palestrina, or the majestic Monte Cavo, in order to absorb into one's soul such images as memory will preserve for ever amongst its noblest and happiest pictures. No; we have no such glories in the North! And at the risk of being laughed at for an enthusiast, I dare maintain that a summer sunset on the Roman Campagna is

BRACCIANO.

the most splendid spectacle which the poetic soul can hope to see. Alas, only very few can enjoy it, however; for at the moment when it is most magnificent, in August, there is no "public" to be found on the Campagna, and Nature plays to empty benches! She pours out her golden colouring in streams, and exhausts herself to produce the most luxuriant splendours in utter solitude. She mirrors herself in the most forsaken of seas, and descends into her bath at night, to rise next day from the waves under the pure rays of the morning sun, in all the loveliness of Aphrodite.

I remember yet, with deep emotion, a sunset such as I have only seen once in all my life. We were returning from the sea-shore, along the ancient Via Ardeatina. It was a rough September evening, towards the end of the month; a cutting cold north wind blew over the open heath, and rustled in the dry shrubs by the wayside, bending them to the earth, and sighed among the sunburnt rushes. A cold, dreary, sullen colouring lay upon the country: a dull neutral tone. The Campagna looked like the countenance of one who has suffered much, and now, at the moment of some new and painful parting, forcibly restrains his tears, or conceals them beneath a mask of cold defiance. It was a spectacle which attuned the soul to deepest melancholy.

The sun hangs yet but a little while above the edge of the sea; but ere it sinks in its last moments, it suddenly pours out a stream of gold over the world—a stream so full and dazzling, that the eyes quiver and close before it. There is no green to be distinguished in the trees or the high reeds, no grey in the walls and fences. Every blade, every leaf is as if cast in burnished metal, and all nature is steeped in one deep glaring yellow. This lasts for fully ten minutes, then—there needs but an instant for the change—a clear joyous rose-colour shines on high; that changes into a solemn, majestic purple, and is in its turn succeeded by deep violet, which, slowly withdrawing across the landscape, seems at length to concentrate itself in the Alban mountains, and to linger there until it melts away from the latest-illumined summit, the Monte Cavo, above which the evening star already trembles.

Was this glaring yellow illumination beautiful? It was wonderful, entrancing, filling the soul with images of another world, another time, images such as seldom visit even our dreams; a universe in flames!

* * * * * *

The landscape stage is so vast, and the incidents enacted in it are so small! We only behold insignificant pastoral scenes; but not in the elegant, pink-ribboned, smiling style. No; these are rough, rude, harsh, though picturesque enough withal. At times that great theatre named the Agro Romano is quite empty—the wild haunt of airy phantoms; and we may wander from the blooming fields of Tuscany, even to the smiling gardens of the whilom kingdom of Naples, without meeting with any life or movement. It is true that many a proud high-sounding name is named to us, and these places look stately enough still on the map. But what to-day is Porto d'Anzio, the ancient Antium, the favourite seat of Nero, Hadrian, Domitian, and of many other famous men who drew the sword against haughty Rome? A beggar crouching on the sea-shore. What is Nettuno? So poverty-stricken, that even its rich, beautiful costumes, the delight of all painters, will, in a few years, have entirely disappeared. Borghetto, old and ruinous, in a desert neighbourhood, with a few hungry inhabitants. Civita Castellana, old, old, only fit to serve as the foreground to a romantic picture of ruins. It is the same with Ronciglione, and Monterondo; all destroyed in the germ, or checked in fuller growth, by the harsh feudal times! Montefiascone, the once flourishing place renowned for its "Est-est," now, alas, *mortuus est!* These and many another proud name we hear, for there were once no fewer than twenty-three flourishing populous cities in the Campagna. But truly this is hard to believe, when the bearers of these proud names are pointed out to us at the present day, a few grey, wretched groups of houses, whose inhabitants are lost in the wide wilderness, and leave no trace behind.

On leaving the green belt of gardens that girdle Rome, where elm and vine still greet us cheerfully above the walls, a brief pilgrimage brings us into the midst of a houseless solitude. No cheerful villages nestle close to the ancient mother. Lapped for long centuries in the pious luxury of ecclesiastical splendour, lazy, loveless, she has let her children perish of famine,—she has murdered them!

ON THE WAY TO CERVARA ARTISTS' FESTIVAL IN ROME.

Not a tile, not a stone, is used to build any new thing on the Campagna. The dwellings that exist, that appear from a distance to offer hospitable shelter, when you approach them, prove to be some mediæval or antique fragment, a piece of fortress wall, to which man has patched on his dwelling, like to the fleeting swallow which the brief

SHEPHERD OF THE CAMPAGNA.

spring brings hither. Those who dwell here have nothing to lose; and the iron bars before the solitary window serve rather for ornament than for security. And yet those are happy who can find a home in even such a *casale* as this; for hundreds of others dwell in the low, damp caves of the brown-red *tufa* quarries, whose walls, blackened by the smoke of perpetual fires, give but a cheerless shelter. Here stand the beds of rough boards covered with fleeces, prepared precisely like the couch which the divine swine-herd Eumæus offered to the home-returning Ulysses.

> "then placed he near to the fire
> A bed well covered with skins of goats, and with sheepskins.
> Here Odysseus lay; and o'er him was thrown a mantle
> Ample, and thick of texture."

The baby rests in a coarse basket placed on wooden rollers. Other furniture there is none in these caves, except guns, agricultural implements, and milk-pans. Some of the peasants encamp themselves in slight huts woven of reeds and hempen cords. But the major part of them spend the night under the serene sky of the Campagna; and the ashes of a burnt-out fire mark the spots where their gregarious life in common has been passed.

The persons whom we meet in such places are very seldom native-born Roman *Campagnoli*. They come down in bands, chased by the poverty that reigns in their sterile mountain homes,—to sow in the spring, and to reap in the summer. Then we behold an army of misery marching silently across the dead plain, from Umbria, from the far Abruzzi, and the Sabine country. They are all lean and famished, with labour-hardened hands, and clad in rags, the immemorial uniform of poverty; rags so wretched, that they are scarce worth putting on, and are therefore never taken off! They carry a broad, heavy mattock over the shoulder, and work the soil under the superintendence of a rough, pitiless, overseer, the so-called *Caporale*. They turn over a thin layer of earth, hastily sprinkle the sods with seed, and then go away to the vineyards, where they labour whilst the corn is growing and ripening. Then they return, at the very time when the Malaria is brooding with leaden wings over the Campagna, and reap a scanty harvest, the profit of which helps to fill the pockets of some rich, lazy, Roman prince or Duke. This life of the peasant is a real campaign; and most of them return home sick and worn, as men do after a campaign, with the scanty wages of their sweat and toil wrapped in a handkerchief, and leaving many a comrade stretched on the great plain under a hillock of wild thyme and heath, victims of the man-killing breath of the swamps. This is modern slavery, and a harder slavery than the ancient.

> "In every furrow of Saturnian soil
> There grows a grewsome weed;—its name is Death.
> When 'neath an over-flood of dazzling light,
> The land lies sad amidst the summer days,
> A thousand reapers sweep down on the plain
> Driven by cruel hunger from their homes,
> And wander o'er it like to banished men.
> Their deep black eyes are dimmed by the foul breath
> Of poisonous airs that stagnate all around.
> And not one joyous bird-note greets the ear,
> No song of home from out the far Abruzzi,
> Revives the melancholy exile's soul.
> In silence do they reap the yellow grain
> For some unknown possessor; and at length
> When all the weary labour is performed
> In silence they depart, even as they came.
> But if perchance they hear the well-known tones
> Of their own native cornamusa sound,
> Their hearts swell high with yearning for their home."—ALEARDI.

In the time of the Roman Republic they were slaves' hands which tilled the soil,

VIA FLAMINIA ON THE ROMAN CAMPAGNA.

MIDDAY IN POUSSIN'S VALLEY.

when it brought forth fruits sixty and a hundred fold, and when the whole of the growing city lived by the produce of the ploughs which furrowed the Campagna. But the slave was the comrade in labour, and the housemate of his lord, and sate with the master's sons around the patriarch of the family, eating from the same board. There is no more pleasant picture that that of Cato's wife suckling the infants of her female slaves, together with her own new-born son. All that, however, was changed in the Imperial times. It was found easier and less laborious to gain necessaries from foreign lands by means of the sword, and the servant became the mere instrument of his master's pride and luxury. The Roman plough rusted before the city gates, and the arable land of the Campagna went to ruin, or at best was covered by pleasure-gardens and luxurious villas.

During the Middle Ages a dozen or two of feudal lords divided the land amongst them; but not even the convulsive efforts of the Papacy could restore the ancient agriculture, and at the present, things are left pretty much to take their chance. Only a very insignificant portion of the soil—still ready to bear fruit under proper conditions—is cultivated. Spring glides over the plain, her hands full of showers and sunshine, but her friendly warmth coaxes forth only briars, thistles, and weeds; which, however, in the abundance of the spring-time, show how willingly the earth would yield a bountiful return to the care of man's hand. Maize and millet seem to grow almost of themselves in the hollows of the plain wherever any moisture remains; and bread, and a kind of porridge prepared from these, form the chief aliments of the few resident peasants of the Campagna. As table luxuries to be added to these come a thin, sour wine, rancid oil pressed from the olives gathered from the poor olive trees, which grow at the foot of the surrounding mountains, and dry cheese made of sheep's or buffalo's milk.

In these caverns, or beneath the shelter of the reed-huts, these people have been educated in the high philosophical school of temperance; other school they know none! Culture moves ceaselessly over the world, travels with the swiftness of the steam-horse, and speaks by means of the lightning; all that is nothing to these men. For a thousand years they have had no part in civilization, and there is nothing to brighten their lives or mitigate their sufferings. Not one joy blooms on their path of life. One must learn to know these hard, stern beings, (ask the painter about them; the painter who really loves them. But you must not confuse them with the dressed up 'models' in the Roman streets, who bear about as much resemblance to the real herdsman as a powdered, coquettish, *bergère* of Trianon bore to a veritable shepherdess of the Black Forest)!—one must learn to know them as they scour these steppes mounted on their lean little long-maned horses. Here are no lyric traits; not one! Their faces are brown, hard, and inflexible as leather, and no smile ever moves their stern features.

Such are the men who have learned to defy the fever and the devil. They do not talk: perhaps they scarcely even think! At all events their range of thought is an excessively limited one. But they make a fine spectacle as they ride over the plain. Accustomed to ride from earliest childhood, and having, as it were, grown up on horseback, they sit their little fiery beasts often without a saddle; sometimes seated on a black goatskin, without stirrups, wrapped in a mantle, their legs protected by hard leather straps up to the thigh, the gun slung at their backs, the lance in their hands, guiding their horse merely with a halter, they thus dash into a drove of wild young horses, or collect together the stubborn white oxen. They are real Nomads, such as poetry and fancy paint them. These are the same breed of black-haired bandits who once followed that antique adventurer of the Palatine, that wild scion of a royal house, Romulus, to welcome deeds of robbery and daring, of blood and death. They should be seen, when, bold and fearless, and unsupported by the applause of a Spanish arena, they master the furious bull, and rush defiantly upon the foaming beast in his wrath. They should be seen, these true sons of the wilderness, chasing the unbroken three-year-old across the downs, and finally catching and taming him. And this perhaps is a delight to them: they certainly have no other. Even love is a stranger to most of them; this flower of life does not flourish here. These men neither laugh nor sing; they are like their land soundless, songless. They belong to the true shepherd breed,[*] and heed not the cultivation of the soil.

"We ne'er will follow the ploughshare here,
We plough the earth with an iron spear."

The flocks and herds which wander over the Campagna are but half tamed, and only obey the iron rule of their rude masters. There are the beautiful greyish-white oxen with their great horns, which we are accustomed to connect with all our mental pictures of the Piazze in Rome, and of the rolling hills of the Agro Romano. But these splendid horns are dangerous, and tremendous combats are fought between themselves by the bulls, the leaders of the herds, in the solitude of the Campagna. The harmless wanderer is not safe from them, and is hopelessly lost if he find himself in the path of a rushing drove far from shelter or any place of refuge.

A cloud of dust arises on the horizon, thick and yellow, till it obscures the sunshine, and whirls on nearer and ever nearer. A wild beating and stamping of powerful hoofs make the earth tremble: here they are! They come, the great strong brutes, foaming, snorting, rushing past with their long sharp horns reared lance-like in the air. Behind them the herdsmen, with flying mantles and long pointed goads, with which they ever and anon prick forward the half mad creatures, and encourage them by their cries to a still more headlong swiftness. We are enveloped in thick dust. A whirlwind seems to have rushed past, a sudden cyclone; for before we can regain our breath, the whole tempest, with its hoofs and horns and dust and cries, is far away, disappearing on the edge of the horizon.

The shepherds, who make their slow migrations across the sunny plain, afford softer pictures to the eye: pictures of peace and pastoral leisure. They make admirable landscape figures, and delight the eye in a great variety of positions. Yonder, in the Via Appia, sits a sun-burned lad perched on a ruined tomb, and there, amidst a shade of myrtle-boughs, he cuts and shapes a simple pipe, and makes melancholy music on it all day long in one persistent monotone. Meanwhile his sheep browse over the graves, or repose, picturesquely grouped, amongst the marble ruins.

It is pretty to see a flock wending its way upwards to the rocky hills which frame in the Campagna. These hills are covered, for the most part, with short, sweet, fragrant, herbage; and when the mid-day breeze blows downward from the mountains to the plain, it brings with it whole clouds of sweet odours. Here the shepherd carries an axe in his girdle, and the *cornamusa* (a kind of bag-pipe) under his arm. For it is necessary, in these parts, to be able to defend the flocks from the cowardly assaults of the lean little wolf of the Campagna, which is still to be met with here and there in considerable numbers, and to call together the wandering sheep by means of the shrill tones of the cornamusa. There lies the happy shepherd, under the shadow of a jutting rock, gazes over the land

---

[*] The men who are accurately described in the foregoing sentences do not belong to the shepherd breed. They are the so-called "butteri," whose business is solely with horses and cattle. The distinction between them and the shepherds of the Campagna is a wide one. And the *butteri* are aristocrats as compared with the shepherd class.—*Translator's note.*

with dreamy eyes and sees the white sails glitter on the distant sea, and men and animals crawling like ants along the high road yonder. There he lies and pipes his ancient melodies with all his soul, until the echoes in the distant valleys are aroused. He is alone. "He looks abroad upon the world, but none can look on him." Only the bees, as they hang on the blossoms of the rose-lipped mountain thyme, buzz around him, or

GOATHERD.

now and then there comes a blue-breasted stone-thrush, perches inquisitively on a neighbouring lentiscus, and gives forth his clear whistle. When the evening light grows red the shepherd collects his flocks, and leads them to some lower meadow in a sheltered spot among the hills. Here he sticks sharp stakes into the ground, connects them together with wide-meshed netting, and folds the sheep there for the night, pressed closely one against the other to gain shelter from the keen mountain air. As soon as the night begins to fall the shepherds assemble together for company's sake, and as a protection against damp vapours from the valley and against prowling wolves, they light huge fires around which they lie or sit in a circle. Then may be heard their melancholy long-drawn songs, chanted to quaint antique melodies. The words are usually about love, and sometimes they even treat the passion in a tone of mockery. But the tunes—whosoever has once heard them cannot forget them : it is as if some long-hidden and inarticulate sorrow of his own had found expression in them.

As the summer advances the flocks mount higher and higher into the hills, and may

SHEPHERD BOY IN THE CAMPAGNA.

be found amidst the well-watered pastures in the neighbourhood of Lago Fucino, and as far as the "Napoletano." In autumn, when the reapers and vintagers return to their mountain homes from the lower Campagna, the flocks, consisting very often of as many as five, or ten, thousand sheep, make their way down to the plain again, in order to pass the winter in the milder climate of the districts bordering the coast. These returning flocks, led by shepherds and their dogs, and with the owner mounted on horseback behind them, offer a new and curious spectacle, and many a road is encumbered for days by bleating sheep, barking restless dogs, and clouds of impenetrable dust.

Such is the poetry of the Roman Campagna. It is ever young, like the poetry of humanity, and if your soul has once been touched by it you can never more forget it. You will hear its old tunes sounding, sounding in your ears; its glowing tints will break upon you amidst the dreamy mists of the North, and fill your heart with longing for a land whose charm is inexplicable even whilst you feel it, and before whose beauty you stand as before some "marble Juno of old Greece."

CECCANO.

FROM THE SHORES OF LAGO FUCINO TO THE PONTINE MARSHES.

> "Ha, dost thou see this garden,—yonder heaven?
> How deeply blue the air! The sun how bright,
> How diamond-clear! No cloudlet to be seen!
> What dullard eye could drowse amid such beauty?
> The sky hangs like a chalice overturned
> Above our heads, and pours down life and joy
> Upon the world, and us. How darkly red
> The grape glows on the vine!"
>
> GRÄSSE.

THE Apennine, divided into three mighty parallel chains, girdles Italy from northwest to south-east. These chains are split by the action of the titanic forces of nature in remote ages; and furrowed by steeply sloping valleys, stony watercourses, and yawning chasms. Here in the province of the Abruzzi, the soaring peaks of the Apennine give the country situated at a considerable height above the sea level the aspect of a truly mountainous land. And its two narrow valleys, cramped in amongst the convolutions of the different chains, are real mountain valleys, and have a stern character which only Italian sunshine can mitigate. In one of the valleys, the valley of the Liris, the fresh green waters of that stream vivify field and woodland. A handsome, cheerful race dwells on the banks of the Liris, and comfort surrounds their cottages. The other valley is the valley of the Imele and the Salto, sterile and stony for the most part. Within it lies the basin of the Lago Fucino, or, as it is now called, the Lake of Celano, that being the most considerable place on its shores. The Lake Fucinus lies in the midst of the Abruzzi, on the western side of the middle chain, which begins near the Umbrian town of Rieti, and reaches its loftiest point in Monte Velino, a mountain nearly eight thousand feet high.

The lake itself lies two thousand and forty-six feet above the sea. Broad and well-kept roads traverse the hills in all directions (advantage being skilfully taken of every natural pass and declivity), and facilitate traffic with Umbria, the lower Roman plains, and the Campagna Felice; whilst the valley of the Pescara leads towards the Adriatic coast. To the west the high land slopes down gradually through the Roman Sub-Apennine to the Tyrrhene Sea. And between the high-lying Lago Fucino, and the flat Pontine Marshes, extending as far as Cape Circello, we have the fine chalk range of the Sabine hills, which are sharply contrasted with the rest of the Abruzzi, both by their form and the materials of which they are composed. Vulcan worked here with a mighty and well-skilled hand, and has produced a great number of varying shapes. The highest points of these hills, which run from the gloomy Valmontone down to the Neapolitan provinces, are the "Mountain of the three frontiers," and the "Donkey's Back," *Schiena d'Asino*.

A pilgrimage from Lago Fucino, through the Sabine Hills to the Latin coasts, offers the sublimest specimens of Italian scenery. Spacious, tranquil, noble landscapes, sunny distances melting into purple haze, open before the enraptured eye. A painter treads these mountain paths with ever-new delight. But, as soon as one leaves the broad high roads they are extremely fatiguing, and offer to the traveller spoilt by luxurious hotel living scarcely anything which can please him, or even satisfy his wants. If you are coming from the blooming soil of Naples and pass through the happy valley of the Liris, by picturesque Arce, and the sombre mountain cities of Civitella, Canistro, and Capistrello, you become gradually accustomed to the total absence of comfort. But any one beginning

CELANO, ON LAGO FUCINO.

his journey from the Roman side must make up his mind to endure many hardships from the very beginning.

The blue lake of Fucino lies in a deep valley-basin, surrounded by golden-brown mountains, piled one above the other, until they disappear behind the silver veil of mist on the horizon. A strange peacefulness seems to brood on the landscape, and the numerous white little villages dotted about on the green shores lie restfully as if they were forgotten by the world, and had been breathed upon by the spirit of old legend. They take a last look at themselves in the sinking waters. Already most of them have come to be far inland, and where a few years ago the boats of the fishermen of Avezzano and Celano floated, where the waves danced in the mountain breeze, little gardens now flourish, young trees spring, and the brown son of the Marsyan soil reaps a Roman

Prince's harvest. For the lake will soon be a myth, a corn-field reclaimed from the watery kingdom of Neptune after a struggle and a combat of a thousand years! It will be a colossal cornfield though; for the lake was three miles long, and in parts as much as two miles broad. A little principality lay hidden in its slimy bottom, and these modern times, for whose enterprise no mountain is too high, no isthmus too wide, have raised it up from the flood and made of it an altar to Ceres.

In ancient times the project of draining the lake had already entered men's heads. In the season when the mountain snows were melting, and in the time of violent rains, the lake swelled and devastated the surrounding country. It even swallowed up several towns, which had in vain endeavoured to defend themselves against its encroachments by building cyclopean walls as dams upon the shore. A century ago, during a very hot, dry, summer, the depths of the lake were revealed, and the remains of these towns were made visible: ancient cities of the Marsii. Marruvium is one of them, and Archippe another, at the same time several marble statues were found in the mud of the bottom.

The lake has no outlet; and Julius Cæsar conceived the idea of constructing an emissary. It was Claudius, however, who carried it out, and celebrated its inauguration by the sacrifice of numerous human lives in a bloody naval battle given in honour of the day! But the lake again grew troublesome. Hadrian made a fresh attempt to regulate it, which attempt failed. After the Roman Emperor, a German one, Frederick the Second,—when he had destroyed a flourishing place on the lake, Celano, which had adhered to the Guelph party,—gave directions for a work of canalisation to be carried out. So also did the French and Spanish kings. But the lake grew more and more menacing, and frequently threatened to destroy the towns and hamlets on its shores;— Avezzano, Trasacco, Venere, Manaforno, Vico, San Venenziano, Luco, Ortucchio, Pescina, and San Benedetto (Marruvium). In this century some works were begun to make the old emissary practicable. But that which baffled Kings and Kaisers was accomplished by the Roman Banker-Prince, Torlonia. He gave his millions; foreign countries—England and Switzerland,—supplied engineering skill, and now the waters of the lake flow in a finely constructed conduit, or canal, through the Monte Salviano, peacefully to the Liris. The dwellers by the lake will soon be high and dry altogether; a scarcity of water has succeeded to its too great abundance, and in Avezzano it has already been found necessary to deepen the wells.

Avezzano, a melancholy looking little town, lies in the midst of a kind of sandy desert. And the pleasant gardens which greenly girdle it round, have been redeemed from the arid soil with incredible pains and labour. It seems to lie still under the ban of the Middle Ages; and, like a sentinel of those times of darkness, there rises close beside it the baronial castle of the Orsini, haughtily towering over the plain. The inhabitants, descended from the ancient Marsii, are friendly people, of a robust and pleasing aspect. But the rumour goes that they have not even yet entirely forgotten the traditions of their savage and ferocious ancestors, and that the knife is to this day their most trusted companion. This was the very centre and focus of the Marsic wars. Here the wild hordes assembled to prepare for a struggle against Rome:—rude brothers-in-arms of these inaccessible mountains, an antique confederation on the shores of this Italian lake, the Marrucini, Æqui, Peligni, Vestini! And not infrequently their rude arms were victorious over the haughty Roman legions.

Here stood Alba; once Alba Marsorum, then an advanced post of the Romans, who kept a permanent garrison there. This was the Marsic Legion, which won Cicero's

BATTLEFIELD NEAR TAGLIACOZZO

brilliant eulogy, and a reward from the Roman Senate. The position of this frontier-fortress was a singularly fortunate one. It was thrust like an iron wedge into the mountains, dividing Samnium from Etruria. It was surrounded by three hills, each of which was surmounted by a strong castle. The remains of these fortifications may still be traced on two of the hills. The grey old Cyclopean constructions rise terrace-wise from amongst the shrubs and bushes. And short stretches of well-paved roads show themselves here and there, leading down to the sandy plain. Within these walls,—from whose summit a beautiful sunny view may be enjoyed of the wide valley and the brown hills,—many enemies of Rome were imprisoned in somewhat later times.

Syphax, the Numidian King, lay captive here, preserved to grace the triumphal processsion of Scipio; also the cruel Perseus, the last king of Macedonia, with his sons Philip and Alexander, the chief of the Allobroges Bituitus, and many others who were not willing to bow their necks beneath the Roman yoke.

The present insignificant little town lies on the Colle d'Alba, and still hides within its narrow lanes, its gardens and its churches, many important remnants of antiquity in the shape of beautiful Corinthian columns, cornices, and inscriptions. Also the remains of a theatre and of an amphitheatre are still to be seen.

Other places also preserve some trace of the names of their original inhabitants; thus at this day there is a Nagliano dei Marsi, a Gioja dei Marsi, and several others. Luco was formerly called Lucus Ancitiæ, and took its name from the ancient divinity, the *Bona Dea* of the Marsii. Her sister Circe dwells on the promontory yonder, and golden magic threads of mythological tradition have spun themselves over the whole country, from Lago Fucino to the sea coast. The mountains around the lake, which to this day abound in venomous snakes and healing herbs, seemed particularly adapted to the mysterious worship of this goddess; and the Marsii long vaunted their charms for exorcising venomous serpents, and their herbs for healing the bites of them. Virgil sings of such a priest of Ancitia, who comes from Fucinus:—

> "Came too, brave Umbro, priest of Marsian race,
> By King Archippus sent ; his crested casque
> With olive wreaths of happy omen decked.
> His was the art by song and touch to lull
> The viper's brood, and ill-breath'd hydra foul,
> To soothe their rage, and cure their venom'd bite."
> Æn. VII. 750 *et seq.*

As in Alba, so also in the vicinity of Luco, there are still to be found many fragments of pre-historic and Roman masonry; even the ruins of a temple, and the foundations of an amphitheatre are extant. But nearer to us than the old myths which still murmur in the reeds by the lake, and the heather on the mountains, is the history of an Imperial house whose ancient glories—like those of the royal race of Macedonia, faded and were finally extinguished on these shores.

To the northwest of Avezzano, about four hours' journey further into the interior of the inhospitable country, we find Tagliacozzo. Here, in the month of August of the year 1268, ended the brave and beautiful race of Hohenstaufen, overthrown, even to the dust, by French arms, which a Pope had consecrated against Germany; crushed in its last hopeful blossom, by a French Prince. Upon this stage, full of Italian charm and beauty, on the poplar-fringed borders of the rivers Imele and Salto, on the high tableland above the lake, Charles of Anjou conquered the valiant, but youthful and inexperienced,

Conradin. The latter fled, accompanied only by a few faithful followers, across the Sabine Hills to Rome, and thence to Astura. There stands to this day the solitary tower on the Latin coast, sad and melancholy, beside the blue waves, which seemed to promise help and safety to the fugitive. The yellow waters of the Salto flow murmuringly on, and could tell many a tale of that sultry summer day on which the flower of German and Italian chivalry fought on its banks against the ragged Provençal troops, and were finally

CIVITELLA.

overcome. Beneath yonder hills shone the watchfires of the victorious Charles of Anjou; the noise of drunken soldiers, and the revelry of victory resounded on all sides; and the gloomy Charles, whom not even victory could rouse from his sullen moodiness, sat in the royal tent and dictated the despatch which was to carry the good news of success to Pope Clement the Fourth, who was anxiously awaiting the tidings in Rome.

A bridle path, only practicable for mules and donkeys, leads from Canistro over the Zoglietta, by the Serra di Sant' Antonio, the well-watered valley of the Geanara, and past Filettino to Trevi and Guercino. It is a lonely and fatiguing ride. There are very few inhabitants among these hills, whose stony soil refuses to nourish corn or vines. Some poor olive trees grow sparsely round a solitary hut here and there. Coarse grass and herbage grow on the little scraps of pasture land, high among the hills, and the sheep of the Campagna climb up hither to pass the summer, which is always cool here. In the green little valley of Trevi the Anio begins its course, which, were we to follow it, would bring us to the rich district of Subiaco with its tranquil mountain monasteries, to the enchanting cascades of Tivoli, and finally to the sacred city of Rome itself. But we will first turn towards the venerable and ancient Alatri.

We have passed through a very beautiful landscape. Every time we look backward from any height we see through some gap in the distant silvery mountains, a golden plain swimming and steeped in sunlight:—that is the Roman Campagna. But soon dark, woody, wildly-shaped mountains rise before us, and the road winds along a precipice and

CYCLOPEAN WALLS NEAR ALBA FUCESE.

enters a hoary ancient wood of oaks and chestnuts, with countless fragments of rock all over-grown with ferns, strewed between the tree-stems. Then all vegetation ceases, and sharp, bluish-grey stones, formed in a thousand curious shapes, are seen all around, and close to the road itself. Poor shepherds and herdsmen, wretched peasants working in the scanty maize-fields, a swift horseman with a great cloak and his gun slanting across his saddle, white, shaggy wolf-dogs, fierce and shy,—such are the only figures which animate this dreary mountain-landscape.

But by degrees the valley grows broader; rich olive plantations, and vineyards surrounded by white walls, begin to be visible. Old watch-towers, overgrown with ivy and wild vine, peep above tall maples. Troops of gaily costumed country folks are seen upon the roads, or climbing to the heights above by green mountain paths. Light two-wheeled vehicles roll past us. A pleasant look of neatness and well-being smiles from field and meadow. A broad, steep hill rises in the midst of blooming gardens, and bears upon its back a town of attractive and hospitable appearance, pressed close together by high masses of antique masonry:—that is Alatri! One of the towns ruled over by the mythological Saturnus; and the walls are the renowned Cyclopean walls, in more perfect preservation than any others in Italian soil.

We are now in Latium, the "land of hiding;" but its towns are by no means hidden. They stand high upon some hill and shine across the plains, visible on all sides to friend or foe. Owing to their position they are greatly isolated—more so than many a far-off island—from the contact of modern culture, which travels more easily on the plain with its rivers and railways. The selection of this sort of site for a town,—which is, indeed, frequent all throughout Italy—probably was necessitated in the days when the "kingdom was divided against itself;" when town fought against town, commune against commune, all made, and broke, leagues of offence and defence, and life and property had little security save beneath the shelter of the walls of an Acropolis, or a strong castle. The houses were crowded closely together within the protecting walls, and were built with as much economy of ground as possible, thus leaving only narrow streets for the use of the inhabitants. Those times are over; but the custom of building on the old sites remains to this day. As the swallow returns year after year to the eaves where her first nest was hung, so the citizen of Latium erects his dwelling to-day, on the same spot where dwelt his forefathers in the ages of grey antiquity.

This tenacity is an almost pathetic trait: for upon these isolated heights, amidst these sterile stones, and on this dry soil, and, often absolutely in want of water for the purposes of life, the inhabitants contend with all kinds of hardship, with cold, with thirst, with hunger! Down below them lie the green luxuriant valleys where vine and corn ripen abundantly, and where full streams and rills ripple all summer through. They look down from their arid eyrie cold, hungry,—and unenvying! Whosoever has seen needy little Civitella above Olevano, San Pietro on the hills behind pleasant Palestrina, or Collepardo deep amid the Hernician mountains, cannot but ask himself wonderingly: "What can these people do up here? How do they live?" For the soil gives absolutely no sustenance; there are stones for bread; no twig blossoms, no bird sings in these deserts; and in San Pietro, mother Earth closes her flinty bosom when she is asked to receive her dead children back again:—the soil is absolutely too hard to dig a grave in!

In Alatri it is better. There gardens bloom around the hill, and fruit-trees climb up its slopes, even to the Cyclopean walls,—even to the streets of the town. And, although they cost much labour to obtain, yet corn and wine are to be had here in abundance, and delicious fruits and clear water refresh the thirsty palate in the summer. Where nature smiles kindly on her children, they thank her by cheerfulness and gaiety. What a lively population is this of Alatri, and what a handsome one! All, men and women, are tall and straight; the men broad-shouldered, the women full-busted, and with great, glorious dark eyes. The men wear a red waistcoat, short black breeches, and a hat adorned with many ribbons and artificial flowers, which sits carelessly on the head as if the mountain breezes had blown it to one side. The women also love bright colours; red or blue petticoats, black bodices, with embroidered shoulder-straps, against which their clean white linen sleeves are pleasantly relieved. The forehead and cheeks are shaded by the white folded kerchief on the top of the head, and the grand Roman profiles stand out splendidly beneath this head-dress. When you see these women returning from the well, with great antique-shaped copper vases on their heads, one hand upon the hip, the other

OLLANTA.

gracefully raised to support the brimming vessel, or else with both arms folded on the ample bosom, you think, as they move past you with slow majestic gait, that they are

CAPISTRELLO, IN THE VALLEY OF THE LIRIS.

daughters of some ancient king, carrying up water to the kingly halls as king's daughters are said to have done in old legends.

Amidst all the cheerfulness of this little mountain population, you can trace a certain defiant scornfulness,—well visible in a tiny line between the handsome black eyebrows, which their race and their history has stamped upon them. Their history is a bloody one.

What the town suffered in classic times, during the civil wars of Marius and Sylla, may have been entirely buried in oblivion, since those sufferings were followed by a long period of rest. But the traces stamped on it by the arms of Germans, Frenchmen, and Spaniards, from the times of the Hohenstaufens down to the great French Revolution, are still distinctly visible.

In these days no one makes war upon Alatri more. The ancient Porta Bellona is now called Porta San Pietro. A few poets and painters climb up hither from time to time, search after the fragments of antiquity, and then sit throughout long sunny afternoons upon the Cyclopean walls which have defied all ravages of time, and gaze into the silent landscape. One might sit here and dream the whole day long, for the view that meets one's eye is wondrous. What peacefulness all around! Roses bloom in the crevices of the wall, the summer breeze whispers among the tendrils of the ivy, and sweet odours are blown from the mountain slopes. The *cicale* chirp their sun-inspired song among the vineyards, and the swallows flit and twitter round the grey old stones. The soul seems to be freed from its earthly shackles, and to float far away on the wings of a dream,—far away through the pure ether to the setting sun, and sink into the purple depths of evening.

Many little towns are scattered over this mountainous district. To the eastward lie Veroli, Banco, Ripi, Torrice, Poffi, Arnara, and Frosinone, the pleasantest of them all; and the mountain tops are innumerable. All these towns and hills and streams and meadows are, as it were, woven in with the texture of old histories:—mostly, indeed, with blood-red threads, and the spirit of these old histories breathes all around us, and transports us far, far back into the youth of the world, into the mists of the past. These walls, whose colossal construction is a mystery to us, were built by mythic Titans, who dared to set their adventurous feet even on the threshold of the golden dwelling of the gods; and who piled up their earthly buildings in imitation of it! The populace ascribes the foundation of Alatri to Saturn, who is said to have also founded Anagni, Arpino, Aquino, and Atina, all in this district. The sickle and the pruning-knife were his attributes; and hand in hand with his wife Ops, he wandered in that golden age among the hills, shedding a blessing over field and vineyard. To this day the blessing of the god has power, and makes the soil bring forth corn and wine abundantly.

If, on looking down from the lofty walls of Alatri we receive an impression of those old god-ruled pagan times, in Anagni, on the other hand, we behold the very form and body of the Pope-ruled Middle Ages. This town, which once played an important part in history, stands on a hill. The *via latina* passes by it; that road along which the Roman troops marched towards the Volturnus. The *via latina* leads through the fine scenery of the valley of the Sacco, from which the Volscian mountains rise on the side towards the sea. Here the peculiar colouring of the Roman Campagna may be enjoyed in perfection. The plain, alternately waste and cultivated, offers every gradation of tint, from a light sunny yellow to the deepest earth-brown. It slopes gently up towards the hills, and on the heights all deeper hues are lost in a pure lucent silvery grey. Over all is stretched an exquisitely clear sky: fit heaven for the gods, who have not yet averted their gaze from their old earthly realm. But human life upon that plain is poor and powerless, even as the gods themselves; especially in the neighbourhood of the Volscian Mountains. Miserable, ruinous towns and villages lie on the sun-baked soil like dying beggars:—Supino, Patrica, Morolo, Scurcola, and others. Their very names are almost forgotten.

The inhabitants of those rocky nests are unspeakably poor, and may well look enviously across at the Hernician hills, where Alatri, Anagni, Ferentino, Veroli, and Frosinone, are surrounded by a green garland of vines and olives. The height on which Anagni stands has many bright flowers woven into its crown of vines. All sorts of fruit

ARPINO.

trees blossom round about Anagni, and there is a veritable wall of foliage through which you pass amidst the murmur of leaves, the perfume of flowers, the humming of bees, and the song of birds, to the gate of the town. This world of greenery is like a veil behind which one expects to see smiling youth and beauty; but, lift it, and you behold a dignified grave matron clad in mediæval garb. On entering the town through the Porta Ferentina, we pass through narrow but clean streets, full of fine old palaces, whose glory has long departed, but which still have an imposing aspect with their time-darkened colouring, and the numerous remains of fine gothic marble-work about their doors and windows. They are for the most part empty: for the great old families that owned them have nearly all died out. "*Le dodici stelle di Anagni*," as the twelve principal families were called, have lost their lustre, and the town is now an unimportant place. Nevertheless it is still one of the most interesting spots in Latium, both from its position and its history.

Its situation is absolutely enchanting, and commands a view over the whole of Latium. The eye roams over the fertile plain of Palestrina even to the Roman territory. The pen is powerless to paint this landscape; even the ablest artist would fail to represent it adequately with brush and palette. For granting that he could faithfully reproduce the noble outlines which melt so softly into one another, could copy all the delicate yet decided forms, could give the harmony of tone which marks the whole, yet can he never hope to catch that inexpressible softness of atmosphere, that aërial vapour which broods over plain and mountain like a breath of ancient Odyssean heroic legend, full of dreamy melancholy. Who has once beheld this picture in the full summer sunshine can never forget it to the end of his life; Gregorovius says: "This view is so beautiful that it transports even those who have seen all Italy from the Alps to the Afric and Ionic seas." And, truly, he is right!

Anagni delights the traveller by a certain, almost Greek, cheerfulness which distinguishes its inhabitants. They are overflowing with health and strength, and enjoy—perhaps even unconsciously—the beauty of their country. Children play joyously in the sunshine; the laugh and song abound, and the stranger is saluted with a cordial greeting. Anagni is a kind of Nuremberg translated into Italian. The whole town is a series of pictures. Travellers are seldom seen here; painters still seldomer. Yet it is certain that both would find much interest and enjoyment in the place. On either side of the great high roads, and hidden deep within classic Latium, lies very much that is worthy of attention.

But we must onward, through Genazzano to Palestrina and Tivoli.

The road now leads through a rich and cultivated country, full of trees and corn and vines and olives. Suddenly we are surprised by a glimpse of a grey old town on a gently sloping eminence behind the green summits of the oaks and chestnuts. This is Genazzano; like Anagni, a mediæval town which has preserved its peculiar character. The ancient fortifications are still standing; there is a strong lofty town-gate surmounted by battlements, and most of the houses retain traces of gothic architecture. The streets are narrow and steep, and all converge towards the palace of the Colonnas, to whom the town once belonged. A world of flowers bloom on the high walls which enclose this proud old castle, and the grey stone-work is clasped by green tendrils. In the interior all is ruinous. The castle is a mere storehouse for grain. In the courtyard, encumbered by piles of wood for fuel, horses and poultry stray about. Very few chambers are still habitable, and the proud armorial bearings of the Colonnas—an upright column with a crown above it—peer out from heaps of dust and dirt. The lofty halls are turned into stables. One saloon serves as a place for storing oil in, and here some dozen or so of family portraits are hanging all in tatters, and covered with cobwebs. The marble statues have lost their heads, and are used as perches by swarms of pigeons.

Behind the castle stretches the Campagna, but divided from it by a deep ravine, which is spanned by a fine bridge giving access to the smiling fertile plain. Seen from this bridge, the ruins of a Roman aqueduct stretching towards a dark grove of secular oak-trees, and the classic character of the landscape, may recall ancient Roman times to the spectator. But the chief builders and rulers here, were the powerful Colonnas; they were the Kings of the Campagna. In the entrance-hall of the upper castle the walls are covered with pictures and inscriptions setting forth the various places over which they ruled. It takes a quarter of an hour merely to read all the names, for their power extended far into

THE ITALIAN FAMILY UMBRELLA.

the Abruzzi, as far as the Neapolitan frontier. At the present day this is all changed. Leaf by leaf, time has stripped the mighty tree; and what remains is but a faint image of former glories.

But the landscape still shines in ever-youthful beauty, and the Italian sun brings yearly the self-same bloom of spring to these well-watered valleys, as smiled in the Middle Ages. Here glows the purple grape whose juice cheered and animated the knights of old; and here the rose still blossoms amidst cypress and laurel. Genazzano seems to be a sort of outpost of the Neapolitan paradise. The eye ranges over shrubs, vineyards, and beautiful groups of trees, to the mountains on the left, dominated by the proud pyramid of Monte Serrone. Gloomy castles, and grey towns, crown the summits of most of the hills, or peep out from green valleys that run from Rome towards Campania. Yonder passed the bold troops of the Hohenstaufens; there the Frenchmen and the Spaniard spurred their chargers; Franks marched by, Goths, Vandals! Now all is still, and Peace lies like

VILLA FALCONIERI, NEAR FRASCATI.

a sleeping shepherdess upon the land. The air seems to vibrate with the sound of bells chiming the Ave Maria. We are in the headquarters of Madonna-worship. Here in Genazzano is her miracle-working picture, which was once, according to Catholic tradition, carried by angel hands from Albania, and borne through the air high above land and sea to Genazzano. A church was built for it, and its fame soon spread through all the hills and vales of Latium and Campania. The poor shepherd of the plain, the dweller amid Neapolitan mountains, the fever-stricken wretch from the Pontine Marshes, the Marsic people of Avezzano,—all, all make a pilgrimage at least once in their lives to this Romish Mecca, to beg for a favourable oracle, and to lay their confessions at the feet of the "*Madonna del buon consiglio.*" They come in crowds:—tottering, whitehaired old men, powerful fellows in the prime of life, brigand-like swaggerers, women and girls in the gay costumes of their native hills, black-haired urchins, and even children in arms,—they come hither to lay their little offerings before the Queen of Heaven, who can help them out of poverty, care, and love-troubles, if she only will! Thousands of lustrous dark eyes are turned towards her, and passionate, wild songs and prayers resound everywhere. These pilgrimages take place twice a year; the first in the early days of spring, the second at the vintage time in the glorious month of September. And whoever wishes to study and enjoy the genuine Italian populace has only to come hither and mingle with the crowd of pilgrims: among whom types of the highest classic beauty are by no means rare.

All the land around teems with rich vegetation. The trees are not only strong and luxuriant, but picturesquely beautiful, and arranged in groups which delight the eye by manifold contrasts of form and foliage. The lively Via Prænestina passes through many

GENAZZANO.

such groups. Now it is a hoary heaven-piercing cypress rising like a pillar from amidst the cheerful chestnut trees: now a group of thick-stemmed stone pines, whose outlines contrast agreeably with the slender vertical poplar: now some elms hung over with bacchic garlands of the vine. But above all, the walnut trees flourish here especially. Beyond Cave the road passes through a hollow way which is almost choked up with bush and shrub and creeping plants. A stream flows through it on the right; and one of the rocky walls which enclose the hollow way, is constantly dripping with tiny rivulets of water, which trickle silverly between the great leaves of the wood-ivy. Here and there the water is collected into stone basins, and, around these, gaily clad women wash and chat: the herdsman or the carter stops his beasts to drink; and slender girls lift up their great copper pitchers to the mouth of the Campagnan farmer as he halts in his ride. It is a series of charming pictures. Presently we meet soldiers on furlough, women with a bundle of freshly cut grass or a basket of fruit on the head, and a sucking infant at the breast, grave, black-robed priests, nuns with downcast eyes, and children at play in the shadow of the trees.

English, German, and French tourists trot by mounted on donkeys or horses, and before us, piled up house above house on the height, appears sunny Palestrina, the renowned city of Fortune.

Five different epochs may be traced in her masonry:—the Pre-historic Period, that of the Roman Republic, of the Empire, and of the Middle Ages; and lastly these modern times are setting their mark on her with gardens, and villas, and summer-houses of the Roman nobles and citizens, hôtels, and other innovations! The entire site on which Palestrina now stands was once occupied by the Temple of Fortune. It was watered with a fearful quantity of blood; for Palestrina, flourishing and powerful, bold and independent, excited every now and then the jealousy of her mighty neighbour, world-compelling Rome. But the most cruel fate was given her at the hands of Sylla. The younger Marius, after the massacre of the Roman senators, fled with his troop to Præneste, and took refuge there, and Sylla left Quintus Ofella to besiege the town. Several armies marched to the rescue of the hard-pressed Præneste, but none succeeded in freeing her. The last of these, which menaced Rome itself, and on which Marius had staked all his hopes, was defeated before the city gate; the heads of the leaders were flung over the walls into Præneste; and then the chiefs, the Consul Caius Marius, and the son of Pontius, understood that all was over, and perished by their own hands. The unbridled hosts of the angry Sylla poured through the gates into the city. With the exception of the women and children, the whole population was destroyed by a bloody massacre, which lasted for days. And then, when there was nothing more to plunder, no one more to murder, they set fire to the town, and left behind them, as a monument of Sylla's vengeance, a smouldering heap of ruins, which covered the Campagna far and wide with a pall of black smoke, and warned the neighbouring cities of the fate they might expect. Norba, the town by the marsh, saw it. The frightful news travelled quickly; and anticipating the red-handed ministers of slaughter, they set fire to their town, killed their wives, their children, and finally, themselves.

Possibly remorse of conscience tormented Sylla in after days beyond endurance; for, as if by way of expiation, he rebuilt the town, and erected in all its glory the Temple of Fortune, which remained for a long period the most renowned sacred edifice upon the Latin soil. By this means the town grew to remarkable prosperity, which was further increased by the circumstance that several emperors favoured it specially. Augustus loved Præneste. Tiberius, Nero, and Domitian dwelt here, and Hadrian built himself an enchanting villa close at hand.

The attractions which drew these Emperors, and many great and powerful Romans besides, to the spot, still distinguish the city: these are air, sunshine, and cool mountain springs. Nowhere is the air purer, the sunlight more genial, than in cheerful Palestrina. From the windows of the town an exquisite view is to be enjoyed. The hill of Palestrina commands the whole Campagna, from the shores of the Liris to the city of Rome, and beyond it. From hence, too, the sea is visible, with distant islands dotting its shining surface.

The solemn, noble, colouring of ancient history and fable, gives its tone to the whole dark plain below us. For let the eye turn where it will:—towards stern Soracte, or the silver chain of the Roman Apennine, to the Sabine Hills, or to those of Latium,—everywhere, from the mountains to the sea, it rests upon spots which belong to the history of all ages. This landscape is a great world's amphitheatre; and we seek out the regions and frontiers of the peoples who acted on it,—ancient nations whom the new and growing Rome found long established on the soil,—Hernicians, Umbrians, Latins, Albans, Volscians, and many more.

Everything shines and shimmers in the beneficent sunlight. The world seems steeped in peace and pleasure. This sky and soil have long forgotten that they once witnessed horrible days here, when the land was filled with blood, and fire, and smoke from burning cities. From the blood, red roses have sprung; from the tears, song-inspiring wine; and for the ruins,—the green hopeful ivy has overspread them with his protecting tendrils. As we look to the west we see a purple mist on the horizon, but from it rises, distinctly visible, the dome of St. Peter's. *Salve!* There then lies Rome the beloved! We can trace the white lines of roads which all lead towards her gates, and the old yearning awakes in our hearts. The sun goes down exactly behind St. Peter's cupola, and an indescribable play of colours quivers over the land. But the purple veil of mist over Rome is lifted, and the Seven Hills show clearly, glowing beneath the farewell kiss of the sun. Great fires are lighted down in the plain, and columns of waving smoke rise up to the clear evening sky, like the smoke of burnt-offerings to Ceres. How fearfully sublime a spectacle must the burning of Rome by Nero have been from hence! What a dread black pall must have spread over the landscape! But this rosy evening light transfigures everything. The Christian bells of the victorious church militant ring out the Ave Maria; and Fortune, the antique goddess, hears the sound from amid her ruined walls, and veils her matron head anew.

Many objects which belonged to her temple are still found here from time to time: such as small terra-cotta statuettes of men and animals, bronze caskets of fine workmanship, tablets with the calendar on them, metal mirrors, heads of marble statues, etc., etc., etc. Near to the cathedral, built into the wall, and covered with modern whitewash, are four Corinthian pilasters. And adjoining these is a very ruinous arcade, under which the modern Fortune, the Italian "*Lotto*" (state lottery) has set up her temple. Amongst the pomegranates and acacias in the gardens, many antique fragments are lying. But the finest of all is the colossal mosaic in the Palace of the Barberini, which surmounts the town like a princely coronet.

You climb up to the highest summit of the Prænestian hill, over a waste of dreary fragments. Here stood one of the oldest fortresses of Latium, whose erection is ascribed to the enigmatical Cæculus. Cæculus, the offspring of Vulcan by a slave, had been found when a child by the Vestal Virgins. He grew up like the sons of Mars, Romulus and Remus, among the herdsmen of the Campagna, and became a shepherd king. He gathered around him a wild and lawless population, and built a fortress on these heights; proving his divine descent from time to time by fire which fell from heaven.

In the sixth century a convent was established near to the ruins of the castle. In the Middle Ages, the fortress itself was rebuilt, and the Colonnas inhabited it. The fierce Anagnese, Boniface the Eighth, in his endeavours to root out the Colonna family, destroyed the *Castrum Montis Penestrini* by the help of the traitorous Guido da Montefeltro. Re-built once more, it has become a ruin again at the present day, and is all draped with ivy, and wild vine, and golden broom, and dog-roses. The wretched village which lies among the rubbish here, sustains a miserable existence. It is called after the ancient monastery, San Pietro; and offers its haggard and hungry inhabitants stones for bread. The view is more extended from hence than from the lower town, stretching out farther to the north-east. We look into a grey, treeless wilderness of mountains, stretching from the dreary Rocca di Cavi, and Capranica, to the distant valley of the Anio by Subiaco. But yonder, where blue Soracte rises, amongst the fair Sabine Hills, lies Tivoli; and there the Anio, gently winding, enters into the Roman Campagna. The richly watered Tivoli invites us :—

> "When weary of voyages, and rambling, and war,
> The evening of life needs some haven of rest,
> In Tibur of old, built by Greeks from afar,
> Would I fain make my rest!"—HORACE.

And truly any one who has been charmed by the position of these hills, and has drunk of the fresh springs where the sirens dwell, may echo these words.

TEMPLE OF THE SIBYL, TIVOLI.

You leave Palestrina by the Porta del Sole, and enter at once into the kingdom of sunshine indeed. The green vineyards, fruit-trees, and flower gardens, are soon left behind, and the road is bordered by a growth of fern and bracken tanned to a reddish brown by the glow of summer. It runs parallel to the ancient Via Prænestina, the polygonal pavement of which—somewhat above the level of the present road—is visible here and there in stretches of considerable extent. Here we have again the real wilderness of the Campagna. The hillocks are covered with dry herbage, and on the flat ground a growth of thistles, as tall as a man, forms an almost impenetrable thicket. The humble weeds and blossoms—such as mint and balm,—which grow among their roots, send out absolutely intoxicating odours beneath the powerful rays of the sun. These rays form a sort of golden network, in whose meshes the blue and white butterflies flutter languidly over the plain. Then comes a bit of oak wood at the foot of a mountain; and on the top of the latter stands an old castle, with blackened walls, which looks like a true robber's den. The old knights have long ago disappeared; and down by the stream yonder, where the cattle are clustered, a mill is working noisily. Now again the sunny plain opens out before us, and thick clouds of dust sweep over it, driven by the midday breeze. The chirp of grasshoppers and cicale fills the air, lizards dart arrow-swift across the road, a bird of prey floats slowly with wide gyrations in the brazen sky,—and that is all the life which animates the landscape.

At length the houses of Tivoli appear over the slope, thickly overgrown with Minerva's tree. Near the Ponte Lucano, close to which stands the tomb of the Plautii, built in imitation of that of Cecilia Metella, the road branches off towards the city. But it makes many a tedious zig-zag as it climbs the hill amid groves of the sad-suited grey olive. All the more striking, after this sober vegetation, is the contrast with the other side of the hill, so verdant and richly watered.

Tivoli!—There are spots which we approach with a certain timidity, on account of their wealth of memories, and of landscape beauty. We fear to become so much attached to them, that a prolonged stay amidst their charms will but make parting at last more

TIVOLI.

difficult. Such a spot is Tivoli. It is best to take but a brief view of its beauties, so that they shall abide in the memory as a beautiful dream might abide there. For this purpose it will suffice to sit beneath the little temple of Vesta, to visit the falls of the Anio, to wander through the gardens of the Villa d'Este, and to see the Villa of Hadrian by way of farewell.

Illumined from morn to eve by the rays of the sun, the charming temple of the Sibyl (or Temple of Vesta), overhangs the ravine perched on its rocky height. To the left, the great fall thunders in the gulf below; to the right, the smaller cascade falls like a silvery veil over the green tendrils of climbing plants. The foreground is filled with a thick wood of various kinds of foliage, from amidst which proud pine-trees and the dark pyramidal cypress rise. At every turn may be found cool, shady, mysterious spots, impenetrable by any ray of sunshine, and dedicated to the nymphs. To the right, on the height stands the cheerful little town. A handsome stone bridge leads to it. Beneath this bridge lie delicious little gardens among the rocks, and cottages built on the edge of the precipice; and the former course of the cascade is still distinctly traceable, together with deep caverns eaten out by the waters. In the background rise the soft outlines of Monte Catillo, clothed with vines and olives. If we descend into the ravine, the picture changes at each turn of the path, and the vegetation grows more and more luxuriant. The spray of many waters fills the air, and there is a cool sweet smell from leaves and flowers. When we enter the caverns, we seem to be penetrating into the very bowels of the earth, and are amazed at the power of the water which has pierced these gigantic veins in the rock. We descend still deeper. Evergreen oaks, and broad-leaved elms, catch the last sun-rays which penetrate this shady region. Here is the grotto of the sirens, where the stream, plunging into mysterious depths, suddenly disappears from our ken. We must retrace our steps.

The whole place is like a garden interspersed with trees; and the foot lingers and hesitates before leaving this perfumed shade, for broad daylight and the work-a-day world. The purple splendour of the violet shines from amid the green, and in the whispering boughs the nightingales sing all the year through. All other sounds are softly mingled with the low thunders of the waterfall, and the soul is spell-bound as in a dream, and would fain fold her wings here, and depart no more from this enchanted garden by the Anio. As we stand at the edge of the great fall, we see the waters come and glide into the gulf: and still they come, unresting, again and again to fall and disappear. A voice seems to sound from the pressing foaming waves:—

"The soul of man is like to water!"

Before the fall, where the flood glides smoothly on, unconscious of its approaching fate, we are in the midst of a charming river-landscape. Here we sit on the bank, in the neighbourhood of the old cemetery, and look into the shining waves. The shrubs and trees seem to press and crowd each other in their efforts to draw near to the cool waters, and mingle with the matted tendrils of the vine, and hang over the stream as though they would plunge into it. There are the poplar, the ash, the oak, willows, and acacias. In the middle of the river, on a tiny islet, stands a hoary weeping willow. Its long light branches droop mournfully over the flood, but little birds sing cheerfully amidst its foliage. The bank is partly overgrown with reeds, but ere they have climbed far up the slope, they are met by a green barrier of vines. Behind all this, rise white gleaming walls, and groups of houses. Butterflies flutter close to the surface of the stream, their tiny shadows dancing on the ripples, and pursued by sunbeams that dart through every opening in the wind-stirred foliage. A blue heaven flecked with golden clouds, is reflected in the glassy waters.

Then the sun begins to sink. Solemn shadows overspread the vale, but the evening purple mingles with them, and dyes the leaves with the wondrous, magic tints of faery. Swarms of swallows play around the stream, or, skimming joyously above it, dip their warm breasts in the golden water, before they fly home to their nests among the ruins of a glorious past. Then night descends upon the branches. The waters sob and sigh as they hasten towards the fall whose rush is heard in this still evening hour; and the moon rises above the tree-tops.

FROM THE VILLA OF HADRIAN, NEAR TIVOLI.

In these evergreen groves, on the cool banks of the Anio, the land was covered throughout the Imperial period with countless smiling villas. The Emperors themselves dwelt here: especially Augustus. And poets thronged to the villa Mæcenas. Here

ROMAN BEGGAR CHILD.

Propertius sang his love-song for his Cynthia, "the golden maiden of Tibur;" here Horace bound his brows with ivy, and invited his friends to enjoy the happy present in intimate communion.

"Huc vina et unguenta, et nimium brevis
Flores amoenos ferre jube rosæ,
Dum res, et ætas, et Sororum
Fila trium patiuntur atra."

Here poetized Statius, the admirer of Virgil, and sang an enthusiastic eulogy of the beautiful classic villa of Vobiscus, whose roof-tree Venus herself had sprinkled with Idalian odours, and endowed with eternal graces and Olympian charms.

> "Whence thou gazest forth on the still and silent woodland,
> Where peace reigns undisturbed, and where, unvexed by storm-winds,
> The night is hushed to rest, and soft murmurs lull thee to slumber."

Here wandered Catullus, Martial, and Tibullus. On the brow of the hill Quinctilius Varus had his home, who exchanged life amidst southern roses, for death beneath the dark northern oaks. Only a few crumbling ruins remain of that home; but it will live for ever in eternal classic songs.

But the works of later times are also falling into decay. In the sixteenth century another Mæcenas built a lordly dwelling here, and another Horace dedicated poems to him. These were the Cardinal d'Este, and the poet Ariosto. The Villa d'Este now belongs to Cardinal Hohenlohe.

How still is all around us here! The rays of sunshine stray and shimmer under the arcades of the courtyard, whose walls are overgrown with creeping plants. Thick dust lies in the chambers, and the foot treads softly as though it feared to awaken a sleeper. We descend a flight of steps, and pass down into the weed-grown, low-lying garden. Here everything seems spell-bound, and Melancholy seems to have chosen it for her silent kingdom. Nature truly is ever busily striving to conceal the universal ruin, to cover it with laurels and roses, and to breathe fresh life into the mouldering stones; but the grave-clothes show through the branches and blossoms, and the tree-tops whisper to each other only of sadness and solitude.

And yet,—how beautiful it is! It is a poet's world; the garden itself is a poem of the highest kind. We wander beneath the shadow of the aspiring laurels; roses kiss our brow as we go, and the fountains murmur in their mossy basins. Up above there the sun pierces with power through the tangled ilex-trees, and white marble statues glimmer amid the green. In the centre of the garden stands a semicircle of hoary ancient cypresses, and there the fountains flash, and the birds sing "so sweetly and so sadly." But the lightnings of heaven threaten even these old symbols of bygone splendour; already one lofty summit has been smitten down, and the days of the noble trees are numbered. The springing jets of water murmur on,—busy, loquacious, and hasty,—as though, like clocks, they had to count the passing seconds, and feared to lose a fragment of time. The prickly cactus-plants stand round them with uplifted spear;—a faithful body-guard steadfastly awaiting the ever nearer approach of Time. His advance is chronicled by the sound of the clock-bell that chimes out mournfully above the dark tree tops. In the wide, overflowing reservoir of water,—once the mirror of Venus herself,—the beautiful villa is reflected. Its once cheerful aspect grows daily sadder and more forlorn. Where is all the clear laughter that was wont to ring here? Where the song and sound of lutes? Where all the gay, joyous masque of revelry? The dry leaves crackle beneath our feet!

Day has departed. The silent queen of night treads through the clouds, and pours her enchanted light over the sleeping garden. The branches shiver, the flowers open their chalices and breathe sweet odours all around, the waters swell and rise as though they longed to reach the stars, and the garden-walks grow animated. The marble statues

SHORES OF LAGO FUCINO TO THE PONTINE MARSHES. 321

descend from their pedestals, and move as gods amidst the laurel hedges. Yonder, where the brooding Sybil sits in the dark bower of planes, the great conches begin to sound, and the dripping river gods, Anio and Tiber, break through their bonds of ivy wreaths and

ROMAN PEASANTS.

step out through the waters. Beneath the shadow of the black cypresses, between leaves and flowers, beautiful Roman girls—the nieces of the great Cardinal—flit and rustle with silvery laughter. The nymphs of the fountain bathe their white limbs among the waving reeds. Oh sweet dream-life, filled with perfume and moonlight! The nightingale sings from the grove on the hill, and would fain pour out all her little heart in song; she sings of love, of nought save love.

How enchanting is the view between the ilex-trees, of the Campagna which lies down there before us like a vast web of moon-rays, looking all the brighter because seen from this dense dark shade! How nebulously are all the mountains transfigured—and above all, the sternly beautiful Soracte! And yonder lies Rome. That white, winding road, the Via Tiburtina, leads through the desolate plain to the Eternal City. And the eye can reach still farther: there is the sea, a shining strip that seems as though it were hanging in the sky, and on its shores lie Civita Vecchia, and Ostia at the mouth of the Tiber. Other cities, too, lie within our view; Frascati stands at the foot of the wood-grown Monte Cavo, and as far as we can see, the Campagna stretches out in a golden glimmer of light.

At the foot of the southern slope of the hill on which we stand, are the ruins of Hadrian's Villa. Here all the splendours of the world once shone in gold and marble and bronze and precious stones. A great lover of the beautiful had ransacked the earth, seeking through all the provinces of the mighty Roman Empire—on the Ebro, on the Nile, in Greece—for beauty, and here he designed his proud Pantheon, and called the Graces to minister to the work. Then all the glories of the world flowed hither; the temples of Athens, of Egypt, of Asia, were rifled, the hands of innumerable masters set in motion, to adorn this place. The villa and its grounds stretched over a space of seven miles, and contained hills and valleys, streams and lakes. Rotundas supported on costly columns, shine with gold, and are encrusted with precious stones. Mosaics cover the walls, the floors, and the ceilings. The wide staircases are flanked by exquisite Grecian vases, and covered with Babylonian carpets. The flowers of all zones bloom around these architectural glories, and mingle their perfume with the aromatic clouds of spicy incense. Greek songs are heard to the accompaniment of flute and harp. Roman warriors flash by in their silver-bright armour. And still new treasures continue to pour in; the Emperor's hands are untiring.

And to-day? You smile as you listen to the chattering cicerone who leads you about, and declares that on this mound the Emperor's palace stood commanding the splendours he had created; that this is the Canopus, on whose bosom he glided in a purple Nile-boat from his palace to the luxurious Thermæ; here flowed the stream of the Alpheus; that field above there, is called the Hippodrome; in yonder hidden depth, lay the gloomy Tartarus, and here bloomed the Elysian Fields. This is the Academy; that, the Lyceum; there the Prytaneum. Those walls formed the splendid Pœcile of Athens; and these next to them the School of Philosophy. Besides all these we find the remains of three theatres, five temples copied from the most beautiful in the world, a Palæstra, libraries, and barracks. When the whole was completed, the Emperor, by the advice of the priests, consecrated it by a sacrifice of Christian blood. The Christian martyrology tells of a Saint Symphorosa, who, together with her seven blooming sons, was sacrificed to the ancient gods near the temple of Hercules. The youthful Benedict, when he fled from the corruptions of Rome to dedicate himself entirely to Heaven in the solitude of the distant Sabine mountains, beheld the magnificent buildings of Hadrian almost uninjured. That was towards the end of the fifth century; and only fifty years later, they were utterly devastated by the savage hordes of Totila. Since that time, the churches and museums of Rome,—and, indeed, all Europe,—have been enriched from this treasure house, and pickaxe and spade have brought to light the antique splendours which now adorn many a distant hall.

The mass of ruins is very confused and intricate, and has been the despair of many an archæologist; but the rich growth of wild plants, and the surrounding Campagna, make the place unspeakably attractive. A whole series of classic landscapes may be

MARINO ON THE LAKE ALBANO.

found here, forming a treasure-store of another kind for the appreciative artist, and one that is eternal and inexhaustible. The cypress with its ancient stem replaces the fallen pillars of the old world of marble; ivy represents the carpets, acanthus the capitals of the columns, instead of incense we have the breath of the wild rose, and in place of the Grecian flutes, the spring song of birds.

In an oblique line across the waving Campagna lies a group of blue mountains. This is the exhausted Vesuvius of the Roman landscape,—the much praised hills of Albano. Vulcan created them, and the foot may yet wander for miles upon the blackened ashes of his strenuous work. But the forge smokes no longer; and where the fire once glowed, and hammer and anvil rang, the silent fishing bark swims on the still, green lakes of Nemi and Albano. Here were the original cradles of Rome; and hither the most modern life of wealthy Rome loves to come. The nobles build proud villas in Frascati and Albano, in whose gardens the shrill whistle of the locomotive sounds at all hours! The painter, the poet, and such-like pedestrian folks, are grateful and glad if they can get a little chamber looking between the vines on to the lake of Nemi.

Shall we explore all the paths that lead through the green ravines, over the wooded sides of Monte Cavo, to Nemi and Albano? Nature paints here with so wondrously fine and vaporous a pencil—and it is Nature alone, without any addition of man's handiwork—that pen-pictures, mere white paper and printer's ink, cannot suffice to re-produce her. We can but pluck a bunch of flowers to stick in our hat, a blossom to put between the leaves of our journal of travel, and for this we shall have opportunity enough on these mountain paths. It were good, too, that we should not look back on Rome; else would our wandering farther and farther from it be too painful. Let us stoop here, then, and gather a nosegay! What a rosy glow amidst the brown fallen leaves! These are the perfumed violets which have not ceased to bloom here since Cicero's time, and take no heed of the changing seasons in this shady grove. They make this place eternally vernal; for a Roman autumn amongst these Albanian hills, looks like his first-born brother, the smiling Spring.

> "The day
> Is wonderful. The very ruins shine
> Beneath its light like spirits glorified.
> Such autumn days belong to Rome alone.
> And, as great Romans did of yore, the land
> Has donned its robes of pomp and victory
> To die!"   GRABBE.

The path continues amidst a thick growth of shrubs, chestnuts, and oaks, where masses of ruin sleep overgrown with ivy. Then we emerge suddenly upon a brown, sun-burned plain, from which naked stony hills rise up, and before us is the wild-looking mountain eyrie of Rocca di Papa. Above it grey mists float around a height whose summit shines in sunlight:—Monte Cavo. Yonder glimmering cupolas belong to the Pope's summer palace, Castel Gandolfo. The path still continues to mount. The foot slips on rolling lava stones, and the way is bordered by the golden broom, and many a bush and tree. The wide sunburned tract we have seen below, bears the name of Hannibal's Camp. It looks like the crater of an extinct volcano, and is covered with a scanty vegetation. It is admirably adapted for a military post of observation, for Rome is seen from hence in its whole extent. Our way leads hence up to the sacred seat of the gods of these mountains of Albano. This is no common road; it is the ancient Via Triumphalis, which led to the temple of Jupiter Latialis, the protecting deity of the Latin Confederation. This road was trodden by the allied peoples when they celebrated the annual festival of the federation, and resounded beneath the hoofs of the Roman horses bearing their warrior masters with myrtle-wreathed helmets, to celebrate a triumph on the sacred hill. These polygonal blocks of basalt pavement, so wonderfully well preserved, were laid by antique hands. Now they are surrounded by woodland; and the whole

CAMP OF HANNIBAL NEAR ROCCA DI PAPA.

landscape in its silence and solitude has somewhat of the mystery of a sacred grove. On the summit of Monte Cavo, we stand before the consecrated portal of a Passionist Convent, from the shrill sound of whose jangling bells, the old gods fly deep into the woods. Within the eighteenth century the ancient temple was still standing in tolerably good preservation; but then monkish superstition suppressed it, and that by means of an Englishman, Cardinal York, the last of the Stuarts, who erected the ugly monastery on the site of the beautiful temple, and dedicated it to the Trinity.

GENZANO ON THE LAKE OF NEMI.

One cannot but regret this barbarous destruction, in looking at the mighty antique blocks which form the substructure of the convent, and enclose a dreary garden where tomatoes are cultivated to flavour the monks' macaroni. On the eastern side of the hill stand huge beeches and elms, whose roots are twined around many a fragment of the temple, and against whose stems we may lean and dream ourselves back into past centuries. The branches rustle mysteriously, Venus's turtle-doves coo tenderly amongst the odorous foliage, and the noise of the modern workaday world is far away. Between the trees and shrubs you can get views over the whole of Latium: nay, if the day be clear, you may see the islands of Sardinia and Corsica floating hazily in the sunset light. The

Mediterranean glitters golden, and its coasts stretch southward in fine soft outlines beyond the headland of Circe. We might name a thousand names that are written in the ancient histories, and the more we gazed the more we should discover. But let us look downward into the neighbouring valleys and enchant our sight with the lakes of Nemi and Albano.

They look up to the blue sky like the eyes of Venus, and are fringed with flowering myrtles. This is a sacred soil; and yonder you can perceive distinctly the site of the

VIEW OF CASTEL GANDOLFO FROM THE VILLA DORIA.

venerable Alba Longa. It stretched in a long line between the mountain and the lake. On the side towards the lake much of the rock has been quarried away by human hands. Somewhere in the immediate neighbourhood was the grove of the presiding goddess of the Latin Confederation, the *lucus Ferentinæ*. Dame Venus dwelt here, and the lake was her mirror, in which she contemplated herself by the light of the full moon.

> "Around the ivied grot luxuriant foliage pressed,
> And thickly rustled the leaves beside the living waters.
> Here was the tendrilled dwelling, whence at hot noon Sylvanus
> With sweetest fluted notes, summoned the herds to drink."—PROPERTIUS.

And we enter this shady "tendrilled dwelling" if we take the woodland path down to Nemi. The wild, fresh Flora of the mountains has adorned these slopes with the gayest of flowers. With the exception of the purple blossoming cyclamen, nearly all the

plants we meet with are found on our northern soil; but here they seem bound to no
special season, and the fortunate conditions of the soil, combined with the southern sky,
make them more rich, abundant, and perfect. The wood is chiefly composed of Spanish
chestnuts, oaks, and beeches, with an undergrowth of gigantic ferns, above which rise the
branches of blackberry and raspberry bushes mixed with the wild rose. Amongst all
these bloom bluebells, primroses, the white and red Scabiosa, convulvulus, dark-blue

NINFA, WITH NORMA.

gentians, foxgloves, and a profusion of strawberries. Ground ivy grows in the shade, and
soft velvety moss near the trickling streamlets. The gay woodpecker, the enchanted
King's son, loves to haunt these woods. Circe, seeking herbs, met him here, and in
vengeance for despised love, transformed him to this shape.

> "He, in rage to find that sudden through Latium's woods
> He wanders, a wingèd fowl, now hacks with his horny bill,
> Wounding the rising boughs, and striking the trees in his fury."—OVID.

But singers, also, dwell in these hidden haunts; and blackbirds, thrushes, and nightingales
animate the solitude of the legend-laden hills with their sweet songs.

On quitting the wood, you find yourself at the edge of the height immediately overlooking the Lake of Nemi. What an enchanting prospect! In the foreground the roofs and the church of the remote and decaying lake townlet, where the grape-vines climb from house to house; beneath, under the blooming terraced gardens, the still, dreamy expanse of water, shadowed by the dark green reflections of the wooded hills around it, and beyond—floating in sunshine—the horizontal lines of the Campagna and the sea, rising like a Fata Morgana above the dark foreground. What is it that draws the soul so powerfully to this Lago di Nemi? The lotos does not float on its bosom, nor does any siren sing on its shores, and yet its image will not fade from the mind, and it draws the heart ever back again to itself. It lies there in its shadowy depths, like a riddle, like a dream of the goddess Venus, and we strive, and ponder, and cannot find the right tone which will awaken a responsive echo on its banks. Schubert has succeeded in finding this tone in his music; and whosoever wishes to get the impression of these mysterious waters, should sing his lovely, pensive song—breathing the very spirit of the water-nymphs—of the "*Erlafsee*,"—the Lake of Erlaf:

"'Tis sweet, yet mournful, here
By Erlaf's quiet mere.
Silence broods among the woods,
The blue lake's breast is all at rest,
Only cloud-thrown shadows pass
Mute athwart the liquid glass."—MAYERHOFER.

At this point the idyll of the Monti Albani, ceases. On the opposite side of the lake lies the domain of Prince Orsini, and the broad Via Appia Nuova leading to cheerful Genazzano and Albano. Along the whole length of this road henceforward we do not lose sight of the sea, which shines beyond the Campagna's edge like a hill of gold. The houses and gardens to the right and the left of us, belong to Roman luxury, and if opportunity favour us we may see the "Nobili" of the Eternal City roll by in stately carriages. Exactly in the same tone as that, in which he describes the ruins of Hadrian's Villa, your cicerone will announce: "These are the Chigis, the Piombinos, the Barberinis, Dorias, Alticris, Rospigliosis, Massimos, Cesarinis, Fianos, and others!" All these families have summer residences here, which they frequent, not for pleasure, but for health. The little wine-shops, and *osterie* are pushed out by pretentious hôtels which promise every imaginable comfort under French or English names. The beautiful women of Albano, and their pleasing costume, have already become rare. The latter are replaced by coloured printed cottons, and as to the former, the legend goes that the modern Quirites are quite as apt as their forefathers to steal their wives from this neighbourhood :—only the theft is conducted according to law!

Albano does not lie on the line of railway, and the road to the station is a somewhat long one. We must take it, however, to reach our goal, the unenticing Pontine Marshes. Then the route passes Civita Lavigna, Velletri,—a shadow in the distance, attractive by its promise of excellent wine grown on the pleasant slopes of the Monte Artemisio,—Valmontone with its old-world feudal aspect, and finally Segni. The train halts at the foot of some rather steep hills. These are the Volscian Mountains, rough, sun-baked, sun-browned, chalk hills, and amongst them lies Segni, formerly Signia, which was made into a Latin fortress or confederate outpost against the unruly Volscians simultaneously with Cora and Norba, but without the rights of citizenship. And thither we climb.

The landscape around consists of dry shrubs and blocks of ruins, gloomy wood, and

ARICCIA.

jagged ravine: all is waste, wild, inhospitable, and desolate. Luxury reigns not in these mountains; here reign only poverty and privation. The gay colours of the garments which we see in the plain,—red, green, and light blue,—are not found here. The race that inhabits these fastnesses clothes itself in sombre brown and a deep blackish blue; sad hues, but yet more really picturesque than the bright and crude ones of the much admired costume pictures. The mediæval baronial castle is deserted. The breed of spiders which once dwelt here has departed, and has left nothing behind it on the barren

LE MAMELLE, NEAR CIVITELLA.

rock, save the wretched dwellings of Segni, like the sucked-out bodies of Volscian flies. There is nothing to detain us here, although from the height of the Cyclopean walls, where the Arx or citadel once stood, we might enjoy a classical view over the whole country we have come through.

Behind Segni, where the spicy sea-wind is blowing, begins the forest,—the primeval forest. We know that beyond these woods the wide plain of the Pontine Marshes stretches to the sea, and that thence we shall behold the sea itself in its sublime beauty and greatness, and we long to add wings to our feet. But this silent, virgin Nature, has its own charms: not those of a soft Venus couched on roses, but the unapproachable, solemn beauty of the northern Valkyrie, who has laid herself to slumber on the woodland moss. The forests of these mountains are so magnificent, so deep, so awful almost,—so solitary and mysterious, solemn and obscure, that we can find no words worthily to paint them. We populate the woods of our own land with fairy figures which trip smilingly over the wild flowers; but here wander antique gloomy Legend, and the witch of these shores, the eerie Circe gathering wondrous herbs, and holding converse with the glittering snakes that bask upon the rocks. Then the west wind touches the summits of pine and beech, and a tone of lamentation sounds through the Volscian land.

The mountain grows ever wilder. Often it throws aside the dark green dress it has brought from the valleys, strips off the leafy robe, and mounts naked and defiant into the clouds, a bold, weather-beaten Titanic form, hurling down huge blocks from its heights, into the lower lands, whereby the wanderer's path is made tedious and difficult. It is a long, long path to traverse; but at length there comes a break in the trees, and a distant silvery gleam fills the soul with delightful anticipations. Yet a little more forest shadow, yet another turn in the path, and lo, the Pontine plain lies before us, swimming in enchanted light, bathed in the soft tints of a summer sun which melts everything into harmony! Above it the sea builds a silver wall, and the glorified blue skies of ancient Rome stretch their vault from south to north. Our spirit seems to dive down into this ocean of beauty: we are confused, amazed, by its fulness. We feel ourselves small and poor, yet great and rich, and unspeakably happy! Only by degrees, and almost with pain, do we resolve to examine the picture more closely and coolly, and to analyse its component parts.

GIRL OF THE SABINE HILLS.

Yes; those are the Pontine Marshes, and, seen from our airy height, the dreaded district appears by no means dreadful. Soft hills alternate with greyish green meadows. The thick dark line of dwarf wood, opposes itself to the white sand dunes from Ostia, past Nettuno and Cisterna, as far as Terracina. Many shepherds' huts and farm buildings appear on the dark background, and here and there we see the shining waters of some buffalo-haunted pool. Streams meander towards the sea coast, but of the marshes we see absolutely nothing; they are hidden beneath a green carpet of vegetation. The landscape has nothing terrible about it,—and yet Death dwells there. After a brief spring-time, he rises with the first glowing rays of the summer sun from his lair in the fens, and mows down human life all along the coast, even to the foot of the mountains. Whomsoever he meets in this plain, as far as Terracina, he greets with a greeting from the world of shadows. The Via Appia from the *Tres Tabernæ*, the Linea Pia which leads to Terracina, pass through the midst of his realm.

We stand upon the Cyclopean walls of the ancient Norba; Ninfa, half buried in ivy, lies at our feet; to our right the castle of Sermoneta. In this semi-circular stretch of sea-coast, the watch-towers erected in the middle ages against the Saracens, stand here and there like solitary sentinels. White lateen sails cut through the waters; and beyond, in the sun-steeped distance, the dark blue islands of Ponza rise from the waves. Yonder grey tower is the tower of Astura, in which the tragic fate of the German Conradin and his friends was fulfilled. The finely cut headland there, against which

Neptune's white-maned horses rage and foam, and where the sea-gulls flutter, is the scene of the legend of Circe's cup. Ulysses gazed out upon it. The footprints of history go from north to south: a history richer both in glory and misfortune than that of any other land on earth. From the wild, sun-burnt herdsmen of the Saturnian age, from the lawless robber bands of these rich pastures, arose a race of heroes whose eagle shadowed the world with his wings. This valiant breed has sunk into its funeral urn; the urn itself has perished, reeds and weeds overgrow its fragments; and in place of the defiant eagle, stands the suffering figure of the Son of Man upon the Cross, before whom the uncivilized nomade of to-day pulls off his ragged hat, and has no glimmering knowledge of the greatness of his ancestors. Where the sword rusts, the cross arises; and where the legions scoured the plain mounted on their war horses, the untamed buffalo lurks sullen in the marshes.

The journey from the shores of the Lago Fucino hither, may be called a passage through the "street of tombs" of ancient history. Although nature clothes this slumbering earth with all the charms of spring, and all the glowing colours of summer, yet the old gravestones will peep through; and amidst all our delight in the enchantments which still remain to the Present, we never lose the sad thought of

BOY OF THE SABINE HILLS.

the lost beauty and greatness of the Past. O land, thou hast been sown for the reaper, Death, and sprinkled with Stygian waters! *Ergo bibamus!* A full goblet to thy thousand charms, thou sacred soil, and to a new race of heroes!

> "See my dusty pilgrim feet
> Plodding on without relief;
> Maiden, bring a flask of wine!
> Cheer me with thy kisses sweet,
> Fill my soul with new belief
> In life's beauty, maiden mine."

MOUNTAIN MONASTERIES AND A PAINTER'S PARADISE.

> "E'en as in Isis' temple proud,
> E'en as in Delphi's forest hoar,
> Sounding thro' tree and stone aloud,
> Or whisp'ring soft thro' leaf and flower,
> Nature still strives for articulate voice.
> Fain would she speak to us now as of yore,—
> Speak to us, live with us, weep, and rejoice!"
> H. LINGG.

FROM the great loom of Rome there stretches out a consecrated thread through the valleys and over the heights of the Sabine mountains, even to the Hernician Wood, and the first outrunners of the Samnite range; and on it are strung, like dark pearls, a series of convents and abbeys which the stormy tide of the Middle Ages once cast upon these shores, and on whose decaying walls the sun of the bright present shines but dimly. Between the dark pearls on this thread, however, we see precious jewels of landscape glitter in green and gold; we see hamlets and little towns whose charm and value age has only increased, and which offer a perpetual feast to the painter and to the eyes of all who love natural beauty.

We will make a pilgrimage from Subiaco up to Monte Cassino, and then, throwing away the pilgrim's staff, we will pass with the swift step of the tourist through the Painter's Paradise. The south greets us with its warm perfumed airs; the clouds and the birds entice us southward. We will let the grave Anio travel on to grave Rome, and hasten to where the bright green Liris leaps to meet us from its smiling banks. The venerable Subiaco stands on the Anio, and the still more venerable Monte Cassino beside the Liris. In Subiaco we still breathe the atmosphere of ecclesiastical Rome; but on Monte Cassino we begin already to feel the delightful influence of Parthenope.

Subiaco and Monte Cassino are the oldest seats of the learned monkish orders in Italy. They were once the holy shrines in which simple piety sheltered the Christian Cross, and watched over it with zeal and love. Blood and fire smoked all over the classic soil; the great migrations of the peoples were achieved amidst wild struggle and strife; sceptres were broken, thrones fell, and the cross itself wavered and seemed about to sink into the slough of history, and to be trodden under the hoofs of the Vandals' horses, when a pious youth took the sacred burthen on his own shoulders and carried it away, far from the slaughter of the plains, to the security of the mountains. He planted it on the still heights, in the valleys, where peace yet dwelt, and which were inhabited by a poor and uncorrupted population of shepherds, who watched with hope and longing for the overthrow of tyrannous, luxurious paganism. The cross brought fulfilment of this hope: before it they could raise their heads bowed in slavery. Benedict of Nursia, the high-minded patrician's son, was the Apostle of these mountains. He left Rome to its hatreds, and carried love into the woody wilderness.

The Roman sun had shed its splendid rays even amongst these mountains of Subiaco. Her most luxurious son, the mighty Nero, had made artificial lakes here, high above the Anio, had built baths and marble villas near them, and carried the bacchanalian torch deep into these remote forests; and the town which arose later in the neighbourhood of his magnificent edifices, was called *Sublacum* or *Sublaquenm*,—"Under the lakes." But at the time when Benedict left Rome to come hither, the lake dams had long been burst, the marble pillars broken; and, as no emperor came to visit it any more, the town had fallen into poverty and decay. A poor population of peasants and shepherds eked out a

SUBIACO.

miserable existence here. They had seen the golden gods of Olympus perish in the dust, they had beheld all the splendours quenched in the lighted temple,—when suddenly there shone from a dark cleft in the rocks by the Anio, a new and eternal ray, and the words of the prophet were fulfilled: "The people that walked in darkness have seen a great light."

The cavern—in front of which a grand monastery was subsequently built—is called to this day the "*Sacro speco*," or holy cave. It lies in a gorge, at that time almost inaccessible, through which a tributary torrent of the Anio pours, between the steep mountains, Monte Calvo and Monte Talco. In this cavern the youthful Benedict became a teacher, and soon was the model to whom thousands looked up: here he gained his first disciples, and consecrated the first little community in the spirit of the Christian dispensation. In this same spirit he built his monasteries amid the mountain solitudes, and along the banks of the Anio. The blessing of labour, no longer the toil of slaves, brought golden harvests, and life returned even to the deserted city, and riches flowed from every side into the new institutions. Benedict was unable to see the full blossoming of his work here; whilst it was still in the bud he was driven away from his convents on the Anio by avarice and hatred, which had slipped into this retreat in the train of wealth,— and the waves closed behind him. The flood of barbarism poured over the land, and covered all traces of that time of love and childlike trust, undermined the foundations of nearly all the old monastic institutions, and only Malice and Poverty saved themselves on the shore. Thus Subiaco is at this day a poverty-stricken city, and the two convents, which alone preserve a few antiquities and souvenirs of old days, subsist but scantily on the allowance doled out to them by government. The original wilderness again overspreads the landscape, and encamps before the doors of the monastery and the gates of the town.

CHARACTERISTIC HEAD FROM THE SABINE HILLS.

We enter the sacred oak-wood of Saint Benedict, whose hoary oak trees are stooping as if in salutation. A beautiful legend of the shepherds tells how they bent their lofty summits in reverence when Benedict passed by, and have remained ever since in that posture. All seems so antique in this wood,—so ascetic, so strange! There is no movement, save when a lizard rustles mysteriously through the fallen leaves. The murmur of the Anio sounds softened and peaceful. What a solitude! We lean on the railing of the little bridge, and see how the great convent rises on the mountain like an enchanted tree growing out of the rock: an enchanted tree with a thousand enchanted blossoms! We pass the portal, we wander through the winding corridors, upstairs and downstairs, and seem to see the realization of a story from the "Thousand and One Nights." Dazzled by the golden splendours of walls, pictures, and images, confused by pillars, and columns, and cloisters, and by the lavish sunlight which gilds and animates the whole, we close our eyes fearing to destroy the delightful dream. And if it were not for the black-robed monk who shows pictures, names names, gives explanations, and continually refers to the self-denying life of the father of the Benedictines, we should expect to see the enchanted daughter of some oriental potentate appear from behind a pillar.

The effect of the whole is indescribable; and the spectator finds it difficult to turn aside from this general impression, in order to examine details. The first thing that you observe is that you are obviously in a Christian place: the walls around you are populated with saints; they look down from the vaults of the ceiling, and wherever there is a flat space, you are sure to find some pious countenance depicted on it. But whatever be the names of all these men and women who once lived in the odour of sanctity, not one of them equalled the holiness of the founder. Thus the chief interest is concentrated on the memorials connected with Benedict himself; and of these the principal are the two caves before mentioned. In one of them, which served the devout youth as a refuge from the world, his statue is seen kneeling in prayer with inspired features, illuminated by the

ROAD FROM CAVI TO GENAZZANO.

faint rays of a lamp that hangs in front of a richly decorated altar. In the other he used to preach, first to the shepherds, and afterwards to the people who crowded to hear him from all the country round. The famous hedge of roses, too, in which, as Gregory the Great relates, "*voluptatem traxit in dolorem*," throwing himself among its thorns, and emerging a victor from his struggle with the temptations of the flesh, is still green, having been preserved by pious tradition.

Another convent lies above this one : it takes its name from Scolastica, the devout, nay sainted, sister of Benedict. The cheerfulness of simple piety does not dwell here. A heavy ascetic atmosphere breathes through these cloisters. Ruin is everywhere around, but some curiosities of antiquity and of the Middle Ages may still attract the enquirer. The German may please himself with contemplating some works of his countrymen, which are over four centuries old. These are the precious specimens of printing by Conrad Schweinheym and Arnold Pannartz of Mayence, who crossed the Alps in the second half of the fifteenth century, in order to introduce Gutenberg's "black art" into the cloisters of the learned monkish orders. They printed here with skill and diligence, and later removed their press to Rome into the palace of the Massimi.

The landscape, around Subiaco along the course of the Anio, is rich and inexhaustible, like all river scenery in Italy. A certain sunny cheerfulness which enjoys the present, mingled with a kind of retrospective seriousness, makes up an expression of serene gentleness, such as may be seen on the face of a man who, after many storms, at length is established peacefully on his own spot of earth, and sings and meditates tranquilly—

> "I've niched myself from the world apart
> In my own sweet rose-grown bower ;
> And sacred peace o'erflows my heart,
> As I rest 'mid fruit and flower.
> And would sun or moon peep where I'm hid,
> For me they shall not be forbid."—L. SCHEFER.

And if the painters would like to come too, "for me they shall not be forbid ;"—at least not the nobler-souled among them. Subiaco knows them well, and has long known. And when once they have come here, they find it difficult to depart, to tear themselves away from these still, richly watered valleys where the heart of Nature seems to beat audibly. Books are no longer printed in these regions ; but, instead, spring, summer, and autumn, are painted in a thousand pictures, good and bad. If the trees still possessed their dryads and hamadryads, those nymphs would scarce know how to hold themselves for sheer coquetry ;—so often have they been counterfeited in every conceivable posture ! And the same fate attends the smoky huts and barns of the town blown crooked by the wind, which seem to crawl wearily up the steep castle hill. The town swarms with "subjects" in brown and grey ; and the very conceptions of vertical and horizontal have departed from its architecture centuries ago ! But the crookeder the better : the more weather-stained the prettier ! It really seems as if the artists expended more zeal and labour on the portrait of one of these mouldy *Sublaquean* edifices, than it cost the architect to build the whole swallow's nest of a city. Amidst the dust and filth of squalid street corners, and waging strife with man and the bristly beast of these mountains, Art celebrates her triumphs here ! Then, when the first withered leaf falls on his hat or painting umbrella, the young enthusiast for mountain scenery returns to Rome with a richly filled sketch-book, and passes the winter in reproducing on canvas the sacred sunshine of these vales to gladden the eyes of the foreigners.

But many great and serious talents have visited distant Subiaco, and honour to all who come hither with earnestness and dignity, bringing the full Olympic enthusiasm of the genuine artist into this grand landscape ! To such the scenes around the Anio will ever, and in all times, reveal their innermost secrets. A path well known to painters leads out of this monastic valley up the mountain to Civitella, that ancient eagle's eyrie in the Sabine Hills. The path leads through thorns and thistles, over stones and weeds, past trees, and jagged roots, but the heart rejoices in the virgin beauty all around, which inspires it with many a fairy-like sylvan dream. This is not the Italy we imagine to ourselves in a lyric mood: the Italy of golden oranges and softly whispering myrtle, of

SAN GERMANO AND MONTE CASSINO.

palaces whose rooftree is upheld by marble pillars carved in likeness of the gods. No; this is the stern, epic Italy, that we picture to ourselves in meditating on far past times, when men first began to forge iron with fire stolen from the gods,—when castles towered high on the mountains in Titanic defiance. The huge fragments of them, stared on by the people as mysterious Cyclopean walls, are still scattered about among the brambles, and beneath dark garlands of ivy. We might believe that History, weary of her wild game at dice down there in the populous plains, from the foot of the mountains to the headland of Circe, had retired hither as into a solitary hermitage; and one can scarcely help expecting to meet the ancient inhabitants of these hills at every moment.

But only poor mountaineers cross our path, with grave and gloomy, or weary and sickly countenances, and wearing the rude costume of the district. Stern, epic Italy, offers to these children of her bosom, a stone instead of bread. Longing and hope have long ago died in these poor souls;—but so, also, has discontent. The curse of an utter absence of wants and aspirations, lies "*like a petrified sunbeam*" upon the whole range of the Sabine Hills. The heart which has been rejoicing in the aspect of this overpowering nature, is chilled on beholding how wretched are the men in its midst. This landscape is only delightful to the wandering stranger who is to return in a few days to the plain where luxuriant cornfields wave beside river-banks, and the joyous grape-vines are slung from the elms ; or to the artist, who enchanted with the soft magical tints in which the southern

PEASANTS OF SORA. SUNDAY REST.

sunshine paints the grand outlines of the hills, thinks not of the stony soil over which the backs of many a generation have been bowed in sterile labour.

Civitella!—Has this rocky peak been always inhabited since the days when Titan hands piled up those walls before its gates? If so we may perhaps understand the attachment to their home of the present inhabitants, who despite hunger and indigence, autumn storms and winter cold, starving or freezing, still cling on here. Civitella is like Subiaco, one of the painter's paradises ; and below Civitella we behold the most famous of them, the much vaunted Olevano. With Olevano in sight we will not tarry long on the steep heights of Civitella; although from thence our thoughts may fly swallow-like to greet the rugged Rojate, the soft Mammelle, the finely shaped Monte Acuto, the white gleaming cheerful Anagni, Gavignano, Pagliano, gloomy Segni in the glimmering Volscian Hills, Monte Fortino, and the mountains of Scrime. We discover some new nest or other in the folds of the hills at every moment ; and, could we soar as high as yonder hawk above us, we should discern the whole vast plain, and in the plain the Eternal City.

But we lower our gaze to where a prettily winding road shaded by oaks and chesnuts leads us down to Olevano. There, rooted in between the white rocks, stand the sentinels of the landscape, the hundred ancient oaks of the Serpentara. Here the great masters

BY THE WELL AT OLEVANO.

of landscape art painted more than a century ago; and here the scholars' scholars of *their* scholars are painting to this day! Here they sit endeavouring to wring from nature the secret of eternity, and to grow as the oak-plants do, that spring up every year among the older trees and draw pith and nourishment from the roots of their predecessors.

But Olevano is moreover a " Poets' Corner;" and many a poet has sat at the host's table in Casa Baldi amongst the painters,—a Saul amongst the prophets,—and has sung the

PEASANTS OF SORA PREPARING POLENTA.

praise of Olevano's beauties to all the world. Casa Baldi stands on a sunny olive-grown hill outside the town, and is a European caravanserai for artist folks of all sorts, who by day roam through the gorges and under the trees of the slopes, or sit on the rocks and gaze over the wide landscape, and sing, and paint, and then in the evening enjoy the purple sunset from the terrace of the inn with wine and jollity. J. B. Scheffel wrote his richly coloured "Departure from Olevano" in this house, and the less known W. Waiblinger sang his enthusiastic lyrics here as long ago as in 1827. But even more in his "Letters from Olevano" than in his songs, shines out the passionate love he cherishes for this happy corner of the earth. He constantly returned hither; and longed to be free and happy that he might dwell here for ever, and he sings:—

> "E'en as the eagle clings, true to his rocky eyrie,
> So would I cling to thee, and set all my joy in thy mountains,
> Living my life in the realms of freshest, purest ether,
> Unseen by the herd of men,—or only in cloudy distance;
> Dwelling beyond the range of humanity's poisoned arrows,
> Safe in this rocky land of the Sabine and old Hernician,
> And ever true to thee, my hidden, secret Tempe,
> My Olevano, ever true!"

The inhabitants of the town, or rather of the heap of mediæval ruins which goes by that name, are a strong and handsome race; and the women are particularly distinguished by elegance of form and majesty of bearing. Most persons have seen in some exhibition of paintings, studies of these Olevanese maidens, either going down to the stream with the great double-handled copper vase on their heads, or lingering in the twilight by the ivy-covered well, or gazing from the mountain's brow into the sunny landscape. Many charming pictures are to be met with in these huts and paths; and it is touching to see how much beauty can be the companion of poverty and toil. For Olevano is poor, and the hard soil demands hard labour, and the greater part of this labour falls on the women. Idle merriment and revelry, and the sound of song and dance are not found here. The towns which Anacreon invited his artist to depict:

"Hear now, hear, thou best of painters,
What the Muse would have thee do!
Paint me cities where gay voices
Laugh and jest the whole day through"—

Such towns are not met with amongst these mountains. The best thing in them is the air, which sweeps over them, but cannot be enjoyed in the streets themselves; for though the name of Olevano may be derived from the olive trees that surround it, it certainly does not come from *olibano*, *i.e.*, incense, or *olive*, denoting a good smell!

A hundred paths lead hence in all directions. And whether we turn our steps towards neighbouring Genazzano and proudly towered Palestrina, towards Tivoli or Anagni, downward across the violet-tinted Campagna to the coasts of the sea, or back again to plunge still deeper amid the intricacies of the mountains to Alatri girdled with Cyclopean walls, or the loneliest woodland monastery of these regions the Certosa of Trisulti, or the Lake of Fucino,—everywhere we wander amidst natural beauties whose varieties of charm and form, changing with the changing lights of the day and seasons of the year, are endless and inexhaustible.

Near the Certosa, that woodland paradise, are found, not only landscape beauties, but natural curiosities. A famous grotto lies among the hills, below the God-forsaken townlet of Collepardo, and where the Cosa leaps foaming over the stones. The grotto's depth is yet unfathomed, and the stalactites within it are of most extraordinary forms. There, too, is the *Pozzo di Santullo*, the "Well of Italy," a natural circular shaft with steep, inaccessible walls, within whose giddy depths there grows a wood with birds building in the branches. Up above on the height, surrounded by a hoary oak-wood, stands the convent, where a branch of the Benedictines, the strict Carthusians, live in pious contemplation, and are the benefactors of the district. The sound of the convent bell ringing across the valley, surprises and moves the soul, and we think we are obeying the very voice of peace, as we climb upward in answer to its summons. We fancy that the most restless heart must become tranquil here, and that we may let fall the rudder which is needed to steer us across the stormy waves of the outer world. And in truth it would be impossible to find a stiller spot, or one more entirely cut off from the rest of the world. The roar of the great tides of humanity is not heard here: the birds sing from the boughs in the rose-scented cloister garden, prayerful voices whisper through the halls, the bell rings in the twilight, or announces dewy dawn,—and that is all! We think we could tarry here for ever, but the purple distance beckons us, the clouds sail swiftly above the precipice towards the immeasurable horizon, and then our wings begin to stir like those of a bird about to leave its cage, and we, too, prepare for flight over hill and dale.

Thus, when the sun rises next, we find ourselves upon a summit of the Samnite mountains. A bright river winds along below us: it is the Garigliano, the *Liris*; in the background the snow-covered peaks of the Abruzzi rise into a bluer heaven, and this vast pile of building here, which we approach beneath a canopy of ilex trees, is the convent of Monte Cassino, and the town nestling in the ravine at its feet is the Oscan, Volscian,

THE SERPENTARA NEAR OLEVANO.

Samnite, Roman, city of San Germano. The service of Apollo was still performed here, and the columns of the temple of Venus were still twined with roses, when Benedict, beginning to grow old, and expelled by the malice of his enemies, wandered hither from Subiaco, to found a home for imperilled Christianity. The convent was built, faithful disciples gathered around the master, and multitudes of worshippers animated the mountain paths. The temple of Apollo was soon deserted, and the roses of Venus were left to wither. Peace reigned here whilst the world resounded with the clash of arms. Vandals, Goths, Greeks, struggled in bloody strife for the crown that had fallen on the earth, and the storm raged even to the foot of the convent hill: for the decisive battle between Tejas and Narses, was fought down there on the Volturno.

During these agitations the needy, the sorrowful, the sick, and the hungry, took refuge with the pious fathers. But not only these: the arts and sciences came too, sought and found an asylum, and dwelt with the brethren in their simple cells, where they were loved and cherished, and faithfully guarded for posterity. This honour belongs to the convent still, and for this reason it was spared in the recent spring storms of new Italian unity; for this reason Protestants as well as Catholics approach it respectfully, and rejoice in the treasures which monkish industry has stored up in its archives. Of the original monastery, as it arose according to Benedict's plan, only a few wall fragments remain. For the fate which the stormy Middle Ages brought to all countries, did not spare it, and more than once the torch of war was hurled into its quiet courtyards. What we see now is a large mass of building, almost like a city, dating from the last century, and allowing free entrance to light and air. But if you step outside the portal, you find yourself at once in the midst of the mountain wilderness, in whose glimmering depths the eye soon loses itself. It is like a dream to see these modern times glide past on iron rails through the valley at our feet; it is like a dream to hear the shrill whistle of the locomotive as it carries a caravan of travellers southward to the distant Naples.

FROM THE BANKS OF THE LIRIS TO THE SHORES OF THE SIRENS.

COMPANION LANDSCAPES.

> "Italy,
> Oh thou art fair! As the maiden
> Mirrors her bridal array
> In the brook, so thou see'st smiling,
> Chased in two seas, thy perfections:
> Fair art thou;—fair beside Naples,
> Exquisite bay, in Tasso's verdant Sorrento,
> 'Mid the lava of thy Vesuvius:"
>
> HALM.

EXCURSION FROM THE GRAN SASSO D'ITALIA TO VESUVIUS.

RISING like a majestic cloud-capped Alpine pillar between the two seas,—the Tyrrhene and the Adriatic,—which girdle the peninsula, and visible from afar over all the valleys of the Samnite country, stands the Gran Sasso d'Italia.

Around this mountain are gathered all the lines of the Apennine, belonging to the provinces of the Abruzzi, converging from every direction. It is the central knot of the tangle of mountains which runs from north to south, and indeed of the whole peninsula. This is the real point of division between north and south: you recognise it in the light and heat, in the vegetation and the animal world, in the speech and manners of the inhabitants—briefly, in everything. The Roman, Etrurian, and Ligurian Apennines, run northward toward the Alps, with the Tuscan and Umbrian ranges parallel to them. The mountains of the Abruzzi sink softly toward the south into the Campanian downs; or run farther into the land as Apulian and Calabrian Apennines, as far as the blue waves of the Faro di Messina, into which they dive to reappear in the Trinacrian islands, and finally to end their course at Trapani.

The three highest peaks of the Gran Sasso rise like pyramids into the air. The principal of them is Monte Corno, next to that Monte Brancastello, and, lastly, Monte di Fano Trojano. The various summits show like a camp of Titans, and the enemy stands opposite on the Majella in the shape of the grand Monte Amaro, who would fain contest with Monte Corno the honour of being the highest in Italy. Somewhat lower than these are the Morrone, Monte Alto, the Scalata, and the Rocca di Lipareto. From the pyramid of the Gran Sasso (which is very seldom climbed), you may behold "all the kingdoms of this world and the glory thereof." And if the enthusiastic traveller breaks out into exclamations of surprise and delight when he catches a glimpse through the figs and olives of the Sorrento hills, of a blue gulf of waters on either side of him, here he

BOY OF THE ABRUZZI.

beholds with a sensation almost of awe, the two mighty seas which rise to meet the sinking sky in the east and in the west. Yonder, over the blue waves of the Tyrrhene Sea, glide sails from the Campanian, Sicilian, Gallic, and Iberian shores; Grecian and Oriental barks plough the Adriatic. Through the lower hills there wind green valleys, and rivers, and roads toward the coast or the interior.

At our feet, where now white towns are glittering, once stood the fortresses of the

Samnite Confederation which defied even Rome. As far as our eye can reach stretched the regions of the Marsii, the Picentii, and the Hirpinii, and of various other tribes. Their once mighty cities, such as Bovianum, lie somewhere in the green wilderness below, mere heaps of grassy ruin. The Capitoline she-wolf has devoured their inhabitants: and

GIRL OF THE ABRUZZI.

Sylla, the she-wolf's son, swung his blazing torch among the woodland settlements, nor rested until the land became a desert, and the dwelling of foxes and owls. Samnium has never entirely revived; her sons, and those of Magna Grecia, are the step-children of Italy. Among the cities that remain, are Teramo, Ascoli, Chieti, Ortona, Lanciano, and Vasto, on the steep but pleasant coast of the Adriatic. More inland lie Aquila (it seems but an arrow-flight away), Popoli, Solmona, Castel di Sangro, and Isernia, past which the mountain road leads southward to the shores of that other sea above whose flood Nature has set the great watch-fires of Etna and Vesuvius.

Even now as we cross these heights, the soft breath of the South breathes on our cheek, and the *Tramontana*—the north wind—falls broken-winged against the stony forehead of the Gran Sasso. As our gaze roams over the last outlines of the hills, melting into purple haze, we dream of the land of delights, of the islands of the blessed, of grapes and roses :

> "The northwind breaks on the rocky stone,
> Soft breezes blow through the valleys lone,
> The moon through the wood gleams fitfully,
> And far away murmurs the foaming sea.
> Ah, far away my heart fain would be!"

So we willingly descend to the frequented roads, and with a quickened pulse, ask our way to the South. We cannot miss it :

> "There the Abruzzian mountains, and here the Pontine marshes,
> Lead from the Land of Art to the Paradise of Nature."—PLATEN.

We fly from the sombre gravity of Rome, which has often oppressed our spirit, from blackened sarcophagi to blooming rose-bowers, from the chanted requiem of the priests to the twang of guitars, the bacchic clash of tambourines, and the gay love-song of a joyous population. The change is by no means sudden and immediate. The feet of the wayfarer have to toil through the dust of many a hill and dale before he reaches Parthenope. It is easier, and makes the contrast more striking, to be carried on steam wings through the Pontine Marshes to Naples. You mount into the train by night, wrap yourself in your mantle and sleep whilst your wild steed careers through the desolate plain, and open your eyes again to see the morning sun redden the peak of Vesuvius, and strew roses over the heights above Naples.

We, however, cling to our pilgrim's staff. This pleasant town is Aquila. She is seated on an airy hill whose sides are decked with cheerful greenery and gardens, in the midst of a great amphitheatre of mountains. She looks gay and bright as a mountain girl in her gala dress ; and wears her best attire, for she has to represent and typify the land of the Abruzzi,—and she does it worthily. She has quite forgotten the old times ;—nay, even the mediæval ones. And were it not for the name, and the Imperial eagle, which still here and there may be seen very crippled of wing carved into a wall, no one would guess that Aquila had been built by a German sovereign. The Emperor Frederick the Second was the founder of the town. In those days ninety-nine communes were united in one enclosure as a frontier-wall against Rome ; ninety-nine fountains flowed in the city, and the bells of the ninety-nine churches summoned the seventy thousand inhabitants to prayer. It sounds like a fairy tale ;—and *is* one, almost. These things have come to be a legend. But a few fountains murmur now, but a few cracked bell-voices call the population,—decimated by mediæval feuds, by earthquakes, and poverty,—to the old worship. A Hohenstauffen built the city, a Hohenstauffen (Manfred) destroyed it. A Frenchman raised it from its ruins, but earthquake after earthquake threw it back again to the ground. So that at this day the houses, with many a stately palace among them, are mostly cracked, or miserably patched up ; and the inhabitants go through the streets looking in each other's faces as though they would ask " Dost thou know of any work for me to do ?" But they are a handsome people, both men and women :—strong and

FALL OF THE LIRIS NEAR ISOLA.

handsome, and well able to bear a good share of their country's fate on their broad shoulders. But for this, it might be well that the earthquake should knock down a few more churches! For Aquila is still, as in the days when it took decided part with the Pope, a remarkably pious city. The numerous churches,—amongst which Santa Maria di

ALBA.

Collemaggio, Santa Maria del Soccorso, San Bernardino di Siena, San Domenico, and four or five others, are the most interesting,—leave no room for industrial buildings. If there were not a little traffic in garden produce and cattle, there would be absolutely no living at all!

A short walk carries us away from the poverty-stricken present, to classic antiquity, a fragment of which remains in the ruins on yonder sunburnt hill. The Aternus flows through the valley, and this was once Amiternum, the beautiful city of the Sabines, now re-christened San Vittorino. What an indigent saint he must be,—or what an ascetic! For the handful of houses which bear his name consist of mud, and broken fragments of antiquity: and the narrow streets are carpeted by manure, a foot deep. In the midst of the dung-heaps lies a colossal, headless Minerva, and the street pigs rub themselves against the folds of her drapery. Down the valley the foundations still remain of the amphitheatre, whose arena is now scarred by the plough; and on the houses and in the houses are stuck countless bits of old inscriptions, friezes, capitals, pilasters, and reliefs. This is the ghost of the beautiful Amiternum, the maternal city of Sallust! Only once a year she still dons her old purple,—in March, at the beginning of Spring, when the blossoming almond-trees cover the neighbouring slopes with a rosy mantle: but it soon falls from her shoulders again!

And this is the condition of all the Roman remains in the Abruzzi which have been left to fall back under the dominion of untamed nature. The names are almost all that remain of them; and later generations, as though they shrank from the curse which seems to rest upon these blood-stained seats of antiquity, have never loved to build or rebuild among the ruins, but have sought more distant settlements. Thus Popoli, a smiling little town on the banks of the Pescara, is built at about an hour's distance from the once strongly walled Corsinium, just as Aquila is from Amiternum. Corsinium, a town of the Peligni, was looked upon by the people who made the war of the Confederation, as an impregnable fortress. New Rome was to arise here, and in this belief it was baptized with blood, *Italica*. The ashes of the confederate peoples are scattered to the winds; and above the crumbling marbles of proud Italica, grows the maize of the Abruzzian peasant, who guesses not the meaning of the grey walls which crop up here and there out of the soil and hinder him in his labours.

But Popoli is flourishing. Frequented roads meet here from all parts, and the modern time rushes past the old ruins on its steam wings. Looking southward from Popoli, you gaze into a grand, beautiful, gigantic landscape. Mountain is piled above mountain in every variety of form and colour. And when dark clouds float around the distant peaks, and the sun sprinkles its gold in between, all seems to live and move as in some migration of Titans. There is the mighty Majella, a mountain mass five miles in circumference; across it, and past its defiant walls the road leads to the south.

Solmona is the next town after Popoli. The landscape grows ever brighter, and you feel the breath of the climate that makes the citrons bloom, and opens the myrtle buds upon the slopes. The clear Gizio pours its quickening stream through the wide vale, and as far as the eye can see you behold corn, and wine, and fruit, and olives, ripening in the sun. In Spring, and at harvest time, the land rings with the songs of a people who sow and reap joyfully. The ancient Sulmo has preserved her renown for fruitfulness: and we may say to-day of her fields what Ovid once sang of them:

> "Rich in Ceres' fruit is the land, yet richer in grape-vines;
> Pallas' berry swells full on the lighter soil.
> Streams glide through the grass, which bends itself, and then rises,
> Lending the moistened earth beneath, a turfy shade."

But dearer than its renown for fertility, is the boast that it is the birthplace of Ovid. Every citizen knows this, and every citizen believes himself to be a descendant of that illustrious equestrian family. Yes; in Sulmo the Singer of Love was born on the twentieth of March, forty-four years B.C., and although no stone remains of the villa where his cradle stood, his spirit breathes still about the place. The most wretched priestling in the town, will proudly take down his Publius Ovidius Naso from the bookshelf, and fingering through the leaves, will refer to this or that passage, and prove to you from the poet's own words, the truth of the statement that he was born at Sulmo. Ovid's countrymen were celebrated even in antiquity, for their energy and love of freedom; but also for peaceable manners and cheerful contentment. They had many hardships to endure:

OLIVE GROVE NEAR VLNAFRO.

Sylla raged among them with fire and sword; then came Marc Antony and barbarous foreign hordes. The Hohenstauffens, too, fired the city, and what the flames spared, the earthquake destroyed. We may well wonder to see it at the present day, an orderly, well-built city. But its walls enclose scarcely any but modern buildings. All that remains of Gothic, is to be found in one or two churches.

Since the opening of new roads of communication, the dark atmosphere of the Middle Ages which reigned throughout all these hill cities, has been obliged to give place to a fresher air. The spell is broken, and if all goes well, a fair future may await these regions, and the pampered populations of the luxurious cities of the plain, may be regenerated by this robust breed of men. A green-and-gold garland of fields and meadows surrounds the walls of the town. Beautiful groups of trees stand beside the streams, and the vine climbs amidst their sunny summits. Yes, thou art fair, thou "Sulmonia third of the realm of the Peligni!" Fair art thou, and worthy to be sung! Here dwells the strength of Italy.

At Pettorano you leave the plain, and enter into the mountain world of the Majella. The dazzling white road continues to climb ever higher among the rocks. They are bare, and shine like gold when the sun touches them, for they have long ago been robbed of their green clothing of forest. The dress of poverty covers their rugged forms :— heath, woodbine, wild balsam, and thyme, in which the bees of Solmona and Pettorano hum busily. The birds, too, are few.

STREET SCENE IN THE ABRUZZI.

You only see the hawk circling above the mountain peaks, or the shy woodlark flit across the deserted path. In winter the bear and wolf show themselves on the heights, and the shepherd exchanges his staff for a long carbine such as the brigands use, who from time to time appear in addition to the four-footed beasts of prey.

Here you may find the genuine shepherd of old times. For more than a thousand years probably nothing has been changed in his manners and customs; for even his Christianity is only paganism slightly varnished over. These Samnite shepherds of the Abruzzi are fine hardy men, strong and handsome, and wonderfully good-natured. They pass the summer under a slight thatch of reeds, with the great shaggy wolf-dog of the Abruzzi as their inseparable companion, a lithograph of Saint Pamphilius pasted up against the rock as their domestic god, and for amusement the screeching *zampogna* (bagpipes) hung up at the door of the hut. The women are occupied in the valleys; the eldest boy is with his father, and looks after the young lambs. Out of their poverty man and wife build themselves a bit of a swallow's nest by the stream where the others dwell, and the joys of the great world without, never peep in at their windows. Out of such poverty,—sheer poverty,—the miserable little village of Rocca Valloscura, in a narrow ravine, has been patched together. No field is green, no garden blooms there; only a couple of old trees make a kind of shelter over the nests of these birds of paradise. And what nests they are! The painter may draw out his sketch-book, the poet string together a little idyll,—but every other human being will hasten away from the place as fast as he can!

The road continues to rise; and, on a sudden, on emerging from the last ravine, you are astonished by the magnificent spectacle of a vast table-land as flat as the floor of a ball-room, and breathed on by the most delicious air from the high mountains around it. But a solitude as of the Steppes surrounds the traveller: only quite at the end of the table-land a hill shows itself crowned with the work of man's hands—a city. This is Roccarasa, the loftiest town in central and lower Italy, and the high plain is called the Piano di Cinquemiglia, so named from its great extent. It forms one gigantic cornfield, on which, after the harvest is reaped, countless herds of horses, cattle, and swine, and sheep are pastured. The air here is wonderfully clear and transparent, but even in August it is sensibly cool, and in winter the north wind heaps the snow up so high as to block up the road for a long time together. In the Middle Ages there was more than one instance of German and Venetian troops succumbing to the rigours of this un-Italian sky.

The people whom we meet here look as stern as the scenes which bred them, and their clothing is sombre. In the Roman and Neapolitan mountains, for example, to the north of Monte Cassino, in Atino, San Donato, and Elia, the women's dress displays bright colours: in the neighbourhood of Solmona the men still wear the scarlet vest; but from this point all grows dark. The stuffs in which the men and women clothe themselves from head to foot are dark blue or dark brown. The light sandals of the land of the *Ciociari* * will not do here; these rough rocks require stout shoes of the hardest leather. And the step of the inhabitants is heavy and ungraceful: elasticity of gait, as well as flexibility of mind, must be sought for in Rome or Naples.

Behind Roccarasa begins a fine oak wood, through which the road slopes gently down to Castel di Sangro. In Italy you may enjoy the beauties of atmosphere and sunshine, sea and sky, almost everywhere, but a wood, nay, a grove, is a rarity. But when we do find one it produces a delightful effect; for the light and colour of a southern climate play

* The peasants of the hills around Rome are so called from the peculiar sort of sandals which they wear: a coarse linen bandage strapped round the leg and foot with leathern thongs.—*Translator's note.*

VAL DI SANGRO.

amongst the branches, and the warmth distils a more aromatic odour from the leaves than is the case with us at home. Then when we hear the song of home birds, or the well-known cry of the jay, and see the dear familiar blue and white butterflies fluttering above the beautiful flowers of this foreign land, the heart is filled with joy. And then our beloved fairy stories arise out of the mossy background, and the sun-woven veils of the woodland elves wave from the dark, lichen-stained rocks. But to the people here, all is dead; nothing moves in stream or fountain, no friendly legend is twined with the ivy on the banks, they have no story to relate about the ruins crumbling among the tree roots. The old heroes, the old calamities, the antique gods,—all, all are plunged in the slumber of oblivion.

The wood ceases at Castel di Sangro. A swelling river, the Sangro, flows here, and on its banks Misery has built herself a temple in the shape of the town named after the stream. There is nothing to detain us here; tedious dulness is encamped in the streets, or stares out of the low-browed windows, in which, however, you may see here and there a slender marble column inserted—relic of the Middle Ages. Now no one can purchase marble to build with here; their riches scarcely suffice to buy coarse bread.

Onward!

Whoever has a last greeting to send to the Adriatic, let him entrust it to the rushing Sangro. This river has but a hard life of it, like a true son of the Abruzzi as he is. His course is long, crooked, narrow, rough,—a mazy, weary road. He was born in Gioja—in "Joy"—up there on Monte Turchio on the south-west shore of the Lago Fucino, presses eastward in meandering curves through the jagged mountain chain, through lonely valleys, to fall wearily into the marshes of the Adriatic coast. Oh if we could but be carried southward by such a stream out of desolation into the pleasant land! This mountain road is never-ending. The hawk overhead looks far and wide over the sunny south, but our view is checked by countless mountain peaks, whose bare sides look inhospitable enough. Wherever there was the possibility of making a human settlement, you find a black, ruinous, *uncanny* looking robber's nest, out of whose doors and windows pale hunger glares, and where all implements are rust-eaten except the musket. Rionero is such a settlement, looking as if it had been hastily heaped together out of stolen materials, piled up crookedly as a shelter against the north wind. A shy population lurks at the house corners, and the eyes of the poorly and thinly clad girls and women gleam with quick uneasy glances.

Down in the woody valley flows the swift Rio, hastening after the Vandra to fall, like it, into the Volturno. These go into the kingdom of Naples, under the walls of Capua, and soon the Samnite region will lie behind us also. Who could tarry in Isernia, Venafro, or Teano,—who could loiter on the very threshold of the goal, after having crossed the Alps, traversed rivers, climbed the Apennine, and plodded through the dust of many a great highway? Yet Isernia might tempt one to stay. This, the ancient Œsernia, is a thoroughly Italian town in the midst of a noble landscape. On one side of it a deep valley opens, furrowed on either hand by countless smaller valleys running down from the mountains in the background. On one slope of the main valley rises a high wall, and above this peep, in picturesque confusion, mediæval houses, villas, and palaces with colonnades in the Italian style. Roof, porch, and window are hung and clothed and wreathed with the tendrils of the vine, whose leaves, moreover, give a pleasant shade, beneath which brightly costumed women sit and spin. Red oleanders and fresh-blown roses greet the traveller; flocks of white pigeons fly across the blue sky;—this is the real Italy, the land of peace and pleasure!

But I would advise the wayfarer only to glance at the picture from a distance, and then to hasten onward, so as to preserve a pleasant image in his memory; for bitter

GRAN SASSO D'ITALIA.

disappointment awaits him in the interior of the town, and the beds of the inn are filled with anything but bright illusions! I must own that the ham in the town is excellent; but, *en revanche*, the animal that furnishes it enjoys the privilege of too unbounded a liberty! Outside the city gates one may enjoy life once more. Silver mountain streams flow on every side, as rivulets or rivers; there is the Lorda, that rises behind Monte Secco, and yonder the Cavaliere waters the well-cultivated plain of San Vito, and these are fed by many sparkling rills. So long as man is able to command and distribute the water, everything is greener and more flourishing under this Italian sun than anywhere else in the world; but when, as is the case in the neighbouring plain, it dashes headlong from the treeless hills, covering the flat fields with mud and pebbles, the thistle flourishes, and even Spring's most genial rays produce only useless weeds among the stones. The cutting down of the forests has been the curse of Italy: and not only of Italy, but of Spain, of Greece, of Palestine, and many other countries. The sins of the fathers are visited upon the children at every autumn storm.

How mournfully they stand in their freezing nakedness, the noble mountain shapes! We look compassionately at the disrobed giants, rising, peak after peak, out of the waving mist. There is Monte Secco, there Coll' Alto, and yonder the noble Monte Miletto, dominating this whole mass of the Matese. They all look down into needy valleys to which they send only stones in spring, and avalanches in winter. Even Venafro, the flourishing, sleek Venafrum of Imperial times, the city of the olive-tree, what is she to-day but an abode of poverty? What a life was lived here in the ancient days! How the oil of the plain and the wine of the slopes attracted hither Rome's luxurious great, for a pleasant *villeggiatura!* More blooming fields than these were nowhere to be found. Horace praised them; and Ovid, and Juvenal, Cicero, Martial, Pliny, Strabo, all vaunted the beauty of Venafrum. It has perished! The numerous temples decayed, the conduits of the baths were shattered, the walls fell in, and the modern Venafro cowers amidst the landscape in the guise of a poor Abruzzian peasant.

A solitary bell jangles from a slender tower. It sounds like the trembling tearful voice of an aged man, telling to his reduced descendants stories of kingly halls, of lute and song. Soon we leave the mountains behind us, the road descends continuously, and down below there, where thick clouds of dust are whirling, extends the flat Campagna, bounded on the west by the sea, on the south by the vineyard-covered Neapolitan hills. At Teano we are on level ground. We mount into the railway carriage rattling on its way from Rome, and it carries us past blooming fields and gardens where sunshine and the labour of men's hands unweariedly bring forth fruit and flowers year in, year out; past cheerful towns, surrounded by golden-fruited orange trees; past Capua, Caserta, Maddaloni, to the smiling shores of the sirens, to the blue sea, to the Joyous City!

"KNOWST THOU THE LAND?"

"The sea swells high, the stars are bright,
Fair Naples' Bay, half hid in gloom,
Before us lies ; and through the night
See Cape Myeene,—Ischia, loom !

And giant-like, great towers stand
And frowning look across the sea,
Stern sentinels that guard this land,
This magic-girdled Italy !"

H. LINGG.

IT is a moonlight night in Spring. A steamboat, coming from the north, glides through the waves of the Tyrrhene sea, past the silent shores of Latium. To the south rise softly outlined heights flooded with moonlight. From the islands lying like cloud-shadows on the sea, beacon fires are glittering, and now and then a sail, driven by the breath of the night breeze, crosses their field of light.

The dreary shore yonder, where the mists are brooding, is Cuma ; and that flat, low-lying islet, which seems to glimmer like a dream across the waters, is called Procida. Over there the waves are dashing themselves against steep Cape Myeene, and their foam, as they break, is white beneath the moonbeams. Lights show here and there to the left, they shine from the fishermen's cottages in Baja. Then again comes a stretch of solitary shore,—the lights from a town upon a rock,—Pozzuoli !—and as the moon

SUMMER NIGHT AT POSILIPO.

declines behind the western mountains, lo, a city rises from the tranquil waters, and we cast anchor before the waveborn, Grecian, exquisite Parthenope!

In Naples the heart leaps with joy to find its dream fulfilled, its old longings satisfied.

GIRL OF THE MOUNTAINS NEAR SALERNO.

Yes; the land that lies before thee on the waters is Naples,—the dreamed of, longed for, Naples! The land of mirth and song, of love and cheerfulness;—the land of the laurel and myrtle, the Greece of Italy! " Knowest thou it well?"

She sleeps still beneath rose-tinted veils of morning, this Venus of the flower-scented shores. But even in slumber a smile of enchantment plays upon her lips, and her breath moves softly over the drowsy waters that bathe her feet, like the perfume of the orange and citron which adorn her luxuriant tresses. Her head reposes on the vine-grown slopes of Posilippo, and the transparent veil which covers her flows out even to the foot of yon fire-crowned mountain, that smokes like her own sacrificial altar. A thousand great stars, far more beautiful than any we behold in the cold north, glide above her head; and at the first joyful breeze of morning her lovely limbs begin to stir, and she opens her eyes beaming with delight and beauty.

Have you seen the Sleeping Ariadne of the Vatican? In her dream she awaits with longing and trembling the kiss of the god Bacchus. Her robe is loose, and her fair bosom rises and falls, yearning for the day and for her lover. The sleeping city of the sirens may be likened to that sleeping Ariadne. And for her too,—lo the god comes!

A streak of light is seen behind the fire-mountain. A long purple line slowly stretches across the sea until it shines rosy. The mountains of Sorrento begin to be coloured. The coasts of Portici and Resina come forth from the mist. Then the first golden shaft strikes down among the roses round the sleeper's head, and she awakes and looks wide-eyed into the day. A soft, sweet air blows over the rocking waves, and wafts away the last gauzy mists that linger to veil Parthenope; and there she stands in full and perfect beauty, and Bacchus, genial god, crowns her golden locks with grapes.

A slender column of smoke rises from Vesuvius, like the smoke of a sacrifice, towards Olympus.

> "Morn scatters roses, smiling sweet,
> O'er isle and city, strand and bay:
> Soft zephyrs flutter round her feet,
> And fan her in their wanton play."—H. LINGG.

Thus Naples awakes, and merry voices echo through her teeming streets. Fishermen and boatmen loosen their craft from the strand, and put out upon the swelling flood with powerful oar-strokes. Their light barks glide in a motley crowd, amongst the great ships and steamers, whose sails and masts are still dripping with the dews of night. All around one hears lively chattering, laughter, and the hoarse cries of the sailors; whilst from the city comes a dull sound like distant thunder:—the roar and movement of a swarming population.

In Rome the roses blossomed over tombs: here they grow on Bacchic soil that bears the grape, and other golden fruits. And still they bloom, for as one full-blown rose perishes, a young bud starts into life. And the Hesperian fruit, too, is eternal here. No sooner does one fall over-ripe to earth, than its neighbour is mature, and near it hangs the hopeful blossom. The withered garland which last night took from your brow, is replaced this morning by one of fresher beauty. Even the weeds of the cemetery are not grey with funeral ashes scattered by the doleful past; no, they are powdered with the sunny gold-dust of to-day, on which the thought of yesterday—be it sad or joyful,—never intrudes.

> "Only the present is fair; only one golden bright moment
> Smiles upon him who is happy. The present delights him alone!"

Did I weep yesterday? Was my heart oppressed with bitter cares? Did I strive in vain for the wreath of fame?—I open my eyes on the morrow, and the troublous thoughts of yesterday are dissipated; joy, and faith in the beauty of life, hover round my couch, kiss my cheeks and brow, and point towards the mountains and the sea. The sea! It lies like a silver girdle around the fair body of the enchanting sirens, clasping all their beauties together as a ribbon binds a bunch of flowers. Smiling cities are scattered all along the shore like pearls and diamonds, from the dark green promontory of Sorrento, to the lovely slopes of Castellamare;—from hence, past the shining Torri, to pleasant Portici; and on the sides of Vesuvius, and the Vomero, and Posilippo,—whither shall we

FOUNTAIN IN THE VILLA REALE, NAPLES.

turn our eyes? How take in all this beauty? Where begin? At Caprera's jagged island, or the bold Cape of Minerva? Shall we hasten to the Greek temples of distant Pæstum? Or wander through the city of Hercules, and the ancient Stabiæ? Or listen for the sybilline oracle in the temple of Cumæ? Yonder the terrors of Vesuvius excite our wonder; here soft memories attract us to the vine-grown tomb of Virgil. In this direction, a jolly company of dancers, excited by wild bacchanalian music, is beating the ground in a shady garden; in the other, a shoal of little boats are rocking in the sunshine on the blue sea. And thou, child of man, standest in the midst and askest thyself wondering, " May I, too, rejoice?" Ah yes; rejoice, thou, also! Stand not on one side like a mute, stupid boy. Thy good mother, thy great, rich mother Nature, takes thee by the hand, and leads thee lovingly into the golden circle of enjoyment. And ye in the North:

"Grudge him not, far-away friends, these moments of pleasure. Oh chide not!
Brief is all human delight; chide not at swift-fading joys!"

Once when Gregorovius was standing in a vineyard high above Naples, and looking at the sea and the islands stretched out below, as in a dream of enchantment—Capri, Nisita, Procida, and Ischia,—and when his heart was full of the spell of this beauty, a common Swiss soldier came up to him, and said abruptly, pointing downward to the paradise beneath, "*Ach es isch zu schön! Es macht ganz traurig!*" "Ah it is too beautiful! It makes one sorrowful!"

And so it is; this overflowing beauty makes us sad at last. At least this sentiment is experienced by the men of northern lands, whose earnest and contemplative temperament is alien to careless gaiety. Even as we utter an exclamation of delighted admiration it seems to be mingled with a sigh. Is it that at such moments we feel more than usual the sense of the brevity of life? Does the thought oppress us that all this glorious loveliness is built up on the ashes of countless generations, and that it will survive those who are to come after, and still smile serenely as it smiles to-day? Or do we feel that our souls are not vast enough to contain so much grandeur? In vain do we say to the passing minute, "Tarry! Thou art so fair!" It may not be. In vain the heart strives to hold this beauty, to make it its own, to clasp it;—we stretch out our arms in yearning, and they fall back empty and unsatisfied, for ever!

FISHERMAN OF GAETA.

The poet and the painter endeavour with warm enthusiasm, and with devoted industry, to fix this grand picture permanently; to reproduce it in its greatness and completeness even as it shone upon their own souls. But what is the result? The same result which happens to a flower in the hands of a botanist, or to a brilliant butterfly in the net of an entomologist;—the dewy freshness fades, the vivid velvet bloom is brushed away, and nought remains save a dry, dead thing. From the golden enchantment of a delicious, warm, perfumed May evening in Naples,—from the violet tints of the distant islands and headlands in the bay, to the blackness of printer's ink, is a long and dreary distance, and the word-pictures look pale and poor in this herbarium of dried thoughts!

Naples is beautiful taken as a whole. It ought to be viewed, like the full-blown rose, in its completeness, and not examined leaf by leaf so as to give no conception of it in its entirety. Even as the rose is the rose by its combination of colour, form, and fragrance, so is Naples only Naples by the combination of land, sea, and city. It consists of these three, and must be looked at in its triple form in order to be thoroughly enjoyed. The land runs back from the shore in manifold varieties of form :—mountain and valley, rock and ravine. But each melts softly into the other. Soft, too, are the lines in which it meets the horizon; there is nothing harsh, nothing rugged; a master-hand has modelled here. You cannot think that this land assumed its present form by the agency of Titanic forces. No, it arose under the fostering care of friendly gods; and even now they tend and cherish it. They have decked their favourite soil of Campania, lovingly, as a bride is decked for her marriage. The vineyards are spread like a network over hill and

TRIUMPHAL ARCH OF KING ALFONSO.

valley down to the very shore. Wherever there is a prop, a tree, a shrub, it is seized on by the joyful and victorious vine. And the most exquisite grapes grow on these vines : —grapes from which the divine juice is pressed that gives Naples its peculiar consecration,—that fills it with the careless gaiety which is for ever alien to the native countries of hops and barley.

Amid the vines are crowded orange and lemon trees, covered in summer with a thousand starry white blossoms, in winter with shining fruit, and surrounded at all seasons

THE BAY OF NAPLES FROM CAMALDOLI.

with exquisite fragrance. There, too, is Apollo's proud and dark-leaved tree, the laurel, beloved of heroes and of artists. On the walls, and the white terraces of the houses, roses bloom even at Christmas ; and at the same wintry season you may find great purple violets half hidden beneath the evergreens. Above the garden walls peers the tall magnolia with its lucent leaves and glorious white flowers. What a contrast to their whiteness, and to the rich green of all the surrounding foliage, is offered by the blossoms of the oleander, which seem to shine and shimmer like thousands of red flames ! But here again, all is mellowed and mingled with loving tenderness. No tree, no shrub, stands alone and makes harsh contrast with its fellows : unless it be here and there a pine or cypress. For creeping plants of all sorts send out their clinging tendrils to bind, to link, and to unite one with another in perfect harmony.

Such are the gardens and vineyards of Naples.

But outside the walls, where the hand of man neither helps nor hinders nature's work,—on the dry rocks baked through and through by the omnipotent glow of summer's sunshine,—among the ruins of ancient buildings,—on the seashore near the lonely fisher's hut, the growths look wild and savage, and display the strangest and most fantastic forms. There stands the silver-grey cactus keeping watch, the Indian fig whose broad prickly leaves show a plenteous crop of this favourite fruit of the populace in the hot midsummer, the bold stem of the agave, like a sea-king's lance-bearer, and the tall, flexible reed swaying and whispering in the breeze. Here too we find the stone pine, the wild olive-tree, the evergreen oak, the strawberry plant, and the wild myrtle and heath, hummed through by innumerable bees; whilst even in the second month of winter the lavish soil teems with anemones, crocuses, and numerous varieties of the lily.

NEAPOLITAN FISHER GIRL.

He who wanders through this rich domain of plants, is constantly surrounded by clouds of aromatic perfumes which arise from leaf and flower; and the vegetation is continuous, although it may often change the form of its manifestations. Its life may stagnate for a brief time, not in the winter, but during midsummer's fierce and earth-cleaving heat. It does but stagnate, however, it does not die: for no sooner does the first autumn shower descend, than it recommences freshly to bud and bloom. And when the earliest snow has fallen in our northern homes, here the young fresh green is shooting from the revived earth. The land here slopes gently downward to the sea as if to bathe luxuriously in its tepid waters. The headlands swimming in golden haze seem bound to the mainland by a green riband; and the islands, although completely separated from it, crowd near to their common mother like a troop of bathing children.

And what a sea it is! Exquisite mirror of an exquisite sky, it almost always shines with reflected beauty. To-day of an intense blue, to-morrow emerald-green, then like glittering silver, purple towards the hour of sunset, dark when storms arise among the mountains,—but always splendid! Always grand and sublime, whether it elevates the spirit, or soothes it with tranquil beauty! It washes the shore in wide and beautiful curves; and the bays of Naples, Baiæ, and Salerno, show in the picture like amphitheatres of Neptune. The sight of this sea inspires cheerfulness and peace. The mind recurs, voluntarily or involuntarily, to this lucent plain which holds no fearful mysteries, no weird secrets in its depths, and which reflects back stars and eyes as smiling and serene as they gaze down on it. What this sea is you learn when you are obliged for a while to forego the sight of it. Your soul grows restless, and yearns to return to it. The poorest fisherman feels this: place him on a sandy heath, on inland heights, among valleys distant from the sea, and he would pine and die like a sea-gull in a cage.

Beside this sea, and on this soil, a careless joy-loving people has built its city:—a city typical of the most childlike simplicity of mind. This people needed but a roof, a shelter for the night, a covering against the rain; and straightway built, with slight care or pains, their unadorned houses, leaving the arrangement of them to chance, and the decoration of them to the sun, the sky, the sea, and above all to the rich vegetation. Who could think of building for eternity in this city where man cares but for the gifts of to-day? Who could believe in the stability of things, on this spot? Who could peer into the future, and carefully provide for posterity? We live for to-day, and build for to-morrow at farthest! Thus it was when the Greek language still sounded in the bay: thus it was still, when the Latin, Saracenic, Norman, German, Spanish, and French tongues were spoken here: and thus it will continue to be. It is useless to expect that heavenward soaring domes should be built in this city. Our eyes roam unchecked over the expanse of flat roofs, and are only held by the three grey castles. These castles are distinguished merely by their strength and solidity; for tyranny once had its stronghold in them, and wished to sleep in security. But even these castles are but a few centuries old. We seek in vain for any important relics of the Grecian period;—all that has perished utterly.

But the sun shines in eternal youth above the city of the present; the moon which transfigures the modern town with its light, is the same which once beamed upon Greek temples on this spot. The scars which history has ploughed upon these lovely shores are hidden by wreaths of roses; where sighs were once heard, merry songs resound; the evergreen laurel grows above the ashes of the dead, even as Vesuvius's gloomy lava-fields bring forth the joy-giving grape. Care has no abiding place in this land.

ANCIENT AND MODERN CAMPANIANS.

*"Homer, arise! Though in the cloudy north
Coldly thou wert repulsed from door to door,
Here find'st thou men half Greeks, and a Greek heaven!"*
PLATEN.

THE stern, iron-girdled, ancient history of the world dwells amidst the ruins of the Seven Hills. The blooming groves of Parthenope are the home of Mythic Legend. Long before history was written in marble, Grecian Legend poetized on these shores; and a daughter of beauty-loving Greek phantasy was the fair and divine maiden Parthenope, who came hither from far-off Hellenic islands, on a ship guided by Apollo's dove, to found the virgin city.

Thus, in later times, wanderers from more easterly shores found Grecian mythology already installed here amongst the blooming fields, and on the myrtle-grown margins of inland lakes, and they saw that it was good to dwell in this land. The people of their homes gave ear to the account of the returning seafarers. They manned new ships, and set sail for the Italian coast. There came the Ionians from Naxos, the Chalcedonians from Eubœa;—they came from all the islands: the Achæans, Locrians, Corinthians, Rhodians, and they founded on these shores, opposite to the blue islands, the strong city of Cumæ (Kyme) the mother city of the Greek settlements in this land.

From Cumæ, the sea-loving Greeks spread themselves along the sunny coast to the bay on whose margin lay the fair Parthenope. They called the original town Palaiopolis, and the new one, built by themselves, Neapolis. A wall divided the two cities from each other, but they were united by one law, one faith, and by their common veneration for the sacred tomb of the divine maiden Parthenope.

Later on, both cities were broken up into companies, or confraternities, formed by the natives of the various nations who had settled here. These unions were called "*Fratriæ*," and were each named after some favourite divinity, or one whose worship was peculiar to the nation composing it. Thus there was the *Fratria* of the Artemisians, the Hebionotes, the Aristæans, etc. At the head of each society there was a Demarch, and the administration of them all was entrusted to Archons, chosen by the people. The constitution of the state was Republican. The Greeks did not land on these shores sword in hand, but bringing with them the soft illumination of Hellenic culture and manners; and this illumination shone for centuries upon the growing city in the bay.

But the city by the Tiber grew faster; and Roman strength was mightier than Grecian culture. Rome's powerful arm subjugated the populations one after another, even to the southernmost point of the Peninsula where the fierce defiant Bruttians, Salantinians, Iapygæ, and Apulians, dwelt. In the year 327 B.C. the hard-pressed Samnites threw themselves into the town of Neapolis. But by the year 290, it was impossible to hold out longer, it was the grand year of victory for the Romans; and in 272 the whole of rich Magna Græcia was a vassal of the Roman Republic.

Naples became an allied city. She sent tribute to Rome, and maintained her own old laws, customs, and language. She kept her faith with Rome, remaining true during

NAPLES, WITH VESUVIUS, FROM POSILIPO.

various trials; and the yoke of Rome was thus always easy upon her. She was treated, indeed, like a favourite child. The Emperors, too, enjoyed the Greek cheerfulness and beauty, which ceased not to reign in Naples. Augustus, who gave so great a preference to Hellenic culture, loved it. Tiberius also delighted in these skies, and lived for years upon his solitary island opposite to Naples. Caligula, Claudius, Nero, Marcus Aurelius, —all these came hither, and received sacrifice after the Grecian manner, in the magnificent temples of Ceres, of Diana, and of Castor and Pollux. Even Constantine, although inclining towards the new faith in the Crucified One, still knelt at the altars consecrated to the ancient gods.

Christianity,—the religion of renunciation,—found at first but few adherents in the pleasure-loving city. It was the time

"When Venus' cheerful temple stood."

The tomb of Parthenope, too, was still standing, and the noble ladies of the city celebrated the Eleusinian mysteries here every year. But when the niece of Constantine—Patrizia, a devout servant of the Suffering Saviour,—came hither, she made with her finger the sign of the cross on the marble, and said "*Hic requies mea!*" Thus at least the pious legend runs. Patrizia departed on a journey: but a storm cast her ship on to the rocks close to the gardens of Lucullus, where the Castel dell' Ovo now stands, and where there is a well that still bears the name of Patrizia, and, dying, she commanded her attendants to bury her body at the spot where the funeral car should stop of its own accord. Two white steers drew the corpse to the tomb of Parthenope, and then stood still, and there she was buried. A church, dedicated to her name, was erected over the ruins of antiquity, and Patrizia's maidens came to dwell near it, and to devote themselves to the service of Him in whom their mistress had believed. Thus at length the old joyous gods were exiled from Naples, their temples fell into decay or were converted into Christian churches, and their very sites are now forgotten.

* * * * "*E copre*
Tutte cose l'oblio nella sua notte!"—UGO FOSCOLO.

* * * * "And all things
Oblivion now has covered with her night!"

Where are the temples of Diana and of Mercury? The legend says that they stood where now the stately church of Santa Maria Maggiore rises. One capital of a column— the only one,—still remains, and serves for a holy water basin. The temple of Castor and Pollux gave place to the church of San Paolo Maggiore, and only two dusky columns, antique *canephorae* of this Christian Olympus, stand upright at the portal where the modern population enters day by day. Moreover, a magnificent horse's head in bronze,—a work worthy of Phidias,—which was formerly the symbol of the city, dates from that classic period so rich in beauty.

Beyond these, little but names remain. When we find a couple of dirty alleys in old Naples designated by the names "*Vico del Sole*" and "*della Luna*," we may conjecture that these are relics of the old time. The same may be said of the names which still cling to the vine-crowned heights of Posilippo, to the delightful road Platamion (called by the people *Chiatamone*), and to the city itself.

The greater number of the names of streets, and other local appellations in Naples, however, have reference to the period of Spanish or French dominion. The name of

Toledo, for example, will never be effaced from the principal street. The Neapolitan nobility, in their love of splendour and festivity, were well inclined to the foreign rulers, and so completely adopted their character and customs, that scarce a trace of their own original strain remained in them: and of the old Greek blood no trace at all remained. This strain was, however, preserved among the populace; and despite all chances and changes, despite the numerous immigrations of stranger peoples which have flooded the land, you may still find here "a Grecian heaven" and "men half Greeks."

Nay, if you seek you may find traces of the ancient *Fratrie* in the *confraternità*,— companies or guilds belonging to different quarters of the city, which cling together with singular strictness. A great number of Greek words still linger in the dialect of the country. They are much corrupted, of course, but easily distinguishable by the learned. Still more striking relics of antiquity are to be found in the manners, customs, and superstitions of the people. The new-born infant is still carried around the purifying fire; he is swathed in tight bands precisely as the Greeks used to do; he is rocked to sleep with the same old long-drawn, monotonous, "*ninna-nanna*" lullaby; his nurse is much such a personage as of old, and so is the pedagogue who accompanies the boys to school. When the children play, they play at a Greek game two or three thousand years old, played with five stones. You may behold it in an ancient Pompeian picture in the museum, representing the children of Medea; and at every street corner among the children of the Lazzaroni! The game consists in throwing five pebbles, or potsherds simultaneously into the air, and catching them again on the back of the outstretched hand. Other ancient paintings show a game still very popular under the name of *Mora* or *Tocco*. From the Greeks—the great masters of the mimic dance—the Neapolitan inherits his expressive tarantella, and the instruments which accompany it are of Greek origin. There is the syrinx or Pandean pipe formed of reeds; the aulos, or flute, of laurel wood; the castanets; the rattling tympanon or tambourine; and even a species of sistron, well known to the children under the name of *tricca balacca*. With these instruments, and hung over with all manner of amulets, the people go to worship their Madonna dell' Arco, and of the Monte Vergine, just as they frequented the orgies of Dionysos and Ceres in Hellenic times. With the same instruments, and by the yelling out of mocking songs, they make a diabolical uproar beneath the windows of any persons who may have been so ill-advised as to marry in the winter of life. This also was a Greek custom.

The antique rhapsodist still plays his part with lofty dignity to the admiration of the populace, on the Molo, or along the shore where the fishermen dwell. He is now called *Canta-storie*, carries a staff like his Hellenic forefathers, and even as those kept alive the songs of Homer, so our canta-storie spreads abroad the lays of Ariosto and of Tasso, to which the poetry-loving people are never weary of listening.

An interior, domestic life, such as the Germanic nations love, is entirely foreign to the Neapolitan's nature. All that is outside of himself interests him; and, in the lower populace, this interest becomes an insatiable curiosity. Two persons are quarrelling over a bargain,—a couple of children at play begin to fight,—a deserted kitten is sitting out in the street,—a canary-bird has flown away,—immediately a circle of curious spectators, often amounting to hundreds, is formed to observe the trivial circumstance and to discuss it in all its bearings with much energy and vociferation! In the same way a bright light, a pretty face, or the rich dresses of the "quality" are subjects of demonstrative admiration and attention. They cannot let their voices stay idle in their throats. They must come forth, and at their full pitch too! Singing and shouting goes on from morning to night;

THE CORSO, NAPLES.

ON AN ERRAND.

and even late into the night. No one is troubled by cares for the morrow; no one is moved by the world-shaking question of the day. A sort of divine carelessness reigns in every mind. And this carelessness reaches to such a degree that the people will sell their most necessary possessions, their very beds, in order to enjoy a festa, or a banquet. This light-mindedness is exhibited in its extremest form among the race of Lazzaroni—the *razza lazzarona*.

The real Lazzarone has passed through the school of Diogenes, and the philosophical schools of the Cynics, and has brought nothing away with him save his basket, with which he earns (when he does earn !), and in which he dwells and sleeps like his great prototype in the famous tub. His clothing consists of a shirt, never changed, of a pair of short breeches bound round his middle by a leathern belt, and a woollen cap which once, many years ago, was red. His ornaments are a number of amulets, and medallions with the image of the Santissima Madonna del Carmine, and the equally holy San Gennaro. He lives on bread and wine and air and sunshine, as temperate as a cicala that sips the dew. He laughs at society, to which he is bound neither by ties of blood nor custom, for which he has neither appreciation nor envy, and whose cares he never participates in. The world exists for him: it is his stage, and he feels himself a king on it. He establishes his palace wheresoever he lists, and a godlike cheerfulness reigns within it. He has songs and aphorisms for ever on his lips, and is as epigrammatic as a Greek. For the most part he remains unmarried : for if he takes a wife he must then take up a fixed calling. This calling is invariably that of a *facchino*, a porter ; and he stands waiting in the market-place until he is hired for a few soldi, or until he finds a permanent post in the precincts of the Dogana. The children of a Lazzarone thus "settled" in life, either return to their father's original condition, or rise a step higher to be stable-boys or messengers. To such as these there opens out the career of a hackney coachman, the driver of one of those light swift *carrozzelle* which ply for hire, or the proprietor of a little stall. The second generation seldom return to the condition of Lazzaroni. They become servants or *valets de place*, or waiters in the various *trattorie* and hotels ; and most of them learn to read and write. But there is no danger that the caste of Lazzaroni should die out. The sun and the air of the south continually produce and foster new ones !

The whole population of the south has something of the Lazzaroni about it !—and by this I would not be understood to say any ill of them. Their life is the very contrary of our sharp-set complicated machinery of existence. The nature around them is very different from the "dreary, stingy, grey, formless and colourless nature of our homes." Their course is widely contrasted with our ceaseless, body-and-soul-devouring exertions, our restless pains and anxieties for every day, amid which life slips away unenjoyed." (*Stahr*, "*A Year in Italy*.") I repeat what I have said in other places, and what I am glad to say once more : go and seek to know and understand this people in their valleys and mountains, on the seashore and among the vineyards, in the islands, amidst blooming gardens, and where the soil demands hard labour ; dwell amongst the well-to-do population of wine-growers, or where the fever-stricken peasant with all his pallid family cannot earn enough by hard year-long toil, to replace his squalid rags by new garments ; everywhere you find one thing which has remained the inalienable heritage of this poor people through all the weary centuries,—*grace*. Grace rules the motions of his limbs, grace gives him courtesy, a courtesy of the heart, a fine sense to distinguish the true from the false, an appreciation of the good and the beautiful, in such rich measure as might make some other peoples—among whom grace has been choked and smothered by coal-dust and steam— envious. To be sure, it is true that with this grace alone,—a grace which reveals itself to the superficial observer merely in music, dance, and song,—it is true, I say, that with this grace alone you will never make a Mont Cenis tunnel, a St. Gothard railway, or a Suez

PORTA CAPUANA, NAPLES.

GROTTO OF POSILIPPO.

canal. Nevertheless it is an important factor in education. And we may hope for better things. When once the two Roman heritages;—the antique Roman superstitions, and the ecclesiastical superstitions, which also have their origin in Rome,—shall have given place to the belief in the light and truth which alone can bring salvation, then the people, not only of Naples, but even as far as Etna, will be acknowledged to be among the worthiest in Europe. Yes; this hope exists, and is well-founded!

Whoever wishes to write the history of Naples must not lose sight for an instant of the *Papal sceptre!* Like a fiery meteor presaging ruin, it shines and floats continually above the rising or falling stars of innumerable houses and dynasties. Throughout all the windings of the "street of tombs" which marks the progress of the lords and rulers of the people, the Pope's influence runs like a clue steeped in blood. And thus the monuments and landmarks of history (nowhere more than here the history rather of the tyrants than of the people) must be sought for the most part in the dimness of the cloister, in sepulchres, and gloomy prison towers. Nowhere more than here do we behold a wild chasing and striving after crowns and thrones:—ambition seeking to gratify itself by enjoyment of the present, and heedless of the future. The history of Naples is full of germs which have never matured into flower and fruit. This is shown in the people, who preserve only the antique intuitions, and in the architecture, which, ever since the Græco-Roman Period, has displayed no originality, no peculiarly national characteristics. Even the rule of the Normans, and of the German Emperors under whom Naples developed into wealth and power, was unable to produce anything of importance. The bud fell unopened from the tree. The Renaissance, so enormously potent throughout the rest of Italy, scarcely stirred the city on the bay with its Spring-like breathings. It only coaxed a few scanty blossoms from this soil. Before any great thing could be produced, all had degenerated into perverted mannerism, and the style of the Renaissance had become *barocco*. Whatever was done in later times was done by the patron hand of the Church; and thus freedom and independence of architectural design were unable to find expression.

What remains from the old times is little more than a name here and there, which we tack to some relic of Greece, Rome, or early Christianity. First of all there is the Grotto of Posilippo,—certainly the oldest tunnel in Europe. It leads under charming vine-grown slopes outside the town, towards the localities of the old Greek colonies, above which rises Cape Misenum, famed in fabulous story. Of these old colonies the poor little fishing town of Pozzuoli is perhaps the most worthy of mention at the present day. More than three thousand years ago the inhabitants of Cumæ and Parthenope worked at digging this grotto of Posilippo, in order to unite the latter city with the Cumæan shores. What centuries, what manifold vicissitudes, have passed between the torches of the Greeks and Romans which first illumined this darkness, and the modern gas-lamps placed here by the last of the Bourbons! How many times has the vine blossomed above this grotto in the sunshine, and yielded the generous wine which enlivened the bacchanalian processions of the antique peoples, even as it enlivens to this day the uproarious autumn festival!

The opening of the huge cavern yawns darkly in the bright daylight, like the gates of Orcus, the very jaws of the all-devouring under-world. The vaulting of the broad tunnel looks like the lid of a coffin, and is tapestried with secular spiders'-webs, and blackened with secular smoke and dust. The finger of history may be traced here too. Greeks, Romans, Spaniards, and Frenchmen have laboured at it. But according to the legend current among the people it is the work of the great enchanter Virgil!

This great enchanter of Antiquity, the Latin Homer, has found a grave among the vines and flowers that grow above the grotto:—a true poet's grave, unmatched elsewhere in the world. He himself desired that his ashes might be carried to Naples, because in that city his most beautiful poems had been brought to maturity, and his Emperor himself

HOME FAR NESTE.

took care that the poet's wish should be worthily fulfilled. What a glorious life it must have been on these shores whilst Virgil, surrounded by a circle of enthusiastic comrades in art and noble friends, passed full seven years of the prime of his manhood in composing his eternal songs!

"Illo Virgilium me tempore dulcis alebat Parthenope."

And Strabo, Horace, and Ovid, joined him in praising the charms of this Grecian Muse. Eighteen hundred years have passed over the sepulchre, the urn has long been broken, and the ashes it contained are scattered to the winds; many a laurel has sprouted on that sacred soil, and has withered and perished; many a one has stood full of enthusiasm beside this grave who was doomed to descend unknown to Orcus; but even as the sea beneath us eternally sounds its majestic music on the shore,—imperishable as the Spring which lingers for ever beneath this sky—so sing and bloom throughout the centuries the creations of the poet, the Georgics and the Æneid!

The remains of the third period of antiquity, dating from early Christian times, belong equally to the subterranean world. They consist of the underground burial places of the first disciples of Jesus in Naples,—the catacombs of Saint Januarius, Bishop of the city. In these grey cold caves of *tufa*, they laid the earthly husk to rest in the hope of a joyful resurrection. The first basilica was formed within these rocks, in whose gloomy and oppressive corridors filled with dust and night, the Crucified One was first adored, and the worshipper closed his eyes on the dazzling world,—on roses, sunshine, and the brilliancy of Olympus. Here moulder the ashes of many thousand human beings. Whole generations appear to have rested here, for the narrow rock-hewn tombs open on every side, unguarded now even by a stone. But it is touching to see how Love descended to these vaults and adorned the tombs with colour, although never a flower might bloom there; and made niches in the wall wherein to insert the little Pompeian lamps which were to shine like stars of hope amid this darkness. Some tombs are adorned with bright mosaics. The traces of this devoted love are innumerable, and speak to us from every wall.

Where have the Greek joyousness, the Roman delight in luxury, vanished to? Christianity refused to accept the smallest heritage from paganism into her new realm.

A poor monk, clad in a coarse robe, with hard sandals on his naked feet, and his forehead smeared with penitential ashes, entered timidly into the gorgeous halls of a Roman imperial palace. He passed through golden portals, heavy curtains of rich silk rustled above him, statues of bronze and marble, wrought by the master-hands of Greece, stood around the walls, and pillars laden with richest ornament rose up to the jewel-encrusted roof. He stood, and gazed, and sighed;—but soon he retired again to his cell, where he dreams in the darkness of all that glory, and only ventures in visions to clothe the beings whom he adores,—the Saviour, His blessed Mother, and the saints,—with the golden splendours he has beheld.

This monk may be taken as an image of Christianity in Italy, in the smiling South, when it first appeared in this world of artistic culture. At first it borrowed nothing,—absolutely nothing,—from this profane world, save perhaps a marble tablet or so on which to engrave some beloved names, unadorned with the poet's panegyric. The sacred grove of Apollo became a wilderness; Virgil's laurel tree, and indeed all artistic laurels in general, were stripped of their green branches, and left to wither. We ask ourselves how it was possible for this smiling art, which still flourished in Pompeii, covering the walls with luxuriant ornamentation, and with figures full of light and life,—we ask ourselves how it was possible for this art to perish and disappear so utterly?

But Fancy is killed; sense is darkened; men strive not after enjoyment, but after suffering. They no longer delight in the sunny aspect of the world, but seek its shadowed side. Mystery affects shadow; self-contemplation loves to dwell in the dark. The light and cheerful colonnades of the ancients have nothing in common with the longing for death. The first Christian temples were constructed underground, mystery was their guest, and the Christian artists were allowed to speak only in symbols. The artist, deprived of all assistance from the graces, rudely scratched upon the rough marble in the glimmering twilight, an olive branch, a bird, a palm tree, a fish, an anchor, the ship of the church, or Christ as the Good Shepherd. All this is purposely simple, plain, and poor; for so the new sect will have it, —the sect which was recruited mainly from among the poor, and which worshipped a Saviour on the cross "who had not where to lay his head."

OYSTER-BEDS AT SANTA LUCIA.

When Christianity emerged from its hiding-places, the seed of antique art which had fallen on the pathway of the great migrations of the peoples, was trodden down, or else lay dry and withered under the ruins of the universal convulsion. The bright soaring butterfly had lost its sunny wings, and crawled about as a poor caterpillar in the dim cloisters of convents and basilicas. A mortal silence reigned everywhere; the noise of the busy chisel had long ceased. Only in the silent catacombs did men paint and scratch a few rude images.

This poverty-stricken art,—and indeed the whole aspect of the catacombs,—forms a striking contrast with the life and the landscape of this busy city. We come out of the

CEMETERY. FEAST OF ALL SOULS, NAPLES.

damp dark passages, and find our eyes dazzled by glorious sunlight. The hedges are
covered with roses, the crimson oleander burns red against the deep blue sky, the leaves
of the palm-trees are stirred by a refreshing breeze from the sea, merry children play in

ZAMPOGNARO.

the gardens, and their hands are full of flowers, the golden orange ripens amidst its dark
foliage,—thus it is to-day; even thus it was in the days when the mustard-seed of the
Gospel ripened in yonder dark caverns, soon to grow into a tree, from whose wood a
great throne was made! A throne whence the destinies of nations were governed with a

tyranny only to be compared to that of the days of Pagan universal dominion—to the hard and implacable rule of the ancient Cæsars.

As we have said before, this tyranny runs like a blood-red thread throughout all the windings of Neapolitan history. The heads of hundreds of rulers, and of many noble men of the nation, are strung on it as beads upon a rosary; and with these a bloody finger reckons off years and centuries of darkness and despotism. Naples is a tragic spot of earth. And it is well that Nature should strew the soil with roses and with all manner of flowers so as to overpower the smell of decay which arises from the graves of the murdered, by the sweet scents of violet and orange flower! Like mists before the wind, like withered leaves in the gales of autumn, thousands of figures pass before our eyes;—all bearing a sword,—either the sword of a brave warrior, or the weapon of the executioner—and all clad in blood-stained garments. The last of the Cæsars, Romulus Augustulus, glides onward, a pale shadow, to die in the gardens of Lucullus at Castello dell' Ovo. From all points of the compass the people came crowding on sword in hand, —Vandals, Goths, Greeks,—all eager to divide the heritage of the Roman Empire. In those days it behoved the dwellers in Naples to go armed night and day, and to keep constant watch and ward from their towers. The Goths are within the city; Belisarius is approaching, to seize upon it for the Grecian Emperor; by means of a water-conduit (the populace call the remains of it to this day, *i ponti rossi*,—the red bridges), he forces an entrance, and then all is bloodshed, fire and plunder. Totila, the great King of the Goths, advances. Famine opens the city gates to him. After him came the Longo-bards. Naples lies like an apple of discord between these monarchs and the neighbouring dukes of Benevento, but the town remains true to the Grecian crown, and willingly receives its ruler from Ravenna. Division, envy, contest, and tyranny are rife throughout Italy, and the Greek diadem is shorn of its brightness; but still Naples remains true to the sinking star. Now the sea is covered with the fleets of Saracenic pirates, the land with thousands of hostile plunderers. Norman pilgrims are transformed into Norman warriors, before whom both Greeks and Saracens have to give way. The Pope calls a German Kaiser to his aid;—new swarms of Normans;—and then Naples falls!

It was in 1130 that the valiant Count Roger founded the proud kingdom of the Two Sicilies, and held sword and sceptre in an iron grasp. His race flourished, and perished. The haughty Hohenzollerns came across the Alps; the Guelphs, the Waiblingen! It is the German sword and the Romish cross,—the Imperial crown and the Pontifical tiara,—hate against hate! The great ones of the earth contend together, and the people bleeds.'

The star of the Hohenstaufen declines, and finally sets in the person of Conradin, whose youthful blood was shed in the Mercato. The race of Anjou mounts to the throne by blood-stained stairs. Blood marks its track, and with blood it is cemented for near upon two hundred years; its footsteps on Italian soil are soaked in blood. But its hour at last approaches: the long-expected hour of vengeance, so impatiently desired and brought on by the house of Aragon, at length draws near, and then that accursed race of Anjou seizes on the headsman's axe to defend itself. Fifty years more are accorded to it by Fate; and at the end of that time the funeral knell of Naples' independence, which it has cost the lives of thousands to maintain, is rung by the bells that peal to celebrate the entry of the Spaniard.

A long line of viceroys follows. Many a proud name is heard:—Gonsalvo, Alba, Toledo, Olivarez, Medina! Two hundred long years of suffering, oppression, and extortion pass by, and history inscribes on her tablets the name of a poor fisherman,—Masaniello. Many grim figures arise out of the mists of those days, but the worst was not yet come. The Spanish war of succession is fought; and now Austria sends her viceroys to Naples. France and Austria take arms against each other, and in the midst of the fray the first Bourbon, Charles, lands on the Neapolitan coast. This is in the year 1734, and then begins the ill-omened rule of the Bourbons. It is interrupted for a brief space by the French Revolution and the French Empire. Joseph, Murat, cross the scene, and then Ferdinand the First—that arrogant lackey of a blood-thirsty papacy—returns and inaugurates the reign of the bayonet, the subterranean dungeon, the unresting weapon of the headsman, and the stealthily gliding, omnipotent Jesuit! But they pass; they all pass away: Francis the First, Ferdinand the Second, Francis the Second,—all are past.

Garibaldi, the hero of the people, comes and brings them long yearned for liberty on the point of his sword!

Years have gone by since then, and Naples is enrolled in the noble brotherhood which binds the Italian nation together from the Alps to Etna. The new day rises enthroned on golden clouds, but they look on it at first with eyes dimmed and dazzled by long imprisonment. However, that which hatred divided, love may knit together again; even although the scars left by the course of history on this unfortunate land may never wholly disappear.

All that remains of the old stormy times are dark walls, castles, and fortresses, which were the tyrants' refuge. Castel Sant' Elmo, Castello dell' Ovo, Castel Capuana, Castel Nuovo, the royal palace, the monuments of rulers whom the Church favoured, because they served the Church. There are proud memorials of triumph, like the arch of the haughty Aragonese, Alfonso the First. And through the echoing halls of the church of the Carmine, where stands the statue of the unfortunate Conradin, the words of the poet sound :

"Love lives but as the grass,
And joy endures not long;
Like weeds they fade and pass,
But hatred's curse is strong!"

THE EVER YOUNG PARTHENOPE.

"One perceives no dissonance, for this Elysian Nature is all harmony; one beholds not a single gloomy or meditative face, for this smiling heaven steeps all in idle ecstasy."—GREGOROVIUS, *Wanderjahre*.

THE poet Waiblinger begins one of his Neapolitan songs with these words :—

"I saunter and lounge all day,
And think of no manner of work."

"I saunter and lounge all day!" Certainly no town in the world is so completely adapted for the delightful pastime of lounging, for idle curiosity, and for enjoyment without exertion, as this Naples is! The stranger, who, in Rome, has been half-smothered in the dust of libraries, or has wandered amid the monuments of ancient art with some dry and learned book as his guide, may here throw aside his classics bound in pig-skin, and, accompanied only by Virgil or Horace, or, perhaps, Anacreon, sally forth to meet the new day which shines above Vesuvius. The painter, with his Roman sketch-book in his hand, would fain set to work :—but all around him are a thousand ever changing forms; he wanders, and gazes, absorbed in pleasant contemplation, and—the morning and the evening are the first day, and many following days, and the canvas remains blank! The poet'—Ah, he is hindered from making the smallest poem, by

ON THE MOLE, NAPLES.

sheer poetry! The poems which Naples has inspired have been mostly dictated in absence by a longing to return to her.

We sit dreaming beneath a slender palm-tree, breathed upon by sweet sea-breezes mixed with the scent of flowers and shrubs, shone upon by quivering rays of spring sunshine. The murmur of the neighbouring sea sounds like the voice of the sirens; cheerful talk and laughter of fishermen strike upon our ear; the eye catches a vision of a Greek temple, and of white statues :—Apollo, Bacchus and his crew, Hercules, gods,

VIEW OF NAPLES FROM THE CORSO VITTORIO EMANUELE.

and demigods, glimmer amidst the evergreens. Has old Hellas risen again from the depths of the Mediterranean?

But no;—the sound of the liveliest dialect in Italy, spoken by well-dressed men and women, wakens us out of our dream. The clash of military music sounds, silken robes sweep and rustle between the flower-beds, dandies in fashionable Parisian costume twirl

GIPSY TINKERS IN NAPLES.

their jaunty canes, flashing glances, and soft words fly hither and thither; everything is bright and smiling,—the sea and sky themselves seem to be full of joy and brilliancy. Modern Naples presses around us; its perfumed waves close above our heads, and we dive deep down in them enjoyingly.

Who thinks of the gray old fortress-prisons, or of the blood-stained Mercato? Who could compare these voluptuous images of pleasure on which the roses breathe their perfume, with the statue of the youthful Hohenstaufen in the grim Carmelite church, half hidden by choking clouds of priestly incense? To breathe and live here, is to breathe airs of Paradise and to exist in the present alone. This garden by the shore, which nature and art have combined to make one of the loveliest on earth, is called the "Villa Nazionale." The warm south wind, and the soft breath from the east which opens the flower-buds, are the only winds that penetrate into this Eden. A line of heights, covered with foliage and pleasant dwellings, protects it against the rude *tramontana* (the north wind).

The highest point of this chain of hills is the gigantic Castel Sant Elmo crowning the city, whose dark yellow walls shine at sunrise and sunset like molten gold. From thence the slopes descend gently, by groves and vineyards to the blue waters of the sea. The populace calls this chain "Vomero" at its beginning ; the Greeks named the portion that touches on the shore "Posilippo." Between the umbrellas of the stone pines, and the dark pillars of the cypress-trees which grow upon its slopes, many-coloured, flat-roofed villas may be seen looking out far over the sea. Yonder black rocks, running boldly out into the Mediterranean, whose waves have foamed and fought with them for ages, bear the Castello dell' Ovo. No sons of royal race pine there now-a-days. Only nineteenth century heroes, blue-coated soldiers of the kingdom of Italy, sit there now, and blow their blaring bugles, or stare across the forlorn ramparts at the great mountain of ashes, which—lava-dark amidst the sunny landscape—stands there and sends up a smoke into the sky like an altar of sacrifice. From those ramparts, too, they can see the range of glistening towns, which bind the heights of Naples and of Sorrento together like a string of pearls. That highest mountain, that looks as if a Cyclopean fortress had been piled upon its summit, is Monte Sant' Angelo, the rocky sentinel over two gulfs.

But one's gaze wanders towards the Hesperian shores of Sorrento :—to its enchanted gardens, its blossom filled groves upon steep cliffs, its peaceful valleys! Our soul floats as on the wings of a sea-gull across the waters to yonder blue, fairy-like island, which lies upon the sea like a vision of old Greece,—the isle of Tiberius, the siren-haunted Capri! Sails glide over the sea looking like water-lilies ; dolphins sport and roll ; little fish leap, and the eager broad-winged gulls dart swiftly after them ; brown-skinned boys paddle in the waters ; fishermen draw up their nets upon the sandy shore ;—and still the gay military music plays, and still the roses bloom. We sit still beneath the slender palm-tree, and enjoy the present.

Equally beautiful with this villa of the living, is the villa of the dead :—the *Camposanto nuovo*. There is nothing here to remind one of the gloom of the grave ; no mournful figures, no dry and dreary wreaths of *immortelles*. Fresh flowers bloom here, and those who bring them remember their departed amidst light and perfume. Modern Naples comes hither also. Silk dresses rustle, and gay voices sound as on the strand below. It seems almost as though Death and Life had chosen this for a pleasant trysting place, and met to enjoy the sunny present together. What a glorious burial-ground is this Camposanto! Art has laboured here with skill and diligence, and Nature has poured her sweetest treasures out amid these temples, chapels, monuments, arcades, and elegantly decorated tombs. True the black cypress throws his shadow across the sunny paths ; but even its darkness is flecked with rose-leaves which the winter strews as freely as the spring. And what a wealth of flowers between these funeral trees ! What a rich perfume all around us ! Those shrubs and thickets garlanded with climbing plants, and where the nightingale sings in May, suggest no mournful thoughts. Rather they seem to invite to some lover's rendezvous. And lo, betwixt the tree-stems where the dense foliage opens, the many-coloured city, the luxuriant Campania, the eternal sea rocking softly in the universal joy of existence ! There, Vesuvius, not stern nor menacing, but breathing peace : yonder the *Paludi*, where an industrious people raises green and succulent plants from the soil ; further down, the swarming Mercato, filled with a roar of many voices that mounts up even to this quiet spot. In the distance the shore, white sails filled with a fresh wind putting out to sea, the light-house, dome after dome, Sant' Elmo, and the convent of Camaldoli sending down a quiet "*Pax vobiscum!*" to the land below. Life,—blooming joyous life is everywhere in the sky, the sea, and the earth!

When the first foundations of this cemetery were dug on the height of Poggio-reale—where once the proud Aragonese had built himself a "lordly pleasure-house,"—the spades of the workmen constantly turned up antique urns, funeral lamps, and coins; and it was found that on this very spot, where the generations of this nineteenth century were to be laid to rest, the original inhabitants of Palaiopolis had buried the remains of their dead three or four thousand years ago! The winds had scattered the ashes of those Greek forefathers, or flowers were rooted in them destined to deck the graves of their remote descendants. And far below the noisy railway-engine goes rattling and steaming.

"Even as the leaves in the forest, so are the generations of men."

Even this city of the dead has its festival. If Naples hold high revels on its riotous Christmas Eve, its noisy Easter-Day, or its bacchanalian festival of Piedigrotta, the second of November (All Souls' Day) is celebrated here with not less noise and show. There are glancing lights, chanting priests, moving masses of people pushing and being

THE CUSTOM-HOUSE DOCK, NAPLES.

pushed hither and thither, and all with flowers or tapers in their hands, inside the cemetery: and thousands of vehicles of all kinds, crowds singing, shouting, playing *mora*, or *boccia*, or drinking in the wine-shops, outside its walls. All Naples is afoot here, come to see how the dead are lodged, how pleasant it must be to rest here, and also—with an intense sense of the present—to remind itself to enjoy life. How true it is, as Ugo Foscolo sings :

> "*All'ombra dei cipressi, e dentro l'urne*
> *Confortati di pianto, è forse il sonno*
> *Della morte men duro ?*"—
>
> "Beneath the cypress shade, or in the urn
> Bedewed with tears, think'st thou the sleep of death
> Is less profound ?"—

"Enjoy life!" Onwards, driver! Carry us onward into the midst of life where it seethes and roars amidst a thousand enjoyments great and small, and where the light-hearted populace leads its careless existence. Onwards, into the palpitating heart of the city!

Here begins the locality known as old Naples; and into its lanes and alleys, its *vichi* and *vicoletti*, the fresh airs of progress have never yet penetrated. In this spot is concentrated all that Naples still preserves of its old original customs and peculiarities, its houses, and shops, and wares, and men. Between these dingy, narrow, enormously lofty houses, of no style of architecture whatever, on this wretched, filthy, ever damp pavement, see what a swarming crowd,—what pushing, striving, pressing forward, backward, up and down, hither and thither, shouting, yelling, calling, from all points of the compass towards all points of the compass! Whatsoever the pastures, gardens, vineyards, or the sea, produce to eat and drink,—all that swims and creeps and flies and runs, is brought hither in barrels and tubs, in nets and baskets, on men's heads or on donkeys or in carts, and lies piled up here. Often the food is offensive to eyes and nose: often the ears are hurt by the wild yells of its vendors: but to the populace it is attractive under all and every form. —stored in tubs, or hung up, or spread out. Here is frying and frizzling in pans and pots, filling of flasks and dishes, tempting of the hungry with what seems to them the highest good on earth.

Who can seize these pictures? What colours would have to be mixed, what forms and figures, what caricatures of mankind, what over-driven beasts, would the pencil have to delineate! But even colours and pencil would not suffice; for noise, and atmosphere, and constant change of grouping, cannot be fixed on paper. Any one suddenly transported from an orderly, cleanly, northern market-place to this spot, would surely believe that a band of suburban vagabonds in full revolution were fighting over the division of the spoils of some huge camp, and were minded to be off again in a quarter of an hour! Envy, hatred, malice, rage, fury, murder and sudden death,—all manner of devilries and maniacal frenzies, seem to roar around him in every direction;—and yet the scene is one of complete peace:—only peace after the Neapolitan fashion! For in truth wherever there is a smell of eating, this people becomes immediately peaceful and good-humoured. All this shouting and shoving put into a few words would run thus: "Buy of me, for I have the best and the cheapest."—" Nay, good friend, I want something yet better and cheaper." And that's all!

Indeed, the best-humoured man screams and yells the loudest, just to express his delight in the profusion of good things around him, or may be to gain an extra soldo on his five halfpence worth of goods!

The houses in these streets,—all expressive of the utmost uninhabitableness, if the word may pass,—are nearly empty throughout the day. A man must be in mortal sickness before he would consent to be cooped up in the hideous little dens there. All throng out into the street. "Out of doors" is the watchword which sounds here at about

PORT OF NAPLES.

five o'clock in the morning;—in the cool seasons of the year, that is say. In the summer time there is no rest or quiet by day or by night. However long your experience

SANTA MARIA IN PORTICO, NAPLES.

of the place may be, you can never finally decide whether the people really do go to sleep here at all. Thus there is, of course, no care expended on the dwellings. Scarcely one whole window is to be seen in them; or if there be one, it is black with the dust of the middle-ages! On the rusty iron-work of the balconies in front of the windows hang the grey banners of Poverty, who is constantly passing in noisy procession through these alleys; and in honour of Poverty there wave all manner of conceivable and inconceivable rags of clothing. Sometimes they are mere heaps of patches just dipped in water, or inscrutable webs, apparently of string, fluttering in the sea-breeze when one chances to find its way into this labyrinth.

The very faces that one sees here seemed patched and faded. The stamp of humanity on them is dulled and blunted; they are distorted, worn, haggard, eager, and hungry. A wolfish craving to be satisfied glares out of many dark eyes; and out of some a reminiscence of the good old Bourbon times of lawlessness and plunder. The fishermen who bring their wares to market here, are the only handsome men to be seen. For the most part they preserve the old classic regularity of features, and a certain dignity distinguishes them from the rest of the clamouring crowd. Here too you may hear the genuine Neapolitan of the Lazzaroni, so difficult to understand. Here you may see the genuine Lazzaroni pantomime,—gestures of hand and finger, and arm and head, bandied to and fro with inconceivable rapidity. And to look and listen here, is as good as a play. Let us take a few specimens!

Here are two vendors of melons whose gaily-painted stalls stand side by side, wildly shouting at the passing crowd. How popular is the juicy water-melon; that fruit which reproduces the Italian tricolour with its green and white rind and dark red flesh. According to the Lazzaroni's proverb, it supplies three wants: "*Cu nu rano magno, vevo, e me lav'a faccia.*" (For a *grano*—less than a farthing—I can eat, drink, and wash my face.) One of these merchants shouts with a mighty voice: "*Castiellamare! che maraviglia! . . . So de Castiellamare!*" (From Castellamare! What marvels! They come from Castellamare!)

But the other overpowers him. "*Mo so benute da la rotta della neve, e so de foco!*" (They are but just come out of an ice-cave, and they're full of fire!)

And now the strife grows loud and swift. "*Oh! oh! che bellezza! Che rrobba! Che rrobba è chesta! E nu sole che mo esce!*" (Oh what beauties! What wares are these! Look, here's the sun just rising!)

"*No, no; ccà staunu li mellune veraci! Chisse lloco è la luna; lu veru sole beditelo ccà!*" (No, no; here are your genuine melons. Those yonder are only the moon. The true sun, behold it here!)

His rival puts one of his highly eulogised fruits on the head of a boy, deftly splits it with one stroke of the knife, and pretending amazement roars out, "*Uh! l'ottava meraviglia de lu munno! bidite, si avite uocchi, bidite! Fuoco, fuoco!*" (Oh! The eighth wonder of the world! See, if you have eyes, only see! Fire, fire!)

"*Vesuvio, Vesuvio!*" shouts the other. To which number two replies with "*Etna e Mongibello!*" But the first still caps him, and screams out, "*E lu ufiernu cu tutti li diavoli!*" (It is the infernal regions with all the devils in it!)

Upon this, his rival lays down melon and knife, sticks his arms a-kimbo, and says, in a kind of envious surprise, "*Bidimmo mò che cci hai da dicere cchiù!*" (Well, let's hear what you've got to say *next*.) And then the war begins all over again.

In the same fashion shout and scream the *Pizzajuolo* (sausage-seller), the vendor of onion cakes, and the greasy woman who sells wafers made of maize-flour. "*Caure, caure, scagliuozzole! Quatto nu suold!*" (Hot, hot, maize-flour cakes! Four for a soldo!) The orange-seller rattles by with his wheelbarrow, and his cry rises above the roofs,

"*Pportovalle de Palermo! Scialate, scialate, ca mo è lu tiempu, scialate!*" (Oranges of Palermo! Feast, feast, for now is your time; feast!) His voice is half drowned by the shrill tones of the ragged woman with maize dumplings boiled or fried: "*Polauchelle*

IN FRONT OF A BAKER'S OVEN IN NAPLES.

tenerelle caude e belle! E cè lu latte! cu lu tutoro d'oro! Polauchelle!" (Little chickens, tender, warm, and beautiful! Full of milk and golden yolk of egg! Little chickens!) "*Chi vo vevere? chi vo vevere?*" yells the vendor of sulphur water in our ears. "*Aequa zurfegna fridda, fridda, uh cumme la tengo annevata!*" (Who will drink? Who will drink? Sulphur water, cold, cold, oh how cool I keep it with snow!)

"*Mupaglia segge!*" screams the maker of straw chairs. "*Mupaglia segge!*" from house to house. *Facchini* with huge loads piled high on their heads push their way through the crowd, and give out their warning cry, "*A nanze, guarda, a nanze!*" (In front there! Look out in front there!) There are the shouts of the coachmen, the donkey drivers, the seller of milk who drives his cow before him from house to house of his customers. Everywhere, in whatever direction you turn your head, you hear prices being roared out; *cinque, tre, sic.* .... All at once the bells, big and little, of innumerable churches and chapels, begin to mingle their shrill cracked voices with the noise of the crowd. This rouses the *Zampognaro*, who in emulation, blows his bagpipes almost to bursting. Then the *Tambarellajo* (player on a species of tambourine) thumps his bacchanalian *tammuriello*, ever louder and louder. One strives in clamour against the other. Youthful female merchants—the egg-woman, the *Mozzamara*, or seller of cigar-ends, the girl with brooms made of reeds, the hair-plaiter, the weaver of ribbons, the knitter of gloves,—all trip along singing and chattering. And amidst the uproar may be heard the popular songs bellowed forth in wild rollicking fashion: "*Te voglio bene assaje, e tu nun pienze a me!*" (So much, so much I love thee! But thou think'st not of me!)

*   *   *   *   *   *

Hold! Here is a row going on! A seller of *ricottelle* (curd cheese) from Massa, a seller of *fraufeliechi* (a preparation of honey), and a seller of lucifer matches, have all been sitting in a corner together playing *mora*. One wanted to take advantage of the other, and the result was a grand conflict. A handful of curd cheese flies out amidst the passers-by; the clumsy lucifer matches strew the ground; the third makes off to save his honey; there are scratched faces and tremendous threats; but—just when you think the fight must begin in dread earnest, behold they are all sitting together again at their game in the most perfect amity! If it happens to be a *festa* day, every dwelling becomes a ball-room. Out of every entrance-hall you hear the thrum of the tambourine, the clapping of the castanets, and the shrill rapidly enunciated song of the tarantella keep time to both. With what enthusiasm yonder girl with her dark hair elaborately piled up high on her head, opens her mouth, and sings, keeping time to the dancers' feet:

LA TARANTELLA.	THE TARANTELLA.
"*E la luna mmiezu mare,*	"'See the moon shines over the sea!
Mamma mia, nozillame tu?'	Marry me, mammy, marry me now?'
'*Figlia mia, chi l'aggio a da?*'	'Daughter, whom shall I give to thee?
'*Mamma mia, pensaci tu!*'	'Think of it, mammy, settle it thou!
'*Si te do nu scarparielle,*	'Should I give thee a cobbler gay?
U scarpariello non fa pe te;	A cobbler would never suit, I fear.
Sempe va, e sempe vene,	He's lounging up and down all day,
Sempe a suglia mmana tene;	His awl in his hand he keeps alway,
Si llo vota la fantasia,	And if his temper went astray,
A suglia nfuccia a figlia mia!'	He might stick the awl in my daughter dear!'"
E la luna mmiezu mare," &c. &c.	See the moon shines over the sea," &c. &c.

How often in the midst of this ever moving throng do the words of Horace recur to us:

"*Beatus ille qui procul negotiis*"—

Yes; blessed, thrice blessed, is he who can from time to time escape from the pressure of busy life, and rest awhile in the bosom of Nature,—here so mild and soft that she cures the pains of mind and body! Happy is the man who can content himself with a rural dwelling on one of yonder soft far-seeing slopes! The noise of busy day does not reach up thither. The waves of life do but sound faintly, even as the murmur of the sea which breaks and foams upon the shore below. All sorts of flowers bloom in these gardens on the heights, and the evergreen trees which shadow the houses with their thick foliage, serve as a shield against the fiery rays of July sunshine, and ward off the hot breath of the south wind. How exquisite is the air upon these hills! The soul seems freed from its corporeal bonds, and free from care, softly breathes away the day with its ætherial joys. The monks who built their cloisters here among the trees, were of a different sort from their brethren who dwelt in the city. In that nerve-exciting, crowded town, vice existed side by side with fanaticism: ambition, tyranny, and avarice, with apparent poverty and abnegation. But, up here dwelt gentleness and mildness, contentment and benevolence. You may see them still, in the eyes of the Benedictine monk who is just opening the little wicket, and giving us admission to his paradise.

We are at Camaldoli.

Between garden walls, with a constant view across blooming, perfumed, flower beds on to the sea and the islands, goes our path. It winds onward and upward through a shady chestnut wood, in whose green moss the purple violet blooms, and where whole choirs of nightingales sing throughout the Spring, to the portal of the often visited convent. It lies here, as though raised halfway to heaven, and happily removed from earth, under its hoary evergreen oaks, breathed on by the divine breath of Spring, and with fluttering wood birds all about it. Down yonder the city spreads its dark stone wings and covers the land beside the shore; and the sea rolls its silver-shining flood between the flowery coasts. It is a picture so grand, so harmonious, so restful, soft, and smiling, that it seems as if all the peace of the world had been poured out here. Scarce a sound disturbs us. Birds twitter in the branches; leaves rustle; butterflies born of light and perfume, flutter in the sunshine; ants silently pursue their tiny paths;—and man, grown silent too, gazes for hours and hours into this vision of delight, touched with ecstatic awe, enchanted, inspired, filled with overflowing love towards God and man. Here every trouble is forgotten, every wish is stilled, every passion slumbers in the heart. Neither the town at our feet, nor the many towns beyond the Alps,—neither the commonplaceness of mankind everywhere, nor aught of all that has once pained us, has power to trouble us here. Our thoughts have become a part of Time itself;—Time that never looks backward, that glides onward, softly and noiselessly. We float along upon a tideless sea, beholding no shore and longing for no landing-place.

But the evening nears; the sun sinks. Already the chariot of the god is falling towards the glimmering islands of Ponza, and he is turning the torch of day downward to be quenched in the waves. Little rosy cloudlets flutter round him over Ischia's lofty peak. They come, too, in crowds from behind Capri's dusky rock, and press across the shining peninsula of Sorrento, across Monte Sant' Angelo, to grim Vesuvius, and crown his gloomy brow with youthful roses. Then they hasten after the sun-god, and dive down with him in the flood. But lo, as by the stroke of an enchanter's wand, the heavens spread out a purple tent above the darkening earth! Sea and sky, mountains and islands appear clad in the clearest, purest, violet. Vesuvius glows like a great amethyst,—half transparent;

> "How grave and still, veiled with a gauzy smoke,
> Vesuvius in his purple-tinted robe!
> The semicircle of the hills lies stretched
> Even to Cape Mycene, like a crown.

> All, all is steeped in one delicious flush
> Of rosy light. What glories glow around!
> And in the evening stillness it might seem
> As though the heavens were leaning down to earth
> To kiss it!"

Then the splendour fades. But ere yet the last gleam departs, the moon rises above the mountain of Somma, attended by a train of great beautiful stars, and then land and sea, mountain and city, put on another glittering robe,—the mantle of the Queen of Night. She glides peacefully above the streets and silent roads, between the tree-stems, gathering perfume from the orange-plants, inspiring hearts with love, and lips with kisses, and from the shining shore by Santa Lucia sounds the song:

> "O dolce Napoli,
> O suol beato,
> Dove sorridere
> Volle il creato!
> Tu sei l'impero
> Dell' armonia;
> Santa Lucia! Santa Lucia!"

THE BEAUTIFUL, DANGEROUS NEIGHBOUR.

> "Lo, Vesuvius the lord, grand in imperial purple!
> Calmly he stands, and looks o'er the battle-field, looks on the slaughtered,
> Hero-like, ruthless, serene; and leans on his spear blazing brightly."
> GREGOROVIUS, *Euphorion*.

NOT all the Cyclopean forges in which superhuman forces once melted, and hammered and shaped our earth-ball into hills and valleys,—not all of these, I say, were extinguished and destroyed on the seventh day of rest. A few were forgotten, and flame on to this day, sending out streams of burning matter to the terror and confusion of the men who dwell in their neigbourhood. There where Nature blooms the fairest, and offers deepest delights, are found these workshops of Vulcan :—here Vesuvius, yonder Etna.

Vesuvius stands upon the smiling bay like a huge enigma that needs Titans to unravel it. It thunders across the sea, and across the dwellings of mankind like an Olympic oracle; and men gaze up at it anxious, fearful,—but none understands it in its greatness. A generation of gardeners and peasants toils and digs around its feet like ants around the claws of a slumbering lion. On a sudden the lion awakes, growls, shakes his mighty mane, treads to powder the tiny swarm beneath his paws, growls once more, and lies down to rest again.——And then the ants come back more numerous than ever!

This is a symbol of the mountain and of the men who live near it, and has been for thousands of years. And had no man written his history, yet Vesuvius has written it for himself in gigantic letters and with a glowing graver on the plains of Campania even to the sea. Thou mayst read them there, traveller, from the ancient records of Pompeii,—from the year of grace 79, down to the date of the latest eruption. Thou mayst read them in the bowels of the earth when thou descendest to look upon the corpse of Herculaneum buried in lava, or in the modern houses of Torre del Greco eight times rebuilt; or of Torre Annunziata, Portici, and San Sebastiano. Thou mayst drink them

THE LAVA COMES!

I COME! Depart from house and hall,
   Nor barn, nor cellar heeding!
Haste, fly! Above the outer wall
I climb and spread a smoky pall,
   Still onward fiercely speeding.

Above the fruitful, vine-grown land,
   Where ripening grapes looked cheery,
I strew hot ashes and burning sand,
I clasp the trees with my fiery hand,
   And leave them black and dreary.

My scorching breath shall quickly blast
   The fount that freshly plashes;
My parching footsteps travel fast;
The grove is shrivelled where they have passed,
   And all is dust and ashes!

in the fiery wine that grows amid the ashes, and trace them in the mobile character of a people that calls itself the "sons of Vesuvius!"

But the history of Vesuvius, like the history of all the great lords over Naples, is but a story of massacre, fire, and spoil. Fire goes before him, and the land lies dead behind him! He has passed like a triumphant Cæsar over the cities of Stabia, Herculaneum, and Pompeii, all unheeding the broken marbles of temple and theatre which his fiery

POMPEII.

coursers crushed beneath their hoofs; treading into dust the poor cottage of the vintager, scorching the trees, and tearing away the grapes from the green vine, with his red hot chariot wheels. High in the air he swings the torch that lights him to his work of destruction, and turns night to glaring day.

"I mock at darkness and night!
I mock at the morning's glow!
My robe glares far and bright;
Its fiery hem for miles doth flow,
And its rustle says 'Death and woe!'"

If you stand on a height to the west or north of Naples, and look across to the plains out of which Vesuvius rises on his throne, there seems to be an everlasting shade of sadness over those blooming fields, so richly cultivated. Dark banners of crape hang from that grim throne over the land. The traveller fancies he sees cloud-shadows, but let him look up: a clear pure ether spreads itself above him, and not a cloudlet swims in the sea of air. No; that which floats around the mountain's summit is born of fire,—is smoke. And those dark streaks he took for shadows on the landscape are streams of lava, whose traces all-healing Nature has not yet been able to efface in all these centuries.

3 D

Yonder places stretching along the coast from Naples,—Barra, S. Jorio, S. Giorgio Portici, Resina, Torre del Greco, Torre Annunziata, with Bosco Tre Case, and Bosco Reale, stand, almost all of them like islands in a flood of lava, on a soil made of lava; their fields and gardens are old and new ash-heaps. Even so it is with those villages which surround the mountain in closer proximity to it: San Sebastiano (the nearest to Naples), Massa di Somma, Pollena, Sant' Anastasia, Somma, and Ottajano, and innumerable other groups of houses to the west. They have all suffered sorely, and the youngest, as well as the oldest, of their inhabitants have many tales to tell of the terrors of the mountain. Within this century there have been twenty eruptions from 1804 to 1872, alone! That the volcano's strength is by no means diminished is proved by the eruption of 1872, the most tremendous on record since that which destroyed Pompeii, with the exception of the eruption of 1631. The mountain poured out nearly twenty millions of cubic metres of lava over the country which was just then full of Spring blossoms; and devastated the greater part of the pleasant villages of San Sebastiano and Massa.

The lava still smokes. You may gather from caverns and gulfs made by the lava amongst the vineyards stones that are scorching hot; and the volcanic mass keeps its heat, in certain places, for centuries. But new and cheerful life returns to dwell upon and between the slowly cooling streams of lava. Those who but a short time since were flying in haste and terror, have long ago returned. They make new roads or uncover old ones with hatchet and spade, tend the vines, and plant young trees, which thrive marvellously, fed on the very heart's blood of the earth. They build up again their swallows' nests of houses close to the mountain, absolutely on the streams of petrified lava, which furnishes them with the materials for their walls and pavements. Thus have their forefathers done for ages; thus they will do Spring after Spring, even though next autumn the mountain should again destroy their property. What a mysterious attraction is exercised by the love of home!

"Dear, beloved native land,
Scarred by many a lava stripe,
Where my grazing cattle stand,
Where my grapes are growing ripe.

"Still my herds shall pasture here!
Here my purple wine ferments!
Whatsoever comes I'll bear;
Meantime peaceful and content."—RÜCKERT.

If we look down from a height upon those houses, they show like white crystals in the dark mass of slag: or like snowy flocks of lambs in the green islands amidst the black lava. As we approach them we find ourselves in a labyrinth of streets and alleys immediately behind Naples, which conduct us gently upward to the well-cultivated fields and vineyards on the lower slopes of Vesuvius. The vine climbs to the summits of the poplars and elms; roses bloom in the hedges; figs and pomegranates display their fruits in extraordinary luxuriance. The rich foliage of the orange and lemon trees is seen beneath the shadow of tall pines and cypresses, almost as though the former sought shelter from the rays of the sun, here so tremendously powerful; in a word, the whole flora of the south is to be found here in glorious abundance.

But those who gather these treasures,—the dwellers on the slopes of Vesuvius, are a poor and simple race. They have been reared in labour and poverty, and ask nothing of life but the barest necessaries. Their vine-grown cottages, which look so pleasant to the passer by, contain nothing of that which the outer world would call comfort; still less the

DRAWWELL AT THE FOOT OF VESUVIUS.

smallest approach to luxury. These rough walls contain but one room, and this room is at once sleeping chamber and kitchen, stable and cellar. The walls inside are black, the floor rough, the beds which serve the family to take their brief repose hard and wretched.

The great wine barrels on huge wooden stands are the chief treasures of the family, and the only playthings of the children, who grow up free and untended as the birds of the air.

The joy of the poor man is his garden with its fruit-trees and vines, the produce of which, however, belongs for the most part to the proprietor in the city. What remains of the crop just serves to provide a scanty subsistence for the peasant and his family.

The joy of the poor man is his garden: and he watches the blossoming of the vines, sees the beans and tomatos flourish, marks the swelling of the juicy fruit among the boughs, with a hopeful heart. Everywhere in these villages you may see faces full of tranquil contentment. The Neapolitan Spring begins to shake his horn of plenty. The sunshine and the warm genial rains combine to draw forth treasures from the carefully tended soil. The perfume of orange flowers fills the air, and the scent of a thousand aromatic plants is borne by the light-winged breeze over the Campanian plains. The days are followed by delicious moonlit nights, and the whole landscape breathes of peace. 'Tis true that from time to time a thunderous sound is heard from the mountain, and echoes growling among the black ravines of the rugged Somma; and the peasant glances up at his dangerous neighbour. But the dangerous neighbour is breathing his bluish column of vapour into the air as peacefully as a sacrificial altar: and careless contentment sleeps again undismayed.

But lo, one midnight, there rises a fierce stormy wind, and with the clapping of doors and windows, and the wild sough of the bending trees, is mingled an ominous roar. That is not thunder,—the heavens are clear and bright with moon and stars;—that is the Mountain! The terrified peasant rushes out;—it comes! In broad rolling waves, like to a fiery serpent, hurrying down the ashen-grey slopes, it comes! The dread destroyer, the lava, comes. The mountain, filled to the brim, has split its chalice with a mighty noise, and is pouring fiery masses down into the vales. The wretched peasant cries aloud; he calls on all the saints to help him; he rouses his wife and children; their only hope of safety is in flight. Already has the flowing lava set its swift feet in the neighbouring gardens. Already it embraces the trees with glowing arms; the flames climb up to the topmost summit of pine and cypress, tear the vines from the burning branches, split the thick stems, and the sputtering and crackling of the all-devouring element is heard even here. There, see, the lava is over the wall of the neighbour's garden, it presses against the house, it yields, falls, and a bright flame shoots up from the ruined roof-tree.

And still the flame-crowned summit of the furious mountain thunders louder and louder. Wild cries resound from all the valleys. Torches glimmer here and there, and the thin terror-stricken voices of the little quavering chapel bells are heard warning all to fly. Hark! already hot cinders and stones are rattling down among the foliage of the garden. To flight, to flight, away! Everywhere there is stir, movement, preparation to depart from the fast approaching danger. Cattle, lowing piteously, are hastily driven out; beds, linen, chests, all the poor household goods and chattels are laden upon carts; the women shriek and cry; the children stand sobbing and staring at the swiftly advancing glare. A second house is in flames; a third;—and now with waving smoke-banners and triumphant detonations, the lava pours into the narrow village lanes, breaking down doors, filling rooms even to the ceiling, carrying walls and roofs before it, overthrowing and destroying all things.

But the houses are already emptied. The little caravans are on their way to the great city, and out of reach of the red-hot flood. They take their way along the deep gullies made by rain-fed streams;—gullies half choked up with fragments of pumice stones, and blocks of lava. New groups join the line, or pass by, weeping or talking. Each one has something to relate; fears or hopes to communicate. In Portici and Resina every window is lighted up, partly with candles, partly by the reflections from the lava. The sea quivers in a purple glow even as far as Capri, and still new streams of fire are poured and run in new directions. Torre del Greco and Torre Annunziata by the sea are threatened and must prepare for flight. Long does the rose-flush of the dawn, rising behind the smoking mountain, contend against the glare of the fire; and long is it overpowered by the latter. But finally the sunshine conquers, and in its radiance the glare is quenched, and only clouds of dark-grey vapour mark the course of the destroyer.

How glorious is the newly risen day! How softly smiling lies the sea veiled with a silver haze within the bright goblet of the Bay of Naples! The oranges smell sweet as ever, the oleander blossoms gaily, every flower shines refreshed with dew; but from the road that leads to Naples,—the beautiful, sea-bordered road,—arise thick clouds of dust, and the poor houseless wanderers from Vesuvius are struggling in it. Their poor belongings are piled on carts and barrows, in baskets and panniers. Each one has to help himself. The way resounds with curses, threats, cracking of whips;—"onward!" is the universal watchword.

> "With weaker beasts of burden
> Some would fain fare slower; others pressed eagerly onward.
> Then arose a cry from the struggling women and children,
> Bleating of flocks and herds, with barking of dogs commingled;
> Rose a wailing sound, the cry of the sick and aged,
> Perched on the high-piled waggons, trembling aloft, and swaying."—GOETHE.

But the rich, also, are abandoning their villas and gardens, and hastening back to Naples, or embarking in their yachts which have been lying ready in the harbour since last night. About midday it begins to be known what amount of damage the lava has done. There are many killed. They have been struck down by falling stones, or scorched by the hot stream. Many persons,—natives and foreigners,—who have been enticed by curiosity as far as the Hermitage, or beyond it, even to the *Atrio del Cavallo*, are missing, and are anxiously enquired after. Once more the night descends upon the Campanian landscape, but rest descends not with her; for the mountain thunders with an ever mightier sound. In Naples it is as if an uninterrupted cannonade were going on, and the doors and windows quiver and clap in all the houses. The populace begins to fear an earthquake, and rushes away from the narrow streets into the open *piazze*, or into the churches, where the bells keep ringing ceaselessly. There is chanting of priests, incense, processions, loud prayers to the patron of the city, the holy Saint Januarius, crowds, and disquietude everywhere. Ever louder thunders the mountain. It is midnight, and again the eastern sky is illumined by a wild glare; again the sea shines red even to its depths;—how slowly pass the hours!

All at once—the mountain is silent; suddenly, instantly! A dread mysterious stillness seems to weigh on every heart. Every one fears the worst, and watches in half feverish, half slumbering anxiety, for the day.

But the day does not come.

The hour of sunrise is long past, but a gray, desolate twilight still broods over the city. Not a sound is heard. The air we breathe is thick and suffocating. Hastily we open the window-shutters and step out on the balcony. Horror! What a sight! Is the dreadful fate of Pompeii about to overtake us? There is no sky, no sea, no earth, no air, to be seen:—the landscape lies before us like a dreary corpse beneath a shroud of ashes. And still they are falling on head and shoulders, filling our eyes, and nostrils,—

IN THE HARBOUR OF PORTICI.

falling, falling, falling in thick flakes like black snow, and rising higher and higher on every flat surface!

Whoever witnessed the last tremendous eruption of 1872, will certainly remember that gruesome Sunday morning (28th of April), when the daylight would never come, as the most terrific of all the experiences of the time.

This rain of ashes usually lasts for days, and the wind carries them to great distances. Stuff from Vesuvius has been known to fall in distant Calabria. But this phenomenon generally heralds the last act of the drama, which closes with tremendous storms born as it were within the crater, when lightnings flash and play around its smoking edge as though Jupiter were hurling Olympian weapons against the Titan Typhœus.

* * * * * * *

Whosoever, for ages past, has visited Rome, has endeavoured to see the Pope; whosoever visits the City of the Sirens on the Bay ascends Vesuvius. Nor is this either a dangerous, or a fatiguing exploit. The lion is slumbering for the most part, and calmly permits the little human ants to crawl about his back. You clamber over blocks of lava, wade knee-deep in ashes, drink a flask of Vesuvian wine, inscribe your name in the strangers' book at the "Hermitage," admire the enchanting view over land and sea,—and if all goes well, can sit comfortably the same evening to see the play in a Neapolitan theatre. This at least is the method of the mere pleasure-seeking traveller. The serious enquirer has much more to do. He has to see the observatory with its fine instruments and rich collections :—an outpost of science that is always in danger. The geologist may peer into secrets of the earth within the crater; its great heart is, as it were, laid bare, and a skilful hand may count its pulses. The learned of all countries have been here, and volumes in all languages have been written about the mountain, so that its literature would fill a library.

Poets too have wandered hither, attracted by the grandeur and wonder of these phenomena. We find their names in the old visitors' books :—Byron, Alfieri, Dumas, and the old Titan, Wolfgang Goethe, 6th of March 1787! Yes, many poets have been here; but it is singular that none of them should have been inspired by the mighty mountain with any exceptionally lofty strains. No song really worthy of the colossus has been sung. And if we seek the cause, we might almost accept Chateaubriand's opinion, that great men and great things, are less apt to awake great thoughts than is commonly supposed. Their greatness lies open to the day; and all words added to the naked fact serve rather to diminish than to magnify it.

Since therefore, we may not hope to crown his ancient brow with praise, we will wave him farewell as the railway carries us across black lava-fields to the resuscitated Pompeii. And we offer him our humble thanks that he has preserved for us beneath his iron wings, a brilliant remnant of antiquity, and we greet him as the faithful watcher over the fair urn of joyous Hellenism, and as the majestic sentinel of the Golden Gulf.

> "Vesuvius, thou keep'st watch and ward,
> Above fair Naples' Bay!
> And Etna, with his breath of flame,
> Stands sentry, too, alway.
>
> "O let beneath your fiery feet,
> Unalarmed the peoples dwell,
> And bear ye, to our absent friends
> A yearning, sad, 'farewell :'"

EVENING IN THE STREET OF TOMBS, POMPEII.

AMONG GRECIAN RUINS.

"Once on a time, I heard a god's lament
From out a star fast to oblivion waning,
'My star,' the spirit cried, 'was passing fair;
Mine own bright world, my star that I created!
Now fading, crumbling, in the self-same air,
Which by its ray, was erst illuminated!"

H. Lingg.

WE pass along the "Street of Tombs" of Italian Hellenism; past Cumae, Pompeii, Pæstum,—and find silence and death everywhere. But under what an amiable image he appears to us here,—Death the destroyer of the peoples! He stands like a genius upon the fair ruins of these temples, with gently drooping torch— the Genius of Eternal Youth! The Beautiful is ever young, and its sweet influence pervades even hoary ruins, fallen columns, and deserted tombs. How different is his aspect in Rome, the mighty Rome! There Death shows like an all-powerful Cæsar. But here:—

"Like to a laughing Cupid,
Thanatos, seem'st thou here, 'mid Pompeii's glittering ruins,
Playing with golden dust, and fragments of broken vases;
Piecing with precious stones, lapis lazuli, maidens' jewels,
Many a fairy tale into funeral mosaics!"—Gregorovius.

We are in Pompeii. We wander over the ancient pavement, through the Gate of

Herculaneum into the Street of Tombs, and sit down upon a stone bench beside the tomb of the priestess Mamia. This is a place for contemplation:—the very spot in which the sweet sadness of the past may sink into the heart. It is so still here! Even in old times

ON THE SHORE OF CUMÆ.

the noise of the gay Greek-souled city did not penetrate hither. Here was heard neither the wild clamour and clash of arms from the dusty arena, nor the babble of the swarming forum. Only the soft tread of a sandalled foot broke the silence. Here the dark branches of the sepulchral cypress whispered mysteriously even as they do to-day.

Evergreen ivy overgrows the crumbling stones of the *columbarium*, and fresh roses nestle faithfully all the year round, close to the urns of forgotten generations. Lizards with keen bright eyes dart across the bending weeds, or over the inscription on some marble tablet. Profoundest silence reigns! The dreaming soul glides away over the graves, over the flowers and the ashes, to unfold its wings above that silvery bay whose waters, on a distant day, washed the walls of a rich and prosperous city whither Greek, Roman, and Egyptian ships brought art and artists from far foreign lands, and luxuries and wealth from many a golden coast. Yonder flame the windows of Castellamare, or Stabia: swimming in sunshine, the promontory of Surrentum with its perfumed orange groves, and olive woods, rises from the blue waters. Where it sinks into the waves at Cape Minerva, behold the rocky isle of Capri like an azure dream woven of light and mist, with many a white sail gliding past it on its southward voyage.

In the east arise wooded hills speckled with glistening hamlets. They stretch towards the distant, rugged Abruzzi,—towards Lucania. And there he stands in defiant strength, the mighty thunderer Vesuvius! His ashen-coloured mantle stretches even to the Street of Tombs, and he stands, the one stern and gloomy apparition in the smiling landscape, which lies at his feet like a flower-crowned captive maid before a conqueror. Little golden cloudlets float dreamily above his head. Is he dreaming of the fair Grecian beauties who once surrounded him in youth and joyousness, and whom he slew in his wild wrath? How fair she was, the blooming city of Venus, how happy were her days! She bathed her feet in the peacefullest of seas, what time her head was crowned with Bacchic foliage and the silver branches of Minerva's tree. Peace, cheerfulness, and golden rest dwelt here. Above the marble temples of Venus, Jupiter, Hercules, and all the gods,—above the echoing public places girdled about with rows of glorious pillars,—above the small and elegant theatre and the great arena,—stretched a sky that was mild in winter, and gave refreshing breezes in the summer. The streets were filled with a people whose busy and skilful hands prepared the costly stuffs brought by the craft that crowded the harbour, mast after mast :—craft from Egypt, Phœnicia, Cyprus, and all parts. Rich merchants came to the city by Vesuvius ; built themselves houses and villas there, and adorned them with all that makes life beautiful and agreeable. The pavements were splendid with mosaics, the walls with the luxuriant colouring and seductive designs of Grecian artists. Every pitcher, every bowl, was a perfect work of art. Beauty was added to beauty, and life flowed by clear and enchanting ; neither foaming turbidly, nor leaving bitter dregs behind it. All the gods and all the muses loved this city, and the great ones and princes of this earth came to wear rosy garlands within her walls :—Augustus, Claudius, and Nero.

Then came a day and a night :—a day of darkness and a night of terror. The mountain gave vent to its long pent up rage, in wildest fury. Vulcan, mad with jealousy of the Roman Mars, destroyed his fair wife, and covered her corpse with a mantle of ashes. The whole country from the mountains to the sea had become a dreary waste of ashes. No tree blossomed, no green field blessed the peasant's view. The sea itself had retreated as if in terror from this fated coast, and no ship could be discerned in its harbour. Such of the inhabitants as had escaped with their lives, wandered far and wide in poverty. The very name of Pompeii died away, and her place was known no more.

Centuries passed over the buried city. Many Springs returned, and with air and sunshine coaxed from the arid soil a scanty vegetation, and a few young saplings. Then men began to return hither. They planted the descendants of ancient vines in the ashes, and made the tree of Minerva shade once again the sunny plain. Ugly dwellings arose on the site of the buried ones, and poor fishermen's huts on the sea-shore. The very language was changed. There, where once Greek and Latin resounded, the speech of Tasso now was heard. How had the world changed! Nearly seventeen centuries had elapsed since that day of terror, before the resuscitation arrived; but then the buried one shook the grave-clothes from about her, and stared,—the beautiful Greek!—into the

TEMPLE OF VENUS NEAR BAIÆ.

strange modern world of the eighteenth century. There she stood, a stranger amidst the crowd of curious enquirers: her tongue unknown save to the learned, her very name a subject of dispute and discussion.

This is Pompeii! How marvellously preserved! A whole antique city lies before our astonished eyes to-day. We wander through her streets, we enter her open uninhabited houses, and cannot help fancying that the population will presently return joyous and full of life, from some festival in the Campanian plains. But all is still desolate. Life has fled, and the fair husk of it alone remains. Moved by a thousand varied emotions, we sit upon the flower-grown mound above the city, and lament with the Italian poet:

"Where now I sit, once on a time there stood
Thy walls, Pompeii, towering loftily!
Now thou art girdled round by many a rood
Of rustic field. All hushed thy minstrelsy,
Thy dance, and song; and o'er thy streets doth brood
A lonely sadness mourning silently!"

And truly from this height the view over Pompeii is not a cheerful one. We see a confused labyrinth of grey, desolate walls, which offer not one picturesque point for the eye to rest upon. But if we call imagination to our aid, and descending into yonder streets, examine carefully every detail,—mentally completing what remains, and supplying what is lost,—and if we return patiently again and again to the task, what a fulness of beauty will reward us at last! We behold the mirror of a culture which,—growing up out of the intercourse with all beauty-worshipping peoples of the earth, out of Rome's imperial sway, hellenic skill in art, and the combined qualities of many various nations,— was on the point of bursting into full and perfect flower when the powers of nature caused it to perish utterly. And therefore the antiquary, the philosopher, the painter, the architect, and the thoughtful traveller are never weary of gazing again and again into this mirror, and penetrating ever deeper and deeper into the secrets of this city of wonders.

Pompeii was certainly not a city of the first rank. It may perhaps be compared with the neighbouring town of Castellamare as to population; but the life and activity of Pompeii were incomparably greater. Its encircling walls, which dated from the Oscan period, could be walked round in three quarters of an hour. They girdled the city in the shape of an oval. The whole plan was an extremely simple one. Two parallel main streets divided the city from east to west, and a longer street cut it in half from north to south. The six divisions thus formed were again intersected by hundreds of narrow lanes and alleys, which allowed the southern sunshine to visit them but sparingly. The chief life of the city was concentrated in its southern portion, where lay its very heart, the great splendid forum, set about with beautiful open arcades. Six streets open into this piazza, which is paved with polished blocks of travertine like a festal hall. Its columns, of Doric and Ionic architecture, have fallen. There was a double row of them on the southern side of the forum. The proud statues of honoured citizens, two-and-twenty in number, are destroyed, and only the empty pedestals remain. It is difficult for the imagination to reconstruct all the old glories.

If you fancy yourself standing at the southern end of the forum, and lay your left hand palm downwards on its pavement, the little finger would point to the wonderful basilica—the oldest of the buildings—the third finger to the fine temple of Venus, the middle finger to the temple of the father of the gods, which completes the northern circuit of the forum, the first finger to the noble Augusteum, whilst the thumb would cover the temple of Mercury and the vast Chalcidicum erected by the priestess Eumachia. Below the wrist joint would be the three curiæ, the buildings for the sittings of the Decurions. Remaining in the same spot and spreading out your right hand to the eastward of the left, it will cover the Triangular Forum with the temple of Hercules; and the most important public buildings are,—counting from the thumb,—the *Curia Isiaca* of the temple of Isis, the great tragic theatre, the small open theatre, and the barracks of the gladiators. The whole of the city stretches to the northward in front of us. This meagre sketch pretends to no more than to give a general plan or outline of Pompeii. To fill it up with a thousand brilliant colours and architectural beauties, must be the task of the imagination.

We must further mention the two great Thermæ or public baths, of which one is situated in the main street running from east to west, and the other in that running from north to south, a little to the northward of the triangular forum.

But the private dwellings of the citizens, the labouring, and wealthy classes, have a

EXCAVATIONS IN POMPEII.

higher interest for us than the public buildings of Pompeii. In Pompeii alone can we find any trustworthy revelation of the daily domestic life of the ancients. These dwellings and arrangements are entirely different from our northern ones. The architecture and mode of life in the south at the present time resemble those of the antique world to some extent; as is, indeed, necessitated by the conditions of climate. We do not divide our houses horizontally, but vertically, building upwards and piling story on story.

Now let us imagine a modern three-storied house, arranged in the following way: On the ground floor a corridor leads from the street into an ample hall, which is surrounded by six or more chambers. On the sides where the house is free, there are shops and magazines of all kinds of dealers, which, however, are not connected with the hall or its surrounding rooms. Above these shops is a kind of *entresol*, called by the Italians *mezzanino*, where poor families live. The hall serves the family of the master of the house for their ordinary sitting-room; domestic business is conducted here; here the mistress sits at work with her maidens, and here stand the money-coffer, the linen chest, and the nuptial bed; and the dead are laid out here. Next to the ground floor comes the first story, which consists also of a central saloon with contiguous chambers. But here is more show and luxury. Ancestral portraits and family treasures are kept here, and here the master of the house transacts his weightier affairs, having at hand his archives and his library. Narrow passages lead from this story to the airy, cheerful, second floor adorned with columns, and adapted for purposes of recreation. Around the central saloon of this floor lie the dining and sleeping rooms, and light and air have free admission. Place now a miniature flower garden on the flat roof, and you have the complete villa, whose arrangement is not very far from that of us moderns.

From what has been stated above, we may be able to reconstruct a Pompeian dwelling-house by the simple process of placing the various floors, not one upon the other, but one *behind* the other, only leaving the *mezzanino* still above the shops. Behind the entrance hall, we put the space occupied by our imaginary first floor; behind this, the second floor; and last of all the tiny garden. Thus on entering the house you pass through three suites of rooms to the garden which closes the perspective as seen from the external door of entrance. It is evident that this arrangement, which permitted pillars and columns to be placed everywhere without danger of over-weight, offered greater freedom of architectural decoration. And the rich availed themselves of it fully. For the same reason it was possible to have all sorts of water-works, fountains, and marble basins for adornment and refreshment during the heats of summer; and in this respect little Pompeii could vie with great Rome.

We enter, then, through the *vestibulum* which was frequently supported on columns, into the *ostium* or hall, where the *ostiarius* (door-keeper) had his cell. Before us lies the *atrium*; if it be an *atrium corinthium* it is richly decorated and adorned with columns: if *tuscanicum* it is in a simpler style. There is an opening in its roof, which opening (*impluvium*) admits the rain, collected in a marble basin placed beneath it. The surrounding rooms are called *cubicula*. Next to this hall comes the *tablinum* decorated with fine mosaics and wall-frescoes; and beyond again, you see the third, and in most cases the largest division, called the *peristylium*, which is not approached direct from the *tablinum*, but by means of the *fauces* or covered corridors. The *peristylium* (called also *cavedium*) is larger than the *atrium*, and its central space, open to the sky, is surrounded by roofed and pillared arcades. There was a marble basin for water here;

and in many houses, elegant springing fountains. Behind this again, and reaching to the furthest boundary wall of the house was the *viridarium* or garden.

Although the exterior of the Pompeian houses—even the richest—displays scarcely any ornamentation, the interior was always splendidly decorated, as is testified to this day by the well-preserved mosaic pavements, formed of marble, pottery, and glass, and by the fine wall paintings. We colder peoples, who live almost divorced from art, can hardly conceive to ourselves how an entire population came to be so penetrated by the

LAKE OF FUSARO NEAR BAIÆ.

love of art and pictures, that in the interior of their houses there was scarcely the smallest space to be found free from artistic decoration.

"The citizen heaps up riches
Then he summons the artist to glorify all his splendour,
And lend to prosaic comfort the forms of ideal beauty."

But not alone the skilful architect, and the painter, were employed to make Pompeii into an asylum of the arts; sculptors and casters of bronze furnished statues for the adornment of temples, halls, and gardens. All trades and callings endeavoured to produce pure and beautiful forms. How happy were those who were permitted to view the city while it was still perfect, resting in the full harmony of its beauty under the soft skies of the south! What an enchanting picture must have presented itself to one approaching Pompeii by sea! He beheld the bright cheerful Grecian temples spreading out on the slopes before him; the pillared forum, the rounded marble theatres. He saw smiling villas descending to the very edge of the blue waves by noble flights of steps, surrounded with green pines, laurels, and cypresses from amidst whose dark foliage marble statues of the gods glanced whitely. And behind this brilliant picture, and enclosing it as in a frame, he saw the grey battlemented walls of the city, from whence the landscape rose in a gentle slope to the summit of the thundering mountain!

Then if he entered a villa, stepping across the smooth mosaic pavement, he perceived glimmering out of the delicious half-twilight of the saloons, the slender forms of graceful dancing girls, and mythological figures which seemed to float in the air. Wherever he turned his eyes he saw form and colour.

> "Here were masks that peeped forth from encircling flowers ;
> There Anacreon's cricket, driving a chariot tiny
> Drawn at sober pace, by a bird of brilliant plumage ;
> Then a group of cupids musing beside a streamlet,
> Out of whose crystal waves they drew up fish with an angle.
> But what most of all enchanted the eye, were yon mænads
> Limned on a sombre ground, floating with veils transparent ;
> Tossing their silken locks for the wanton airs to sport with,
> Upward gazing, inspired, as though winging their flight to heaven."—GRILLPARZER.

What a wealth of splendid vessels and utensils was contained in the chests and closets! Gold, and gilded ivory, pearls and precious stones, were used to decorate tables and chairs, vessels for eating and drinking. Elegant lamps hung from the ceiling, and candelabra and little lamps of the most exquisite shapes illuminated the apartments at night. What a fairy world! How grave and old and grey we feel as we stand gazing into these ruins, once the abode of pleasure adorned by joyous-souled Greeks! This dead world seems like a long past dream of our youth. What remains, moves us like "some poem dimly understood," and the heart is oppressed with sorrow for the setting of their sun. We muse and muse, and cannot understand why all perfection must be followed by destruction ; why the Grand and the Beautiful are doomed to death for ever and ever. We yearn after the old days, and would fain cry to them, "Come back, come back, and bring happiness to this weary, busy, modern generation!" How willingly would we dream ourselves back into Pompeii's palmy days, and what wealth of materials for the poet are contained in these silent ruins. To the poet, indeed, they belong in their length and breadth ; and he is a faithful watcher of the dead. Lingg, in his charming verses "To my Pompeian Lamp," has expressed somewhat of this dreamy sentiment :

> "Dost thou recall thine ancient dwelling?
> From out a mask, of marble made,
> A sweet-voiced crystal stream came welling,
> And murmuring through the night it played
> In the arcade.
>
> "Dost thou recall the student hoary,
> Who held thee when he stooped to seek
> The rolled papyrus' treasured story,
> Broke seal-wax, and was wont to speak
> In classic Greek?"

Pompeii was the fair daughter of a Grecian mother. The daughter perished in her bloom, struck by the lightnings of Jove : the mother grew old and older, and bewailed her tragic fate through centuries of slow decay. Her name is Cumæ, and she sits far away yonder on the western shore, where solitude reigns supreme, where the sea sand is drifted over ghastly dunes, and malaria lurks upon the spreading flats. Here was the original seat of Italian Hellenism, and here it had already grown to be great and powerful long before Rome had built her capitol or sallied forth to conquer the world. At the present day her very name is but dimly remembered, and only a few ruins arise amidst the weed-grown fields to testify of the past.

The road from Naples to Cumæ passes over the Phlegræan Fields where once Vulcan's fires glowed in countless forges; now they are all extinguished; the Solfatara alone still breathes a fiery breath, and the extinct craters are filled with marshy lakes, such as Astroni, Lucrino, Averno, and Fusaro. Now Bacchus reigns, with vine-crowned thyrsus, over these shores; and where once flourished the Falernian grape (whose habitat

IN THE STREET OF TOMBS, POMPEII.

was the low hills close to the sea) rich vines still ripen, warmed by the powers of the volcanic soil. The road passes by the northern slopes above Avernus, which lies silent amidst the green encircling hills, unfathomable, mysterious, as a secret of the under-world. The ruins of a temple still stand on its margin, but the god who dwelt there is no more: he has succumbed to the dreary loneliness of the place, and the shuddering melancholy of the past. Funeral urns are found here, and tombs lie hid beneath the long, sighing grass. Here was the entrance to the lower regions, and here the dark Cimmerians dwelt.

One conspicuous remnant of antiquity surprises our eyes: a huge archway—the *Arco Felice*,—standing on a height above the former territory of the town of Cumæ. The peculiar, antique looking landscape is set in it as in a frame. We look across vineyards and wild shrubs, into a grand and beautiful solitude. The sea marks the horizon on which the rocky island of Vendutena looms, and where white sails glance across the blue. On the drear sea-shore, the grey, ruinous Acropolis rises like an enchanted castle

in a fairy tale. Dædalus alighted here when he had taken flight from the kingdom of
Minos, and here he built the temple of Apollo, and adorned it with fair mythic figures,
and with the image of his unfortunate son. Here too is the theatre of the hoariest
Grecian antiquity: the stage of the oldest Odyssey, and the scene of the Æneid. In
the spacious caverns of these rocks, the Cumæan sibyl uttered her oracles, the Erythræan
virgin who carried hence the new rolls of sybilline leaves to Tarquinius Superbus.

In those days Græco-Roman legend knew and named every stone, and even to this
day the grand landscape is steeped in the magic of that legend. The glamour of the

TEMPLE OF NEPTUNE AT PÆSTUM.

heroic times is over it all, and in imagination we see the old lofty shapes which live
eternally youthful in epic song, rise again out of the mists. What a landscape! What
a change after only a few hours' pilgrimage! Are we still on the blooming soil of Naples?
Where is the joyous populace, living only in the present?

All that is small and pitiful in these modish modern days is far, far from us here, and
our lyre sounds no more sweet lays about the love of one heart, or the sorrows of one
insignificant individual. The whole of the great antique world seems to be expressed in
grand solemn chords, and the soul, filled with sympathy for that greatness, is ravished
away from the present, and looking forth from the lonely heights of the Acropolis would
fain spread the wings of Dædalus and fly away over the golden-purple distance:—would
fain fly to the wave-bordered Cape of Circe, the tomb of Elpenor rising near Terracina,
beyond the seas which the bold Tyrrhene people ruled under the valiant sons of
Odysseus! Not a human being is to be seen as far as the eye can reach. The few
fever-stricken peasants sit in their scattered smoke-blacked huts, and wait for the scanty

grapes to ripen. No one ascends hither to the hill of the gods; only painters and poets worship here now.

There is nothing more delightful than to pass a day in this solitude. The hot summer is brooding over the land and over the lakes of Licola and Patria. The mountain thyme and aromatic wild mint send out their fragrance all around us. Not a sound reaches the ear. The sea heaves in long full respirations, and girdles the amphitheatre of the coast with a bright band of silver: only from time to time we hear the fierce cry of the osprey, as he floats with motionless wing through the air, or the humming of golden bees. If we descend from the height, we find everywhere the 'traces of man's disposing hand.' Blackened marble capitals lie half hidden amidst the acanthus plants, ivy clothes the ruinous aqueducts, and the wild fig tree grows in the clefts of fallen sepulchres. Again, we come on the remains of a temple; and everywhere upon the soil overgrown with lupins and the red-blossoming clover, are found innumerable fragments of pottery, glass, and mosaic; with here and there a coin, a finely carved stone, a little lamp, a few words of an inscription, broken sarcophagi, and bas-reliefs in terracotta. But there have been discoveries of more precious objects made here, and they fill a large room of the Museum in Naples.

All these things are of Grecian workmanship; and Greeks were they who first made these coasts productive. Ionians from Naxos and from Chalcis of Eubœa came and founded the first Grecian city on the island of Ischia towering out of the sea before our eyes, and opposite to the site occupied later by Cumæ. The latter city was built up larger and finer on the shore, and flourished mightily, and came to be the mother of other cities all along the coast as far as Naples. From Cumæ, Grecian culture, Grecian institutions, and soft Grecian manners, spread themselves over the western shores of lower Italy, and made them charming. Subsequently the fate of the city was linked with that of Rome. Happier had it been for her, if in the full bloom of her prosperity the sudden fate of Pompeii had overtaken her. She was, however, destined to sink gradually and to perish miserably. Her sad existence was prolonged into the Middle Ages. Her temples, her very walls, were broken down; not a column was left standing upright, and gangs of vile robbers and vagabonds were her latest inhabitants. At the present day there remains scarce the shadow of a shade of Cumæ. There are huts instead of temples, dry herbage instead of roses, malaria and desolation instead of sybaritic luxury, and Corinthian cheerfulness. Nature herself is poor and languid here; and filthy ragged beggars, like creatures bred out of decay and corruption, press around us on the very spot, perhaps, where silken robes once rustled to the banquet.

Moss and weeds instead of roses!—Where are the roses of proud Pæstum?*

> "When the Olympians were flown, the departing goddess of beauty
> Took from the savage soil even her own fair roses;
> Twined them to form a crown for the head of that race immortal,
> Who once to eternal gods had raised up temples eternal."

These are temples of the city of Neptune on the Bay of Salerno; majestic witnesses to the greatness of the past, and built, in truth, for eternity.

From the Hellenic city of Sybaris on the eastern coast a bridge was thrown across to the westward, in order to connect the Campanian country with Magna Græcia; and at

---

* The far-famed roses of Pæstum have not, however, all disappeared. The present writer has seen them growing and blooming in lavish abundance on the road between Salerno and Pæstum, in the middle of January.—*Translator's note.*

the end of this bridge was situated Posidonia, which had been founded five hundred years before Christ, by a Sybarite colony. Sybaris is now a swamp, and the other city which she founded has disappeared from the earth; only the magnificent lines of columns, in the three Doric temples, remaining to testify that a wealthy people once worshipped the Greek gods in this place. The shores of Pæstum are more melancholy than those of Cumæ; and the waste which stretches from the very thresholds of the temples to the foot of the mountains, more desolate, dreary, and fever-stricken. Nature here is like a corpse, dried up by the man-killing South winds; and poison and pestilence reek around her. Yet the temples,—especially the temple of Neptune,—are the noblest works of men's hands to be seen throughout the whole of the peninsula and Sicily. They also, together with the temple at Girgenti, and the Roman Pantheon, are the best preserved monuments which have been saved from out the stormy centuries to the present day.

This temple of Neptune seems to have been built for the gods of Homer; and the pillars, lighted up by the gold of southern sunshine, are ranged around the sanctuary like strophes of the Iliad. Standing here in the purple light of the setting sun, surrounded by the silence and solitude of this wilderness, we feel a sentiment of awe,—almost of worship. If amid the ruins of Pompeii we realize the charm and sweetness of that past and gone youth of humanity, here, on the other hand, we are sensible of greatness, and genius inspired by the father of the gods. It is impossible to imagine a higher effort of man's creative genius than this temple of Neptune. Six-and-thirty Doric columns seem to grow out of the earth, and rise light and free as lily-stems, towards heaven. They raise aloft their burthen in the cheerful and unforced service of the god;—nay, it scarcely seems to be a burthen, but a sacrifice, towards which celestial hands are eagerly stretched from above. To the south and the north of Neptune's temple stand the basilica, girdled by fifty columns, and the smaller temple of Ceres, which belongs to a later period. The gods have preserved what was their own here, in unadorned simplicity, and have given over man's portion to the powers of destruction. The city walls are only partially preserved; the towers and gateways ruined, and only the gate towards the rising sun is at all perfect. But no fair new day will make his triumphal entry through this arch for evermore. All the rest consists of unimportant fragments, broken stones overgrown with thistles and dry shrubs, and haunted by the weasel and the fox.

The sea-wind sighs through the grass, and we feel the chill breath of mortality,—or of eternity. For:

"Still th' unbroken columns stand!
Since those Doric shafts first stood,
A thousand years with storm and flood
Have fiercely swept across the land.
But, like the sea to which they're vowed,
On those marble summits free
Calmly breathes Eternity!"

A SEA VOYAGE FROM BAIÆ TO SALERNO.

> "I saw the queen enthroned on high,
> On the hem of her robe I passed by.
>   *   *   *   *
> Headlands rocky and manifold,
> Sloping hills with fold on fold,
> Grassy lawn and tendrilled vine,
> Here a palm tree, there a pine,
> And houses scattered 'midst wood and wold,
> Of every fashion, new and old !
> From the sea upriseth a ruin hoary
> Telling a tale of departed glory."—RÜCKERT.

THE beautiful Tyrrhene sea stretches along the land in a series of grand curves from Cape Misenum, with its light-crowned head and sea-bathed feet, to the distant headland of Licosa, forming three bays, of which the smallest is the Bay of Pozzuoli. But upon this part of the coast antiquity displayed her richest luxury; here joyous Grecian legend, and grave Roman history, wandered together in a sisterly embrace ; here lay the Elysian, and the Phlegræan Fields, whose soil, where the numerous craters almost touch each other, is furrowed by volcanic forces, as if gigantic moles had been burrowing there ; here was the dark lake of Acheron, and the cheerful, luxurious Baiæ ; here, in Puteoli, landed the chosen instrument of the Lord, the Apostle Paul ; and here now, alas ! life has decayed, and a thousand ruined fragments of a world that has passed away, strew the shores of the little Bay of Pozzuoli !

Next to it extends from the Punta di Caroglio,—the rocky outpost of Posilippo,—to the lonely Cape of Minerva, the animated and magnificent Bay of Naples, a vase full of beauty wreathed round with vines, and adorned with shining towns and villages ;—Portici, Resina, Torre del Greco, Torre Annunziata, Castellamare, Vico, Meta, Sorrento, Massa !

Then comes the widest are, the spreading Gulf of Salerno. One of its coasts (that which is contiguous to the headlands of Sorrento) belongs to the living world. It contains the picturesque, rocky cities of Positano, Amalfi, Atrani, Majori, Minori, Vietri, and Salerno, where fishermen, sailors, and gardeners dwell, whose industry divides the booty of the sea, and the harvest of golden fruits. The other shore of the Gulf, stretching from Salerno to the desolate Cape of Licosa, contains the ruined temples of Pæstum, and is a great, fever-haunted desert,—a realm of Death.

Thus the Bay of Naples lies like a blooming garden between two mournful graveyards ;—the shores of Baiæ and Cumæ, and the gulf of Salerno : or like a beaker of foaming wine between two poisoned chalices. And the islands which press around its sunny strand, smile with new charms upon the mainland. It is intensely delightful to float in a light sailing bark upon the shining flood, cutting through the blue waves as though we were traversing the heavens with a sea-gull's flight.

"È il cielo, o il mar?"

How enchanting is a moonlight night in Spring upon these waters ! Our bark glides slowly past the black hulls of the ships in the harbour, with the water lapping softly against

PINE-WOOD NEAR TORRE DEL GRECO.

their keels. The lamps on the shore throw their yellow light far over the sea, where it mingles trembling with the blue rays of the moon. From the teeming city there comes the dull roll of wheels and the roar of voices. But by degrees the noise dies away; the lamps grow fainter; the most distant of them dip down into the waves,—others follow them,

ON THE SHORE AT BAIÆ.

—the last disappear,—and then only the moonlight trembles on the sea, and the waters shine beneath our keel like the fiery track of a comet. Capri lies upon the watery plain, like a phantom of the mist, and a diadem of stars glitters above her rocky brow. The shores seem to move and live in the clear light of the mild planet overhead, and to swim after the little frail boat full of mortals, and the ancient legends of the sirens are revived. The night is dreaming a royal dream, and the scent of orange-flowers perfumes her sleeping mouth.

By degrees the sky sends out pale streaks seaward from behind Vesuvius. Morning is beginning to dawn; and soon she stands upon the mountain tops clad in bright robes of saffron, and descends to the sea, to the waves which are still gliding sleepily towards the shore, and decks their curling crests with golden spangles. Yonder is Baiæ, with its crumbling castle above, and the beautiful ruins of its temple of Venus below. Poor, sunburnt fishermen offer us baskets full of fragments of marble and mosaic, as we land, or flowers, violets and pinks, bound together with ivy from the ruins. Wherever you set your foot, ruins, nothing but ruins! The whole range of heights behind the strand seems like one huge work of men's hands, for the original soil is scarcely anywhere to be seen; it is covered, to the last ridge, with cut stones, which either still stand firm, or are heaped in ruinous masses. Remains of fine *opus reticulatum* reach to the very edge of the sea: nay even beneath the water, half covered by seaweed, one may see the foundations of baths and villas deep in the fine sand.

The shores of Baiæ have not that character of grand and historic tragedy which affects us so powerfully in Cumæ; they are less solitary, less imposing. Yet its decay may excite solemn reflections on the brevity of sensual enjoyments:

"Learn ye to choose delights that, fading, still are sweet."

The ruins lie on the dried up soil like the flowers and ornaments trodden into the dirt after an orgie. This is no longer the golden shore of the goddess of Love, where she had her stolen interviews with Mars. Festal crowds streamed hither from distant Rome, and in summer time the Via Appia was constantly animated by travellers to Baiæ, and the marble city by the soft sea wore a gay holiday garment. That other city, too, which looks at us from the opposite side of the bay, was once splendid, although now so poor and beggarly. Puteoli,—now Pozzuoli,—was, during the imperial times, the first harbour in the Roman empire, and sheltered a world of ships and treasures. The strand was covered with gigantic warehouses; and in these magazines were stored the corn of Egypt, the wine and oil of Iberia, copper, tin, iron, costly Syrian carpets, linen from Alexandria, incense from Arabia, and all the productions of the East. The merchants of Puteoli were proud and rich lords, who dwelt splendidly and luxuriously in the villas which crowned the soft hills overgrown with vines and roses. All languages of the world were heard here, all races of men were represented, and the various modes of worship were countless. Science and art, too, flourished in Puteoli.

Now, the traveller who sails along this coast sees Poverty glaring hollow-eyed from the windows of a town built on a crag; filthy mud soils his feet in the narrow streets, and the importunate voices of innumerable beggars, and the general squalid aspect of the population, offend his ears and eyes. Swarms of officious *ciceroni* drag him to look at the testimonies to bygone splendour, which still lie miserably scattered amid the neglected vineyards.

Upon the height stands the once grand amphitheatre, capable of containing thirty thousand spectators. It commands a wide view over land and sea, and pines and cypresses stand sentries at its entrance. Down on the shore is the much defaced temple of Serapis. A Bourbon king robbed the Egyptian god of the columns which adorned his house, in order to place them in his own theatre at Caserta; and the walls have long been stripped of their marble lining. It is no longer possible to distinguish what was the original use or destination of the ruins, which the chattering guide points out to you as the temple of Honour, of Diana, or of Neptune. The numerous tombs, too, have been irreverently mutilated and destroyed. During the time of the Emperors an artistic temple of Augustus rose on the highest point within the town. Victorious Christianity erected a tasteless cathedral on its foundations, dedicated to Saint Proculus. But a few and insignificant craft lie in the harbour; the mole has been destroyed by winds and

A VILLA AT SORRENTO.

waves centuries ago; and the little, brown, dreary town is only interesting to the antiquarian or the painter.

Leaving the deserted western coast in its solitude and sadness, our little bark flies before the wind that blows from the island of Ischia,—the fresh wind called the *maestrale*—towards the smiling settlements on the eastern shore of the bay, which stretch from the foot of Vesuvius to the edge of the sea. In these localities modern Naples holds its

ROAD NEAR MASSA. VIEW OF CAPRI.

villeggiatura during the flaming summer heats; inhabiting pleasant country houses whose airy chambers are traversed at all hours of the day by cool sea-breezes. We contemplate this landscape from the water, and receive an impression of cheerfulness and peace. An active population drives its carts and beasts of burthen through the streets, works and sings on the flat roofs and before the doors, gathers fruit in the gardens, or casts brown nets into the flood. Close to the villa of the rich man stands the low hut of his humble vintager, half concealed by a broad-leaved fig tree; and where the garden ends, the brawny but handsome fisherman has built his nest among the reeds. Lava is the material of the villa, as of the fisherman's cottage; lava borders the strand from Portici to Castellamare, and if we look down from our boat to the sea-bottom we perceive the dark streaks of lava gradually losing themselves in the depths. They tell of the wild conflict between two elements, the struggle between Vulcan and Neptune, in which the coast city of Hercules at length perished.

The pearl of all these cities is Castellamare, the ancient Stabiæ. It lies in a sheltered corner of the bay, where the mountains in its rear begin to slope downward toward Sorrento, at the foot of Monte Sant' Angelo. An industrious population lives here from day to day. It has long ago forgotten the old histories,—how it was once devastated by Sylla and overwhelmed by Vesuvius; forgotten, too, that it owes its second foundation to a German Emperor. Who thinks here at this day of Frederick the Second and his "Castle by the Sea,"—whence the name of the town originates? In the valleys which gradually rise into the midst of the mountains from the steep streets of the town, blooms a perpetual Spring; nightingales sing in the shadow of the tall-stemmed trees, and the breast, oppressed by the dust of cities, breathes a balmy and health-giving air. Yes; here one gains health, and a king has named his villa on the heights *Qui-si-sana*.

From hence to Sorrento begins the realm of the olive tree, which clothes the feet of the hills. Greyish-yellow rocks, silver-grey foliage of the olive, dark green groups and groves of orange and lemon trees, white, sunny townlets,—Vico Equense, Meta,—all with flat-roofed houses, steep cliffs, shrub-encircled inlets with gaily painted fishermen's houses, a blue sky above, a blue sea below,—such is the character of this exquisite coast scenery! Idyll follows idyll, but the most charming of all is Sorrento. It speaks to the heart like a joyous poem of Anacreon inscribed in silver letters on a golden ground.

> "See the children of the Springtide,
> See them, fresh, abundant roses!
> See how on the azure ocean
> Peaceful shining calm reposes!
>
> "Houses glisten in the sunshine;
> There the olive bendeth lowly;
> 'Mid the vine-leaves' green recesses
> Grapes are growing purple slowly."—ANACREON.

Fair Sorrento! Delightful life of Sorrento! To revel in air and sunlight on the high mountains with a noble bay on either hand;—to dream upon the softer slopes where the laurel and olive are mixed together, of peace and beauty, and all things which delight the soul,—to rhapsodise in shady bowers beside the beloved maiden of your heart, surrounded by the intoxicating perfume of orange flowers,—this, this is the life of Sorrento! And if there be persons for whom all this is a little too much,—why, there are excellent hotels in the town, where you may drink Rhine wine, and have broken English or French talked to you by the waiters! And for those who find the little narrow paths through many a cool mountain gorge overhung with ivy too steep, there is a long and admirably kept road between the houses all the way to Massa.

But all of us,—we in the leafy groves, or on the flat roof of the humble vintager, and those yonder in the "first-class hotel,"—all think, after our different fashions, of the ill-starred Tasso, whose songs, like those of Byron and Goethe, are the common property of all nations. We see the singer of the "Gerusalemme Liberata" returning pale and miserable from the world, from the struggle for fame, to where roses bloom and grapes ripen and careless peace is reigning; and the words rise to our lips, "Live, oh heart! Take heed to live!" And Tasso's verses recur to our memory:

> "Thus passes, like the passing of a day,
> Of mortal life the freshness and the flower;
> Nor, though the Spring return to earth, can May
> Make our lost youth rebloom with bud and bower.
> Gather the dewy rose whilst morning's ray
> Adorns it, 'ere the noontide's scorching power!
> Gather love's rose whilst ye can taste its sweetness;
> To love beloved again, is love's completeness."—TASSO.

FROM A VILLA, CASTELLAMARE.

Sorrento, too, lives but in the present. Those who come hither seem to look into the face of Spring ; and no one would think of raising the veil of ivy from the forehead of some crumbling temple, to explore the secrets of the past. Already in the later days of

GORGE NEAR SORRENTO.

the Roman Republic, the proud inhabitants of the capital came to this city, which boasted of the special protection of Bacchus and Venus, to enjoy sunny leisure. And at the present day the sons and daughters of the green islands of Britain, sick children from distant Russia, and people from all the ends of the earth come hither. A path leads down from the steep and lofty cliffs on which the town is situated, through a narrow gorge, to the sea-beach, where, on a strip of sand between the waves and the vineyards, the fishermen's houses stand. This spot is the haunt of mirth and jollity on festivals and summer evenings; the people sing and dance to the rhythmic beat of the tambourine, and their brown faces glow with enjoyment and wine, which beams red and clear in huge pitchers. The fine ladies on the terraces above,—for the most part delicate, fragile, sickly-looking creatures,—and the spruce gentlemen, eye-glass in eye, lean over the balcony of the hotel,

TASSO'S HOUSE, SORRENTO.

and wonder where these active lads, and dark-eyed lasses, get the strength to dance on as they do, hour after hour!

From Sorrento, four boatmen row us in a couple of hours to Capri, which rises siren-like and enticing from the waves. But we mean to double Cape Minerva; we are bound for Amalfi :—a strong epic after a sweet lyric! A stern Odyssean landscape after the enchanted gardens of Armida!

Beyond Sorrento the shore grows more and more deserted; but numerous remains upon the rocks half eaten away by the sea, indicate the former existence here of busy and prosperous life. There are fragments of baths and villas, the most poetical of which is the Bath of Diana : a miniature haven, a still, calm basin between walls of natural rock, and of masonry which has become as hard as the rock itself. Elsewhere, the waves may foam and toss, but here they hold their breath and listen to the bathing nymphs. Outside,

BATH OF DIANA.

the waters dash themselves in spray over the stones covered with sea-weed, creep sobbing and sighing into clefts and caverns, and sink below the broad line of red coral-growths. From the open sea between the Cape, and the island of Capri, broader waves roll in and dash themselves against the naked rocks on which Ulysses once erected a temple to the protecting Minerva. In the Middle Ages a bell-tower stood here, whose brazen tongue warned the inhabitants of the coast of the approach of Saracen pirate ships; whence the other name of the Cape: Campanella.

The Saracens founded their kingdom on the other side of the Peninsula; and from

RAVELLO.

Amalfi down as far as Salerno we find numerous traces of the Moorish splendour. The latest historic monuments which were erected here, are the indiscribably picturesque towers standing singly and solitary along the coast, where they seem to belong as naturally to the landscape as the cactus, pine, or agave. They are called by the people, Norman, or Saracen towers; and were built for the most part in the time of Charles the Fifth, as a protection against the continually renewed incursions of Moorish pirates. Many are altogether in ruins; but some of them have been repaired and made habitable, and poor fisher people, or equally poor coastguard-men of the new kingdom, live in the dreary tower chambers. In the loopholes where formerly the warning cannon sounded, or on the battlements whence arose the smoke of signal fires, crimson carnations are growing, tended by the wives and daughters of the present inhabitants; and where once bearded warriors gazed from under their rusty helmets across the sea to Sicily, black-eyed children peep out smiling into the sunshine. The ships cruising out at sea yonder are no pirate craft; they are fishing barks, and the procession even now descending from that old sea-robbers' nest, Positano, to the shore, is about to bless the boats, the nets, and the fishermen. The chanting of the priest is heard across the waves, the little bell of the chapel sounds, and the fishermen pause on their oars, pull off their red caps, and repeat the words of the prayers in reverent faith.

May Mary, the golden star of these sea folks, be gracious to this coast! For when the *Scirocco* blows, the waves beat here with resistless fury against the land, and there are but few spots to which the little boat tossed between sea and sky can run for shelter; perhaps, indeed, only one,—the little creek of Prajano; and then further on at the end of the range of rocks before Salerno, the harbour of Vietri. The fisherman of Amalfi knows this danger, and is at once more skilful and more bold than the mariner of the soft Bay of

SALERNO.

Naples. To this strength and boldness of character was due the founding of the Republic of Amalfi, which once gave laws (the *Tabulæ Amalphitanæ*) to the Mediterranean waters as far as Byzantium, and possessed colonies on the distant soil of Asia and Africa. The flag of Amalfi was respected, and her sword feared, on every coast. But Pisa at length broke the sword, the Genoese tore down the flag, the sea broke devastating into the town, —and, from a population of fifty thousand inhabitants clad in gold-embroidered robes, and living in marble palaces filled with the treasures of the East, the town diminished to a population of five thousand, who carry on a modest trade in fruits, carobs, and wine, and above all in the celebrated and excellent Amalfi maccaroni.

The present town is poor and dirty; but the traces of its noble descent are still to be seen in it. Its origin dates from the earliest period of the Middle Ages, and its chief prosperity was about the year 1000. The churches still bear record of this date, especially the fine cathedral of St. Andrew. It is built in the Norman-Byzantine style, and has preserved many precious ornaments from its youthful days; for example the fine Byzantine bronze doors, the side-posts of the central entrance with their rich scroll-work, the mosaics of vivid colouring. But also Pagan antiquity has contributed many objects to these sacred

VIEW OF AMALFI FROM THE CAPUCHINS' GARDEN.

aisles; such as columns brought from Pæstum's Grecian soil, vases, sarcophagi, and marble panels with fine bas-reliefs. From the exterior portico, supported by pillars, you look across the busy market-place, and the maze of streets, and dark alleys, to gardens pressed against the rocks, and to vintagers' huts and ruined castles perched on the summit of the cliffs.

It must have cost no trifling labour to squeeze all these houses together in this narrow gorge,—which they fill to the giddy summit,—and to connect them by means of staircases, bridges, and paths over, under, and behind each other, all cut in the living rock. One house sits on the shoulders of another and looks down its chimneys! Here it is essential to keep on good terms with one's neighbours; for a dispute about boundaries could scarcely be decided by the keenest lawyer in Naples! The most flourishing little gardens are perched on the house roofs, and orange, lemon, carob, and fig-trees, stretch their hands filled with delicious fruit even into the kitchens and bedchambers. You have but to shake the boughs to send down this noble dessert on to the table of the dwellers in the second or third story below, as they sit eating their maccaroni!

And yet the population is poor and ugly, exhausted by severe labour in the mills of the *Valle dé Molini*, and by insufficient nourishment; and they have none of the gaiety of the Sorrentians. Nevertheless, the hardships of life are softened and consoled even here, by the sweet melodies of Italian popular songs; and all those who have sailed with the fishermen of Amalfi must remember with pleasure their four-part songs, sounding across the water and keeping time to the oars.

"*'Ncoppa la montagnella* (bis)   "High up upon the mountain,
Ddél stanno li pastor,   Where flocks and shepherds rove,
Nce stanno tre sorelle (bis)   There once did dwell three sisters
E tutte e tre d'ammor.   All fair, and ripe for love.

"*Cecilia la schià bella,*   "Cecilia was the fairest,
L'olitte navigâ;   And she put out to sea;
Ppe vedè, poverella!   To seek—the simple maiden!—
Fortuna de trovâ.   Her fortune, forth rowed she.

"*Bello pescaturiello,*   "Oh fisher youth so handsome,
Vene a pescà 'cchiù cèà!   Come fish more near to me!"
  *   *   *   *   *   *   *   *

The whole splendid coast viewed from the sea, seems to inspire song. It is the most enchanting of all the Italian shores. But to those who handle a sword better than a lyre, it seems to invite conquest, and they woo the beautiful sea-bride with manly prowess. This is the old charm of the Sirens, against which the companions of Ulysses had to stop their ears lest they should yield to the spell and forget their homes; to which the valiant Moors of the Middle Ages succumbed; and which drew the fierce desires of the mighty Normans, again and again. Look up towards yon high rock turned to the seaward, which towers above Atrani built in the ravines and on the lower spurs at its feet. You see gardens, and singularly formed masonry, and towers, and ruins lying under the clouds there;—that is Ravello, once a Moorish eyrie. And the remains of buildings half hid among the gardens there are all Moorish: Moorish towers, Moorish columns, Moorish window arches covered with fantastic arabesques, and thickly overgrown with roses which bloom luxuriantly up aloft there. But a perfect *Alhambra*, the wonderful Palazzo Ruffoli, is still preserved in its completeness, and in its chambers one can easily fancy oneself back in the days when Poetry wandered with sword and lute over the blooming earth.

The same dream recurs in ever changing images, on the shore. How they rise up, the charming poems, full of enchantment and paradisiacal repose! There are Minori and Majori; from the white sea-sand the fishermen's cottages mount up to the hanging gardens; above the gardens lie pleasant houses; between the houses gush out foaming, cloud-fed mountain streams plunging down to the waves beneath, and above all an ancient castle towers into the sky. If the eye wanders over the sea, it beholds Capri's rocky crown, the curiously formed cliffs of the Faraglioni, nearer the isles of the Sirens, and in the extreme distance, bathed in light, the coast of Pæstum to the lonely Cape Licosa, behind which the sea loses itself in the south. After Majori comes Cetara, and as our gaze, wearied with sunshine and beauty, falls upon this singular little fishing village, we feel inclined to retire altogether from the world, and, hidden amongst the vines in the rich gardens, to pass the rest of our days in the mere delight of looking!

But onward!—past Vietri,—Salerno,—and now life and the present claim us again. For in Salerno, despite the fine remains of past times enclosed within its walls, despite the beauty of its situation, we find a modern town; and if we come from Amalfi bearing a vision of Paradise in our hearts, we are shocked by the roar of the market-place and the whistle of the locomotive which is to bear us back to noisy Naples. Salerno has nothing to do with that song of the Sirens to which we have been listening in joyful forgetfulness all along this divine coast.

THE THREE SISTER ISLANDS.

"Without thee, oh Vesuvius, and ye, most lovely islands,
Scarcely would Naples' self seem Naples unto me!"
WAIBLINGER.

NISITA, Procida, Ischia, the pearls of the western sea, rise from the waves like beautiful legends of old or dreams of Elysium. We are in beautiful Neapolis, but we are not content; we would fain go farther into new distances. And there are the enticing islands, swimming in haze and looking as if in their world-forgetting solitude, they must hide that secret of happiness which we fail to find amidst the shriek of steam-engines, the clatter of printing-presses, and the restless tramping up and down the dusty highways of our modern civilization. The islands grow out of the water like care-destroying lotos blossoms, and we hasten thither with the wish:

"To bide here plucking the lotos, forsaking our homes for ever."

Even Emperors have felt this longing. How Augustus loved his Capræa! And how we love our maiden Procida, the '*Isola incantata*' this enchanting and enchanted island! Like a shy virgin she hides her charms from the great world, and lies coyly with her face turned towards the blue sea, only friendly to her friends. And then Ischia, exquisite Ischia!

The boat carries us past the villa gardens of Posilippo, and just opposite to where its rocks sink into the sea, lies the first and smallest of the three sister islands, Nisita, soaring boldly out of the sea. Waiblinger the German poet sings of her:

"Like to a lovely child, smiling with roguish dimples,
Yet too timid to stray far from its mother's side,
So thou turnest in play from the sportive waves around thee,
Pressing with child-like fear, close to thy mother-land!"

But a hard fate was reserved for this "lovely child;" for sickness and crime dwell here. After the great pestilence of Messina, Philip the Fourth of Spain, built in 1624, a lazaretto and quarantine establishment on the *mole* of the island. And on its summit where once Queen Joanna, and after her the Dukes of Amalfi, inhabited a splendid castle, the Bagno now stands; and *camorristi*, and brigands from all the provinces of the kingdom, enjoy a glorious view from its windows! In ancient times the island was the

ISCHIA.

abode of luxury, and the remains of the buildings of Lucullus, are still distinctly to be seen on the strand, and under the water. Cicero came to live in this villa of the wealthy Roman after his expulsion from the capital which followed the fall of Julius Cæsar. Here he met Brutus who had flown hither to wait after the great deed, and these rocks witnessed weighty negotiations.

When you row past Nisita in the stillness of a summer afternoon, you hear the clanking of the prisoners' chains, and feel no desire to land here. We will steer for Cape Misenum, to the flat shore of Miniscola, and beckon the brown fishermen of Procida across to us from the island. The fair and peaceful day has smoothed the sea into a golden mirror; it spreads between the curving coastlines like a flood of wine in a shining chalice. Peace and happiness seem to overspread the mainland and the island, which looks enticing, and smiling as the face of a friend who greets us. *Prochyta*, as it was called in Grecian times, was once a Grecian colony. The Hellenes lived here after they had founded Cumæ; and any spot in which they have once dwelt is ennobled and consecrated for all time. The population of Procida, like that of Ischia and Capri, is said to be of Grecian origin, and where once the Ionian lute sounded, there still lingers some Ionian softness in the speech of the people. The poor folk of Procida and Ischia speak very differently from those of Naples or Pozzuoli; although perhaps the *marina* (sea-beach) of our little island is an exception to this rule, owing to the number of the coasting sailors from all the neighbouring shores, who meet here. Singular houses with arched arcades, and strange-looking Saracenic cupolas stand here. The sails of the ships flutter close to the arcades, and the roar of the waves lulls the fisherwife's infant to sleep. This population earns its bread solely by the sea; the young men go forth into foreign waters, to Africa, or the coasts of Sardinia for the coral fishery, come back, buy a few feet of land, and marry a daughter of the island. It is not on record that any one of them has brought back a foreign wife from his voyages; and the gay coloured silk handkerchiefs which the girls and women wear on festal days, are presents brought home by the sweetheart or husband. At times the island is almost exclusively inhabited by women, who cultivate the gardens, and on holiday evenings sit on the roofs or walls of the upper part of the island, and gaze over the sea where the ships come and go. Or else they sit before their doors erect and silent, like the daughter of Icarius, spinning and awaiting the return of the sea-traversing Ulysses. These women are for the most part handsome, and of gentle manners. Waiblinger must have been in a bad humour when he accused them of "incredibly brutal obtrusiveness and rude audacity."! So too when he declared that "the island in itself affords nothing picturesque, except a few points of views, of which the western one looking towards Ischia is the finest." Yet every painter must have been enchanted not only with the views, but with the charming "bits" and "motives" with which every road and lane in the island abounds. If you mount up from the Marina and lose yourself in the delightful maze of vineyards which cover the maiden isle as with a veil of greenery, what a splendid vegetation spreads around you! And amongst it what a variety of little dwellings, abodes of content and bacchic enjoyment! A thick cloud of perfume rises from the blossoms of countless *agrumi* (lemon and citron plants) in the spring; in summer the trees are more heavily laden with golden fruit than even those of Sorrento; and in autumn the rich abundance of grapes demands the labour of all hands to make and store the excellent Procida wine. Then the air is so pure, the sound of the waves so soothing and dreamy,—oh this island is a little paradise! The view from the heights of the castle, over the roofs of the upper and lower town, is very striking; a few palm trees, together with the cupolas of the roofs, give it the aspect of a Moorish city.

The Saracens have indeed been here, and did much mischief in the island in the time of the Spanish viceroys: especially under the leadership of the fierce Barbarossa. The history of the island furnishes another name connected with the annals of the Hohenstaufens: Giovanni da Procida. He was the originator of the Sicilian Vespers, in which he would fain have washed away in torrents of French blood the stain of Conradin's execution, which he witnessed in the market-place at Naples. He was a nobleman of Salerno, and the island of Procida belonged to him.

From the last gardens of the island we look upon the desert little islet of Guevara, which is only a bit of the wall of an extinct crater sunk in the sea between it and Procida, and further still we see Ischia towering up into its mountain of Epomeo. The fields spread dark blue along the sides of this mighty mountain, and numerous hamlets peep forth hospitable and inviting from the shade of groups of trees. So farewell, fair Procida! Thy more perfect neighbour invites us; and we exclaim by way of adieu:

CORAL FISHING

> "I would compare thee to some youthful nymph
> Whose maiden charms are scarcely yet matured.
> Still might thy budding beauties chain my heart,
> But that thy sister's full perfection wins me."

The sister is Ischia, and Ischia is perfection!

The radiant island smiles at us across the waters, and draws our boat as if with magic bands nearer and nearer to its shores. These shores are girdled with black lava, over which the waves break in white foam. Dark brown crags rise from these blocks of

POZZUOLI, WITH CAPO MISENO AND THE ISLANDS OF PROCIDA AND ISCHIA.

lava, bare, or only clothed with coarse plants that love the sea; but at their feet, like a golden hem on the maiden's robe, blooms the luxuriant yellow broom. From hence the land slopes gently upward to the middle of the towering Epomeo, and is covered to the remotest corner with pleasant vegetation; the whole land is a pleasure garden. When the sun shines on Ischia, you can distinguish from the sea the various forms and species of trees. The olive tree is contrasted with the vine, and this again with darker foliage, all harmonizing exquisitely with the light brown tufa soil, and forming a thousand gradations of light and shade; and nowhere are the habitations of men, vintagers' cottages, and villas, so bright-looking as in this island, which enjoys an immunity from dust!

Ischia is now the fair realm of Flora and Pomona, and no one considers that it was once a masterpiece of Vulcan's handiwork. At his behest and by his power, it rose by degrees out of the waves, higher and higher until it almost touched the dwelling of the gods with its burning forehead. The very foundation of this island is a volcano, Monte Epomeo, which stands in the centre of it. Fiery masses flowed out in broad streams from its vast crater, and spreading into the waters below, formed the flat circumference of the island. From its volcanic architect it received the form of its main outline,—a circular one. Other and subordinate powers added the jagged ornamentation. These were the clefts or gullies of lava which opened in the flanks of the mountain after the higher crater had cooled, and pushed themselves out into the sea so as to surround the island with a series of capes and points. There are nine-and-twenty of these lava ornaments; and the principal of them enumerated by the Ischian fishermen are Punta di San Pancrazio, Punta Sant' Angelo, and Capo Negro, in the south ; Punta dell' Imperatore and S. Francesco in the west ; Punta Caruso, Cornacchio del Lacco, della Scrofa, and S. Pietro, in the north ; and to the east the rock on which Ischia's ancient castle stands.

AT THE WELL.

You land below this castle in the charming harbour of Ischia made by Nature herself, as if in sport, by sinking an old crater and filling it with sea-water. It is quite circular, and as still as a mountain tarn ; not a wave is felt to move here. Rosy flowering oleanders surround it with southern profusion, and gleaming white houses, and gardens filled with fruit, come down to the water's edge. From hence a good road made of volcanic materials conducts us along the seaboard to the little town of Ischia. This road crosses a stream of lava, which suddenly and unexpectedly—in the year 1301, in the reign of Charles the Second of Anjou—poured out of a cleft beneath Monte Epomeo, after the volcano had been silent for nearly seventeen hundred years. Numerous blooming gardens which lay in its path were burnt up, the villas of the nobles (who preferred this side of the island to the other, on account of the protection afforded by the neighbourhood of the castle) were destroyed, and the devastating stream fell into the sea at length close to Punta Molina. The lava has long ago grown cold ; but the adjacent vegetation has never recovered the effects of this terrific scorching: the lava still presents a blackened and barren mass. The people call the upper part of the stream *Cremato*, and the lower *Arso*—both names alluding to its fiery nature.

There are more than twelve craters visible on the island, all clustered round the great crater of Epomeo like children round a parent. The foot of the latter is reached by traversing great wastes of lava, and blocks of lava are the materials of which the walls are

COURTYARD IN ISCHIA.

built which surround the numerous vineyards: for the industrious people have planted the grape wherever the surface of the lava has become rotten and soft by the action of centuries. The road winds between these vineyards to the summit of the mountain pyramid. We ride along under chestnuts and fig trees, and look down between the branches upon the sea as deeply blue as the sky, on the delightful shores of Sorrento slightly veiled in haze, on the fairy-like, glimmering Capri, on the flat little sister island, on Naples dimmed by grey vapours, with Sant' Elmo, the Castle, and Camaldoli glittering in bright sunshine. On reaching the village of Moropano, the limitless expanse of the sea stretches before us. Many a sail glides over the silent plain, and up here the chirp of the sun-loving *cicala* is the only sound to be heard.

Then the narrow road cuts through some rocky cliffs; the land is a wilderness, and only a few arid weeds feel the influence of a brief Spring-time. The whole landscape has a yellow tone, dazzling the eyes, and awing the soul with its savageness. Here, two thousand feet above the level of the sea, lies the highest village on the island, and above the village, five hundred feet higher, the mountain terminates in a sharp jagged peak, in whose tufa a little chapel and the dwelling of a sunburned hermit have been scooped. From hence one looks down like an eagle from his eyrie over the garden of the island, and sees the nests of men peeping forth singly or in groups from the dark green foliage. Then we gaze over the sea, and —— no, it is too vast, too glorious! more than one pair of human eyes behold, or one human heart receive!

The traveller lays his pen down, unwilling to wrong the grand picture by cold and insignificant words; it must be seen, and can never be described. An extract from a letter written on the summit of the mountain to a friend, may serve to close the sketch of Ischia, since I can find nothing better to say now than I did then:

"I have received one more image of pure beauty into my soul; one of those which remain for ever in our memory like the sunlight of Olympus—which carry us back to the paradise we dreamt of in our innocent youth. I know I am not saying too much. I, who know Italy so thoroughly, am well aware that there are grander landscapes—as, for example, in my beloved Latium, and in Syracuse, which influence the mind by sublime historic associations. But the soul is constantly drawn back to the Odyssey, and here is spread out before us the wave-resounding theatre of that most delightful of all fables; and the breath of old Legend blows from these shores and fills us once more with the sweet awe and wonder of our childhood. Here the atmosphere is full of serenity and joy."

THE ISLAND OF TIBERIUS.

"Lo! there rises not far from Naples the sunny island,
Crowned with Dædalian rocks. There in the sapphire grottos
Cupid delights to dream; and to dwell in the sirens' chambers.
There the phosphoric wave whispers in luminous ripples,
There the love-drowsy air quivers in azure twilight."
GREGOROVIUS.

THE island of Capri lies in the Bay of Naples like a precious pearl in a goblet of wine, shining and enticing from afar. Sirens once sang from its rocks melodies that entranced the senses, to the southward sailing Ulysses, and seduced the Grecian sailors. Then there came men from the distant coast of Leucadia, seeking a new home, and bringing with them the exquisite grape of the wine-yielding soil, the gods and the sonorous speech of Hellas. On the sandy, open shore of the northern side of the island, they furled the wings of their *phaseli* and pushed up their boats on the beach. And so Capreæ became a Greek island.

The new comers planted the vine and the olive in the clefts of the rocks, and built two cities, one named Capri, the other on the heights, Anacapri. Thence they looked across to the brilliant mother-city on the Bay, the fair and flourishing Neapolis; they were speedily united with it by the bonds of common laws and customs, and lived a peaceful existence for centuries.

Then it chanced that Augustus—that lover of hellenism—weary of life and the bustling capital, seeking for peace in the remote solitudes of the southern sea, set his foot on this rocky shore. Scarcely had he done so, when there reached him the joyful news

CAPRI, FROM THE HOTEL PAGANO.

that an oak dry with age, had put out new shoots on his landing, and the auspicious message was communicated to him by the mouth of one Eutychus, which name signifies

OLD "SCALINATA" IN CAPRI.

"child of good fortune." Moreover a flock of doves flew down to meet him; and the dove was sacred to Venus, the ancestress of the Julian race. All this endeared the island to him at once, and he obtained it from the city of Neapolis, by exchanging for it the whole of rich Ænaria. And thus Capreæ became the property of the Roman Emperors.

Augustus, who cared not for the splendour and the restraint of marble palaces, built himself simple country houses on the peaceful island, and adorned them, not with costly statues and pictures, but with flowers and shady plantations, bowers of vine, and pleasant pathways. He enjoyed, like a private amateur, the collections of antiquities and rarities which he increased here by the gigantic bones of some land and sea monsters. His mode of life was simple; his bed, his coverlets, his table, his meals, resembled those of a well-to-do country gentleman. The garments he wore were spun and sewed by the women of his household. In summer he slept near the open door: often, indeed, in the peristyle overgrown with creeping plants, lulled by the murmur of the fountain. Pure air and repose were all he craved for in his latter days, and where were both to be had in fuller perfection than on the lonely island?

If he looked out from the terrace of his house across the sea, from the towering peak of Ænaria to Pæstum, and as far as Cape Licosa, what a glorious world revealed itself to his contemplation! How warmly and luxuriantly pulsed the waves of life on yonder thickly populated shores! There lay the delightful Prochyta, and opposite to it the proud promontory of Misenum, the Portus Misenus where the world-compelling Roman fleet rode at anchor. The luxurious *Sinus Bajanus* was filled with pleasure boats in a gay and many-coloured swarm, and the city of Baiæ with stately marble palaces. Behind it stretched the Phlegræan Fields so rich in legends, bounded by the Mons Gaurus overgrown with vineyards, at whose foot lay the wealthy mercantile city of Dicæarchia, or Puteoli! Then came Palæopolis, a collection of villas near the spot where the Pausilypus fell into the sea, and then—palace joined to palace—Neapolis! Further on there were ranged under the shadow of Vesuvius, which was overgrown to its very summit with vineyards and fruit trees, the cities of Resina, Herculaneum, Oplontiæ, Pompeii, Stabiæ, and many others, even as far as Surrentum,—as Cape Minerva, with its temple whose marble colonnades still stood in all their pristine splendour, and where the protecting Pallas Athena still received daily sacrifice.

So the Emperor, as he grew old, lived many happy days upon his island; and it was granted to him to pass some of the last days of his life here in undisturbed serenity. He came from Rome. As he sailed past the harbour of Puteoli he was recognised by some Greek sailors and travellers from Alexandria, who celebrated a joyous sacrificial feast in honour of the protector of Arts and Commerce, in the graceful Grecian fashion. This came like a sunbeam into the evening of his days; and he went on to Capri, there to continue the cheerful festival with the gymnastic games of the youths; with banquets among whose rose-crowned guests were many of the inhabitants of his island; with songs and all manner of entertainments. Once more his spirit flickered up brightly, so that he himself recited some Greek verses. Four times he saw the sun rise behind Vesuvius, and then he departed—led by the hand of death—for the mainland. In Nola the fatal hour struck him down.

Twelve years have passed by. In the year 26, there lands a gloomy man, one at war with the world and with the gods, in Capri.

> "See'st thou the smooth and shining rocks there!"—"Yes."—
> "And there Sorrentum standing like a wall."
> "—And the sea rolls between them."—"Aye; whoever
> Should leap into it there, would scarcely swim
> Safe to Sorrentum."—HAUCH, TIBERIUS.

This dialogue is supposed to take place between Tiberius and his astrologer

Thrasyllus on the scene of the former's orgies, the villa which he built at Capri. He came like a huge spider, and spun a network of gorgeous pleasure-houses over the twelve summits of the island. And like a spider he sat within this net, whose threads extended to Rome, and all the corners of the earth, and from hence he ruled Rome and the world. Peace was banished from the island, and dark passions took up their abode in the golden palace chambers. A curse rested like a cloud upon these rocks, and when the lightnings flashed from it, they portended death in some part of the kingdom. This lightning from Capri struck at length the all-powerful Sejanus.

Thus passed away eleven years. The Emperor's brain was disordered with gloom and madness. The sight of humanity was loathsome to him. He sat in the gardens of his "Villa of Jupiter," and fed with senile superstition his favourite serpent. Then he called down the curse of the gods upon his own head, as is written in his letter to the Senate: "May all the gods and goddesses make me perish yet more miserably than I feel myself perishing day by day, if I—" and the curse was fulfilled. As Augustus once received omens of peace here, so Tiberius received omens of destruction. The splendid light-tower of his Villa, vaunted as the "rival of the moon," suddenly fell down without any discoverable reason; and his pet serpent was found by the solitary maniac, lying dead in a garden-path, and covered with a swarm of ants. Then, as if driven by mysterious powers, he departed to the mainland, and at Cape Misenus was struck down amongst the shades. With Tiberius, History also left the island, after having inscribed in her records: *Sed tum Tiberius duodecim villarum nominibus et molibus insiderat*. So says Tacitus; and we may stand at the present day on the ruins of the twelve villas which tradition says were dedicated to the twelve principal divinities. No one can distinguish their names with certainty now. But the name of Tiberius still sounds like that of an evil spirit, through the songs and legends of the Capriote people. Eighteen centuries have not sufficed to efface the memory of this blackest of all the Cæsars.

So the Cæsars and the sirens abandoned the island, and left the little Greek colony to itself. Once more the population enjoyed peace upon its own soil, having saved out of the golden days of antiquity only its inborn grace, the beauty of its women, the fiery Leucadian wine, and the joy-inspiring tarantella. The tarantella is an inheritance from the Sirens! So at least declares popular tradition: for when the sirens had in vain tried to entice Ulysses with their songs, they besought the graces for a new gift to charm unwary mariners. The graces taught them the tarantella; but neither the tarantella nor any other dance was exactly suited to the forms of the sea-women, and in despair they killed themselves! But the daughters of the fishermen who lived on the shore had heard and seen all, and they practised the tarantella under the grape-vines in their gardens. By degrees the inhabitants of all these coasts learned the tarantella, but its headquarters was and is Capri, the Isle of the Sirens, where the lithe maidens had learned it of the Graces!

A painter once found this out; and then went and blabbed the secret. And from thenceforward Capri became the *Painter's Island*, the property of colour-loving masters and pupils; and so it remains to this day. But poets come there also, and travellers who have read of its beauties, and are curious to behold the wonders of the Blue Grotto. Countless are the boats, and barks, and sailing vessels, and steamships, which come across from Naples and Sorrento, bringing cargoes of foreigners to spend a few days at the hotels on the island. As in the time of Tiberius there were twelve villas dedicated to the gods, so now-a-days there are twelve inns on the various points; and the adventurous voyager is received by a crowd of black-coated waiters, whose seductions have superseded those of the sirens.

In the height of summer, however, the painters are lords of the isle, and enjoy themselves mightily. They remain here for months together, and then return again the following year.

NATURAL ARCHWAY.

They are never weary of drawing the wonderful lines of the overhanging rocks, and the cliffs rising sheer out of the sea; nor of painting the million-fold play of colours made by a southern sun in the clefts of the heights, in the gardens by the sea, on the waves themselves which play upon the beach with ceaseless change and variety from glimmering dawn to golden evening, and roll away towards the purple horizon. Truly the blue grotto is not the most beautiful thing in Capri, great though its reputation may be. The beautiful here is not hidden in caves and grottos, but lies open to the day, now amazing us with grandeur, now enchanting us with softness, but always new. No one who has passed a fair May or August day upon the island can ever forget it. It remains in the memory with siren-like sweetness.

A cheerful population — chiefly women and girls — living in the fishers' cottages on the narrow strip of shore called the Marina—receive the traveller when he lands with childlike curiosity. He will probably not discover many who can be called beauties among them; for these mostly hide themselves in the little town of Capri, or else up aloft in Anacapri, under the bowers of the vineyards. The road to Capri from the shore is narrow and incommodious, made up of all manner of stones and rubbish. Nevertheless, the light, gazelle-like maidens of the island clamber up and down it many times a day, bearing huge burdens on their graceful heads: great pitchers full of water, wine-casks, heaps of fruit, stones, boards, and other building materials. It is astonishing to see such slender, lithe forms, such graceful figures, able to carry such elephantine loads. But they step on before you as you toil painfully upward, light and elastic of step, chattering, jesting, and laughing as though they had nothing heavier than a basket of Cupid's roses

A GARDEN SPRING IN CAPRI.

on their heads. They wear his arrow passed slantingly through the Grecian coils of their black hair, and his roses glow on their brown cheeks, and he shines in the bright gleam of their dark eyes. Their features are usually fine, and in some exceptionally pure types you may see distinct traces of their Grecian origin. Their teeth seem, like the pearls of their necklaces, to be taken from the jewel-case of the sea-born Venus, the Anadyomene. You are not treated as a stranger amongst them; you are received as a friend and brother,

MARINA, CAPRI.

admitted into the family circles, allowed to hear their little troubles, and partake their modest joys, on the sole condition of becoming once more a simple, light-hearted child. The old father, whose face expresses good humour in every line of it, will carry you to see his little garden on the mountain; will show you the olive tree full of fruit, the vine heavy with grapes, and the carob laden with dark pods. The mother leads you into her chamber, where, on the walls, in baskets, on tables and benches, the silver-grey silk-worm lives, in whose prosperity you are expected to take the heartiest interest. The daughter will take the stranger to her little patch of garden full of rosemary, and gather a rosebud and a fragrant sprig or two for his button-hole. Or else she sits and spins whilst you entertain this maiden Penelope with your best jests about her spinning and her sweetheart. In the porch in front of the house formed by a trellis of vines, the little son sets his straw-bottomed chair for a table, and on green leafy dishes, he and his little sister bring you golden figs and purple Capri grapes. And you enjoy the feast; you feel at home there; you return again eagerly expected and pleasantly welcomed. Then when the day grows cool, and the swarms of cicale have gone to sleep in the crevices of the old olive tree, the girls who have been toiling under heavy burdens all day, come within the broad-leaved cactus hedge of the garden, attracted by the thrum of the tambourine, and the tarantella begins;—a fairy tale, or rather a drama, in miniature!

Dolci ire, dolci sdegni, e dolci paci;—jealousy, love, grief, all the passions of an enamoured soul are represented in turn. And the two partners dance on like two hearts that love each other, and quarrel, and are reconciled. They fly apart, then embrace, then kneel, and then seem to faint with rapture. One might fancy that the altar of the goddess Venus stood between them, and that a great flame arose from it in whose glow they flutter and perish like unwary moths. The grandmother beats ever louder on the jingling tambourine with her hard brown hands; the girl seated on the threshold of the door screams out her tarantella tune ever louder and with more bacchanalian wildness, into the evening air; the guitar twangs, the castanets click, the asses returning from their labour to the field below, set up a loud braying which is echoed from rock to rock—all Greek antiquity seems to live again, and the idyll of the world's springtime once more inspires our souls for a few brief hours. Another graceful round dance, performed by four or eight couples, is called the *Trescone*, and is only known on this island.* The Greeks called it *Ormos*.

When the eye is weary of gazing out over the entrancing sea-view, and the foot of clambering over the rough paths which are sometimes scarcely practicable except for the mountain-goats which browse there, we return with pleasure to the peace of these lowly roofs, where the heart almost forgets that outside in the world there, such things exist as dusty highroads, and anxious crowds. No longings stretch their wings beyond the limits of this island; they have already made their nests within it, and chosen favourite spots, of which there are plenty here. It is singular, however, that these favourite spots are invariably those where the villas of the frenzied Roman Emperor once stood. They are Damecuta, Monticello, Timberino, Capodimonte, Palazzo a Mare, Ajano, Castiglione, San Michele, Unghia Marina, Tuoro Grande, and—by far the finest of all,—the cliff on which the poor little church of Santa Maria del Soccorso now stands, the former site of Tiberius' Villa of Jupiter.

It lies to the eastward, opposite the bold headland of Minerva; and if you peer over the myrtles, thistles, and rosemary, which clothe these chalk cliffs, you may look sheer down a thousand feet into the sea. From hence you may perceive how grandly the waves pour into the Bay of Naples from the open sea, how they foam against the towering walls of the Cape of Minerva, and how they surround the island of Capri in alternate combat and sportiveness. White-winged ships looking like the seagulls that build in these rocks, glide into the harbour of Naples, or Castellamare, or make for the more distant Calabria. Steamships, too, cut through the waves, and leave long trailing black veils behind them on the blue sea. They come from Africa, Sicily, or the French coast. The travellers on deck gaze up curiously at the rock of Tiberius; but the sailors look at it mistrustfully, for they know that in foul weather it is dangerous, and has often been fatal to shipping.

Bright sunlight illumines all the landscape, and Vesuvius, and the fine lines of the distant Apennine, are clearly relieved against the azure background. Only above the

---

* The Trescone, although now become obsolete, was, a generation ago, perfectly well known and frequently danced by the peasants of Tuscany.—*Translator's note*.

ARRIVAL OF A MARKET BOAT, CAPRI.

marshy shores of Pæstum broods the misty breath of summer noon. The shrill chirp of the cicala sounds from tree and bush, lizards glide swiftly about on the fragments of grey masonry, and blue butterflies hang poised on the bright red carnations which grow upon the seaward edge of the cliff. Except a distant waft of song from the vineyards on the opposite coast, there is no token of human neighbourhood. Absolute stillness! The

ROCK OF TIBERIUS, WITH THE JUPITER VILLA, CAPRI.

leaves of the olive are motionless, and a trembling air scarcely stirs the blades of brown herbage.

By degrees it grows dark behind Vesuvius, and night seems to invade the blueness of the sky and cast deep shadows over the sea. There is lightning,—a brief peal of thunder,—a puff of wind upon the waves,—and then a sudden blast that storms against the rocks and sets the boughs waving with a soughing noise. The chirp of the cicala is dumb, and with a hoarse cry the sea-gull swoops from the cliff down on to the foaming waves. More thunder, echoed and re-echoed by the rocks and mountains; the black cloud mingles its rainy edges with the waters of the sea, and long flaming flashes of lightning seem as they would pierce its very depths; and there in the midst of the crash of the elements, goes the little bark steered by human hands, her sail slanting and dipping down into the foam, making for *terra firma*.

It is a wild sight. The daughters of Nereus raise themselves up out of the flood, and the sons of Æolus bend down to them from on high for fierce embraces. The sea mounts up to the heavens; the heavens plunge down into the sea; and mighty waterspouts whirl and spin in frenzied dance around the island to the sound of the rolling thunder. At such times the cowardly Tiberius was wont to creep into the asylum of the temple, and press the divine laurel tremblingly against his forehead, that so he might ward off the bolt of the angry Thunderer. Now-a-days the hermit of the mountain sounds the bell of the chapel of Santa Maria del Soccorso, Our Lady of Succour, whose holy shrine was erected on this blood-stained spot in expiation of the guilty deeds performed there.

The remains of the ancient buildings are more numerous here than in any other point of the island; and enable you to distinguish, if not the original plan of the Villa, at least its extent. This is attested by the numerous remains of chambers, vaults, staircases, Mosaic pavements, fragments of columns, and crumbling walls, half hidden in foliage and vegetation. On several pieces of the wall the rich Pompeian colouring,—red, blue, and yellow,—may still be seen. And it is possible that these heaps of rubbish still conceal many buried treasures. Several beautiful things have been already found here. The ruined palace was doubtless a marvel of the splendour of those days, built at the command of an arrogant and powerful Cæsar. But Nature has created greater marvels in the silence and solitude of this island. On the south-eastern side of it she has piled mass upon mass, rock upon rock, hung colossal cliffs leaning over the verge of a precipice, raised pyramids, and crowned her titanic sport with a gigantic natural triumphal arch, overlooking the solitude of the sea! There it stands, a wonder to this day, the marvellous *Arco Naturale* towering up from a chaos of sharp cliffs. You look through it into the vast expanse of the sea, and the sensation of solitude becomes almost overpowering.

Lower down you descend into the evil-omened Cave of Mithra, where dark and mysterious rites were performed in honour of unknown powers. Human blood has flowed in that cavern. Yes, in truth this is the Isle of Tiberius! Wherever we turn we meet with some record of that gloomy spectre.

Anacapri may perhaps be excepted. It lies still nearer heaven, on the western side of the island which rises in Monte Solaro to the height of two thousand feet: about twice as high as the eastern side. The giddy stairway consisting of five hundred and thirty-six steps, cut in the rock, which formerly led up from the *Marina* to the upper town, has recently been destroyed. A good road has been made by cutting and blasting the rocks, on which prosaic folks may comfortably ride up on donkeys,—perhaps before long there may be a drive with hackney coaches!—instead of poetically and pantingly clambering to the heights as was formerly the case. What splendid pictures one used to see on the rocky stairway! How magnificently picturesque especially were the groups of women going up and down with pitchers and burthens on their heads! Or else pausing to rest and leaning over the parapet to gaze after the distant ships at sea! And the women of Anacapri are of purer race, and therefore handsomer and prouder than those of the lower town.

Up here in Anacapri the air is deliciously pure, and the soil produces all kinds of treasures in rich abundance, such as the hill districts of the *Napoletano* alone can boast of. The people, however, are poor but contented; and if there be still a paradise on earth, it is Anacapri. What does it know of the changing years?—what of the bustles of the world? But the happiest man of all Anacapri is the hermit, who passes his existence on the highest point of the island! The hermitage is perched on the summit of Monte Solaro like a falcon's nest, and the solitary man sits up here like a sentinel of Olympus, surrounded by winds and clouds, and sees the earliest gleam of the sun behind

ENTRANCE TO THE BAT GROTTO.

the Lucanian Apennine, and his latest rays as he sinks into the western sea. He is used to these grand spectacles; but to us, beholding it but for once, it seems to fill the soul with a flood of beauty.

Shall we descend once more into the shining sea-chamber of the Blue Grotto? Shall we listen to the secret of the waves, and try to paint these mysterious splendours?

A TOILET IN CAPRI.

In vain! The palettes whence the old painters drew their glorious tints are dry and empty, and a pen-and-ink sketch cannot attempt to reproduce them. But let me repeat once more, that the Blue Grotto is by no means the most beautiful of all the beautiful things to be seen in Capri.

So we depart from the island. We take leave of the jolly company of artists who live year in, year out, in the palm-shaded Hotel Pagano, or the Albergo di Don Luigi on the height; we take leave of the natives with their Greek cheerfulness, and wish to each and all on the dear island, health and happiness. Hear the blessing of the strangers whom ye have received beneath your roofs, or under the shelter of trellised leaves, and feasted with your bread and your wine in the true spirit of hospitality! Hear the blessing poured out upon your wave-kissed shores: May the kind god of the grape grant to you throughout all future years, to celebrate your cheerful festivals, and to enjoy a liberal vintage after hopeful toil!

But we must depart also from the Bay of Naples and the landscapes of Campania. Joyous land beside the heaving sea, with thy sunny shores, and blissful isles,—farewell!

FROM THE SHORES OF THE SIRENS TO THE MOUNTAINS OF CALABRIA.

GRÆCIA MAGNA.

"Beauteous world, where art thou? Nature's Spring-time ;
Freshly blooming time, oh come again !
Only in the poet's fairy kingdom
Do the traces of that time remain.
Dull and dead the landscape lies forsaken,
No divinity mine eyes behold ;
Out, alas ! Of all that life-warm picture
We inherit but the shadows cold !"
SCHILLER.

A PROCESSION ACROSS THE COUNTRY.

PENTECOST,—pleasantest of festivals,—is here. Shot after shot sounds through the slumbering streets of Naples ;—from Borgo di Coreto, from Pendino, from the narrow alleys of the quarters of the Molo Piccolo, Chiaja, and Stella, and thus awakened, the populace pours out in holiday trim into the streets and piazzas. Carts and vehicles of all sorts clatter over the pavement of the eastern suburb, and congregate in a motley throng, upon the wide space before the Porta Capuana. There are callings and shoutings, and songs, and the sounds of musical instruments, and fresh explosions of gunpowder. The noise grows louder and louder. Hundreds of vehicles adorned with barbaric gaudiness and filled with human beings of all ages, are assembled here in the early dawn. The drivers crack their whips, the horses stamp on the dusty ground, and as soon as the sun peeps up behind Vesuvius, they set off in mad career along the road to Nola. This is on the Friday night, and Saturday morning before Whitsuntide ; and on Whit Sunday the population of Naples celebrates its favourite festival away there on the eastern hills by Avellino, on the 'ancient and sacred Monte Vergine':—the festival of the *Madonna degli Angeli*, and, on the same day, that of the *Madonna dell' Arco*.

This mountain, which stands isolated from the Neapolitan Apennine, was deemed sacred by the first Grecian settlers. The temple dedicated to the virgin Diana stood here on the centre of the mountain ; and the road which led to it from the Grecian city on the shore, was still called in the Roman times "*Ad matrem magnam.*" From the summit of the mountain they looked eastward during their devotions and sought " the land of the Greeks with their soul." On the plain below there was a temple of Apollo, the village of Mercogliano is said to derive its name from *Mercurii ara*, and a meadow hard by bears to this day the name of Vesta.

From a very remote antiquity, numerous Christian churches and chapels have stood in this neighbourhood; and they owe their fame to the antique traditions of Diana the

MONTE VERGINE.

Helpful, in whose footprints on the steep, treeless, chalk cliff, Our Lady of Succour has trodden. In honour of the latter a famous convent has been erected on the ruins of heathendom; and thither goes the Pentecost procession.

All Naples and the adjacent towns and villages gird themselves up for this procession. Piety and wild jollity are mingled with keen love of gain, which urges the dealers and pedlars with their carts hung with bells, and with stores of dainties, and toys, and wine, and water, to be early on the spot. The tambourine seller must not fail either; nor those who sell flags and fireworks, guitars and castanets. For after the church ceremonies follow dance and song and bacchanalian orgies; and for the due supply of these latter, are needed the hundreds of moveable kitchens and cellars with abundant store of provisions, which precede the locust-like advance of the pious and jolly Whitsuntide pilgrims.

Here they come! The devout carry presents for the shrine, of wax or metal, each one deeming himself bound to give a thank-offering for past favours,—the cure of severe sickness and the like,—or to propitiate the giver of favours for the future. They bring great bundles of wax tapers, silver lamps, light and heavy, silver hearts, and gold chains and clasps, which are all ostentatiously displayed during the journey in glittering show. Here, too, are the most popular singers and reciters of the city, the foremost *improvisatori*, —" *Canta-figliole* " the common people call them,—who challenge and try to surpass each other in screaming out long-drawn *ritornelle* in honour of the Virgin, with a never-ending "*figlio-o-o-le*" at the termination of each verse. Hundreds of ducats are expended on the decorations of the waggons, horses, and drivers, as well as on personal adornments. Poor persons will sometimes half starve themselves for a year in order to obtain the fleeting intoxication of this festival!

A thick cloud of dust rises on the highway and above the beautiful cemetery of Naples, over the walls of which, as the crowds hurry past, fly cries of greeting and prayers for the poor souls in purgatory. On they go, past Cisterna, Marigliano, Pontecicciano, and the evening halt is made at Cimitile. The name of this place reminds us of the dead who rest by thousands underneath the turf here; for we are encamped above the catacombs of Nola. But those who tread the turf now are engrossed with life, and merrymaking resounds through the night. It is the same in Monteforte, where tents and barricades are erected for the pilgrims who pass the night here. Some go on to Avellino, whose houses and courtyards and staircases are crowded with sleepers; and Mercogliano affords similar nocturnal pictures. Great fires glare through the darkness, and around the fires the wine-cup circulates, the jest and song and twang of guitars are heard amidst the groups lighted up by the glare of the flames, until at length they subside into a murmur of prayer, and the noise gradually dies out with the dying fire.

Movement begins again whilst it is still dark. Torches are lighted, and by their blaze the procession begins to ascend the winding way which leads up from Mercogliano to the mountain. Banners flutter in the red torchlight, and gay costumes and faces of men and women are seen strangely illumined. The glare flickers up among the summits of the hoary oaks and chestnuts which border the road, interspersed with masses of rock. The night breeze carries the hymn to the Madonna,—now loud, now faint,—over the slumbering land, from whence at intervals the clang of a chapel bell is heard. The procession disappears behind a rock at a turn in the round, and, when it next is seen, has mounted higher up among the trees. Higher it goes;—higher yet!

On the summit a crowd of poor people lies sleeping, stretched on the convent steps. They are awakened by the great bell ringing out in festal tones its "*Salve Regina!*" through the dewy morning air. And then the voices of those in the procession advancing from below chant in answer,

"Salve regina,
Mater misericordiæ!"

The portals of the sanctuary are opened, and the crowd pours into it tumultuously, with outstretched arms, praying and praising and uttering vows to the Queen of Heaven. High mass is celebrated with the profoundest devotion, the church is filled with clouds of incense, and the bright summer sun sends down his golden rays through the windows, upon the dense, kneeling, many-coloured crowd. The poorest throws his mite, and the rich man his gold, behind the grating of the chapel of San Guglielmo, the founder of the church. He erected it in the year 1125, on the threshold of the deposed goddess Diana.

The Hohenstaufen Emperor, Frederick the Second, twice visited the church, and the ill-starred Manfred appointed that his monument should be erected here. After he had fallen at Benevento, however, Charles of Anjou caused the tomb to be destroyed, and had

MILL NEAR ARIANO.

his own crest of the three lilies sculptured on the marble of the church. So that there are manifold traces of history to be met with on this rock.

After the completion of the religious ceremonies, the people descend from the mountain, and then begins the unbridled bacchanalian revelry. Cherry and ash trees, ivy and vine are plundered to make green wreaths for the revellers, who are merrymaking amidst the tents and booths decorated with banners. Shouting, singing, the braying of trumpets, the thrum of tambourines, the clinking of glasses, and the clattering of plates are all mingled in one wild uproar. Later on they hear mass once more in the Vescovato, and then proceed on their way to Saviano and Sant' Anastasia. The maidens of these villages meet them half way with waving banners, flowers, and music; and if it be possible that there should be a *crescendo* to the wildness of the revelry, one may say that the *crescendo* continues until the return home of the pilgrims on Whit Monday. On that day the crowd breaks up; and any one coming from Naples amongst these mountains on the afternoon of that day, would meet nothing but tired, sleepy, dusty creatures, plodding back in silence to their homes.

The last pilgrim has disappeared. We stand alone upon the sacred mountain, and look down at the quiet, beautiful landscape below us. Yonder rises Vesuvius, dark blue with a diadem of silver cloudlets on his brow. That town is the ancient Benevento; that other Ariano. There lie Bisaccia, Caudano, Arpadio, Monte Sarchio, and Sant' Agata de' Goti. The great Apulian plain stretches to the east, and southward through the wooded country of the Irpini, runs the chain of the Lucanian Hills towards Calabria.

LUCANIA, APULIA, AND CALABRIA, IN THE PAST AND THE PRESENT.

"Sing we the mountain groves . . ."
VIRGIL.

TWO mighty groups of mountains in the west, and a vast plain to the eastward, form the foot of Italy which is bathed in two seas;—the Tyrrhene and the Ionian. The northernmost of the two mountain groups is the Neapolitan Apennine, which stretches southward as a continuation of the Abruzzi, from the hills of Sorrento; extending in many jagged branches. The country occupied by it is called the Basilicata, or Lucania. The latter name is probably derived from *lucus*, a grove; for deep woods, often even yet virgin forests, cover its slopes, and grey inhospitable townlets and villages nestle at their foot, or crown the summit of some height. These places and their half savage inhabitants are alike untouched by civilization. The first chain of mountains reaches to the Ofanto (formerly the Aufidus), and in it, too, rises near Melfi, the well-known, mighty Monte Vulture. A second branch leads to the Bay of Policastro, and the chief points of this range are Monte Acuto, Monte Papa, and Monte Rosaro. From the latter various broken lines run out to the eastward, and lose themselves in the Apulian plain. The cities of this district are Potenza, Brienza, Accerenza, Matera, Lagonegro, and above all the historic Melfi, and Venosa, the birthplace of Horace.

The Apulian plain, or Tavogliere di Puglia, is flat throughout, with the exception of a few low terraces of land which rise in it. It bears a strong resemblance in appearance to the Roman Campagna; only that its horizon is formed by the Ionian Sea. All the southern provinces might bear the plough and the shepherd's crook in their coat of arms, for they live but by the produce of field and pasture. Corn and maize grow in every part of the plain, whilst a fiery grape ripens on the sunny slopes, and in the gardens along the coast all manner of southern fruits are produced in incredible profusion. Sheep are pastured during the winter on the wide grass lands extending for many a mile, and in summer they are driven up to the hill pastures and far into the mountains, and their

BATTLEFIELD OF CANNÆ.

shepherds are savage-looking fellows, whose half barbaric costume has been made
familiar to us by the pictures of brigands : for in these parts brigands and shepherds are
pretty closely related ! In order to know these nomade herdsmen and shepherds, one
must cross the Tavogliere di Puglia. Hundreds of thousands of sheep wander across
the baked chalky plain towards the western mountains with their promise of fresh water,

PETRA ROSETI, ON THE CALORE NEAR BENEVENTO.

or to the isolated mountain mass of Gargano, which shows blue and tempting from the Gulf of
Manfredonia. The plain is abandoned almost entirely to the shepherds; but on the edge
of the coast there is a series of young and growing cities. They have dedicated themselves, as it were, to the sea, and seek their chief sustenance from sea commerce, like the
Greek settlers of old time. In the three provinces of the Capitanata, Terra di Bari, and
Terra di Otranto, from the steadily increasing town of Foggia down to Taranto, may be
reckoned a number of cities such as Barletta, Trani, Bari, Brindisi, and Lecce, which all
strive with each other for pre-eminence.

Under the same degree of latitude as that in which the Puglian plain runs eastward
of the Gulf of Taranto towards the Ionian Sea, the mountains of Calabria begin their
course to the west of the same gulf. Each of the three provinces of the Calabrias
(citeriore, and ulteriore first and second) is marked off by an isolated mass of this

mountain chain, the centre one of which is the great mysterious range of the Forest of Sila. And Calabria is the most interesting part of all the south!

It rises stern and wild, bold and defiant, torn and jagged with a thousand inaccessible mountain valleys, girdled by the Tyrrhene and Ionian seas, guarded like a fortress by

RUINS OF THE ABBEY OF THE HOLY TRINITY, VENOSA.

many a rocky cape and headland which advances boldly into the blue waves. In the winter and spring the waters of the Crati, Amato, Corace, Niete, and Metramo hasten through the narrow rocky valleys to end their short course in the neighbouring sea; whilst in summer their wide beds are dry and dusty. The same blue heaven smiles here as above the Campagna Felice, the laurel and myrtle bloom,—but the Calabrian landscape is silent, almost sullen. Sullenly the poverty-stricken inhabitants gather the gifts which the sun and the rain and the dews bestow on them. These gifts are so numerous that they might fill the country with prosperity and riches and happiness; and yet throughout Calabria poverty weeps in the valleys and on the hills, or else embarks in foreign ships and departs for America. The province is becoming depopulated; and yet nowhere is there more need for agricultural labour.

LUCANIA, APULIA, AND CALABRIA.

These three districts, Lucania, Apulia, and Calabria, once belonged to the beautiful and much praised Græcia Magna, of which there remains scarce the shadow of a shade.

"Beauteous world, where art thou?"

Where are the noble cities for whose favour an Alexander, a Hannibal, a Pyrrhus,

CATACOMBS OF SIPONTO NEAR MANFREDONIA.

have striven in past times?—cities which produced an Agathocles, a Zaleucos, a Charondes,—which heard the teaching of Pythagoras as he paced their marble streets, and were praised by Pindar and Demosthenes,—where are they? Where, too, are the days when Cicero landed on these shores to meet Brutus, the days of Alaric and his iron Goths, of Otto the Second, Frederick the Second, and all the great figures which once trod this wondrous stage?

They have passed like a dream. All is covered with the dust and decay of centuries, and only here and there some crumbling ruin, some tradition half transformed into the semblance of a Christian legend, or some lonely column, speaks faintly to us of the glorious days of Græcia Magna.

Much of what remained was destroyed later by the sword of the French. What they had spared was devastated by nature herself in repeated earthquakes, which have their home beneath the soil of the Basilicata and the Calabrian Apennine. And last of all—when scarcely anything remained save misery, tears, and sighs, after the cities were desolate and their sites strewn with salt, came the Bourbons, and planted amidst tears and sighs the poisonous, but rank and luxuriant, weed of a priesthood greedy for blood and booty; a priesthood which was able—like the brigands—to draw excellent nourish-

STREET IN MONTE SANT' ANGELO.

ment out of the last sap of the dying oak. The country—with the exception of the commercial cities on the eastern coast—will not speedily rise to prosperity again.

To one travelling from dirty Benevento (which, however, still possesses one of the most beautiful objects in Italy in the "Golden Gate" of Trajan's arch above the banks of the Calore) through Ariano, Foggia, and Manfredonia, towards the south, the landscape forms the chief object of attraction;—there the grand mountainous district, here the charming coast scenery. All the villages and towns become more repulsive and inhospitable the farther one advances southward; therefore the country is still almost unknown. Very few strangers' feet explore the abundantly rich scenery of Monte Gargano. Everyone shuns the dirty and disagreeable quarters to be found in such places as San Severo, Apricena, San Nicandro, Cagnano: all of which are blighted by the malaria exhaled from the swampy lagoons which border Monte Gargano to the north and south. But from every one of these places the distant view is enchanting, whether we gaze from San Nicandro upon the blue islands of Tremiti, or behold the azure waves of the lake of Varano, in which a city is said to have sunk centuries ago, or the Lago di Lesina. Nature seems here and there to make an effort to deck herself with southern richness, as where she surrounds Ischitella, throned on its rock, with a splendid orange grove; but for the most part her robe is poor and scanty. Vico, Peschici (built in to the rock on the stony coast), Rodi, precisely resemble the miserable nests of the Sabine mountains, and

JEWISH CATACOMBS NEAR VENOSA.

would probably excite the enthusiasm of a painter. The coast is bordered by lemon and orange groves; but at the foot of the Gargano begins the primeval forest. A true primeval forest really does still grow on these heights. There are oaks of a thousand years, hoary beeches, fallen trunks, from whose decay a young generation of trees arises, climbing plants, which mount to the highest branches, and fall again to earth, thorns and thickets, which afford a safe retreat to the wild woodland animals, and likewise to the brigands, who need fear no myrmidons of the law in these forests. The flocks and herds of Apulia are pastured on the cleared spots, and the shepherds' fires shine amidst the shadows of the foliage.

From hence you can pursue your way through the woods to Sant' Angelo, and descend by winding paths to the ancient Sipontum. It was colonized by the Romans; but in consequence of the fever which prevailed here, the town was rebuilt by Manfred under the name of Manfredonia, on a site somewhat higher, and nearer to the coast.

In Santa Maria Maggiore di Siponto, a ruined cathedral, and extensive catacombs still remind us of the fact that an important city once stood here.

The dreary flat coast landscape to the south of Manfredonia, exactly resembles the Pontine Marshes; and the neighbourhood of Cannæ on the Ofanto is of the same character. Intense melancholy broods over these dreary plains, and of Cannæ (which,

CANOSA ANTICA.

however, was but an unimportant city) no vestige remains. Now and then, perhaps, the peasant's hoe strikes against a fragment of marble, or turns up coins, and pieces of armour from the swampy soil. The greatest drama of ancient history was played on this spot; and the back-ground of the stage is formed by the exquisitely curving Gulf of Manfredonia, and the dark woody heights of the Gargano rising above it.

The road passes through Canosa with its Mediæval fortress on the height, along the Ofanto, through Lavello to Melfi and Venosa. Who would not feel some enthusiasm at the name of Venosa, which is associated with the amiable Venus, and with Horace, whose birthplace it is? *Venusia*, the famous city of antiquity! It was situated at a very important point in the Roman world: the boundaries of Samnium, Lucania, and Apulia, and on the great road between Samnium and Tarentum. And when the Romans put twenty thousand colonists into the town about the year 291 B.C., and, a year or two later, strengthened it in other ways, Venusia became a formidable check upon the neighbouring districts, even to far into the south. Near at hand rises Monte Vulture with its double peak; an ancient volcano, extinct for the present, but probably not for ever. In the

THE LAKES OF MONTICCHIO.

course of time it has been covered by woods and luxuriant vegetation. It is the same Vulture of which Horace so pleasantly narrates that in his childhood,

> "Me fabulosæ, Vulture in Apulo,
> Altricis extra limen Apuliæ,
> Ludo fatigatumque somno
> Fronde novâ puerum palumbes
> Texere;" &c. &c.

On the slopes of the mountain lie the little lakes of Monticchio in the hollow of a crater, and a few villages niched among the rocks. The view from the summit reminds us of that from Monte Cavo, and a romantic monastery (San Michele) serves to increase the resemblance.

From Barletta you traverse the flat line of coast to Taranto, and from the latter place you behold all the swampy shores on which some of the most famous of the Grecian cities once stood. They all owed their existence to the ruler of the seas, as did Taras, or

Tarentum, founded by a son of Neptune, and Greeks were their first colonists. Tarentum however, was colonized by Dorians. The oldest of these cities was Heracleia, built on the site of the venerable Ionian Siris. Heracleia was situated at the mouth of the Achiris, and became so flourishing, that it for a long time enjoyed the honour of being the city

TAVOLA DE' PALADINI.

where the congress of all Græcia Magna was held. The painter Zeuxis was born here. The site of Heracleia is marked now by the village of Policoro half sunk in the marshes.

To the north of it lay the mighty Metapontium. Nestor built it; or else Sinon, the contriver of the Trojan horse. The Lucanians destroyed it. The Sybarites rebuilt and fortified it. The Romans subdued it in the war against Pyrrhus. Later it passed to the Carthaginians, and thenceforward disappears from history. A swamp occupies the site of it. Farther to the south the names of Sybaris and Croton sound like a faint echo from old times. Sybaris to which in that dim antiquity five-and-twenty important cities were subject even as far as Poseidonia, which could bring three hundred thousand men into the field, and was inhabited by a hundred thousand luxurious Greeks,—Sybaris is now a miserable village; Palinore, and its marble palaces are buried in the swamp. Croton too with its boasting proverb " The last of the Crotonites is the first of the Greeks," of which it was said :

"Aliæ urbes, si ad Crotonem conferantur, vanæ nihilque sunt."

Croton, too, (or Cotrone as it is now called) is but the shadow of a shade. It is built close to the waters of the Ionian sea, and seems to be slowly dying of dulness. The only remnants of bygone splendours are a solitary Doric column, and a bit of broken masonry

ON THE BUSENTO NEAR COSENZA.

at Cape Nau, where around the lighthouse are grouped a few villas of the Crotonese who come there for the summer.

These are all abodes of melancholy. And what is the posterity of the Achaiens and Spartans like? Who among them knows anything of the school of Pythagoras? What has become of the wise and beautiful laws which Croton obeyed in purity of morals? The sullen peasant, his pointed brigand hat on his head, a gun at his back, slinks through the fields of an alien master, and cowers with his fever-stricken family in a wretched mud hovel, leading an almost inhuman existence. The Calabrese of the present day,—the great mass of the uncultivated population,—displays no trace of Hellenism. He might well derive his rude manners and customs, his tendency to blood and murder, from that rough and barbarous people the Brettii, the disloyal deserters, who were declared by the Romans to be slaves of the State.

The Calabria of to-day shows a terrible lack of cities or important hamlets, in the interior. What there are, especially on or near the Sila, are mere disorderly, miserably built groups of houses called *Casali*. These look as if they had been arrested in flight half way down some mountain slope, or on the edge of a precipice ; they lurk half hidden behind bush and shrub, and far from roads or paths. They seem to tell of a time when the frequent incursion of Vandal, Goth, or Saracen, drove the trembling people from the coast, to take refuge in the mountains, and so formed these temporary settlements.

REGGIO CALABRO.

Others speak of the dark feudal days of the Middle Ages, for above them towers the moss-grown ruin of some baronial fortress, or the walls of a convent or monastery. The towns and villages themselves, are destitute of all attraction ; the houses, clumsy, windowless piles of stone ; the streets, unpaved dung-heaps where squalor and poverty sprout up. If Cosenza, Nicastro, Catanzaro, and above all, Reggio, appear somewhat more pleasant seen from without, yet within all present the same picture of misery, decay, and hopeless poverty.

But poetry and poverty almost always go hand in hand ; throughout Italy they are sisters, and in Calabria twin sisters ! Let us take the hand of the more cheerful of the two, and descend to the strand at Reggio. We will part from the mainland with some pleasant pictures.

It is the time of the vintage! A joyous, festal time! In the grey dawn they come from the mountains, the sun-burned girls with great black eyes, clad in their gay and becoming costumes, and carrying baskets on their arms, and larger baskets on their heads. They appear at different turns of the road, now singly, now in groups. In the neighbourhood of the wine-press they sit down on the ground, and breakfast with many a merry jest. But by the time the sun has dried the dew on the grapes the work begins.

FISHERMAN'S COTTAGE.

They scatter themselves over the vineyard like a flock of birds. Some gather the fruit, others carry it to the wine-press, supporting the load on their heads with brown strong arms. The gay blues and reds of kerchief and petticoat glimmer through the green, and merry "*canzoni*" resound on all sides. Shots are heard; the noise and jollity grow louder; one vineyard answers and emulates another with song against song. Then comes a troop of young men under the pretext of paying their respects to the owner of the vineyard, but in reality to "*far gli occhi dolci*" ("make sweet eyes") to the girls, and indulge in a little flirtation. By the evening the work must be completed, and each girl receives her scanty pay and a basket of grapes. Singing and chatting they return in the twilight to their homes, and many a one carries back with her the rose of Love hidden amongst the berries of Bacchus.

Perhaps the olive harvest is still prettier on this olive-grown coast, where so many rich oil-growers dwell. It takes place in October and November, and women and girls from all the mountain districts of Calabria attend it. All sorts of types, costumes, dialects, and popular songs are represented here. What pictures are to be seen in single figures—or groups of girls under the shadow of the softly-tinted olive-trees! They sleep at night in little huts around the oil-press, but they spin and wash for hours before going to rest; and chatter and sing unceasingly. But on Sundays they devote themselves to enjoyment, dance, sing, and play the castanets and the clashing cymbals.

These are truly the only joyous days in the life of this poor people: days when they pour out their hearts in song, and are carried on wings of poesy far away from the dusty paths of their weary lives, away from hunger and care to the shining summits where flows Olympian nectar! As we prepare to depart, a farewell song echoes in our ears from the Calabrian shores:—

"*Sia bineditta chi fici lu munnu!*	"Oh blessed be He who hath made the world!
Sia bineditta chi lu seppe fari!	Blessed be He for making it so rarely!
Fici lu cielu cu lu giru tunnu,	He made the sky in a great circle curled,
Fici li stilli pe' ci accampagnari,	And made the stars to glitter in it fairly.
Fici lu mari, e poi ci fici l'unnu,	He made the sea, and then the waves that move,
Fici la varca, pe' ci navicari,	And then the bark upon their breast careering,
E poi facetti a tia janca palummu,	And then made thee, thou snowy-plumaged dove,
Chi puerti i corti di lu navicari."	That bear'st the charts to guide the shipman's steering!"

This "snowy-plumaged dove" of poesy guides our way towards the ancient land of fable, Trinacria, and towards our final goal, the mighty, lofty, uttermost sentinel of Italy,—the flame-breathing Etna!

FROM THE SILA TO ETNA.

SICILIAN LANDSCAPE.

"———; tribus haec excurrit in aequora linguis;
E quibus imbriferos obversa Pachynos ad Austros;
Mollibus expositum Zephyris Lilybaeon; et Arcton
Æquoris expertem spectat, Ioniaeque Pelorus."

OVID.

THE ISLAND UNDER THE VEIL OF LEGEND AND HISTORY.

SICILY is the golden fairy-land of the antique world, and, like curious children attracted by strange tales, the nations came from the north and the south, and the east and the west, to behold the wonders of the sunny island, on whose meadows blooms eternal spring. During the pre-historic period, when the earth was convulsed with mighty throes, gigantic powers fought and strove here, and it was the Titans who hurled down this mass of earth to lead an isolated existence, breaking it off from the towering rocky mountains of the mainland, and opening out a passage from the western Italian sea to the waters of Greece. Then they heaved up the land by the power of fire, and made it tower high above the bosom of the sea, and piled great mountains one on the other, and spread out the volcanic coasts widely to the south and the east. For majestic light-houses and watch-towers of the land, they set Etna flaming in the east, and in the north, the volcanos of the Æolian islands.

But then came the kind Ceres, friendly to the race of men, and dwelt in the interior of the land, and the lovely Spring spread his carpet of flowers over the blackened and burning soil. Through the silver veil of Legend we discern the fair daughter of the goddess,—Persephone, sporting in innocent happiness with her companions upon the violet-breathing meads of Enna. Athena, with a troop of cheerful nymphs, guardians of the warm springs, dwelt near Himera; and Artemis, at the mouth of the Anapus, on the island of Ortygia. They were all three bred up in Trinacria, and loved the island above all things.

All around the flowery meads of Enna the cornfields are laden with a rich harvest, and the gods have descended to earth for the joyous feast of Ceres. When lo! the earth opens, and the ruler of the lower regions arises to seize upon Persephone, with her crown of blossoms, and drag her down into his gloomy kingdom. The mother comes, seeking her beloved child, but no one reveals to her what has befallen. Then, wrapped in dark mourning robes, she searches wildly through the island, from sunrise to sunset, and when

night falls, she lights two pine-stems at the fires of Etna, to flame as torches over the
dark earth, as the Greek tragic poet sings :—

> "In sorrow for her daughter lost, she goes
> Seeking and wandering through many lands,
> While from the depths of Ætna, streams of fire
> Impregnate all the Isle of Sicily,
> And the earth groans aloud :—"

In the neighbourhood of the spot where the noble city of Syracuse afterwards stood,
Pluto had sunk again into the earth; and here, in honour of his lovely prize, he caused

STRAITS OF MESSINA.

the blue fountain of Cyane to gush forth. Only after the bereaved mother had traversed
the earth far and wide, in her car drawn by dragons, and after she had made the Athenians
participators in her noble gifts and mild laws, did she discover the abode of the long-lost
one, and by her entreaties, obtained from Jupiter the boon that her daughter should be
allowed to return to her every Spring, and abide with her till harvest-time. And so she
rises every year, and strews violets and roses, and brilliant blossoms over the land, and
blesses the fields with abundant harvests. And for many centuries the people were wont
to celebrate the festival of the goddesses every harvest-tide, and decked their hair with
wreaths of wheat-ears and corn-flowers, as Ceres had adorned her golden tresses in the
joy of being re-united with her child.

Thus Sicily owed her wealth and civilization to the beneficence of the kind divinity.
And even to this day it is distinguished above all lands for the gifts of Ceres. But also
the swarms of shining lizards which we see darting out their rapid tongues, and flashing

swiftly over the old walls on every road in the island are creations of Ceres. Their ancestor was a brown vintager's boy who mocked at the goddess as she was drinking hastily in her flight, and whom she sprinkled with the dregs of her draught, and thus transformed him into a restless wall-haunting lizard. Enna, where now Castro-Giovanni stands poor and wretched on its brown, steep rock, became the holy central point of the island—"the navel of Sicily," as the Romans called it. And, in truth, one looks hence

RUINS OF THE ANCIENT THEATRE AT SYRACUSE.

over the whole island with its wild green valleys, rugged hills, and blue glimmering mountains. Here Gelon, after the great victory near Himera, built a splendid temple to Ceres.

The shores of the island, before agriculture accustomed men to softer manners, were inhabited by wild people. Near Etna were the Cyclops, the "lawless" crew of Homer, amongst whom the companions of Ulysses met with a tragic fate. Later they dwelt inside Etna, and in the volcanoes of the Lipari islands, and forged thunderbolts for Jupiter, and armour for heroes. Also the ferocious and gigantic Læstrygonians lived a wild life in their city of Telepylos, and cruelly opposed the landing of foreign ships.

Around the Æolian islands the winds blew boisterously from the sea, and the fire of their volcanoes glowed far and wide across the waters. These islands were once waste and empty; when Liparos, the son of King Anson, being banished from his home on the mainland, wandered hither, and one of the islands was named after him. He had already grown to be an old man, when Æolus, son of Hippotes, landed on Lipara with a troop of followers, and wooed the old man's daughter, the fair Cyane. He became king

3 M

of the seven islands, and his splendid palace shone across the sea with brazen walls. To him arrived Ulysses, and found him in a splendid hall where the music of flutes resounded, surrounded by lovely sons and daughters. And here, on his departure, Ulysses received the gift of the wind-bag so fraught with fate. The sons of Æolus afterwards divided amongst themselves the command over the Sicilian and Southern Italian coasts.

All these legends have sprung from the natural peculiarities of the wondrous Trinacria. They are "Nature-myths;" for the island is made up of the blooming meadows and cornfields of Persephone and Ceres, of the rough, inaccessible, rock-strewn coasts of the Læstrygonians and Cyclops, of mysterious subterranean powers, and terrific volcanoes, the whole surrounded by a stormy sea. The island by its position between Europe and Africa, and midway between the eastern and western portions of the Mediterranean, has always served as a stepping-stone, or bridge for the nations; whilst its beauty and riches have made it also the frequent subject of strife and contention. Even as the waves of the sea encompassed and beat upon its shores from all sides, so did the peoples come from north, south, east and west to gain a footing on the favoured island. The three mightiest people of antiquity,—the Hellenes, Carthaginians, and Romans,—met sword in hand in Sicily, struggling for the mastery of the world.

In a short time the population of the island received the appellation of "the triple-tongued," *trilinguis*, because three languages, the Sicilian, the Greek, and the Phœnician, were spoken there. But this denomination soon became inadequate. The original inhabitants (within the historic period) were the Sicanians, from whom the island received the name of Sicania. The Siculi crossed over from the mainland and settled here; and they came in such numbers as to push the aborigines out to the westward. These Siculi formed a number of small principalities, and cultivated the land from the northern coast a good way into the interior. The Phœnicians also landed on sundry points of the island which advance into the sea, and founded many maritime cities on the steep coast, and the smaller islands, as a protection for their fleet. But it was reserved for the Greeks fully to develop the resources of the island. Hellenism was transplanted to this favourable soil, and grew and flourished with almost more strength and beauty than in its mother earth. The population of the island proved docile to Grecian culture; and Theocles,—the first Greek who landed here,—met with no opposition in founding Naxos and Catana, and Lentini, with his troop of Ionians from Chalcis.

The Ionians were succeeded by the Dorians, and these latter became even more important and powerful. Syracuse arose in Corinthian splendour. Men of Megara and Rhodes founded Gela, Acragas, and Selinus. The original inhabitants had become the servants of the new-comers. During more than two centuries the Greeks continued to prosper and increase, and the island was covered with beautiful cities, and fine masterpieces of art and architecture. A new Hellas had arisen from the waves of the western sea; but their good fortune was by no means unalloyed; a bond of union was wanting amongst them, or if it existed was corroded by internal dissensions. Then the Carthaginians landed at Panormus; but in the face of the enemy the different tribes forgot their civic disputes, gave each other the hand, and the Punic forces, led by Hamilcar, were utterly defeated near Himera by Gelon, in 480. After that the prosperity of the island reached a pitch of the greatest luxuriance.

But Athens fell; and her fall determined the fate of Sicily. The Carthaginians once more advanced in devastating force from the west of the island, where they had obtained a firm settlement, and conquered Acragas, Selinus and the strong Panormus also fell into their hands. Then both the first and the second Dionysius, favoured by the general confusion, seized all power in their own hands, to the destruction of liberty; and the cruel Agathocles raised himself from the humble position of a potter, to be a tyrant. Thus the Greeks and Carthaginians struggled against each other with varying success.

The Second Punic War had already begun when the Carthaginian party in the island made a league with Hannibal, thus drawing on themselves the avenging sword of the Romans. Marcellus appeared before Syracuse with the Roman legions. He besieged it

SHIPPING OFF CAPTIVE BRIGANDS.

for two years, and then it fell, the strong Agrigentum,—and the fate of Sicily was decided. It became and remained a Roman province: the first which the Romans added to those on the Italian peninsula, and, in fact, the corner-stone of the subsequent colossal edifice called the Roman Empire. This occurred in the year 210 B.C.

Stern and avaricious governors at once began to drain the new, rich, land in the cruellest manner. They cared nothing for Hellenic art and culture, nor for the ancient rights and laws which existed before their time. The noble sea-cities fell to ruin; the people were oppressed and crushed into abject slavery, and their daily task thenceforward was to fill the grain ships of their Roman tyrants with corn. Sicily came to be the granary of distant Rome,—and nothing else; for arts, industry, and commerce ceased there. All the cultivated land fell into the hands of rapacious Roman knights, who speedily found themselves unable to manage properly their unwieldy possessions; and thus by degrees more than half of the magnificent arable land degenerated into desert plains, where bands of runaway slaves, and others who had fled from oppression, led a wandering and precarious existence. The harshness of the Romans, who drove the Sicilian plough by means of the sword, exasperated the sufferers to rise in those hideous servile wars, in which three Roman armies were consumed, but in which also the greater part of the old industrious population was extirpated utterly. Then a deadly quiet fell on Sicily, the land sank deeper and deeper into misery, and its ruin was completed by the two rapacious Prætors M. Æmilius Lepidus, and the still more terrible Verres, who with impious hand plundered the ancient shrines, and took away all the precious statues and other works of Grecian art. Poor island! It lay writhing like a dying creature. Augustus attempted to infuse new blood into its veins,—too late! The vital forces of the land were gone for ever.

Then Christianity came to the island; but it did not appear as a deliverer from oppression. Sicily was a ball tossed from one ruler's hand to another. The storm of foreign incursions raged over it and devastated it:—barbarians, Vandals, Goths. History began her cycle anew. As once the Siculi, Hellenes, Carthaginians, and Romans, followed each other, so now pressed on, in quick succession, the Germans, Byzantines, Saracens, and Normans. Ever wilder and swifter the wheel of history turned, and crushed peoples and heroes who had thrown themselves amidst its spokes to check, or guide it. Of the Ostrogoths and Longobards no trace remains, save one or two philological curiosities in the dialect of remote valleys. The Byzantines too have disappeared, —the noble Norman race is gone,—gone too, and forgotten the proud handsome Hohenstaufen Emperor,—the French stock which once ruled arrogantly here is rooted out,— Arragonese, Spaniards,—gone, all gone! The unhappy country lay constantly between two,—sometimes three,—sharp sword-points; and at length it ceased to complain, suffered with apathy, and gradually sank into a state of social stagnation.

And at last came the Bourbons, like owls and foxes that love to dwell amid ruins. And there came too, earthquake, volcanic eruptions, cholera, and scarcity.

At length, though late, the spirit of the people awoke; and it was a grand and heroic spectacle to behold how in their ever repressed but still surviving longing for independence, in their glowing enthusiasm for their country, and their no less burning hatred of their tyrants, they sacrificed their blood and their sons' blood without a murmur. It was reserved too for the island to strike the first decisive blow for the unity of Italy, and to tear asunder the dark cloudy veil which had overshadowed the fair land of sunshine for centuries. She accomplished this under the leadership of the valiant hero of Nice, who landed with his famous "Thousand" at Marsala, the site of the ancient Lilybæon. This was on the eleventh of May, 1860, and with this spring the tree of liberty bloomed anew, and the purple mantle of the bigot king fell from his shoulders like a beggar's rags. The hymn of freedom sounded over the stormy straits to the mainland, and freedom herself leaped across them. A new life burgeoned from the ruins, and the island sowed the seed of hope upon her fields and plains.

She lives now upon this germinating hope. Will the blossom unfold itself at last in all its old glory and fullness? That lies still in the councils of the gods!

So the population of to-day is the child of a changeful story. But antique blood no longer flows in its veins. Two races divide the possession of the island; all the others having been sifted out: these two are the Italian race in the north and east, and the African Saracenic in the south; but even these two have not remained quite pure and unmixed. In both races both faults and virtues are more strongly and sharply marked than in the Italians of the continent. A fiery passionateness is the essence of their

PLAYAS NEAR MONTALLERO.

character. Love is a fierce passion with them: hatred, mockery, song, dance, patriotism, all spring from a never-resting volcanic force in them which too frequently shoots out far beyond the limits of beauty and order. The Sicilian is a true son of his native land; and as the latter can boast that it never knows a day entirely without sunshine, so your genuine Sicilian is never utterly depressed and cast down to earth even in the season of his deepest sorrows. Poetry comes to his aid and helps him to endure, even as she helps his much more unhappy and gloomy neighbour, the Calabrian, over yonder. To no country on earth can the poet's words be better applied, when he says:

> "Amid the ruins sprouts a tender green,
> And the cicala shrills his clearest strain.
> Aye, in the midst of ruin oft resounds
> The cheeriest shout of joy!——"

A VOYAGE ROUND THE ISLAND.

> "Tenderest fleecy clouds float o'er the snowfields of Etna,
> Clear as a mirror and bright shimmers the sea at our feet;
> Rises the steep-piled town high above convent gardens,
> Cypresses, tall and dark, shadow the blossoming vine.
> Yonder beneath the sun Italy's coasts are glowing ——."
> PLATEN.

HIGH over the bare crags, and the lofty table-land of the Calabrian Sila, the wind is roaring. Ancient weather-beaten pines, oaks, and beeches that have struggled through many a hard winter, bow and bend before the blast. Streams that were born in the snow-filled crevices of the rocks dash down the steep precipices, and many a wild river foams along towards the shore of the Ionian or Tyrrhene Sea, stretching to the west and the east in a sheet of silver. White-winged sailing ships cast themselves loose from their anchors and sail away to the north, to France and Spain, or else to neighbouring Greece, or the coasts of burning Africa. The heart is filled with longing by the fresh breath of the sea wind; it saw the sun rise out of the Grecian waters, and shine above the summit of Sila, and incline westward towards Sicilia's isle.

There it lies,—there stretches its legendary jagged coast glimmering in the blue of the mid-day haze. It seems to us like a new piece of earth, like a paradise hidden amid the seas, as we descend the steep, rugged, woody cliffs of Calabria facing it, and come down to the little Calabrian coast towns and fishing villages perched like sea-birds' nests in the clifts of the rocks. The poor people look wistfully across at the sunny island, from which they are separated only by a narrow strip of sea, but which enjoys a far softer climate and offers less harsh conditions of existence than their own land. Once upon a time these people stretched a hand of brotherhood to each other. They both were sprung from the same mother, the noble Graecia Magna, and lived in harmony together. But now they are strangers; the Sicilian looks coldly and contemptuously across to the coast of Calabria, which he can overlook from Cape Vaticano to Cape Spartivento, and on which the poor villages glitter white as pearls on a dark thread. The Sicilian will not be an Italian: and his island, however near it may lie to the mainland, is clearly not Italian soil. The Italian character here is mingled with a singular oriental, Arabian element; and, in truth, Sicily belongs much more to Africa—only a few hours distant—than to Italy.

The sun of Sicily is different from that of even the warmest parts of the continent: the soil and the configuration of the land are different: the vegetation far more luxuriant than even that of Naples, and often wonderfully varied within quite narrow limits of space.

Here is the true bright realm of summer; and his African offspring, the slender palm tree, is no alien here, but stands and grows strong and vigorous among the other plants which unfold their brilliant colours in this pure light. Winter scarcely touches the island at all. He passes with a hasty foot over Etna, leaving a trace of his flight in the

THE ROADSTEAD, NEAR LICATA.

perpetual snows on the volcano, whose lava walls and heaps of ashes bring forth splendid chestnuts, oaks and beeches. In the evergreen valleys at its foot the roses bloom all the year round, and in the hollows of the crumbling volcanic soil wheat grows in glorious abundance. Near to the corn, the vine is slung from one mulberry tree to another. From these grapes is pressed the golden wine which seems to be compounded of Etna's fires and summer sunshine, and which inspires the people's popular songs. Olives too are here, old and hoary as one never sees them on the mainland, and oranges and citrons are at home here, glowing like gold, and full of exquisite juice. Wherever we turn our steps we find lavish abundance, a luxuriance of plenty poured out with open hands. The carob overshadows the dazzling yellow slopes of the hills, the broad-leaved fig-tree peers above garden walls. And everywhere,—in places where more delicate vegetation shrinks from the broad blaze of sunshine, the parched lava of the ground is covered by the victorious Indian fig, whose red-gold fruit offers refreshment in the sunniest desert. Its standard-bearer is the bold Agave that often marches on in long lines across the naked rock, or stands sentry round some ruin of the Grecian times. These plants, together with the palms and olive trees, and the stiff reeds that clothe the lower lands with their sad grey

ON THE ORETO IN THE CONCA D'ORO NEAR PALERMO.

colouring, give the whole landscape a strange, outlandish character, and make the traveller
fancy himself in another quarter of the world.

Wherever the land slopes down and is cut through by singular water-courses, the
natives plant cotton, rice, and the sugar-cane. Herds of cattle and horses wander over
the hilly pastures of the interior; the Sicilian horses were famous in antiquity. The
coasts are inhabited by a bold and adventurous race of fishermen and sailors, who live in
villages or isolated huts, and—wherever the conformation of the shore, which, for the most

NEAR ALCAMO.

part, descends steeply in the water, permits,—they lead a remote and obscure life, far from
the world, but rich in reminiscences of antiquity. Their chief booty is the clumsy tunny,
or the sword-fish, and the fishery takes place in the spring, when the markets of Palermo
and Messina are filled with the fresh fish, and young and old subsist on it for many
weeks.

The dark sunburnt coral fishers boldly defy wind and weather, and pass long months
on the sea between Sicily and Africa in miserable leaky little vessels, to drag up the bright
red coral from the deep; whilst their brothers at home labour within the entrails of a
volcano to gain the gold of Sicily, the much-prized sulphur, and have a hard life of it with
heat and dust and fever. The seaports offer a picture of busy life and activity, and one
can distinctly trace in them the various periods of Sicilian history, Greek, Roman,
Saracenic, and Norman; classic Antiquity, and Mediævalism, are mixed up with showy
modern life, and an oriental element is strongly manifested throughout the whole. It is
manifested not only in the position and architecture of the towns, but perhaps still more

markedly in the manners and customs of the inhabitants, who are entirely different from those of the mainland. You may know Italy if you have traversed it from the Alps to Reggio; but you can draw no conclusions thence respecting the life and landscape of Sicily. Sicily is altogether a peculiar world, and as such it struck the Romans, who visited it to enjoy and admire the wonders of Nature there, its mild springlike winter, the beauty and historic grandeur of its marble cities. Ovid speaks of the *Palicorum Stagna* —the sulphureous lakes near Palica—as wonderful; and also of those of Enna, of the fountains of Cyane, and of Arethusa near Syracuse, of the Anapus, and, above all, of Etna, frequently ascended by the Romans; for at that time Vesuvius still slumbered.

Numerous roads—eleven hundred miles of roads—traversed the island in those days, and united not only all the principal points on the coast, but Syracuse with Catania, and the latter, by way of Termini, with Panormus (Palermo); whilst another road led from Panormus to Girgenti. At the present day a journey across the inhospitable interior of the island does not belong to the category of pleasant things: indeed it must frequently resemble an African expedition more than anything else! There are no roads, and if a sudden shower should fall, the *fiumare*, or water-courses, which intersect the country in all directions, and are usually half dried up, are all at once transformed into turbulent rivers, and the traveller stands helpless on the brink:—

"And the wild stream becomes a raging sea."

Then again, if the sultry scirocco blows from the African Desert, across the narrow seas, not a drop of water is to be found among the parched pebbles. These are the same obstacles which present themselves to the progress of the traveller in Schiller's poem, and they result here from the peculiar geognostic conformation of the land, and from the extremely scanty rainfall. Moreover, the island is almost entirely girdled with threatening rugged coasts, which fall steeply into the sea; for only a few stretches on the south-eastern and western coasts are absolutely flat. The granite-bound coast on the east, from Cape Faro to Cape Alessio, and the black volcanic line of the lower slopes of Etna, look sullenly at the mainland opposite.

Farther to the southward the shore grows flatter, and is divided into a great variety of bays and creeks and harbours, with seaports:—for example, Augusta, Syracuse, Noto, and the little peninsula of Santa Croce; Cape Passero forms the southernmost point. If from the latter you were to draw a line running east and west, and parallel with the thirty-seventh degree of latitude, it would cut deep into Africa, and pass only a very little to the north of Cape Matapan, the most southerly point of Europe. The south coast of the island is rocky, but presents few indentations; it formerly boasted of the noble Agrigentum, whose name is faintly echoed in the modern one of Girgenti. Its little rivers, the Biagio and Drago, were called in ancient times Acragas and Hypsas.

The western promontory of the island advances into the sea under the name of Cape Bono; and opposite to it, like an advanced guard, are posted the Ægatian or Goat Islands, whose antique name has fallen into oblivion long ago. They are now called Favignano, Maretimo, and Levanzo, and they witnessed 242 years, B.C., the great victory of Lutetius over the Carthaginians, and in modern times the daring landing of the hero of freedom, Garibaldi. To the north-west lies Trapani, a Carthaginian city at the foot of the Eryx, on which a temple to the famous Erycinian Venus once stood. Here too, as on Monte Vergine, a wonder-working Madonna has replaced the ancient goddess. At Trapani begins the north coast, running in many a lovely line of curving bays. At Cape

San Vito, the fine bay of Castellamare runs deep into the land; it continues in one great arc to the Cape Zaffarano, in the Bay of Palermo, whose waters wash the Conca d'Oro, the blooming and luxuriant pleasure gardens of Palermo. The beauties of this bay vie

LATOMIE DEL PARADISO, NEAR SYRACUSE.

with those of the Bay of Naples, and many a one has hesitated to which to award the palm. From thence, however, past Cefalù, from Cape Orlando to Milazzo, the shore loses all charm; it is rude, deserted, steep, and rugged, and not till we reach Messina do we again behold the rich luxuriance of southern beauty.

The traveller, looking from on board ship outside the harbour at Messina, sees some dark uncouth masses of rock, like sea-monsters, rising out of the waves, which seem to guard the entrance to this paradise. These are the Lipari Islands, which formed the kingdom of Æolus. We are

> "Here in the realm of storm ; in Æolia, home of the south wind.
> Here in his cavern vast, King Æolus, mighty ruler,
> Quiets the restive winds, and tames the loud-howling tempest."

Stromboli, formerly Strongyle, is the first to show itself through the haze of distance. It sends up a smoking cloud high into the air, thus bearing witness to subterranean fires even in the midst of the water. Then come Lipari, and Volcano, the ancient Thermosia, pouring out dark smoke over the sea. This is the home of Vulcan, of which Virgil sings :

> "Insula Sicanium juxta latus Æoliamque
> Erigitur Liparen, fumantibus ardua saxis :
> Quam subter specus et Cyclopum exesa caminis
> Antra Ætnæa tonant ——."

Ericuso, Diæyme, and Phœnicusæ were the ancient names of the sister isles.

From this position the eye embraces that watery way which has cleft the Apennine and pressed itself in between the Calabrian chain on the one side, and the Peloritanian mountains—a continuation of the Calabrian range—on the other. But the separation does not appear to be quite complete. The sea looks like a magnificent bay entirely shut in from Capo Vaticano to Milazzo, having Capo di Faro and the rocks of Scylla, with other mountains towering behind them, for a background. It is only when the ship approaches close to Messina that the sea opens out to the south.

In Messina a new scene displays itself to the traveller. There is a stronger impulse of life here than in the harbour of Naples ; and indeed this port seems better adapted than any other for a world-wide commerce. What position could possibly be more favourable ? It is separated but by the breadth of a river from the mainland, but this stream opens into two seas ; so that the town is in almost immediate communication with the continent, whilst at the same time her harbour is a central point for shipping of all countries. A great wealth of inland produce is piled up here, and is constantly being laded by an active and busy population. All languages resound on the quays, in boats, and barks, and towering merchantmen. The stranger from the north is chiefly attracted by the golden southern fruits, which lie here in basketsful by the million ; he snuffs the scented breeze that carries the perfume of their blossom seaward, and gazes at the gardens which produce them, and which rise high behind the bright cheerful town, advancing with a row of palaces almost to the water's edge. The hills rise terrace-wise above the town ; palaces, towers, villas surrounded with palm-trees, garden houses, vintagers' cottages, are mingled in picturesque variety, the latter half buried in the foliage of the vine. The whole is surrounded by a thick green garland formed of the famous orange-groves of Messina, and here and there may be seen a relic of the Monkish Middle Ages, in the shape of some white convent, the finest of which is that upon the Monte dei Cappuccini, commanding a magnificent view over the town and the sea.

The town truly belongs to the sea ; and towards the sea all her energies are concentrated. From the long tongue of land, at whose extremity a light-house now stands, the town was anciently called Zancle. Its inhabitants have proudly given it the name of "*La nobile*," as Genoa, its north Italian sister, is called "*La superba*." Messina is proud of her history, which goes back to a remote antiquity. She flourished when the Hellenes were lords here; and even the conquering Romans admitted her to be the second city in the island. She was a favourite child of the Arabs, who decked her with the richest architecture after their manner. The Normans came, and Messina was the jewel in their ruler's crown. All the nations wooed the enchanting sea-siren, and so she grew spoilt, capricious, and haughty, and at the present day is somewhat unwilling to abandon her bridal finery for the work-a-day garb of a good housewife. But "La nobile"

RUINS OF THE TEMPLE OF HERCULES, NEAR GIRGENTI.

must learn to become a *bourgeoise*, and then a fair future lies before her. Her population is prouder and more dignified than that of Naples.

Palermo has perhaps understood her modern mission better than Messina, and has been labouring actively for some years past to render herself more and more worthy of it. And truly her efforts are seconded by the sea and the land, the mountain and the plain, the sky and the soil. The plain, enclosed by a semi-circle of hills, is named from its singular form and luxuriant fertility, the *Conca d'Oro*, the Golden Shell; and within this shell lies Palermo, like a splendid pearl. *Panormus*, the haven of havens, unites within itself everything needful to become a Garden of Eden, if man would but have it so. To the eye, however, it must ever appear a landscape paradise. Comparisons are odious; and if you gaze at Naples from the sea, or look from its shore across at Vesuvius, or the smiling Sorrento, or that blue dream of the waters, Capri, nothing can be finer than Naples. But when you behold Palermo spreading out upon the fruitful plain, her towers and cupolas, her palaces, and quaint curious houses, her two sphinx-like rocks advancing into the sea,—Catalfano on the left, and on the right Pellegrino,—with the wild mountains in the background; or when you lean upon the balustrade and gaze from the town over the unbroken expanse of sea, which breaks with a dreamy murmur almost at your feet,—then you forget even beautiful Naples, and give the crown to the city by Monte Pellegrino!

Palermo is made up of the same elements as Naples; sea and land, and the work of

CONVENT OF SAN MARTINO, NEAR PALERMO.

man's hands. But the sea appears vaster; the land, although not so varied in its outlines, has grander forms, and is incomparably richer in its products; and the edifices of the city and on the hills around it, have preserved the characteristics of the various periods of its history (the same as those which Naples passed through) far more strikingly and perfectly than its rival on the mainland. In Palermo you realize the ideal of a south Italian city more completely than anywhere else. Everything seems to have been

PALERMO.

produced by the spirit of sunshine. The life of the city is essence of sunbeams; it moves and roars and breathes and works enjoyingly, whether in luxurious saloons or on the steps of the gaudily decked-out churches. In brief, it is a life of full, complete, intense enjoyment. This seems very strange to us northern folks, who work hard all the week,

CATHEDRAL OF PALERMO.

and only venture on Sundays to blink timidly at a ray of pleasure. Even in Palermo we work,—and extremely hard too!—at sight-seeing; seeking out from morning till evening the mediæval treasures of which the city is full. Examine the various remains of Roman, Byzantine, and Saracenic architecture, which the Palermitan builders seem to have shaken into ever new and charming combinations, as in a kaleidoscope: wander through the Palazzo Reale with its renowed Capella Palatina: stare at the wonders of the cathedral of Santa Rosalia: the churches of La Martorana, San Giovanni, Santa

Maria della Catena, San Giuseppe, the church of the Dominicans, the palaces of the rich: make an expedition to the royal Favorita, or to Monreale, where another cathedral will enchain your admiration:—stay! stay here days and weeks, and look and enjoy!

We fly in thought southwards over the soft rolling landscape of Alcamo. To the right, amongst wild and rugged hills lie the ruins of the hoary antique Segesta, whose Doric temple of Ceres was built for eternity. By the sea, far away to the south, is her rival sister Selinus, a few remnants of whose ancient splendour may still be descried in the modern town of Castelvetrano. Acragas, Agrigentum,—a mighty queen throned upon the southern sea-shore! Girgenti,—a wretched, withered-up old beggar woman, cowering on the steps of her former throne! The old gods have long departed hence, and left their lofty marble houses, where joyous Greeks once sung hymns of praise, to crumble sadly to decay, and be wondered at by the generations of a later time. We pass by the temples of Proserpine, of Jupiter, of Juno Lucinia, where once Zeuxis' wondrous statue of Venus stood, to the temple of Ceres, and everywhere from ruins and rubbish, from thistles and weeds, blooms out still the beauteous flower of Grecian Art. The landscape too, the delight of painters, is thoroughly in harmony with that art; but at the present day it affords only a glorious frame for a solitary world of ruins.

This is the abiding charm of the Syracusan remains. The beginnings of the town founded by the Corinthians, are to be sought on the island of Ortygia, which lies in a beautiful, still bay opposite to the promontory of Plemmyrion. From this island the town grew and spread to the westward, across the plain and even into the mountains, and became a gigantic city, whose walls were many miles in circumference, and whose population was counted by hundreds of thousands. The Syracuse of to-day has retreated timidly back to the island whence it took its origin, and encircled by the melancholy ruins of the past, it leads a poor existence beside a harbour choked with sand, and amidst the poisonous exhalations from surrounding swamps. But the Syracusan is proud of his past history; and wears the remembrance of it as a beggar might wear a player king's robe. In his pride he maintains that Syracuse possessed the papyrus plant long before Egypt did! And declares that it still grows beside the stagnant stream called La Pisma,—once Cyane. Proudly, too, he leads the stranger to the ancient fortifications,—of which some important fragments still remain,—to the amphitheatre, to the tombs, to the wonderful *latomie* (marble-quarries) and the catacombs. The Grecian theatre resembles in its position that of Taormina; it is hewn in the rock; and from its height the Greeks once looked over their beautiful city, and the richly blooming landscape around it, and the harbour swarming with ships. So that the theatre served at once for the enjoyment of art and nature. To a still greater degree was this the case with the theatre of Tauromenion, which even to-day, in its decay, appeals to the heart like an enchanting poem. The exquisite charm of the view hence, the landscape glories from the harbour of Ulysses to the smoking mountain in the background, are indescribable. Sicily possesses an abundance of splendid ruins, but the Theatre of Taormina is the most wonderful, the most captivating of them all! The spirit of Homer still wanders here at broad noonday, and the very stones re-echo the song of the poets of the Sicilian island, beloved of the Muses:—the isle which

> "Filled Epicharmus once with festal strains, and melodious.
> Here Stesichorus sang, and Simonides too; and yonder
> Ibycus holds thine urn, oh Æschylus! Pindar, the godlike,
> Hymned his mighty odes; Theocritus strayed 'mid the shepherds,———"

Here, as in so many other parts of Italy, we clearly realize what we have lost by the destruction of that "beauteous world."

We have flitted across the island with a hasty flight, and must leave it to the painter to give distinct form and colour to these rapid sketches.

We leave Taormina, carrying with us a delightful impression of Greek antiquity, and retrace our steps along the dusty roads from Giardini to Catania, having the giant Etna before us in all his glory. Boldly he sets his foot in the blue sea; we are in his dominions; the black masses of rock in the sea eaten into wonderful shapes by the salt foam,—the great blocks that lie dark amidst the green of the land,—all have been scattered by his mighty force. What lies between these is Modern Sicily, and the *modernest* of its towns is Catania, which, although more than once betrayed, returns again and again to nestle beside the mountain, and builds palaces for its children's children, unheeding that to-morrow one movement of the giant may destroy them. Several times already the lava has flowed through the streets of the town, and even into the harbour; but as often as this happened the town was rebuilt on the ashes. But, in compensation, when the latest buildings of Catania have come to be fifty years old, its gardens have produced within those fifty years, more than those of other places in two hundred! A careless sense of enjoyment pervades the scene; Catania troubles herself not about the past, but celebrates the present with libations of the fiery blood of her grapes grown in the ashy soil.

TO ETNA.

"Degravat Ætna caput ; sub qua resupinus arenas
Ejectat, flammasque fero vomit ore Typhœus.
Sæpe remoliri luctatur pondera terræ,
Oppidaque, et magnos evoluere corpore montes.
Inde tremit tellus ;———"

OVID.

OUR feet are dusty with our wanderings. Upon the distant Alps approaching winter spreads wider and wider his white mantle of mist and snow, and lets it flow down even into the southward valleys. The northern winter calls us home.

So we take up our staff for the last time to reach the goal of our pilgrimage from the Alps to Etna,—to climb the old fire-mountain which we behold from the vine-grown gardens of Catania, far-seeing and far-seen, rising into the air with graceful, gently sloping outline. Many a thousand years have laboured to build him higher and higher; for many a thousand years has the fire been seething and glowing in his mysterious depths, and ever and anon with titanic thunderings he hurls out burning floods over the sand. The earth around is drenched in its own blood ; but from this blood spring up Earth's glorious children, corn and wine. Truly we behold a picture of destruction in these huge blocks of black lava scattered amid the grass of the earth and the waves of the sea ; the gloomy mantle, whose hem flows out even to the peasant's gardens and the streets of the town, is a warrior's cloak. But Ceres touches it with her magic wand, adorned with wheat and flowers, and underneath its folds begins the sprouting of seed, and the budding of blossoms! Minerva sets her peaceful silver-grey olive on it ; the cactus and agave rise triumphant over it; the roots of the lofty pine split the volcanic rock and strew its crumbling fragments to manure the surrounding soil. In all those portions of the island where chalk and lime-stone predominate, nature is far more niggardly than where Etna's hand has fertilized the ground. And Etna's realm is a princely one.

Reckoning the volcanic region of Sicily to extend from the Punta delle Correnti across Etna to the islands of Volcano and Lipari, the volcanic circle around Etna alone,

PALAZZO CORVAJA, IN TAORMINA.

is six miles in diameter. The line of its circumference runs from the mouth of the Cantaro in the east, all along the lava-bordered banks of that river to the mediæval mountain town of Randazzo, which has frequently—and even in recent times—been injured by the subterranean powers; then the line rises higher to Maletto and Bronte, whence the mountain falls steeply to the west, and where the lava streams are most perilous; then downward towards the lower terraces of Etna, through Aldemo, Paterna, Catania, and along the sea-coast formed by blocks of lava. The realm is a princely one; and cheerful well-to-do populations inhabit for the most part the numerous villages and towns of Etna: especially to the south and west, as far up as Nicolosi, a singular little place, which is passed in making the ascent of Etna. Zaffarana, Annunziata, Trecastagne, Signagrossa, and others, lie nearly all of them at least two thousand feet above the sea level. But they are thickly populated, and surrounded by beautiful gardens, whose produce both from blade and tree is double that of the mainland. The people are happy subjects of a mighty king!

How grand he looks on his throne in the early spring, clad in his shining white snow-mantle, whilst the fields are rosy with almond blossoms and adorned with the delicate cyclamen! Then the woods around his throne are covered with rich foliage; the smothered heat bursts forth, the snows melt, turbid streams dash down the precipices, and around the monarch's head soft clouds flutter, or float in tattered banners through his dark

EVERGREEN OAKS, NEAR SCIACCA.

ravines. Sometimes he groans up to the face of heaven with titanic breathings; or his seat trembles and shakes as, musing on past times, he proves the strength of his arm by hurling down red-hot stones upon the puny human creatures below. Then again he sinks into a long long dream, and the corn is sown in the folds of his robe, and young saplings sprout up close around his feet.

Eruptions of the mountain are chronicled in the earliest legends of the island. And although Homer does not mention these, yet the terrific Cyclops who flings rocks at the little Grecian ships, and whom they are forced to flee from, is probably a personification of Etna. In later times there have been recorded about two eruptions in each century, and many towns have suffered by them: especially Catania, which rises again and again like a phœnix from its ashes.

In ancient as in modern times the colossus has often been ascended by curious travellers as well as serious men of science. Nay, there stands immediately beneath the chief crater a grey fragment of masonry of great antiquity, called by the people the Torre del Filosofo. It may be either the observatory of Empedocles, who in order to make a mysterious exit from the world threw himself headlong into the crater,—or a lodge built by Hadrian, who took a fancy to see the sun rise from the summit of Etna. A good deal has been recorded respecting the natural wonders, but very little has been written of the glorious view from the summit; from which we may conclude that the ascents were chiefly made for scientific purposes. Seneca begs his friend the Imperial Procurator Lucilius, to climb the mountain; and in all probability it was this Lucilius who wrote a poem full of physical science, about Etna. Strabo narrates that the ascent was always begun from the little town of Etna, and that the traveller descended again to the same point. At the present day you ascend from Catania, by a long winding road bordered by gardens. A rich vegetation peeps over the walls made of blocks of lava,—olive and carob trees, groves of oranges and lemons; and amongst them black little gardeners' or vintagers' huts also built out of the produce of the mountain, and overgrown with vines. Then follow wide cornfields bordered with cactus, and buildings ruined by earthquakes, covered with creeping plants. Then come stretches of lava not yet conquered by vegetation: dreary black or reddish brown fragments, or heaps of dusty ashes; and so the road winds along through the gardens and villages of Pasquale, Gravina, Torre di Grifo, all inhabited by healthy, cheerful, and industrious populations.

At length we reach Nicolosi, in front of whose territory a broad, desolate lava-field stretches, the result of the eruption of the year 1537. Not far from Nicolosi rises the double peak of Monte Rosso, whose reddish rocks form the rim of a crater. From this point the view over land and sea is very fine. The eye ranges along the jagged coast from Messina to distant Syracuse, or loses itself in the leafy gardens of the Piano di Catania. Higher still, begins the monarch's own peculiar domain. The hoof of the climbing mule slips and scrambles over sharp stones and crumbling lava, or sinks deep into the ashes. Yet even here man has dared to strew seed-corn, and has reaped an abundant harvest. Where the cornfields cease, the woody region begins, and rises to a height of five thousand four hundred feet. But on this side only a few trees have escaped the destroying axe or flame, and these lonely outposts stand defiantly, buffeted by wind and weather, amidst the lava. The latter grows harder and more solid, and is split here and there into gullies filled with sharp pointed stones. Only in a few sheltered corners do you find a handful of soil where the wild myrtle and yellow broom grow, or coarse hard grass spreads a scanty oasis. When you look to the south and south-west into the amphitheatre of mountains, you perceive with astonishment how the followers of the great monarch press around his throne with crater after crater. Every one of these has served at one time or another to form the land below, pushing it far out into the waves, and narrowing the straits. The king thundered up aloft, and his servants carried their flaming torches down into the plain. From this spot as many as fifty subsidiary craters can be counted.

ETNA FROM THE SOUTH.

At about eight thousand five hundred feet above the sea vegetation finally ceases, and the region of snow begins; which, however, is nearly all melted in summer, or limited to the shadiest hollows. Here, at an altitude of eight thousand nine hundred feet, stands the Torre del Filosofo; and at about nine thousand two hundred feet, the Casa Inglese, the highest building on the island. Sideways, to the east, the huge, terrific hollow called the Val di Bove sinks down suddenly. It is at least a mile in diameter, and is awful in its solitude and desolation; the eye plunges awe-stricken into its depths, and when the wind howls in it you might imagine yourself to hear the yells and cries of dying Titans.

ON THE ROAD FROM MESSINA TO TAORMINA.

But peaceful, serene, and unspeakably sublime is the view of all that lies below us in clear sunshine, and of the tender blue lines of mountains swimming in the haze of distance. Trinacria lies spread out beneath us like a splendid jewel set in the Mediterranean, whose silver foam dashes over the lava-bound coast. The land looks like a pleasure garden lifted out of the sea by Vulcan's mighty hands as a gift for Venus. Wherever we turn our gaze, towns, villages, dark valleys, blue or silvery mountains, the sea, the vaulted sky,—all seem to be as strophes of a sublime poem. There to the north are the Peloritanian mountains, and fair Messina, with the straits whose waters roll like a strong river from sea to sea! Yonder is the stern Calabrian range, clothed with dark woods, and seamed with many a black ravine. To the west the honeyed Hybla stretches his soft slopes; to the east and to the south,—down there, sheer below us, falling steep into the sea,—the lava coast, the deep bay of Augusta, the storied harbour of Syracuse, the blue lakes of Lentini, gardens, rugged mountains, wooded vales, all traversed by white gleaming roads, and enlivened by a hundred towns and hamlets! Further still, the eye turns dreamily towards Malta and the African coast, and the soul hovers over the Ionian Sea towards the shores of Greece, and loses itself in visions of the wondrous past.

The mountain thunders out a greeting to the gods to whom this island once was consecrated. A thick cloud of smoke rises into the crystalline ether, and for sacrifice we offer up a joyful song of praise. Blessed, thrice blessed is he to whom it is given to behold this glorious land in the sunlight and the starlight. With a spirit exalted and enriched by divine memories, he returns to his northern home, bearing with him many treasured pictures of that beauty which is "a joy for ever."

Addio,—addio, bella Italia! We have heard the last song of the nightingale in thy groves, we have gathered our last rose from thy gardens. A less brilliant Spring awaits us,—but it is the Spring-time of our own home. And we take the poet's words to comfort us:

> "Not alone by southern waters
> Doth the springtime hold his feast;
> Nightingales here in our northland
> Joyful build the vernal nest.
>
> "Grieve not for the glowing summers
> O'er Vesuvius' crest that roll;
> Trill, ye nightingales full-throated,
> Sun-fraught songs that warm the soul!"

We lay down our pilgrim's staff on the altar of our northern household gods. The painter closes his sketch-book, and puts by his busy pencil. What we have seen, the blossoms we have plucked from Hesperian gardens, are here bound together in a wreath:

ITALY:
A PILGRIMAGE FROM THE ALPS TO ETNA.

THE END.

BRADBURY, AGNEW, & CO., PRINTERS, WHITEFRIARS.

www.ingramcontent.com/pod-product-compliance
Lightning Source LLC
Chambersburg PA
CBHW021219300426
44111CB00007B/354